SUPER AUSSIE SOAPS

BEHIND THE SCENES OF
AUSTRALIA'S BEST LOVED TV SHOWS

ANDREW MERCADO

PLUTO PRESS AUSTRALIA

First published in 2004 by
Pluto Press Australia
7 Leveson Street
North Melbourne Victoria 3051
www.plutoaustralia.com

Copyright © Andrew Mercado

Design and typesetting by Justin Archer
Edited by Chris Mikul
Production co-ordination by Kathryn Lamberton
Printed and bound by Griffin Press

Australian Cataloguing in Publication Data

Mercado, Andrew.
    Super Aussie soaps : behind the scenes of Australia's best loved TV shows.

    Bibliography.
    ISBN 1 86403 191 3.

    1. Soap operas - Australia - History. 2. Television actors
    and actresses - Australia. I. Title.

791.45750994

CONTENTS

DEDICATION

This book is dedicated to all the hard-working crews – writers, technicians, caterers, production runners, in fact everyone – who quietly worked behind the scenes to get all these soaps on air. Their contribution and mateship are very much appreciated.

FOREWORD

Amanda Keller wishes she was a *Number 96* sexpot.

Thursday was my favourite day of the week. That was the day Mum did the grocery shopping at Carlingford Court, and brought home the latest edition of *TV Times*. I would devour every morsel of information about my favourite soap stars. I knew their birthdays, their favourite colours and who they dated on screen and off.

I seemed to have a different crush every week, from a young Mark Holden in *The Young Doctors* to Andrew McFarlane in *The Sullivans*. I was hooked, and desperate to be part of their orbit. My only claim to fame was that a woman my mother used to work with was the sister of Barry Creighton from *The Mavis Bramston Show*. I'd never seen the show – but who cared – I almost knew someone who'd been in *TV Times*.

Like many kids my age, I wasn't allowed to watch *Number 96* or *The Box*, so it all started for me with the *Class of '74*, without doubt a far racier and drama-prone school than Carlingford High. It certainly made me wonder what really went on in the staff room. It was the first time we, as a nation, clapped eyes on Peta Toppano (or as she exotically called herself then, Pieta). I thought she was the most beautiful woman in the world and *TV Times* kept me up to date with her courtship and subsequent marriage to the equally gorgeous Barry Quinn from *Prisoner*. I think the magazine had folded though by the time they were divorced.

The mother of all soaps for me was *The Young Doctors*. I was allowed to watch this before dinner, after which came homework, so it was the shining light in my day. I don't remember any medical procedures taking place, but that hospital was certainly bursting at the seams with romance. I'm sure many people my age entered the medical profession solely for a chance to crack on to major spunks in bars like Bunny's that were surely part of every medical establishment. The show finished each night with a bit of a cliffhanger and there's one I particularly remember: the episode ended with the kettle boiling and Dr Denham's secretary, Helen Gordon, saying 'I'll get it'. Even though I was only 14 or so, I knew writer's block when I saw it.

I don't know what I found more terrifying in *Prisoner* – the steam press, the women or how high they wore their pants. Then there were the clouds racing across the sky during the opening titles of *The Restless Years* ... the shock of Grace Sullivan being blown away in London ... and Jeremy Sims's backside in *Chances*. So many memories, so little time.

The thing that's so wonderful about all these shows is their unadulterated 'Australianness'. Here we were in all our glory ... bad hair, high pants, dodgy sets and all. I chart my teenage years through my viewing of Aussie soaps, and I don't apologise for it for a minute. And now as an adult watching old episodes of *96* and *The Box*, I'm shocked by what they got away with.

Reading this book I've relived my teenage years, remembered my favourite episodes and characters, and reignited my desire to watch these classic Aussie soaps – again and again.

Umm ... err ... I think I hear the kettle boiling ... I'll get it.

Amanda Keller

ACKNOWLEDGEMENTS

This book would not have been possible without the support of many generous people – let's start with the fabulous actors like Rowena Wallace, Paula Duncan, Rebecca Gilling, Judy McBurney, Jackie Woodburne, Lorraine Bayly, Lynda Stoner, Tina Bursill, Louise Crawford, Tory Mussett, Simone Buchanan, Melissa Tkautz, Vivienne Garrett, Maggie Kirkpatrick, Joan Bruce, Judy Nunn, Joanne Samuel, Elspeth Ballantyne, Judith McGrath, Kate Ritchie, Kimberley Joseph, Raelee Hill, Kate Raison, Marina Finlay, Kimberley Cooper, Brian Meegan, Patrick Ward, Danny Roberts, Martin Henderson, Damien de Montemas, Alan Hopgood, Peter Flett, Adrian Lee, Jeremy Sims, Michael Smith, Toby Truslove, Ron Graham, Peter Mochrie, Damon Herriman, Lloyd Morris, Peter Kowitz, Terry Norris and Paul Kelman.

Thank you to those producers, directors, writers and creative people behind the scenes, such as Bevan Lee, Jock Blair, Bruce Best, Peter Pinne, John Holmes, Jason Herbison, Jan Russ, Gwenda Marsh, Lynn Bayonas, Mike Lilley, Adam Bowen, Alan Coleman, Jimmy Thomson, Gretel Killeen, Roger Simpson, Jo Porter, Oscar Whitbread, Alan Bateman, James Davern, David Sale, Nancy Cash, Ken Lord, Ian Bradley, Rick Maier, John Edwards, Forrest Redlich, Leigh Spence, and Hal and Di McElroy.

How could I have done this without the full support of our National Screen and Sound Archive, *ScreenSound*? Huge thanks to Simon Drake, Jane Adam, Carla Teixeira, Joanna Fleming, Tina Fiveash and Anna Kamasz.

Production company-wise, from Crawford's, thanks to Nick McMahon, Don Samuelon and Carol Matthews; from Beyond, Rhiannon Haughee; and from Screentime, Bob Campbell and Marietta Delvecchio.

To those at the networks, thanks to Sasha Mackie, Victoria Supple, Linda Calkin, Steve Murphy, Tony Stower, Janeen Faithfull and Bec Barnett from Seven; Andrew Stewart, Sonya Fera and Irene Doel from Nine; Tim Clucas, Grant Gillies and Belinda Wong from Ten; Ian Phipps, Genevieve Walkley-Reid and Anna Sorensen from SBS; Julie McCrossin, Richard Glover, Noel Debien and Guy Tranter from the ABC; and Brian Walsh, Elizabeth Hunter, Greg Crockett and Shirley Kennard from Foxtel.

I would never have been given the opportunity to write this book if it wasn't for Vesna Petropoulos and everyone at *TV Soap*; Selena Crowley from TV1; and Barry Chapman, Sally Burleigh and Valerie Larnach (ex-Channel [V]). Thank you all for believing in me.

I would also like to acknowledge the following organisations for providing the photographs appearing in the book: ABC, Australian Consolidated Press, Beyond, Cash Harmon Productions, Crawford Productions, Fox Australia, Nine Network, Pacific Publications, SBS,

Screentime, Seven Network (Operations) Limited, State Library of NSW, State Library of Victoria and *TV Soap*. Thank you also to the ABC, Seven Network (Operations) Limited, Nine Network and Ten Network for permission to reproduce their soap advertisements.

And let's not forget Amanda Keller, Michael Idato, Barry Humphries, Ali Montgomery, Judy Steeves, Cristel Lee Leed, Andrea Black, Liza Lakusa, Paula Mansfield, Andy Purcell, Victoria Buchan, Karl Schmidt, Loyce Cox-Paton, Robert Paton, Samantha Woodruff, Wade Goring, Sanchia Bull, Paul Dillon, Chris Corradi, Di Campisi, Georgina Harrop, Joanna Harrop, Ian Skillicorn, David Byak, Kim Jennings, Leanne Kingwell, Rob Pullan, Donna Barton, Shane Kennedy, Emma Markestyn, Amanda West, Tim Elkington, Dino Scatena, Rachel Newman, Michael Bodey, Michaela Boland, Michael Jackson, Mark Berridge, Jason McArthur, Margee Brown and Benjamin Tunstall.

Of course, big thanks to Tony Moore, Sarah Crisp, Brendan O'Dwyer, Justin Archer, Jude Fowler Smith, Kathryn Lamberton and everyone else at Pluto Press who have made this book happen.

Special thanks to the Buckner family – Kevin, Norma, Christopher and Andrew – who hid me away in Canada while I tried to finish writing; Elizabeth, the incredible psychic who predicted this book over ten years ago; and my mother, Bryanne, who proofread every chapter.

As for these last two people, well they truly went above and beyond the call of duty. Thank you Nigel Giles for your endless enthusiasm and newspaper scouring and Martin McDowell for continually mailing me tapes and information all the way from Ireland. Quite simply, I would still be writing this if it wasn't for the pair of you.

I hope I haven't forgotten anybody...

Andrew Mercado

INTRODUCTION

Welcome to the wonderful world of Aussie soaps. A world of knicker snippers, pantyhose stranglers and suburban discos. Where the female cops are more glamorous than the crims and every hooker has a heart of gold. Where a bride can arrive at her wedding in a ute, give birth to twins in a barn and still be on speaking terms with her pet wombat. Where hospitals and jails can be fun places and a cup of tea solves every problem. Where neighbours become good friends and teenage delinquents are rehabilitated in a seaside set. Australia has been making TV serials since 1958 and many of them have passed into TV legend. Everyone has a personal favourite, whether it be *The Sullivans*, *The Restless Years* or *Sons and Daughters*. Fans even have a favourite bomb (and not just the one that went off in the *Number 96* deli) and can recall with a smile *The Unisexers*, *Arcade* or *Holiday Island*.

Christine Stephen-Daly, Andrew Mercado and Lloyd Morris at the filming of a *Pacific Drive* wedding.

It's a great unsung Aussie tradition that has never been properly celebrated – until now. Along the way as we check out every soap made, in chronological order, we'll also see how they are a barometer for Australia's changing morals and attitudes. Not to mention becoming one of our great export industries.

Soap shouldn't be a dirty word, but in the heady world of popular culture, it's considered a much lesser art form than theatre or film and rarely worthy of discussion (except when a few academics theorise on why the Brits love *Neighbours*). Even television types convince themselves that self-contained episodic drama is much more prestigious than a never-ending soapie. Yet, all over the world, in practically every single culture, continuing TV serials are viewed by more people than any other form of entertainment. Such popularity does not sit well with the elite art police who consider it all nothing more than cheap diversion for the masses.

Australia has a love-hate relationship with its homegrown soaps. It seems like every kid in the schoolyard is watching when they are growing up, with some of the more obsessive fans (such as myself) cutting and pasting pictures from magazines like *TV Week* and *TV Soap* into scrapbooks and onto bedroom walls. For many, a lifetime habit has been bred and their fandom knows no limits.

However, soaps become an underground activity for some who keep watching into adulthood. It's perfectly acceptable to discuss the latest art-house movie at a dinner party but social suicide to admit to following a serial. It's even more difficult for those who work in the medium. Hard-working actors are generally sneered at while they appear in a soap, yet when they make the break and move into film or theatre (like Guy Pearce, Radha Mitchell or Simon Baker) suddenly it's patriotic to laud their talent.

Television snobs prefer short films and motion pictures, yet most of what the heavily subsidised Australian film industry churns out is ignored by audiences, both here and abroad. Unlike those little-seen, pretentious local movies though, international audiences from Iceland to Zanzibar have been lapping up our serials since the early 80s and providing some serious export dollars for Australia.

Aussie soaps are loved abroad and still command huge audiences. Yet each time another country discovers one of our soap gems, we question why they would want to watch such 'rubbish'. We convince ourselves that overseas viewers only watch our soaps because they covet our swimming pool lifestyle. Even if we can't quite understand the international obsession, nearly everybody has a favourite soap from years gone by that they have loved. This book will take you from *Bellbird* to *Prisoner* to *The Secret Life of Us*, and hopefully you will come to the conclusion that, collectively, Australia has made, and continues to make, bloody good television shows.

The Aussie soap isn't unique, but we have been clever enough to combine the best qualities of the shows produced by our American and British cousins. Essentially, we sped up the storytelling, because American soaps moved too slowly, and, like the Brits, we preferred to balance our melodrama with a good deal more comedy. What emerged was a winning formula about middle-class folk who didn't take themselves too seriously. The model we created to pump out five nights of prime-time soap has since been used as the blueprint for local soap production all over Europe and Asia. They adapted our shows for their own audiences and it required Aussie talent to go over and teach them how to do it.

Rather than pat ourselves on the back for teaching the rest of the world how to make TV, we choose instead to deride our local soap makers. Such critics often have no concept of the skill and hard work required to meet deadlines, week in and week out, year after year. Actors need to be word-perfect and nail their moments with minimal takes and little rehearsal. Soap writers must constantly be thinking up simultaneous storylines for a large cast who all need to figure in the action every week. There's not a lot of money for big-budget stunts so it's usually the deceptively simple but often complex storytelling that keeps viewers hooked and entertained. It's all too easy to sit on your couch and mouth off that you could write better – try hammering out an episode yourself or plotting a week of soap action and you'll discover that it's not as easy as it looks.

Serials are not a recent phenomenon. Hundreds of years before the invention of television, people were already listening to open-ended stories. In the 15th century *Arabian Nights*, Princess Scheherazade avoided being beheaded by weaving a continuing story over 1001 evenings. During the Victorian era, novelists, most notably Charles Dickens, serialised their stories in magazines and newspapers. By the 1930s, American radio coined a new term, soap opera, in a nod to the sponsors who advertised their washing products during the long-running melodramas. Meanwhile, cinemas were running their own weekly serials (like *Batman and Robin* and *The Perils of Pauline*) as a prelude to the main feature.

The advent of television refined the genre further. The first ever TV soap, *Faraway Hill*, was made in 1946, for Washington and New York transmission only, for just $300 a week. In 1952, *The Guiding Light*, a radio staple since 1937, was adapted for American daytime television. It is still on air today and is the longest-running soap on the airwaves.

Across the Atlantic, English audiences embraced their own soaps, first on radio (*The Frontline Family* and *The Archers*) and then on TV. The first was 1956's *The Grove Family*, but it was the groundbreaking *Coronation Street*, launched in 1960, that became an institution for night-time audiences. By 1964, Americans were obsessed with their own prime-time soap, *Peyton Place*. Australia was already experimenting with daytime versions, unaware that one day we would challenge both countries for soap supremacy.

This book is the history of every Australian soap since 1958. Soap is the term I am choosing to use for any drama or serial that is mostly propelled forward by never-ending stories that will only end when the audience drifts away. There are many, many Australian television shows that have adopted soap storytelling (such as *The Flying Doctors* and *McLeod's Daughters*), but their major plotlines each week are self-contained tales. So, for the sake of space, and my sanity, they are all ripe to be explored more fully in another book.

I have been a fan of Aussie soaps ever since 1972 when I first saw an ad on TV for a new show called *Number 96*. It fascinated me but alarmed my parents who forbade me to watch the adults-only show. I grabbed snatches of it at a neighbour's house and eventually wore my parents down. They bought another TV so I could watch it and all the other serials it began to spawn. Not only have I watched nearly every show in this book, but my own television career started as location manager on *Paradise Beach* and later as the unit publicist for *Pacific Drive*. Being a fan and working behind the scenes has, hopefully, provided me with a unique perspective on this subject.

When working on both those soaps, I was struck by a real sense of family, created by the cast and crew who toiled together for 12 hour days all week and then got together every weekend to party. Not surprisingly, this sense of family often translates to the small screen. Even though television soaps are heightened reality, a rare familiarity and empathy exists within this genre because of the frequency of watching night after night, year after year.

So whether you've been an occasional viewer or a dedicated fan, I hope this book brings back some good memories for you about your favourites. Sadly, many of these shows are languishing in forgotten vaults and deteriorating to the point where it may not be possible to screen them again. Network television sees no value in nostalgia and subscription TV also believes there is no audience for our classic programs. By buying this book, I think you've just proved them wrong, and hopefully we might see all these soaps, good and bad, back on our screens soon.

Andrew Mercado

AUTUMN AFFAIR

PREMIERE: **1958** EPISODES: **156** NETWORK: **SEVEN** FINALE: **1959**

Meg (Janette Craig) admires Steve's (Leonard Bullen) weapons.

When television in Australia started transmitting in 1956, the Seven Network was the first commercial station to make drama a priority. Based at ATN studios in Sydney, and under the leadership of General Manager James Oswin, their first in-house soap was on air within two years. Produced and directed by David Cahill and written by radio playwright Richard Lane, it was originally to be called *Julia: An Early Autumn Affair*, but the title was shortened before its premiere to just *Autumn Affair*.

As in many other countries, Australian audiences had shown a healthy appetite for radio serials since the 1940s. There had been over 200 of them, including *When a Girl Marries*, *Martin's Corner*, *Crossroads of Life*, *Mary Livingstone MD*, *Hagen's Circus* and the most popular of them all, *Blue Hills*. *Autumn Affair* would owe a lot to these predecessors, particularly since this early production was not much more than a radio soap with pictures.

Autumn Affair began in October 1958, with a voiceover from the central character as she was first seen writing in a notebook and thinking out aloud…

'I'm writing it all down just as it happened. I think of it as an early autumn affair, first because that was the season when it all began, but very soon I began to see this accident of season as something significant. I, Julia Parrish, am now 43, the early autumn time of life, the season of pastel shades, quiet memories, or so I said to myself, but now I don't know. Looking back on what has already happened it could be that this was the most important time of my whole life. The bewildering sequence of events that have turned my life from a quiet sheltered stream into a racing torrent began when Mark arrived back from his overseas trip. The happiness I always knew at seeing him again after such an absence was there as Mark's plane touched down, but the moment I had driven him from the airport to my home the old problems started again...'

Julia Parrish (Muriel Steinbeck) was a successful authoress who had been widowed for fifteen years when the tangled story began. For the last seven years, she had been dating businessman Mark (John Juson), which seemed to involve smoking many cigarettes and drinking cocktails. Sex, apparently, was a no-no, or at the very least, not talked about in public.

Julia's modelling daughter Meg (Janette Craig) was well-known enough to worry about her reputation – like, what if she was seen in the same outfit twice in the social pages! Consequently she was often disappearing to 'change outfits', in what was a precursor for the fashion-mad divas of 80s soaps such as *Sons and Daughters* and *Return to Eden*.

Julia's life was turned upside down when photographer Steve Meadows (Leonard Bullen) took snaps of her for an article he was doing on women in the arts. Her secretary Julie (Diana Perryman) was quick to note that Steve was 'attractive' and so did fashionable daughter Meg, who quickly found a reason to visit Steve when her mother chose to go off on a country drive with psychiatrist Larry Muir (Owen Weingott).

So began the tortured romantic storylines as Julia's Irish housekeeper (Queenie Ashton) let it be known that she didn't approve of such goings-on, particularly after a neglected Mark flew back to England. Later, Steve announced he wanted to marry Julia, and Larry became 'violent' at the news, which probably meant he slammed his drink down onto the bar instead of placing it there gently. But not *too* hard, or the primitive set might have collapsed onto him.

Not only were the sets basic by today's standards, they were also somewhat politically incorrect. To illustrate that Steve Meadows was successful and suave, an entire wall of his lounge room was devoted to a display of guns, mounted from ceiling to floor. Outside everybody's windows were hand-painted landscape backgrounds that, not surprisingly, looked a little fake. However, they were no less convincing than the dreadful full-colour photographs that would populate the backgrounds of Aussie soaps for years afterwards.

Autumn Affair screened just three times a week at 8.45 in the morning. It was undemanding viewing for housewives as the action was propelled mostly via two-way telephone conversations. And long conversations at that. In his book, *The Golden Age of Australian Radio Drama*, writer Richard Lane explained that 'Muriel had to learn many, many words each week' since 'she was in every episode'. Muriel herself admitted that the marathon sessions required to film three episodes in one day took their toll. 'My dear, it nearly killed me!' Although not once, Lane noted, did her good demeanour falter. Chosen because of her 'mature beauty, her intelligence and her charm, as well as her acting background', Steinbeck turned out to be 'a very happy choice'.

Queenie Ashton's role was less demanding, allowing the already veteran actress to do double duty on both *Autumn Affair* and *Blue Hills*. Ashton originally appeared in the ABC Radio serial playing doctor's wife Mrs Gordon. After being written out, Ashton was helping new actors audition by reading the part of a still-uncast new character, Granny Bishop. Writer Gwen Meredith decided she was perfect for the 86-year-old Granny character, even though Ashton was a good 40 years younger at the time. Long after *Autumn Affair* had disappeared off screens, Ashton was still playing Granny on the radio, and she even uttered the final lines of dialogue when Australia's best-known radio soap finally ended in 1976: 'We don't have to see or hear people every day of the week to remember them in their surroundings. It isn't really so hard to say goodbye … and God bless!'

After saying goodbye to *Autumn Affair*, several actors admitted that they had received little or no direction on their first television production. Their enthusiasm for the new medium was quite obvious, even when viewed today. Perhaps it was the dialogue that kept the show lively ('You're in a gay mood!' 'Oh, it's the silly season – autumn'), more likely it was the thrill of doing it all for the very first time.

As a first drama effort, *Autumn Affair* was an 'experimental investment' as Seven hoped the soap might get itself a sponsor. It didn't, but Shell's

Julia (Muriel Steinbeck) began each episode by writing in her journal.

London office was impressed enough to fork over some dollars for a future anthology series for the network based on what they had done with *Autumn Affair*. It was also a major training ground for the crew, still trying to figure out the unfamiliar equipment. They quickly learned that the primitive cameras, for example, got so hot they had to be switched off and allowed to cool down between takes.

Autumn Affair ended after 156 episodes and Seven immediately began planning their next morning serial, to be called *The Story of Peter Grey*. It had been a start and nothing to be embarrassed about, even today. It was also a valuable learning experience for the fledgling network, which would continue to be at the forefront of soaps and drama for many years to come.

THE STORY OF PETER GREY

PREMIERE: **1961** EPISODES: **164** NETWORK: **SEVEN** FINALE: **1962**

Peter (James Condon) encourages two parishioners to light up.

After *Autumn Affair* finished, Seven were already at work on a replacement morning soap to be called *The Story of Peter Grey*. This time the action, if you could call it that, centred on a church minister. Written by Kay Keavney, the serial was produced and directed by Ken Hannam, who would go on to make the seminal Australian movie *Sunday Too Far Away* with Jack Thompson.

Clergyman Peter Grey (James Condon) had a 'neurotic, haunted, yet loving wife' called Brenda (Lynne Murphy) who made sure her husband always had a good cup of tea and lovely sandwiches cut into triangles. She talked about her mother, worried about her mother and lied about writing letters to her mother.

Friend Jane Marner (Diana Perryman) was being wooed by Tony Beaumont (Walter Sullivan) who was very suave, and such an important businessman he had two phones on his desk. He appeared to work at Circular Quay, pre Sydney Opera House, and got himself into trouble when he referred to Jane as 'My dear Louise'. This 'slip of the tongue' did not go down too well, giving Jane an excuse to stare wistfully into the distance and wonder who Louise was. Anne Vail (Moya O'Sullivan) looked after Peter Grey when his wife was off visiting her mother, and she

 SCHOOL/UNI
 SEX & SIN
 PERIOD
 MEDICAL
 POLICE
 HOLIDAY
 GAOL
 RICH
 SUBURBIA
 SHOP
 LEGAL
 RURAL
 NUDITY
 TV STATION

kept the triangular sandwiches coming and the cigarettes lit, sometimes devouring both at the same time. She also eavesdropped when Peter was called upon to help out 'new Australian' Paul (Robert McDarra) when the migrant needed help with his love life and proper use of the English language.

Each episode of *The Story of Peter Grey* never seemed to have more than four characters who moved listlessly around sets constructed by Cul Cullen (before he started acting in *The Box*). It plodded along for 164 episodes and the most interesting thing about it today is the credits. Frocks were by Horrockses Fashions and foundation garments by Berlei. You could certainly tell Jane was outfitted in one hell of a girdle, if not a pair of control pants as well, to give her that controlled hips look.

Since times were still innocent for this soap, it's fun noting the change James Condon would go through in the following decade. In 1974, he would return to the genre in the *Number 96* movie, playing a randy politician, Nick Brent, who ended up marrying resident agony tart Vera Collins after his bikie son had raped her. Despite Vera's past, the movie would end with him becoming prime minister. Perhaps the voters forgave him because he had been a churchman first.

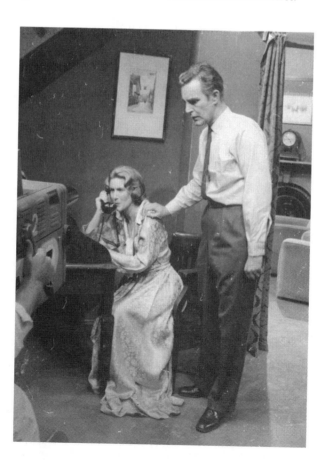

Peter tries (unsuccessfully) to get wife Brenda (Lynne Murphy) off the phone.

BELLBIRD

PREMIERE: **1967** EPISODES: **1697** NETWORK: **ABC** FINALE: **1977**

In the pub. L-R: Quinney (Maurie Fields), Mary (Beverley Dunn), Joe (Terry Norris), Olive (Moira Carleton), Colonel Emerson (Carl Bleazby) and Marge (Carmel Millhouse).

Australia's national broadcaster, the ABC, had already proved it could create a successful serial – at least on radio. *Blue Hills*, first known as *The Lawsons*, began on 23 February 1944 and aired at 1pm for farmers to eat their lunch to. Before too long it was being repeated at 6.45pm so city folk could listen in when they returned home from work. While it was originally created to impart thinly-veiled government messages about new farming techniques, the personal dramas of the Lawson family (John, Eileen and teenager daughter Sue) soon took over and radio's longest running soap had been born.

When *The Lawsons* morphed into *Blue Hills* in 1949, new characters were introduced to broaden the show's scope, including Jack (Peter Whitford, then John Ewart), Granny (Queenie Ashton), Mabel (Hilda Scurr), Meg (Ethel Lang), Fleur (Julianna Allan), Old Davey (Max Osbiston), cook Hilda (Nellie Lamport) and niece Emmy (Gwen Plumb). Writer Gwen Meredith wrote every one of the 5,795 episodes, and the serial only stopped when she decided to retire. It was last heard on 30 September 1976.

With the advent of television, ABC-TV had started off by adapting old stage plays for the new medium. Then ex-BBC man David Goddard was hired as Head of Drama, and when market research indicated that a serial would help increase audience figures in the early evening, *Bellbird* was commissioned as a lead-in for the 7pm national news bulletin. Four 15-minute episodes, in black and white, were to be screened at 6.40pm, Mondays to Thursdays.

With the popularity of *Blue Hills* on radio, it was decided that the first ABC-TV serial should also have a rural setting. Author Colin Free based the concept on an enclosed community like the Megalong Valley. He called it *Bellbird* after he heard the familiar 'ting ting' of the bellbirds near his home in the Blue Mountains.

Bellbird was fictionally situated on the Weewrang River, 200 miles from Melbourne (with the show's opening credits being filmed in Daylesford, Victoria). The television country town had a population of about 3,500. There was a shopping arcade (with 'Ye Olde Coffee Shop' at its entrance), a 'boutique', a railway station, a bowling green, a football oval, a showground, a drive-in, a golf course and just one licensed hotel. It was the sort of place where you could leave the house unlocked if you needed to pop out for a visit.

When it all started on 28 August 1967, *TV Times* described it as a 'typical Australian country town', in other words, a place where gossip could make or break you. Top of the busybodies' list of targets was librarian Lori Chandler (Elspeth Ballantyne), a descendant of one of the district's original settlers. She lived in a stately eight-bedroom home, Bellbird Station, and it was customary for any schoolteacher (usually a woman) to board with her. There was outrage when the new appointee turned out to be a heartbroken man, Michael Foley (Bruce Barry), and the unmarried Lori still let him stay in her house! There was even more chatter when it was revealed that Michael's first wife had been murdered by one of his students.

Bellbird's most tart, tongue-tied tattler was Mrs Phillips (Joan Macarthur) and next in her line of fire after Lori was sweet blonde Rhoda (Lynette Curran), the teenage daughter of Rose (Dorothy Bradley) and Gil Lang (Keith Eden). Rose was a bit of a snob (she was from Sydney, you see) and Gil was the town solicitor. Rhoda's crime, in Mrs Phillips's short-sighted eyes, was in getting a bit too friendly with crop-dusting pilot Tony Buckland (Clive Winmill).

Meanwhile, Glenda Chan (Anne Lucas) found out that her land, which she thought had been handed down to her by her grandfather, still belonged to the council. Upset, she took an overdose of sleeping tablets. Later, Lori Chandler would discover that her father had never officially deeded it over to 'old Chan', so she insisted Glenda move in with her.

Bellbird was also home to the reclusive, widowed Colonel James Emerson (Carl Bleazby) and wily real estate agent Charlie Cousins (Robin Ramsay). By the end of the first week, Lori was infuriated by his dishonest antics, but within the year she would be engaged to him.

Early critics of the show were outraged at the English accents in the Aussie bush. 'If scriptwriter Barbara Vernon wishes to make good the claim that *Bellbird* is an Australian town, she should set the scene unmistakably by using kangaroos, billabongs, nulla-nullas and other snippets of Australiana,' *TV Times*' F.C. Kennedy wrote after the first couple of weeks. 'In *Bellbird*, most well-educated women speak fluent London shopgirl; upper class men talk suspiciously like Oxford drop-outs and Charlie Cousins, a fair dinkum Aussie con-artist, has the odd habit of ending most sentences with "then" – in the manner of Alf Garnett in *Till Death Us Do Part*.' Kennedy had a point, especially given that the show's first-ever line of dialogue was 'Get away from that car. Cor!' Clearly the ABC's cultural cringe to Britain has a long pedigree.

Bellbird was, F.C. Kennedy concluded, 'a disinfected *Peyton Place* or a *Coronation Street* without slums'. At least one *TV Times* reader agreed that 'the characters are an unlikely lot. A visit to the barber would make them more believable'. Phillip Adams was another unimpressed critic, declaring it 'not so much a drama as a reassuring habit, like thumb-sucking'. He also thought a more appropriate title for the show would be *Plaster Duck*.

Luckily for the ABC, the positive reviews were soon outweighing the negative ones. Mungo MacCallum praised the show for 'presenting country townsfolk of 1967 who can talk fast and grammatically and don't wear bowyangs'. Meanwhile, the cast waded through the reviews and tried to figure out if they were doing the right thing or not. 'Nobody had a clue if *Bellbird* would be a hit,' remembers Elspeth Ballantyne. 'We thought the country people would like it but nobody knew how many of them would actually have television.'

They needn't have worried. It soon became obvious that a veritable army of *Bellbird* devotees was forming and they would spend the next decade endlessly debating and dissecting its merits, not to mention the occasional lapses in social etiquette. Until the show caught hold, however, a few scripting problems had to be sorted out.

After the first 13 weeks had been scripted out of Sydney, the ABC's David Goddard decided to move the writing department to Melbourne. The show's first story editor, Barbara Vernon, had barely finished the first season before suffering a nervous breakdown. 'There was a serious problem with the first scripts because nobody knew how to do it,' remembers James Davern, who directed the pilot and later became the soap's producer. 'There were lots of writers but no continuity.'

Barbara Vernon would eventually recover and go on to write two best-selling novels based on the serial, while all the time denying that she was basing *Bellbird* on her home town of Inverell, New South Wales. She always insisted it was a composite of many towns.

Executive producer Brett Porter hired a new script editor, Janet Kehoe, after Vernon's departure and a completely new set of Melbourne-based writers also came on board. Once again, the show began to fall apart because of continuity problems – they were all writing scripts independently of each other. James Davern discovered one week there was no script for him to direct and, at the request of the ABC, he 'decided to give it a go. I wrote it out in longhand over five days and my wife Philippa typed it out.' When the script was accepted, Davern was asked to write another one. And then *Bellbird*'s second script editor also had a nervous breakdown.

Forced to go into hiatus, David Goddard flew down to Melbourne for crisis meetings. 'He was determined not to see *Bellbird* fail,' recalls Davern, 'and he appointed me as the new script editor. I said, "Just a minute here – the last two have had mental breakdowns. I've got a wife and three kids at home."' Goddard told him if he didn't take the job, production on the show would cease, so Davern went home and told his wife to make sure their medical insurance was up to date. He then tried to figure out how to be a script editor.

'Of all the Melbourne writers, I found six that I thought were pretty good,' says Davern. 'I got them all together and, as a group, we devised the storylines for a week, in synopsis form. One writer then went away to write them all and the following week we all got together for another week of synopses and a different writer started on them. That way, everyone had a five week turnaround, and eventually we started to get it happening.' The first-time writers for television would quickly catch on and continue in the industry for decades, particularly Judith Colquhon, Ray Kollie, Peter Pinne, Don Battye and Oriel Grey.

Davern and the writers started going out on research trips to actual country towns. They talked to farmers to get ideas for *Bellbird* and the hard work began to pay off. At its height, *Bellbird* was said to have 3 million viewers and reach more than 35 per cent of the available audience in Tasmania, Victoria and Queensland. This was all achieved in the early years on a budget of just $4,000 a week.

After its shaky first few months, *Bellbird* returned in 1968. Bad boy Charlie Cousins had become insanely popular but actor Robin Ramsay

The cast circa 1969.

decided to go to Japan to play Fagin in a stage production of *Oliver*. That was the end of any plans to wed Lori (Elspeth Ballantyne), and the press dutifully reported that Charlie Cousins would be gone within nine weeks. Despite the warning, viewers went into shock at what happened next – *Bellbird*'s most infamous moment.

Charlie Cousins slipped while on top of a wheat silo and fell to his death. 'It was dreadful,' actress Lynette Curran told *TV Times*, recounting how she and Elspeth Ballantyne went out on location to watch the stunt. 'We felt silly afterwards because we knew what was going to happen, but when we saw that horrid dummy falling to the ground, we both started to cry, and ended up sobbing our hearts out.'

Viewers also sobbed, unprepared for the first death of a favourite TV drama character. Director Oscar Whitbread filmed the shock sequence with just one camera and then edited it sharply to accentuate the horror. ABC-TV management were concerned it was too frank for the early timeslot. 'I even had an argument with management because they didn't want me to put in a scream,' Whitbread remembers.

The screaming continued after the show aired. Lynette Curran was refused service by an upset shopkeeper in protest, and hundreds wrote in or telephoned to lodge complaints. Actor Robin Ramsay would never live down the incident, and during the initial outcry, scriptwriters briefly considered bringing him back as Charlie's twin brother. Luckily for the show's credibility, Charlie stayed dead.

Instead, along came property owner Max Pearson (Terry McDermott), old Molly Wilson (Stella Lamond, mother of Helen Reddy and Toni Lamond) and Constable Des Davies (Dennis Miller). Des would marry artist and boutique owner Fiona Buckland (Gerda Nicolson) after her brief affair with Duncan Ross (Ken Shorter).

Most memorably, there was also a new 'baddie', cranky John Quinney (Maurie Fields). He was a money-hungry stock and station agent with a controlling interest in the nearby *Riverdale Examiner* newspaper. Quinney didn't show his soft side often, but every now and then viewers were reminded that he had brought up Constable Des, who had been orphaned as a young lad.

Bellbird Hotel was taken over by former cop Jim Bacon (Peter Aanensen) and his wife Marge (Carmel Millhouse) after they won the lottery. Jim was always there with a cold beer and a shoulder to cry on, while Marge ran around trying to get her own way as President of the Women's Action Movement. Other new characters included a clumsy police constable, Steve Kowsowski (David Phillips); a nursing sister, Wendy Robinson (Anne Charleston); a doctor, Liz Sinclair (Margaret Cruickshank) and her spunky younger sister, Anne (Camilla Rountree).

Running the district's boarding house were truck driver Joe Turner (Terry Norris) and his wife Olive (Moira Carleton). Terry Norris had originally popped in to play neurotic handyman Kevin Porter but producers later decided to cast him in a longer-running role as cranky Joe. Pretty soon though, Joe lightened up and became one of the serial's most

Bellbird's most infamous moment – Charlie Cousins slipped while on top of a wheat silo and fell to his death.

An African American soldier on leave from Vietnam upset the locals when he danced 'strenuously' with Rhoda.

popular characters. 'It's something about the air,' Terry Norris said at the time about the mythical town of Bellbird. 'Once over the bridge and you're in Brigadoon.' As Joe became increasingly lovable, he took over the local petrol station but, lovable or not, something continued to bother one viewer – his hat. 'I watch *Bellbird* with avid interest every evening and of all the people and events which make it an interesting serial, one thing stands out like a sore thumb,' a concerned citizen wrote to *TV Times*. 'I am positive that Joe must wear that ubiquitous hat in bed, but does he wear it in his bath? I am willing to bet that he does. I've noticed that he wears it to the breakfast table and also at counter lunches at the Bacons' pub, so I am sure it would be more than he could bear to part from it even for his ablutions.'

Social niceties aside, at least Joe looked the real deal. Some of the others still annoyed F. C. Kennedy when he re-visited the show for *TV Times*. 'Though *Bellbird* purports to be the story of people in an Australian country town, its squatters, policemen, shopkeepers and other rural citizens look and behave like a colony of actors. This leads to such ridiculous spectacles as supposedly horny-handed sons of the soil, dressed in with-it gear straight from a fashionable boutique – cravats, high-heeled boots, trousers with front pockets, long lapelled shirts and flashy gents-jewellery. The ladies of the cast go about *Bellbird* looking like actresses making a screen test – complete with false eye-lashes, after-five make-up and daring neck-and-hemlines.'

While *Bellbird* probably was a little too modern for a small town, its stories were groundbreaking. When Oscar Whitbread returned from England and became the show's new executive producer, he noticed a change in the writers and in the audience. 'Aussies were finally proud of their heritage instead of suppressing it. *Bellbird*'s writers picked up on that. They were proud to be Australians too.'

Top of the to-do list was showing how migrant characters could become part of the community. There had already been Chinese residents (Glenda Chan and family), now it was time to introduce some Germans. August Grossark (Kurt Ludescher) and daughter Ruth (Lynda Keane) arrived and widowed relative Maggie Haesler (Gabrielle Hartley) soon followed. Maggie worked as a secretary, model and interpreter before marrying Colonel Emerson at his property, Namguyah.

Some viewers disliked Maggie's 'exaggerated' German accent and, in 1971, the press luridly reported on a 'death threat' she received. 'I have had obscene suggestions made over the phone before but this time the caller said he intended to kill me,' Hartley told *TV Times*. Other migrants in the community included Italians George (Frank Rich) and Anna Maria O'Lini (Rosie Sturgess) who had a small farm out past the stockyards. Luckily, nobody rang those actors with any death threats.

Eventually, *Bellbird* became the first Australian drama to tackle, as *TV Week* described it, the 'explosive – and sensitive – theme of racism'. An African American soldier on leave from Vietnam (and not, like the rest of his battalion, hanging out in Kings Cross) upset the locals when he danced 'strenuously' with Rhoda. Eventually he had a beer with the local boys, which convinced them he was OK. It was a one-off appearance for actor and dancer Ronne Arnold, but a few years later he would take part in Australian TV's first-ever interracial kiss in *Number 96*.

In 1969, *Bellbird* got an Aboriginal lawyer, Gerry Walters (Bob Maza), and some viewers didn't like the idea of him being married to a white girl. Disturbingly, the most racist letters came from viewers who were described by James Davern as being 'highly educated'. Indeed, even F.C. Kennedy thought the show was grandstanding about issues such as 'The Colour Problem' and 'The New Australian Problem'.

Kennedy also felt the scriptwriters had created 'a very peculiar town inhabited by two sorts of people: Sensitive, articulate, analytical citizens capable of conveying to viewers the private opinions and finer thoughts of the writers, and walking caricatures of lower-class Australians, created for the express purpose of mirroring the writers' contempt for people who do not attend art shows, drink red wine with the beef, or wear cravats after five. This division of its citizens into two sharply defined classes made *Bellbird* a highly unlikely town. The fact that the classes mixed chummily made it even less believable.'

However, Kennedy admitted that the writers' 'crusading spirit' seemed to have been 'dampened by the grim necessity of churning out four episodes a week'. Recent programs had been confined to 'showing the effects of flood, finance and falling prices on a rural community. It may be that this switch to bread-and-butter situations has robbed *Bellbird* of the high drama of yesteryear, but it has made the serial more credible.'

Now filming extensively on location, cast and crew were lucky if they got bread and butter for lunch. 'We went out on location with just a three man crew and a trailer full of batteries because we didn't have a generator,' says producer Oscar Whitbread. 'Catering was an unknown word then, and the ABC accounts department would get up in arms asking why we were having free tea and biscuits!'

Back in the studio, it was also kept to basics, even when a scene called for Colonel Emerson to impress a lady with a sumptuous meal. The budget would only allow for ABC-TV canteen food, leaving the actors struggling to keep straight faces as cold spaghetti bolognaise, a la Channel 2 canteen, was supposed to be a gourmet's delight.

God knows what the actors got to eat if there was a wedding, but *Bellbird* loved to splash out on one every now and then. Dr Liz (Margaret Cruickshank) married stock and station agent Bob Wright (Mark Albiston). Lori Chandler (Elspeth Ballantyne) proved she really was hopeless at picking men when she married conman Tom Grey (Tom Oliver), only to become a 'prison widow' when he was jailed. There was an even more momentous wedding in real life when Dennis Miller married Elspeth Ballantyne. Any *Bellbird* wedding, real or fictional, was swamped by fans.

'The ABC would tell the newspapers where we were going to film the weddings,' remembers Elspeth Ballantyne. 'Then the fans would be out-

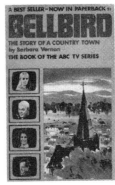

Two spin-off books were written, the second forming the plotline for the *Bellbird* movie.

side the church in droves.' Ballantyne soon learnt that if she was driving from Melbourne to Adelaide to visit family, it was easier to pack her lunch than stop for it at a country town and end up being mobbed.

'Once Dennis Miller and I were sent to Bega to open the Bachelors and Spinsters Ball,' says Ballantyne. 'We were driven through the city in the back of a sports car and I said to Dennis, "Wave to the crowd", and he said he couldn't. I said, "You have to, I'm doing it! Don't do a royal wave, just motion up and down." That night at the ball, Dennis had to dance with 180 spinsters and I had to dance with 180 bachelors and it nearly killed us both.'

Bellbird's younger viewers were also besotted with 21-year-old Gary Gray who played Colonel Emerson's nephew, the leather jacket-clad, motorbike-riding David. Amongst his fan mail was a letter from a convent schoolgirl who told him that, while she and her friends all loved him, 'white socks do nothing for your image. White socks are sissy.' Another woman admitted 'my husband would kill me if he knew I wrote letters to you.' Let's hope she was never caught.

By now, *Bellbird* was said to have an audience of 1.2 million every evening. Indeed, on Friday nights when the show didn't air, ABC-TV was lucky to scrape up half that number. It was such a success in rural areas it was no surprise to learn that the Cairns Water Board advised that water consumption in Far North Queensland fell to nil whenever the show was airing. Given its short running time, even the most elderly fan (and there were plenty) could last the distance without needing a toilet trip. Indeed, *Bellbird* even finished at 6.55pm, giving everyone a five-minute break before the evening news.

TV Times became the unofficial magazine for the show, mostly because it was part owned by the ABC, while *TV Week* ignored most of its goings-on. That left *TV Times* to run a competition where winners won a day on the set and a copy of creator Barbara Vernon's first hardcover book, *Bellbird – the Story of a Country Town*. It was based on *Bellbird*'s first 20 episodes and became such a big seller, it was later re-released in paperback.

It seemed the public were willing to snap up anything *Bellbird* related, even if it wasn't real. When the plot called for a fictional novel to cause a censorship row in the show, a library in South Australia reported that over 50 high school students had requested to see the non-existent book in the hope of finding something 'indecent' to read in it.

A much younger group of children, on an excursion to the set, were traumatised when they saw supposed wowser Mrs Phillips lighting up a cigarette. Actress Joan Macarthur was forced to explain to them that she smoked but her character didn't. When Gil Lang, the town solicitor, was swept away in a flood, a Melbourne child became 'hysterical' on seeing the actor Keith Eden walking down the street and ran screaming to his mother. Gil's drowning was an early end-of-season (and for Australia that meant Christmas) cliffhanger and one viewer didn't appreciate the timing. 'For days after, I felt depressed and miserable, as did most of my family – as though we had lost a beloved friend.' She probably didn't appreciate the irony when *Bellbird* opened a memorial swimming pool in Gil's honour.

Fans were now taking it all very, very seriously. Another *TV Times* reader thought that everybody in her small country town watched it, since if town meetings 'get a bit dull, I only have to say, "What do you think of so-and-so in *Bellbird*?" and wow, people can't talk fast enough. It is amazing what a hold it has on people.'

From Queensland came this cry: 'Since retiring to the Sunshine Coast, I used to have a late afternoon walk, but this is out of the question now as it is the hottest part of the afternoon. By the time it is cool enough to walk, *Bellbird* is on and I have to miss it. Why have this scheme thrust on us when there is already plenty of sunshine?'

And another, after Colonel Emerson wore his gumboots into his (shock, horror) lounge room: 'The Colonel is portrayed as a leader in *Bellbird* society and he should show a better example to the lower strata.' From Lismore came this simple request: 'We enjoy *Bellbird* but please, someone straighten the baize on Mrs Wilson's kitchen shelf.'

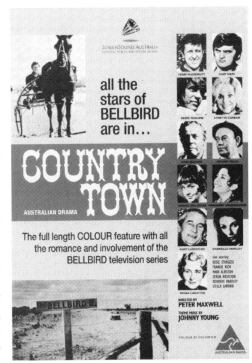

The *Bellbird* movie.

Even the closing credits of the show could upset fans, and not just because they appeared so soon after it started. One viewer complained: 'John Quinney [Maurie Fields] is a hard-headed businessman, not the monster the citizens of *Bellbird* dub him, but the cruellest blow comes with the credits. All members of the cast are mentioned by their Christian names, with the exception of John Quinney who is simply called Quinney. Fifty years ago this type of thing may have been accepted but not today.'

In 1971, creator Barbara Vernon released her second hardcover novel, *A Big Day at Bellbird*. This time, the story was a continuation of the first book and did not follow what had happened on the TV series. However, a portion of the book's plot became the basis for a movie version of *Bellbird* called *Country Town*. The novel was re-released in paperback to tie in with the movie's release.

Without the consent of the ABC, actors Terry McDermott (who played Max Pearson) and Gary Gray (David Emerson) formed Outback Films to make the movie (and ensure they got top billing in the credits). *Country Town* premiered in Mildura on 19 June and made its capital city debut in Brisbane on 21 October. It was received surprisingly well by critics ('Highly enjoyable entertainment for the whole family,' said *The Courier Mail*) but box office takings were dismal in the bigger cities, which were not the audience base for the TV serial.

In the days before colour television, TV series were made into movies so fans could see their favourite characters in colour. Unfortunately, the

TERRY NORRIS as JOE TURNER
in BELLBIRD ABC-TV
6.40 p.m. MONDAY to THURSDAY

BRIAN HANNAN as ROGER
in BELLBIRD   ABC-TV

drab-looking movie version of *Bellbird* was set against the worst drought in the recorded history of the town. Ironically, the filmmakers struggled against unseasonable rain while trying to shoot the film over four weeks in rural Victoria.

Gary Gray left *Bellbird* to promote his film in regional centres but, sadly, *Country Town* failed to turn a profit. Undeterred, Gray tried to get another movie off the ground while his character, David Emerson, was shipped off to what must have been the longest agricultural college course ever, as he didn't return to *Bellbird* for five years.

Meanwhile, Elspeth Ballantyne was asked to return to the TV show she had left to give birth to her first son, Matthew. She was back barely a month when she found herself pregnant again. Producers decided the character of Lori could have a baby and, furthermore, Ballantyne's real-life baby could play the part. 'How Lori got pregnant was a bit of a mystery since her husband was in jail so I guess they must have had an interesting contact visit!' says Ballantyne. 'As for using my own child, I agreed only on the condition that he not be used too often.' After giving birth to Tobias, Ballantyne was horrified when the baby decided he didn't like acting. 'Every time I took him into the studio he would start to scream and it upset me enormously. I immediately gave in my notice and asked them to write me out again as soon as possible. Acting came second to motherhood.'

When *Bellbird* returned to the ABC in 1972, fans were anxiously waiting to see if Rhoda (Lynette Curran) was going to get married again. Her first (shotgun) marriage to Ron Wilson (Sean Scully) had ended in divorce after the birth of baby Jo-Liz (no wonder they split up if they gave names to their kids like that), but now Rhoda was getting hitched to journalist Roger Green (Brian Hannan). Despite their wedding breakfast being interrupted by a bushfire that eventually burnt down their house, the town and the marriage survived and Rhoda began working with Roger on the local newspaper, *The Clarion*.

Rebel Marcus Lloyd (Christopher Pate) had to leave town after a marijuana scandal, and Joe and Olive Turner's nasty daughter Cheryl (Jill Perryman) arrived to cause some heartache for her poor parents. Actress Jill Perryman was still getting grief from irate fans five years later when she moved to Perth. 'One day a woman in the supermarket came bristling up and told me I should be ashamed of myself for the way I carried on,' she told *TV Times*. 'I was stunned when I realised what was upsetting her. Then I was thrilled. I was in *Bellbird* for only six weeks, and Cheryl is about the only bitch I've ever played.'

Bellbird High now had a new schoolmistress, Elaine Thomas (Julia Blake, real-life wife of Terry Norris, who played Joe) and a new English teacher, Adam Lockhart (Bryon Williams). Fifteen-year-old orphan and pupil Sally Morris (Marilyn Vernon) had a crush on Mr Lockhart but Adam was in town to woo his former girlfriend, nurse Wendy (Anne Charleston). The reignited romance didn't please Bernie Austin (Syd Conabere) who had fallen in love with Wendy himself. Love was also in the air for widow Rose Lang who was moving on from the sudden death of Gil by dating writer Ian Bennett (Brian James). And Joe Turner's look-alike brother turned up (in a dual role from Terry Norris), which confused poor Olive terribly.

In April, 52 episodes were sold to Thames Television for daytime viewing in the London viewing area only. Thames asked for more, with an eye to expanding it throughout the UK. Supposedly, Actors Equity intervened in the next set of negotiations and insisted the ABC jack up the price to include residuals for the actors. This was all done without the knowledge of the cast, who were later furious to discover that the increase in cost had caused Thames Television to pass on buying any more episodes. 'We all felt it was more important to get the show onto the world stage rather than haggle over prices,' Alan Hopgood (Dr Matthew) says. '*Bellbird* could have been a forerunner to *Neighbours*.'

For *Bellbird*, it was back to doing what it did best for its Aussie audience – gossip, weddings and the rural recession – while still acknowledging that times were changing. *Listener In-TV* magazine asked in August 1973: 'Brawling bikies … illicit love … divorce … and now kidnap, all on one TV show! *Number 96*? No, *Bellbird*.' Yes, things were hotting up in *Bellbird* but everything was still suitable for the family timeslot.

New doctor Matthew Reed (Alan Hopgood) was having an illicit affair with Maggie (Gabrielle Hartley) who, desperate to have a baby, resorted to kidnapping one from an unmarried girl. Out on the Coonah farm, Leo Hill (John Stanton) was forced to turn his family farm into a piggery, insisting that younger brother Terry (Ross Thompson) get a job at the abattoir. Unhappy, Terry joined the Stoneyvale bikie gang which led to the wrecking of Quinney's new sawmill.

So realistic was the 'vandalisation' filmed on location at Gembrook that a neighbour phoned in a complaint and a police riot squad was sent racing down from Melbourne before a local cop discovered it was just *Bellbird*. When the episode aired, the ABC was bombarded with protests about the bikies getting away without being punished. What they thought of the sexy Abigail Crane (Natalie Mosco) getting hooked on drugs is probably unprintable.

Leo and Terry fought over the affections of Ginny Campbell (Penne Hackforth-Jones) who lived on the neighbouring farm, but it was Leo who married her in the 1972 Christmas finale. Within a few weeks of the show returning in 1973, he had been killed when a tractor rolled on him. Happier times were ahead though, as *Bellbird*, and Australian TV, were about to get their first ever birth and, a few weeks later, 1,000th episode of drama. It was now being watched by nearly 2 million viewers.

In April, Constable Des (Dennis Miller) and Fiona Davies (Gerda Nicolson) had their long-awaited baby, and it was the first childbirth filmed for an Australian television drama. The filming, which took place at Dandenong and District Hospital, was only possible because of a recent change in the Victorian child welfare laws. On a previous occasion, a crew had travelled interstate to film a sequence involving another infant.

'Brawling bikies … illicit love … divorce … and now kidnap, all on one TV show! Number 96? No, Bellbird.'

Molly (Stella Lamond, mother of Toni Lamond and Helen Reddy) and Rhoda (Lynette Curran).

In June, the 1,000th episode aired during a gala 'Back to *Bellbird*' week. There were lots of returning favourites, like Max Pearson (last seen heading off to a horse stud in Western Australia), Lori Chandler (now living in the city) and David Emerson (finally graduating from that farm school). Even actor Robin Ramsay, whose character Charlie had fallen off the silo years earlier, returned to play a new role as a pageant director. The reunion also included a parade and cabaret at the Mitchell homestead. Only a royal visit could have been bigger.

Sadly, just a few weeks later, actress Stella Lamond died at her Melbourne home. Most of the cast and crew from *Bellbird* attended her funeral and the ABC provided a police escort to the service and the cemetery. Daughter Toni Lamond, in her autobiography *First Half*, admitted that her mother, supporting a sick husband who suffered from uncontrollable rages, 'had long since retreated into alcoholism but was functional. *Bellbird* was what gave her a reason to get up in the morning.'

During the show's previous Christmas break, 16-year-old actress Louise Philip had been paralysed from the waist down as a result of a car accident outside Wagga. Coincidentally, Terry Norris was doing a personal appearance in the same town. 'I got a message that someone from the *Bellbird* cast had just been brought to the Wagga Base Hospital,' Norris remembers. 'I was still in Joe's costume with the hat and moustache and I dashed to the hospital just as she was being told she'd broken her back and would never walk again. It was one of the most tragic reunions ever. Seeing her as she was then, I could not have imagined she would go on to re-establish her career the way she did, with such determination and courage.'

In September 1973, Louise Philip returned triumphantly to *Bellbird* playing the same character, Christine Jackson, who was also now in a wheelchair. When Joe (Terry Norris) and Olive Turner heard that Christine, previously their ward of the state, had been paralysed, they visited her in hospital and brought her back to their home for a two-week visit. Louise Philip would return to the show full-time the following year, and be reunited again with Terry Norris on *Cop Shop* from 1977, where they played father and daughter for many years.

As *Bellbird* moved into 1974, some cast regulars tired of the grind and asked to be written out of the show. Rhoda (Lynette Curran) had the most tragic exit when she ended up under a train at a level crossing, but within a couple of months, Constable Des (Dennis Miller), Fiona (Gerda Nicolson), Terry (Ross Thompson), Maggie (Gabrielle Hartley) and Rose (Dorothy Bradley) all left. To replace them, back came widow Ginny (now played by Brenda Addie) from overseas, while the Colonel got himself a new Irish housekeeper (*Coronation Street*'s Sandra Gough).

As 1975 rolled around and the show began filming in colour, *Bellbird* was still 'honest, clean and wholesome', but the raunchier antics of commercial TV's soaps were getting much better ratings in the capital cities – except in Hobart, where *Bellbird* rated higher (43 share) than *Number 96* (33). The ABC serial tried to get some sexy stars out on the farm and *Number 96*'s Abigail came close to signing as a guest love interest for John Quinney (Maurie Fields). Instead, Abigail made a disastrous decision to do *Class of '75*, and *Bellbird* had to settle for *The Box*'s Helen Hemingway as Quinney's businesswoman niece, Caroline.

There was a new constable, George Cooper (Warwick Randall); a rough-and-ready career woman, Harriet Downs (Marion Edward); farmer Robbie Campbell (Bruce Kilpatrick) and his mother Mary Campbell (Beverley Dunn), who would go on to marry the Colonel. Doctor Matthew Reed (Alan Hopgood) was shocked when his estranged wife Georgina Moorhouse (Maggie Millar) reappeared to patch up their marriage. Georgina was also a doctor and they would later share a clinic and a receptionist, paraplegic Christine Jackson (Louise Philip).

Radical Ritchie Bates (Peter Dahlsen) started work at *The Clarion* with Roger Green, and bikie Mike Cochran (Stewart Faichney) cleaned up his act, particularly when brother Jerry (George Mallaby) arrived. *Bellbird*'s big wedding that year was between the Colonel's latest housekeeper, Kate Murray (Anne Phelan) and police sergeant Russell Ashwood (Ian Smith).

Nineteen seventy-six got off to a shock start with a camping holiday that nearly ended in death for the Turners (Terry Norris and Moira Carleton) and the Quinneys (Maurie Fields and Margaret Reid) when they almost drove over a precipice on a narrow mountain road. The Colonel was struggling to keep new manager Chris Lang (Gregory Ross) in line, while Scott Leighton (Rod Mullinar) was floored to see Claire (Briony Behets) in town. Jim Bacon and John Quinney teamed up to open a Friday night cabaret at the Bellbird pub, and David Emerson (Gary Gray) was elected to Federal Parliament.

While bikies and radicals were always good for a bit of generation-gap drama, an unconventional new Catholic priest was too much for some viewers. Fr John Kramer (Mike Preston) gave a sermon about the differing attitudes between drinkers and drug users, which saw young people being condemned for smoking marijuana, while the older citizens of town were potential murderers every night while driving home drunk. 'I know *Bellbird* is fiction, but I cannot understand how the scriptwriter and the producer failed to realise that the episodes shown on March 8 and 9 would be objectionable to most viewers. I have watched *Bellbird* from the beginning but I will not see it again,' a Terrigal viewer wrote.

Other *Bellbird* fans were also giving up their nightly fixture, so the ABC decided a radical change was in order. In April, they announced that the serial would become a weekly one-hour drama. The regular cast of 14 would be cut in half, but the self-contained episodes would allow for more guest stars. Staying were Joe and Olive Turner, Marge Bacon, Dr Matthew and Dr Georgia, Colonel Emerson and his new wife Mary.

For years, fans had been begging the ABC to lengthen the show from its often-too-short 15-minute running time per episode. One clock-watcher even noted that the show could run two to three minutes short every night, thereby depriving viewers of up to ten minutes of drama every week. Yet the new concept for *Bellbird* was not welcomed by the majority of its viewers.

'My family and I were horrified – to say the least – to learn of *Bellbird*'s change of format. Please, ABC-TV, leave *Bellbird* as it is,' begged an Attadale watcher. Another from Peterborough struggled to stay ladylike. 'I have felt hostile to ABC-TV since they decided to change *Bellbird* and had to scrap two letters I wrote about it, because they would have been unprintable.'

Even the actors were dubious enough to suggest that the proposed changes would lead to the death of the series. 'The success of the show is that it is a meandering story with no climaxes,' former *Bellbird* regular Terry McDermott told *TV Times*. 'Putting it into a one-hour once-a-week format changes the whole nature of the show. I don't think the people who have followed the show for years will stick with it.'

The first one-hour episode screened on 3 August at 6pm and featured Quinney having a heart attack (so actor Maurie Fields could leave the show for 15 weeks to make sitcom *Bobby Dazzler* with John Farnham and fellow *Bellbird* actor Terry Norris). Adam Lockhart (Bryon Williams) was back, but this time as the headmaster of Bellbird High, and he was trying to cope with anti-Semitic feelings about a new Jewish-American exchange teacher (Jillian Archer of singing group 'The Glitter Sisters'). Next, pub-lican Jim Bacon dropped dead, leaving wife Marge to run the Bellbird Hotel with barman Bob (Bob Horsfall). Long-time fans began to get very, very nervous.

Executive producer Patrick Barton told *TV Times*, 'Some people who have been involved with the serial for a long time persist in prophesying doom (about the format change), but we're confident it will go well.' It didn't. Despite the return of the Turners' unpleasant daughter, Cheryl (now being played by Lesley Baker), and the arrival of a new migrant family, the Lusics (David Ravenswood and Jennifer Hagan), the show continued to slip. After 40,000 viewer protests, the ABC capitulated and decided to move the show to the later timeslot of 6.30pm for 1977, and air *Bellbird* in three half-hour episodes each week.

As the show's 10th anniversary approached, new executive producer Keith Wilkes refuted suggestions that the ABC undervalued the show. 'The fact that the serial is being extended, getting a bigger budget and going back to three evenings a week, shows the faith the commission has in it.' An English migrant couple who had been involved in a recent '*Bellbird* gets flooded again' episode, Cliff (John Murphy) and Janet Sutton (Felicity Gordon), were going to stay around as regulars and guest stars would include Terry Donovan and Alwyn Kurts.

After 40,000 viewer protests, the ABC capitulated and decided to move the show.

The first three-parter aired at 6.30pm on 1 March 1977, and involved Cliff Sutton's runaway tractor. But Maggie Millar (who played Dr Georgia) was worried about the constant timeslot changes. 'People watch the show because they regard the characters as friends, but suddenly it's a whole new ball game with people viewers don't know doing extraordinary things. In my opinion, the ABC doesn't take enough notice of country viewers. The city ratings for *Bellbird* are laughable but if they took the country ratings it would be one of the top-rating shows in the country.'

Brian Hannan (who played Roger Green) agreed the show was still an enigma to viewers in the capital cities, but insisted it didn't deserve derision. 'People joke about the quality of *Bellbird* but, in fact, it is notably high. The shows which have relied on sex and violence have blown themselves out. They are under the hammer while *Bellbird*, with its slice of everyday lifestyle, continues on. There have been times when I felt the show could be more controversial and there have been times when it has strayed off into drunks or bikies or something like that, but it soon comes back on the course the viewers want.'

In a bid to recover the lost youth audience, *Bellbird* needed to do something a bit more hip, so in came some hippies. A commune on the outskirts of town was supposedly going to 'shock many of the older towns-people with its free and easy lifestyle'. In came commune chicks Linda Rodin (Barbara Llewellyn) and Kelly Jameson (Penny Downie), as well as an itinerant family, the Carters.

In June, the show celebrated its final wedding as widower Roger Green married new veterinarian Frances Byrne (Laurel Burton). Upon reaching its 10th birthday that August, *TV Times* revealed that most of the actors were still only being paid about $400 per week. And since the show was only on for 30 weeks of the year, its regulars received the grand sum of $12,000 a year salary.

Worse, they were all about to be unemployed. As past and present actors gathered to celebrate the milestone, many realised that they were also at a wake. Within days, it was decided production would finish in November. One cast member said there was a 'stunned silence' after the announcement during a rehearsal afternoon. Maurie Fields (Quinney) told *TV Times*, 'They claim it didn't rate in the city, but I've just returned from Proserpine, where about 90 per cent of people are *Bellbird* fans and I can say it's still as strong as ever in the country.' After the final day of filming, there was only a low-key 'break-up' party at a Melbourne restaurant.

'There were 70,000 letters of protest,' says Alan Hopgood. 'The cast split them up and read them all, then put the best ones forward to ABC management. I don't think they even read them. Someone had decided it had been tying up resources for too long. I think the ABC started *Bellbird* as an experiment and, like Frankenstein's monster, it became bigger than they anticipated.' Terry Norris remembers reading letters from 'light-house keepers, the bishop of Bathurst and a convent of nuns who had altered their prayer times to watch. They were such fantastic letters we even considered publishing an anthology of them.'

On 23 December 1977, the final episode aired, ironically titled 'Time for a Change'. There was one last peace offering for devotees, the surprise reappearance of reformed bikie Mike Cochran (Stewart Faichney, now the host of an ABC-TV sports show). Pulling her last beer at the pub was Marge Bacon, the longest-running character. Actress Carmel Millhouse recalled that it had taken her two years to learn how to pull a beer, and that her worst memory of the show was being trapped in an old gold mine with Quinney after a cave-in. 'That was dreadful,' she told *TV Times*. 'I had to be doused in dirt about six times a day. The script called for me to kill a spider and I am petrified of spiders and snakes. It took six takes of my killing spiders before the director was happy with the scene.'

Bellbird's fans were inconsolable as they poured their hearts out to *TV Times*. 'With neighbours miles away, and no-one to chat to till meal time, *Bellbird* would come on and the men would down their tools,' lamented a South Australian. 'I don't know how I'm going to go through 1978 without *Bellbird*,' wondered a Queensland viewer. 'It was the highlight of my day; the best program TV has ever produced.'

Within a few months of the show ending, Moira Carleton (Olive Turner) died, and many blamed the death of *Bellbird* for the death of the veteran actress. 'Moira had suffered a lot of ill health over the years,' remembers Terry Norris. 'Yes, she was a chronic asthmatic with a pacemaker who also suffered from arthritis, but she also used to say, "This show keeps me alive Terry!" In a way, Moira ceased to have any reason to keep going when *Bellbird* finished. Moira was at least 25 years older than me but she was never a complainer. She was a trouper of the first order, a real professional.'

Bellbird is remembered today as the first truly popular Australian soap and proved to be an invaluable training ground for writers and directors, just as the ABC had always intended. Many of the actors went on to work for years afterwards, even some who didn't speak a word of dialogue. Before *The Sullivans*, Andrew McFarlane's first television role was as an extra in the Bacons' pub.

Bellbird's first director, James Davern, was inspired enough by the ABC serial to remake it, somewhat, as *A Country Practice* in 1981. It became such a hit, particularly with city viewers, that another rural serial was mooted. In 1983 former *Mike Walsh Show* producer David Price revealed his plans for a grand soap based on the radio serial that had inspired *Bellbird*. *Blue Hills* never made it to the pilot stage, but *Bellbird* was re-made, in a manner, as *Something in the Air* at the turn of the century.

Before, during and after *Bellbird*, actor Alan Hopgood (Dr Matthew Reed) wrote plays (*And The Big Men Fly*), movies (*Alvin Purple*) and continued to act (in *Prisoner* and *Neighbours*). Having been one of the original scriptwriters who planned the serial back in 1967, along with Barbara Vernon, Michael Wright and Jeff Underhill, it was perhaps no surprise that Hopgood would revisit it over three decades later.

In 2003, Alan Hopgood decided to write a play set in the mythical town that fans had never forgotten. *Back to Bellbird* opened at the

Local cop Russell
(Ian Smith before
Neighbours) marries
Kate (Anne Phelan
before *Prisoner*) as
Joe (Terry Norris)
grabs some bubbly.

Kingston Arts Centre in August and alongside Dr Matthew for the two-hander play was his wife Dr Georgia Moorhouse (Maggie Millar).

Twenty-six years after the last episode, the (still squabbling) pair had left their medical practice in Melbourne to put their country home onto the market. 'Georgia has become very aware of how the rural crisis is affecting Bellbird so she's coming back, ostensibly to sell the house, but in actual fact she's planning to rescue the town,' Hopgood told *The Age*. The play was well received and Hopgood and Millar hope to tour it in regional centres throughout Australia where *Bellbird*'s fan base still remembers the show fondly.

In all, 1,697 episodes had been made of varying length (1–1,508 as 15-minute shows, 1,509–1,562 as one-hour episodes and 1,563–1,697 as 30-minute shows). Sadly, the ABC erased over eight years worth of *Bellbird*. 'All these years later, wherever I go, *Bellbird* follows me,' says Hopgood. 'And yet the ABC taped over the master tapes. They never seemed to realise what a national institution it was.' Terry Norris agrees – 'It is a blot on the historical records of Australian television that eight years is gone forever.' All that remains of Australia's first big soap is the final two years of colour episodes and its unauthorised film spin-off, *Country Town*.

'The ABC thought every Australian's dream was to live in the great outdoors and that it'd be urban dwellers who would watch *Bellbird* and dream of living in a country town,' says Terry Norris. 'Instead, city people could have taken it or left it. It was the country folk who loved watching us because we were depicting their lives.'

4

MOTEL

PREMIERE: **1968** EPISODES: **132** NETWORK: **SEVEN** FINALE: **1969**

Politician Paul Drennan (Brian James) has an affair with secretary Liz (Gaye Anderson).

In 1968, the Seven Network decided to try and make its own version of British soap *Crossroads*, which was set in a motel. Since *Crossroads* hadn't been seen in Australia, *TV Times* tried to explain to its readers that it would be 'the Australian *Peyton Place*', referring to the then popular night-time fixture on Nine. Despite Seven pulling 'a shroud of secrecy over the series', the magazine was able to reveal that there would be a regular cast of 16 players and nine full-scale sets, including a minister's office in Canberra. 'A high budget has been allocated for the series and the series should get an "adults only" label despite its daytime slot, due to its earthy nature. The first of the five half-hour episodes already completed concerns an eminent politician who acts indiscreetly by taking his secretary to the motel.'

Richard Lane, who had been responsible for Seven's first daytime soap, *Autumn Affair*, and had also just penned the very controversial *You Can't See Round Corners* (in which Ken Shorter had put his hand up Rowena Wallace's skirt), headed up a group of writers for the new serial. *Motel*'s producer was Graham McPherson and its first director Kevin Burston, both of whom were already working on Seven's big daytime talk-show hit, *Beauty and the Beast*.

Produced at ATN Sydney, Australia's first half-hour serial should have been a huge improvement, production-wise, over Seven's first two soaps nearly a decade earlier. Yet the early camerawork in *Motel* was even shakier and more unfocused than either *Autumn Affair* or *The Story of Peter Grey*. One improvement, though, was the use of location filming to move the action outdoors. And its storylines were much more adventurous than the earlier serials. A whiff of scandal would always be in the breeze at this highway motel just outside Canberra.

Greenfields Motel was run by the Gillian family. At the reception desk were 'weak but likable' Hal (Walter Sullivan) and his 'strong but lovable' wife Mary (Brenda Senders). Both were always ready with fake smiles plastered across their faces and oh-so-pukka British accents, but away from the desk, they had their hands full dealing with a brood of troublesome children.

Eldest son Rod (Noel Trevarthen) ran a Sydney advertising company but was financially dependent on his wanton wife Gaye (Jill Forster), who slinked around with a memorably high 60s hairdo while bundled up in fur coats and sports cars. Press

Rod (Noel Trevarthen) and wanton wife Gaye (Jill Forster) with her father (Tony Bazell).

kits trumpeted her as 'a model-like beauty but a bitchy, vicious wife who is frequently and blatantly unfaithful to her husband and who is always seeking the high life and pleasure'. This drove her neglected husband to turn his attention to migrant and motel maid Maria (Margot Reid), probably because her hair required minimal attention. When Gaye found out about the stolen kisses, though, she behaved as all good soap bitches would – by being as vile as possible to her rival.

Eldest daughter Liz (Gaye Anderson) worked for Government minister Paul Drennan (Brian James) and was kissing him passionately within the first week, even though he was old enough to be her father. Liz, it appeared, liked her men 'distinguished'. Her sister Sue (Janne Walmsley) lived nearby as the wife of the local chemist. This husband was played by Jack Thompson and *Motel* was the legendary actor's first regular television role. Thompson only got the part after producers told him he needed to get a haircut first.

But it was the Gillians' youngest son Chris (Gregory Ross) who kicked the series off in dramatic style by hanging out with the local hoons led by the leather-jacket-wearing Bruce Jackson (Harold Hopkins). Other regulars in *Motel* included Hal's golfing pal Tony Cranwell (Allan Lander), who was the district's property-owning playboy; motel worker Janie (Maggi Gray); motel chain owner Alec Evans (John Faassen); the local church minister (Ross Higgins) and vet Andy Maxwell (Stuart Finch).

The breakout character, however, turned out to be the oldest person in town. Bunty Creighton was the 'grand old lady of the district' and was played by 80-year-old Enid Lorimer (a veteran of Aussie radio serials and best remembered as the doc's wife in *Doctor Mac*). 'I'm horrible!' Lorimer enthusiastically told *TV Week*, which reviewed her character as 'a fair-dinkum tartar – acid tongued, straight-shooting, opinionated and nosy'. Bunty was based somewhat on the cantankerous Ena Sharples from *Coronation Street*, but in the translation to *Motel* she had become a fourth-generation descendant of 'good convict stock' who could be heard to proclaim that 'No Creighton was ever hanged!' One of the early plotlines revolved around someone trying to kill Bunty, but Enid Lorimer wasn't concerned. 'They can't kill me. I'm under contract,' she told *TV Week* with great satisfaction.

The show began on air at noon on 27 May 1968. *TV Week* was 'yet to see the searing, sordid aspects that *Motel*'s pre-publicity promises' but thought the new show 'should have hooked midday viewers from the word go.' *TV Times* thought that 'any viewer who assesses the production with a critical eye will arrive at the pleasing conclusion that he is watching professionals at work'.

The 'searing, sordid aspects' of *Motel* were mostly restricted to Gaye (Jill Forster), who fell pregnant and was determined to get rid of it, since she was too busy hatching plots with her influential father Mark (Tony Bazell) to destroy migrant Maria and her family. The only other 'sordid' storyline was Paul (Brian James) and Liz's illicit love. As their affair continued, he asked his mentally ill wife for a divorce, but then worried who had started sending him poison pen letters.

TV Week continued to be impressed that Seven was spending 'some real money in catering for afternoon viewers. Sad to think that should it succeed, as I suspect it must, it will probably be given an evening timeslot and the poor old afternoon viewers will once again suffer nothing but the cheapest and least inventive of programs.' By August, however, Seven had moved the program to 1.30pm weekdays to become a lead-in for hit talk show *Beauty and the Beast*. By September, the network was taking the advice of *TV Week* and trying out some episodes in prime time. Several repeat episodes were tried out at 9.30pm on Wednesday and Thursday nights.

At this point, the show's plotlines had Bruce (Harold Hopkins) attempting to force Bunty (Enid Lorimer) to accept his courtship of Janie (Maggi Gray), which resulted in Bunty having a heart attack. Meanwhile Gaye (Jill Forster), astonished and delighted at the sight of Rod (Noel Trevarthen) standing up to her father, had fallen in love with her husband all over again. These developments weren't enough though, up against Graham Kennedy's *In Melbourne Tonight*, and by October, *Motel* was pushed back to 11pm on Wednesday nights only. Unable to secure a decent enough audience in either daytime or night-time, *Motel* became a casualty of a wide-scale production switch Seven made from drama to light variety entertainment.

As ambitious as this soap was, it had missed making much of an impact. Perhaps its opening and closing credits were a stumbling block to viewers, since they must still hold the record for being the longest ever

Gaye (Jill Forster) and 'grand old lady of the district' Bunty Creighton (Enid Lorimer) discuss how high 60s hair can get.

filmed for a soap. Each episode began and ended with a boring drive as a car meandered past golf courses and horses trotting through fields for well over three minutes. Little wonder that *Motel* shut down after just 132 episodes.

After it had finished, Jill Forster said she had never received any mail from viewers who had been disturbed by Gaye's unscrupulous ways. 'They all said they loved her – men and women,' she told *TV Times*. 'I think one can rather underestimate the intelligence of an audience.' In 1970, the glamorous actress was hospitalised with a viral infection and an old co-star from her *Motel* days dropped by. Actor Tony Bazell, who had played her father, caused quite a scene when he tried to get into Forster's hospital room.

'I'm afraid you can't go in,' Forster's real mother told him. 'Jill isn't feeling too well.' 'Dammit, a father has every right to see his daughter,' exclaimed Bazell as he brushed past her. Forster's mother, who had just arrived from Britain and had never seen an episode of *Motel*, was speechless. 'You can imagine Mum's astonishment,' Forster told *TV Times*. 'There she was, confronted by a total stranger who claimed to be my father.' Jill Forster went on to star in many more Aussie soapies, but hopefully her mother watched them and never had such a shock again.

5

NUMBER 96

PREMIERE: **1972** EPISODES: **1218** NETWORK: **TEN** FINALE: **1977**

Diana (Rebecca Gilling) and Jack Sellars (Tom Oliver)
get it on and get it off for the movie.

If *Bellbird*'s mild ratings success signalled there was an audience for a local soap, albeit a wholesome country tale, imagine what might happen if a more ambitious, sexy, city version was told? The sexual revolution was now in full swing and, with a change in government, censorship had been relaxed. Nowhere would this be more noticeable than in the nation's very own lounge rooms, every weeknight at 8.30pm.

In 1971, the Ten Network was considered a poor cousin to the longer-established Nine and Seven networks. Ten's advertising revenue was minimal and they were unable to compete with their rivals when it came to buying new American shows. In sheer desperation, Ten decided to risk everything with a new adults-only, night-time serial. Ten's Sydney program director, Ian Holmes, who had to satisfy the Broadcasting Control Board's order for an increase in Australian drama content, had witnessed the enduring popularity of soap with his programming of *Coronation Street* while working at Nine. Together with director of production Peter Skelton, they approached producers Don Cash and Bill Harmon, who had just made a well-received 13-episode sitcom for Seven called *The Group*.

Holmes wanted the action to be set in a high-rise apartment block in the inner city of Sydney. American born Bill Harmon and softly spoken Englishman Don Cash agreed the content would have to be hard-hitting. Nudity would be an initial drawcard and differentiate it from the competition, and the publicity about it wouldn't hurt either. Cash and Harmon turned to scriptwriter and budding author David Sale to think up all the characters. 'Bill and Don gave me a lavish lunch then showed me the Moncur Street block in Paddington,' says David Sale today. 'They told me I could take it from there and do what I liked.'

Sale was due in London for his first book launch so he wasn't all that interested in the task at hand. He sat down with a bottle of scotch and wrote the basic concept in just three hours, selecting names by jabbing a pin into a phone book. 'I also supplied three pages of plotlines that were still being utilised two years later,' Sale recalls. 'I don't know who I was channelling that night!' He innocently came up with the salacious title because he thought it sounded good. *Number 96* was just about ready to become Australia's most notorious address.

Ten got so excited by the package, they suggested the unthinkable – instead of bi-weekly, they wanted to strip it five nights a week. With *Bellbird* only making one hour of soap a week, the Cash-Harmon creative team were flabbergasted at being asked to do two and a half hours. Cash and Harmon immediately expanded their production team by hiring directors Peter Benardos and Brian Phillis and production co-ordinator Bob Huber to help with the unprecedented workload. Extra script-writers, hired specifically for their comedic talents, joined David Sale, and former *Coronation Street* scriptwriter Johnny Whyte was hired as script controller. Together they began to churn out plotlines.

'Bill Harmon and Don Cash were buccaneers and not afraid to push boundaries of convention back then,' says David Sale today. 'Their synergy made them a totally compatible and complementary twosome. Bill was brash, showbiz and full of chutzpah, with an unerring instinct for spot-on casting and detecting script weaknesses. He was tough and direct but underneath he was a softie who did innumerable good turns in secret.'

'Don Cash was the cool, laid-back numbers man who organised the finance, contracts and schedules. It was Don who originated the system of shooting five episodes at once in the shortest possible time, a system that became standard Aussie soap procedure and still used today. Don's system involved shooting a week's worth of scenes, out of context, in apartment one, then moving on to do the same in the next set. At the end of the week, the footage was all edited together into their correct places in the five episodes. At the time it was revolutionary.'

Sadly, Don Cash died in 1973 of cancer just as the show was hitting the heights of its popularity. 'Don and Bill each had individual skills that made them unbeatable as a team, but after Don died, no other Cash-Harmon productions worked. Bill was lost without him.' Ever the gentleman, Bill Harmon continued to pay Don's widow half the profits Cash-Harmon made for all the years of *Number 96*. 'I always had great respect for both of them and I think it was them giving me absolute freedom at the creative stage that really fired me in coming up with those characters,' says Sale.

'Bill Harmon and Don Cash were buccaneers and not afraid to push boundaries of convention back then,' says David Sale today.

Abigail and Joe Hasham in the first night ad.

Nearly every working actor and actress in Sydney auditioned for the 14 regular characters. Many blithely signed a nudity clause assuming they'd never be asked to strip, especially since no other TV show at the time got away with such flagrant displays. They were all about to receive a nasty shock.

Actress Vivienne Garrett's first meeting with Bill Harmon had been at her NIDA graduation performance. Taken over to supposedly meet the producer, she was humiliated when he (literally) brushed her aside and said, 'Oh no, not her, the good-looking blonde up the back,' referring to fellow graduate Pamela Stephenson. Consequently, when Garrett attended the cattle call for *Number 96*, she was blasé about the audition. 'I guess I must have stuck out from all the others desperate to impress,' Garrett says. More likely, Bill Harmon realised he had finally found his rebellious, wayward teenager, Rose Godolfus, and after a screen test, Garrett was asked to sign up. Unaware of what would come next, the actress put aside her theatre ambitions and joined up.

Number 96 premiered at 8.30pm on 13 March 1972, with full-page newspaper ads proclaiming 'Tonight at 8.30 Television loses its virginity!' Some newspapers refused to run the advertisement and changed the wording to 'Tonight at 8.30 Television loses its innocence!' As it turned out, the outrageous by-line wasn't that far off the mark. From night one, *Number 96* established itself as a controversial taboo-breaker that proved to be years ahead of its time.

The first movie-length episode (three half-hour shows tacked together – and many disgusted viewers did brand it tacky) shocked the nation. Only Sydney viewers got to see horny husband Mark Eastwood (Martin Harris) groping under the skirt of his eight-months pregnant wife Helen (Briony Behets). Everywhere else, the bottom half of the TV screen was blacked out, leading viewers to imagine much worse was going on. After being rejected, Mark popped downstairs to the deli where he saved nice Jewish girl Rose Godolfus (Vivienne Garrett) from being raped by a bikie. Rose repaid Mark's gallantry by sleeping with him. When Helen discovered them in her bed, she ran out in shock, fell down the stairs and lost the baby.

Number 96's first bedroom scene was filmed on a supposedly 'closed set' – that is if you ignored the fact that countless 'executives' were watching the action live on closed-circuit monitors within the building. Vivienne Garrett drew the line at jumping out of bed nude, so producer Bill Harmon suggested the sheet fall away, revealing her breasts. When Garrett tried reasoning with Harmon by telling him she didn't even have big breasts, Harmon responded with, 'They're lovely. They're pear-shaped.' Then, just before they went for a take, he told Martin Harris to 'tweak her nipples'. Harris turned to his co-star in horror, and Garrett didn't hesitate in telling her new boss to 'get real'. 'Those guys would try anything in those days,' says Garrett. 'Today you'd be up for sexual harassment.'

In the end, the nude scene only went to air in Sydney, and was edited out by the time the show was broadcast to the rest of the country a week later. It actually made Vivienne Garrett the first actress to go topless on Australian television, even though most people assume that honour belongs to Abigail.

Despite her history-making moment, Garrett broke her contract within a few months. The staunch feminist was outraged when constant victim Rose was gang-raped by a group of bikies and the script actually called for her to be enjoying it. Garrett asked friend Vince Gil, who was playing the head bikie, if he would support her refusal to do the scene as written. He and the other male actors involved stood by her, and production was halted until a re-write was done. When Garrett asked to be let go from the show, producers agreed, no doubt hoping to replace her with a more willing performer. Rose was married off to a good Jewish boy in 96's first wedding.

Number 96 had a total of eight flats, with two downstairs shops for all the residents to mix in (the delicatessen and a chemist that would soon evolve into a wine bar). A multicultural group was assembled without the slightest hint of cringe. Deli owner Aldo Godolfus (Johnny Lockwood) was Jewish Hungarian. Alf and Lucy Sutcliffe (James Elliott and Elisabeth Kirkby) were English migrants. Alf was a typical 'whingeing Pom' while Lucy quickly became *Number 96*'s long-suffering earth mother. Over the years she went through it all – blindness, suspected breast cancer and a menopausal baby. Her portrayer, Elisabeth Kirkby, went on to become leader of the Australian Democrats in the NSW Legislative Council, forever recognised and proud to be remembered for *Number 96*.

Lucy and Alf's next-door neighbour was the unlucky-in-love, South African born Vera Collins (Elaine Lee). Vera was separated from her alcoholic husband and forced to make ends meet with dressmaking and telling fortunes. Over the years, her tarot cards would warn of impending doom, especially in her own bedroom where she would bed an endless array of disastrous lovers. Sadly, the cards didn't let her know she was going to be raped several times – first by returning husband Harry (Norman Yemm), then by her stepfather who flew all the way over from South Africa, had his way with her, then went straight back home.

Number 96 would always bring onto the canvas any ethnic performer available – there was never a White Australia policy in this show. Just a few weeks after premiering, black American Chad Farrell (Ronne Arnold) was romancing the very white Sonia (Lynn Rainbow). Their cliffhanger smooch was the first interracial kiss filmed for Australian television, a full three years before the Federal Government introduced a Racial Discrimination Act.

Also living in the building were Herb (Ron Shand) and Dorrie Evans (Pat McDonald). They lived in Flat 3 rent-free because they had originally owned a house on the plot of land the building now occupied. Henpecked Herb was the building's caretaker, while Dorrie considered herself the unofficial concierge (or as she pronounced it, 'consurge'). Despite her insatiable busybody ways and constant shrieking, Dorrie would soon become one of the show's most beloved characters.

Vivienne Garrett was the first actress to go topless on Australian television.

Actress Pat McDonald would win the ultimate popularity award in television, the Gold Logie, as well as several Silver Logies for Best Actress. McDonald swore she was never once abused in the street or received an obscene fan letter. Instead, the fans would gush, 'You keep that Herbie under the thumb, don't you?' When the fans ran up to Ron Shand, though, it was: 'How do you put up with the silly bitch?'

Later, Pat McDonald suggested bringing another actress, Bunney Brooke, into the mix. Originally written as a nemesis for Dorrie, Flo Patterson moved into the Evans' flat (with budgerigar Mr Perky) when her own burnt down. She became the perfect comic foil for Dorrie. To the public, in magazine at-home spreads, McDonald and Brooke were simply good friends sharing a house together. It never occurred to anyone that the pair were actually lesbian lovers.

When Pat McDonald won her first Logie for best actress in 1973, she refused to take all the credit. 'When I was singled out I handed the Logie over to its rightful owners, and its home is now the set of *96* in the Channel 10 studios,' she told *Woman's Day*. 'If you watch very closely you can sometimes catch glimpses of it sitting on the set. We leave it there during filming and it's flashed up a couple of times on screen. But I don't feel it's mine. It belongs not to me, but *Number 96* – from the person with the humblest job right up to the top writers and producers. Everyone, little and big, is pulling for the success of the show as a whole – not just for himself or herself.'

Number 96 cast photograph from 1972.

FRONT L-R: Lynn Rainbow, Joe James, Pat McDonald, Abigail, Elisabeth Kirkby, James Elliott, Bettina Welch.

BACK L-R: Briony Behets, Martin Harris, Ron Shand, Robyn Gurney, Joe Hasham, Harry Harris, Elaine Lee.

Pat McDonald's most touching personal moment occurred towards the end of the series' five-year run when an old lady at a charity event asked her how many scenes she had filmed as Dorrie Evans. Pat made a quick calculation. 'Well,' the lady said, 'do you know that you and I have been together in my lounge room over 3,000 times yet I only see my son twice a year?'

Number 96 also introduced the Australian public to an unknown actress with just one name – Abigail (who never revealed her family surname was actually Rogan). Just 23 years old, she played Bev Houghton, who, despite professing to be a modern girl who knew everything about sex, was actually a virgin for the first few months of the show.

Bev would eventually be deflowered by Jack Sellars (Tom Oliver) but only after she convinced him that she and her crippled brother Rod (John Benton) weren't having an incestuous affair. Bev and Rod's childhood alliance was actually a result of the many battles they had with their snooty mother, Claire Houghton (Thelma Scott, who played the title role in *Big Sister*, the first daytime radio serial designed for women in 1942). Later, when both kids were long gone from *Number 96*, Claire would continue to be a recurring character, and one who particularly impressed Dorrie Evans because of her upmarket address in nearby Point Piper.

Abigail became Australia's first fair dinkum sex symbol goddess and she had an immediate impact on thousands of Aussie men and schoolboys. Was it the carefree attitude, her extra long blonde hair or those voluptuous breasts that left viewers still thinking they saw her cavorting stark naked throughout the entire series? In fact, she never did full nudity until after leaving *Number 96*. Such was the power of her appeal, however, that if she did show a flash of bottom or breast, viewers always imagined they had seen much more.

Abigail's popularity was so phenomenal that, for once, the tight-knit cast turned nasty, with some cast members jealous of her popularity and critical of her late arrivals on set and propensity to wear see-through garments. She was 'temporarily written out' of the show for several weeks, and when she returned, was permanently sacked soon after (although Abigail insisted she left to make a movie). To this day, rumours continue about why she was sent packing, but the real story, according to David Sale who was in the office when Bill Harmon fired his biggest star, can finally be told.

Abigail had left a handbag behind in a taxi that contained a roll of undeveloped film that featured her in some very compromising situations. How the photographs got into circulation remains a mystery but the fact that they were doing the rounds was enough for Bill Harmon to decide enough was enough. 'Nobody is indispensable' was a favourite saying of Harmon's, and by getting rid of the show's biggest star he proved he wasn't joking. 'Honey, I can make you walk into a room one night and the next night a different actress can walk out and nobody will care!' yelled Bill Harmon as Abigail withered in her chair.

Australia's first sex symbol, the one and only Abigail.

Abigail's bestselling book cover was shot in front of her lounge room curtains.

Her firing was (literally) front-page news across the country, so viewers were glued to their sets for her final episodes when she returned briefly from Tuesday, 12 June 1973. Bev had now acquired an American husband, Earl Goodman (Richard Lupino) and a couple of weeks later, just as Bill Harmon had threatened, Bev Houghton walked into her bedroom, only to emerge the next night being played by Vicky Raymond (real-life sister of actress Candy Raymond, who was already steaming up *Number 96* as wild child Jill Sheridan). The 24-year-old Vicky was promoted in *Listener In-TV* magazine as having a '37 inch bust, 24 inch waist and 36 inch hips'. She was blonde and sounded similar to her predecessor, but it just wasn't the same. Bev was shot dead six months later in the summer cliffhanger.

'That stoopid broad's gonna end up strippin'!' Bill Harmon predicted and within months, she was. Abigail was treading the boards in a 'bawdy musical romp' called *The Saga of San Peel* at the Barrel Theatre in the red-light district of Kings Cross. Nearly all the cast were nude at some point, but despite playing a puritanical evangelist out to convert all the girls in the Mexican brothel where the play was set, Abigail managed to take a bath on stage. She would emerge from the tub for a full frontal audience flash, twice nightly, six nights a week (and all for a rumoured $800 a week). 'The bubble bath scene is just something I do to wash the Mexican dust off me,' she told *Australian Post* at the time, which also reported that taxi drivers were giving tourists a choice of two Sydney attractions: 'The Opera House or Abigail in the raw?' Abigail would end up back on TV in soap (*Class of '75*, *The Young Doctors*, *Sons and Daughters*, *Neighbours*, *Family and Friends* and *Chances*), rather than washing in it, but Bill Harmon had been proved right, yet again.

Even without Abigail, *Number 96* continued to set new standards on Australian television. The Broadcasting Control Board demanded to watch all episodes before they screened and occasionally ordered cuts. It was the first time in the history of TV they had invoked this power. The Ten Network originally trod lightly with *96* but as the show continued to go from strength to strength, the Board was forced to relax its rules and let the public watch what it wanted to see. Not even stern warnings from church pulpits could halt the show's meteoric rise to the top.

The only time the producers ever felt they overstepped the mark was with a black mass sequence. Vera (Elaine Lee) was trying to give up smoking by going to hypnotherapist Vernon Saville (Peter Reynolds), unaware that he was also a Satanic High Priest called De Como. When he discovered that Vera had psychic powers, and that her neighbour Bev (Abigail) was still a virgin, he realised this pair were the key to his coven's summoning up the devil himself! Consequently, undercover lesbian witch Karen Winters (Toni Lamond) moved in with Bev and began to insinuate herself into Bev and Vera's lives.

For the black mass sequence, Abigail was required to lie nude on an altar and Toni Lamond also needed to be topless. In Lamond's autobiography, *First Half*, she described how her son had advised her to 'lose five kilos' while Abigail had reassured her by saying, 'You've got a better pair than I have.' The dialogue required Lamond and Peter Reynolds to recite the Lord's Prayer backwards, but Lamond refused to memorise the blasphemous dialogue and asked for cue cards instead. 'I felt it was dangerous and that it could attract negative vibrations with which I would prefer not to meddle.'

Actor Peter Reynolds was also uncomfortable about learning the lines, but was told he would have to. Against his better judgement he did, and within two years he had died in a suspicious fire at his home. To make things worse for the superstitious actors, the controversial black mass sequence was filmed in a derelict Redfern church on Friday the 13th. Although Jack Sellars (Tom Oliver) broke in at the last moment to save Bev and Vera, the episode was deemed so close to the bone it only screened uncut in Sydney before being heavily edited everywhere else.

Naturally, the critics of the day hated it all, describing 96 as 'childish tripe', 'unreal' and 'television's most backward step'. F.C. Kennedy from *TV Times* was one of the few who dared to suggest the show had a winning formula. He called it a 'dicey bid to rope in two seemingly incompatible audiences – the sentimentalists who dote on soap opera and the fundamentalists who 'haunt' R certificate movies'. He suggested cutting out the spicy bits and running them later at night as *The Naughty 96s*, which he felt would leave 'the best human-interest drama yet produced in Australia' for an earlier timeslot.

For some viewers, the sexiness was apparently part of a larger conspiracy. One deluded soul wrote to *TV Week* stating, 'I'm certain that programs like this are part of a gigantic Communist plot to take over Australia after all morals have been destroyed. If Mr. Menzies were still Prime Minister I'll bet he would soon put a stop to depravity in television programs.' Menzies was long gone by this stage and Australia's current Prime Minster, Gough Whitlam, was said to be a fan along with wife Margaret, who had gone to school with Pat McDonald. The cast of *Number 96* made it known they were fans of the PM by appearing in political ads for the Labor Party.

Most confronting to critics of the show was when survey after survey revealed *Number 96* was the favourite TV program of teenage and preschool children. Even Abigail was shocked to discover a fan letter from a four year old who had just learned how to write. Whilst kids loved the characters as much as their parents did, there was no denying that an entire generation of Australians learnt about sex much earlier than planned. Day after day, schoolkids were chatting endlessly about what had happened the night before in *Number 96*, and for those forbidden by their parents to watch, there was always at least one kid who could report on events. Other children hid quietly behind couches, determined that what was good enough for Mum and Dad was good enough for them. Sooner or later, every kid found out what a virgin, a knicker snipper and a homosexual were.

In *Number 96*, the homosexual was Don Finlayson (Joe Hasham), and what a positive role model he turned out to be. He was a well-adjusted,

The stars were rushed into recording studios.

upstanding lawyer and the first regular gay character in a TV series anywhere in the world. Breaking down such stereotypes was a priority for *Number 96* producers from day one. Don wasn't a limp-wristed, mincing caricature but a hero who would help out every other character on the show.

By being portrayed as the gay man next door instead of a freak, Don struck a chord with audiences everywhere (even though hundreds of female fans wrote in begging for the chance to turn him straight). Eventually even little old ladies on buses could be heard chatting about his love life, even when he had a live-in relationship with the decidedly camp Dudley Butterfield (Chard Hayward).

Homosexuality wasn't the only taboo being smashed in the nation's living rooms. There was candid exploration of adultery, rape within marriage, domestic violence, drugs, alcoholism, breast cancer, racism, transsexual romance, prostitution and nymphomania. Yet beneath all of this, it was *Number 96*'s characters who really caught on with middle Australia. For all its raunchiness, in some homes three generations of a family would sit down to watch. Thousands were hooked and it became the most popular show ever seen on Australian television up to that point.

The huge gamble paid off handsomely for the Ten Network. In 1972 it recorded a profit of just $100,000. On the strength of *96*, this had risen to $1.5 million within two years. In 1973, *Listener In-TV* reported that each episode of *Number 96* cost $9,500 to make while the regular actors only took home $15,000 a year in salary.

Rival networks were left struggling in the wake of *96*'s extraordinary popularity. To compete with the show's half-hour domination every weeknight at 8.30pm, the Seven Network programmed British comedy repeats while Nine countered with American sitcoms. By mid-1973, Nine was even using Graham Kennedy to give away $20,000 worth of prizes every week if viewers watched their channel instead of the sexy soap. *Number 96* demolished every show in its wake, including *Please Sir, The Odd Couple, $25,000 Great Temptation* and an ill-fated Seven talk show, *J.C. at 8.30*.

Number 96's actors became phenomenally popular. Before the show they were mostly fading vaudeville comics or unknown theatre actors, but from the moment they appeared on the sexy drama, they were superstars. When the entire cast travelled overnight on a train from Sydney to Melbourne to attend the Logies, railway platforms were packed at every country station throughout the night. By the time the train rolled into Melbourne, there were more people waiting at Spencer Street Railway Station than there were to see the Beatles a few years earlier.

Merchandising spun off everywhere. There were nine paperback tie-ins, a lurid Abigail autobiography, and *TV Week* published special commemorative magazines every Christmas to keep up with demand. *Family Circle* published the *Number 96* cookbook with Joe Hasham's favourite Lebanese dishes, Johnny Lockwood's rabbit pie and a *Number 96* iron-on transfer to make your very own T-shirt.

The stars were also rushed into recording studios. Abigail recorded an album with a heavy-breathing, best-selling single, 'Je T'aime'. Pat McDonald and Ron Shand's album was titled *The Old Fashioned Way*, while Norman Yemm, in character as Harry Collins, released a single dedicated to his on-screen wife, 'Darlin' Vera'. Joe Hasham meanwhile nearly got swept out to sea while recording a musical TV special for his album, *New World*. While the magazines and books flew off the shelves, record sales were more patchy, although none ended up in the discount bins more quickly than *Number 96 Party Music*. Meant to cash in on the ill-advised 'disco period' in the show's fading years, even the most devoted fan baulked at buying a cover of 'Shake Your Booty' by Duddles Disco's in-house band, The Executives. Despite the poor record sales, The Executives continued their soap career by recording the theme for *The Young Doctors*, and stuck around as the house band at the hospital watering hole, Bunny's.

Even English gentry stopped by to visit, although newspapers at the time referred to them as royalty. In 1973, the Duke and Duchess of Bedford had cameos playing themselves. What they were doing in Norma's Wine Bar was never quite explained, but it made perfect sense for Amanda (Carol Raye) to recognise them. As well as being Don's aunt, the Baroness Von Pappenburg was the most likely character to belong to the same social strata. The nude portrait of Norma that always hung in the Wine Bar was removed before the special visitors arrived for taping, although the Duchess seemed not to care about such things. 'I'm all for undressing providing it's necessary to the action,' she said. After completing their scene in three takes, *TV Week* reported that they 'piled into a mustard coloured MG and took off at great speed'.

Since the first three years were broadcast in black-and-white, a movie version was rushed out to show fans what it looked like in colour. *Number 96 – The Movie* was filmed during the show's Christmas break in 1973 in eleven days. The budget was rumoured to be just $100,000 and the cast were paid only an extra week's salary (supposedly all of $400 each). The movie was released just in time for school holidays and became a smash hit, due in part to 20-year-old drama student Rebecca Gilling who was seen naked in bedrooms, showers and psychedelic dream sequences. Full-frontal nudity was still unknown on TV in 1974 (it would become ho-hum on the show circa 1977) so Gilling was naked for most of the movie.

If indeed there was a cinema patron who wandered in having never seen the TV show, they sure caught on quick when Vera Collins (Elaine Lee) was pack raped by bikies within the film's first two minutes. Don (Joe Hasham) was also taking advantage of the more liberal cinema censorship, getting naked with his new boyfriend Simon (John Orcsik) and kissing him! The lip-lock, however, was mysteriously excised from the print after the Sydney season. 'One critic said it was only the second homo kiss in screen history after *Sunday, Bloody Sunday*,' says writer David Sale. 'I remember taking my parents to see it in the second week and dreading the kiss scene but they didn't bat an eyelid!'

There was a series of lurid novels.

Number 96 movie ad.

Other happenings in the two-hour movie included Dorrie encountering a bunch of nude fellas in the new sauna in the basement (and her underwear inexplicably falling down throughout much of the film). Aldo's flat caught fire but since this was Australian cinema's cheapest ever blaze, all that got singed was his mattress. Original character Sonia (Lynn Rainbow, by now Tom Oliver's real-life wife) returned only to find her new on-screen husband Duncan (Alistair Smart) was trying to kill her, with the help of evil air hostess Diana (Rebecca Gilling) who was carrying on with Jack Sellars (Tom Oliver) as part of the con.

After a fancy dress party for Dorrie and Herb's 40th wedding anniversary, there was one last outrageous moment for the finale. Vera had discovered that the head bikie who had raped her was actually Tony Brent (Patrick Ward), the son of her new politician boyfriend Nick Brent (James Condon). After he died in Australian cinema's cheapest ever car crash, the movie finished with a tickertape parade. Nick Brent was the newly-elected Australian prime minister, and riding alongside him was his new wife, Vera, despite her chequered past.

Film critic Mike Harris slammed the film in national newspaper *The Australian*, but had to admit that he had never been in a cinema before where every character's first entrance got a roar of approval from the crowd. To this day, *Number 96* remains one of the most profitable Australian films ever made, even though it was shot on 16mm and blown up to 35mm for national release. Never before and never since has such a popular Australian film been released looking so shoddy. When it screens occasionally on television today, there are many moments of political incorrectness for modern audiences to gasp at, but none more so than Claire Houghton's immortal line: 'We all feel as deeply as you do about Aboriginals, just so long as they don't move into Point Piper.'

Number 96 always juxtaposed its melodrama with humour. David Sale's original roster of characters was cleverly developed to be split between heavy and light storylines. While Vera, Bev and Don would be involved in some tragic affair, Dorrie, Herb or Aldo could offset this with a few laughs. Johnny Lockwood referred to it as 'dramatic vaudeville'. Soon, other comic characters such as Arnold Feather (Jeff Kevin); Les Whittaker (Gordon McDougall); Norma Whittaker (Sheila Kennelly); and Edie (Wendy Blacklock) and Reg McDonald (Mike Dorsey), or Mummy and Daddy as they called each other, were introduced. Soon the series was getting more laughs than gasps and while Australian TV remained bereft of situation comedies, the madcap antics of *Number 96* became true comedy classics.

Much of the hilarity sprang from the outrageous script conferences in the Cash-Harmon offices which were situated over a funeral home in North Sydney. Script controller Johnny Whyte insisted upon uniformity amongst all the scriptwriters (who got paid $350 for each 30-minute script and that was pretty good for its day) and instructed them all on signature expressions for each character, including how they were to address one another. Vera Collins referred to everyone as 'darling' while Norma

The controversial Black Mass sequence with Bev (Abigail), naked under the sheet, Satanic priest Vernon Saville (Peter Reynolds), Vera (Elaine Lee) and lesbian witch Karen Winters (Toni Lamond).

Whittaker (who wore a wig while working behind her bar) addressed everybody as 'duckie'. Aldo's wife Roma (Philippa Baker) would say 'This I cannot believe', Les would mutter 'All in good time', while Arnold would say 'If I may be so bold' and 'In point of actual fact'. Meanwhile Bev's mother Claire Houghton (Thelma Scott) would bring any subject to a close by declaring 'Allow me to be the best judge of that!'

Wine Bar chef Dudley talked endlessly about old movies, often asking 'Did you see it, ooh it was ever so good!' Flo Patterson used old wartime lingo such as 'hubba hubba', 'fair crack of the whip' and 'tickety-boo', while Herb summed up everything with 'more or less'. Dorrie Evans, however, was responsible for the show's most remembered expressions and malapropisms. Her wit and wisdom included 'ardamant' instead of adamant, 'bony fido' instead of bona fide, 'beresk' instead of berserk and the much-repeated catchphrase 'Why wasn't I told?' If Herb was sick, he had 'orgasms' running through his body instead of organisms, and when Dorrie had a sore foot, she announced she was off to see a 'pederast'. In the movie, she even referred to her 'last will and testicles'. All became cult sayings and some Aussies still refer to a local gossip as a 'Dorrie'.

Number 96 also established a new rhythm for soap opera. Unlike the commercial-free *Bellbird*, scriptwriters were instructed to plot a mini-cliffhanger for every ad break. A major cliffhanger was saved for the end of every episode and particularly compelling disasters were planned for summer breaks. Years later, the Americans would assume they invented the summer cliffhanger when *Dallas*'s 'Who Shot JR' became a major worldwide obsession.

Number 96's most infamous moments revolved around three notorious villains – the knicker snipper, the hooded rapist and the pantyhose

NUMBER 96
VICKI RAYMOND
as
BEV HOUGHTON

VICKI RAYMOND
SHERMAN in
NUMBER 96

ELAINE LEE IS
VERA COLLINS in
NUMBER 96

JAN ADELE as
TRIXIE O'TOOLE in
NUMBER 96

BETTINA
WELCH as
MAGGIE
CAMERON
in NUMBER 96

strangler. The knicker snipper broke into girls' apartments, rifled through their underwear drawers and cut holes in their panties and bras. Viewers only once glimpsed his hand when it crept out from under the bed of Georgina (Susannah Pigott). Dorrie and Herb's niece was home alone undressing for a shower and, as she peeled off her panties and left them on the floor, the hand slowly crept out from under the bed to snatch them away. It was *Number 96*'s first big whodunit and pubs and clubs across the country had to install TV sets in their bars to keep their punters from going home to find out who it was (it was actually a minor character played by Mark Hashfield, Abigail's then-manager and fiancé).

A hooded rapist also ran amok in the building. Aboriginal hairdresser Miss Rhonda pretended to be an early victim in an effort to drum up publicity for Dudley and Arnold's new hair salon, before being raped for real by the masked man. Played by Justine Saunders, she was the latest in a long line of sex symbols that followed in the wake of Abigail. The indigenous actress had already been raped in many of her early roles, particularly in colonial dramas, but at least in *Number 96* she was playing a modern girl in another taboo-breaking storyline.

Impossible to top though was another lover of ladies' apparel, the pantyhose strangler. With an unknown blonde being killed around the corner (off-screen), and Vera Collins having premonitions of death, the stage was set for the kinkiest villain of them all. Wine Bar waitress Lorelei Wilkinson, whose signature line was 'that would be quite congenial', was probably anything but when she became the first victim. Actress Josephine Knur, who played Lorelei, had been told on her first day of shooting to play dumb, pull her tummy in and keep her chest out. She was outfitted with an uplift bra that added 8 centimetres to her own bust, making the measurement an even 96. After being discovered dead on the Whittakers' couch, Knur went straight into another Cash-Harmon soapie, *The Unisexers*, that was strangled after just 15 episodes.

After nurse Tracy Wilson (Chantal Contouri) survived an attack, the next victim copped it in the 1974 summer cliffhanger episode. This time it was Arnold Feather's wife Patti (Pamela Garrick). The couple had recently married after meeting when Arnold had his leg blown off in the letter bomb blast cliffhanger the year before. Patti was the nurse assigned to help Arnold get used to his artificial leg. Actor Jeff Kevin limped around on the show for a few weeks pretending to have a fake limb, but one day Bill Harmon decided it was slowing down the action, so the peg leg was conveniently forgotten. In a continuing in-joke, the artificial leg was always lying around in the mess that was the Whittakers' flat, and it was last seen being auctioned off for charity, along with a swag of other memorabilia, on a live TV auction after the show had finished. As for Patti Feather, she would be the first resident of *Number 96* to have an on-screen burial.

Finally, Marilyn McDonald (Frances Hargreaves) was alone in the laundromat when a pair of gloved hands holding pantyhose came towards her. 'Oh my God – it's you!' she screamed in a sensational Friday night cliffhanger. On Monday night the killer was finally revealed to be Tracy, who had faked her own attack in order to draw suspicion away from herself. She blithely told police (who had been following her in an undercover sting) that she killed her victims for 'being too nice'. Escaping from police custody, she was dead by the end of the half-hour episode, jumping head first from the top floor flat where boyfriend Andy Marshall (Peter Adams) lived.

It's the bomb blast in the deli, however, that is the series' best-known moment and it only happened in a blind moment of panic. In 1975, producer Bill Harmon sensed the show was in trouble so he threw out 13 weeks worth of completed scripts. All the scriptwriters agreed that some characters had run their course so a bomb blast seemed the quickest way to get rid of them and freshen up the cast with new members. Rumours also ran rampant that some of the actors were getting difficult about re-signing contracts and Harmon had decided to 'blow them all up'.

First for the chop were Aldo and Roma, since scriptwriters had been complaining for months about how hard it was to sustain their bickering storylines. Regrettably, they also felt that Les Whittaker's crazy inventions were making his character more and more unbelievable. He had bred cockroaches in the cellar to use their urine as petrol, and invented an automatic sausage making machine, an automatic wine pourer and a confetti dispenser. All of his contraptions ended up spewing their contents all over the building. The ultimate irony is that Les Whittaker ended up all over the delicatessen when the bomb exploded on that dreadful 'Black Friday' night in September.

The bomb episode was a major publicity coup. A veil of secrecy was pulled over the show, although newspapers couldn't wait to print the list of the dead as soon as the victims were revealed. Advertisements for the episodes outrageously compared the events at 'Australia's most famous address' to real-life tragedies suffered in Belfast and London. Aldo, Roma, Les and a minor character, Miles Cooper (Scott Lambert), were revealed to have died in a special one-hour episode the following Monday. Sadly, *Number 96* would never be quite the same again, and even though it lasted another two years, its audience gradually fell away. Producers soon regretted dumping so many beloved older characters as the new younger ones never quite caught on. Actor Gordon McDougall was eventually brought back as Les's Scottish cousin, Andrew, but he never caught on either – with viewers or the widowed Norma.

As for the revelation of who planted the bomb, well, that resulted in the departure of another fan favourite. Power-hungry and terminally bitter bitch Maggie Cameron (Bettina Welch) had always wanted to redevelop the site *Number 96* sat on, and foolishly thought a bomb might give everyone a good scare and send them packing. Even though she had never meant to kill anybody, she was classified as insane, shipped off to Silverwater Women's Detention Centre and released just in time to return for the show's final episode two years later.

Outrageously comparing a fictional TV address to real-life blasts in Belfast and London.

Anya Salecky as Jaja.

Despite reaching 1,000 episodes, and a format change to two one-hour episodes per week, by 1977 *Number 96* was in serious ratings trouble. Script controller Johnny Whyte decided to see if audiences could still be shocked, but what was there left to do? First up was introducing teenage Debbie (Dina Mann) to heroin. Years before, the Control Board had insisted that Rose Godolfus (Vivienne Garrett) get sick after trying marijuana. Now, at the request of the NSW police force, a hooked-on-heroin storyline was meant to put kids off ever trying the drug. Unfortunately, it also played as a lesson on how to shoot up. Hopefully, impressionable kiddies kept watching long enough to watch Debbie's hysterical slide into rehab.

Over the years, the show had been relying less and less on nudity, so much so that when new blonde bombshell Anya Salecky (who played Jaja) burst into tears after seeing her first nude scene, she pleaded for her 'must strip' clause to be removed from her contract. Producers agreed and quietly slipped in the show's first full-frontal nude scene with a bit player. Lindi Mason, playing a nurse in bed with the newly straight Dudley, ran naked down the stairs when his flat caught fire in November 1976. On the way down, the towel she was holding for modesty blew up in the air, revealing all, even if it was only a glimpse.

The producers decided to include full-frontal nudity, with no mere glimpses, from May 1977. A new character was introduced, described as a Lady Godiva-type with an aversion to wearing clothes. Miss Hemingway (Deborah Gray) was a patient of the building's new resident psychiatrist, Harold (Dave Allenby), and would flounce into his consulting room and throw off her fur coat to stand naked in extended sequences. In the past, nudity had caused network switchboards across the country to light up, but the Aussie audience was now so blasé, the full-frontal Miss Hemingway received just three complaints. The *Number 96* deathwatch had begun.

Series creator David Sale was outraged by the direction the show was taking and quit, warning that the increasing reliance on nudity and violence would backfire. He was particularly referring to a Nazi-loving bikie gang so over the top that they crucified Giovanni (Harry Michaels) in one sickening sequence. A group of real bikies threatened retaliation, despite never having previously objected to being depicted as sadistic rapists in both the show and the spin-off movie.

Number 96 really lost the plot in late 1977 when it converted Norma's Wine Bar into Australia's first suburban disco, Duddles. As the audience drifted away to cool new American shows like *Starsky and Hutch*, the series sank to even lower depths. Its low point was undoubtedly a *Jaws* rip-off in which Debbie (Dina Mann) watched both her parents get eaten by a shark. Fake fins wobbling unconvincingly should have been banned from all Aussie soaps at that point, but a decade later, on a *Sons and Daughters* Christmas cliffhanger, it was still just as laughable.

Finally, after an action-packed five and a half years, Bill Harmon, seeing the writing on the wall, scrambled to keep his production company alive with a spin-off series. He desperately wanted a sitcom to rise from the ashes of *Number 96*, believing that this was where he next needed to revolutionise Australian television. Within the framework of *96*'s regular shows, he tried out *Mummy and Me*, which had Reg and Edie McDonald going to work for an advertising agency; *Fair Game* with Elaine Lee (back as Vera Collins), *Bellbird*'s Lynette Curran and Abigail as three saucy divorcees; and *Hope'll Help* with American *Laugh-In* star Chelsea Brown. Despite *Number 96*'s great comic timing, none of them got off the ground since the comedy seemed too corny without the drama in between. A Don Finlayson private investigator drama, *A Law unto Himself*, fared no better, probably because they were rumoured to be turning the gay boy next door into a tough straight man.

In the ultimate irony, after having produced Ten's greatest ever drama hit (up to that point), Bill Harmon would return to the network in 1980 with *Arcade*, still the biggest soap flop of all time. Still, it's a testament to his popularity with the cast that all the *96* regulars were part of *This Is Your Life* when the American producer was honoured. Host Roger Climpson snuck onto the set by telling Harmon they wanted to surprise Ron Shand (Herb), but the actor was in on the gag and turned the tables on his boss.

Number 96's final episode brought all the storylines to a happy ending. At the start of the final hour, Dorrie and Herb had just signed a contract that would finally see the building knocked down for redevelopment. At that moment, in swept mad bomber Maggie Cameron, revealing herself to be the mystery buyer. When a clerical error made the contract invalid, the Evanses refused to sign again. The building and its residents would stay right where they were, and it appeared from Maggie Cameron's wry smile that she had planned it this way all along. As the residents gathered in Duddles Disco for Arnold Feather's third wedding reception (marrying Vicki after second wife Liz had tried to poison him), Maggie arrived with a huge wedding present as a peace offering. Her gift was accepted in a new spirit of reconciliation as a final toast was raised, although nobody bothered to check if there was another bomb ticking away inside.

In the show's final scene, Edie McDonald sat down at a typewriter upstairs to write her first novel. 'Once upon a time there was a building called Number 96…' she typed. As befitting the grand-daddy of all Aussie soaps, and with a nod to its vaudeville and theatrical background, a voiceover then announced that as many actors as possible from the series would return to say goodbye in the 'traditional manner'. So began a roll call of more than 50 familiar faces from over the years. The final shot was from overhead as Ron Shand silently walked through the sets and switched off all the studio lights.

By the time episode 1,218 of *Number 96* had finished, close to $20 million had been pumped into its production. Over 6 million words had been written by over 43 scriptwriters to create 609 hours of television. Parents everywhere had been forced to talk about sex with their kids, and Australian networks were all forging ahead with new home-grown dramas now that *96* had proved there was an audience hungry for them.

The American *Number 96*, advertised as 'The Series They Tried to Ban in Australia!'.

And 1,300 actors had been employed, many of whom would continue in television for years afterwards.

At the height of its success there was talk of selling *Number 96* internationally, but apart from screenings in Italy and Canada, there weren't really that many markets that could handle the show's permissiveness and nudity. One country that refused flat out was America and it wasn't because of the sex, it was that interracial romance and kiss from the early months.

Time magazine had run a story on the show in June 1972, reporting that 'even at posh parties, hostesses expect half their guests to hover around the set while the show is on'. While America could not cope with the original, they did buy the rights to make their own version. Stupidly, they decided to re-make it as a one-hour sitcom – complete with dreaded laugh track.

The Americanisation was set at 96 Pacific Way, West Hollywood, and premiered on NBC on 10 December 1980. It was launched over three consecutive nights in the hope that audiences would get hooked and keep watching every Friday night at 9pm. NBC President Fred Silverman was prepared to try anything to get *Number 96* to work, since the bottom-rated network was desperate for a hit.

It was promoted as 'the series they tried to ban in Australia!' even though most Americans, pre-*Crocodile Dundee*, didn't even know where Australia was, and the Australian scripts and characters had been replaced by a completely new set of residents and situations. Like the original, however, most of the cast were unknowns.

Number 96, American Style, premiered on 10 December 1980 and was an instant flop. It was NBC's lowest-rated show that week, and lasted for less than two months. Apart from trying to launch a comedy about 'wild California sexcapades' during the family-friendly TV time of Christmas, the hype fooled nobody. 'The most outrageous group of TV characters ever collected under one roof! Is the newly-arrived bombshell an X-rated star? Why has Marion taken up derriere painting? And does the newly-divorced travelling salesman make a sale at home?' Full-page ads in *TV Guide* with these headlines only showed how desperate the new version was.

By all reports, the show was neither funny nor revealing, and it probably never stood a chance of succeeding. Several years later, however, another show about a West Hollywood apartment building emerged. This time it seemed to be heavily based on the Australian version of *Number 96*, with a blonde bombshell, a virtuous gay man, psycho killers and a huge bomb blast. *Melrose Place*, anyone?

In September 1990, *TV Week* reported that Ten was considering resurrecting *Number 96* by signing up some of the original cast and recruiting new ones. At the time, Ten was in a ratings hole and apparently some executives thought an adult drama might work again for the ailing network. Luckily, sanity prevailed and the show never eventuated.

It's one of the great tragedies of Australian television that, just like *Bellbird*, over two years of *Number 96* has been lost forever. Despite the

The final episode of *Number 96* featured a calvalcade of 50 former stars in a 'traditional' farewell.

show's unprecedented success, nobody had the foresight to keep master broadcast tapes of it. The Ten Network actually unspooled months of the show to make a foyer display out of used videotape. Lost forever is the hugely controversial black mass sequence, Arnold Feather's porno movie and the highest-ever rating episode when Lucy Sutcliffe found out the lump in her breast was benign. After repeating the series at midnight during the early 80s, Ten gave the master tapes to Australia's National Screen and Sound Archive, ScreenSound, which continues to keep every colour episode as well as a handful of black and white ones.

Many of the actors, especially those who believe in the superstitious elements of showbiz, refer to the cosmic force that launched their careers as 'The Spirit of *Number 96*'. Ron Shand was always certain about why it worked – 'Perfect casting and giving the public what it wants.' An original scriptwriter, Eleanor Witcombe, remembers it as being 'the most professional, well-organised and integrated show' that she had ever worked on.

What was originally slammed by critics and detractors as being too ridiculous to be real now stands as an amazingly accurate social document of Australia in the 70s. Made before the young and the beautiful would take over television, it is a more real depiction of Australia than any soap that followed. The notorious *Number 96* was multicultural, non-ageist and non-judgemental, and there's never been anything quite like it since.

6

CERTAIN WOMEN

PREMIERE: **1973** EPISODES: **166** NETWORK: **ABC** FINALE: **1976**

Jane (Joan Bruce) and husband Alan (Ron Graham) fire up the barbie.

While the commercial networks were trying to replicate *Number 96*'s sex 'n' sin formula, the ABC was determined to keep it clean. With an increased budget and a mandate to produce more Australian drama, the national broadcaster set about developing an inner city based serial (perhaps mindful of the fact that *Bellbird* didn't rate very well in the cities). Their first attempt was 1972's *Lane End*, focusing on the Pappas family and their corner store in Balmain. Except for the shop, migrant clichés were avoided, and Aussie neighbours included John Meillon as a used-car salesman and Carole Skinner as his blowsy wife. After a seven-episode run in 1972 though, the ABC discovered they had a much more interesting proposition.

Certain Women began life as a six-part miniseries on 14 February 1973. It was written by Tony Morphett, with each television 'play' focusing on a different female from the multi-generational Lucas family. Teenage schoolgirl Gillian Stone (Elisabeth Crosby) couldn't make up her mind whether she should stay at school and study or leave and take up modelling. The next week, the focus shifted to eldest sister Marjorie (Judy Morris), who was married to Carl Faber (Peter Sumner) and found herself pregnant just when her job was starting to become interesting.

Their university student sister Helen (Jenny Lee) found herself on the outer when her radical ideas clashed with those of her conservative family. She decided she would have to move out of home, even though she could barely afford it. Not surprisingly, this episode was written by seminal playwright David Williamson and it was his first ever television script.

Next up was the sisters' mother Jane (Joan Bruce). When her 'battler' husband Alan Stone (Ron Graham) lost his job, she decided to return to teaching, even though it would dent her husband's pride. Jane's sister Freda Lucas (June Salter) didn't want to give up her career as a solicitor and opted instead for a casual relationship with lover Duncan (Charles Tingwell). Her dilemma arose when Duncan wanted to get married and Freda wanted to keep her independence.

Finally, there was Jane and Freda's mother, Dolly Lucas (Queenie Ashton). Her personal drama, in the last of the original six episodes, affected everybody when her husband of 50 years, Fred (Jack Fegan), died suddenly. 'It's a beautiful series,' Fegan told *TV Times*. 'Its message is a simple one, but vital in today's society. It is this: Whatever travail, hardship, loss or difficulties people may have they will survive provided they have a meaningful place in society – such as in a family group – to fall back on.'

With good critical reviews (Sandra Hall described it as a 'cleaned-up *Number 96*') and a positive response from the audience, the ABC decided that the Lucas family would make an even better continuing serial. However, when Tony Morphett found out, his first response was one of regret. 'All we could think was: "But we've killed Jack Fegan!" It was a good, strong story for one of a series of six plays, but a terrible mistake when it became a long-running series,' he told *TV Times*.

Returning to the ABC on 10 October 1973, *Certain Women* became a Wednesday night fixture at 8pm, and for those viewers who missed it, there was a repeat late every Sunday night. The new serial kicked off with widow Dolly upset because her husband had left their house to the children to avoid double death duties. While the family tried to reassure her, Dolly wasn't happy about being dependent on them. Marjorie found it tough going with a small baby when she and Carl were forced to move into their derelict terrace house to avoid it being vandalised. Helen, meanwhile, started to fall for her university flatmate Julius, or as he was better known, 'Big Julie' (Bruce Spence), and Freda got herself an ex-army boyfriend, Barry (Brian Wenzel).

Some fans of the miniseries weren't impressed with any new character that threatened the original characters' motivations. 'Dear Tony Morphett: Why don't you call your show *Certain People*?' asked a *TV Times*

Those Women are back

"Certain Women" was one of the most successful dramatic series ever presented on ABC-TV. Because of its popularity a new series has been produced—but in a totally different format—as a continuing serial. In the first episode Dolly learns that her late husband, Fred, has left the house to the children —in order to avoid death duties. She feels hurt and rejected as now she is totally dependent on her family. The problems that the situation creates unfold, and affect the lives of all around her.

"Certain Women" tonight at 8.00 on ABC-TV. (repeat next Saturday 9.45 p.m.)

the good looking Australian ABCtv

reader. 'Where are your two "liberated" women disappearing to? I could not stand it if Helen became the ultra-feminine Girl-Friday to big, strong, dependable "Big Julie". And Freda – please let her remain a person who is independent and stable and don't turn her into a neurotic woman. Let this program remain one about six *Certain Women*, who do have more challenges in their lives than making curtains for the front room of somebody's new house.'

Another wrote to say she was 'disgusted by the way Tony Morphett has changed the roles of every one of the women (except the grandmother and the youngest daughter) into those of subservient, mindless, illogical twits. Alan Stone now has no apparent feeling for the women in his family – laughing at Gillian's wish to be a solicitor and causing his wife to withdraw from her occupation as a teacher.' Those ABC-TV viewers who particularly came to dislike the show began referring to it as *Cretin Women*.

Regardless of the extra men now required to keep the series going, sharp-eyed viewers should have noticed that the women still ruled the roost every time the show ended. The lead actresses were all listed first, then, after a credit that said 'and also...', the male actors' names would appear. And top of the list for a return credit was Jack Fegan whom creator Tony Morphett regretted killing off. Fegan returned briefly as Fred's brother Tom Lucas. Tom arrived unexpectedly from America with son Peter (Christopher Pate) in tow, and the family was soon scandalised when Peter and cousin Gillian fell in love and ran away together.

After 23 episodes, chronic bronchitis forced actress Elisabeth Crosby out of the series and Christine Amor took over the role of Gillian (who suddenly went blonde). Judy Morris and Peter Sumner also chose to leave the series at this point, with some newspapers suggesting they were bored with their roles. Tony Morphett wasn't worried and told *TV Times*, 'I keep in touch with the cast and I usually know when they're being misquoted.'

Actor Peter Sumner was possibly tiring of viewers who took it all too seriously, especially after an old lady abused him in a city street for the way he was treating his 'wife'. After being told that Marjorie was stuck in the house all day washing nappies, while he was out carrying on with 'fancy women', Sumner tried to explain to her that he was just an actor, but the avid viewer refused to listen. When she started hitting him with her handbag, Sumner was forced to flee.

Marjorie and Carl moved to Melbourne and Helen's now de facto 'Big Julie' also left to go to America and study. They were replaced by new family members and new neighbours (the Stone family had moved from Lidcombe to Dundas). Among the new cast were relatives Heather (Betty Lucas) and Barbara (Anne Haddy), and neighbours Paula (Kate Fitzpatrick) and Norm Coburn (Don Barker), Father Michael (John Stanton) and dress designer Kenneth Price (Wallas Eaton), who ended up buying into Alan and Barry's used car yard.

To celebrate the show's conversion to colour in 1975, Alan and Jane went on a second honeymoon 'to the seaside' and met up with old wartime friends Horrie (Vincent Ball) and Alice (Diana Perryman). Freda contemplated leaving Barry for businessman George Lindsay (Richard Meikle). Gillian's photographer boyfriend Steve Williams (Eric Oldfield) caught Helen's attention when he came for a family dinner, but ended up getting it on with Helen's flatmate, librarian Beth Pearson (Carmen Duncan). That left Helen free to marry university tutor Michael Fraser (Ivar Kants) in 'a church wedding to please the families'.

Now firmly established, the show briefly travelled to England. Thames TV bought one series of *Certain Women* for screening on the ITV network, which was already screening ABC-TV's other popular soap, *Bellbird*. 'We were told it was getting quite popular in the UK,' says Joan Bruce, 'but the ABC had already wiped some master tapes so it mucked up the continuity of what could be sold overseas.' When the actress travelled to the UK not long after it had aired, many Brits did a double-take upon seeing *Certain Women*'s Jane walking through the streets of London.

Joan Bruce and Queenie Ashton attend a function.

June Salter, in her autobiography *A Pinch of Salt*, recalled how she was inundated with mail when Barry moved in with Freda. 'They finally accepted him "if it made Freda happy"!' Salter was already fielding her 'professional advice on legal matters, especially from pensioners who couldn't afford expensive solicitors. Freda was radical (which I'm not), self-sufficient and independent (I fall down there, too) and a feminist (which I'm certainly not!). She also vowed she would never fall in love or marry!' To prove how well she could play against type, Salter would go on to win Penguin Awards for *Certain Women* in 1975 and 1976.

After one Darwin viewer lost her home in Cyclone Tracy, she wrote to Salter wondering if the plans for Freda's new house could be forwarded to her so she could re-build her new home just like it. And since Darwin only had black and white TV, she also asked nicely for interior colour schemes!

Joan Bruce had an equally bold fan letter after the Stones moved house and didn't take their fridge with them. A Queensland viewer asked if the Stones' old refrigerator was 'just sitting in a shed doing nothing' and, if it was, they would be more than willing to buy the handle. It seems their own Kelvinator had been missing its door handle ever since their four year old had broken it, so here was an opportunity to do some home repairs, courtesy of *Certain Women*.

At the heart of the series were the problems of typical Aussie couple Alan and Jane Stone. *TV Times* complimented actors Ron Graham and Joan Bruce who could 'anticipate each other's responses in the telepathic way of old married couples'. Their private night-time chats in

Some fans weren't happy when Freda (June Salter) got a boyfriend, Barry (Brian Wenzel).

bed together struck a chord with viewers who loved their intimacy and honesty. 'We had worked together on the stage and so we knew each other very well and just sort of relaxed into the roles,' says Ron Graham. 'I'd already played dear Ronnie's mother, wife, sister and lover before *Certain Women*,' remembers Joan Bruce.

Teenage son Damon (Matthew Crosby) began to figure more in the story as he hit puberty and started showing an interest (sadly unrequited) in neighbour Vicki Mitchell (Sally Cahill). Marjorie returned (now played by Diane Craig) but husband Carl never did – he was killed in a plane crash flying home from Japan.

When Alan lost his job – again – Jane was forced to go back to work. Faced with having the head of the family on the dole, the Stones took on more relatives to help out with expenses. Down from Dubbo came nieces Michelle (Vynka Lee-Steere) and Caroline (Joanne Samuel). Aunty Eileen stormed down soon afterwards, facing a crisis when unwed daughter Caroline announced she was pregnant. Some *TV Times* readers were disturbed when Eileen was unforgiving about the scandal, but as time wore on, she had an about-face and 'took the errant Caroline to her bosom'.

The storyline was necessitated by actress Joanne Samuel's real-life pregnancy with then *Number 96* actor Vince Martin. 'They were very cross with me,' remembers Samuel, although the unplanned storyline probably saved her character from terminal boredom. 'Caroline was so insipid and so sweet that you couldn't really take her anywhere. Having a baby on the show was probably a bit too much for everybody though so they had to send her back to Dubbo!'

Despite the slow pacing, Joanne Samuel loved working on the show, even if her rebellious nature got her on the wrong side of some of the older actors. 'The ABC crew went on strike because they had to wait weeks to get paid so I went on strike too. I was pretty left wing in those days and Juney Salter got really cross with me that I would actually stop performing for a strike with the crew. She felt that you had to keep working regardless. I can see her perspective on that now but in those days I was young and vocal, despite my real respect for her.'

As the series moved into 1976, Freda and Barry got over her flirtation with another man and moved into a new house together while Alan got work, first as a taxi driver, then a parking inspector (the dreaded 'brown bomber'), then a colour TV repairman. Marjorie's landlord Peter Clayton

(Shane Porteus) had everyone wondering if he might become more than just that, especially when he separated from wife Christine (Kris McQuade). Even Dolly got a bit of romance when wealthy Arthur Baxter (John Dease) worked his way into her affections. They eventually left the series together for an extended holiday in New Zealand.

Finally, after six series and 166 episodes, an ABC spokesman told *TV Times* that after 'budget cuts in ABC-TV drama', *Certain Women* would come to an end that December. 'It was still going very well, so it was a bit of a shock to us all,' remembers Ron Graham (Alan). 'I remember June Salter was very upset about the axing. The cast were really like a family, we all used to look forward to coming in to work.'

For the finale, Alan and Jane retired to a country property at Blights Creek, which is where Marjorie married Peter in the grounds of their new home. It would never have been believable if Dolly hadn't been there for her granddaughter's wedding, and sure enough, she rocked into town and even caught the bridal bouquet. *Certain Women* ended with happy endings all round.

Long-time fans weren't too happy though with 'their' ABC. 'I could get over 200 signatures from local people demanding the return of the most popular show we had but would they be of any use?' asked a *TV Times* reader from Blackheath. 'How can they justify the cancellation of this good, wholesome show because of lack of finance when they produce such inane programs as *Alvin Purple*?' asked a Port Pirie viewer. 'This serial deals with social issues and always retains interest. ABC-TV should make a film of *Certain Women*, not axe it.'

ABC-TV controller John Cameron wrote to all the cast and Joan Bruce still has her letter. 'That *Certain Women* has been a happy and successful show is due to the cast members and notable amongst them, yourself,' he wrote. 'The quality of your performance has been a continuing strength and it's a great pity that we have been obliged to take the programme off air purely for reasons of cost. I sincerely hope that we will continue to see you on the screen with lucrative frequency, but your Jane will always be remembered by the ABC and by me and its viewers. With many thanks for a lovely characterisation from a charming artist, John Cameron.'

Despite the letters of thanks and protest, *Certain Women* was gone. No more would the Stone family resolve any crisis by putting the kettle on. 'When we finished, we went out on a high but it's never been given a great deal of publicity or credence since,' says Joan Bruce. 'The critics thought the ABC needed to move away from the "washing-machine culture" but I always thought *Certain Women* was a lovely show and a good quality soap.'

7

THE BOX

PREMIERE: **1974** EPISODES: **335** NETWORK: **TEN** FINALE: **1977**

Clueless actor Tony Wild (Ken James) with
flamboyant director Lee Whiteman (Paul Karo).

As *Number 96* became a huge hit and turned around the fortunes of the Ten Network, Australia's other two commercial networks, Seven and Nine, watched on in horror. Their first strategy against the monster soap was to milk the controversy the show was causing over its sexual content. Supposedly voicing 'community concern', they petitioned the Minister for the Media, Senator Douglas McClelland, to remove one commercial television licence – and they certainly weren't nominating one of their own. When this bid failed to gather much support, it soon became obvious they would have to invest in a little home-grown soap of their own. And bugger any 'community concern' over its content.

In 1973 Nine approached Melbourne-based Crawford Productions to come up with ideas for a rival serial. Crawford's were keen as they were concerned their long-running police dramas (*Homicide*, *Division 4* and *Matlock Police*) might be running out of steam. They dug out an old story outline company director Ian Jones had once written and, together with scriptwriter Tom Hegarty, began re-working the story of what went on behind the scenes of a television station, calling it *The Dream Makers*.

By now Seven were also scratching around for a soap, so Crawford's came up with one for them too, called *Saints and Sinners*. Specifically conceived for actor George Mallaby, who had just left *Homicide* and was still on a two-month holding contract, *Saints and Sinners* appeared to be a strange hybrid of *Number 96*, *Bellbird* and *The Story of Peter Grey*. It was to be about a swinging country Protestant minister, and Seven were, understandably, somewhat underwhelmed.

When Nine passed on *The Dream Makers*, Crawford's offered it to Seven, as negotiations about possible changes needed for *Saints and Sinners* had stalled. Seven also knocked back *The Dream Makers*, with *The Bulletin* reporting that Seven's chairman, Rupert Henderson, ordered it 'out of his sight' due to its explicit content. Just as George Mallaby's contract was about to lapse, Crawford's dropped a bombshell. The television station soap, now called *The Box*, and starring George Mallaby, had been sold to Ten and would screen back-to-back after *Number 96*. 'They must have been dreaming,' was Ten's response to Seven and Nine letting *The Box* slip through their fingers. 'They must have been sound asleep.'

The publicity machine began to crank up. *TV Times* reported that Bert Newton and Jack Thompson were offered leading roles, although neither signed up. Crawford Productions were so certain they had a hit on their hands, they spent half a million dollars in production before one episode had been aired. Religious and family groups, however, began flooding the family-owned company with complaints about the 'bombardment of nudity, obscenity and smut'. Concerned, Hector Crawford, the company's founder, took out newspaper advertisements defending *The Box*. 'I believe our responsibility is to the TV audience at large, not to vocal, and sometimes highly organised minority groups which try to dictate what people should be allowed to see on their screens.'

A religious newspaper was quick to point out that Hector Crawford had a somewhat different opinion back in 1971, after an overseas trip revealed a new wave of permissiveness in cinema and the theatre. 'Personally I found a lot quite disgusting,' he said back then. 'We have to refine our censorship laws. We have got to stop this awful stuff coming here.' *The Catholic Advocate* headlined their story 'Methinks he doth protest too much', and they were right to be concerned. Just a couple of years later, topless women were paraded down the city streets of Melbourne wearing sandwich boards to advertise the premiere of *The Box*.

'TV's Hottest Show' and 'TV's Most Expensive Production', as it was now being called, exploded onto the air in a 90-minute extravaganza in

February 1974. As promised, life behind the scenes at UCV-12 was indeed uninhibited. Variety show compere Gary Burke (Peter Regan) discovered a naked girl in his dressing room between takes of his live show, 'Big Night Out'. Rather than return to the soundstage for his next cue, he made love to her in the shower, only to miss an entrance for his show. Watching from home and rushing in to find out what happened was recently appointed station programmer Paul Donovan (George Mallaby). The revelation that the temptress was a 15-year-old schoolgirl called Felicity (played by 20-year-old Helen Hemingway) made for one hell of a first commercial break cliffhanger.

Paul struggled to keep the scandal from leaking to the press but sniffing around was the man- (and woman-) hungry TV columnist Vicki Stafford (Judy Nunn) who wrote for 'Teleview' magazine. She seduced dopey actor Tony Wild (Ken James), the star of Channel 12's police drama 'Manhunt', in an effort to get the full story. After tracking down Felicity and using her in a nude centrefold with Tony, Vicki kissed Felicity. Australian TV's first lesbian kiss was another scorching cliffhanger.

Meanwhile, Paul's first staff appointment, the extremely camp Lee Whiteman (Paul Karo), arrived to help lift the station's ailing ratings. Station manager Max Knight (Barrie Barkla), married to Marion (Margaret Cruickshank), the daughter of Channel 12's owner, Sir Henry Usher (Fred Betts), was threatened by Paul and uncomfortable with Lee's overt sexuality. Lee insisted on using Gary's warm-up guy Eddie Holliday (Cul Cullen) on 'Big Night Out', but a jealous Gary plotted to get the former alcoholic drunk before the show. Stage manager Don Cook (Graeme Blundell) was roped in to distract naïve secretary Cathy Holliday (Kay McFeeter), who was trying to make sure her father didn't mess up his last big chance.

Max's sexy secretary was Kay Webster (Belinda Giblin) and she was soon flirting with Paul, even though he had a neurotic wife Judy (Briony Behets) at home. However, Kay already had her own secret lunchtime rendezvous. The scenes showing Kay with her lover were shot from the lover's point of view, with a disturbing, hand-held camera. The lover was eventually revealed to be Max, although Barrie Barkla was only seen with her in bed once. 'It was a big secret too long. She did it all with the camera. It was six or seven months into the series before I got into bed with her and in the same episode I was quickly out on my ear,' he later told *TV Times*.

The Box received mostly good reviews from the critics. The much-ballyhooed sex scenes were offset by the sharply-written characters, talented cast and technically superior production values. Hundreds of viewers rang Channel 10 to complain about what one reviewer had counted as 'five nude scenes, eight buttocks, one drunk, two lesbians and only one homosexual', although Publicity Director Tom Greer took great pleasure in noting that all the calls were made during commercial breaks or after the show had finished. Brisbane morals campaigner Alan Russell, who was also a dentist, was outraged by the open-mouthed kiss-

Hundreds of viewers rang to complain about what one reviewer had counted as 'five nude scenes, eight buttocks, one drunk, two lesbians and only one homosexual'...

ing scenes. 'I wouldn't open-mouth kiss a woman for all the money in the world,' he screamed to *The Sunday Sun*. 'If those actors only knew the interchange of bacteria that occurs.'

Sydney's Anglican bishop, the Very Reverend Lance Shilton, despaired that Australia was turning into a nation of peeping toms, and ratings confirmed his worst suspicions. The new serial was a smash hit in all markets, particularly in Sydney where its premiere had achieved a remarkable 46 share, although it had slipped to a still respectable 33 within a few weeks. After the fuss subsided, *The Box* settled down to respectable ratings, even though it never again out rated its lead-in, *Number 96*.

Bisexual reporter Vicki Stafford, played by Judy Nunn.

For a while there was some rivalry between the Melbourne-made *Box* and Sydney's *96*. Newspapers could not wait to play it up, with one referring to it as 'The Battle of the Boobs'. Making their series in the more established production house of Crawford's, the cast of *The Box* naturally considered theirs the more prestigious series. Crawford's played up the distinction, insisting they were making 'quality drama', not soap, and they would continue to say this with every soap they made thereafter.

'We take our clothes off only when it is integral to the plot – never just for the sake of showing some naked flesh. In *Number 96* they make excuses so people can go naked,' Judy Nunn said at the time.

Today she laughs at the comment. 'We were all theatre actors and a little bit up ourselves back then,' Nunn says. 'You have to remember that the show could be taken on two levels – as a soap or as satire. It was a real send-up of what went on in TV.'

Playing bitch Vicki Stafford was a world away from her later role as maternal Ailsa on *Home and Away*, but as *The Box* progressed and relied less on titillation, bisexual Vicki was soon enjoying domestic bliss with Gary Burke. *The Box* settled down too, into the very rhythm established by *Number 96* – a balanced mix of drama and comedy – but the satirical side of the show was always there if you knew where to look. Frank Thring, the legendary theatrical actor who would later blast away at soaps in his *TV Week* column, was apparently a huge fan of *The Box* for its satire and high camp moments.

Over the years, its camp characters proved to be the most memorable. Mousy secretary Jean Stafford (Monica Maughan) was followed by the even more prim and proper Enid Parker. Unlike her previous soap incarnations in *Motel* and *Number 96*, actress Jill Forster disguised her glamour behind glasses and an old-fashioned hairdo, although she eventually let it all hang out and slinked around in a fur coat as Enid's nefarious sister, Emma. Channel 12 also had an outrageous make-up lady, Magda Palmer (Nina Gregory), fix-it man Mick Maloney (Luigi Villani) and Sir Henry's potty sister, Hester Davenhurst (Davina Whitehouse).

Such was its reputation that, when *The Box* was finally sold to New Zealand television, the press seized upon the potential scandal during an election year. Local moral watchdogs went berserk, with one demanding that Parliament 'immediately stop New Zealanders' taxes and licence fees being wasted on such tripe'. However, if the campaigners had read past the lurid headlines, they would have learnt that *The Box* was being screened from episode 254 onwards, when nympho underage schoolgirls were well and truly gone from the show. At some point, the New Zealanders may have raised an eyebrow at the Channel 12 staff picnic that somehow ended up in a nudist camp but, since such scenes were now being played strictly for laughs, the country seemed to survive the 'Australian soap opera shocker'.

The disclaimer 'The characters and events depicted in this serial are fictitious' is usually seen at the end of shows, but each episode of *The Box* actually began with it. After that, a huge exclamation mark appeared on screen as a television set featuring a topless girl exploded. The inside joke was that most of the characters and events depicted were far from fiction. Producer Jock Blair, who wrote the storylines for the first 200 episodes, admitted nearly all the characters were based on real people. Even today, he won't reveal their identities because some are still alive (and presumably still clueless about their alter egos).

What is known is that Mrs Hopkins (Lois Ramsey) was based directly on Crawford Productions' own tea lady, Mrs Carter. Just like in *The Box*, the Crawford's tea lady ruled the roost and spoke her mind, aware that she was the one person everyone wanted to keep in their good books for fear of missing out on a cuppa. So it was with Mrs H, although in true, sexy soap fashion, when her son was released from prison he had an affair with Lee Whiteman (Paul Karo) before drowning.

More drama ensued when Judy Donovan (Briony Behets) became increasingly despondent over not being able to have children, which she blamed on an abortion she had had years before. Judy left her husband and moved in with Lee Whiteman, while Paul (George Mallaby) allowed the marriage to fall victim to his job. 'Like Paul Donovan I am an idealist and I can be ruthless when I have to be,' Mallaby told *TV Times* in 1975. 'I'm a Scorpio and I'm sure Paul is too, he has all the characteristics.'

Channel Nine owner Frank Packer assumed Sir Henry Usher (Fred Betts) was based on Ten's owner, Reg Ansett. Ansett in turn would roar with laughter every time he watched the show, convinced they were getting Packer down to a tee. Hector Crawford thought he had the inside info and, assuming the character was Reg Ansett, passed on stories about him to help the scriptwriters. Jock Blair finally admits today that they were re-creating just one television mogul – Hector Crawford – but always done with great affection.

With *The Box*, fiction was always in danger of merging with real life. When TV actor Tony Wild was written out of 'Manhunt', real actor Ken James thought he was being axed too and reminded producers he had a contract that couldn't be broken. Actor Peter Regan, who played variety show host Gary Burke, ended up hosting his own variety show, *Quest*, on the ABC after leaving *The Box*. Blonde sex symbol Cheryl Rixon, whose character Angela was always being asked to disrobe for the cameras, ended up becoming American *Penthouse* Pet of the Year.

In 1975, the year after the film of *Number 96* had proved to be a cash cow in cinemas, *The Box* was also made into a feature film. Once again, reel life reflected real life, with the major plotline being the filming of UCV-12's police series 'Manhunt' for the big screen. Special Guest Graham Kennedy played himself, brought to Channel 12 to host 'Big Night Out', and just as Kennedy was looking to move into acting in real life, so too did he request a role in the movie version of 'Manhunt'. It turned

The Box movie ad.

out to be a comic disaster, but in real life Kennedy would indeed find a new career as an excellent actor, turning up in *Don's Party*, *The Odd Angry Shot* and *Travelling North*.

The movie also saw the return of Kay Webster (Belinda Giblin), who fell straight back into bed with old lover Paul Donovan (George Mallaby); and an old girlfriend of Vicki Stafford's, S.M. Winter (Cornelia Frances). Mrs Hopkins was given the sack by the station's new efficiency expert, but reinstated when it was revealed she was a major shareholder in the channel (just like the real-life Crawford's tea lady). 'Manhunt' the movie turned out to be a disaster but ended up being sold to Asia as a comedy, thereby saving Channel 12 from financial ruin. And in the film's finale, Tony Wild, at the helm of an out-of-control speedboat, crashed into Sir Henry's houseboat, leaving the drenched cast to swim to shore and watch their leader 'go down with the ship'.

Like the *96* movie, there was plenty of nudity, particularly full frontal and particularly from Marilyn Vernon as dancer Ingrid O'Toole, who frolicked naked throughout most of the movie. 'I auditioned for a part in *The Box* series but told them I wouldn't strip, so I missed out,' Vernon told *TV Times*. 'I thought hard about it before the movie came up, and when they asked me again if I would strip I said yes straightaway. It's an important part of the story.' And quite a change for the actress who had played a schoolgirl in *Bellbird*, too.

Filmed in three weeks and written by the TV series' new executive producer, Tom Hegarty, *The Box* did poorly at the box office, despite a live half-hour telecast of the Brisbane premiere featuring 'the arrival of the

Underage schoolgirl Felicity (Helen Hemingway) causes somewhat of a scandal in the first episodes.

stars and the variety pageant'. Opening in cinemas six months after colour TV started in Australia probably didn't help its cause. About the only good thing to come out of the movie were new sets, incorporated into the series after a scripted fire destroyed the old ones.

Back on the TV show, Gary Burke (Peter Regan) drowned in Max's pool. Lee (Paul Karo) fell in love with John (Donald MacDonald) and helped him come out of the closet. Horrie Weatherburn (Maurie Fields) challenged Sir Henry's ownership of Channel 12. Sports reporter Vern Walters (Syd Heylen) sweet-talked his way into town, while producer Walter Freeman (Phillip Ross) and younger wife Becky (Sonia Finn) arrived with stepdaughter Trish (Anne Lambert) in tow. Trish thought their family was cursed after her mother had died while making a documentary, and she blamed Becky for the death. It was later revealed that the culprit was not Trish's stepmother, but her father.

New program manager Nick Manning (John Stanton) lost his wife Carol (Barbara Ramsay) and child in a level crossing accident, after he had supported her through a suicide attempt, a near- abortion, drug addiction and incarceration in a mental home. You would think that would have put him off any more relationships, but in his grief he turned to Enid Parker (Jill Forster) for comfort, although their one night stand was kept a secret to viewers until she revealed she was pregnant.

Tony Wild (Ken James) became paranoid about new actor Monte (Tony Bonner), but when 'Manhunt' was cancelled it was Tony Wild who got the lead in Channel 12's new colonial drama. Madcap Deidre Matthews (Isobel Kirk) was the disaster-prone daughter of Channel 12's managing director, and Greg Patterson (Tom Richards) became the newsroom chief. Kids show host Johnny Masters (Don Barker) arrived with son Kevin (Rod Kirkham) who hooked up with production assistant Barbara MacArthur (Barbara Llewellyn). Director Brian Colson (Roger Newcombe) and dancer Yvette Monchamps (Christine Broadway) got married in a splashy church ceremony, as did Mrs Hopkins (Lois Ramsey), getting hitched to former conman Donald Hawker (Ted Ogden). Even newly married, she was still Mrs H.

Not only did *The Box* provide a change of pace for Crawford's roster of policeman-playing actors (George Mallaby, John Stanton, Gary Day, Don Barker, Tom Richards and Charles Tingwell – the latter also occasionally directed), it also launched the television careers of musical theatre star Geraldine Turner (who played, in her own words, 'boring' secretary Lindy), Noni Hazlehurst (as production assistant Sharon Lewis) and Tracy Mann (as innocent wardrobe assistant Tina). Years before *A Country*

Practice, Shane Porteus (playing male chauvinist David Warner) had to do a nude love scene with Belinda Giblin, but admitted to *TV Week* that there was nothing intimate about the shoot. 'The scene was done at six o'clock on a rainy Melbourne morning. And I can assure you, at that time of the day, after dashing to the studio through the pouring rain, neither of us felt in the least bit sexy.'

It was also the first acting role for former Queensland television weather girl Delvene Delaney, who was the first to ask for and receive a special no-nudity clause in her contract to play wardrobe assistant Penny O'Brien. Delaney wasn't kept past her initial eight-week contract amidst rumours that she could have stayed longer if she'd stripped. In contrast, 19-year-old Vanessa Leigh took it all off several times while playing Channel 12's weather girl, Fanny Adams, but she wasn't heard from again after leaving the series. Delaney returned to soap in *The Young Doctors* and became a regular on *The Paul Hogan Show*.

The Box ran out of steam in 1977, just three months before *Number 96* did. It too had become a victim of its own permissiveness, no longer able to shock its audience. Sir Henry had already been stabbed to death by Max's secretary, Louise (Roberta Grant), who had gone psycho after having an affair with Max. In the final episode, Max was finally able to convince his wife to drop her investigation into the murder, thereby keeping his extramarital fling a secret forever. And Mrs Hopkins died in her sleep after, ironically, nodding off in front of the TV. As the entire cast gathered for her wake in their local hangout, the Commodore Chateau bar, Donald raised a glass as Mrs H appeared one final time as a ghostly vision, seen only by her husband, and the viewers.

The Box had saved Crawford Productions from going under when all its police shows were axed, enabling it to rebuild and move onto the next phase which spawned *The Sullivans* and *Cop Shop*. Crawford's even sold the show to Germany and it was believed to have reached into some parts of Russia. What they made of it is anyone's guess. Today, libel laws and political correctness make it unlikely that there will ever be another series like it again in Australia.

The Box *had saved* Crawford Productions *from going under when all its police shows were axed.*

8

CLASS OF '74 / '75

PREMIERE: **1974** EPISODES: **290** NETWORK: **SEVEN** FINALE: **1975**

Strung-out student Peggy (Anne Lambert) and school janitor
Hubbard (Gordon Glenwright) at Waratah High.

After passing on *The Box*, the Seven Network approached Grundy Productions to develop a night-time soap for them. Reg Grundy, whose production company had been making quiz shows in Australia for over 20 years, was keen to expand into drama, so he leapt at the opportunity Seven offered. Former Crawford's executive John Edwards came up with a serial set on a university campus, but Reg Grundy suggested a high school instead and *Class of '74* was born.

Seven issued a 'no nude scenes' ultimatum as they planned to run their new show five nights a week before 8.30pm. 'Before that time you simply can't get away with some of the show-it-all sensation of *Number 96*,' a Grundy's source told *TV Week*. 'But, take it from me, you will see everything else up to the point where the last garment is shed.' Naturally, the Australian Broadcasting Control Board went on full alert. Nudity might have been a no-no but storyline-wise, there was plenty to be concerned about. Producer John Edwards was already promising to *TV Times* that *Class of '74* was to 'feature young girls who are very pretty and very sexy'.

TV Week launched the show with a sizzling two-page spread entitled 'Schoolroom Scandals Shock The Censor!' The 'nubile young schoolgirls' were pictured in bikinis or in hockey skirts with a split up the leg, and there wasn't a male student to be seen. Actor Leonard Teale defended the show, saying, 'Sex is not the reason for the show. It is a genuine problem in some schools and *Class of '74* deals with it as it would with other problems such as drugs, if they should arise.'

The swinging co-educational Waratah High crammed the early episodes with as many sexual situations as possible. Within the very first episode there was a student/teacher love affair as sweet Julie Armstrong (Carla Hoogeveen, 25) whispered to hunky Gary Evans (Vince Martin), 'I love you … Sir.' Bikie student Greg Simpson (Chris Cummings, 21) was deflowering virgin Nora Hayes (Barbara Llewellyn, 21) in a tent, and a search of student lockers uncovered *Playboy* magazines. The Broadcasting Control Board was unimpressed and ordered several cuts before it could be screened at 7pm around the country. The deflowering did not survive when the show went to air.

Class of '74 premiered on 18 March 1974. All the advance publicity and advertising teasers ('Which girl is having an affair with one of her teachers? Is it true that some of the pupils are practising black magic? Who posed for pornographic pictures?') resulted in a record-breaking opening night. Monday night's rating of 37 was the highest ever recorded for a 7pm show. Despite the sensational figures, however, the future of *Class of '74* hung in the balance after the Broadcasting Control Board ordered another two minutes cut from the second episode, and then ordered the third episode could only be screened after 7.30pm.

Sydney immediately moved the first two weeks of the show to 8pm while Melbourne moved it to 7.30pm for the same period. Seven weren't happy as their contract with Grundy's had stipulated that the program be G-rated, mainly because they didn't have anywhere available in their schedule for an adult-rated serial. Emergency talks were held between Grundy's, Seven executives and the Broadcasting Control Board with Reg Grundy personally flying down to persuade the board to reverse its ruling. He took with him audience research material that showed that kids were already watching *Number 96*, which probably only alarmed the Control Board further about what was happening to Australian television in the 70s.

The Control Board secretary told *TV Times* they objected to the general tone of the new soap. '*Class of '74* seems to be developing an immoral tone with a bit of sex, which is unsuitable for that timeslot when impressionable children are watching. One particular scene we objected to was where the pupils put nitric acid on the principal's car.' Critic F.C. Kennedy, however, thought that 'armchair peeping toms must have been sorely disappointed with the premiere'. He thought 'nothing very spicy' was ever going to occur, especially when the teacher in love with his student asked her to marry him. 'As everyone knows, immorality vanishes at the very mention of matrimony.'

Nevertheless, from that point on, *Class of '74* was heavily monitored and Grundy's had to fall into line. The early suggestion of devil worship

'Which girl is having an affair with one of her teachers? Is it true that some of the pupils are practising black magic? Who posed for pornographic pictures?'

In Brisbane, the show aired even earlier than in Sydney, outraging the censors.

quickly fizzled. The fluttering eye contact between priest Father Paul Kennedy (Allan Lander) and teacher Mary Dunstan (Jeanie Drynan) bit the dust as the would-be lovers became just good friends. And the forbidden student/teacher love affair was all over when Mr Evans was killed in a rock cave-in. Poor Julie, devastated by the loss of her hairy-chested tutor, ended up (temporarily) paralysed in a wheelchair.

Forced to now submit scripts in advance to the Broadcasting Control Board, the writers found they were even forbidden to use the expression 'Oh my God'. They began writing 'flexible' scenes that could be toned down if the board objected. One saucy storyline that did survive, however, was that of pregnant coffee shop waitress Evie (Gaynor Sterling) who proclaimed to have no idea who the father of her baby was and, most shocking of all, didn't seem to care. At least scriptwriters had resisted starting the show with Sterling playing a pregnant schoolgirl as had originally been planned. Within a few weeks, most of the sexual content was phased out in favour of more traditional schoolyard drama with the odd dash of comedy.

Homicide veteran Leonard Teale was the backbone of the series, playing headmaster Charles Ogilvy (nicknamed 'The Ogre' by the students). His deputy was history teacher Donald Blair (John Hamblin) who was unhappily married to alcoholic wife Maureen (Janet Kingsbury). Kingsbury was originally told her character would be a rich bitch, but a lonely housewife was much more interesting, especially when she started flirting with Italian delivery boy Tony Bianco (Adrian Bernotti, 24) who was a student of her husband's (their planned affair became another victim of the board clampdown on unsuitable storylines). Even more disconcerting was the fact that Kingsbury and Hamblin still paired up each week on ABC-TV's *Play School* which must have proved very confusing to any preschoolers who watched *Class of '74* and saw their favourite couple hurling abuse at each other.

These 'acting oldies', as *TV Times* called them, were necessary to help the somewhat inexperienced younger cast, including Ann Watson (Megan Williams, 17), school magazine editor Barry Collins (John Diedrich, 21), Peggy Richardson (Anne Lambert, 18) and boxer John Ward (Kevin Wilson, 23). American teacher Glen Turner (Chuck Danskin) was an 'oldie' but he became one of the soap's first casualties when he started freaking out every time somebody mentioned 'the war' (he was a bit touchy about Vietnam). More cast axings were to come.

In May, Grundy's announced that half of the regular cast weren't going to have their contracts renewed after the original 15-week agreement expired that month. Ten of the original 17 permanent actors were free to take other jobs but all were told the storyline department might get them back in the future. Carla Hoogeveen, one of the actresses being 'rested', tried to look on the bright side. 'We were all worried about the money angle at first but after the plan was fully explained to us, we agreed it was better to be put on a freelance basis.'

Twenty years later, Carla Hoogeveen realised the cast changes ruined the show. 'It all got a bit lost then,' she told fanzine *TV Eye*. 'What they decided to do was rotate the regulars like me and Anne Lambert, on for three months and off for three months, and it just pulled it apart really. Initially the series was quite well prepared but I think when a serial gains momentum it is quite difficult to maintain it.' Hoogeveen and Anne Lambert used their break to study acting with visiting New York drama coach Stella Adler.

Back on the show, *Class of '74* swelled its corridors with new students and teachers. Adult student Heather Jones (Jessica Noad) enrolled and faced a hostile reception from her much younger classmates like Wayne Elliott (Mark Hollis), Carlo Soporetti (Terry Camilleri) and Patti (Margaret Nelson). New teachers included about-to-retire Mr Finlay (Edward Howell) and Elena Kyriacos (Derani Scarr).

One of the most successful new characters was schoolgirl Trina Campbell, played by Grundy's receptionist Claire Hale. She had been working on the front desk at Reg Grundy's Chatswood office before successfully auditioning for *Class of '74*, and

Temporarily paralysed Julie (Carla Hoogeveen) meets movie star Janet Henderson (Margo Lee), an old flame of Principal Ogilvy's (Leonard Teale).

was given six weeks leave of absence to play the part. When she made the catchphrase 'Don't anybody move!' famous, screamed out whenever Trina lost one of her contact lenses, Hale found herself written back into the show for another eight-week stint.

For the show's 100th episode, the students discarded their regular school uniforms to substitute them with period dress of the 19th century. Then, in a nice bit of Grundy's and Seven cross-promotion, new student Tim (Chris Benaud) appeared on the quiz show *Great Temptation*. This was probably done as a favour as the long-running quiz show, hosted by Tony Barber, used to comfortably occupy the 7pm timeslot until *Class of '74* came along. Moved to 8.30pm up against *Number 96*, it needed all the help it could get to survive the year against Australia's top-rating show.

Larrikin pupil Peter Cooper (Jeremy Chance) got a shock when his politician father died. In real life, actor Jeremy Chance also got a shock when he dislocated his shoulder and had to tell producers he would be wearing a sling for a few weeks. Producers hastily rewrote scripts to incorporate his injury into the show, so consequently, Peter fell over in a mad scramble to see the coffee shop's foxy new waitress Gloria (Carol Lane).

Actress Joanne Samuel, the youngest in the cast at 16, remembers filming as being pretty rough and ready. 'We were really close to the bone of producing and going to air. We were told it had to be a major problem to stop tape, so to get them to stop you had to look down the barrel of the camera and say something really bad!' Samuel also got to play bad on-screen as head girl Sue Taylor, particularly when the rebellious schoolgirl posed for a nude photo atop Ogilvy's desk (off-camera of course). Sue was unmasked as the cheeky chick because she forgot to take off one identifying piece of wardrobe – a ring.

Amidst all the comings and goings, Joanne Samuel and Megan Williams were the only schoolgirls seen on air for the entire year. 'It was a really, really fun show to make,' Joanne Samuel says, 'and I met terrific people that remain friends even today.' Back in the show's heyday, a generation of kids wished that they too could hang out with the swinging students from *Class of '74*, and TV magazines rushed to capitalise on its wild popularity.

When *TV Times* ran a contest asking viewers to suggest storylines for the show, the winning entry came from Brisbane's Tony Crossley who suggested that school janitor Hubbard (Gordon Glenwright) should have an accident and suffer amnesia. He would then develop a grudge against Mr Ogilvy, the upshot of which would see the crazed janitor chasing the frightened principal around the school. The 14-year-old student won a trip to the Sydney set to watch *Class of '74* being filmed. 'I don't think there's enough action in it,' Crossley told *TV Times*, 'although it's still a pretty good show with a lot of good actors.'

The schoolboy would never get his wish to see more action at Waratah High, as romance was a much higher priority for the scriptwriters. Ogilvy (Leonard Teale) enjoyed a brief fling with movie star Janet Henderson (Margo Lee), an unhappily married Australian actress who was also an old sweetheart. The school was agog at seeing their principal with a 'fillum' star but when she returned to Hollywood, Ogilvy wasn't alone for long as his daughter Jill (Jennifer Cluff) turned up and announced she was marrying 'self-made man' Sam Wandsworth (Patrick Ward). It was another on-screen father and daughter reunion for actors Jennifer Cluff and Leonard Teale, who had just acted together in the acclaimed ABC drama *Seven Little Australians*.

Another reunion took place when actor Vince Martin rejoined the show. Even though he had died on-screen five months earlier playing Julie's naughty teacher/boyfriend, producers hired Martin again, this time to play a new tutor called Jack Christianson. This time round, Julie did not fall for him (nor did she seem to notice the resemblance). In real life, however, actress Carla Hoogeveen, who had recently returned to the show after a three-month break, finally did start to notice the actor. They revealed to *TV Times* that they were dating but the affair didn't last as Martin moved on to have a child with another *Class of '74* actress, Joanne Samuel. Back on the show, his character also became known as a ladies' man, so much so that little old ladies in the street started warning actress Jeanie Drynan that her on-screen boyfriend was not to be trusted.

In August, another cast shake-up saw the departure of Ann (after she had become rivals with Patti and Julie over an acting role in an American movie) and John was sent off to prison. New additions to the show included Donald's younger brother Graham Blair (Greg Apps), student Freddie Randall (Graham Bassett) and a new family. Mother Ruth Howard (Judy Ferris) was a teacher at the school while her two kids, Jackie

About as politically incorrect as you can get – school headmaster Charles Ogilvy (Leonard Teale) frolics with his bikini-clad students (L-R): Julie (Carla Hoogeveen), Peggy (Anne Lambert) and Ann (Megan Williams).

(Sharon Higgins) and Dean (Greg Bepper), were fifth-formers in the year below the *Class of '74* regulars.

School janitor Hubbard (Gordon Glenwright) fell for the new manager of the school canteen, Madge (Beryl Cheers), and their romance was going well until a tea-leaf reading friend advised them never to get married. The students refused to accept this and brought in their own psychic who told the couple to go ahead. They married on-screen in November, just as talk was beginning about *Class of '74* returning the next year as *Class of '75*. A Grundy spokesman said it would be 'more of a family show, with more interest to grown-ups as well as youngsters, but it will remain strictly 'G' in its classification. There will be some new characters, obviously, because this year's sixth formers will have left, but all of them will be brought back at various times for brief periods.'

As 1974 drew to a close, *Class of '74* came to an end with episode 191 on 4 December. A mysterious poisoner was finally unmasked and teachers Jack and Mary got engaged. Ogilvy was going to America with Laurie Wandsworth (Bernadette Hughson) while Ruth Howard was undecided about moving to Fiji with her boyfriend Jean-Pierre (Kevin Miles). Just as all the students left on a bus to travel around Australia for the summer, Patti's hysterical mother ran in demanding that the group had to return because she feared that her daughter had secretly married student Mike (Terry Peck).

Class of '75 could now start filming in garish colour and with a completely new concept. George Mallaby wisely turned down the chance to appear in the 'new-look' show but his sultry *Box* on-screen wife Briony Behets signed up, along with *Number 96*'s Abigail. They weren't there to disrobe, as they had done on their Network Ten shows, but to prove they

Abigail in disguise
as undercover cop/
French headmistress
Angelique Dupree.

could be funny. Spicy situations were dropped in favour of broad comedy. 'I'm proud to bear the title "sex symbol" but there are things beyond that waiting to be used, particularly in the comedy field,' Abigail told *TV Times*. 'In the French farce vein, for example.' The only French farce about to come was her appalling French accent.

If Abigail was looking to highlight her comedy chops, *Class of '75* wasn't the show to do it in. The attempt to get more laughs, at the expense of the formula *Class of '74* had comfortably settled into, was a complete disaster. From the first episode on 27 January 1975, the exaggerated comic sequences failed to raise a smile from even the most undemanding pre-schoolers, let alone its supposed 'grown-up' audience. Nubile young schoolgirls were out, yet in a strange role reversal, the teachers were suddenly all hot to trot.

Waratah had now become a wacky co-educational boarding school. Students arriving in the first episode included the unbearably snobby Jane Potter (Angela Punch before she became Angela Punch-McGregor), whiny mummy's boy Dennis Braithwaite (Peter Bensley), identity swapping Tom Carter (Marty Rhone) and neurotic nerd Loretta Day (Bronwyn Winter), who couldn't complete a sentence without a fake-sounding sneeze, because she was allergic to everything around her including, wait for it, oxygen.

Also appearing in her first major television role was Peita Toppano (before she dropped the 'i' to become Peta) playing Italian actress Gina Ferrari, who one student remarked was so sexy she made 'Sophia Loren look like Snoopy'. What a movie star was doing hiding out in a badly designed suburban Sydney school only underscored how ridiculous the show had become (although it had always harboured a fascination for international movie stars). Gina had a bodyguard called Luigi who dressed like a gangster and ducked in and out of bushes to *Benny Hill* style music. He even chased everyone around the school with a gun, the joke being that it wasn't loaded. If only the gun had been loaded, Australia could have been spared everything that followed.

Overseeing this turgid turmoil was the most unlikely bunch of teachers ever assembled on Australian television. There was phys ed teacher Jorja Jones (Briony Behets) who got the hots for polyester clad Rick Harris (Peter Flett), and a new professor called Grimble (Phil Ross). While Ogilvy attempted to fly back to Australia in a light plane and ended up 'missing at sea' for three weeks, the school was run by a mysterious new French headmistress, Angelique Dupree. Abigail was unrecognisable, hidden behind glasses and a Princess Leia black wig, but for the show's first cliffhanger, she removed her disguise, shook out her long blonde hair and dropped the put-on French accent to breathlessly announce to herself, 'Well, I'm in. And it looks as though it's going to be a cinch.'

If only it had been. Abigail wasn't in for long, and after some ridiculous undercover intrigue, she disappeared to be replaced by Faith Adam (Anne Charleston). Not surprisingly, viewers had also disappeared. Within a few months, Seven's Melbourne station sounded the death knell by dumping it to an 8am Saturday morning slot. The move took Grundy's by surprise, especially since the Control Board had just relaxed the restrictions it had placed on the program in the early days. Students were finally allowed to kiss and use the word 'pregnant' instead of 'having a baby'.

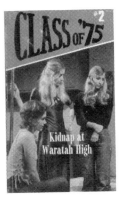

Class of '75 novel.

While there were very few laughs to be had on screen, behind the scenes the cast were having a riot. Actor Peter Flett (Rick Harris) remembers a particularly wild birthday party he had at his flat where he snuck up behind Abigail and undid her halter top, in the hope that her breasts might be revealed. Abigail, however, caught the top before anything spilled out, and turned around and slapped *Number 96*'s Julian Rockett for the incident. Flett owned up and took the blame while explaining to them both that it had all been a joke. He assumed that was the end of it.

The following Sunday, however, his parents rang to ask if he'd seen the morning newspapers. Splashed across them were lurid details that made out Flett had thrown an orgy, complete with nude skinny-dipping, even though he didn't have a pool! The Abigail incident was now being referred to as an 'attack', allegedly courtesy of her fiancé, Mark Hashfield, who knew a good publicity opportunity when he saw one.

Back on the set, *Class of '75* experienced major production delays courtesy of a NSW power industry dispute. The long hours were nearly disastrous for one actress. Angela Punch, who was also appearing every night on stage in a play, fell asleep at the wheel of her car at 'twenty to eight at night'. She told *TV Times* it had caused her to re-think her priorities and she quit the show soon afterwards.

'When they offered me the part I thought of all that lovely money I would earn and then I wondered what the scripts would be like. Through no fault of the producers or the network, I was disappointed in some ways,' Punch diplomatically told *TV Times*. 'I blame censorship for the serial's trite, cute stories that have little relevance to present-day activities in a high school. The actors have to try some real characterisations within the framework of unreal situations and this causes frustration among the cast.'

There was more frustration – or maybe relief – when Sydney moved *Class of '75* from its 7pm weeknight slot and replaced it with repeats of *Bewitched*. 'If it works at the new time of 5pm we would still be interested in renewing the show when the present agreement with Reg Grundy Productions runs out in eight weeks time, but we can't renew the show if it fails to pull an audience,' an ATN spokesman told *TV Times*. It failed to pull an audience in its new timeslot and was finally put out of its misery.

Class of '75's final episode was spent busily patching up the show's many romances. Jackie (Sharon Higgins) and student Archie (Stephen

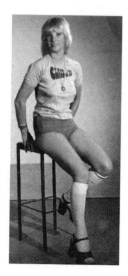

Brioney Behets.

McDonald) reunited, while Ogilvy (Leonard Teale) announced he was going to marry Sharon's mother Ruth (Judy Ferris), who was down in the rec room showing off her tap-dancing skills. For some bizarre reason, the saga was about to end with a musical variety finale. Tom was leaving school to become a pop star, giving actor Marty Rhone a chance to croon an acoustic version of his then Top 10 hit 'Denim and Lace'. Pop turned into vaudeville as the cast moved on to 'Roll out the Barrel' before shedding tears singing 'Auld Lang Syne' over the credits. After 290 episodes, it was a most inglorious finish to what had once been a very edgy, ground-breaking show. As soon as ratings finished that year, Seven repeated *Class of '75* in 90-minute blocks at 2.30pm every weekday, probably in a bid to torture its school holiday audience who had given the show a big thumbs down.

Today, *Class of '74/'75* is best remembered for its punchy theme song, written and performed by Brian Cadd (who also did the music for the *Alvin Purple* movies). It was voted the number one theme of *TV Times* readers when they got to vote on which tunes would appear on the magazine's theme songs record. Perhaps the show should be remembered, though, as the forerunner to *Neighbours* as Grundy's had stumbled onto a winning formula of young spunky kids backed up by older and more experienced actors.

Grundy's went back to school one more time with *Glenview High* in 1977. Costing $1 million for the first 16 one-hour episodes, it starred Grigor Taylor, Elaine Lee, Ken James, Camilla Rountree and Rebecca Gilling. Newcomer Brandon Burke was promoted as being Australia's answer to *Happy Days'* Fonzie and the show was shot on location in a real school that had been made available by the NSW Education Department. It was sufficiently classy enough to erase the memory of *Class of '75*, but when it didn't rate in Melbourne, the Sydney-based show was all over after 39 episodes.

9

UNTIL TOMORROW

PREMIERE: **1975** EPISODES: **180** NETWORK: **SEVEN** FINALE: **1976**

Local shop owner Bill (Ron Cadee) with
neighbourhood gossip Marge (Hazel Phillips).

After *Class of '74*, Grundy Productions and the Seven Network partnered up again for a daytime soap they hoped would 'walk the same successful road'. *Until Tomorrow* was described as 'an Australian version of a blending of *Days of Our Lives* and *The Young and the Restless*' and it began production during the first week of December 1974. The Brisbane-based serial was to follow the lives of several families who lived in suburban Vale Street.

Brisbane already had a healthy local TV scene, but they had never produced a home-grown drama for a national audience. Given that the 1974 Brisbane floods had devastated the city the previous Christmas, was it bad luck to begin every episode of *Until Tomorrow* with an aerial shot of the now quiet Brisbane River, snaking its way around the city? Was it a metaphor for the heartbreak and danger lurking in even the quietest Brisbane street? Or would the show end up stinking like the mud left behind by the floodwaters?

Until Tomorrow was the first Aussie soap creation from Brisbane-born Reg Watson, the man who would later be nicknamed the 'Godfather' of Aussie soap. He had previously written and produced the British serial

Crossroads and was brought home to make the first ever soap in his former home town. He wrote the first episodes, supervised casting and stayed on board as the serial's executive producer for the first few months. It was a shaky start, but Watson would end up masterminding many more soaps for Grundy's, including every one of their international successes.

Until Tomorrow was the fourth attempt by Seven to crack the daytime market. It was also, quite possibly, their cheapest yet, with just 10 regular characters, unknown actors and only interior sets. In comparison, 1968's *Motel* had been a mega production with 16 regulars, big name actors and extensive outdoor location footage.

The only recognisable face in *Until Tomorrow* belonged to Hazel Phillips, a favourite of the blue-rinse set for her 60s afternoon chat show *Girltalk* until her 'shocking strip' for the daring, but laughably inept, 1970 movie *The Set*. 'The press came out like vultures and I really regret doing that movie. It was the worst thing I've ever done,' Phillips later admitted to *TV Soap*. After another controversial gig, as a lesbian peeping in on Vera Collins showering on *Number 96*, Phillips was playing it safe with *Until Tomorrow*. The only shenanigans 'vicious gossip' Marge Stewart would get up to was forcing herself upon her messed-up neighbours for another interminable chat.

Brisbane audiences recognised two other performers – Muriel Watson and Ron Cadee – from regular appearances on local Grundy QTQ-9 quiz shows *I've Got a Secret* and *Play Your Hunch*. Both appeared regularly on the cocktail hour shows alongside the future Mrs Reg Grundy, Joy Chambers, who had the good sense to stay out of *Until Tomorrow* and wait for *The Restless Years* to launch her acting career.

Until Tomorrow began (very slowly) with listless Laura Mitchell (Muriel Watson) arriving at the Vale Street house of widowed Judge Jackson Kerridge (John Nash). She was fresh out of prison for the murder (which she didn't commit) of her husband, and was planning to shoot the judge for his part in sentencing her. When he answered the door, he didn't recognise her because he was now blind. Jackson assumed she was answering his ad for a new housekeeper and, confused, Laura accepted the job. They fell in love, he shuffled around (looking more like a Thunderbird puppet than a blind man), and she cleaned the house.

Jackson's daughter Sue McKenzie (Sue Robinson) wasn't too thrilled about daddy's new washerwoman, but she had bigger problems of her own when her womaniser husband Trevor (Barry Otto) pushed her down the stairs when she was pregnant. The then unknown Otto was thrilled to be playing a cad or, as he described it to *TV Times* at the time, a four-letter word they couldn't print. 'He's a ****, terribly ambitious, the type that shouldn't be married,' Otto said. 'He doesn't want any children and he sells cars.' A bastard, misogynist and a car salesman – could Trevor have been any more sleazy? 'I don't think [*Until Tomorrow*] is as sexy as *Number 96* or *The Box*, but I think the mums will get involved.' Wishful thinking, as the only mums who would get involved were the really, really bored ones.

Trevor's neglected wife Sue embarked on an affair with Doctor Warwick Curtis (Harry Scott) who was young, spunky, recovering from a broken engagement and renovating his own home. While Sue and Dr Warwick played 'hide the hammer', Trevor had an affair with Angela Wainwright (Kaye Stevenson), the slutty bitch wife of dopey local shop owner Bill Wainwright (Ron Cadee).

Angela blamed Bill for the death of her younger sister and had been torturing him for years. When Bill finally collapsed with a heart attack, Angela stood by and did nothing, hoping he would die. He was certainly in no danger of being discovered by a customer as the budget didn't extend to any extras popping in or out of their corner shop.

Upon recovering, Bill was accused of the murder of Laura's son, Kevin Mitchell, who had previously killed his own father and let his mother take the blame. Also injured in the melee was wife Angela, who got amnesia. Psychiatrist Dr Janet Kingsford (Elaine Cusick) was called in to treat the problem and ended up turning Angela into a decent person. Bill was cleared of all charges but remained suicidal, terrified his wife was only pretending to be nice. Dr Janet hung around, moping and hiding (as all good soap psychiatrists do) a secret bigger than any of her patients.

Then unknown actor Barry Otto with Sue Robinson filming in the Brisbane studio.

Another miserable specialist in the serial was Dr Grant Roberts (Robert Quilter) who was completely dominated by his rich mother Charlotte (Babette Stephens). Sixteen years earlier, she had broken up his romance with Valerie Vernon (Cynthia Cooper) and pushed him into a more desirable (but disastrous) wedding to psycho Mary (Berys Marsh). Valerie skipped town, leaving behind a baby girl with her worldly-wise mother Daphne 'Gran' Gilchrist (Jean Jarrott). Guess who the father was.

It took 16 years for vague Valerie to pop back 'from abroad' and blonde bombshell daughter Sharon (Rosemary Ricketts) wasn't that thrilled to see her (would you if your internationally-travelled mother's wardrobe was as dreary as all the neighbours?). Sharon was far more interested in eyeing up Dr Warwick and his toolbox while her secret father, Dr Grant, was eyeing up Valerie again.

Until Tomorrow began on air in February 1975, at 2.30pm (up against *General Hospital* on Nine). Ron Cadee, supposedly 'Brisbane's own Liberace', had convinced himself that it was preferable to such American shows. 'In my opinion, the quality of *Until Tomorrow* is superb,' Cadee told *TV Times*. 'Something new happens every day – not like some American series that you can miss for three years and pick up again easily.'

Until Tomorrow may have moved a tad more quickly than its American counterparts, but technically and acting-wise, the quality of *Until*

Tomorrow was not superb. If anything, missing a day was actually a relief, especially when actors like Ron Cadee were (literally) walking into the furniture and stumbling over their lines. Perhaps they were just uncomfortable having to recite the florid dialogue. As an example, here is the special moment when everyone in Vale Street threw a surprise farewell party for ex-con turned cleaner Laura, who was leaving town because she thought she wasn't good enough for Judge Jackson. The assembled guests, all on the verge of tears, peppered their conversation with mock courtroom expressions as a nod to the blubbering judge.

> DR GRANT: 'It is the considered opinion of this court that you are guilty of being an honest, cherished person. A woman of great courage and humility.'
> DR WARWICK: 'Laura Mitchell, your friends condemn you to a life of happiness and love with Jackson Kerridge.'

(And, after much crying all round)

> LAURA: 'I am going to accept your sentence with honour and give this man all the love that I've had lying around all these years. You don't realise what you've done for me.'

Yes, but what was it doing to the audience? By July, amidst rumours that its days were numbered, the show was moved back to 11.30am as a lead-in to the midday movie. 'We are still fighting like mad to improve the ratings on the show,' BTQ-7 publicity manager Robbie Lonergan told *TV Times*. Despite another murder mystery (killing off another psychiatrist who was taping all his patients' secrets and then blackmailing them) and Jackson's sight being restored (so he could see how 'beautiful' Laura was instead of just fingering her face), the series plodded along to a crashing halt after 180 episodes. None of the stories ended with any resolutions.

'It is understood that Brisbane and Adelaide wanted to continue with the serial, but we were not supported by Melbourne or Sydney,' Lonergan admitted later to *TV Times*. 'Perhaps too much plot development was inserted in too short a time. In imported soap operas, things just seem to drift along.'

Actress Cynthia Cooper thought 'a lot more money could have been spent promoting the show. We have had competition from other serials which have been running for some time, and the attitude of some Queenslanders hasn't helped. They think that nothing good could come out of their state.'

Actor Barry Otto was loyal and respectful right to the end. 'Perhaps the script was sometimes overwritten but the writing never at any stage embarrassed me as an actor,' he told *TV Times*. 'But maybe it's a good thing in that I will move to Sydney sooner than I would have if the show had continued.' It turned out to be a very good thing, and after his breakthrough role in *Bliss* in 1985, he won the AFI Best Supporting Actor award in 1992 for *Strictly Ballroom*. Daughter Miranda Otto would also become an actress, appearing in *The Lord of the Rings* blockbusters.

Scriptwriter Ken Lord always felt sorry for the actors. 'They got one walk-through and just one rehearsal before being thrown to the wolves amongst the cardboard sets. Their make-up was slapped onto them and then they ended up with shadows all over their faces because of the 1959 lighting grids. We used to sit there holding our breath from 7am till 7pm every day wondering if that day's episode would get done.'

The actors also had to deal with constant script inconsistencies as the writers never sat down together to ensure any uniformity. 'Gran was originally written as a Catholic, then the next writer turned her into a Methodist and still another pegged her as Salvation Army!' Lord laughs today.

That might explain why *Until Tomorrow* was often appalling, and it wasn't just the bad acting or sparse sets (where doctors' surgeries had just a lone eye-chart on the wall). Its soundtrack was also dire, using the same ear-piercing, oboe-screeching snatch of dramatic music over and over again. It must have sent many housewives rushing for the Valium.

'To be honest, I think Grundy's were ironing out the bugs in Brisbane so they could get it right with their new Sydney productions,' says Ken Lord. Halfway through *Until Tomorrow*, Reg Watson moved down to Grundy's Sydney office where they began to plan much grander things.

Until Tomorrow may have helped bring about the next wave of Grundy's soaps, but more significantly, the dull but neighbourly Vale Street might have been the genesis for Reg Watson's creation of *Neighbours'* Ramsay Street a decade later. Perhaps Vale Street is where Scott and Charlene now live, along with the rest of the banished-to-Queensland ex-*Neighbours* characters. Somehow, it seems only fitting.

THE UNISEXERS

PREMIERE: **1975** EPISODES: **15** NETWORK: **NINE** FINALE: **1975**

Angus Melody (Walter Pym) lectures the most
well-behaved hippies ever seen on TV.

By the mid-70s, Ten had *Number 96* and *The Box* and Seven had *Class of '74*. Nine needed its own soapie to compete so they commissioned several pilots in search of the perfect show. South Pacific Films came up with *Secret Doors*, which starred Gerard Maguire, *Number 96*'s Norman Yemm and Candy Raymond, and Rebecca Gilling. It was to be an adults-only saga set in a small country town, and sounded very much like *Bellbird* with nudity. Nine passed and kept looking.

Grundy's had offered two pilots. One was a 'clean' serial called *The Martins and the McCoys*, about two families who lived next door to each other. Widower Nick McCoy (Jimmy Hannan) had three children, one of whom was adopted, and next door lived deserted wife Jane Martin (Annie Brisk) with three kids of her own. It all sounded suspiciously like *The Brady Bunch* down-under.

'I'm not recognisable as Jimmy Hannan – all teeth and smile and flashing lights. It's different and at times quite heavy,' the Grundy's quiz show host told *TV Times*. 'Nick McCoy is a lovely, family part; not a rape, a drug or swear word in sight.' Other characters in the sickly sweet premise included a 'mischievous' five year old called Mr Smith, corner shop owner George Evans (Willie Fennell) and policeman Ted Williams (Tex Morton). Perhaps sensing that one *Brady Bunch* on TV was more than enough, Nine seriously considered Grundy's other pilot.

That was *Two Way Mirror* which Nine claimed would be the most daring soap on television. They bravely touted it to run directly opposite *Number 96*, five nights a week. Their serial was set in the cosmetic and fashion industry, with the show's title referring to a mirror where characters could watch nude photographic sessions going on next door. So far, so good, but wouldn't the voyeuristic premise get a bit repetitive? And could an entire series be built around one mirror?

The pilot featured Tristan Rogers, Jill Forster and Anne Charleston. A decade before becoming grandmotherly icon Madge on *Neighbours*, Charleston was philosophical about stripping. 'It's a thing that does worry me but if the role is good enough to warrant it, I would be quite happy about it,' she told *TV Times*. 'It might be a problem for [young son Nicky] with the kids at school teasing him about having his mother naked on TV.' Luckily for Nicky and future fans of *Neighbours*, it never came to that.

Producer Alan Coleman recalls a deliciously over-the-top Bette Davis type character, played by Brisbane actress Babette Stephens. He particularly remembers a scene where the camera pulled back from some rude goings-on to reveal how someone was watching from the other side of the two-way mirror. It was the series' wicked matriarch and as she turned around to reveal her face for the first time, viewers would be alarmed to see that she wore a patch over one eye.

Sadly, this outrageous moment never made it to air because, in the end, Nine settled for a faux hippie serial called *The Unisexers*. The announcement was front-page news in Sydney and the tabloid press started salivating over the possibilities. Would there be experimental drug use? Communal nude bathing? Of course there would be, because it was all coming from the makers of *Number 96*, Cash Harmon Productions.

The Unisexers' title actually had several meanings. Firstly, it referred to the brand name of the denim clothes the characters were going to produce while living and working together. Secondly, it referred to the growing fad where boys and girls were able to wear the same clothes. Finally – and probably most importantly for shows from this era – the title had the word 'sex' in it. If this had actually been in the show, it might have helped what was a pretty dreadful concept.

Retired English professor Angus Melody (Walter Pym) and his dreamer wife Dora (Jessica Noad) lived in a rambling old mansion in Paddington, Sydney (the same suburb as *Number 96* but, for this show, a world away from the raunchy apartment block). They were lonely because their seven children had grown up and moved away. In *The Unisexers*' opening scene, they were having high tea with commune mastermind Cornelius 'Corny' Hastings (Patrick Ward) and passionate but practical Julian 'Tinsel' Tinsley (Steven Tandy), and discussing their exciting new business venture in the rag trade. Without hesitation, the Melodys agreed to let the well-dressed boys move in with all their friends. Comedy was

The premiere was ruled unsuitable for a family timeslot.

meant to ensue when a kombi van pulled up during the credits and badly-dressed hippies began pouring out the back door.

The 'crowd from TV's kooky commune', as *TV Times* called them, included former university student Felicity aka 'Flick' (Tina Bursill); earnest Monica Parry (Michele Fawdon); her lazy, cynical brother Brian (Scott Lambert); suburban Sally Pickles (*Number 96*'s pantyhose strangler victim Josephine Knur); rich girl Deirdre (Anne Grigg); optimistic accountant Benjy Lewis (Tony Sheldon) and clumsy Humphrey 'Humph' Brown (Hugh Logan).

There was also Brigitte (Sonia Hoffman) and Eustice (John Paramor) who were always getting hot and heavy with each other. This was an absolute no-no for the ridiculously chaste commune, where boys lived on one floor and the girls on another one below. When the pair were caught slipping into a bedroom (on their own!) they had to come clean and admit they were a secretly married couple. Although it was against the rules of the clan to engage in such an outdated concept, the Melodys insisted the young couple be allowed to stay. Actually, dopey Dora referred to them as 'the children', which wasn't far from the truth.

The 'children' cleared out a storage room to convert into a workroom and its contents were strewn all over the house. In some very strange (or maybe just cheap) art direction, the hippie palace now featured a kids' swing, rocking horse and a suit of armour. More comic hijinks were supposed to derive from the making of the jeans, particularly since one of the girls had to sit in a bathtub full of water to shrink every pair.

In doing so, 'a girl wearing only bra and panties who used strong language' upset the Broadcasting Control Board, which gave Nine an ultimatum to censor the show or move it to a later timeslot. Originally planned to screen at 6.30pm on Sundays, against *Disneyland*, Nine was forced to bring the premiere forward to 7.30pm on Friday, 7 February 1975. For once, the Board was overreacting, but probably getting in early in the fear of worse goings-on to come. If only they knew there was no need for concern from this commune.

The pilot also introduced the Melodys' cranky housekeeper, Mrs Tripp (Dolore Whiteman), who was horrified at the new 'combine' (a horrid attempt to create another character who mixed up her words just like *Number 96*'s Dorrie Evans). Ridiculously, Mrs Tripp had a complete change of heart by the next commercial break when she was asked to model in jeans for a senior citizen photo shoot with the Melodys. Since the young girls had all displayed un-hippie-like behaviour in wanting to be the prettiest model, the 'older generation' were chosen to wear the clothes for the first newspaper shoot. By the end of *The Unisexers*' first hour, this plot development had sapped the series of any last bit of credibility. Hippies that didn't have sex with each other were hard enough to swallow, but the sight of the retirees and their housekeeper swanning around in the ugly jeans was too much.

Given that there were limited storylines about making jeans, the commune lifestyle was actually meant to be at the heart of the show's concept. Sadly, this made it one very annoying concept. Everyone referred to each other as 'brother' and a gong was comically sounded every time they needed a group discussion. Lacking any sexual tension, the series was supposed to survive on 'generation gap' comic situations, which hardly seemed possible given how accommodating the oldies were proving to be.

'We were the most conservative bunch of hippies ever seen on screen and the show ended up naïve and bland,' says Tina Bursill today. 'Not only did everyone speak in an appalling "educated Australian accent", in no way did it represent the culture of the time, particularly when compared to how we all were when away from the set.' Off-screen, most of the actors were drinking, smoking pot and sleeping with each other, but none of this was allowed to happen on the show.

Regular *Number 96* writers such as Derek Strahan, Johnny Whyte and the lady who dreamt up the doomed series, Anne Hall, were hampered by the 6pm timeslot which the show was given after its premiere, and which would not permit any situation that involved sex, violence or 'anything that could inspire fear'. After the pilot had been shot and the regular episodes began being made, the restrictions meant that was the end of the married hippies ever referring to the Pill again, as they had during the 'strong language' of the first hour. And Flick (Tina Bursill) never would strip down to her underwear again.

Indeed, given that the debut of *Number 96* had been promoted as 'Tonight at 8.30 Television loses its virginity!' one wag from *The Sunday Telegraph* suggested the ridiculously innocent *Unisexers* warranted the proclamation 'TV Regains Its Virginity!' Bill Harmon claimed he didn't find out just how tough the Broadcasting Control Board was going to be until after the series went into production. 'Here was a show about a group of young kids sharing a house and we couldn't even have a bottle of wine on the table,' he told *Cleo* magazine. 'Everything that we could have fun with was taboo, we were left with nothing to play with.'

Not only that, but some much older characters were about to arrive and none of them looked as if they were going to provide much joy. Melody's brother, Reverend Gerald (Redmond Phillips), was a former missionary just beginning to have memory lapses (sounds like a barrel of laughs) while Benjy's mum and dad (Brian Moll and Toni Lamond) were Orthodox Jews who provided endless Jewish parents' clichés. The only positive aspect for Toni Lamond was acting for the first time opposite her real-life son, Tony Sheldon, who played Benjy.

Given its predominantly kids-only audience, the show had given them nobody to identify with, so Cash Harmon Productions announced to *TV Times* that *The Unisexers* would gain a 'godson'. Fifteen-year-old Ashley Grenville (from comedy series *The Godfathers*) was to play a Canberra boy who visits Sydney. 'His experience was an important consideration because our tight production schedule won't allow any coaching,' a spokesman told *TV Times*.

The Unisexers' production schedule should have been able to accommodate the odd spot of drama coaching, since the cast worked six days a week for up to 16 hours a day. Conditions in the shabby studios that would next house *The Young Doctors* were nothing short of appalling. 'There was no air-conditioning, no dressing room and no green room,' recalls Bursill. The actors considered a stop-work meeting to improve conditions but, like the fictional brotherhood they were playing on screen, their off-screen union effort proved to be just as fruitless. After sweltering away in 45-degree heat, everybody was probably too exhausted to keep up the fight.

In the end it hardly mattered since Nine's expensive 'experiment' bit the dust after just three weeks on air. 'The ratings crashed,' Bill Harmon explained to *Cleo*. 'After a short meeting with Channel Nine it was mutually agreed to get it off. Fast!' *TV Times* advised that the chairman of the network, Kerry Packer, who had personally given the series its green light, cancelled it on 27 February. Nine's Sydney program manager, Lynton Taylor, said the program had been 'a $1 million experiment'.

'A friend of mine from Kings Cross had a clothing manufacturing company and he put out a line of jeans to match the show,' remembers actor Patrick Ward. 'He lost a lot of money, poor bastard.' Ward, who played Corny, always liked working with producer Bill Harmon because he was 'brash but down to earth. He gave me a lot of work.' When Ward crossed over to do *Number 96*, Harmon intervened when it came time to shoot a fight scene with actor Max Cullen. 'He came down onto the set and said, "Patrick can take a hit!" and he punched me in the stomach really hard. Max has never gotten over it. He still talks about it to this day.' Realising that Ward could take a good kick to the guts, Harmon made sure that the actor was part of his biggest disaster years later, *Arcade*.

Bellbird's Camilla Rountree, who joined the show in its dying days, told *TV Times* that *The Unisexers* was 'exhausting, even nightmarish. We worked with new colour equipment that had just been delivered and nobody was too sure how to use. It would have had to be a cross between Disney and *The Partridge Family* to have been successful [but] I'd love to know how the ratings were done. I still see lots of kids with *Unisexers* stickers on their cases, and they are always talking to me in the street. Obviously they watched it, but I bet they weren't consulted in any surveys.'

If they had been consulted, it appears that many were secretly wishing for the return of an American sitcom favourite. 'I wish to condemn Channel 9 for replacing *Happy Days* with a load of rubbish called *The Unisexers*,' one irate schoolchild wrote to *TV Times*. 'Channel 9 claims *Unisexers* has wide family appeal. Well, I can prove this is wrong. To start with, I hate it (I'm 16). My brothers and sisters hate it (their ages are 13, 9, 6 and 5) and my parents don't watch it either. Most of the kids at the school I go to are avid *Happy Days* fans and we all used to watch it every single night.' Luckily for all those kids, the editor was able to break good news – 'Ed: Channel 9 brought back *Happy Days* to replace *The Unisexers*. That's showbusiness.'

11

THE YOUNG DOCTORS

PREMIERE: **1976** EPISODES: **1396** NETWORK: **NINE** FINALE: **1983**

Nurse Tania (Judy McBurney) marries Dr Garcia (Tony Alvarez).

'I'll never forget you, Nurse, you know that.'
'And I'll never forget you, Doctor...'
That's how it all started in the first scene of the first episode of *The Young Doctors*. Dr Craig Rothwell (John Walton) was leaving one hospital to start work at another, the Albert Memorial, and as the camera pulled back to show him and his lovelorn nurse entwined on top of an operating table, two strange doors could be seen in the background. Were there really Gents and Ladies toilets in an emergency room? No, it was just the edge of the Bunny's set, the neighbourhood bar that would be at the centre of the love action for nearly 1,400 episodes.

The Young Doctors was a popular success, but lightweight enough never to win any award during its long run, peer- or public-voted, except from the medical fraternity. For the record though, its producers never claimed it was anything more than pure entertainment. Medical accuracy was not a priority – this was no *E.R.*, *Casualty* or even *All Saints*. Its early evening timeslot meant blood and gore were a no-no and, besides, this was a hospital you wouldn't want to have ended up in if you were sick. Patients were often non-speaking extras and their ailments merely background action to a never-ending series of love affairs.

Ironically, The Young Doctors *debuted on air the same week as* The Sullivans.

Ironically, *The Young Doctors* debuted on air the same week as *The Sullivans*, in November 1976. Nine was determined to succeed with their own local soap, and by chance they were trying out two simultaneously. Reg Grundy and Reg Watson had already been discussing a medical series when they heard Nine wanted such a show. Watson, who had worked on the popular English medical series *Emergency Ward 10*, knocked off 12 months of projected storylines.

Nine was impressed enough to give the green light for 13 weeks of episodes and recruited Alan Coleman (*Class of '74/'75*) as its producer since he had worked with Watson on the British serial *Crossroads*. Australia's first medical series was a goer, although Seven had nearly beaten them to it with one called *Casualty Ward* 18 months earlier.

The show began with a group of new interns beginning work at the Albert Memorial (and discovering the hospital wasn't all that big, given it contained just a couple of sets in the early days). To get things rolling, the aforementioned playboy Dr Craig Rothwell spent next to no time 'catching up' with lonely Laura Denham (Joanna Moore-Smith). She was the neglected wife of new hospital superintendent Dr Brian Denham (Michael Beecher), and with her husband in New Zealand at a medical conference, she slipped away for a night of passion with the much younger doctor, leaving young son Toby in the care of a seriously dated hippie babysitter. Finding himself alone the next morning, Toby set off in search of his mother only to be hit by a car for the show's first cliffhanger.

Other core characters included Dr Denham's dependable secretary Helen Gordon (Lyn James), her sweet daughter Nurse Jill Gordon (Joanne Samuel), busybody kiosk attendant Ada Simmonds (Gwen Plumb), the debonair (but only if carnations in the top pocket impress) Dr Raymond Shaw (Alfred Sandor), the charmless Dr Graham Steele (Tim Page), the fun-loving Dr Greg Mason (pop singer Mark Holden), the over-achieving Dr Gail Henderson (Peita Toppano), nerdy orderly Dennis Jamison (Chris King) and the series' most memorable bitch, 'Dragon Lady' Sister Grace Scott (Cornelia Frances). For sex appeal, there was also Nurse Jo Jo Adams (Delvene Delaney) who could be seen exuberantly disco dancing (with boobs a-bouncing) in the show's opening credits.

Naturally enough, the critics were horrified ('Medical Misfits Are a Terminal Bore' said *The Daily Telegraph*), particularly since they were impressed by the much more lavish *The Sullivans*. Perhaps anxious to keep the more prestigious production, Nine decided not to take up an option for more episodes of *The Young Doctors* and a *TV Week* announcement about new cast members became a post-mortem instead ('Abigail's Sad Comeback'). In her autobiography, *Plumb Crazy*, Gwen Plumb recalled abusing Nine's director of programming, telling him 'none of you people in positions of making decisions walk along a street, shop in a supermarket, go to restaurants or sporting fixtures where you are recognised and spoken to. We in the cast of *Doctors* get first-hand what the public think about the show – and they love it. It's already catching on like fire and it will be big!'

As it turned out, a private ratings survey confirmed Ada was right! In an amazing about-face, Nine reversed their decision and the announcement was made at what was supposed to be the series' wrap party. It proved to be a very wise decision on the part of Nine, who got themselves two popular soaps for the next six years. The celebration also began a long tradition of wild cast and crew parties, usually held on the set of Bunny's. After one such event, cast and crew arrived at work the next day to find one of the leading actresses, naked and asleep, under a car with a cameraman. If that's what was going on behind the scenes, no wonder it translated into outstanding ratings.

Dr Greg Mason (Mark Holden before judging *Australian Idol*) with nurse Jo Jo Adams (Delvene Delaney).

Within a year the show had an average rating of about 20 in Sydney and close to 30 in Melbourne, screening at 6pm. In Brisbane it aired at 7pm and was the city's number one show, rating in the high 30s. Yet Adelaide, which aired it twice a week instead of stripping it five nights, could only muster a 15.

Safe from the axe and ensconced in an early evening timeslot, the young doctors and nurses came and went with alarming regularity. Doctors included Chris Piper (Bartholomew John), Mike Newman (Peter Bensley), Peter Holland (Peter Lochran), John Forrest (Alan Dale), Ben Fielding (Eric Oldfield), Tony Garcia (Tony Alvarez) and Rod Langley (Chris Orchard). Suave Dr Shaw, meanwhile, tried to hide some 'mysterious wartime activities' and wondered if he could ever operate again with an injured hand, while Dr Denham found himself back on the 'singles' market after his wayward wife Laura ran away to Spain with Dr Garcia's father.

The female doctors, however, could be counted on the fingers of one hand. After Gail Henderson failed to return from delivering the world's longest lecture on microsurgery (in reality, actress Peita Toppano was leaving to do the stage musical *A Chorus Line*), there came Susan Richards (American-born Judy Lynne) and Robyn Porter (Joy Chambers). In the absence of any hunky male nurses, they both fell in love with male doctors.

The problem was, all of the male doctors were already entangled with the always available female nurses. On standby for a bit of slap and tickle were Sister Vivienne Jeffries (Diana McLean), Sister Evans (Jeanie Drynan), Sister Eve Turner (Anne Lucas) and Sister Suzanne Gibbs (Susanne Stuart). These senior nurses were only mildly less horny than the nurses they bossed around – Sherry Andrews (*Playboy* centrefold Karen Pini), Liz Kennedy (Rebecca Gilling), Lisa Brooks (Paula Duncan), Kim Barrington (Lynda Stoner) and fan favourite Tania Livingstone (Judy McBurney).

Now came the mix and match to ensure plenty of dating mishaps, love affairs, engagements, weddings and near-weddings, with all receptions to be held at – where else? – Bunny's. Divorce was decreed a series no-no so as not to upset younger viewers, although rapes, shootings and bombs were considered acceptable. According to Alan Coleman, Nine was always telling him to 'push the envelope'. Still, courting *Young Doctors* style couldn't have been more chaste. After a come-on in the supply room

Sister Grace Scott (Cornelia Frances).

or right in front of their patients, the couple would head off to dinner at Bunny's, the only venue in town, and afterwards they might retire to someone's flat, where interior design usually only extended as far as a spice rack on the kitchen wall.

In this crazy world of love, Sister Scott was the first to be raped and the first to be jilted at the altar (she was raped three times all up, stalked twice and charged with murder just once). Other wedding disasters included that of Dr Russell Edwards (Peter Cousens), who was about to marry Julie Holland (Lisa Aldenhoven) until a gunman opened fire inside the chapel; and the cancelled wedding of Dr Chris (Bartholomew John) to Kim (Lynda Stoner) after she was shot dead. The wedding of Dr Fielding (Eric Oldfield) to Liz Kennedy (Rebecca Gilling) was interrupted when Dr Forrest (Alan Dale) stood up and declared his objection, apparently unable to 'forever hold his peace'. Then, when Liz finally did marry him, she was electrocuted on her wedding day by a faulty light fixture.

While the sexy brigade couldn't find true love, the plain Janes found happiness with their even plainer husbands. Caroline Fielding (Kim Wran, daughter of the then NSW Premier, Neville Wran) had been originally introduced as the slinky mistress of mogul Philip Winter (Noel Trevarthen). He checked into hospital accompanied by Caroline and his buxom executive secretary Hilary Templeton (Abigail). Later in the show, Winter dumped Caroline and she was rushed to the hospital after a suicide attempt. In an unusual soapie reversal, actor Kim Wran was ordered to cover up and wear unflattering spectacles. Transformation complete, Caroline found work at the Albert Memorial front desk, found herself a husband, then found herself a widow after he was killed in a bank robbery just after she'd given birth. Eventually she married dopey hospital orderly Dennis (Chris King).

Another tragic couple was Dr Steele (Tim Page) and Eve (Anne Lucas), who were allowed to stay married but suffered several offspring catastrophes. Their first baby miscarried, the second was killed and the third kidnapped from Grace's office. Even though the baby-snatching occurred the same day as poor Tania was hit by a truck while crossing the road to Bunny's (happening off-screen of course) the cast reacted to both tragedies with as much emotional intensity as if Ada's kiosk had run out of sandwiches.

One wedding that did make it through the vows was the hugely hyped Tony and Tania tizzy. After nearly marrying Lisa Brooks (Paula Duncan), Dr Garcia's marriage to Tania Livingstone on 7 March 1978 was the 'TV surprise wedding of the year'. Grundy's splashed out and hired a Rolls Royce for the bridal vehicle. Dr Shaw (Alfred Sandor) gave Tania away, while bridesmaid Caroline Fielding (Kim Wran) was allowed to look as glamorous as possible for the high-rating event and *TV Times* colour spread.

To celebrate, Nine took actors Tony Alvarez and Judy McBurney on a whistle-stop tour around Australia. In full wedding regalia, they hosted a wedding reception in every capital city for a room full of competition

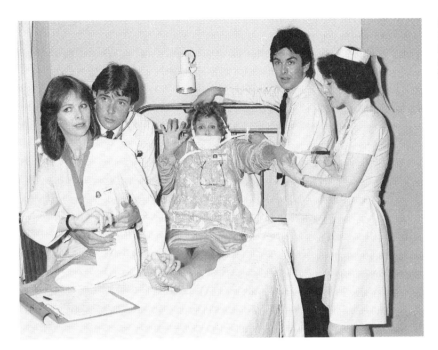

Rebecca Gilling, Peter Bensley, Gwen Plumb, Peter Lochran and Susanne Stuart fool around on set.

winners. The couple were mobbed in every location and given real wedding presents by besotted viewers. Tony Alvarez and Judy McBurney bemusedly split the gifts up between them. 'There were lots of salt and pepper shakers, doilies and toasters,' McBurney remembers.

After all the fuss, Tony Alvarez decided to leave the series, so the happy couple were broken up. He moved to Hollywood where he appeared in *The Mambo Kings* with Antonio Banderas. He returned to Sydney to die tragically of cancer at just 41 years of age. Lynda Stoner, who shared a house with Alvarez and John Dommett while making the show, remembers him with great affection. 'I had some of the best and funniest times living there and it was a wonderful experience,' Stoner recalls.

Judy McBurney originally signed on for just two weeks, but ended up staying for six years. 'Tania was always having affairs or being engaged,' says McBurney. 'I think she was probably a little tart but she was so sweet and gorgeous, I liked her a lot.' McBurney resisted scriptwriters' attempts to promote Tania to head nurse because she hated the bigger head wear required of the new position. So Tania kept failing her exams until scriptwriters eventually insisted Nurse Livingstone couldn't remain a third-year nurse forever.

While Tony and Tania's nuptials would become the show's best-remembered wedding, one moment is more infamous – the night Sister Scott plummeted down the elevator shaft. Grace, delivering a stinging barb to Nurse Gordon (Joanne Samuel), forgot the lift was broken and stormed past the repairmen into thin air. The nasty fall failed to do in the old battleaxe and Sister Scott recovered and got promoted to Matron before leaving the show.

In 1991, American television producer David E. Kelley (*The Practice*, *Ally McBeal*) would mark his arrival on American television using the same storyline when bitchy lawyer Roslind Shays (Diana Muldaur) fell down the *L.A. Law* elevator shaft. Kelley would be praised by *TV Guide* as a 'wildly unconventional force' for scripting such an event. No such recognition was given to the *Young Doctors* scribes.

Since there was limited editing time available, *The Young Doctors* would shoot episodes in sequence, which is rarely done in the world of movies or television. With the operating theatre set doubling as the casualty ward and patients' rooms, the art department crew would be busy re-setting this room whenever the action switched outside to the reception hallway. The only editing that needed to be done to an episode was if location footage needed to be spliced in – and that was infrequent, since most of the action stayed strictly indoors.

Not that the viewers seemed to mind how cheap the show looked. Gwen Plumb once received a 10 cent coin in the mail, because the writer had noticed that Dennis had forgotten to pay for a paper from Ada's kiosk. *TV Times* reported that Plumb put the coin into a charity collection tin. Meanwhile, actress Lyn James (Dr Denham's secretary Helen Gordon) made an appearance at a charity fete and was asked three times by different people about job vacancies at the Albert Memorial Hospital. Strangely though, nobody ever wanted to work in Bunny's.

Hospital staff always congregated in one of two spots to discuss their tortured romances – Bunny's restaurant/cocktail bar/nightclub or Ada's hallway kiosk. Opposite the hospital's front desk, Ada got to hear most of what was going on, and was able to wring from her customers what she hadn't yet figured out. Her own life was sketchy and her major dramatic moment was when her ailing, arthritic husband Arthur (Willie Fennell) drowned in a fishing accident when he was supposed to be putting up her new wallpaper.

One of the show's long-running inside jokes was a stuffed parrot that could be glimpsed inside Ada's refrigerator whenever she reached in to get a cold drink. Sometimes it was re-positioned to hang just on the edge of the framed shots. Viewers were so engrossed in the action, however, they always failed to see the gag. There was also a stuffed calico dummy known affectionately to cast and crew as 'Fred'. 'Most of the time he was used as a non-speaking patient in a bed in the background,' laughs Peter Pinne, 'but the actors used to have a lot of fun with "Fred", frequently erotic!'

As well as her aforementioned autobiography, Gwen Plumb also penned a spin-off *Young Doctors* recipe book, *What's Cooking With Ada?* 'I learned a lot from her even though she was incredibly bossy,' remembers Lynda Stoner. 'She was also very funny and very professional and she had no time for "youngsters" who came on set not knowing their lines. She was someone we looked up to and respected.'

If staff weren't hanging out at Ada's kiosk, they were usually at Bunny's. Bunny was played by comedian Ugly Dave Gray, who dropped the 'Ugly' from his name for this rare dramatic role. He told *TV Times* when the show started that he couldn't see himself doing the role for long. 'I couldn't be serious all day, it would drive me round the bend.' He wasn't joking – Bunny died soon after of a heart attack but Ugly turned up (with every old joke in the book) as a regular panellist on another Grundy smash quiz show, *Graham Kennedy's Blankety Blanks*. Bunny's was taken over by Anne Marie Austin (a thankless role for Judi Connelli who went on to become a major star in cabaret and musical theatre).

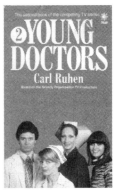

Other well-known names to end up in the Albert Memorial were a teenage Russell Crowe as a shirt-shedding patient; Serge Lazareff ('fake' doctor Ian Parish), Lois Ramsey (Winnie Parsons, a cooking rival of Ada's); Mark Hembrow (pop star Georgie Saint); John Jarratt (chef Ben Stone); a prepubescent Gerry Sont (years before he'd start flashing his arse on *Chances*); and Iain Finlay (a current affairs reporter from *This Day Tonight* who played villain Frank Curtis).

Most of the Sydney-based cast of *Number 96*, by this time out of work, also popped up, including Joe Hasham (this time playing a heterosexual baddie, Ken Hansen); Deborah Gray (keeping her clothes on as a wheelchair-bound patient); Bunney Brooke (as a cleaning lady/clown with an analgesic addiction) and background group The Executives (who provided music to boogie to in Bunny's that was even more bogus than their efforts in *Number 96*'s Duddles Disco).

TOP: Paperback.
ABOVE:
1,000th episode commemorative magazine.

The Young Doctors ended up being screened in Canada, France, Angola, Barbados and Trinidad, not to mention the UK where it topped daytime ratings. A Young Doctors Appreciation Society had over 8,000 members at the height of its popularity but this was in the 80s, long after the show had finished production. Not that a bit of overseas money would have beefed up working conditions behind the scenes, because this show enjoyed possibly the worst conditions in Aussie soap history.

When production began, the Mitchell Street studios, ironically rumoured to be a former sausage factory, had no air conditioning. Crew wiped asbestos off their cameras every morning before starting work. They were the original cameras bought by Nine for the start of television in 1956, and they often broke down and rarely matched. Peter Pinne, who started off as a writer, then script editor and finally associate producer, was under no illusions while making the show. 'Nine only agreed to do the show because it was cheap and they had to produce a certain amount of drama. *The Sullivans* cost at least three times as much.'

'Nine were a difficult network to work with,' says Peter Pinne. 'Ada's kiosk used to sell magazines, but the only ones we could display were those owned by Consolidated Press, which was owned by Nine. If some other mag was there, we had to re-shoot the scene.' As for the carefully plotted end-of-year cliffhangers, they never worked because of live broadcast of cricket matches. 'Then Nine would complain that the ratings weren't the way they used to be. You could never win.'

The network also wasn't above ripping cameras out of the *Young Doctors* studio whenever there was a sports broadcast mishap. 'If one of the cameras broke down at the cricket, they'd just take away one of ours. The poor director would be there with all his scenes planned and all of a sudden a van would pull up and we'd be a camera short! We were low down on the priority list,' laughs Joanne Samuel (Jill Gordon). The actress also remembers how good producer Alan Coleman was to her when another *Young Doctors* actress, Rosie Bailey, was injured while making the movie *Mad Max*. Coleman didn't hesitate in letting Joanne Samuel leave the show immediately so she could take over the cult role of the road warrior's doomed wife.

At least she was away from the dilapidated studios where crews froze in winter and mopped up rain when it leaked through the roof. In summer, actors' make-up sweated away under the hot lights. 'We had to keep changing our hospital uniforms because of perspiration,' says Judy McBurney, remembering that they also had to change in the ladies' loo. 'Someone had to dry our wet-with-sweat hair with hairdryers. After about four-and-a-half years they finally put in air conditioning.' Joanne Samuel remembers having to change into her nurses' shoes on the studio floor. 'You had to walk in galoshes from wardrobe to the studios because the wardrobe room would flood whenever it rained.'

For years, this mopping up was supervised by chief make-up lady Patricia Hutchence, who was given a cameo appearance in the final episode. She was the mother of Michael Hutchence, lead singer of INXS, and yes, the infamous band did play at a wild cast party.

Regular actors made the most of any staff party because they were paid only $588.50 a week if they made four episodes or $377 for a two-episode week (reduced to about $250 after tax and agents' fees). In October 1980, *The Sun-Herald* printed these figures in a news story about cast angst over wages. They had just taken particular offence at finding out how much more the actors were to be paid on the still unscreened (and spectacularly unsuccessful) male version of *Prisoner, Punishment*. It was years before things would improve behind the scenes, and indeed, location shoots and new sets only became the norm in the show's dying days.

Amongst the frequent wobbly cameras and boom shadows, acting from the regulars was minimalist to say the least, while guest stars often appeared to be taking the piss. One example was the usually dependable Carmen Duncan camping it up outrageously as an oversexed patient. Told her operation time had been changed, she responded to her handsome doctor with 'As long as I don't have to wait … too long for it.' Add in a few toots and whistles and it could have been *Carry On Matron*. 'I confess we did get into the laughing gas that was on set as a prop when things got a bit boring,' admits Rebecca Gilling.

It's no real surprise that the nurses were getting into the laughing gas since medical accuracy wasn't a priority. 'We did have a medical advisor who was a real nurse,' remembers Joanne Samuel (Jill), 'but you could see there was a point where she gave up trying to tell us what to do. You know, if it didn't fit the shot or the drama, then the medical procedure was out!' Rather than get frustrated, the show's medical officer became an extra and eventually even got a speaking role.

In June 1982, the cast congregated to celebrate a major milestone – episode 1,219. At that point, *The Young Doctors* had become the longest-running soap in Australian TV history, having surpassed the record set by *Number 96*. Sadly, it was also to be the beginning of the end. Original producer Alan Coleman, as well as many of the show's favourite characters, had tired of the grind and left to move on to new projects. Nine was also tired. With the onset of summer and their relentless programming of cricket, the show would not survive the ever-changing timeslots.

When Judy McBurney (Tania) resigned, producers asked if she could stay on for just a couple more months. 'I think they knew the end was coming,' says McBurney. 'I thought it was a beautiful ending though, so sweet.'

In 1983, the final shows were quietly hidden away at 2.30pm weekdays. For the second to last episode, sweet Tania was dumped yet again, this time by a racing car driver who wore a lurid Grand Prix jacket in every scene. Ada (Gwen Plumb) and Helen (Lyn James) schemed to get long lost love Peter Holland to phone Tania from Turkey. He did and then proposed. Tania thought about it for two seconds and then agreed to fly off the next day to marry him. In reality, actor Peter Lochran wasn't around to supply his voice since he was in America playing Prince Ali Mamoud in daytime soap *Capitol*.

The Albert Memorial was to be shut down, leading to many of the long-serving cast members staring off into the distance while having flashbacks to past episodes. The new cast (which now included 'Totty' Goldsmith, Graham Harvey, Genevieve Lemon and Julie Nihill) dressed up for a farewell party at Bunny's, which remained open despite the loss of every one of its customers. They sang 'Auld Lang Syne' together while Ada walked through the empty hospital corridors. As episode 1,396 came to an end, she turned the lights off for the very last time.

Although it was fitting for that honour to go to Ada (of course the kiosk lady would shut down a major city hospital, wouldn't she?), it did leave the impression that Gwen Plumb was the show's longest-serving actor. Technically speaking, Ada hadn't appeared in the one-hour premiere, so that left Dr Graham Steele (Tim Page) as the lone survivor from the first episode. He has not been heard from since and is probably having a good lie down.

12

THE SULLIVANS

PREMIERE: **1976** EPISODES: **1114** NETWORK: **NINE** FINALE: **1982**

Dave (Paul Cronin) and Grace (Lorraine Bayly)
farewell son Tom (Steven Tandy) off to war.

Hector Crawford, the head of Crawford Productions, never did like the term 'soapie', particularly when it was applied to one of his own shows. When it came to *The Sullivans*, he referred to it as a 'meticulously researched period drama'. Considering that it only made it to air after an idea for a show about an undercover nun was rejected, *The Sullivans* was at least able to wear its quality as a badge of honour.

Producers Jock Blair and Ian Jones originally pitched *The Sullivans* to the Seven Network, and in one of those decisions executives would regret for years afterwards, Seven told the pair they hated the idea of a wartime family drama. So off went *The Sullivans* into a Crawford's filing cabinet to gather dust.

A year later, Blair and Jones were pitching the undercover nun story to the Nine Network. Not surprisingly, Nine's Jim Mackay was underwhelmed and asked instead for a show about a family you could care about, possibly in the vein of their successful American import *Little House on the Prairie*. Blair and Jones took one look at each other and promised they would return. Back at Crawford's, they pulled out the original outline for *The Sullivans* and did a quick edit on the front page, asking

Hector Crawford's secretary to type 'For the Nine Network' on it instead of Seven. 'Gentlemen,' Blair remembers saying, 'Do we have a show for you!'

This time Nine was excited, so excited in fact that they asked for it to be on air within three months. Hector Crawford was dubious they could meet the deadline (and privately thought the show would be lucky to last three months on air once it began). Given the detailed period re-creation, the new team did need longer than three months in pre-production, and they ended up taking about twice that long. Blair and Jones were also working feverishly on the scripts, although neither had any real idea what was going to happen. 'It was all an amalgamation of Ian's childhood and mine and what we remembered about the war,' says Blair today. As they recalled their youths, the characters began to come alive on the pages.

Lorraine Bayly, then in her 30s, was playing an old woman in a Sydney play when she got a call about the role that would change her life. She flew down to Melbourne that night and washed the grey out of her hair in preparation for the audition the following day. Arriving at the studio early next morning, having made herself look as pretty as possible, she read the script and learnt that she was going for the role of Grace Sullivan, a 40-year-old mother. She cursed having changed her hair colour, and rushed off to the bathroom to remove most of her make-up. 'I got out my brown eye shadow and put it under my eyes for some shading and I quickly pulled my hair back into a bun,' Bayly recalls today. The aging-up worked and after three anxious days waiting by the phone, Bayly was told she had the role.

Grace Sullivan was about to become an iconic figure in Australian television history, but Bayly had no idea that the show was going to last much longer than the initial order of 13 weeks. 'It wasn't considered a serial, it was just going to be a drama piece on the war.' Bayly, a single woman who couldn't cook or clean in real life, based her characterisation on her mother. 'I wore my hair in a victory roll I copied from my mother. Having studied theatre make-up, I used to put fine lines under my eyes so it didn't look so smooth on camera.' For six months, Bayly would refuse to allow any photographs taken of her out of character until the series was established.

The Sullivans were to be an average Aussie family living at 7 Gordon Street, Camberwell, Melbourne. Grace Sullivan was married to Dave (Paul Cronin) and they had four children – medical student John (Andrew McFarlane), Tom (Steven Tandy), Terry (Richard Morgan) and baby sister Kitty (Susan Hannaford). Dave had a larrikin brother Harry

The Sullivans. A new TV series as big as this Australian land.

The Sullivans. An Australian family you'll come to know and love. Australian television comes of age with this series in the tradition of "Upstairs, Downstairs."

Premieres tonight at 8.00

Promoting the first night even though it was beginning in a non-ratings period.

Horse trainer Ben Dawson (Sam Neill) was Kitty's (Susan Hannaford) first big romance – on a special location shoot in Sydney.

(Michael Caton) who was married to Rose (Maggie Dence). Their idyllic world, although quaint and old-fashioned, was nevertheless fascinating for viewers of the 1970s, and a world away from what they were used to seeing in serials.

The premiere episode kicked off the story on 1 September 1939, and ended with every character listening grimly to their radios as British Prime Minister Neville Chamberlain declared war on Germany. While Grace looked nervously at her husband and sons, down the road the German shopkeepers were sobbing openly at how it would affect them in their adopted country. Audiences watched in nostalgic recognition or wonder, depending on their age group. War was about to change everything in the Sullivan family's world.

Hans (Leon Lissek) and Lotte Kauffman (Marcella Burgoyne) ran the local corner store and approved wholeheartedly that their sweet daughter Anna (Ingrid Mason) was in love with the upstanding John Sullivan. Then came the announcement of war and almost immediately the innocent family were copping abuse and harassment. Eventually Hans was sent to an internment camp for aliens and Lotte chose to go with him. Hans died there, leaving the shop to be run by Harry and Rose, and Lotte returned briefly to farewell John as he went off to war.

Anna married John but was so traumatised about her parents' detainment that she couldn't make love to him. 'From the wedding night, poor old John wasn't getting any and he had to talk to his mother and she had to talk to the local priest and I think that was when John started hitting the bottle,' remembers Andrew McFarlane. 'Well, you would, wouldn't you?' Anna then contracted polio and was dead by Christmas, leading viewers to send in real-life cards of condolence and flower arrangements. By the time New Year's Eve had rolled around however, John was making goo-goo eyes at Nurse Sue Marriott (Belinda Giblin, who was Andrew McFarlane's real-life flatmate).

Living next door to the Sullivan family was a gossipy neighbour, Mrs Jessup (Vivean Gray, who would go on to play virtually the same role as Mrs Mangel in *Neighbours*). As the series began, she was taking in two boarders from the country, the sleazy Bert Duggan (Peter Hehir) and his downtrodden wife Lill Duggan (Noni Hazlehurst). While Grace would be traumatised as each of her sons went off to war, Lill was probably relieved to see the back of her yobbish husband even though she was left pregnant. Bert got killed after standing on a land mine and Lill returned to Burrabrai with baby Albert.

The local pub, The Great Southern, had a female publican, Maggie Hayward (Vikki Hammond). She was open about being a divorcee, despite the gossip and innuendo, but she kept quiet about being a former flame of Dave's. Maggie was ably assisted in the pub by the reliable Jack Fletcher (Reg Gorman).

As Grace held back the tears and watched the first of her sons go off to war with his mates, the action swung to battlefields around the world. Tom, Bert and Dave's former World War I mate, Norm (Norman Yemm) were soon donning army greens as the show re-created battle scenes in Yugoslavia, Crete, Holland, Greece, Egypt, North Africa and South-East Asia. Crew members referred to these characters as 'The Three Musketeers'.

This world travelogue, all filmed within driving distance of Melbourne, was supplemented with the use of actual newsreel footage, blended seamlessly into the action. This meant some scenes were shot in black and white for continuity. Israel was replicated in one square mile of sand. A Melbourne orchard became a traditional Palestinian hora. A craggy location near the town of Little River was covered in tonnes of rock salt and styrofoam pellets to recreate a European winter. A lone olive tree in Sunbury was photographed from all angles to resemble Crete. The Dandenong Ranges, where it was usually freezing cold, became the tropical Kokoda Trail.

One exception was an overseas shoot in Holland for a storyline involving the German occupation. After a week, it was back to the freezing Victorian seaside where Queenscliff's railway museum was transformed into a Dutch train station. Norm (disguised as a Nazi) and Tom (dressed as a woman) slipped into town to elude capture, as the show slipped dangerously close to *Hogan's Heroes* territory.

TV Times writer Eric Scott spent a freezing day on set as an extra in 1979, as the show re-created tropical Changi in a derelict gas works near the Yarra River. Scott had already been given $4 from petty cash to get a '*Sullivans* special' haircut (short back and sides) before arriving at 'the dressing rooms – a converted bus and a caravan'. After being covered in make-up, fake suntan and petroleum jelly (to resemble sweat), he worked all night in the wet and cold with 'specially selected skinny extras needed to portray starving inmates of the camp'. Scott decided he didn't have 'the stamina to become a TV star' and couldn't wait for his hair to grow back to normal so he could 'socialise again'.

The original newsreel footage also helped disguise the show's relatively low budget. For scenes that required hundreds of soldiers, shooting through a long lens disguised the fact that only a handful of actors were actually marching in shot. Not only did it save money, but Melbourne had a limited number of 'skinny extras' that could survive the rigours of filming every week.

Meticulous re-creation was a key element in the success of *The Sullivans*. Art department crews scoured second-hand stores and jumble sales across Victoria in an effort to keep absolutely every prop authentic. Every piece of furniture, every bottle label and even the wedding rings were authentic, whilst wardrobe and make-up insisted on nothing but

The paperback and 'Songs of *The Sullivans*' album.

carefully copied looks of the 1940s if real items of clothing could not be located.

The regular viewers who became hooked on the show loved this incredible detail. 'Obviously people wanted to go back,' says Jock Blair. 'It was a very personal journey for the audience.' This was never more apparent than when a fire accidentally destroyed half the set of the Sullivan home. Several important period props were destroyed, including what was thought to be a rare sewing machine from the era. After Nine's night-time news ran a story on the fire, 45 offers of a replacement sewing machine were received the next morning. Every single piece of burnt memorabilia was replaced by loyal fans.

Sometimes the viewers would give *The Sullivans* original costumes from the era. *TV Times* reported in 1978 that a Mrs Emmett of Victoria had offered her own wedding dress from 1943. Costume designer Ron Williams grabbed it for Alice Morgan's (Megan Williams) wedding to Michael (John Walton) and only had to design a Juliet cap to go with her white veil.

Andrew McFarlane, who grew up close to the exterior locations used in *The Sullivans*, was able to stay at his parents overnight if he had an early morning call at John's house. 'I used to shop at the Kauffman shop as a kid and buy sweets on the way to school,' he remembers. 'I remember Terry Donovan, a good mate from *Division 4* days, watching filming one day and he brought Jason (later of *Neighbours*) who was only about six. Because the shop was still functioning on the days we weren't filming, I bought him an ice-cream from inside.'

Back in the studio, however, eating the props became a bit of a problem. 'There were huge jars of sweets everywhere and Marcella Burgoyne was the worst culprit. Playing Lotte, she owned the shop, so she felt it was her right to eat those sweets!' McFarlane laughs today. Finally, the art department sprayed all the goods with insecticide, which had a triple benefit. 'One, it stopped the flies. Two, it stopped the actors eating them, and thirdly it made them look more shiny and glossy for TV.'

As the war rolled on, some characters were doomed, and not just those who ate the poisoned lollies. The lovable Aunty Rose (often used as comic relief as Maggie Dence's breakthrough role had been in the 1960s satirical sketch comedy series *The Mavis Bramston Show*) unexpectedly drowned in the Yarra River during a picnic. Dence was the first of the core cast to leave the show, tiring of the weekly commute from Sydney to Melbourne. Harry would eventually remarry army Sergeant Lou (Annie Byron). Michael Caton left the series in 1978 in search of a film career, which didn't pay off until over a decade and a half later when *The Castle* became a smash hit.

Often the stories would be based on real people and incidents from the time. Aboriginal war hero Reg Saunders (himself immortalised in the series by being played by his own son, Christopher Saunders) advised on adapting the story of Vasaliki Sagarakis, a partisan woman who aided allied soldiers. Saunders told *TV Times* she was 'the most fabulous woman of all time'. In *The Sullivans*, she became Melina (Chantal Contouri) and ended up married to Norm Baker. While the men tried to escape Crete, Melina was tortured by a Nazi soldier, Krull (Burt Cooper), who was hell-bent on finding the Aussies.

In one of the most graphic episodes filmed, Melina was executed by a German firing squad after refusing to divulge her husband's whereabouts. Watching on in horror with the other villagers was a disguised and helpless Norm. He didn't rest until he tracked down Melina's murderer, Krull, and exacted revenge, even though it took him several years and about 500 episodes. In between, Norm made it back to Australia, fell in love with barmaid Maggie and married her.

John Sullivan also had a tortured love life, but it was his brief flirtation with communism that caused Andrew McFarlane's real-life father to wonder if his son's career was heading in the right direction. 'He wasn't too sure about that, but he didn't say anything when John became an alcoholic and had illicit sex with Nurse Sue in the Dandenongs.' McFarlane has one clear memory of filming that love scene with Belinda Giblin. 'One of the unwritten laws of Crawford's was if it was high summer in Melbourne, it was winter in the show you were doing. Subsequently, it was winter in real-life so therefore it was the height of summer in *The Sullivans* world. Poor Belinda was sucking on ice cubes to counteract the freezing mist that comes out of your mouth when you speak, but I couldn't say anything because my lips had gone numb.'

Eventually John lost the lusty nurse and stood across the road watching as she married Corporal Sam Kendall (Sean Scully). Shattered, the one-time pacifist joined the Australian Medical Corps where he transferred overseas and was reported missing in action. McFarlane had actually left to make *Patrol Boat*, so when that was finished and he agreed to return to *The Sullivans*, Crawford's took the unusual step of commissioning a spin-off telemovie, *The John Sullivan Story*, to explain where John had been all that time. The feature followed him from a sinking troopship in 1942 to his eventual rescue by Yugoslavians. He would fight and work as a medic in their war-torn country, as well as getting married to a local girl. After being injured in a bomb blast, John suffered temporary amnesia.

Back in *The Sullivans*, Dave was itching to fight for his country again, but an old war injury ruled him unfit for service. The factory where he had worked all his life was now making much needed supplies for the troops overseas, so Dave felt he was contributing to the war effort. Then Norm told the family that a mystery man had been found with amnesia and it might be John. Norm took Grace on a secret trip to check it out, while telling the family she was just slipping away to visit her sick sister.

When they reached London, Grace was thrilled to find her eldest son still alive, and stayed on to nurse him back to health. It was now time to deal with what would be the series' biggest loss, as Lorraine Bayly wanted to move on. 'It wasn't exhaustion, it was just that I had no life.' From the moment she had allowed herself to be photographed without her Grace garb, Bayly couldn't go anywhere without being mobbed. Not that there

'One of the unwritten laws of Crawford's was if it was high summer in Melbourne, it was winter in the show you were doing.'

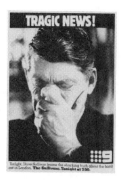

TRAGIC NEWS!

Tonight, Dave Sullivan learns the shocking truth about the bomb blast in London. **The Sullivans**, Tonight at 7.30.

Grace is dead!

was much time to go anywhere – shooting *The Sullivans* was as never ending as the war.

'I remember at the end of one day's filming, at about 2am in the morning, Henry Crawford came down with a bottle of champagne to celebrate that I had just set a record for doing the most scenes in one day – 26, back to back,' Bayly recalls. 'I used to stay up till all hours of the night learning my dialogue. I was missing theatre work. And I had met a man I was interested in but I didn't have any time to see him.' Producer Jock Blair took her to lunch and slapped an open chequebook on the table, asking Bayly to name her price to stay on. 'For the first two years I got about $370 a week, then a bit more after that. I could have made a fortune, but my mind was made up.'

Crawford's were keen to downplay her departure and decided to delay it for as long as possible. Before departing Australia on a long holiday, Bayly filmed a series of scenes that were strung out for over six months as she stayed in London nursing John back to health. Meanwhile, Bayly was living the good life in Brazil. 'I think Crawford's were hoping that I would change my mind and when I didn't, that's apparently when Hector said, "Kill her off then".'

Usually such a departure would be a *TV Week* cover story, but in this case the press were tight-lipped. Episode 598 ended with Grace clutching John as the eerie sound of a falling bomb could be heard. Newspaper ads on the following Monday hinted at what was about to come next. 'Tragic News! Tonight, Dave Sullivan learns the shocking truth about the bomb blast in London.' As John stepped off the plane to greet his father back in Australia, Dave was devastated to see a coffin being offloaded. Grace Sullivan was dead, a victim of the London Blitz.

'We filmed the bombing scene in a set at Abbotsford but when it came to the actual explosion, we were replaced with two inflatable sex dolls with the wide open mouths,' explains Andrew McFarlane. 'They dressed Lorraine's in a hat and dress, while mine was wearing a sports jacket.' Distraught viewers who mourned Grace's untimely death had no idea that a blow-up really had blown up in the name of art.

The show wisely decided not to rush Dave into a new romance, although Ilona Rodgers joined the cast as Mrs Jessup's new boarder, Kate Meredith. Since it was too soon for Dave to even think about another woman, Kate ended up falling for returned prisoner-of-war Christopher Merchant (John Waters). It took a full year before Dave started romancing war widow Elizabeth Bradley (Maggie Millar) and then it never went anywhere anyway.

By now, many more relatives were arriving to beef up the dwindling cast. There was Jim Sullivan (Andy Anderson), Steve Sullivan (David Clencie) and adopted Sullivan orphan Geoff (Jamie Higgins) who lost his last remaining relative, brother Jacko, fighting alongside Tom. Marrying into the family was Caroline (Toni Vernon, then Genevieve Picot) who had many ups and downs with Terry; Patti Spencer (Penny Downie) who married Tom; and Robbie McGovern (Graham Harvey), the man who finally turned little Kitty into a woman.

Norm (Norman Yemm) faces a firing squad.

Kitty grew up to work as a nurse and began courting young boys as soon as she lost the pigtails. She was briefly involved with Lill's brother, Eddie Paterson (Andrew McKaige), but it was Robbie who would make her a wife and mother to baby Gracie. Their nuptials were promoted in *TV Times* as 'The Wedding of the TV Decade' as Kitty wore her mother's wedding dress, flanked by bridesmaids Alice and Sally (Lisa Crittenden). The couple departed for a happy honeymoon at Mt Macedon, but the union would end tragically when the traumatised Robbie committed suicide after witnessing the horrors of Hiroshima first hand.

Behind the scenes it had been a frustrating time for actress Susan Hannaford. Aged 24 when she first had to play the 13-year-old innocent, the actress was frustrated at being so far removed from the character. When she did a sexy shoot for *TV Week*, proclaiming herself a fashion designer, bosses weren't impressed. She wasn't allowed to do another one until after Kitty had married on-screen. It was also a mini-scandal when Richard Morgan (who played Terry) was photographed wearing an earring during a public appearance. The show's makers didn't like the youngest Sullivan children straying too far from their carefully cultivated television images, even though everyone else their age was strutting around with long hair and the fashion mistakes of the late 70s and early 80s.

Another actress who inadvertently caused a scandal was Megan Williams (who played Alice). Already referred to as 'something of a teenage sex symbol' because of her schoolgirl role in *Class of '74*, she was caught sunbathing topless on a Melbourne beach and the pictures became front-page news. 'I was upset because I don't think it was the kind of publicity a show like *The Sullivans* needed,' Williams told *TV Times*. 'But

I wasn't embarrassed by the photograph. It was an invasion of my privacy, but it wasn't a national disaster.'

Back in the 1940s, John left the series again in search of his Yugoslavian wife; Maggie discovered that alcoholic Alice was her long lost illegitimate daughter; and Terry eventually got old enough to go off and fight. He ended up in Changi with Tom and Danny Chapman (Jeff Kevin) and didn't fare too well upon his return to civilian life, resorting to petty crime. Mrs Jessup married Arthur Pike (Wallas Eaton) and had a visit from a sister she hadn't seen in 25 years, Laura Watkins. She was played by Myra De Groot. Several years later, Vivean Gray and Myra De Groot would be reunited as gossips on *Neighbours*.

For its first years on air, *The Sullivans* grew from strength to strength, eventually becoming the number one show in Australia. Emboldened by its success, the Nine Network switched it to the already crowded 7pm timeslot, up against the incredibly popular game show *Graham Kennedy's Blankety Blanks* and current affairs show champ *Willesee at Seven*. The critics predicted that the quiet wartime series would not survive in such a competitive timeslot. As usual, the critics were wrong. More popular than ever, a soundtrack album of 1940s songs was rushed into stores, and a paperback novelisation also appeared. 'Even in the delightfully unpredictable world of television, there can rarely have been a phenomenon quite like *The Sullivans*,' Hector Crawford wrote in the book's foreword. 'This universal acclamation is, of course, most welcome and warming.'

It won a swag of awards, both peer voted (Sammys and AWGIES for scriptwriting) and from the fans (*TV Week* Logie Awards). Lorraine Bayly was always a shoo-in for Best Actress, winning three trophies, while Paul Cronin won many times for playing dependable Dave. Other actors to be

L-R: Jack (Reg Gorman), Dave (Paul Cronin), 'Horrible', (Nick Waters), Maggie (Vikki Hammond), 'Urger' (Peter Harvey-Wright), Mrs Jessup (Vivean Gray). FRONT: Maureen (Fiona Paul) and 'Magpie' (Gary Sweet).

honoured included Michael Caton, Vivean Gray, Andrew McFarlane, Chantal Contouri (Melina), Andy Anderson (Jim), Vikki Hammond and Gary Sweet (whose first TV role was as Leslie 'Magpie' Maddern).

'Everyone working on the show had something that's unheard of today – integrity,' Jock Blair recently declared. 'I remember so many people coming on saying, 'Well, I don't approve of war, I don't want to work on this show.' After about six weeks though, they'd take on the personas and ultimately it became *the* show to work on. It attracted the best people.'

Australia's best actors were indeed lining up to have a short-back-and-sides haircut or put on a foreign accent. Tracy Mann, who played the only innocent girl in *The Box*, stretched her wings as a Cairo callgirl. Sam Neill played horse trainer Ben Dawson, who was Kitty's first big romance as the show went on location to Sydney. Mel Gibson played naval lieutenant Ray Henderson, and the show also featured the first screen appearance of a prepubescent Kylie Minogue as a young Dutch girl called Carla.

As the years rolled by on screen, producers wondered if *The Sullivans* should finish with the end of the war. Jock Blair remembers this as always being a contentious point. 'We always felt that's where it should end but there was no way the network was going to agree to that.' When World War II did finish on screen, the action-starved show sent poor old Norm off to the Dutch East Indies before the country became known as Indonesia. The little-known battle between Dutch rulers and the local people saw Norm facing a firing squad one last time.

When actor Paul Cronin announced he was leaving after six years, Crawford's insisted *The Sullivans* could continue without him. Actor/Director Charles 'Bud' Tingwell was the series' fifth producer (after Henry Crawford, Jock Blair, John Barningham and Alan Hardy) and he told *TV Week* he was enthusiastic about new storylines based around the Snowy Mountains Scheme, the Korean War and the controversial Petrov Royal Commission. To facilitate this, the series was planning to jump in time to the 1950s with number two son Tom becoming the new *Sullivans'* patriarch.

Actor Steven Tandy, who slipped away for a quick holiday before the extra responsibility, received a nasty shock when flying home. An air hostess informed him that *The Sullivans* had ceased production after 1,114 episodes. The reality of Paul Cronin's decision to leave, together with falling ratings, resulted in the show shutting down on 10 July 1982. The serial would end with Dave getting hit by a car and dying.

'In hindsight, one of the big mistakes we made was killing the pivotal characters,' says Blair today, 'unlike the Americans where they just "lose" the characters. Consequently we are unable to do *Brady Bunch* type reunion specials.' The Nine Network agrees and privately wishes the wartime family could have been re-visited over the years. Back when *The Sullivans* was being made, however, no network executive could have foreseen that telemovies like *A Very Brady Christmas* would tap into nostalgia-starved audiences and top ratings.

Lorraine Bayly, however, has figured out a way to play Grace Sullivan

The show also featured the first screen appearance of a prepubescent Kylie Minogue as a young Dutch girl…

again. Sort of. With Kitty's baby Gracie being born at roughly the same time as Bayly herself, and the possibility that Kitty reverted to her maiden name after her husband's suicide, Bayly could play a grown-up Gracie Sullivan in any story set in the present time. And if Gracie had a son, producers could stage the ultimate reunion by casting Andrew McFarlane as Lorraine Bayly's on-screen son again.

Even as a one-off, such a telemovie would be a delicious prospect for anyone who ever watched the serial. With 1,114 half-hour episodes in the can, *The Sullivans* became Australia's first globally popular soap, in many ways paving the way for *Neighbours*. In the UK the show found an immediate audience on ITV and became a daytime fixture for well over ten years. It eventually screened in over 30 countries including Israel, India, Iceland, Ireland, Bahrain, Costa Rica, El Salvador, Chile, Italy, Malaysia, South Korea, Peru, Portugal, Zambia, Zimbabwe and Canada. It was screened in America on the PBS network and became the top-rating show in Lebanon. 'I think any family that's lived through a war and sent their kids to a frontline identified with *The Sullivans*,' says Blair.

'I really had such respect for the show because it gave younger people and older people a greater respect for days like Anzac Day and Remembrance Day,' says Bayly today. 'Crawford's did a magnificent job. I will always feel very proud to have been part of it.'

Whilst the show was and is still loved all over the world, ironically it was never seen in the island state of Tasmania. Before network aggregation, some regional centres in Australia missed out on certain soaps, and Tasmanian viewers still don't realise what they missed. From the history to the acting to the meticulous re-creation, *The Sullivans* will always be remembered as a class act. And just think, it may never have happened if some fool had liked the idea of an undercover nun.

Now retired, Lorraine Bayly is prepared to revive Gracie Sullivan in a one-off telemovie, but she also wonders whatever became of that under-cover nun series. 'Why not make her deaf and dumb too and then I'd have no lines to learn,' she laughs. 'No dialogue and no costume changes. Now that's the perfect role!'

13

COP SHOP

PREMIERE: **1977** EPISODES: **582** NETWORK: **SEVEN** FINALE: **1984**

The policemen and women of Riverside Police Station.

SCHOOL/UNI

SEX & SIN

PERIOD

MEDICAL

POLICE

HOLIDAY

GAOL

RICH

BLOCK

SHOP

LEGAL

RURAL

NUDITY

TV STATION

Before soaps took hold, most of the Australian dramas seen on air were police shows. The first was *Homicide*, which began on the Seven Network in 1964, while Nine had *Division 4* from 1969, and Ten took on *Matlock Police* in 1971. All were made by Crawford Productions and all finished up in 1975. As each of these series was made up of self-contained episodes in which a villain of the week was captured by show's end, there wasn't a lot of time spent on the private lives of the police officers.

That all changed with the debut in 1977 of Crawford's and Seven's *Cop Shop*, originally to have been called *Palace Guards* or *Saints and Sinners*. Not only were the policewomen given equal billing with the men, but Riverside Police Station was also a mix of uniformed and plain-clothed detectives. And by heading into their homes when off duty, the stories would also include the officers' families, friends and lovers.

Staff at Crawford's were initially not that enthusiastic about doing another cop series. 'Hector Crawford loved his cop shows but all the other staff wanted to do something different,' remembers story editor Gwenda Marsh. Grundy's and other production companies were all pitching to the networks and Crawford's were planning to outgun them all with a pilot about a priest called *The Mission*. 'At the last minute, Hector decided to put in another cop show and the staff all groaned. I didn't think it would last longer than 26 weeks but I ended up doing 400 hours!'

Cop Shop covered a different crime storyline every week in two one-hour instalments. While each case would be neatly wrapped up each week, the personal lives of the cops were never-ending.

Having headlined in *The Box*, George Mallaby returned to Crawford's to play Detective Sergeant Glenn Taylor, the Criminal Investigations boss. In episode one, he was back at work after recovering from a gunshot wound received in the line of duty. His neurotic wife Pamela (Rowena Wallace) was not a happy camper and before that first hour was over, she was conniving with her father, Edmund Eliot-Smith (Walter Sullivan), to get Glenn out of the police force. They failed and she began to drink heavily, often losing her temper with their precocious teenage daughter Gail (Jo-Anne Moore).

Glenn was ably assisted by Detective Don McKenna (Tony Bonner) and the troubled Tom Foster (Peter Sumner). Newly widowed and ashamed of his gay teenage son (Andrew McKaige), Tom was bashing homosexuals, and the victims, upon seeing him in the police station, were too frightened to name their attacker. When Tom's crime was revealed, he left the police force on 'sick leave'.

Next in line was larrikin cop Detective Jeff Johnson (Peter Adams), or J.J. to his mates. He was a first for Aussie cop shows, a hard-drinking, heavy-smoking gambler, liable to lose his temper at any moment but fearless in the line of fire. J.J. was as believable as he was unpredictable. He met stripper Valerie Close (Joanna Lockwood) during the gay-bashing investigation and asked her out to dinner in the middle of their first official police meeting. They fell in love, she gave up stripping, and they married and had a baby girl. The union was as fiery and volatile as its partners were, and after many arguments and misunderstandings, Valerie fled to America in search of an acting career. J.J. left the show but returned to retire and walk away laughing in the final episode.

Downstairs in the 'Cop Shop', the charge counter was run by crabby Senior Sergeant Eric O'Reilly (Terry Norris) with junior cops Senior Constable Tony Benjamin (Gregory Ross) and Constable Peter Fleming (Patrick Ward). Tony was eventually promoted upstairs to become a detective and later fell in love with Claire (Louise Philip), O'Reilly's wheelchair-bound daughter.

The most interesting thing about Constable Fleming was his vegetarianism, so he was quickly replaced by the nerdy and pompous Constable Roy Baker (Gil Tucker). Together with O'Reilly, they became quite the comic pair. Roy could be overly officious and spineless, but like all the other cops, he eventually got himself a personal life. There was a disastrous affair with Jenny McGregor (Anne Lambert), who had more of a fascination for police uniforms, guns and handcuffs than poor old Roy himself, before he met and married the girl of his dreams, Melissa (Rosie Bailey).

O'Reilly, meanwhile, married Valerie's mother Lorna Close (Moya O'Sullivan), and continued to run the watch-house until actor Terry Norris was elected to the Victorian Parliament. He was replaced by

Homicide veteran Alwyn Kurts, although Norris returned for the final episodes.

'I didn't think it would look right to be in parliament while acting in a cop show, so I decided to donate my wages to a nursing hospital in my electorate,' says Terry Norris. 'By using the money for a charitable endeavour, it was an easy way to buy some extra hospital beds and it got me out of any hot water I may have encountered in the electorate!'

After a long courtship, Tony (Gregory Ross) and Claire (Louise Philip) got married, and in one of the series' most inspiring episodes, Claire gave birth to a healthy baby girl. Sadly, after that high there had to be a low point, and that certainly came in 1980 when Claire took delivery of a new motor scooter to replace her wheelchair. The couple had borrowed money from loan sharks to pay for it, and the chief baddie (John Stanton) kidnapped Claire when they couldn't make the repayments. It all culminated in a car chase – as most Crawford's cop shows did – before another *Cop Shop* villain realised it was almost suicidal to threaten the wheelchair-bound wife of a Riverside policeman.

Not long afterwards, Louise Philip decided to leave the series and her character was killed off in a bus accident, although baby Prudence was thrown clear and survived. Her funeral scenes were a trying time for the cast, being filmed just a week after they had all attended the funeral of actor Bill Stalker.

Tragically, Stalker, whose Peter Fanelli character had transferred to Riverside from *Skyways'* Pacific International Airport, had just filmed his last *Cop Shop* scene when he was killed in a real-life motorcycle accident. Fanelli's final moment in the show involved him getting married and taking off with his new bride (Annette Andre) to live in Darwin.

'Hector Crawford was always against killing off your heroes,' remembers Gwenda Marsh, which is why many *Cop Shop* characters left Riverside by their own choice rather than in a coffin. In the very early days of the show, the Crawford's boss had made his displeasure known when *Cop Shop* lost its first detective. 'The night Tony Bonner's character was killed off, my phone rang as soon as the show was finished. I thought Hector was going to have a heart attack, he was so furious.' After that, the scriptwriters thought carefully before losing a cop in the line of duty.

Marsh enjoyed writing for all the comic characters, and particularly for Roy. 'I'd ask Gil Tucker what he did on the weekend and then I'd put it all straight into the script. Gil was a natural showman and storyteller.' Hector Crawford challenged Marsh to get *Cop Shop* to beat *Charlie's Angels* in the ratings. 'I took the bet but I didn't think we would beat them. But in the end, Nine had to move *Charlie's Angels* to another timeslot!'

Cop Shop's policewomen were a first for Aussie TV. Up till then, they had always been uniformed and only seen dealing with minor offences. In *Cop Shop*, the girls were front and centre, starting with Danni Francis (Paula Duncan). Danni was smart, tough, sexy and able to take the men's good-natured jibes. She was soon joined by the blonde and busty Amanda King (Lynda Stoner). For a time, the show even

The most watched Cop Show on TV.

COP SHOP

They hide behind their uniform and their gun, but they're people with their own loves and their own hates, and this is their story. Australia's Top Rating Police drama series continues tonight.

8.30 TONIGHT ⑦

introduced a third policewoman, Olga Tamara, as Detective Constable Julie Mitchell, but despite Hector Crawford's possible wrath, she was quickly killed off in a car chase.

'Originally I had to audition for a bisexual cop and I had to toughen up and play it with my hair pulled back,' remembers Paula Duncan. 'After the third audition, they asked me to try it with my hair down, then they came back and said they were going to rewrite the role of Danni Francis for me.' Women were taken off the menu, and instead Danni had a succession of male lovers. First was Detective Don McKenna (Tony Bonner) until he took a bullet, then Detective Tom Foster (Peter Sumner) who returned after being on 'sick leave'. When he took off for Scotland Yard, there was Catholic priest Father Joe Coral (Neil Fitzpatrick) and then conman politician Philip Hardy (Alfred Bell). Next was a secret love affair with the much younger Constable Sam Phillips (Nicholas Eadie), until he too was killed in the line of duty.

While Duncan freely admits to being besotted while working opposite Nicholas Eadie, she couldn't stand John Orcsik when he arrived to play Detective Mike Georgiou. 'Joanna Lockwood came up to me and said you're going to hate this bloke, he's got chains and he drives a beaten up Monaro and you will hate him. And I did,' says Duncan. Orcsik detested her just as much and the actors continually argued about scripts and anything else they discovered they disagreed on.

'There was, however, this amazing chemistry that existed and we fell deeply in love,' admits Duncan. 'On screen we would give looks where they weren't necessary. He was also looking at me physically from behind so there was a lot of stuff going on underneath that we created. The writers picked up on it and wrote for it. But I believe we invented our love affair.' The actors married in 1982, and their characters followed suit in 1983. Duncan gave birth to Jessica and, in the final episode, Danni had her first baby, also a girl. The romance became high-priority fodder for the press and the couple soon found they couldn't move from their front door without being mobbed.

'We were all very glamorous with very glossy lips, there was lots of sexual innuendo, the men wore very tight pants, we didn't wear bras, and there we'd be running around in high heels with the Farrah Fawcett hairstyles,' laughs Duncan. 'It was a bit of a scream and we desperately wanted to be credible but the public believed it. People wrote to Danni when they needed help and when they were suicidal.' After one such letter, Duncan had Crawford's track down the woman and stop her from killing herself. It started her off on a lifetime of charity work.

The cast from the final episode.

FRONT L-R:
Alwyn Kurts,
Gil Tucker,
Alan Fletcher,
Christine Jeston,
John McTernan,
Lynda Stoner,
Gregory Ross,
Peter Adams.

BACK:
Paula Duncan,
John Orcsik,
John Lee.

Lynda Stoner's real life also eerily mirrored her 'reel life'. After living with actor John Walton for two years, her character Amanda married him on-screen when he played Terry Lindford-Jones. This *Cop Shop* marriage, however, didn't last. 'It was one of my most gruelling weeks on the set when he got shot dead,' remembers Stoner. 'It was pretty raw to do.'

One actress missing out on all the action was Rowena Wallace, who complained in an interview that her housewife character Pamela only ever seemed to pour cups of tea for her policeman husband. Crawford's promptly sacked her for putting down the show but, amazingly, reinstated her a short time later. 'The beauty of it was I started getting better scripts, with things to do,' Wallace remembers today. 'Sometimes it helps for actors to complain.'

And complain they did, although this time a united cast pushed for better working conditions for all actors. 'As much as we loved Crawford's, there were things that had to change,' Lynda Stoner says. 'I'd been involved with Actors' Equity with other casts but when push came to shove nobody except just a few people were prepared to go the distance. But with *Cop Shop* we all stuck together and we were prepared to walk to get better working conditions – like not having to change in the back of cars and public toilets. And not having to finish at night at 11pm, learn your lines and then have to be back on set first thing the next morning.'

Eventually their efforts resulted in the creation of the ten-hour turnaround, meaning cast and crew had to have at least a ten-hour break before filming could begin again the next day. By standing together and being honest with each other, the *Cop Shop* actors had forever changed the industry. 'We even all knew what the other was earning,' remembers Duncan. 'We were a real family.' And despite having to stand up to

Crawford's, the cast still loved the company. 'We were spoiled and protected and nurtured and it's one of the most precious times in my life,' says Stoner.

As well as dealing with the death of Bill Stalker, the cast also helped out during another tragedy for one of its own. Gregory Ross and his family lost all their possessions when their house burned down in Victoria's devastating Ash Wednesday bushfires. It was a bad year for Ross, who also missed out yet again in his bid to enter politics (ironically he was campaigning for the Liberal Party while co-star Terry Norris was strictly Labor). And just as he began to re-build the family home, the axe fell on his regular job in *Cop Shop*.

As the series began to wind down, Terence Donovan (father of Jason) arrived as the surly and aggressive new chief, Vic Cameron. He was another cop with an obvious drinking problem, but it was soon revealed that he had a few personal demons of his own, like a dead wife and a neglected daughter. He also had a sister, Liz Cameron (Liz Burch).

'Once we rated 48 in Melbourne,' Paula Duncan remembers. 'Those are astronomical figures. They cancelled us on 26 which also seems incredible today, but both Lynda and myself were pregnant and planning on leaving the show and maybe they felt it couldn't be sustained.' By the time the series ended after 582 one-hour episodes, only two actors had gone the distance – Paula Duncan and Gregory Ross.

'It was so diverse,' Paula Duncan sums up. 'You had action and car chases outside, comedy downstairs on the charge counter, drama upstairs in the detective's office and a soap after hours when we went home.' Crawford's tried going back to conventional, self-contained, one-hour police dramas (*Special Squad*) but none would ever match the success of *Cop Shop*. Rival production company Grundy's would even try to re-make *Cop Shop* with a younger cast several years later. *Waterloo Station* never did amount to much and neither did the police-themed *Richmond Hill*. *Cop Shop* would turn out to be one of a kind.

14

THE RESTLESS YEARS

PREMIERE: **1977** EPISODES: **780** NETWORK: **TEN** FINALE: **1981**

The original school-leavers: Barry, Penny, Alan, Alison and Peter.

The Ten Network wasted no time in getting a replacement soap on air after *Number 96* and *The Box* finished. Noting that the teenage and twenty-something audience had been the first to desert those serials, they asked Grundy's to create something that would have lasting appeal with that age group. Grundy's realised they couldn't do another schoolyard drama like *Class of '74*, as they were already doing that on Seven with *Glenview High*. So instead, creator Reg Watson wondered what might happen with a group of young (and spunky) adults after they left school. Reg Grundy came up with what turned out to be a more than apt title, *The Restless Years*. Nobody quite realised it at the time, but it would become a seminal program in the annals of youth-based melodrama.

The Restless Years debuted in the quiet non-ratings period of December 1977. Newspaper advertisements proclaimed it would be 'the action-packed story of what happens to today's school leavers when they go out in the world to try to get jobs'. 'Action-packed' turned out to be quite a prophetic description, as *The Restless Years* was about to become one of

Leaving school.
Unemployment. Frustration.
Young love. The journey
to adulthood.

The Restless Years

From the studios of the O-10 network, a brand new
Australian drama series. A series that examines the turmoil
of a group of young people facing the realities of life in
the seventies.
Their families. Their friends. Their love and hate. The
first episode stars 1977 Sammy Award winner June Salter

as Miss McKenzie, their dedicated school teacher. It also
introduces five stars of tomorrow: Deborah Coulls,
Julieanne Newbould, Sonny Blake, Nicholas Hedstrom
and Graham Thorburn, as the five teenagers facing the
restless years.

**At last an Australian television drama
that deserves the title drama.**

7·30 Tuesday ❶   PREMIERES TOMORROW

the most turgid and convoluted soaps ever created. Even the scriptwriters would admit to being confused when asked to recall in which order the tragedies occurred.

It all opened innocently enough, if you could call two teenagers waking up in bed together innocent. The lovers were Penny Russell (Deborah Coulls) and Alan Archer (Sonny Blake, later known as Jon Blake and, tragically, irreparably brain damaged in a 1986 car accident). Penny and her elder brother Bruce (Malcolm Thompson), a doctor, were orphans who had been brought up by family friend and schoolteacher Miss McKenzie (June Salter).

At school, Alan and Penny hung out in a clique with their friends, the ruthlessly ambitious Barry King (Graham Thorburn), sweet but naïve Alison Clark (Julieanne Newbould), and class clown and rebel Peter Beckett (Nick Hedstrom). They were seen in their school uniforms just long enough to receive their high school diplomas. It was also to be the last time in school for Miss McKenzie, who was being forced to retire due to ill health. Feeling useless and unloved, and thinking her condition was life-threatening, she decided to gas herself in the oven.

Peter, upset at her scathing but honest refusal to give him a reference, stormed over to have it out with her but ended up saving her life. Despite this, the two continued to bicker for years as they worked together in a youth refuge, Beck and Call. Viewers soon learnt the source of their friction and the series' longest running plot secret. Peter was Miss McKenzie's illegitimate son to Senator Ross Lindsay (Richard Meikle) and had been adopted out at birth. Neither of them would find each other until the final instalment, some 781 episodes later.

TV Times' F.C. Kennedy thought the show couldn't work. 'I am convinced that it is impossible to make a drama based on teenage problems that is acceptable to discriminating adults. But keep an eye on it from time to time, for, who knows? Somebody in the Grundy organisation may have the good sense to take the emphasis off the young and leave the drama to (older) professionals.' Grundy's wisely ignored the advice, having discovered a formula using mostly young people that could be adapted time and time again, eventually ending up as *Neighbours*.

Within just a few months, *TV Times* was forced to eat its words when the show became the biggest new Aussie show of the year. By March 1978, it was on the cover and Nick Hedstrom (who played Peter) was being referred to inside as 'a younger, blond Marlon Brando'. Hedstrom seemed uncomfortable with the hype, saying (and probably quite rightly, too) that 'to some degree, I'm playing myself'. As the show was still supposed to be about the unemployed young, Hedstrom then said, 'The scripts are pretty accurate regarding the dreadfulness of job interviews and the awful frustrations of job-hunting.'

The reality of the unemployed, however, would soon be overtaken by the show's more melodramatic aspects, like prostitution, blackmail, miscarriages, abortions and murders. High school students who watched it could have been forgiven for abandoning all plans of entering the workforce if the characters on the show were anything to go by.

Before falling in love with Dr Bruce, Alison was raped, forced into prostitution and accused of murdering her boyfriend. Just after she accepted Bruce's proposal of marriage, he was swept out to sea and pre-sumed drowned, but was in fact washed ashore with amnesia. Viewers then spent months waiting for him to re-discover Alison. When they finally did run into each other (in front of his old surgery, for God's sake), there was another delay while he struggled to remember she was his fiancée. They finally married, but then Alison miscarried after a writer of poison pen letters tormented her with a runaway pram. When actress Julieanne Newbould decided enough was enough (as many of the over-wrought cast would), Alison was dispatched on the world's longest cruise.

Months later, Bruce and Miss McKenzie went off to search for her after news came through that her Asian tourist bus had been attacked by terrorists. Upon finding her grave (with a headstone that read 'Alison Russell – Australian') in the city of San Ching (actually shot on location in a nearby Sydney national park), Bruce returned to suffer even more complicated love liaisons until the end of the series. Actor Malcolm Thompson would be the only thespian brave enough to see out *The Restless Years* to its final moment.

Penny and Alan's relationship broke up soon after she went into busi-ness with the dreaded go-getter Barry. So too did the relationship between Ten and actress Deborah Coulls, who was fired from her role for allegedly turning up late for publicity appointments. Her dismissal was also seen as a warning to any other misbehaving actors. Actress Sue Smithers took over the role and, as Coulls was a brunette, Smithers's first lines were about Penny's new blonde hair colour.

One thing you could rely on in *The Restless Years* was the quality of the baddies, and none were nuttier than Rita Merrick. This twisted madam was played by Reg Grundy's real-life wife, Joy Chambers, who had previ-ously been a regular panellist on his Brisbane quiz shows. For *The Restless Years*, she would don a curly black wig (was it an Afro?) and, voilà, she was the demented Rita. (Without the wig, she played nice, first on *The Young Doctors*, then years later as cute but cunning Rosemary Daniels in *Neighbours*.)

Apart from tormenting Alison and her former school friend, Olivia Baxter (Zoe Bertram), Rita Merrick had a grudge against Miss McKenzie and plotted with David Harker (Chris Bell) to pose as the long-lost son she had given up. David ended up doing the dirty on both women, pushing Rita down the stairs and trying to kill Miss McKenzie in a bid to get to her money. In the 1978 Christmas cliffhanger, it looked like he had buried Miss McKenzie alive, but six weeks later, viewers were relieved to discover that Rita had actually saved her nemesis from the coffin before it had been buried.

Desperately trying to get off the game, Olivia (the classic soap hooker with a heart of gold) fell for Peter, but he had major issues dealing with her sordid past. Their on again-off again relationship saw Olivia nearly murdered by a deranged former client and Peter falling for his unknown half-sister, the daughter of Ross Lindsay. Olivia was nearly raped by Craig Garside (Vince Martin) and kidnapped by an insane neighbour of Miss McKenzie's, Lee Prentice (Mark Lee). In an obvious *Psycho* rip-off, Lee talked to an unseen mother and then dropped dead of a brain tumour just as he was about to knife Olivia to death.

The 1979 summer cliffhanger inspired one *TV Times* reader to wonder if the producers 'could produce a huge tidal wave and kill off the whole cast? Craig has been shot; Trish chased by a band of killers and her baby ready to be born in the middle of nowhere; Peter grabbed by one of Barry King's deadly men; Olivia run down by a car in the park; Julie (plus brother Tim) in danger from a circus owner; and last, but not least, Jeff Archer bombed in his car, and the rest of his family burned in their chairs. The last night of *The Restless Years* was supposed to be one of the most dramatic experiences but in my living room there were tears of laughter and people rolling on the floor.'

Back for a new year, Olivia had a nervous breakdown but recovered so she could go back to work for, of all people, Craig Garside, just as Rita Merrick returned with a new plot to frame him for murder. After more double-crossing, the only man left for Olivia was her former best friend's husband, the newly widowed Bruce. They married, but when Olivia fell pregnant and discovered she couldn't give birth due to a medical condition, Bruce was forced to arrange her abortion. Afterwards, Olivia cracked up and blamed Bruce for murdering their unborn child. She left him and the series – and viewers breathed a sigh of relief.

And so it continued, year after year, with cast members coming and going at an alarming rate. Some of the series' more memorable characters included its first bride, wacky Raeleen (Victoria Nicolls), who worked as a barmaid at the local watering hole, Thommo's; the slutty Susie Denning (Penny Cook); cute but dim Mickey Pratt (Tom Burlinson); saintly Julie Scott (Kim Lewis) and the often abused Robyn Hunter (*Australian Playboy*'s Playmate of the Year, Rosemary Paul) who was locked in a burning shed for a Christmas cliffhanger because she wasn't proving to be a good enough prostitute.

An unusually long-running couple was schoolgirl Diane Archer (Lenore Smith) and swimmer Rick Moran (Peter Mochrie). Written as a replacement for Sonny Blake, Rick Moran's name was an amalgamation of two of the scriptwriters' names, Rick Maier and Maureen Moran. Today, Peter Mochrie credits June Salter for giving him the good advice to study acting at NIDA after *The Restless Years* and make a career of it.

The Restless Years was a valuable training ground for many of Australia's best-known actors, and launched the careers of Peter Phelps, Rebecca Rigg, Michael Smith, Warren Blondell, Sally Cooper, Martin Sacks, Di Smith and David Franklin. Even Kerri-Anne Wright could be seen in a dramatic role, years before she became the queen of daytime television as Kerri-Anne Kennerley. She played ugly duckling Melinda Burgess who, like the bubbly entertainer herself, emerged from her shell to become a glamorous diva.

Since *The Restless Years* was the first soap to feature such a top-heavy younger cast, more established actors were required to shore them up, particularly since some had never acted before. The 'elders' included Jeff and Carol Archer (Noel Trevarthen and Peggy Thompson) and John Hamblin (as milk bar owner A.R. Jordan, who eventually started up 'The Refuge' for homeless youngsters); Jill Forster Stanton (Heather Russell, Bruce and Penny's aunt who died soon after marrying Jordan) and Lynette Curran (as sexy secretary Jean Stafford).

June Salter was often allowed time off for theatre roles, particularly *Crown Matrimonial* with John Hamblin. At one stage, both actors were doing double duty, recording the soap during the day and appearing on stage at night, leading *TV Times* to observe their relationship while lunching together in the Ten canteen. June Salter 'picks at her salad lunch, while Hamblin smokes innumerable cigarettes with his coffee. "Why are we actors?" asks Hamblin.'

Miss McKenzie (June Salter) and Bruce (Malcolm Thompson) farewell Alison (Julieanne Newbould) on the world's longest ocean cruise, unaware that Olivia (Zoe Bertram) will replace her as the next doctor's wife.

Eventually running out of ways to torture the trusting matriarch character, Miss McKenzie was let go, although Salter kindly agreed to return for the final episode. Loyal viewers were still waiting for the stubborn schoolmarm to find her real son. As the series struggled with its increasingly tortured plotlines, exhausted scriptwriters were probably dreaming of bringing it all to an end with the mother-son reunion.

The series had enjoyed healthy ratings for its first two years but when they started to slip, Ten began to bounce the show around its schedule. Instead of two one-hour episodes a week, four half-hour episodes began airing at 7pm on weeknights, before being moved to an even earlier timeslot. This proved not to be the wisest programming decision when a typical *Restless Years* murder (Speedo-clad villain Gary Fisher being stabbed in a pool) aired uncut in an early family timeslot. Amidst press anger at the unwholesome content, Ten quickly moved the series back to 7pm where it began to peter out. So determined were they to finish it up before a new ratings year began, the last shows were lumped together as a three-and-a-half-hour Friday night finale in Sydney.

For the final ever episode, *The Restless Years* went back to where it all began – graduation day at the local school. Peter Beckett (Nick Hedstrom) returned and walked through the schoolyard as he flashbacked to his last time there four years beforehand. Dropping in to see his former teacher before he left town, he casually mentioned that he had discovered who his real father was. Finally, Elizabeth McKenzie had found her son and they embraced amidst long-awaited tears. Even Dr Bruce Russell looked like living happily ever after, engaged again, this time to Charmaine (Mary-Lou Stewart). Final freeze frames reminded viewers of every regular character that had lived out their restless years – well, the young ones, that is.

While many viewers have trouble remembering the twists and turns of the complicated plots, most can remember the theme song, which charted when recorded by legendary blues singer Renee Geyer. After a quick recap, each episode began with fast-rolling clouds flying across the screen as the theme song serenaded, 'It's only a journey through our restless years, let our hearts run free.' If only life had been that simple for its much maligned characters.

The Restless Years may have been melodramatic and trite but it was never boring. It was also the beginning of a major shift in focus for Aussie serials. The mix of mostly young actors, together with a few oldies, would be repeated in many more soaps to come. Take away the outrageous storylines and it isn't difficult to see how this format would one day morph into *Neighbours*.

SELLING THE FORMATS OVERSEAS

How did *The Restless Years* end up translated into Dutch as *Goede Tijden, Slechte Tijden* and German as *Gute Zeiten, Schlechte Zeiten* (both mean 'Good Times, Bad Times')? The Grundy organisation began producing its Aussie formats overseas after Netherlands production house J.E. Entertainment tried to buy an established format to make Europe's first soap opera. Grundy's refused to sell unless they could produce the new show themselves. So began the international arm of Grundy's, which has seen Aussie production teams create the new shows and teach the locals the ins and outs of soap producing, directing, lighting and writing.

Old scripts from *The Restless Years* (and later *Sons and Daughters* and *Neighbours*) were dusted off and re-jigged to fit in with their new locations. In most cases, the Aussie scripts served as the basis for the first year of the shows. Afterwards, the established series then took the characters into their own storylines, based on local popularity and direction. Soon, Grundy's were producing soaps in Sweden, Italy and Poland. As Aussie soap folklore spread, China even developed their own version of rival *Neighbours* soap, *Home and Away*.

Producer Alan Coleman (*Class of '74/'75*, *The Young Doctors*) was employed as a consultant for the Grundy International Company and sent to Amsterdam in 1989 as executive producer of *Goede Tijden, Slechte Tijden*. Despite not speaking the language, he wrote and directed the serial. 'I learnt that you don't actually direct to the spoken word,' says Coleman. 'You direct to inflection, to body language.' In re-making *The Restless Years* for Dutch consumption, certain events and locations had to change to suit the new country. Because Olivia threw herself off Sydney's North Heads at the end of the first episode, Coleman remembers driving around looking at Holland's dykes wondering how they could be threatening. Instead, the Dutch Olivia threw herself off a roof. A similar problem arose when it came time for Mickey to get his driver's licence. In the Australian version, he kept failing because he couldn't do hill starts. With Holland being so flat, that had to be changed to him being unable to do a three-point turn. As for the long-running storyline that involved boats and fishing, what was a legal job in Australia became an illegal activity in Holland. Because the characters were now breaking local law, they had to be punished and so the Dutch Barry's dinner party was ruined when his guests got sick on poisoned fish.

Coleman also worked his magic on *Unter Uns* ('Between Ourselves'), which appeared to be a German version of *Number 96*, even though that show wasn't Grundy property. Like *96*, there were lots of raunchy goings-on, particularly in the top floor penthouse where three girls shared with a guy who pretended to be gay. Used to shooting nude scenes on closed sets back in Australia, Coleman asked for the same on *Unter Uns* but was met with blank looks. None of the crew seemed to know what he was talking about, and all insisted they were 'essential crew'.

Adam Bowen, who also worked for Grundy's on their European soaps, found it difficult teaching writers how to keep European soap light and frothy. 'German TV had only been going seven years and their government TV writers wanted to do Kafka,' he remembers.

'I created the first Italian soap *Un Posto Al Sole* ('A Place in the Sun') and there was a doctor who was a reclusive alcoholic. The Italians didn't understand that. Italians drink because they enjoy it, they don't drink because they're miserable. Their culture already has so much more eating and sex and looking good, we had to think up new stories there.'

European soaps, Aussie-style, continue to thrive, which means there is less of a demand to buy new Australian series when they can all make their own. Aussie audiences may one day end up watching dubbed European soaps, unaware they've probably seen it all before.

15

PRISONER

PREMIERE: **1979** EPISODES: **692** NETWORK: **TEN** FINALE: **1986**

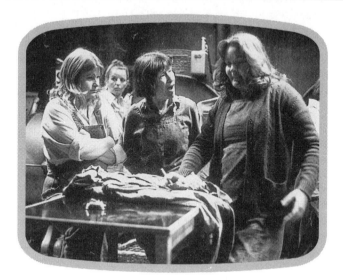

Doreen (Colette Mann), Lizzie (Sheila Florance)
and Bea (Val Lehman) fire up the steam press.

While many Aussie serials have serious cult followings, only one has been elevated to iconic status. That's because only one has been repeated constantly in both Australia and England for the last two decades. It would appear that each new screening hooks another generation of fans who fall in love with a group of denim-clad prisoners and their officious warders. That show is, of course, *Prisoner*, or as it is known outside Australia, *Prisoner: Cell Block H*. Not only does its appeal appear to be timeless, but it is also unique for its predominantly female cast, several spin-off stage productions and its brief but nevertheless astounding success in America where it out-rated the legendary Johnny Carson.

Prisoner was the brainchild of Grundy's Reg Watson and was originally conceived as a gritty 16 part only series. Watson had been a fan of an earlier women's prison drama, Britain's *Within These Walls*, but felt that it had ignored major story potential by focusing only on the lives of the officers. By 1977, Reg Grundy had also been convinced of its potential.

The content would obviously be controversial, but the Ten network had been down this road before with *Number 96* and *The Box*. Research had proved that lesbianism, drugs and crooked officers were commonplace in many prisons and would need to be addressed. Life on the inside was bleak and violent and the series' first 16 episodes did not shy away from such unpleasant truths. Before its more popular characters would be fleshed out for laughs, Wentworth Detention Centre was home to a tough lesbian bikie (Franky Doyle), an unforgiving 'top dog' (Bea Smith) and a Gestapo-like prisoner officer (Vera Bennett, aka Vinegar Tits).

Casting began with actress Val Lehman beating Betty Bobbitt for the role of Bea (Bobbitt was instead brought back a year later as Judy Bryant). Colette Mann became child-like Doreen after testing with Lehman and Sheila Florance (Lizzie Birdsworth). Elspeth Ballantyne (Meg) didn't think she'd be employed for long. 'I never thought *Prisoner* could possibly be a winner,' Ballantyne says today. 'I thought it would revolt everybody.'

'Melbourne was a Crawford's town at the time and Hector Crawford reportedly put the word out that anybody who worked for me would never work for Crawford's again,' reveals Ian Bradley who came on board as *Prisoner*'s first producer and head writer. 'Ironically, I was later to become CEO of Crawford's but, at the time, it meant that we had to do everything ourselves. We just couldn't get enough experienced people to work for us. Reg Watson told me he found it very difficult to write because it was so depressing and actually only wrote the first two hours. So I taught my actress wife Anne Lucas (*Bellbird* and *The Young Doctors*) to script edit and assembled a writing team. We brought in trainee writers like Dave Worthington from as far away as Brisbane and also put on trainee directors like Peta Letchford, Marcus Cole, Leigh Spence and Michael Pattison.'

Unfortunately, the Ten network were so aghast at the first episode, they flew in an American TV executive from *Days of Our Lives* to tell Bradley what was wrong with the show. 'She told me the lighting was too dark, the sets too drab, the uniforms too unflattering and the women wore too little make-up and weren't attractive enough. The show was also too violent and the pace of the show was so fast nobody could follow it.' Bradley ignored her and, under pressure from the network to re-shoot, enlisted the support of Ten's Neil Harold, who liked the show just as it was. 'Neil was obviously persuasive because, apart from re-shooting a scene for sound reasons, the episode stayed intact. The show was market tested and then launched to instant success and suddenly everybody forgot that they ever doubted.'

Everyone, that is, except for officers from Melbourne's Fairlea prison who were assisting Bradley with his research for upcoming stories. 'We were able to placate Victorian prison officers by telling them that all the original research was done in Sydney's Silverwater prison and NSW was responsible for giving prisons a bad name,' reveals Ian Bradley today.

Prisoner premiered in February 1979 and critical reaction was mostly favourable. *TV Times* saw it 'destined for success' but couldn't help taking a few potshots. '*Prisoner* could be described by the uncharitable as *The Young Convicts* or *The Restless Lags*, but in truth it is a slickly made tear-jerker. Old master Reg Watson can't have had as much fun since he helped create *Crossroads*. If you think there is some similarity between *Prisoner* and Googie Withers's British-made series *Within These Walls*, forget it. In many ways, it has more affinity to *Porridge*.'

> 'I never thought Prisoner *could* possibly be a winner. I thought it would revolt everybody.'

First night ad: If you think prison is hell for a man, imagine what it's like for a woman.

While the show might have descended into Ronnie Barker sitcom territory in later episodes, its two-hour opener was a scorcher. It commenced with the arrival of two new inmates at Wentworth, Karen Travers (Peta Toppano) and Lynn Warner (Kerry Armstrong). Karen had killed her abusive husband, while country girl Lynn was a true innocent, framed for the kidnapping of a baby (which had actually been buried alive by its demented mother). Lynn was soon incurring the harsh wrath of Bea Smith, who burnt her arm in the steam press, while Karen was set upon by Franky, in a new variation of love at first sight.

Wentworth's staff was represented by immaculately coiffured Governor Erica Davidson (Patsy King), caring warder Meg (Elspeth Ballantyne), who had been born in a prison, and her psychologist husband Bill Jackson (Don Barker). Bill was killed by Chrissie Latham (Amanda Muggleton) during the series' first riot, thereby setting widow Meg up for a never-ending parade of ill-matched suitors who would either dump, wed or rape her during the series' eight-year run.

And then there was Vera (Fiona Spence). Miss Bennett was nicknamed 'Vinegar Tits' by the women and the expression caught on quickly. After just a few months on air, reports filtered back that schoolkids had started using the name to refer to their least favourite teachers. Like *Number 96* before it, children had unwittingly become regular viewers of another series they weren't supposed to be watching and it was hardly surprising that schoolyards, which operate on the same power dynamics as a prison, ended up with students calling their teachers the same names they saw the TV prisoners calling their warders.

Subsequently, the show would be watered down, and despite research showing that most female prisoners were incarcerated for drug offences, the impressionable underage audience meant that *Prisoner* would always carry an anti-drugs message. Bea Smith had already been set up as a leader who would not tolerate illicit substances, her own daughter having died from a heroin overdose while Bea was locked up.

'The anti-drug stance taken by Bea was part of the moral stance we originally created for the show,' says Ian Bradley, 'and the original cast made the characters an extension of themselves. This to me was the strongest reason for the success of the show, along with our concept that, simply put, everybody is a prisoner of their own environment.'

The early episodes also featured two underdeveloped characters who would soon dominate the show. Doreen Anderson (Colette Mann) was first seen as a thumb-sucking, teddy bear-hugging lesbian lover of Franky Doyle, while Lizzie (Sheila Florance) was a cranky, chain-smoking kleptomaniac, incarcerated for life after poisoning a group of shearers who had complained about her cooking. As the series developed, Doreen, Lizzie and Bea became the show's most beloved characters and, behind the scenes, were nicknamed 'The Three Musketeers'.

Doreen and Lizzie's first meaty storyline came when they escaped with Franky over the prison fence. Lizzie's old age (and 'dodgy ticker') meant she had to be returned to the front gate almost immediately, while

Doreen and Franky went on the run, even donning nuns' habits at one point. Most *Prisoner* escapes would end with re-capture, although the killing of Franky Doyle by police was an exception. Actress Carol Burns couldn't imagine doing the demanding role with a double workload when Ten decided to air two hours of *Prisoner* weekly, so she decided to leave the show.

'Writer Denise Morgan was particularly concerned about showing that Franky's self-violence emanated from something other than her sexuality,' says Ian Bradley. 'Franky wasn't just a vicious crim, she was crying out in agony because of her low self-esteem caused by her deprived childhood and illiteracy. She was actually intended to get an education as the series progressed and go on to lead a useful life in prison reform and become a hero.'

Instead, later that year after Franky had been blasted out of the show, her best moments were re-edited into a two-hour telemovie, *The Franky Doyle Story*, and like the series, the movie was another

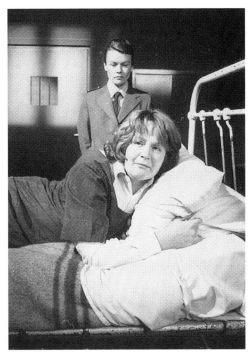

'Vinegar Tits' Vera (Fiona Spence) refuses to let Bea (Val Lehman) go to her daughter's funeral.

huge ratings success. The actors, however, weren't impressed, and took Grundy's to court for not paying them for the new movie. Colette Mann (Doreen), representing the cast, realised they had won their case when the judge addressed her by her character's nickname of 'Dor'. That was the end of the cheap telemovies, but nobody missed them as the show took off in a country nobody ever dreamed would be interested in watching an Aussie soap.

As *Prisoner* became a popular success at home, Grundy's took the unprecedented step of deciding to try to sell the show internationally. After being shopped around at a Las Vegas show convention in April 1979, Los Angeles independent station KTLA-5 bought the 26 episodes. With a title change to prevent confusion with British cult classic *The Prisoner* (which starred Patrick McGoohan), *Prisoner: Cell Block H* premiered in America in August 1979. US critics howled about its sleazy plots and cheap production values, but Californians were fascinated and began to switch on in increasing numbers. Soon it was the second highest-rating show in its timeslot (Wednesdays, 8pm), beaten only by *Charlie's Angels*. A cult had been born.

Not only that, but Americans were actually prepared to listen to the show with the original Aussie accent. Around this time, *Mad Max* had only been released into cinemas after every actor had been dubbed with American voices, including Mel Gibson. The women of *Prisoner*, however, got to speak in their native twang.

When the series first began, American lesbians picketed the television station, concerned that Franky was going to be yet another negative portrayal of a gay woman. They soon changed their mind as each new episode unfolded and Franky's softer side emerged. By the time the character died on-screen, a group of real-life bikies drove to KTLA to lay a wreath at the station door for their favourite character. By 1980, the show was screening in 35 American cities including Chicago, San Diego and Albuquerque, but not without its detractors. *TV Guide* slammed the independent stations that screened it in early-evening timeslots (Minneapolis at 6.30pm, Philadelphia 5pm), claiming it wasn't suitable for family viewing, and, given America's prudish network standards at this time, the show must have been a shock for unsuspecting viewers. In New York, *Prisoner: Cell Block H* was served as a late-night treat but nobody dreamed it would best Johnny Carson's long running *Tonight Show*. At the height of its popularity, even *Saturday Night Live* did a send-up, and several years later it was revealed Sammy Davis Jr was a major fan. When he visited Australia and requested a tour of the set, he begged producers to write him in for a cameo. Amazingly, conflicting schedules prevented this from happening.

No Australian TV series had ever hit the big time in America (and no soap has ever since). Inundated with fan mail from America, not to mention Aussie letters of support, the hard-working actresses began to moan about their relentless working conditions and pay rates. Not surprisingly, the ringleader was the actress who played Wentworth's 'top dog', Bea Smith. Val Lehman took her role as Actors Equity rep seriously, and wasn't above telling the press how little they got paid, especially in light of their American success.

The pay may not have been much chop, but when it came to award ceremonies, riches would rain down upon the *Prisoner* gang. The year Val Lehman won dual Logies for both Best Lead Actress and Most Popular Actress, she was philosophical about the show's success. In front of her peers she said, 'I would like to thank Grundy's for giving me the opportunity of bashing almost every other actress in Australia.' Lehman was only half joking. Bea Smith was at the centre of the action for 400 episodes and practically every working Australian actress went through the show, many returning again and again to play multiple roles.

Between takes, the actresses would hang out in a downstairs green room of Channel 10 at Nunawading nicknamed 'The Tunnel'. It was a dark corridor with no air or outside light, leading some wags to joke that they felt like they really were locked up inside a prison. Rowena Wallace, who relished her role as nutter Anne Griffin, re-christened the actresses' hangout as 'The Vivisection Tunnel'. 'I've never heard so many people torn limb from limb in all my life,' Wallace laughs today. 'It was hysterical. I was always gobsmacked listening to it, but I loved doing the show.'

'We had some enormous egos but they were also marvellous, loud, intelligent, feisty ladies who all had an opinion,' says Elspeth Ballantyne. 'The odd chap was there, but if he had any sense, he would go hang out with the crew.' Maggie Kirkpatrick, who would join the show in 1981 playing 'The Freak', thought that some of the 'original prisoners' made it difficult for new actors, particularly some of the younger ones. 'It's extremely nerve-wracking to go into a long-running series as a guest because you need to be able to slot yourself in quickly and work under pressure with people who are already used to working together,' Kirkpatrick says. 'And I have to say that there were some people who made it very difficult for young people to feel any comfort whatsoever, either in the studio or the green room.'

At one point, Maggie Kirkpatrick and Carole Skinner (who played the murderous Nola) bought flowers and a bottle of champagne for an actress finishing up a six-week stint. 'One of the "old lags" asked why, and I said because she's young, she's frightened, she's had a shit of a time down here and she needs to go home to Sydney feeling that not all of Melbourne is against her! I never saw *Prisoner* as a competition, and I like a good gossip with the rest of them, but the putdowns from certain actresses were unnecessary.'

Tina Bursill (who played ice queen Sonia Stevens) also found the show somewhat depressing to make. 'The actresses, who shall all remain nameless, were either separated from their husbands, jumping the fence and becoming lesbians or talking about food or macramé. There were certain days that were "food days" because we all had to eat in the dining room, or look as if we were, and of course you'd be bored so you would eat and eat and so some women were becoming enormous. What had happened was the rhythm created in making the show seeped into how they behaved behind the scenes. I saw a lot of people ostracised and a lot of bitchery.'

Tina Bursill tried suggesting Sonia become a vegetarian so she would not have to eat the awful mince served out to prisoners, but the request was ignored and the slop kept being served. And despite a silly storyline about tough Sonia being scared of a snake (that somehow found its way into the prison), Bursill still thinks the show is an incredible achievement. '*Prisoner*, to this day, is the most remarkable piece of television. I think it's absolutely fantastic that women at that time could hold their own with great storylines and performances.'

When called for filming, actresses would slip on their denim uniforms and head off to the set, with minimal make-up. Val Lehman never wore any make-up on the show, even if the steam press made her look hot and sweaty. One Friday afternoon, however, the actresses were preparing for the Logie Awards and as each returned to the set with more and more make-up, the director was forced to put a stop to all the glamour in the name of continuity.

When the series began, Bea Smith, a former hairdresser, was being released after serving ten years for murdering her husband's mistress. After spending the night in a luxury hotel, Bea shot her hopeless husband dead for allowing their daughter to become hooked on heroin. Back in Wentworth, 'Queen Bea' returned to her position behind the steam press in the laundry room. Throughout the series, Bea had to fend off contenders for her crown of 'top dog' (like Franky Doyle, Marie Winter, Sandy Edwards, Nola McKenzie and Sonia Stevens).

'The rhythm created in making the show seeped into how they behaved behind the scenes. I saw a lot of people ostracised and a lot of bitchery.'

Doreen (Colette Mann) and Lizzie (Sheila Florance) were also kept busy in the early years. Both were paroled but neither could cope with life on the outside. Doreen was reunited with her long lost mother Alice (Anne Haddy) and married Kevin Burns (Ian Gilmour). Lizzie was pardoned for her original offence after a deathbed confession revealed that someone else had poisoned those shearers, but she missed her mates on the inside so much, the old rascal set about committing petty crimes so she would be put away again.

Actress Sheila Florance was just as memorable off-screen as she was on, even if she was frail enough to be knocked over by a breeze. On one freezing morning, she stepped out of a taxi only to be blown to the ground, and laughed so hard she wet her pants. The cast all decided that it was at least ten degrees cooler filming way out in Nunawading, particularly first thing in the morning and last thing at night.

On one occasion, the actors were cursing at having to do a late night outside shoot in the middle of winter. As prison officers lined up with guns aimed at the door, Lizzie was supposed to emerge from a riot-ravaged Wentworth, wave a white flag as a sign of surrender, and complete just one simple line of dialogue. Yet, take after take, Sheila Florance, couldn't nail the line. Finally she emerged, waved her white flag and uttered the immortal clanger, 'Nuna-fucking-wading! Let's give it back to the Aborigines!'

By now the show was so popular Ten even managed to wring a one-hour variety special out of it by sending the actresses into Melbourne's real-life Pentridge prison. Inside, the women performed a concert for the inmates under a huge marquee. Lizzie sang 'Steam Heat' while sitting in a laundry basket, while Bea, Judy and Doreen did a burlesque

Chrissie (Amanda Muggleton) and Bea (Val Lehman) give Margo (Jane Clifton) a good bashing!

version of 'Give Them What They Want'. The worst rendition by far, however, was 'YMCA' with Bea as the construction worker, Doreen the cowboy, Judy the Indian and Lizzie an unlikely leatherwoman. The actresses had discovered how well they crooned together during production breaks, but even they now cringe at this unfortunate musical interlude. Up front as lead vocalist was Jane Clifton, who played Margo Gaffney, and went on to have a top-selling single, 'Girl on the Wall'. And while Jane at least could carry a tune, there was no excusing Betty Bobbitt's dismal attempts at dancing, which looked more like an attempt to dislodge a nasty case of constipation.

JUDITH McGRATH
as Colleen Powell
PRISONER

Real chart success, however, belonged to Lynne Hamilton who sang the show's haunting theme song, 'On the Inside'. A modest hit in Australia when the show first began, the single went Top 5 in England in 1989. Ten years after recording the track, Lynne Hamilton was flown over to perform the song on English institution *Top of the Pops*. Once again, that should have been the end of it, but throughout the 90s and into the new millennium, DJs revived it in dance track remixes. American soap star John Wesley Shipp (*Dawson's Creek*) even sang a cover version for his album *Images*.

In 1980, possibly in a nod to US viewers, the Bea-Doreen-Lizzie trio was expanded to include an American character, Judy Bryant (Betty Bobbitt). The butch taxi driver intentionally got herself imprisoned to be near her lesbian lover, Sharon Gilmour (Margot Knight). Although initially butting heads with Bea over Sharon's drug crimes, Judy would soon become an ally, particularly after Sharon was killed by evil warder Jock Stewart (Tommy Dysart). Upon her release, Judy would run a halfway house, which provided a point of interest outside the prison walls for storylines (and quite possibly, the scraggiest bunch of housemates ever seen on TV, barring *Big Brother*).

MAGGIE KIRKPATRICK
as Joan Ferguson
PRISONER

Fan cards for Po-Face and The Freak.

Another prisoner to come and go on the whim of scriptwriters was Chrissie Latham. Despite having killed Meg's husband in an early episode, potential had been spotted in actress Amanda Muggleton, so Chrissie expressed remorse for her crime and was forgiven by Meg. Chrissie was soon tugging at viewers' heartstrings when she gave birth to a baby girl, Elizabeth (played by the son of producer Ian Bradley and Anne Lucas). Mother and daughter were separated regularly and, despite Chrissie's best efforts to be a good mother, she was last seen being transferred to Barnhurst prison, in much the same way most of the *Neighbours* cast retire to Queensland.

During this time, the official ranks were swelled by Deputy Governor Jim Fletcher (Gerard Maguire) and Officer Colleen Powell (Judith McGrath), or as the prisoners would call them, Fletch the Lech and Po-Face. Representing 'the Department' was Ted Douglas, played by Ian Smith. When Douglas was caught red-handed in a scandal, Ian Smith went behind the scenes on *Prisoner* as associate producer. Vera Bennett (Fiona Spence), once viewed as just a sour authoritarian, was later revealed to be a sad, lonely spinster nursing her demanding, housebound

Paperbacks were
rushed into print after
the show became a
hit in America.

mother. When she died, the inexperienced Vera embarked on a series of disastrous love affairs (one such lover being legendary Aussie actor Bill Hunter) until episode 224 when she left the show to become the governor of Barnhurst.

'I'm a well-known laugher, and Fiona Spence and I were always in strife for getting the giggles,' reveals Elspeth Ballantyne (Meg). 'The more they told us how many thousands of dollars it was costing every time I laughed, the more it made me laugh. After Fiona Spence left, it was Judith McGrath (Colleen) who would make me laugh.' With so much fun to be had off-screen, what *Prisoner* needed was another nasty screw to sober the inmates up. Enter Joan Ferguson, aka 'The Freak' (Maggie Kirkpatrick).

'I used to look at long-running shows like *Number 96* and think, oooh, that'd be nice!' says Kirkpatrick who was mainly a theatre actress at the time of casting. 'I actually auditioned for Vinegar Tits when the show started, but then in 1981 some friends told me I was going to be offered a role. They said I would be asked to play a bull dyke screw and I thought, charming! Is that what they think of me? So off I went on what was supposed to be just a 13-week stint.'

Joan Ferguson arrived in episode 287 and, by episode's end, had revealed herself to be a corrupt, leather-glove-wearing, marauding lesbian making the moves on new prisoner Hannah Simpson (Julieanne Newbould). 'The minute I slicked back the hair and put the uniform on, there she was,' remembers Kirkpatrick. 'I was so terribly nervous that first day on set, the menacing stillness was born because I was absolutely rigid with fright. Before the episodes had even gone to air, I was told the character would be continued. So began the mad roller coaster ride for four and a half years.'

Joan was far more ruthless and corrupt than Vera Bennett ever was, and had the character not proved so popular, her wrongdoings should have been her undoing much earlier on. Instead, Joan achieved cult status and almost superhero powers in staying one step ahead of the prisoners and her fellow officers. No matter how many times she was bashed, set up or caught red-handed, The Freak would come up smiling and continue to run amok in the prison corridors. Her evil deeds would go unpunished until the final episode many years later.

'I felt that Maggie was terribly lucky to be so evil, particularly when you had to start work at 6am in the morning,' says Elspeth Ballantyne. 'Maggie could be as nasty as she liked whereas I had to wear the halo!' Maggie Kirkpatrick agrees that Ballantyne had the harder job playing 'Saint Meg'. 'It's true, she had to come up smiling, even after gang rapes, bashings and seeing Joan Ferguson every time she walked into that staff room.' Kirkpatrick admits that it was even OK to look rough first thing in the morning because 'even if I'd had a big night and looked like a dog's breakfast, it didn't matter because any harsh look suited Joan.'

'I think I went a little crazy,' admits Kirkpatrick today. 'I guess it was having all that money and not having had it before.' As for leaving the character behind after hours, Kirkpatrick could 'glamour up' to avoid looking like Joan, but one thing always gave her away. 'No matter how girlie I made my hair, the minute I opened my mouth, the voice gave me away.'

Joan was always out to control the women her way, and if she didn't have her own 'top dog' in place, she was out to destroy whoever was there. Naturally then, her first major battle was with Bea Smith. For the 1982 cliffhanger, they were engaged in a fight to the death, while a fire, lit as a diversion, burned out of control. When the show returned in February 1983, two inmates had been burnt alive – Barbara Fields (Susan Guerin) and Mouse (Jentah Sobott). And in an ironic twist, Bea and Joan had been forced to help each other to safety. Other memorable summer cliffhangers were Roslyn Coulsen (Sigrid Thornton) being broken out of jail by a group of terrorists, who then took a shot at Erica (1979), and the pantomime tunnel cave-in that almost buried alive Doreen, Judy and Lizzie (1980).

During one of Bea's three escapes from Wentworth, she reunited with Doreen, who was paroled and living in Sydney. Although *Prisoner* continued to be a ratings success all around Australia, the show often struggled in Sydney, and this location shoot was an obvious attempt to increase its profile there. Unfortunately, the overkill of having the Harbour Bridge and Opera House in nearly every outside shot probably did nothing to endear it to Sydneysiders. Another Sydney shoot a couple of years later, with Bobbie (Maxine Klibingaitis) working as a prostitute on the infamous streets of Kings Cross, was similarly obsessed with the harbourside icons.

As *Prisoner* began to rehash storylines at an alarming rate, the core cast slowly began to depart. Not long after Erica Davidson was replaced by Governor Ann Reynolds (Gerda Nicolson), the unthinkable finally happened – Val Lehman called it quits. In episode 400, Bea Smith was abruptly transferred to Barnhurst. Lizzie only lasted a few more months, with word that actress Sheila Florance was despondent at the loss of her old mate. Even 'Po-Face' Colleen (Judith McGrath) retired from Wentworth to travel overseas. Many fans deserted the show at this point, and as ratings slid, several Australian country stations removed it from their schedules. While hardcore fans would stick around, the show would never again reach the heights of the Bea Smith era.

Prisoner struggled to stay afloat as a rash of new characters arrived. Judy Bryant, convicted of the euthanasia killing of Hazel Kent (Belinda Davey), was sent back inside to become a temporary 'top dog'. Scriptwriters tried desperately to replace audience favourites with thinly veiled replacements. Their most disastrous cloning came when trying to recreate Lizzie, but neither Dot (Alethea McGrath) nor Ettie (Lois Ramsey) had the Birdsworth magic. Instead of becoming lovable old-timers, they just came across as annoying over-actors.

'It got really silly
towards the end.
For a while there it
started to look like
Saint Trinians!'

In desperation, an earlier character from a prison reform group, Myra Desmond (Anne Phelan), killed her husband and was sent inside to become the new 'top dog'. The comparisons to Bea Smith were obvious, yet this time the scriptwriters saved the daughter. Upon learning that her teenage girl was hooked on heroin, Myra broke out of jail to help her go cold turkey. Conveniently, this also kept Myra as anti-drugs as Bea had been. The character was certainly popular and Myra worked the steam press until yet another terrorist group infiltrated the prison. This time they began killing inmates, and in a shocking and memorable *Prisoner* moment, when ordered to nominate a prisoner for execution, Myra selflessly took a bullet herself.

Having spent so long establishing Myra as the new 'top dog', viewers were mystified when she was allowed to die. Anne Phelan revealed on a DVD release of classic episodes that it wasn't merely a whim of the scriptwriters, but more to do with a demand to be paid more. Aware that Betty Bobbitt (Judy) was leaving, Phelan asked for her salary to be increased to match that of the longer-serving actress. When knocked back, Phelan resigned and, according to crew gossip, it cost the producers more to stage the terrorist sequences (with stunts and helicopters) than keeping her on at the higher wage.

Unaware that the show would live on in endless repeats, producers marred its timeless appeal by introducing a character obsessed with the pop group of the day, Culture Club. Lexie Patterson (played by Pepe Trevor, daughter of executive producer Marie Trevor) dressed in the style of Boy George, and while her character was a hit with fans, from this point on the series would always appear very 80s. Whilst some of the hairstyles, fashions and décor all seem hilarious when viewed today, the prison uniforms, which are seen more than anything else, keep the series somewhat timeless. Until special appearances from Aussie celebrities of the day rock up, that is. English audiences will forever wonder why an elderly and mumbling marathon runner, Cliff Young, popped into Wentworth, and the less said about TV chef Peter Russell-Clarke's appearance, the better.

There was even a desperate attempt to cash in on the glory years by remembering the original characters courtesy of a flashback episode. Soon after, a group of new prisoners arrived from the burnt-down Barnhurst prison and revealed that Bea Smith had died in the fire. Their references to Bea and Governor Vera Bennett only seemed to highlight how badly the show had slipped from its glory days. When Paula Duncan came on board to play a prisoner called Lorelei Wilkinson, *Number 96* fans wondered why scriptwriters were so bereft of ideas that they had to steal the name of the pantyhose murderer's first victim.

'It got really silly towards the end,' says Maggie Kirkpatrick. 'I thought it started to make prison look very glamorous with everyone in pretty dresses and make-up. For a while there it started to look like Saint Trinians! When it started it was very gritty and nasty and not some place some teenager would want to go to.' Worse was to come when scriptwriters suggested that The Freak should get a boyfriend.

'We nearly parted ways over that. I'd spent the best part of four years establishing her sexuality and they were going to make a complete mockery of it. I refused to do it, so the writers asked what I could suggest to make Joan's life more interesting. After ballroom dancing was suggested, I said, look, if you want Joan Ferguson to go out and meet people then how about she take up golf? I actually thought I might have scored myself a brand new set of golf clubs, but then I got the script and it said that Joan had "found these old sticks in the garage". And that's what I got, an old set of golf clubs from the floor manager! They thwarted me!' laughs Kirkpatrick. 'Joan did meet a male companion and there was golf and dinner but that's as far as I would let it go. Joan wouldn't jump into bed with some chap at her age, no matter how lonely she was.'

Finally, after many cast shake-ups, the show hit on a winning formula in late 1985 with the arrival of bikie Rita Connors (Glenda Linscott). She proved to be a formidable force in the show's final year, particularly for Joan Ferguson. Like all good 'top dogs' before her, Rita had to become anti-drugs, so within a couple of episodes, the pot-smoker had read some propaganda leaflets and changed her ways. The lazy character change proved the series was running out of steam and Rita was too little, too late. With the continuing audience erosion, Ten finally announced the show was ending. With eight weeks of production still to go, scriptwriters were able to resolve all the storylines as well as plan a big finish.

'When they decided to finish it up, I thought they handled it very well,' says Maggie Kirkpatrick. 'The writers were given ample opportunity to come up with some really good scripts. I think they did a great service ending it the way it did because the public wanted to see Joan get her comeuppance.'

Ann (Gerda Nicolson), Rita (Glenda Linscott), 'Lurch' (Lois Collinder) and Meg (Elspeth Ballantyne) finally put Joan (Maggie Kirkpatrick) behind bars in the last episode.

In the final episode, diagnosed with inoperable cancer, the dying Rita pulled off what no other character had been able to do – she exposed The Freak for the evil bitch she had always been. Rita pretended to form an alliance with Joan over a haul of stolen cash, but it was a set-up designed to catch Joan Ferguson in the act. Logistically, there were a few loopholes in this final set-up but nobody seemed to care, especially when The Freak was hauled out to a police car in the show's final scene. The prisoners were last seen celebrating on the lawn as the car took the hated screw away.

Just one original regular remained from the early days, Elspeth Ballantyne. Veteran extras Barbara Jungwirth and Hazel Henley had also been quietly muttering away in the background of the jail from beginning to end.

By the time the show finished, the cast had included nearly every working actress in Australia. Lynda Stoner, Briony Behets, Judy Nunn, Penny Downie, Tracy Mann, Olivia Hamnett, Lisa Crittenden, Caroline Gillmer, Arkie Whitely, Judi Connelli, Liz Harris, Judy McBurney, Janet Andrewartha, Virginia Hey, Maggie Dence, Debra Lawrance, Jackie Woodburne, Vivean Gray, Jill Forster, Pat Evison, Anna Hruby and Zoe Bertram all got their chance to slip on a denim uniform.

Although *Prisoner* used 6,480 actors, many played dual parts, some even appearing in three roles. Belinda Davey was a Wentworth nurse in the first episode, while a few hundred episodes later she was tragic prisoner Hazel Kent. Lesley Baker arrived in episode 15 as Monica Ferguson, and came back as bikie Tinkerbelle. Lois Ramsey appeared as dotty social worker Agnes and Lizzie wannabe Ettie Parslow. Julieanne Newbould played The Freak's first object of lust, Hannah, and returned four years later as undercover cop Wendy Glover. Diane Craig played prison escapee Jackie and nun Sister Anita Selby. And Julia Blake, Anne Charleston and Kirsty Child all played three roles each.

None, however, could beat Peter Flett who played five roles in *Prisoner*. 'First I was Lizzie Birdsworth's lawyer, then I was a psychiatrist,' remembers Flett. 'Next I played this bizarre religious cult leader called Brother Red Earth, then I was a television reporter helping Judy Bryant escape. Finally I played Alan Maxwell, husband of Kath (Kate Hood). People watching in overseas countries must have thought we had a shortage of actors down here in Australia!'

Ray Meagher could only manage three roles during the series' run, although he did get to always play baddies. His first incarnation, demented Vietnam vet Geoff Butler, sent a letter bomb to his former wartime buddy Jim Fletcher. Tragically, Jim's wife and two boys took delivery of the parcel and were all killed instantly when it exploded. In *Prisoner*'s most outrageous plot rehash, another screw, Colleen Powell, lost her husband and two children when a car bomb killed all of them. It was also unforgivable when not one but two male serial killers began working their way through the female prisoners. One was prison nurse Neil Murray (Adrian Wright), killing prostitutes who had been on the inside, while the second psycho, officer David Bridges (David Waters), hid his victims' bodies all over the prison before being caught.

Filming finished at 7.15pm on Friday, 5 September 1986, but within just a couple of months rumours sprung up about a follow-up show. *TV Week* reported that pre-production had begun on *Barnhurst* and Reg Watson revealed it would be a prison drama with a difference – possibly with male and female prisoners together. In the end though, *Barnhurst* never made it past the presentation reel.

America's love affair with *Prisoner: Cell Block H* didn't last either, and the show gradually disappeared from screens there. New York cancelled their order after 274 episodes, although Philadelphia kept the habit until 1984. In 1991, however, Grundy's convinced the Yanks they could make their own version, *Dangerous Women*. The syndicated series was basically a reworking of early *Prisoner* scripts. Bea Smith was reincarnated as Rita and Karen Travers was now known as Maria Trent. The end result, a very poor imitation of the original, was not a success.

In 1987, just as the last episode was going to air in Australia, England bought the show and began screening it around the country in varying late night slots. Just as in America, the series exceeded projected audience figures everywhere it was screened, and the show soon had an audience so huge it went beyond cult. By 1990 it was so popular that four original cast members (Val Lehman, Sheila Florance, Amanda Muggleton and Carol Burns) were shipped over to appear on English talk shows and tour the country in a unique chat show style theatre event called 'The Great Escape'. Everywhere they appeared, they caused a near riot with hordes of screaming fans. The city of Derby even hosted a civic reception for Bea, Lizzie, Chrissie and Franky.

Next came a stage version of the play, written by Reg Watson, with Patsy King back as Erica the governor and Elspeth Ballantyne as Meg. Glenda Linscott, yet to be seen in most parts of the country as Rita, played a new character called Angela (a 'Chrissie Latham type') while UK actresses Joanna Monro and Brenda Longman played Franky Doyle and Bea respectively. It premiered at the Wimbledon Theatre on 21 September 1989,

'On opening night, I walked on stage and got the biggest fright of my life,' remembers Elspeth Ballantyne. 'The audience all stood up and cheered and screamed. The noise was deafening and it just went on and on. At the end of the show, I asked someone what the clanging noise was and was told there were people dressed in chains and wearing convict uniforms!' Afterwards, the actresses couldn't get out of the stage door for screaming fans and similar hysteria was repeated every night in every location as the show travelled through the UK.

Mobbed by fans, Ballantyne had to disguise herself with a beanie and a scarf to cover her face. She went everywhere with (the very tall) Glenda Linscott who became her bodyguard. 'I just went under her wing everywhere,' says Ballantyne. 'I never spoke. I'd just whisper any questions through Glenda. I got to the stage where I was desperate to meet somebody who had never seen the damn thing and could talk to me about something else.'

Depending on the location, the audience would boo and hiss panto-style, or sit in solemn silence taking it all very seriously. So seriously in fact, the play was revived in 1990 with Fiona Spence (Vera), Jane Clifton (Margo) and Jacqui Gordon (Suzie).

The *Prisoner* phenomenon now spawned its most unusual spin-off. On 29 October 1995, *Prisoner Cell Block H: The Musical* opened at the Queen's Theatre in London, later travelling throughout the UK on a national tour. Emphasising the camp values of the show, this latest version featured Maggie Kirkpatrick as Joan Ferguson and, playing herself, English drag comedian Lily Savage (Paul O'Grady), who is thrown into Wentworth for a crime she didn't commit. Played strictly for laughs, this version had intentional overacting and sets that really did wobble (even though it was an urban myth that *Prisoner*'s rock solid concrete and brick prison cells shook on-camera).

Prisoner Cell Block H: The Musical was written by Peter Pinne and Don Battye. Australian fans assumed the smash hit would make its way down under, but both writers agreed that the pantomime aspects of the show were unique to an English audience. There was also concern as to who could play the lead in a down under version. 'We altered the concept to accommodate Lily Savage,' says Peter Pinne, 'but there was nobody in Australia who could have put bums on the seats the way Lily Savage did.'

'I did a number at the Royal Albert Hall just prior to us opening, on the same bill as Elton John and Kylie Minogue,' remembers Maggie Kirkpatrick. 'I walked on and 5,000 people starting hissing. So I just strode up and down until they finished and then there was this roar of applause! The play was a load of old schlock but people shrieked because it was adult panto and the Brits love all that. It never would have worked in Australia though, it would have just been seen as bad theatre.'

To this day, there are still *Prisoner* fan clubs all over the world and over 50 websites dedicated to the show. It's all done with good humour too as fans continue to debate over who had the most laughable hairstyle, which was the most poorly-choreographed fight scene and what was the most ridiculous storyline (the overweight lesbian Judy Bryant moonlighting as a prostitute perhaps?).

Elspeth Ballantyne credits *Prisoner* with giving her and her two (non-theatrical) sons a very stable lifestyle. While it was being made, she decided that they were both too young to watch it. Years later, her grown-up son Matthew travelled overseas. 'One night he rang me from Ireland at 3am in the morning,' says Ballantyne. 'He kept saying how he'd made a terrible mistake and I was fearing the worst.' It transpired that the family he was staying with were major *Prisoner* fans and after one beer too many, he had told them he was Meg's son. 'The mother became hysterical and forced Matthew to ring me on the spot because Meg was her favourite character. She got on the phone and I couldn't understand a word she was saying because of her accent and all the crying!'

Judith McGrath and
Maggie Kirkpatrick
during a break in
filming in the front
reception set.

Television shows about prisons continue to be fascinating viewing, particularly for *Prisoner* fans looking for copycats. Is the psycho bitch warden of America's *Oz* based on The Freak? And was the commissioning of *Bad Girls* an English attempt to replicate *Prisoner*'s success? In all, the Aussie soap has screened in over 40 countries including Barbados, Ecuador, Hong Kong, Poland, South Africa and Brazil, and one of its most recent signings was to a new gay Canadian TV network, Pride, where it is known as *Caged Women*.

Prisoner has also been dubbed, screened and repeated in Sweden under the title of *Kvinnofangelset*, while in Germany, Grundy's has remade the series locally as *Hinter Gittern* ('Women Behind Bars'). The German version is the most hardcore yet, with more dykes and more bashings. One character even had a tattooed head!

During the late 90s, Grundy's and Ten toyed once again with the idea of making another women's prison drama, but production was pulled just before a pilot was due. In 2002, word got out that Grundy's were still exploring the possibility of making another American version of the show. The failures of both *Dangerous Women* and *Punishment*, the 1981 all-male prison drama, proved that Reg Watson was unable to replicate his prison franchise without the original *Prisoner* creative team or that fabulous group of actors. 'They were great times, great ladies, the best companionship and the best laughs in the world,' says Elspeth Ballantyne. 'I wouldn't have swapped it for anything.'

16

SKYWAYS

Louise (Tina Bursill), guest star Bunney
Brooke and Mandy (Gaynor Martin).

Emboldened by the success of *Cop Shop*, Seven decided to do another soap. *TV Times* had an inside report that it was headed for the 6pm slot, but they couldn't have been more wrong. The network needed something to run after *Cop Shop* at 9.30pm to put a dent in the ratings of Nine's variety winner *The Don Lane Show*. For a while, they flirted with the idea of horny truckies in a pilot from Harrow Films called *Roadhouse*. But when explicit nudity was too much even for Deborah Gray (who told *TV Week* that she didn't want to be typecast after her full-frontal antics in *Number 96*), it was back to the drawing board.

Crawford's came up with the ambitious idea of setting a new serial at an airport and calling it *Skyways*. Arthur Hailey's novel *Airport* had been turned into a successful film franchise but creator Jock Blair had no intention of adapting anything from the book or movies for the new local soap. They would, however, use jumbo jets in storylines so they could rightly claim that *Skyways* used props worth $42 million. Convinced they were on to a winner, Seven bought 78 episodes, sight unseen.

Journalists from all over Australia were flown down to Tasmania for a glamorous launch at Hobart's Wrest Point Casino (perhaps chosen because every new Australian drama was a gamble). In a taste of how much alcohol was about to be consumed on-screen during the series, actor Tony Bonner invited the journalists to his room for more drinking.

'More champagne, more brandy, more vodka, more everything, come on you lot, let's get into it,' he bawled cheerfully, giving, according to *The Sunday Telegraph*, a convincing if largely unintended impersonation of Errol Flynn. When reminded that he had a 5.30am shoot he came back with, 'What the hell, you're only young once, darling. Come on, drink up, there's a ton more where that came from.'

Sadly, Bonner wasn't quite so animated in the show. From the first episode he displayed, as *TV Times* put it, 'a tendency to military stiffness'. Paul McFarlane (Tony Bonner) was next in line to be appointed head of Pacific International Airport. The retiring Harold Forbes (Charles Tingwell) did the dirty on him and recommended an Englishman, Derek Powell (Ron Falk), instead. Derek flew in with wife Jocelyn (Cecily Polson) and turned out to be arrogant, pompous and rude. Within a few episodes, Harold had buckled under the pressure and Paul was installed as the boss.

Paul had teenage twins, no-hoper Alan (Andrew McKaige) and perky Mandy (Gaynor Martin). It wasn't too long before their errant mother Elaine (Carmen Duncan) turned up. She confessed to abandoning her family, but blamed it on her own abandonment by Paul who was 'married' to his career. Elaine had turned to drink and younger men and had been caught in the act with both by Alan, who took a bit of time re-connecting with his mum. Elaine soon discovered that nothing had really changed with Paul or his job so she walked out again, leaving him to be romanced by Trans-Asia assistant manager Christine Burrows (Belinda Giblin).

Back at the airport, Paul's assistant manager was the ruthlessly ambitious Louise Carter (Tina Bursill) who made no secret of wanting Paul's job. Although remembered as a screen bitch, Tina Bursill still defends Louise as a strong career woman who was just trying to get ahead in a man's world. She also has an interesting take on the elegant outfits she got around in. 'Power dressing and the shoulder pads of the 80s allowed women to don their suit of armour to go into a corporate world. It was a very hedonistic time in the 80s and I knew those women existed.'

Nevertheless, Louise wasn't above sleeping with the higher ranking and much older David Rankin (Fred Parslow) in the hope that it might further her career, but she never did get Paul's job. In the last episode she allowed herself to be swept away by pilot Tim (Kit Taylor), but only after he regained his sight. Well, you wouldn't expect Louise to marry a blind pilot, would you?

Airport security chief Peter Fanelli (Bill Stalker) was tough but fair and lived with the sassy Faye (Kris McQuade). Faye was a former heroin junkie and prostitute whom Peter had saved from the streets. She worried that airport gossip (and the occasional former client turning up) would damage Fanelli's credibility but they had the support of Paul McFarlane. She got a job in the duty free store at the airport and eventually married Peter (in her lounge room) with all their work colleagues in attendance. Taking up skydiving, Faye plummeted to earth when her parachute failed to open. A despondent Fanelli left the airport, only to reappear on *Cop Shop*. Because of differing production schedules, for a while he was seen on both shows.

Up in the air traffic control tower, naïve Simon Young (Ken James) was calm and confident while directing planes, but the rest of the time he was a ridiculously overplayed mummy's boy. Still a virgin, he fell in love with the airport's information girl, Kelly Morgan (Joanne Samuel). Mother interfered with all the subtlety of a jumbo jet. Convinced an Aussie girl wasn't of the right breeding, Mrs Young (Irene Inescourt) took to her sick bed with fake 'attacks' and even reported Kelly's 'loose morals' to George Tippet (Brian James) in an effort to get her sacked. For some bizarre reason, the supposedly liberated Kelly fell for Simon, even agreeing to wear a bra to meet the old bitch for the first time. Well, the show did need its first wedding.

'Ken and I did not get on,' remembers Joanne Samuel. 'We were like chalk and cheese. It was really hard to be married to him for 18 months but the audience loved that relationship.' It's a credit to both actors that they were convincing as a happy couple. Sadly, the pilots and air hosties were somewhat less convincing.

Trans-Asia Airlines had macho Captain Doug Stewart (Bruce Barry) who had deserted his wife Wendy (Anne Charleston) so he could get stuck into the chicky babes on his international flights. After many sleazy come-ons, he eventually got down to it with air hostess Jackie Soong (Deborah Coulls) in Hong Kong (cut to stock footage of Hong Kong street life before ending up in a crappy 70s motel set). Surprise, surprise, after calling his Asian porter 'Charlie Chan', boofhead Dougie couldn't get it up.

Jackie Soong was a triumphant return to television for actress Deborah Coulls after her shock firing from *The Restless Years* for allegedly being late for publicity commitments. 'The incident was very upsetting to me at the time and I probably deserved what happened,' she told *TV Week* on being signed to *Skyways*. 'I doubt that it will ever happen again.' Producer Jock Blair never regretted hiring Coulls and cast her again over a decade later in *Paradise Beach*. 'Even when she was difficult it was hard not to like her,' Blair says.

The same probably applied to the location, Melbourne's Tullamarine Airport. Essential to getting the show made, airport staff couldn't have been more helpful. 'They were very keen to get the publicity and saw it as a positive thing,' remembers Blair. The show was given unheard of access to the airport and its surrounds even after early location shooting proved disastrous when Crawford's video cameras scrambled the radar.

Tullamarine wasn't the most glamorous place to be on a cold Melbourne morning. 'I had hot water bottles strapped to my back because I'd always be wearing silk dresses to look like it was summer,' recalls Bursill. The drive to and from location was an hour each way, which didn't help an already long weekly schedule.

Skyways premiered in July 1979. Publicity trumpeted it as the night 'Adult TV Drama Takes Off'. Seven was a very different network to Ten though and didn't want to stuff the show with nudity like *Number 96* and *The Box*. 'I think they thought they were above it,' says Blair. 'For them, a man and woman unmarried in bed was very adult.'

One particular unmarried woman in the early days of *Skyways* wasn't interested in sharing her bed with a man. Federal Airlines had an air hostess, Robyn Davies (Judy Morris), who was gay and deeply ashamed of it, often referring to herself as 'camp', a term any self-respecting lesbian would roar laughing at. The depiction of lesbians in *Skyways*, however, was no laughing matter. At the show's launch, Blair had told the press that lesbians had previously been portrayed as hard-bitten ladies who drive trucks. 'There are warm, caring people who happen to be lesbians,' he told *The Sun-Herald*, but something still got lost in his well-meaning translation.

Robyn had already been abandoned by one lover, Chris (Lisa Dombroski), before moving in with the Eurasian Jackie Soong. While pilot Nick Grainger (Bartholomew John) tried to turn Robyn onto men ('Let me make you whole again'), she ignored his advances to concentrate on moving in on the straight Jackie. For further torture, she was also trying to escape the clutches of an older marauding dyke who wouldn't take no for an answer. ('You play ball with me and I'll do everything I can to

Deborah Coulls
and Debra Lawrance
(playing air hosties)
with director
Bud Tingwell.

help you win over Susie Wong. Who knows? The three of us together could be quite entertaining.')

Not surprisingly, Robyn was punished for strange sexual proclivities by being brutally stabbed to death in the shower, a la *Psycho*. With every lesbian in town suspected of the murder, it actually turned out to be a wacky heterosexual, Fiona (Dina Mann), a demented stalker in love with Nick. The traumatised captain then flew off to charter a plane to Tasmania with Bryan Johnson (John Walton), but crashed with a full load of explosives. Only on *Skyways* could both pilots crawl away from the 'inferno', although Nick was traumatised enough to be scared of flying again (or perhaps it was the fear of messing up his hair).

Skyways was the first soap to use chroma-key backgrounds. It enabled the airport manager's window to look out onto the tarmac, with planes taxiing past. Unfortunately, it always looked very dodgy, and Jock Blair remembers it with a shiver. 'Absolutely the silliest thing ever done,' he says today. 'It cost hours and hours which then meant the really good stuff had to be dropped or raced through.' And Tina Bursill says, 'It was a nightmare because you couldn't have a hair out of place so your natural hair would have to be sprayed into a helmet. And for what? The chroma-key just made us all look like *Thunderbirds*!'

On any one workday, a regular *Skyways* actor could be filming moments from one of six shows. There were the two one-hour episodes being filmed in studio that week, location filming for the following week's shows and pick-up shots for the two eps from the previous week. 'We had so little time to learn our lines at night that we'd have them plastered on our desks, so whoever got the moves walking around the desk would catch the lines and read from them,' remembers Tina Bursill. 'I remember many times finding a reason to look down, like picking up a pen, to read the lines, but not being able to find my line amongst the jumble. We often got the giggles because we were so demented from exhaustion.'

'I was paid $2,500 a week, which is unheard of today, but for that money I was selling my life because they were paying me for overtime up front.' Eventually it all became too much for the actress. 'I had a breakdown and actually collapsed. Hector Crawford gave me two weeks off to go and recuperate. I was so tired I would fall down asleep during a scene. I was young and burning the candle at both ends. I was finding it necessary to take things to sleep at night because I was so hyped up from learning lines. And the trappings of pills is then not being able to get up. I had to be up at 4.30am every morning and looking good and I never shirked on that responsibility, but I played as well. It caught me out and didn't do me any good and that was the beginning of alternative medicine for me and becoming a fitness freak.'

As with *Cop Shop* before it, each week's two-episode arc contained shorter, self-contained storylines about East German defectors, Arab sheiks, assassins, armed robbers, drug smugglers, dying kids, stowaways and runaways (including runaway cows). There was also the first television pairing of two future *Neighbours* superstars – Kylie Minogue and Jason Donovan – before they were even teenagers.

There was also the first television pairing of ... Kylie Minogue and Jason Donovan.

Despite the guest stars, lesbian killings and frequent Pommy-bashing (Derek Powell and Mrs Young), the Melbourne-based soapie didn't rate as well in the all-important market of Sydney as it did in its home-town. 'There was close consultation with Seven which was always very positive,' says Blair. 'They commissioned a lot of market research into characters and identified which ones were really hot and which were lukewarm.'

The critics weren't kind about the show. Those who were resorted to more clichés than an average *Skyways* script. 'Fasten the seat belts,' said *The Sydney Morning Herald*. '*Skyways* might be a long, long flight.' 'This one is up, up and away,' predicted *TV Times*. Adelaide's *Advertiser* was less kind. 'If anyone thought Skylab counted as more than our fair share of rubbish from the skies they were wrong – they hadn't seen *Skyways*. Let's pray for a fast crash-landing with no survivors before it puts Australian TV drama into reverse thrust permanently.'

As the series moved into its second year, the Seven Network began trumpeting it as *Skyways '80*. The show introduced new characters, including Trans-Asia manager Gary Doolan (Gerard Kennedy) and Peter Fanelli's country niece Angela Murray (Kerry Armstrong). It was just as well they had arrived since many of the regulars had started to bail out. Having knocked *The Don Lane Show* about a bit (although it would stay on air until October 1983), Seven decided that after 188 episodes, it was time to bail out too and close *Skyways* down.

Simon and Kelly's marriage had finally unravelled after she had a miscarriage and she departed the show towards the end, probably hoping to never end up with such a loser again. Despite their father's move to London (or maybe Paul McFarlane had just blended into the wallpaper), Alan and Mandy stayed on. He hooked up with Angela while Mandy got engaged to Nick who was overseas training for NASA in the hope that as an astronaut he might be able to blow up an even bigger rig.

In the last episode, stupid old George Tippet organised a royal reception for the Prince and Princess of Wales, but a sudden rainstorm (while the sun continued to shine) meant umbrellas could hide how bad the Diana impersonator really was. The show ended with a montage of clips featuring extraordinarily insignificant moments from its 188 episodes. There was no public outcry over its axing and it lived on in overseas sales to screen throughout Europe, Kenya and Zambia.

'It always amazes me that anyone remembers it at all,' says Blair today. 'Hey, it was not great television in the way that *The Sullivans* was great, but it had its moments and it was one of the few upmarket Australian shows to actually get an audience.'

If *Skyways* is to be remembered for anything in soapie history, it should probably be for its outrageously high alcohol intake. 'Would you like a drink?' had to be the most uttered line throughout the series. You could get pissed in the cocktail bar, visit Louise Carter's flat which contained endless bottles of booze in every room, or head to the airport manager's well-stocked bar. There was no crisis which could not be solved by offering everyone in the room a stiff drink. If only the audience had been given some too.

SAME CHARACTER, DIFFERENT SHOW

In a first for Australian soaps, one *Skyways* character was so memorable he moved on to *Cop Shop* as soon as the airport drama was axed. Peter Fanelli (Bill Stalker) returned to the police force and was posted to Riverside Police Station. The character fitted into the new show seamlessly, although it was sometimes confusing for viewers. Given different production schedules, Fanelli appeared in both shows for a few weeks. Tragically, Bill Stalker died in a motorcycle accident just one week before he was due to leave *Cop Shop* in 1981.

A second *Skyways* character to live on in another Crawford's soapie was administrative officer George Tippet (Brian James). George was a regular pain in the arse as he was actually a male version of a soapie stalwart – the gossiping old woman. When *Skyways* wound up, George had just been promoted to assistant airport manager ahead of Louise Carter (Tina Bursill). It was an unsatisfactory ending for the female viewers wanting Louise to get ahead and, as fate would have it, Tippet would be moving interstate within the year, so maybe Louise did climb up the ladder in his place.

For reasons best known only to the scriptwriters, Tippet took long service leave (and I mean long) on *Holiday Island*, another struggling Crawford soapie. Actor Brian James was hesitant to resume the role, telling *TV Week* that he had always thought Tippet 'a pompous idiot. I'd always disliked him. It wasn't until the end of the series that I realised he was a very lonely and vulnerable old man. And since *Skyways*, a lot of people have approached me in the street to say they sympathised with old George and liked him.' Unfortunately, not enough people liked the show, and Tippet was finally retired for good when the island serial closed down.

17

ARCADE

PREMIERE: **1980** EPISODES: **49** NETWORK: **TEN** FINALE: **1980**

Joey (Greg Bepper), Miriam (Peggy Toppano) and Molly
(Lorrae Desmond) at work in their newsagency.

rcade gets a special place in the Soaps Hall of Shame, because no other Aussie soap was built up to be such a blockbuster only to become such a megaton bomb. What seemed like a sure-fire hit in the pages of *TV Week* became one of the biggest and most notorious television disasters of all time. The first serial totally produced in-house by a network wasted over $1 million on the set alone.

It all started midway through 1979 when the Ten Network, bereft of Australian drama content, passed on producing a series about horse racing called *Centaur*. Desperate for a replacement, the channel's director of programming, Pal Cleary, recalled an earlier story outline for a soap set in a shopping arcade. Together with a bunch of other network executives, they set off on a long business lunch, jotting down ideas on paper napkins and drink coasters, obviously all under the effect of too much alcohol.

After initial storylines that involved a massage parlour peephole enabling the neighbouring photography shop to film porno movies, the good time boys came to their senses and realised they weren't up to making the show without some outside help. It was also decided to drop the sexual aspects and concentrate more on comedy. The next day they contacted *Number 96* producer Bill Harmon and brought him on board as a special consultant to turn *Arcade* into reality.

'Arcade will be the biggest and most ambitious show ever made in the history of television.'

Bill Harmon may have saved Ten in the 70s with *Number 96*, but his track record outside of that show should have set off alarm bells. Four *Number 96* spin-offs had amounted to nothing and his previous early evening serial, *The Unisexers*, had been a colossal flop for Nine back in 1975. But Ten execs were on a roll, dreaming of recapturing the glory days of *96*. They obviously assumed Bill Harmon and his assembled team, which now included *96* writing stalwarts Johnny Whyte and David Sale, still had one more hit left in them. They ignored the very telling fact that while the *96* writers would stay on with the series, Harmon insisted on leaving the producer's chair once the opening telemovie had been made.

Within one week of the long lunch, Ten bosses had decided to go in hard and strip *Arcade* five nights a week in a desperate bid to cancel out the two hugely popular shows that were in the 7pm timeslot – the prestigious *The Sullivans* and long-running current affairs show *Willesee at Seven*. Big mistake. Wanting the series on air by the following January, they decided not to bother making a pilot. Bigger mistake.

Executive producer Peter Benardos could barely contain his excitement as he proclaimed that '*Arcade* will be the biggest and most ambitious show ever made in the history of television. It will do for the industry during the 1980s what *Number 96* did for it in the 70s and, as did *96*, help pioneer a whole new era of local stars and pride in our home-grown product.' Big, big mistake.

By August 1979, *TV Week* was helping in the search for new talent to audition for over 21 regular roles. Harmon told the magazine that he was seeking experienced actors together with 'actors with limited experience, such as those in suburban and country dramatic or musical societies'. Once the series began it would become obvious that actors with limited experience would not look out of place in *Arcade*.

One of the few bright spots was a catchy theme song sung by Doug Parkinson and written by Mike Perjanik, whose theme for *The Restless Years* had become a Top 10 hit for Renee Geyer. With lyrics such as 'Take a look at the world around us, all the people hurrying by, maybe you and I, we're just walking through an arcade', this song would not even reach the Top 40.

While a TV technicians' strike held up pre-production, Ten forged ahead building the elaborate shopping arcade set, the biggest and most expensive yet built for one TV series. There were to be dozens of shops constructed for over 150 extras to browse through every week. Cremorne Shopping Plaza was picked for exterior shots as three entire production crews slaved seven days a week to re-create everything down to the very last detail. Finally the first big gun in the 1980 ratings battle was wheeled out in a 90-minute movie premiere on Sunday, 21 January, and the shopkeepers were revealed to a breathless nation.

First shop on screen was the Bookworm, run by goodtime gal Molly Sparks (Lorrae Desmond) and her prissy busybody sister Miriam Buxton (Peggy Toppano, mother of *Prisoner*'s Peta). Molly's fast-talking son Joey (Greg Bepper) thought nothing of begging his mother to prostitute

herself with the sleazy complex manager Mr
Henderson (Allan Penney) so he could get a job as
his new assistant.

Across from the newsagency was Kitty's Record
Bar, owned by former nightclub singer Kitty
Adams (Joy Miller). She was separated from her
husband Duncan (Danny Adcock) and had a
retarded child hidden away in an institution,
brain damaged after a drunk Duncan had bashed
her when she was pregnant. Down at Flash Back,
the local pinball parlour, former navy man Vic
Marshall (Mike Dorsey) fussed over his independent daughter Tina (Christine Harris), who was
confined to a wheelchair but remained bubbly
nonetheless.

At the Aristocrat Dry Cleaners, secret alcoholic
Walter Blair (Syd Heylen) hid his booze in the
neck of his tailor's mannequin, and obviously
drank to cope with his unbearably snobby wife
Joyce (Aileen Britton). She often referred to being
brought up in the upper-crust suburb of Toorak,
which was the Sydney-based show's one bid to
appease Melbourne viewers.

Madcap gift shop
manageress Magda
(Anne Semler) and
dry cleaner Walter
(Syd Heylen).

The Wan Soos ran Toby's Delicatessen, which served only Aussie tucker
(ironic, hey?). Mother Si (Lucy Taylor) and champion swimmer Phillip
(Raymond Nock) were dealing with the recent arrival from Hong Kong
of Si's long lost daughter Mee Ling (Sinan Leong). Even though *Arcade*
producers had insisted there would be no controversy, they couldn't
resist a bit of incest over dinner as Phillip fell in love with his new sister.

The *Arcade* gym was run by widow Iris Pendleton (Maggie Stuart) and
her brother-in-law Norman (Garth Meade). Unlike Iris's late muscleman
husband, Norman was skinny and effeminate. To further emphasise the
comic aspects of the gym workers, Norman hired a jolly fat girl for the
front desk, Consuela McPhee (Coral Kelly before she became soap
scriptwriter Coral Drouyn). Meanwhile, Iris was getting it on with another
bodybuilder, Len Crosby (Bill Charlton), who was, naturally, incredibly
stupid.

Next came the zany gift shop manageress Magda Yokochek (Anne
Semler, wife of Academy Award winning cinematographer Dean Semler)
who was referred to in press kits as a young Zsa Zsa Gabor. *Penthouse*
magazine's review noted that 'many of Miss Semler's scenes revolve
around her breasts, which are indeed ones of some distinction', but as she
'babbles in broken English at such a rate, it is almost impossible to understand her, which could well be an advantage'.

Finally, there was Surf n' Ski operated by egotistical model Craig
Carmichael (Patrick Ward). His well-educated (and secretly rich – don't
ask) girlfriend was Di Smith (Olga Tamara), who immediately became

Somewhere that weekend in Sydney, some very expensive barbecues were being lit.

suspicious of Craig's newly arrived brother, Robbie (Jeremy Kewley). By the first commercial break, she became convinced that he was a hitch-hiker murderer. By night two, viewers should have been relieved to learn that Robbie was just an innocent country boy, but by night two, hardly anyone cared.

Amazingly, viewers failed to respond to a show that was supposed to be as familiar as a trip to your local mall. Wasn't there a slut, an old maid, a paraplegic, a snob, a drunk, an Asian family, a bitch, a poof, a fattie, a drongo, a blonde with big tits and a male chauvinist serving behind the counters of every suburban shopping centre in Australia?

Well, maybe not, but at least the shops themselves were realistic, with actual goods, and if the audience wasn't buying it, at least the extras were helping themselves to everything they could get their hands on. Theft was so rife on the set, security guards were on guard full-time protecting the shop items. And while a horde of extras made the arcade look crowded, their constant walking to and fro was so noisy it was almost impossible to hear the dialogue over the din. But did anyone really want to hear it as the clichés continued to pile up every night?

As the weeks dragged on, producers gamely introduced new characters and even more ridiculous situations. Walter and Joyce's hippie daughter Suzie (Tracy Mann) turned up after fleeing a religious cult, only to fall back under its influence upon hearing a Mr Whippy ice-cream van. Yes, a Mr Whippy van. Lilian Gasinskayay, the 'red bikini girl' who jumped into Sydney harbour to avoid going back to the U.S.S.R., played herself and offered illegal immigrant Magda advice on how to pull a similar scam – dialogue in Russian, with English subtitles of course. And Mee Ling was married off in a pre-arranged Chinese wedding to Chang Li (Adrian Bernotti) to stop her getting into her brother's pants.

By now, it was all irrelevant – *Arcade* was a disaster. *The Sullivans* and *Willesee at Seven* had actually increased their audience and, worst of all, *Arcade* was even trailing the usually last-rating ABC News. In Sydney, the show was delivering a measly 7.5 share when 20 was considered to be the lowest acceptable figure. Within minutes of the first official ratings survey being released, Ten made a snap decision to shut down their beleaguered *Arcade*. Just 49 episodes had been produced, and only 30 aired.

Actor Syd Heylen admitted to *TV Week* he had been 'broken-hearted', thinking 'at last I've made it, my head's on the billboard and they're all saying it'll run for years'. His on-screen daughter was less complimentary. 'It was a pretty dreadful show. I'm glad for the sake of Australian television that it folded,' said Tracy Mann. 'Everyone worked so hard on it but the scripts weren't very good and the finished product left a lot to be desired.' Having had to recite the line 'Yes, Father of the Heavenly Night Sky, it shall be done as you command', it's no wonder Mann thought the scripts were crap. She went off to Bali with her pay-off cheque, probably hoping never to hear a Mr Whippy van again.

With the show unceremoniously yanked off air, to be replaced by Ten's old standby, *M*A*S*H* repeats, all that was left to do was to dismantle the elaborate sets which 'really were amazing' according to Patrick Ward (Craig) today. 'They pumped so much money into them, we were all convinced it had to be a tax dodge.' Technical director Mike Lilley last saw them all stacked up behind Channel 10 with a sign that said 'Free Firewood'. Somewhere that weekend in Sydney, some very expensive barbecues were being lit.

'In 1980, people didn't hang out in shopping malls the way they do today so the show never rang true,' reflects Patrick Ward. He has a point, but even if society behaved differently back then, would it have resulted in better stories? 'I'm not trying to excuse my participation, but with Bill Harmon gone after the pilot and Johnny Whyte in full charge of the scripts, I had no back-up strength,' recalls writer David Sale today. 'I remember Patrick Ward looking at me before having to say "she's a real movin' chick" or some such outdated cliché, and all I could do was shrug.'

Three days before the axe fell, Sale walked out on the production after a fatal argument over the increasingly ludicrous (and old-fashioned) storylines Johnny Whyte was insisting upon. Ironically, Sale had left *Number 96* in similar circumstances just before that show was cancelled. This time, however, there was no joy in being right again about impending doom. After a 13-year working relationship, David Sale and Johnny Whyte never spoke to each other again.

Whyte returned to England where years of heavy drinking finally caught up with him. After he had a massive stroke which resulted in a leg amputation, Sale relented and recorded messages of support from all the *Number 96* stars who had known him in better days. The recording was sent to friends in London to pass on to Whyte in hospital. Sale was later told that the partially paralysed and speech-impaired Whyte had played the tape endlessly while lying in his hospital bed, and could often be seen clutching the cassette in his hand before he died. It was a poignant end to a turbulent friendship, but it's not surprising that Whyte spent his final hours being reminded about the glory days of *96*. *Arcade* was, understandably, not mentioned. Poor Johnny Whyte had already suffered enough.

Australia's newest television series reveals the private lives-the behind the scenes dramas of the people in a modern shopping arcade.

Arcade

MOVIE LENGTH PREMIERE TONIGHT 7·30 PM CHANNEL TEN

18

PUNISHMENT

PREMIERE: **1981** EPISODES: **26** NETWORK: **TEN** FINALE: **1981**

Mel Gibson and Mike Preston look thrilled to be behind bars.

In 1980, buoyed by the success of *Prisoner*, Grundy's and Ten decided to try an all-male version of the show, to be called *Punishment*. KLTA-5, which had broken *Prisoner* in America, was an interested party and supposedly keen to back a pilot. Ian Holmes, president of Grundy's, told *TV Week*, 'Normally we make a pilot after being commissioned by a local network, but this time we'll make the product and then try to sell it here and overseas.' It proved to be an unwise decision.

Creator Reg Watson started working on the concept and borrowed heavily from his original blueprint for *Prisoner*. East Sydney Technical College, once a colonial prison, and Gladesville Psychiatric Hospital were picked as the exterior locations for Longridge Prison, a fictional gaol supposedly 90 miles from an Australian capital city. Eighty-five thousand dollars was spent on elaborate double-storey interior sets at Ten's Sydney studios, and the cell furnishings down to the bedding, linen and uniforms were exactly the same as those used in NSW prisons.

A top-notch cast was assembled including Mel Gibson, already a superstar after *Mad Max*, playing prisoner Rick Munro. Singer Barry Crocker, once the beer-swilling Barry McKenzie, played it straight down the line as the academic prison governor, Superintendent Alan Smith. His officers included conservative Wally Webb (Brian Wenzel), 'bleeding heart' Mike Rogers (Ross Thompson), dedicated and kind Russell Davis (Ralph Cotterill) and redneck nasty Jack Hudson (Ken Wayne).

The prisoners included a father and son, Sam and Paul Wells (Brian Harrison and Michael Smith). Paul was in on a manslaughter charge for killing the cop who came to arrest his drug-trafficking father. Sam got off on the wrong foot by lagging on the other prisoners and was duly ostracised, even by Paul, who shared a cell with armed robber (and bisexual) Arthur Willetts (Jon Ewing).

There was also habitual escapee David 'Robbo' Roberts (George Spartels), institutionalised since childhood Larry Morrison (Mike Preston), likable American Andy 'Pop' Epstein (Arthur Sherman), nasty Gary 'Gazza' Cooper (James C. Steele) and loner Timothy Jarrett (David Spencer).

Sounding familiar yet? Yes, it was all a thinly-veiled attempt to clone *Prisoner*'s most enduring characters. Officer-wise, Mike was Meg Morris and Jack was 'Vinegar Tits'. *Punishment*'s 'top dog' Arthur was a dead ringer for *Prisoner*'s Bea Smith while Robbo and Larry were meant to be the male versions of Doreen and Lizzie. Paul, the naïve prisoner who would quickly learn to toughen up, was based on *Prisoner*'s Karen Travers (Peta Toppano) while Timothy was innocent of the crime he was accused of – just like Lynn Warner (Kerry Armstrong).

Bearing in mind the huge female audience of *Prisoner*, *Punishment* tried to beef up its female cast. Playing the long-suffering wives of prison warders were acid-tongued Julie Smith (Julie McGregor) who would stop at nothing to get a 'fashionable promotion' for her husband, including having an affair, and Heather Rogers (Penne Hackforth-Jones) who got herself pregnant to stop her husband quitting his job.

There also Kate Randall (Kris McQuade) who, despite the disappearance of boyfriend Rick (Mel Gibson, who wisely decided not to stick around for the whole series and fled straight after the pilot), continued to figure in the action after she stole a purse and found a key to a safety deposit box full of cash and heroin. Meanwhile, Timothy's girlfriend Roslyn Rowney (Lisa Peers) tried to find new evidence to prove he was framed on his murder charge.

Alice Wells (Anne Haddy), the wife of Sam and the mother of Paul, was a constant visitor to Longridge until Haddy was stricken with abdominal cancer after completing just six episodes. She was replaced by Cathy Wells (Cornelia Frances), Sam's sister, who flew in from America upon learning that Alice had to (unexpectedly) go home to run the family business. Anne Haddy was deemed well enough to return after an operation, until she fell over and broke her hip. Given her medical history (which had also included a massive heart attack just a year earlier), producers wisely decided to keep Cornelia Frances on as a regular and wish Anne Haddy a speedy recovery (she would eventually recover from all ailments and spend many years in *Neighbours* as Helen Daniels).

Producer Bruce Best, who was brought on board after the pilot episode had been shot, soon discovered that no thought had been given to what would happen after it. With a background in BBC and ABC drama, he decided to make *Punishment* more realistic than *Prisoner*. He took a team

It was all a thinly-veiled attempt to clone Prisoner's most enduring characters.

of writers off to Parramatta Gaol to talk with some real-life inmates and officers, and hired a senior prison officer as an adviser to keep the show real. In the original press kit, however, he admitted having to make one concession for a suburban audience by not over-emphasising two of the routine aspects of prison life – violence and homosexuality.

'We couldn't ignore homosexuality but there is no undue emphasis on it,' Best said at the time. 'It is implied – a glance, a hand on the shoulder … that sort of thing.' This led to one actor playing that he was in a gay relationship while his 'partner' tried to pretend it wasn't happening. Only with hindsight does Best now admit that everything else in the show was probably too gritty, although at the time he was amazed at the lack of communication from Grundy's and Ten about the direction he was taking. 'We didn't know if they liked the show or hated it,' says Best. 'They all simply said nothing.'

The producer was also determined to re-invent the soap production wheel by filming with single cameras. Up till then, many soaps were shot with multi-cameras while a vision switcher in a control room switched back and forth, selecting the best angles. Shooting with a single camera made it easier for actors, but became a nightmare for editors, especially in the days before computers and digital editing. 'I ended up working 22-hour days,' shudders Best. Despite the extra workload, he continued to make his next two soaps (*Family and Friends* and *Pacific Drive*) using the same technique because he believed it led to better performances from his actors.

By the time *Punishment* aired on 20 February 1981, Ten obviously felt they were stuck with a downer, regardless of how good the acting was. With little fanfare, *Punishment* premiered on a Friday night, second only to Saturdays as Aussie TV's least watched night. After three episodes, it was dropped. Its final 23 episodes weren't screened until the end of that year's ratings period in November.

'I have a feeling it didn't work because the audience knew they were watching a clone,' says Michael Smith (Paul). 'How many nights do you really want to sit at home watching people in prison?' In its bid to be more realistic and authentic, *Punishment* left *Prisoner* viewers taken aback by its unrelentingly grim and heavy-handed plotlines. Fan letters from Australia were almost non-existent but when mail started arriving from Italy, its bemused actors wondered if Grundy's was trying to recoup its losses by selling to countries that weren't familiar with *Prisoner* and there-fore unaware of the cloning and overkill of two prison soaps.

Punishment's failure proved three things. Firstly, television audiences don't really want to know the truth about what happens inside jails. Secondly, women coping together on the inside are far more appealing than men. And lastly, even Mel Gibson in his prime can't save an unoriginal soap. In the final episode, the prisoners revolted and trashed Longridge Prison. Had the viewers been given a chance, they probably would have done it too.

19

HOLIDAY ISLAND

PREMIERE: **1981** EPISODES: **64** NETWORK: **TEN** FINALE: **1982**

Skyways' George Tippet (Brian James) discovers how cold Melbourne pools can get as Kylie (Gaynor Martin) and Wally (Tom Oliver) look on.

When *The Box* was cancelled in 1977, the Ten Network and Crawford's began work on a replacement soap, *Hotel Story*, which would star American import Richard Lawson, Terence Donovan and Carmen Duncan. With just seven episodes in the can, however, a change of management at Ten saw them dump *Hotel Story* mid-production. It turned out that a contract had never been signed between the two companies, and consequently Crawford's had no comeback.

The decision to axe the unseen series caused an inordinate amount of publicity and, having already spent a rumoured $285,000 on production costs, Ten decided to air the opening episode and milk the controversy. Newspaper ads asked the viewing public to decide whether or not *Hotel Story* was up to scratch. Ten's switchboard received a phenomenal number of calls, with the majority of viewers saying they liked the show. It was too late for *Hotel Story* to rise from the ashes, but the seed had been sown for *Holiday Island*.

Instead of a Melbourne hotel, *Holiday Island* was to be set on an island resort on the Great Barrier Reef, somewhere off North Queensland. Like *The Love Boat*, a cast of regulars would be joined every week by a

Sun, seduction, secrets, wait for you.

What ever you want, what
ever you need, you'll find it
on a gentle island paradise in
the sun called Holiday Island.

**STUNNING NEW SERIES
TONIGHT AND TOMORROW NIGHT
7·30 CHANNEL TEN.**

different set of guest stars. There would be palm trees swaying in the breeze, babes in bikinis and sparkling tropical waters. No expense was to be spared, although the money wouldn't stretch to heating what was going to become a very cold swimming pool.

Cast and crew were flown to the resort of Tangalooma on Moreton Island near Brisbane to begin shooting the pilot. In what was perhaps an omen of things to come, it rained non-stop. 'Everyone sat in the bar while Hector Crawford kept ringing wanting to know how much it was all costing!' remembers producer Gwenda Marsh. Because there was no infrastructure in Queensland at the time, a news crew from Ten's Brisbane station were sent over on a ferry to facilitate filming. Unfortunately, they had no idea how to do anything except shoot news, and they certainly didn't know how to lay camera tracks in sand. Marsh had to get her husband, who wasn't in the film business, to show them how to do it so filming could finally commence when the sun came out.

While the production was taking a bit of poetic licence, with Moreton Island being nowhere near the Whitsundays where the show was supposed to be set, at least the location was semi-tropical. Unfortunately, with a few establishing shots in the can, the production returned home to Australia's least tropical city, Melbourne, where the remainder of the series was to be shot. Ten had splurged and built an in-ground swimming pool at the back of their Nunawading studios. The backlot was already being used for *Prisoner* exteriors, but while a bleak Melbourne winter suited that show, it was hardly appropriate for *Holiday Island*.

Built in just three weeks for a rumoured $300,000, set designer Brad Russ explained how he was going to overcome Melbourne's cloudy winter skies. 'I designed everything on the set with canopies over overhangs,' he told *TV Week*. 'The cameras should never have to shoot the sky.' Cameramen and other production crew from *Prisoner* were already lining up to work on the show as its bikini-clad girls were far more appealing than the denim-covered slappers in Wentworth Detention Centre.

'Ten were so proud of the grown palms brought in all the way from the nearby suburb of St Kilda,' remembers Gwenda Marsh, 'but when the Nunawading "Island" was publicised in the newspaper, I believe the public began to scoff at the concept. From that point on, they never believed it was real.' Rather than downplay the unfortunate setting, the publicity department seemed to think that any story might translate into respectable ratings. So when it became obvious that actors would have to suck on ice cubes before delivering dialogue (to hide the cold breath coming out of their mouths), this too became another press release that was killing the show before it even aired.

Holiday Island premiered around Australia in June 1981. Within weeks, some wags were referring to it as *Horror Day on Iceland* or *Arcade with Palm Trees*. As with all good soap premieres, newspaper ads played up the supposed raunchiness, with the show's title splashed across a wet T-shirt-clad set of breasts. One advantage to filming in the cold, it seemed, was a nice pair of erect nipples. Launching the supposedly sun-drenched show in the middle of winter must have seemed like a convenient ploy, until viewers started noticing that there was steam coming out of the actors' mouths.

Episode one started out like every good Crawford series. 'Hector loved a car chase,' says Gwenda Marsh, who was more concerned about the message the show was sending. 'Here was a show supposedly about people going on holidays, but first up there's a character escaping to hide out somewhere.' *Holiday Island*'s new resident bad boy, Jason Scott (Steven Grives) was fleeing gambling debts and running back to the wife he had deserted, Angela (Caz Lederman). She was now working on the island with his brother Neil (Nick Tate) who ran the resort, and staff had already noticed that she was romancing her boss.

The motley group of island staff included Wally (Tom Oliver) who drove the ferry and loved slapping girls' bikini-clad bottoms as they stepped aboard. Zack Zachorakis and Liza Kendall (Peter Mochrie and Alyson Best) did everything from marrying holidaymakers to organising surfing contests (even though there was no surf where the island was supposed to be because of the Great Barrier Reef). Should a child get trapped when a sand tunnel collapsed, they would also be required to become lifesavers.

Bartender Dusty Davis (Marilyn Mayo) served fruity cocktails with little umbrellas in them while Banjo (Frank Wilson) ran the island shop in an old shipwreck. Kylie McArthur (Gaynor Martin) was a spoiled brat forced to work as a housemaid, and island owner Emily Muldoon (Pat Kennedy) was a prime candidate to be worked over by the snivelling Jason.

Meanwhile, a slew of guest stars with fake tans came and went. And shivered. They included radio funnyman John Blackman (who, not surprisingly, never acted again), Anne Phelan, Rebecca Gilling, Maurie Fields, Ray Meagher and Judy Nunn. 'It was absolutely insane,' guest star Rowena Wallace remembers, 'but the people I felt the most sorry for were the extras. Those poor girls in bikinis turning blue, purple and rigid as we watched. It was so ridiculous it was surreal. And the scripts were dreadful – we all knew it was never going to work.'

Beset by all these problems, even the simplest special effects also began to fail. To re-create a cyclone, the Ten News chopper hovered overhead to cause a windstorm while fire hoses drenched the shaky set. 'All this money was being spent on special effects and yet they couldn't get a seagull to crash through the windows,' Gwenda Marsh recalls. 'The special effects guy was supposed to shoot the window followed closely by

Wags were referring to it as Horror Day on Iceland *or* Arcade with Palm Trees.

the fake seagull. But the glass wouldn't break because the art director had put in triple safety glass in all the windows! The set designers and the builders had to remove the window, put in another one, and then the helicopter was sent back overhead to get this one tiny scene right. Can you imagine how much money was spent that day?'

Luckily, chroma-key backgrounds, so unconvincing in *Skyways*, worked a bit more successfully in *Holiday Island*, although the view from the resort rooms out onto the pool still looked fake if people walked by 'outside'. Somehow though, Banjo's shop inside the shipwreck looked as if a real ocean was just outside the door.

Some soap stars were now working both in front of and behind the camera. Brian James was drama coach until producers brought his *Skyways* character George Tippet onto the island, and *The Young Doctors'* Anne Lucas was one of the script editors overseeing the increasingly wacky scripts, which included bodybuilding contests, native witchcraft symbols, hang-gliding accidents, kidnappings, magicians, rock stars, illegal immigrants, sunken Portuguese treasure, card sharks, real sharks and, of course, nudists.

Although critics were surprisingly kind about the show, 64 episodes later it was failing to attract enough regular viewers. When the announcement was made to sink *Holiday Island*, production stopped right there and then. This meant the show's final episode failed to tie up all the loose ends. Angela was long dead, but her slimy ex-husband was still around causing trouble. Jason was trying to stop Emily Muldoon from changing her will, as the old lady had finally figured out she was about to leave all her fortune to a conman. As she struggled to phone her lawyer, she suffered a heart attack and Jason left her to die. As everyone on *Holiday Island* sobbed at her funeral, it looked as if Jason was going to inherit all her money, which was hardly an ending long-term viewers would have wanted.

Peter Mochrie can't remember doing as much publicity for any show as was required on *Holiday Island*. More revealing is his recollection that the wrap party was a very happy affair as relieved actors celebrated never again having to run around in shorts in the middle of winter. With production finished, the *Holiday Island* set was left to rot away, with only the occasional *Prisoner* actress dropping by to exercise in the pool. Finally, it was re-designed to become the Lassiters set in *Neighbours*, although the pool, now dressed to resemble a small lake, is strictly not for swimming anymore.

Amazingly, *Holiday Island* was sold to Austria, Mauritius, Switzerland, The Netherlands, and both East and West Germany (as they were then). When Hector Crawford proclaimed that his company's most amazing triumph was the sale of miniseries *All the Rivers Run* to American network HBO, a colleague reminded him that selling *Holiday Island* anywhere was a far more remarkable achievement. Hector Crawford, apparently, was not amused.

20

A COUNTRY PRACTICE

PREMIERE: **1981** EPISODES: **1088** NETWORK: **SEVEN/TEN** FINALE: **1994**

Vicky (Penny Cook) and Simon's (Grant Dodwell)
first date ends in disaster.

In 1979 the Ten Network ran a script-writing competition. James Davern, who had directed, written and produced *Bellbird* for the ABC, decided to write another series based around a small country town. He submitted *In General Practice* and waited to see how it would fare. Meanwhile, the Writers Guild became incensed at the notion of Ten executives judging such a contest. Ten crumbled and brought in some 'notables' to pick a winner. Predictably, two one-off plays won first and second prize because they were 'artistic', while Davern's entry came in third.

At the end of a three-month option, Ten decided to give *In General Practice* a pass, so Davern took the script to Ted Thomas, then General Manager of the Seven Network in Sydney. 'I was getting a bit pissed off with all the waiting,' remembers Davern, 'so I rang and asked him if he'd read it yet. He said he'd only read half, but he liked it and wanted 13 more.' Amazed, Davern quickly hired Lynn Bayonas and Moya Woods to help him write the scripts, and as he thought it needed a little comedy, brought in Hugh Stuckey to inject some laughs.

Now known as *A Country Practice*, the serial revolved around Wandin Valley, a community of approximately 3,000 people about 700 kilometres

First night ad.

drive inland from Sydney. The 'general practice' was run by Dr Terence Elliott (Shane Porteous) and the newly arrived Dr Simon Bowen (Grant Dodwell). Their freethinking receptionist Shirley Dean (Lorrae Desmond) was the mother of town vet Vicky (Penny Cook), and was being romanced by old-fashioned policeman Frank Gilroy (Brian Wenzel). Matron Marta Kertesz (Helen Hough Scott) ran the small hospital frequented by both doctors.

Realising there weren't quite enough characters to sustain a series, Davern asked his co-writers who else they would add to the town. Lynn Bayonas liked the idea of a young couple fresh from the city. Brendan Jones (Shane Withington) would be a male nurse while his wacky wife Molly, real name Melissa Louise (Anne Tenney), was leaving behind a career in high fashion for life on a farm.

By episode four, jack-of-all-trades Bob Hatfield (Gordon Piper) started figuring in the action, and by episode six, busybody Esme Watson (Joyce Jacobs) was sticking her nose into everybody's business. Together with Vernon 'Cookie' Locke (Syd Heylen), who was introduced in episode 17 running the Wandin Valley RSL Club, these three old-timers would become quite the comic team.

Before anyone had been cast, however, Seven asked James Davern to attend a network meeting where the various state managers were supposedly deciding on whether or not the show would go into production. Each state manager had a different view on the first 13 scripts – one thought there weren't enough cliffhangers, another didn't like the characters. In the end, Davern remembers, 'Ted Thomas said he wanted it put on record that he believed this series was going to be a winner.' The Sydney verdict ruled – within an hour Davern received news that *A Country Practice* was going into production for an initial 52 hours.

Filming commenced in August 1981, and the show premiered in the non-rating summer period on 18 November. *TV Week*'s original double-page spread focused on 'Australia's Miss Piggy', referring to Molly's pet pig Doris (who was originally played by a porker nicknamed Suzi Quatro). While animals such as Fatso the wombat would prove to be popular characters in their own right, magazines such as *TV Week* quickly learnt that the human residents of Wandin Valley would become their future big-selling cover stars.

Part of the show's massive success was because there was nothing else like it on television at the time. It was gentle instead of violent, and was dealing with real social issues rather than who was sleeping with who. Amazingly, after two years of rating between 30 and 36, *ACP* surged further to become Australia's number one show. In short, it was a phenomenon.

A Country Practice would be similar to *Cop Shop* and *Carson's Law* in that two one-hour episodes would tell a story each week with a supporting guest cast. Meanwhile, the regular characters' adventures would stretch out over longer periods of time. The very first two-parter featured 15-year-old Jenny (Arkie Whiteley) wanting to go on the Pill and have sex

with boyfriend Tony (Ric Herbert), against the wishes of her father, Hal
Secombe (Tom Richards). *ACP* immediately established itself as a show
that would not shy away from difficult issues.

The only thing that seems to have changed after the first episode was
the dropping of the ridiculously huge nurses' headwear worn by Judy
Loveday (Wendy Strehlow). Apart from that minor detail, everything
was set for 12 years of crises, love and hijinks. Very quickly, the growing
audience warmed to the initial regular cast, who all seemed to have plenty
of secrets tucked away for future drama.

Joyce Jacobs

Initially, Dr Terence Elliott was a loner who drank excessively, but
eventually he dealt with the fact that misdiagnosing his own son had led
to the boy's death. His estranged socialite wife Rowena (Carmen Duncan)
visited, as did heroin-addicted daughter Sophie (Katrina Sedgwick), who
would tragically die from AIDS. Son CK (Nicholas Rigg and later Peter
Phelps) had little in common with his father and eventually went off to
live in Europe with his mother.

Not surprisingly, workaholic Terence always seemed to find love in or
around the hospital. There were many candle-lit dinners with Marta until
old boyfriend Bela Szollos (Barry Otto) whisked her back home to
Hungary. Terence's marriage to Dr Alex Fraser (Diane Smith) came
undone with the premature birth of baby Laura, who later died, and Alex
left the Valley to work on an Aboriginal mission in the Northern
Territory. Terence reluctantly granted her a divorce.

Syd Heylen

A much more successful marriage – the show's first – was Shirley and
Frank. One of the secrets to keeping this couple entertaining was that
they were complete opposites. Widower Frank pursued Shirley with a
vengeance until she fell in love with him, but even then they were still
diametrically opposed on most issues. Shirley meditated under a pyramid
while Frank pottered around his rose garden. She believed in reincarnation, he bought matching plots at the cemetery. Eventually they began to
board troubled children, starting with punk rebel Gabrielle Baker, better
known as Gabe (Rebecca Rigg).

Meanwhile, another pair of opposites was circling each other in the love
game. Spoilt rich boy Simon was strangely attracted to the no-nonsense
Vicky, but she fought his advances and insisted they remain just friends.
After ratings plummeted when Vicky had an affair with a Frenchman,
James Davern decided to be more vague in the future with unmarried
couples' sleeping arrangements. 'The audience hated it so we pulled
back very smartly,' Davern told *Time*. 'We have never let it happen again.'

Instead, Vicky was moved into a flat to share with Simon and Fatso
the wombat. The writers kept the unresolved sexual tension at boiling
point – between Simon and Vicky that is, not Fatso. Could the city doctor,
who always said he was just in Wandin Valley for a few years' experience,
ever settle down with the vet who seemed determined to stay in the
country? And did the fans want a wedding? Well, what do you reckon?

During a Brisbane telethon, viewers rang in to say they would only
donate money if the TV medicos kissed on air. Penny Cook and Grant

Penny Cook films TV's
'Wedding of the Year'.

Dodwell ended up raising $4,000 with just one quick peck, so it was obvious what had to happen next. Their first kiss together on *A Country Practice* made front-page newspaper headlines around the country.

TV's 'Wedding of the Year' aired on Wednesday, 26 October 1983 to record ratings for the soap. Just like their first date, which had ended with both of them stripped to their underwear and pulling a cow out of a muddy dam, Vicky's love of animals caused chaos when the bride was called away to attend to a gored racehorse. And then when Frank got a flat tyre, the bride had to be driven to the church in the back of Bob's utility truck, her dress billowing behind her.

Wandin Valley's second most popular couple were Molly and Brendan. At first the locals thought the strangely-dressed Molly was mad, particularly when they noticed she had moved her mother's gift of a chandelier into Doris's pig pen. It also didn't go down too well when she started becoming the voice of environmentalism, once chaining herself to a fence to stop loggers. Despite her ways, the character proved a favourite in the town and with viewers. When Molly became pregnant, *TV Week* ran a competition to name the little girl, with responses ranging from Murgatroyd to Rickie Lee.

The Jones baby was eventually named Chloe (Emily Nicol), and the tiny actress picked to play the part turned out to be a natural in front of the camera. 'I wanted a parent who knew what they were getting themselves into,' remembers producer Bruce Best, 'and finding a baby whose mother was a doctor and father was an entertainer really guided our decision.' Maryanne and John Nicol's third child literally grew up in front of the nation on *A Country Practice*, not to mention having an extra set of parents whom she called Molly-Mum (Anne Tenney) and Bren-Dad (Shane

Withington). Unable to pronounce Frank and Shirley, Emily called them Fink and Surley. 'She was one smart little kid,' says James Davern.

Molly and Brendan also wanted a son, but the premature birth of Christopher ended in tragedy when the baby died soon after. Brendan blamed Molly for the accident since she had fallen while decorating the nursery. For a while, their marriage was on shaky ground, but just as they put it behind them, even worse news was about to come their way.

After four years, Anne Tenney wanted to leave the show, and script-writers knew her character would never give up her family willingly. Hence the decision was made to have her die slowly and give viewers plenty of time to prepare for the tragic event. Molly refused chemo-therapy in order to live her brief life to the fullest, but eventually she fell ill with pneumonia and retired to her beloved farm to spend her final days.

The only problem was, Seven realised her death was about to occur during a non-ratings period. Several 'best of' episodes were hastily inserted so that the nation-stopping event could garner maximum bene-fit for the network. On 5 June 1985, as newspapers carried full-page ads with a simple tagline, 'Thanks for everything Molly', a generation of Australians began to weep as Molly took her last breath while watching Brendan and Chloe playing with a kite. By the time Bob Hatfield was reading the poem 'Mad Molly Jones' over the credits, a nation was in mourning.

While it was traumatic for many of the younger viewers (which par-ticularly concerned Anne Tenney), it was doubly so for tiny Emily Nicol who was told that 'Annie' was away on a holiday. 'How do you tell a three-year-old about death?' Maryanne Nicol asked *TV Star*, while also trying to set the record straight about how old her daughter really was. So con-vincing was Emily's performance, one columnist thought that the child had to be at least seven years old instead of three. Molly-Mum never did return to the *Country Practice* set, but Annie continued to see her special friend. 'Anne and Shane came over for dinner the other night and Emily was in seventh heaven,' her mother told *TV Week* in 1986. 'When Emily and Anne see each other they get very teary.'

The tragedy of Molly's death was offset a few months later when Vicky gave birth in a barn to twins Charlotte and Tom, but more shocking news had slipped out about the future of *ACP*. Penny Cook and Grant Dodwell had also quit the show. 'We are losing Simon and Vicky but we are not los-ing them from television,' Lynn Bayonas told *TV Soap*, revealing JNP Films were preparing a sitcom about the couple and their twins based around a medical practice in Sydney. Worried that spin-offs rarely work, James Davern decided not to proceed with the idea.

So, Vicky and the babies left the show at the end of 1985 after she was offered post-graduate work in America, and Simon followed a few months later. In April 1986, Brendan and Chloe were also gone, the wid-ower having found love again with relief schoolteacher Sarah Anderson (Lisa Green). The prophets of doom began to circle. 'A Country Crisis,' cried a *TV Soap* headline. The absence of the show's four major stars would 'definitely bring about the end,' insisted a former producer to *TV Star*.

James Davern and Seven remained optimistic. 'After nearly four years on air you've got to expect people to leave, others to join,' Davern told *TV Star*. 'But a good show will survive on its overall appeal and strength.' He was proved right, even though the first replacement characters didn't come close to achieving the popularity of Vicky, Simon, Molly or Brendan. While Jewish vet Ben Green (Nick Bufalo) caught on with his alternative treatments for animals, brash reporter Kelly Shanahan (Annie Davies) didn't. She was quickly sent back to Sydney to become a TV reporter.

Meanwhile, actors Shane Withington and Grant Dodwell were signed up by retiring *ACP* producer Lynn Bayonas for a new comedy show, *Willing and Abel*, in which they played houseboat buddies who would do anything for money. The series was, unfortunately, an unpopular flash in the pan which quickly floundered on Nine. James Davern's fears about spin-offs, even unofficial ones, had proved to be correct.

Showing there were no hard feelings, Penny Cook returned for a visit to *A Country Practice* within the year, as did Emily Nicol, who got to stay with Shirl and Frank while Brendan had a belated honeymoon in New Zealand. *ACP* had proved it could weather the loss of fan favourites, so new regulars kept arriving to take their place.

Judy's schoolgirl sister, Jo Loveday (Josephine Mitchell), eventually married nurse Michael Langley (Brett Climo). Teacher Peter Manning (Mark Owen-Taylor) was briefly engaged to Alex (before she married Terence), while sister Donna (Caroline Johansson) was the rare nurse not afraid of the formidable Matron Maggie Sloan (Joan Sydney). Peter went

Molly (Anne Tenney) dies at home and a nation mourns.

to live in Victoria, Donna died in a car smash, and Jo and Michael moved to Armidale.

Ranger Cathy Hayden (Kate Raison) found it tough promoting conservation to old-time farmers, and found it even tougher finding a man who agreed with her strong principles. Eventually she married palaeontologist John Freeman (William McInnes) on the edge of a National Park bluff.

After Ben left town, Matt Tyler (John Tarrant) bought his veterinary practice and was revealed to be a former surfie boyfriend of Cathy's. They were now just good friends, which allowed him to fall for nursing sister Lucy Gardiner (Georgie Parker), who had flirted briefly with radical doctor Cris Kouros (Michael Muntz) before marrying Matt. Lucy struggled to conceive but eventually gave birth to a son, James, before leaving with Matt to live in Vietnam. Cris's daughter Jessica (Georgina Fisher), with a little help from Esme, tried her hand at matchmaking her second-generation Greek dad with Director of Nursing Ann Brennan (Mary Regan).

Meanwhile, Frank and Shirley took on another troubled boarder, street kid Luke Ross (Matt Day). With their support, Luke studied to become an airline mechanic, and fell in love with Ann's half-sister Steve Brennan (Sophie Heathcote). She tried to hide her true feelings for Luke and naïvely went after the newly arrived Dr Harry Morrison (Andrew Blackman), but after he set her straight, she decided she really did love Luke. But then she was mistaken for a gypsy while out riding her horse, and when a farmer fired a shot at them, she fell off and broke her neck. A grief-stricken Luke found her dead body. Never quite recovering from his loss, he joined the air force to become a pilot.

Tie-in paperback books.

Matron Maggie Sloan (Joan Sydney), who, it turned out, played a mean game of poker, met her perfect man in rich grazier Lachlan Morrison (John Ewart). He whisked her away to travel the world gambling, so she was replaced by Matron Rosemary Prior (Maureen Edwards) who was fresh off the plane from Africa. Wandin Valley also acquired a new nurse, Kate Bryant (Michelle Pettigrove), and a new environmentalist, teenager Darcy Hudson (Kym Wilson), the granddaughter of potato farmer Percy Hudson (Allan Penney)

ACP also had its share of semi-regular characters who came and went as the story demanded. Among the most memorable were corrupt Councillor Alf Muldoon (Brian Moll), who was always trying to overdevelop the valley and rip off its residents, and Burrigan Hospital's Matron Hilda Arrowsmith (June Salter), who was an old rival of Matron Sloan's in the health profession and on the bowling green. There was also Bev Little who ran the manual telephone exchange. Although everyone spoke to her, and she was said to be a 'giant', she was never seen, even when she checked into the hospital for a tonsillectomy.

By now it was 1991 and *ACP* was one of Australia's most enduring series, celebrating ten years on the air. But while Seven was supposedly celebrating the milestone, behind the scenes they were concerned about

The final night.

the audience demographics. Long-time viewers were growing older and younger viewers weren't so keen on the show anymore. A disastrous decision was made to get rid of some of the older characters and replace them with younger versions.

Cookie and Bob had been the backbone of most of the show's comedy sequences from day one. Cookie always had some tall story or get-rich-quick scam, and had even come close to marrying Esme until it was revealed he already had a wife. Bob watched his wife die of cancer and didn't cope too well in the aftermath, so his 'little mate' Cookie moved in and never got round to leaving – until Seven decided the odd couple had to go for the good of the show.

'I should have fought harder to keep Bob and Cookie,' James Davern now says. 'When they left, we didn't really have the comic relief as catharsis from all the drama. I should have found some other way to introduce younger people but after ten years, we were all getting pretty tired.'

So too was original cast member Lorrae Desmond who refused point blank to die a long, lingering death like Molly had. 'I hate to freak kids out,' she told *TV Week*, 'so I asked to decide my own exit. The last thing I wanted them to see was Shirley laughing.' So Shirl kissed Frank goodbye, waved as the taxi sped away, and died in an off-screen plane crash. In her will, she insisted that Frank strip in some deserted bushland and dance naked on a clifftop as a celebration of her life.

Frank retired from the police force and took over the running of the RSL club, but actor Brian Wenzel was concerned about the direction the show might be heading in without the older regulars. 'Where is the comedy going to come from?' he asked *TV Week*. 'I can't turn turtle from being a straight man to being an out and out fool.'

So along came some new characters, even though the audience continued to drop away. Racing cyclist Hugo Strzelecki (Gavin Harrison) arrived and fell for Darcy, who also had to cope with the arrival of her hippie mother Bernice (Judith McGrath). Harry and Kate married, and new vet Anna Lacey (Anne Looby) got to marry new cop Sergeant Tom Newman (John Concannon) twice after it was discovered that their Christmas Eve wedding wasn't legal, leading to another, more intimate ceremony on Christmas Day.

Finally, after 12 years, 29 Logie Awards and 1,058 hour-long episodes, Seven announced in July that it was bringing the curtain down on *ACP*'s historic run. 'I've been in other shows that have been axed and allowed to dribble away, particularly *Number 96*, and the feeling was of depression and despondency and it was awful,' Shane Porteous told *The Herald Sun*. 'But because we've had such good episodes to go out with … we're going out on a high.'

As part of the final three-hour extravaganza on Monday, 22 November 1993, Wandin Valley was razed to the ground by a bushfire. After the hospital burnt down, Terence and Rosemary were married by civil celebrant Bernice, with special guests Vicky (Penny Cook), Luke (Matt Day) and Maggie (Joan Sydney) in attendance. Afterwards, a behind-the-scenes one-hour special reminisced with many of the actors, including the show's longest-serving cast members, Shane Porteous and Brian Wenzel. To the tune of a Mariah Carey ballad, a clips montage recalled the show's many great moments and its army of guest stars.

Guest star Nicole Kidman as a frizzy-haired seductress.

There had been Nicole Kidman as a frizzy-haired seductress; Miranda Otto giving birth; David Wenham as cop Scott Galbraith, who thought that kids' flour bombs had contained cocaine; Ruth Cracknell flashing at a group of shocked church ladies; Lorraine Bayly as the mother of an AIDS victim; Maria Venuti as a snake charmer; Andrew Denton as a harassed courier; Richard Wilkins as a hitchhiker in tight acid-wash jeans; ballet legend Sir Robert Helpmann playing a ballet legend; and director Baz Luhrmann, in his acting days, as a rough-as-guts yobbo. Appearing as themselves were singer Paul Kelly, country legend Smokey Dawson, jockey Shane Dye, artist Pro Hart, ocean liner the 'Oriana' and even the Prime Minister of Australia, Bob Hawke.

Surrounded by eight personal bodyguards and secret servicemen, 'one-take' Bob nailed his scenes perfectly after paying his ten dollars to join Actors Equity. His appearance in the show was at the written request of Jo Loveday (Josephine Mitchell), who wanted Wandin Valley to be declared a no-nuclear zone. Airing in 1986, the International Year of Peace, the episode won a United Nations Media Peace Award. 'Hawke did it in one take because he didn't have time to do anything more,' remembers James Davern. 'Anyway, he was a terrible ham. Bloody good prime minister but a real ham.'

Apart from the other ham, Doris the alcoholic pig, animals also turned into regular characters in the show. Most memorably there was Fatso the wombat who regularly bit any actor who came near him. The cast often had to stand on chairs in their green room to avoid the marsupial nipping their ankles. It was also a running joke that, while the cast had to drive themselves to studio and location, Fatso always had his own limo. Well, taxi.

Even the show's oldest actors were at risk. Poor Joyce Jacobs was scratched by a koala and bitten by a chimpanzee, but such accidents were never shown on screen. Instead, it was endless ooh-ing and aah-ing over Cuddles the snake, Spike the echidna, Rhett the rooster, Donovan the goat and Dog the dog. Not surprisingly this constant array of animals proved to be endlessly entertaining to millions of viewers outside Australia.

In Germany it was known as *Das Buschkrankenhaus* and in French Canada it was *A Coeur Ouvert*. It became an afternoon favourite in the United Kingdom, but different screenings in every region of the country worked against the show getting any national publicity and becoming a bigger hit. In America, it bombed after test runs in Los Angeles and Boston, but it worked a treat in Indonesia, Spain, Sweden, New Zealand and Swaziland.

How it got to air in Burma was another story. The Australian ambassador, perturbed at all the American shows pouring out of the new

LP record and 10th anniversary magazine.

Burmese channel, rang James Davern and begged to be given 100 hours – to air for free. 'He wanted us to do the decent thing as "honourable" Australians,' laughs Davern. 'So I talked to the actors and they said OK so I sent the ambassador a message – it's on its way, please send elephant.' It was meant to be a joke but the Embassy had the last laugh when a carved wooden elephant really did turn up, inscribed 'With thanks from the Australian Embassy in Burma.'

There had also been constant praise for the show's treatment of medical and social issues, many of which were seen and discussed on Australian television for the first time. These included brain death, voluntary euthanasia, organ donation, anorexia, Down's syndrome and obsessive-compulsive disorder. 'We had three ex-nurses who were our researchers and they had a hotline to and the support of the major teaching hospitals in NSW,' recalls Davern. Subsequently, the Federal Government and the Australian Medical Association used *ACP* as a vehicle to get messages across to the audience. *ACP*'s skill was in keeping the positive propaganda entertaining.

'I had three female story editors with six divorces between them so they were pretty keen on feminism as well as being pretty sympathetic to homosexuals,' says Davern. That meant that *A Country Practice* also did stories on gay bashing, HIV, child abuse, spousal abuse, alcoholism, breast cancer, vasectomies and rape. Critics and academics praised the show's treatment of social issues.

Unfortunately the airing of controversial issues backfired several times. 'The copycat effect wasn't known in those days,' explains Davern, 'which is where a percentage of the audience will regrettably experiment with what they see on TV, even if you're trying to warn them against it.' In 1986, a 14-year-old boy from Melbourne hanged himself after an episode dealt with teen suicide. 'We were very careful not to show the character hanging but it was enough to trigger something in a boy who had schizophrenia. That burdened me for a long time.'

Naturally, the press went into a feeding frenzy about the incident – 'TV soap sparks boy's suicide' – but only because the family show rarely inspired any negative publicity. However, in 1990 they pounced again after three Gunnedah teenagers tried to make a gun after an *ACP* episode dealt with that issue. 'The police had come and asked us to do a story about home-made explosives so we did one, but unfortunately at one stage on the screen we showed him making it before blowing his hand off,' shudders Davern. 'Two days later we get the report that some kid had seen the show, made a gun, fired it and blew half his hand off. It was another low point in my production life.'

Unfortunately there was one more sad legacy of *A Country Practice*, when it was regrettably resurrected on Ten. The network that had let it slip through their fingers over a decade before decided they wanted to take the show over, just as they'd done with *Neighbours*. 'I didn't want to do it, to be quite honest, but Ten waved a lot of money in front of us saying they needed the show,' says Davern. 'We thought we would try and get

The ill-fated Ten cast.
BACK L-R:
Paul Gleeson,
Claudia Black,
Vince Colosimo,
Andrew Blackman,
Joan Sydney.
FRONT:
Jane Hall,
Joyce Jacobs,
Laura Armstrong.

back to the old concept which was very serious subject matter with lots of comedy.' However television, and particularly network executives, had changed a lot since the early 80s.

'In the first ten years I was never queried on a single script. Seven said you're the producer, you do it and if we don't get the audience we'll try to figure out how to make them watch it. That doesn't happen anymore,' says Davern sadly today. 'You get television executives who don't know their arse from their elbow. They tried turning *ACP* into more of a soap with lots of love affairs and who's sleeping with whom and I think we lost a bit of heart. We did our best but it had lost its vitality and life.'

A Country Practice 2 had only a brief 30-episode run on Ten in 1994. As production had moved from Sydney to Melbourne, location filming for Wandin Valley was switched from Pitt Town and Ebenezer in NSW to Emerald, just outside Melbourne. It was disconcerting to say the least, even though a bushfire had razed the town of Wandin Valley a few months before in the final episode on Seven.

Kate (Michelle Pettigrove) had left Dr Harry (Andrew Blackman) and returned briefly to tell him their marriage was over. Maggie (Joan Sydney) was back as Matron, and short-lived *ACP* regulars Nurse Claire Bonacci (Claudia Black) and park ranger Ian McIntyre (Paul Gleeson) had also moved south. All the other regulars were missing in action and never referred to again. Instead, there was Constable Danny Sabatino (Vince Colosimo) and Maggie's veterinary stepdaughter, Jess Morrison (Jane Hall).

Dumped out of prime time onto Saturday nights, the series made no impact whatsoever. So when it came time to end it again, there was no need to spend any money for an on-screen wedding, even though a pregnant Claire was marrying Danny. Instead, Jess and Harry ended the saga as they fell off their horses and into a passionate kiss together. And even though Esme (Joyce Jacobs) was the longest running character to switch networks, she failed to qualify as the show's longest running character as she had only become a regular in episode 99 on Seven.

A Country Practice continues to live on and on, as it is one of the few Aussie soaps to be continually repeated. Seven had the rights to repeat the series three times and they did just that, and the serial lives on in subscription television. Much of the merchandise from the show, including paperback tie-in books, soundtrack records and commemorative magazines, is still floating around flea markets.

'I don't think *A Country Practice* has ever been matched when it comes to serial television,' says Kate Raison (who guested as cowgirl Dolly McCoy before being asked to join the regular cast as ranger Cathy Hayden). 'They didn't have to tackle all of those social issues but they did. When you came into the cast, you were immediately looked after by the older actors and everyone who worked on the show cared about the product. It wasn't glamorous, don't get me wrong, but it was the best time I've ever had on a TV show.'

VALE, MAD MOLLY JONES

'Mad,' we said, 'Mad Molly Jones'
But then we didn't know
The kindness that was hers to spare
The joy that she took everywhere
We simply didn't know.
'Mad,' we said, 'Mad Molly Jones'
But then we hadn't heard
How she could fight to save a flower,
And give each man and his dog
His hour
We simply hadn't heard.
'Mad,' we said, 'Mad Molly Jones'
But then we hadn't seen
That she could make a dull day bright
That she was the colour warmth
And light
We simply hadn't seen.
Molly Jones, it's over
Yet we cannot say goodbye:
For all the loveliness we knew,
And love of life, and friendship true,
And laughter brave, once dwelt in you
And how can such things die?

The poem Bob Hatfield read when Molly died.

Reprinted by courtesy of writer Judith Colquhoun.

21

SONS AND DAUGHTERS

PREMIERE: **1982** EPISODES: **972** NETWORK: **SEVEN** FINALE: **1987**

Twin sisters Pamela Hudson (Rowena Wallace) and Alison Carr (Belinda
Giblin), formerly Patricia Hamilton Morrell, aka 'Pat the Rat'.

Once upon a time there were twin babies who were separated at birth.
The infant girl was whisked away by her social-climbing mother,
while the boy was left with his working class father. Twenty years later
they would unexpectedly reunite and, unaware they were brother and
sister, tongue-kiss each other on their first date.

So began the torrid tale of *Sons and Daughters*, another original concept from the fertile imagination of Reg Watson, who had also created
and plotted *The Restless Years*, *The Young Doctors* and *Prisoner*. Obviously
exhausted (and who can blame him), this time Watson handed over the
storyline reigns to an up-and-coming trainee script editor from *The
Restless Years*, Bevan Lee. Together with Maureen Ann Moran, John
Allsop and Ray Kolle, they began to plot what would turn into one very
convoluted drama about two families, with many, many more to come.

'Reg Watson basically delivered us a South American telenovela,' says
Bevan Lee, referring to the over-the-top soaps hugely popular south of
the U.S. border. 'I think Reg is the great unsung hero of Australian television drama, a man whose shows trail-blazed overseas sales for our
drama. It is indicative of the industry's elitist attitude to serial drama that

BROTHERS AND SISTERS
USUALLY FIGHT.

THESE TWO ARE IN LOVE

7

'Sons and Daughters' premieres tonight at 7.00.

First night ad – and all at the family-friendly timeslot of 7pm too!

he is not given the hugest praise for his contribution, whereas much lesser lights who have trotted out the odd thing for the ABC are lauded as the great ones. They are not the toenail on the foot of Reg's statue.'

Sons and Daughters offered a unique location premise, and one that would finally overcome a long-standing problem with the two major television markets of Australia. With Melbourne-based shows never able to rate as well in Sydney, and vice versa, the new Seven Network show would locate a core family in each city. And while one twin's family would be wealthy (the Hamiltons), the other would definitely hail from 'Aussie battler' (the Palmers).

The first episode, screening in January 1982, was an instant success in both Sydney and Melbourne. Starting with a flashback to 1962, a young and pregnant Patricia (Jackie Woodburne) and David (Rhett Walton) checked into the Sydney boarding house run by former madam Fiona Thompson (Pat McDonald). After giving birth, Patricia fled with her daughter, leaving David a note which read, 'I'm taking the girl. You can have the boy. Whether you have him adopted or not is your problem. I never want to see either of you again.'

Baby John was left in the care of Fiona for the next five years until David (Tom Richards), now happily married to Beryl (Leila Hayes), dragged the screaming tyke to his new Melbourne home. Years later, after being accused of a murder he didn't commit, grown-up John Palmer (Peter Phelps) ran away to Sydney and his Aunt Fiona, who was conveniently still living at the same Manly address. John left behind in Melbourne brother Kevin (Stephen Comey) and sister Susan (Ann Henderson-Stires) who was about to marry Bill (Andrew McKaige), unaware he was the real culprit for the crime John was accused of.

Enter twin number two – Angela Hamilton (Ally Fowler). She had grown up as the privileged daughter of Gordon Hamilton (Brian Blain), and a stepsister to the nefarious Wayne (Ian Rawlings). Angela's mother Patricia (Rowena Wallace) had married well in her bid for financial security and social standing, but a blast from the past was about to shatter her marriage of convenience.

While John quietly celebrated his 20th birthday 'on the run' with Fiona, Angela's celebrations were splashed across the social pages of the Sydney papers. After recognising her as the girl he had dreamt about all his life, John drove around her exclusive suburb until he spotted her riding a horse. Unaware of why they had such a powerful attraction to each other, they were about to hop into the sack when Fiona was forced to tell them the truth about how they were related.

Nobody was as gobsmacked as wicked mother Patricia, or as she would soon be known all around the world, 'Pat the Rat', an expression coined by actor Peter Phelps. There had been soap bitches before her (*Number 96*'s Maggie Cameron and *The Young Doctors*' Sister Scott) but none would ever dominate a show like Rowena Wallace ended up doing. From the endless moneymaking scheming to the obsessive love affairs, breakdowns, addictions and facial reconstruction, *Sons and Daughters* eventually became all about 'Pat the Rat', the Queen of Aussie television in the early 80s. Like *Dynasty*'s Alexis, her children were her weakness, and she was out to control their lives as much as possible. In their best interests, of course.

When originally auditioning for the role, Rowena Wallace thought Patricia Hamilton was a 'boring role – a cardboard cut-out, two-dimensional society bitch. I wasn't excited about it at all and certainly didn't expect to get the part.' Once cast, however, she realised the character would never work unless she became more rounded to offset the evil side. Working closely with the writers, they turned Patricia into a character 'everybody sort of knew. People would say to me, she's just like my mother, my wife, my daughter, my mother-in-law. There was something that the audience identified with in her.'

After an obligatory open-mouthed gape, Patricia eventually accepted John as her long lost son, seducing him with her lavish Sydney lifestyle. Angela stormed off to live with David in Melbourne, where Beryl's house dresses were about as sophisticated as it got. Much to Patricia's horror, Angela eventually married the worst sort of partner imaginable – not only was he poor, he was Beryl's brother, Rob Keegan (Noel Hodda). Left with just juicy John to marry off, Patricia schemed to fix him up with Prue Armstrong (Gaynor Martin).

Feeling needy one day, as all good soap bitches do, Patricia revisited her past and set about seducing David. After a scandalous affair in which she fell in love with him again, he revealed a long-held grudge to get even, and chose to return to Beryl. Eventually ostracised from both families, leaving only vapid but lovable Charlie Bartlett (Sarah Kemp) on her side, Patricia crashed her twins' 21st birthday, to which she had not been

A typical *Sons and Daughters* disaster with Sean Scully, Pat McDonald, Leila Hayes and Tom Richards.

If you thought Pat was a Rat, you haven't seen anything yet! Tonight 7.30

Sons & Daughters

Tonight, Abigail makes her debut as Caroline – Super bitch! ⑦

invited. In a recrimination-laden first summer cliffhanger, she told David that he wasn't the twins' real father.

Come the New Year there was a new family, headed by John and Angela's real father, Martin Healy (Paul Sonkkila). As befitted the show's title, he also had his own son Peter (Brett Climo) and daughter Jennifer (Jodie Yemm). After a few months back with Patricia though, he shot himself in the head. Always the opportunist, Patricia used his suicide note as a blackmail opportunity, and also to frame David for murder.

With brothers, sisters, nieces and illegitimate children arriving on every doorstep, the complicated family tree grew. So too did the frequent flyer points. With everyone flying back and forth from Sydney to Melbourne as if they were popping down to the corner shop, the only respite was the Hamilton country estate, Woombai, overseen by dowdy Rosie (Anne Haddy). Like all the sets in the show, it was very, very beige.

Meanwhile, with not one but two hookers with hearts of gold, Fiona and Jill Taylor (Kim Lewis), early storylines had plenty of possibilities. 'Reg Watson not only put in the classic bitch goddess,' says Bevan Lee, 'but had the balance in Fiona being Patricia's foil. It was a great departure for the great Pat McDonald, even though at times of stress she'd fall back into her Dorrie Evans-isms from *Number 96*.'

It was certainly stressful when Fiona discovered her long-mourned son Terry Hanson (Andrew Clarke) wasn't really dead, so scriptwriter Bevan Lee decided to experiment with a bit of audience manipulation. 'I don't look back on it with pride,' says Lee, 'but I had a bet with someone that I could turn a rapist into a hero within ten weeks.' So Terry Hanson raped Jill Taylor.

Not even ten weeks later, publicity girls watching advance episodes complained about the rape storyline implications. They hated the show being so horrible to Terry. 'For God's sake,' one actually said to Bevan Lee, 'he only raped her.' 'There should have been an outcry from the audience but instead, the women felt sorry for him,' shudders Bevan Lee today. 'It wasn't very politically correct, but nevertheless we got some great story possibilities out of it.' Jill's reluctance to let Terry see baby Fee eventually pushed him to kidnap his child.

With the show expanding from four to five half-hour episodes per week, another new family was introduced, the O'Briens, who lived next door to Beryl. There was Mike (Ken James), Heather (Rona Coleman) and their two children Jeff (Craig Morrison) and Katie (Jane Seaborne). Ditching David, Beryl was briefly romanced by Mike's brother Jim (Sean Scully), while Gordon Hamilton settled down with Barbara Armstrong (Cornelia Frances).

Milking it for every bit of delicious irony she could muster, Patricia pissed off Barbara by marrying her brother, Stephen Morrell (Michael Long). Then up popped his daughters Amanda (Alyce Platt) and Samantha (Sally Tayler), before former wife Caroline (Abigail) swept into the show as 'Caroline the Cat'. By the time every Morrell family member had arrived, Stephen had come to his senses, divorced Patricia and run away with Jenny Turner (Joanna Lockwood), even though she was dying. Obviously a terminal illness was preferable to spending more time with Patricia.

Somewhere during all of this, Beryl also reunited briefly with David and became pregnant. After falling down an unused mine shaft (as you do) she gave birth to a baby, Robert, but he was kidnapped by David's supposed niece Leigh Palmer (Lisa Crittenden), who was actually his illegitimate daughter. Leigh then faked her own death while on a cliffside picnic with Charlie's son, Adam Tate (Adam Biscombe). David also managed to have an affair with Patricia's sister Margaret Dunne (Ilona Rodgers) before she was killed in a plane crash.

Meanwhile, Wayne was blackmailed into marriage by a new 'super-bitch', Karen Fox (Lyndel Rowe), while former lover Jill watched on as a bridesmaid. Ex-wife Amanda Morrell was kidnapped, never to be seen again, and Irene Fisher (Judy Nunn), a boarding house buddy of Fiona's, suddenly revealed herself in a medical emergency to be a doctor.

Businessman Roger Carlyle (Les Dayman) had now arrived on the scene, bringing along his dodgy son Luke (Peter Cousens). Patricia, never one to miss a business deal, or sleeping with a businessman to secure one, tried on both, but it was really the beginning of the end. After 540 episodes and countless Logie Awards, Australia's favourite actress was exhausted. Rowena Wallace breathlessly announced to *TV Week* in July 1984 that she would be leaving the series.

'It wasn't just that the work was so hard,' Wallace remembers today, 'although one particular day I remember running all day to complete 28 scenes in a row. It was more the nature of the character. Patricia was always so manic, forever crying, one month an alcoholic, the next a drug addict.'

'When you're pulling on your emotional self five days a week, it starts to feel very weird. I just didn't have the energy to do it anymore.'

Rumours were also rife that some of the other actors were jealous of Rowena becoming the star of the show. 'I couldn't help the fact that the character became popular,' Wallace recalls. 'It wasn't my fault. It was a combination of writers, directors and the other actors, and the way viewers responded to the character. Sometimes I did get the impression that I was hated for it.' Oddly enough, Rowena was never once abused by a viewer during the entire run of the show. 'They'd say to me, "G'day, Pat, oh, you're a horror, aren't you? What happens next?"'

What happened next was that producers decided Patricia Hamilton Morrell was too good to lose. And so, suspected of murdering Luke Carlyle (when it was really teenage alcoholic Jeff O'Brien), 'Pat the Rat' fled to Rio de Janeiro with new 'boyfriend' Roberto Quinteros (Peter Flett). After one too many tequilas, he beat her up, landing her in hospital. While a bandaged-up double (certainly not Rowena Wallace) spoke with some very dodgy dubbing, 'Patricia' ordered the doctors to give her a new face. Yes, it was time for the 'new identity from plastic surgery' loophole, meaning another actress could assume the role.

While such a storyline was and still is commonplace in American soaps,

Viewers seemed not to notice that Belinda Giblin sounded nothing like Rowena Wallace (as well as being noticeably shorter).

Aussie critics howled at the outlandish twist. Head storyliner Bevan Lee has never understood the controversy. 'In a world where a Seventh Day Adventist goes to Ayers Rock, gets her baby stolen by a dingo and has her life destroyed in a huge murder trial that splits the nation, what's so hard to swallow about *Sons and Daughters*?' he asks, referring to the Azaria Chamberlain case. 'Life is melodramatic!'

Enter Belinda Giblin, previously seen in *The Box* and *The Sullivans*, although just five years earlier she had told *TV Week*, 'I couldn't bear to do another long run in a soapie for as long as I live. I find TV in that sense extremely boring and depressing to do.' 'Pat the Rat', now calling herself Alison Carr, must have been considered neither.

Sweeping out of Sydney Airport into a waiting limousine with her new identity and look, viewers seemed not to notice that Belinda Giblin sounded nothing like Rowena Wallace (as well as being noticeably shorter). 'Everyone laughs about it now,' remembers Bevan Lee, 'but Belinda sort of looked like a re-constructed Rowena – although possibly with a thyroid condition because of her poppy eyes.' Whether the viewers were laughing was irrelevant, as a surge in ratings indicated the re-cast was a success. Temporarily that is.

Meanwhile, back in Rio de Janeiro (actually the Seven backlot where the graffiti was spray-painted in some strange language, although certainly not Spanish) David's search for Patricia led to an amnesiac who just happened to have undergone facial surgery at the same hospital. Assuming she was Patricia, dopey David married her and paraded her to everyone in Australia in the hope it might jog her memory. Alison Carr kept her true identity secret for as long as necessary, although Charlie's pet pooch, Isabella, wasn't fooled.

As the months wore on, the cast began to turn over at an alarming rate. Everyone from Barbara (who, like *Dallas*'s Pamela Ewing, ran away after suffering horrific injuries in a car accident) to the entire O'Brien family slowly began to disappear, to be replaced by far less memorable or downright annoying characters like Spider (Willie Fennell). Bevan Lee, who stopped plotting the show after 600 episodes because he was 'ready to go insane', felt the new writing team lost sight of the show's original premise, and that fine line between the mundane and the ludicrous.

While *Sons and Daughters* cleverly locked into the era's hunger for sex, money and big business (just like *Dynasty*), there was one clear sign that the 80s were coming to an end. As with *Number 96*'s disastrous foray into disco at the end of the 70s, Charlie Bartlett's gymnasium, 'Bumps n' Grinds', an attempt to mirror the 80s aerobics craze, was another story-line bust. As the show grew more desperate to reclaim its glory days, some viewers noticed a few more similarities to *Number 96*. Both shows started off stripped over weeknights in five half-hour episodes before being re-jigged for two hour-long episodes each week. Pat McDonald, who played Dorrie Evans and Aunt Fiona respectively, was on board for the entire run of both soaps. When joined by *96*'s sexpot Abigail, both actresses lashed out at reports that they never spoke to each other because of a feud dating back to 96's early days. 'It's all totally made up,' Abigail told *TV Week* in 1985. 'Pat and I get on like a house on fire.' Only when they were spotted partying together at the Logie Awards did the 'feuding' rumours finally stop.

Indeed, the cast and crew of *Sons and Daughters* prided themselves on the 'family' atmosphere behind the scenes. 'It was the best atmosphere on a set I've ever known,' says Rowena Wallace. 'I remember so many times if I had a difficulty, the cameraman or the props guy might come up and offer a way to do it differently. It really was fantastic teamwork and we had so much fun. Every Wednesday night, we'd have a CTR – the cold tinnie run – and all sit around drinking.'

Rowena Wallace and Ally Fowler shared a harbourside unit, and an impromptu singalong during a party at Peter Phelps's house led to a cast record album. *All My Friends* featured Pat McDonald and Rowena Wallace singing 'Bosom Buddies', Peter Phelps and Kim Lewis warbling 'The More I See You' and Tom Richards and Leila Hayes duetting on 'Behind Closed Doors'. On the flipside of the album, the cast of *A Country Practice* did their best to murder some classics of their own.

To the public, it seemed as if the two successful Seven shows did everything together, but behind the scenes it was quite a different story. Just like the tension between Nine's *The Sullivans* and *The Young Doctors* a few years before, the cast of *A Country Practice* felt their series was of a higher quality. 'We all knew they thought our show was less sophisticated than theirs, but it didn't worry us,' remembers Rowena Wallace.

Meanwhile, the show's storylines were becoming increasingly desperate. For the 1987 summer cliffhanger, Alison was flying off to stop Wayne from marrying Mary Reynolds (Tessa Humphries), the daughter she didn't know she had, and who (in a spooky re-hash of the near-incest between John and Angela) also happened to be his half-sister. Given that Gordon's drunk brother James (Nick Tate) was piloting the plane and running low on petrol, it was hardly surprising that they crashed in the middle of nowhere. Jealous housekeeper Doris (Carole Skinner) was threatening to kill Beryl's baby, Robert; claustrophobic Caroline (Abigail) was locked in a wardrobe after witnessing a robbery; Leigh was on trial for the baby kidnapping and Fiona (Pat McDonald) had been diagnosed with cancer.

A year later, the end-of-year cliffhanger was even more ridiculous. Andy (Danny Roberts) was kicked in the head by a horse, and Alison broke into Wayne's safe only to find a snake inside that bit her. She had already schemed with a cruise skipper (what, no Gilligan?) to keep Wayne on an island for a week, giving her enough time to destroy his business. On the island, Wayne's supposed son, Tick, accidentally fell on a knife, and in a bid to get help, Wayne jumped into the water to swim to shore, only to be followed by a huge shark.

Come the New Year, Wayne escaped his cheap *Jaws* rip-off by simply hitting the shark on the nose, while Alison just happened to run into someone carrying a vial of antivenom. Andy got up off the ground and

Tie-in paperback books.

Alison (Belinda Giblin) is bitten by a snake in a ridiculous Christmas cliffhanger.

remarked what a close call the hit in the head had been. Bevan Lee, watching from home, realised the show was in serious trouble.

'You utterly believed, in some strange shape or form, the human truth of *Sons and Daughters*,' he insists, 'at least for the first three and a half years. People believed it because it was almost like reading a novel. Other serials were patchwork, but we had this rich, ongoing saga. We downplayed the melodrama because if you believed everything these silly people were doing, it was bound to work.' But after the ridiculous shark/horse/snake cliffhanger, Lee knew the show had lost the plot. 'The audience gets to a point where they won't invest emotional energy in the show because they're always getting burnt.'

Actor Danny Roberts (Andy), who'd been whisked across to the show after the failure of another Grundy's soap, *Waterloo Station*, desperately wanted to leave *Sons and Daughters* before another horse kicked him in the head. 'Every Monday, if your pigeon hole [mailbox] was full and another bag of fan mail was sitting on the floor, your contract was going to be renewed,' says Roberts. 'I became more and more popular so they couldn't kill me off, even though I started speaking out, saying that the character wasn't doing anything and I was bored shitless. I was a bit antisoap at that point but I was making a lot of money – especially when compared to what they're making today. You basically played yourself and I found that really hard because I wasn't hiding behind a character.'

The serial bravely struggled on, doing what it did best – marrying everyone off to each other. 'Caroline the Cat' (Abigail), now about as bitchy as a pussycat, got hitched to businessman Doug Fletcher (Normie Rowe) four times (although two weddings were halted before the vows); Wayne headed off to the altar again with Susan Palmer (now being played by Oriana Panozzo), and boring Beryl married boring Gordon. As the ratings continued to slide, producers came up with one last humdinger to lure the faithful back.

In August 1986, *TV Week*'s cover story revealed the 'Return of the *Real Rat*', with Rowena Wallace announcing exclusively that she had expressed interest in reviving the character. Grundy's and Seven found the idea 'appealing', although producer Don Battye admitted it would be a 'scriptwriter's nightmare' to unravel why Alison Carr wasn't Patricia after all this time.'

Fearful of another disastrous *Dallas* scenario, where Bobby Ewing's return was explained away by a season-long dream, they turned to Bevan Lee. He came up with the idea of putting Beryl into jail where she came face to face with a dead ringer for Patricia, a long-termer called Pamela Hudson. With sly nods to *Prisoner*, Pamela was Bendala Detention Centre's 'top dog', even resorting to the steam press to dish out punishment. Conveniently, Pamela was also about to be released, and naturally Beryl suggested her good friend Fiona's boarding house should be the first place she should go.

Rowena Wallace

Rowena Wallace fan card.

Seven's promos promised a showdown between Pamela and Alison Carr, while stopping short of revealing which one was actually Patricia. 'The sparks are flying when "Pat the Rat" meets a tougher rat,' screamed the ads, 'as Rowena Wallace reclaims her title of "Superbitch" (and all in the family-friendly timeslot of 6.30pm Sunday nights too). As it turned out, Pamela was actually Patricia's identical twin sister who even had – wait for it – twin children herself, Greg (Tom Jennings) and Sarah (Melissa Docker). When Pamela discovered she had been given away on a toss of a coin because their parents couldn't afford to bring up both daughters, she was understandably quite bitter. 'Superbitch' bitter, actually.

Unfortunately, Rowena Wallace's return was too late to save the show from the axe. *TV Week* supposedly broke the news of *Sons and Daughters'* demise to the actress, leading her to quip 'Was it something I said?' Today, Rowena Wallace doesn't remember the incident, nor does she believe the magazine would have been able to get through to her on set. 'It's a good quote though. I wish I had said it.'

Belinda Giblin, meanwhile, refrained from saying she would never do another soap again, but did admit to *TV Week* that she 'was going to leave anyway. It's time for a new adventure. I've got nothing but good things to say about the show … but I will miss the money.' Leila Hayes (Beryl), one of four actors to go the distance, along with Ian Rawlings (Wayne), Brian Blain (Gordon) and Pat McDonald (Fiona), found it 'extraordinary' that the axe had fallen five years to the day that she had taped her very first episode.

Rowena Wallace, who had only been re-contracted to the show for ten weeks, now considers her return one of the worst career moves she ever made. 'I'm not sure why I did that,' Wallace laughs today, although it was 'probably the lure of the money. I was having a lot of trouble with my back and taking cortisone and I think my decision-making wasn't very clear.'

Reduced to just one hour a week for its dying days, the final episode screened in Sydney in January 1988. Alison tried to kill Wayne with a car bomb but had to emerge screaming from nearby bushes when best friend Charlie got into the vehicle at the last minute. Finding alternative transport, Charlie whisked Isabella the Maltese terrier off to the beauty parlour to be groomed for its part in her wedding party as she married Todd Buckley (Paul Dawber). Back in Melbourne, Beryl was waxing lyrical about being happy as a housewife, while Gordon was getting teary-eyed that baby Robert had just called him 'Daddy' for the first time.

Caroline, pregnant and reunited with Doug, was shocked to discover he had bought a fish and chip shop for them to run. Susan, who had faked her own suicide to get away from what had indeed turned out to be a disastrous marriage to Wayne, returned one last time to goad him, but she went too far. She was last seen lying dead on the Dural mansion floor as Wayne called the police to turn himself in for strangling her.

Alison, destitute and reduced to living in a cheap motel, was at her lowest point ever until a knock at the door revealed the long-departed David (Tom Richards). Her first true love swept 'Pat' into his arms, kissing her passionately. Dopey David obviously still thought they could live happily ever after, despite the disasters of the past.

In the final scene, a couple arrived at Fiona's boarding house just as the pregnant woman went into labour. In an exact repeat of how the series began, Fiona asked the young man if he wanted a boy or a girl. 'Oh, I don't care,' he said. 'Good,' she replied, 'because you've got one of each. Twins.' Heaven forbid, but the series could be revived in 2007 with this new family, as the next generation of twins are about to celebrate their 20th birthday.

As the credits rolled over snapshots of all the show's previous characters, a Seven voiceover man couldn't help slapping the network on the back. 'Well, that was the last in the record-breaking run of *Sons and Daughters*.' Exactly what was record-breaking was never revealed, as with just 972 half-hour episodes it was hardly the longest-running series, nor the most awarded. Ironically, the voiceover went on to announce the show's replacement, *Home and Away*, a soap which *would* be long running and award winning.

Sons and Daughters then travelled the world, even being re-made for certain foreign markets. The series screened throughout Belgium, the Netherlands, New Zealand, Spain, Ireland and The Azures. Three years after the show had finished production, Ian Rawlings (Wayne), Leila Hayes (Beryl), Tom Richards (David) and Danny Roberts (Andy) were flown to Brussels where the show was a big hit screening in prime time.

'We got off the plane and there were limousines, thousands of fans and the Lord Mayor waiting to welcome us,' recalls Danny Roberts. 'We would do appearances where we would go onto stage and be interviewed, then sing songs they taught us in Flemmish! When I came home via

England and immediately got work in a pantomime, I realised I'd missed an opportunity by going off to America after the show had ended. Had any of us known, we would have all gone to England and Europe where we were so well respected.'

In Germany, the show was re-made as *Verbotene Liebe* (which translates as 'Forbidden Love') and was so successful it ran nearly twice as long as its Aussie parent. In Sweden, it became *Skilda Varlda* ('World Apart') and in Indonesia *Belahan Hati* ('Divided Hearts').

Sadly, many of the actors involved with *Sons and Daughters* have since passed away including Brian Blain (Gordon), Pat McDonald (Fiona), Michael Long (Stephen) and Anne Haddy (Rosie). Other actors who appeared in the show included Noel Trevarthen, Anne Phelan, Vince Martin, Simone Buchanan and Tom Oliver, but despite their best efforts, the show received one long slagging in the press.

'Right across the board the critics said, "We don't possibly see how this could last more than six weeks", but very few of them asked why it turned out to be such a high rater,' remembers Bevan Lee. 'I get very cross at snooty reviewers who put the genre down. Soaps only became acceptable in Australia when they began to be sold overseas. This country is still riddled with cultural cringe.'

'Pat the Rat' couldn't have said it better herself.

LP record.

22

TAURUS RISING

PREMIERE: **1982** EPISODES: **21** NETWORK: **NINE** FINALE: **1982**

They're rich, they're related, they're unhappy.

Knowing *The Sullivans* was on its last legs, Nine needed a big gun for the 1982 ratings year. American night-time soaps *Dallas* and *Dynasty* were the latest rage and filthy rich families seemed to be what viewers wanted. Grundy's and its prolific creator Reg Watson had just the concept. *Taurus Rising* was grand, lavish and expensive, and Nine hoped it would become the next big thing. It was big all right – a big disaster.

It appeared to be jinxed right from the start, and calling it *Taurus Rising* didn't help. 'The name did confuse people,' remembers Damon Herriman (Phil). 'I constantly had to explain in interviews that it had nothing to do with the zodiac or astrology.' Even Nine was unclear as to what their new show was about. At an elaborate launch for it, one network executive was asked to explain. 'Taurus rising from the ashes?' he supposedly guessed. He should have known that the title actually referred to the luxury Taurus building that would be the centrepiece of the series as two families fought each other tooth and nail to construct it.

'We always made sure we didn't refer to *Taurus Rising* as a soap,' says Herriman. 'It was to be called a 'quality drama' and fair enough too, since it was totally shot on film and just about every other show of the time was shooting on video.'

Damon Herriman was just 12 years old when cast in *Taurus Rising*, and he had to leave his family behind in Adelaide and board with a family in Sydney for the seven-month shoot. Familiar to audiences from his starring role as a cheeky (but lovable) kid in *The Sullivans*, he welcomed the opportunity to play against type. His new character, Phil Drysdale, would be front and centre as a misunderstood yet spoilt brat whom everyone wanted custody of. 'Children didn't dominate TV back then, like they do today with *Neighbours* and *Home and Away*. At that age, I wasn't aware of the responsibility that came with having a major role like that. It was more about having fun for me since I was like a kid in a candy shop. My character had a massive train set and it was mine to play with. Atari video games were all the rage and the props buyers would ask me which games I wanted to order.'

Whilst the toys on set were fun, Herriman also enjoyed the excitement of being part of a secret conspiracy. 'Before it aired, we were not allowed to say anything about the show. We did a telethon in Adelaide just weeks before the first episode and I had to keep apologising for being so secretive about it. I remember thinking how were people going to watch if they didn't know anything about it.'

Nine was obviously keen for viewers to find out, as they rushed it onto air earlier than originally planned. This unexpected move resulted in much re-shooting which didn't help the already troubled production. Major delays were being experienced because of the unfortunate studio location picked to film interiors in. Sydney's Bijou theatre had been converted specifically for this purpose, but filming had to stop every time a plane went over (nobody had noticed it was under a flight route) and when the nearby Balmain Town Hall clock chimed (every half hour).

Taurus Rising opened with a series of flashbacks set 60 years beforehand. After being jilted by boyfriend Harry Brent, bitter and heartbroken Isabella had entered into a loveless marriage with James Drysdale and bore him one son, Ben. The Drysdales and the Brents had then spent the next few decades as bitter rivals in the construction business.

Flash forward to the 80s and Harry Brent (Gordon Glenwright) was about to die while the now-ruthless tycoon Ben Drysdale (Alan Cassell) was gloating about the imminent demise of his major business rival. Ben got a nasty shock, however, when he discovered that Harry's long lost daughter Jennifer (Annette Andre) was returning to town. In a classic *Romeo and Juliet* scenario, they had fallen in love 26 years previously, but Ben's formidable mother Isabella (Georgie Sterling) had forbidden their marriage. Jennifer arrived at Harry's deathbed with a son that nobody knew existed. Mike (Andrew Clarke) was 26 years old, so guess who wondered if he was the father.

Ben Drysdale had a son of his own, but Keith (Andrew Sharp) had been a disappointment, preferring to turn his back on the world of high finance for a life playing the tennis circuit. A failed marriage had left him with a young son whom Ben demanded custody of in return for financing Keith's sporting aspirations. Consequently, child prodigy Phil

Filming had to stop every time a plane went over (nobody had noticed it was under a flight route)...

(Damon Herriman) had been brought up thinking his real father had deserted him.

Overseeing this horrific family was Ben's long-suffering wife Faith (Betty Lucas). Years before she had accidentally killed their other child, Jamie, when her car slid off a wet bridge into a river. Her loveless marriage with Ben now mostly involved him torturing her. Indeed, in *Taurus Rising*'s opening scene, Ben introduced Faith to finance reporter Libby Hilton (Diane Craig) before whisking his secret mistress away in his Lear jet for a dirty weekend. Faith, who recognised what was being done to her again, was left on the verge of a nervous collapse.

Meanwhile, Phil was locked in the family mansion as he was considered a target for kidnappers. Bored and lonely, he copied his grandfather's behaviour and did a little torturing of his own. In great soapie tradition, however, he softened towards new tutor Alice Blake (Linda Newton) who managed to turn the little monster into a nice boy. However, when she convinced Faith to let her take Phil off the grounds for an excursion into the real world, a shifty security guard pounced and kidnapped the pair for a $3 million ransom.

There was also a Drysdale daughter, Elizabeth (Marina Finlay), who returned from her own overseas shenanigans to fall for Drysdale associate Sam Farrer (Michael Long). A love triangle was soon heating up between Elizabeth, Sam and Mike, who turned out not to be Ben's son (any incest between brother and sister was saved for that other Grundy's show, *Sons and Daughters*).

Taurus Rising premiered with much fanfare in a two-hour episode on 27 July 1982. Unfortunately, it fared badly in the ratings against the final episodes of *Brideshead Revisited* and another Grundy's ratings powerhouse, *Prisoner*. Without a huge audience for the first episode, *Taurus Rising* was doomed for any new drop-in viewers. All the good acting in the world couldn't help a complicated premise or the fact that hardly any of the characters were likable or distinguishable from each other.

In particular, housekeeper Marie (Jessica Noad) looked so much like her employer Faith (Betty Lucas) that some viewers must have thought they were sisters. The two younger romantic leads, Sam (Michael Long) and Mike (Andrew Clarke), also looked like brothers, and perhaps future episodes would have revealed that both these couples were long-lost siblings.

Most disappointingly though, amongst the seemingly endless scenes of family feuds and power struggles, there wasn't a touch of comedy or camp. *Taurus Rising* took itself far too seriously and was badly in need of some tongue-in-cheek. The mansions were drab, the Rolls-Royce was overexposed and even the constant champagne seemed to lack bubbles. Had nobody realised that part of the appeal of *Dallas* and *Dynasty* was the sheer outrageousness of it all?

Instead, *Taurus Rising* tried to keep it real, but it seems that Aussie audiences didn't want to watch a show about Aussie millionaires. 'I can't think of any show where rich Australian characters have been warmly

TAURUS RISING.

A gripping new series of two Australian business empires. Built on love, hate and revenge.

And two families that will do anything to cause the other's downfall. **Special 2 hour premiere.**

Tonight 7.30 pm.

embraced,' says writer Rick Maier. 'The two exceptions have been *Carson's Law* and *Sons and Daughters*, but they were both always balanced by the working class half – and the rich guys were the bad guys in both shows.'

Even the actors seemed nervous about what a local audience would make of the show. 'I don't like my character but I love the part,' Alan Cassell (Ben) told the *Australian Women's Weekly*. 'I know the JR comparison is going to be made although I'm sorry it will be. None of us wants this series to be compared to *Dallas* or *Dynasty* but I'm afraid it is inevitable because it is probably the first television series made about wealthy Australians. All we can try to do is make our show even better.'

Nobody wanted to be compared to the bigger budget American shows, but behind the scenes it was a different matter. 'I was told to approach my character as if she was a young rich bitch in the style of *Dynasty*'s Joan Collins,' says Marina Finlay (Elizabeth) today. 'It was an extraordinarily big budget show, the most spent on a drama up to that point. The scripts weren't that stimulating but at least we were paid well!'

Despite costing a rumoured $2 million, Nine quickly dumped the show from its Tuesday night prime time slot of 8.30pm and banished it to Friday nights at 10pm. It was replaced by repeats of *The Love Boat*. The press could barely contain their glee, re-naming it *Taurus Flopping/ Sinking/Falling* or whatever other smart title they could come up with. Rival production company Crawford's had their own name for it – *Pisces Plummeting*.

Cast and crew were about halfway through shooting the series when the timeslot change finally signalled that the network had lost patience with their expensive new soap. Damon Herriman became, understandably, protective of the show if anybody tried to tell him it had been canned. 'No, no, it didn't get axed,' he would say, 'They only ever intended to make 21 episodes!'

One lucky by-product of being in production when the axe fell was scriptwriters being given enough time to finish the series properly. While Alice (Linda Newton) inexplicably fell in love with the insipid Keith (Andrew Sharp), Libby (Diane Craig) did the dirty on her former lover by writing a tell-all biography of Ben (Alan Cassell). Desperate to escape her husband's machinations, Faith (Betty Lucas) faked her own death and made it look like Ben had done her in. Hiding out and wearing a wig to disguise herself, she fell in love with Malcolm Adams (Vic Hawkins), which gave her the courage to head back to the mansion and reveal that she was still alive.

After making sure grandson Phil (Damon Herriman) was moving far, far away with Alice and Keith, Faith signed over all her shares in the business to Elizabeth (Marina Finlay), giving her daughter the balance of power in the company. As every member of the family, and even the hired help, deserted the Drysdale mansion, Ben was left with just his dragon of a mother. *Taurus Rising*'s final moment would rob the mean mogul of her too. Isabella (Georgie Sterling) dropped dead on the marble stairs, probably at the sheer inanity of it all.

After the show had ended, Grundy's needed to make up the shortfall on their most expensive production, so it slowly began to be sold around the world. Within six years, it had become the number one show in Turkey. Several of the cast were reunited for a photo shoot after a Turkish newspaper flew a reporter to Australia to feed the demand for information about the show.

Taurus Rising was also sold to cable television in the USA where it received a favourable review from *People* magazine as a '21 hour mini-series'. So complimentary was the review, it was repeated for trade advertisements in *Variety*. Perhaps if Australian audiences had been able to read this first, they may have been more willing to watch.

'What a kick, what a hoot, what a treat! Here's Australia's answer to *Dallas* and *Dynasty* – a "soapie" (as they call it) with warring families and wads of wealth. "Where there's money," says a line in the script, "there's muck." There's also affairs aplenty (though not much flesh), a grand old dame, a devil baby, two kidnappers, a slut reporter, a sweet teacher, an evil businessman, a superb death bed scene – everything you've ever wanted on a soap. But mostly there's plot – a tangled, tawdry tale that'll keep you coming back, as Lifetime re-runs the full series daily and again nightly at 11pm over the two weeks. Our own soaps, daytime and night-time, could learn a few things from this Aussie copy – namely, how a good story is better entertainment than even the best wardrobe. Grade A-.'

23

WATERLOO STATION

PREMIERE: **1983** EPISODES: **52** NETWORK: **NINE** FINALE: **1984**

The cast optimistically tip their police hats at the show's launch.

The Melbourne-based Crawford Productions had established itself with a trio of successful police dramas (*Homicide*, *Division 4* and *Matlock Police*), then struck gold by soaping up the formula with *Cop Shop*. Everybody recognised that cop shows were Crawford's specialty, but Grundy Productions thought it could improve the formula by combining it with what they did best – a spunky youth-orientated cast.

In December 1982, *TV Week* ran the headline 'Nine Pins Hopes on Harbour Cops'. The show in question was *Harbourside Force* and it was to be a new soap, to air as two hour-long programs a week. Created by Reg Watson, it would be about a group of Sydney-based police trainees, and it had already started filming in the studios recently vacated by *The Young Doctors*.

By the time it got to air the following February, it had been re-titled *Waterloo Station*. Police Academy instructor Jack Edwards (Ron Graham) was welcoming a new group of trainee officers, including his daughter Sally (Sally Tayler) who had shocked her parents when she decided to enter the police force. Mother Liz (Pam Western), a former nurse, was trying to keep the peace at home because husband Jack was not only against Sally's career move, but also his daughter's toughest teacher at

the police academy. All Sally had to rely on was the support of cop boyfriend David Keller (Malcolm Cork).

Liz's sister Ann (Jenny Ludlam) was also married to a cop, Detective Sergeant George Logan (John Bonney). He was a workaholic who neglected his wife, and Ann was also bitter because she couldn't have children. That made her fair game for the attentions of cockney Steve Colby (Steven Grives) who was really a hired assassin out to kill both detectives. George, unaware of the danger, continued to work the beat with his womanising partner, Detective Tony Harris (Bartholomew John).

In the Bondi boarding house run by the theatrical Mrs Wallace (Jennifer West), a motley group lived together. There was former alcoholic comic Harry McDowell (country singer Robert 'Tex' Morton); trainee cop Rick Thompson (Gerry Sont); a 'hooker with a heart of gold', Stacey Daniels (Julianne White); and two young boys, Joey Daniels (Paul Smith) and Trevor Brown (Danny Roberts). The kids were always trying to figure out why Mrs Wallace regularly disappeared into her basement. They were right to be suspicious, since she had a secret stash of cash down there.

'We think it's going to be a smash,' a Nine Network spokesman told *TV Week*. 'There's lots of soap opera and, because most of the characters are young trainees, we can get into many of the problems that face young people today. It's set in Sydney but it really could be anywhere. There's a good deal of police action but there's also a lot of human drama and comedy. There's something for everyone.' To finish off, *TV Week* wished the show success by describing it as a cross between *Sons and Daughters* and *Cop Shop* with a dash of *The Restless Years* thrown in.

The next week the magazine kept up the positive spin by doing a profile on blonde 21-year-old actress Sally Tayler. 'Toss in your badge Pepper Anderson (*Policewoman*'s Angie Dickinson) – and your guns and handcuffs, Danni Francis and Amanda King (*Cop Shop*'s Paula Duncan and Lynda Stoner) – Sally Edwards is set to become TV's most popular female cop. Well, that's the advice of the Nine Network.' Tayler was enjoying working on *Waterloo Station* because 'it's a small, core cast and there is more attention paid to detail in the scriptwriting so the characters aren't so one-dimensional'.

After viewing the first episode critics delivered their verdict, and as expected with any new soap, they thought the characters were very one-dimensional. Fiona Manning wrote that 'some real moments of tension come when two constables are beaten up and one is viciously murdered by a group of young thugs. The impact of this moment is spoiled in the next scene when the surviving constable (Malcolm Cork), who has been beaten, kicked and bashed with a baseball bat, is seen happily chatting with not a single bruise in sight except for a plaster over one eyebrow.'

One star, however, was singled out for his performance. 'It was hard not to squirm with embarrassment at some of the dialogue and cast performances but one real star emerges – Danny Roberts, the young Perth actor. His performance is superb and a bright spot in a potentially dull program.' Jacqueline Lee Lewes agreed. 'The camerawork is pedestrian, the lighting harsh and the script full of clichés and although the main concept of this series is interesting I'm tempted to say it's a load of predictable rubbish. But there's a character called Trevor Brown. He is the future star of the series.'

'It was completely overwhelming because one week I was a 17-year-old kid with nothing, the next I was on a plane to Sydney with a stack of scripts,' says Danny Roberts today. 'I was on cloud nine, it was like winning Lotto. Trevor was a rough kid because his mother didn't want him and his foster parents treated him worse than a dog. I wasn't exactly living on the street like he was, but I was able to identify with some of his problems.'

Despite all the publicity (which was a good deal more than Nine's next ill-fated soap, *Starting Out*, would get a few months later), *Waterloo Station* didn't score high enough ratings in Sydney, particularly when programmed directly against two more established soaps, *A Country Practice* and *Carson's Law*. In Adelaide, Perth and Brisbane, however, the show was a smash hit, especially when the young actors visited the cities for promotional tours.

'We rocked up to the Queen Street Mall in Brisbane and there were over 4,000 people there,' remembers Danny Roberts, who travelled to the city along with Sally Tayler, Julianne White and Malcolm Cork. 'We had no security and when the guy on the microphone said everyone could get autographs, the crowd surged towards us and pushed us up against these glass shopfronts. Next thing, there were hands all over me with someone undoing my pants and I had to push, punch and kick my way out. I was absolutely petrified.'

Despite the hysteria, the failing ratings in Sydney caused *Waterloo Station* to lose the battle. Perhaps it might have had more luck in attracting viewers if it hadn't been jinxed by its title. 'Like Napoleon, the Nine Network has been defeated at Waterloo and axed its poor-rating police series,' *TV Week* wrote. A network spokesperson told the magazine, 'Viewer reaction to the series has not been as good as we anticipated and regrettably we are unable to continue the program with its current ratings.' The show was yanked off air as soon as the cancellation was announced, except in Brisbane, which continued to showcase the local actor Malcolm Cork (previously a doorman at a popular nightclub) who had hit the big time down south.

Production ceased on 13 May after just 52 episodes, and some of the remaining shows were screened in the non-ratings period the following summer. Before *Waterloo Station* wrapped up, new cop Brad Stevens (Eric Oldfield) saved the life of undercover cop Chris Cooper (Andrew Clarke); Jack (Ron Graham) was dead; George (John Bonney) and Ann (Jenny Ludlam) had broken up; Sally (Sally Tayler) and David (Malcolm Cork) were about to marry; and Mrs Wallace's (Jennifer West) mystery in the basement was revealed when she and Harry (Tex Morton) were charged with the murder of Mr Wallace. Grundy's whisked Sally Tayler and Danny Roberts across to *Sons and Daughters*. Tex Morton died soon afterwards. Malcolm Cork went back to tending the door at Rosie's nightclub.

24

CARSON'S LAW

PREMIERE: **1983** EPISODES: **184** NETWORK: **TEN** FINALE: **1984**

The Carsons in court – Jennifer (Lorraine Bayly),
Godfrey (Kevin Miles) and Robert (Ross Thompson).

Ten may have been responsible for the Aussie soaps boom after *Number 96*, but the network was hardly known as the home of classy fare. Nine had re-defined the genre with *The Sullivans*, and now Seven was receiving accolades for the socially aware *A Country Practice*. It was time for Ten to have its own quality production, and Crawford's were keen to work their nostalgic magic again. They had also created the perfect vehicle to lure *Sullivans* 'mother' Lorraine Bayly back to the small screen. It was the first time an Australian television series had been created around an actress, and this time Bayly would get to play more than just a housewife. Jennifer Carson was to be based on one of Australia's first female solicitors.

Carson's Law, which hit the airwaves in 1983, was set in Melbourne during the 1920s. The influential and wealthy Carson family was presided over by the domineering Godfrey Carson (Kevin Miles). He ran his family, household and law office with an iron hand. Script editor Gwenda Marsh remembers getting Terry Stapleton's first script and realising the Carsons were based on the real-life Crawford family. 'At the first reading, I was terrified thinking Hector Crawford would either kill or sack us all,' says Gwenda Marsh. Instead, Hector waited till the end

On the set of *Bellbird* at the ABC's Melbourne studios with Rhoda (Lynette Curran) and Ron (Sean Scully) and their chooks.

Number 96's Dorrie Evans (Pat McDonald) dreams she is being romanced by Les Whittaker (Gordon McDougall) – and since it's her dream, she also makes sure 'that painting' of Norma, usually topless, is discreetly covered up.

Tony Wild (Ken James) accidentally drops his towel in front of wardrobe assistant Tina (Tracy Mann) in the movie version of *The Box*.

Schoolgirls Peggy Richardson (Anne Lambert), Sue Taylor (Joanne Samuel) and Ann Watson (Megan Williams) precariously balance atop their clog heels for the *Class of '74* pilot, alongside Joe Wright (Zoltan Kent).

The *Prisoner* cast circa 1982.
BACK L-R: Meg Morris (Elspeth Ballantyne), Margo Gaffney (Jane Clifton), Steve Faulkner (Wayne Jarratt), Judy Bryant (Betty Bobbitt), Joan 'The Freak' Ferguson (Maggie Kirkpatrick), Colleen Powell (Judith McGrath) FRONT: Mouse (Jentah Sobott), Lizzie Birdworth (Sheila Florance), Governor Erica Davidson (Patsy King), Bea Smith (Val Lehman), Chrissie Latham (Amanda Muggleton).

It's the *Prisoner* Variety Special as Betty Bobbitt, Colette Mann and Val Lehman perform inside Pentridge prison in what was obviously punishment for the real-life inmates.

A male stripper inspires everyone in *E Street* to get their gear off, including L-R: Harley (Malcolm Kennard), Paul (Warren Jones), black stockinged Lisa (Alyssa-Jane Cook), fully dressed Megan (Lisbeth Kennelly) Toni (Toni Pearen), Chris (Paul Kelman) and Max (Bruce Samazan) in his white Y-fronts.

Hang the expense! Let's have even more balloons and streamers for *Sons and Daughters* with Gordon (Brian Blain), Irene (Judy Nunn), Barbara (Cornelia Frances), Fiona (Pat McDonald), Andy (Danny Roberts), Beryl (Leila Hayes) and Jill (Kim Lewis).

Policewoman Dannii Francis (Paula Duncan), Constable Roy Baker (Gil Tucker) and Senior Sergeant Eric O'Reilly (Terry Norris) fool around on *Cop Shop*.

A Country Practice cast circa 1989. BACK L-R: Cookie (Syd Heylen), Luke (Matt Day), Cathy (Kate Raison), Jessica (Georgina Fisher), Terence (Shane Porteous), Cris (Michael Muntz), Bob (Gordon Piper), Frank (Brian Wenzel). FRONT: Esme (Joyce Jacobs), Maggie (Joan Sydney), Lucy (Georgie Parker), Matt (John Tarrant), Shirley (Lorrae Desmond).

Pacific Drive's spunky young things. BACK L-R: Bethany (Melissa Tkautz), Joel (Adrian Lee), Tim (Darrin Klimek), Zoe (Libby Tanner), Rick (Andre Eikmeier), Brett (Erik Thomson), Anna (Simone Buchanan). FRONT: Amber (Christine Stephen-Daly), Martin (Joss McWilliam), Luke (Steve Harmon).

Something in the Air's Emu Springs footy team. L-R: Ryan (Jeremy Lindsay Taylor), Stuart (Frank Holden), Joe (Vince Colosimo) and Wayne (Sullivan Stapleton) hold up Father Brian (Steve Adams).

Before *Kath and Kim*, there was *Fast Forward*. L-R: Nikki (Magda Szubanski), Dannii (Gina Riley), Shelley (Marg Downey) and Bobby (Jane Turner) are all trying to marry Craig (Steve Blackburn) as Bob Hatfield (Geoff Brooks) and Reverend Bob (Michael Veitch) look on in *Dumb Street*.

The Midday Show's Friday afternoon send-up, *A Town Like Dallas*, had regulars Raymondo Trotter (Host Ray Martin) and wife Sylvia (writer Gretel Killeen) and welcomed guest stars every week such as *Dynasty*'s Catherine Oxenberg and singer Barry Crocker.

Craig (Patrick Ward) and Vic (Mike Dorsey) push Di (Olga Tamara) and Magda (Anne Semler) around as they prepare for the launch – and very quick demise – of the biggest soap flop of all time, *Arcade*.

Starting Out finished up before anyone barely noticed, although Peter O'Brien (bottom right) would find himself back in his swimming togs as diving champion Shane Ramsay on *Neighbours*.

before he announced to everyone, 'Don't think I don't know what you're doing.'

Hector would provide inspiration for Godfrey Carson as he had once done for Sir Henry from *The Box*. Whenever Godfrey referred to Jennifer Carson (Lorraine Bayly) as 'that woman', Gwenda Marsh would giggle. 'Hector used to call me that because I was a bit of a feminist. But he'd known me since I was ten years old and we actually got on extremely well.' To avoid the press catching on, they were told the Carsons were based on the American Kennedy dynasty, and that was particularly true when it came to storylines involving reckless sons.

In the very first episode, Godfrey Carson gathered the family together to announce his engagement to the much younger Felicity (Christine Amor), the daughter of his friend and business associate Sir Humphrey Moore (Kevin Healy). Felicity obviously had a daddy complex to have fallen in love with such a stubborn and chauvinistic man, although to be fair he was very much a product of his conservative era. Like all good soap patriarchs though, he really did love his family, even if it was always a very tough love.

Carson's Law

A distinguished landmark in Australian television.

With a brilliant cast starring Lorraine Bayly and Kevin Miles.

Tonight [10] 7.30

Youngest son Tommy (Chris Orchard) was a gambling, womanising playboy but got away with it because he was Godfrey's favourite son. The middle brother, ignored and taken for granted, was Robert (Ross Thompson) who was married to the neurotic Margery (Louise Pajo). She nagged him incessantly to be more forthright, but he had wearily resigned himself to copping it all day at work and all night at home. They were also childless, and snobby Margery feared they would never get their fair cut of the family fortune.

Robert also lived in the shadow of his even more dependable older brother, Bill Carson (Jon Sidney), who was married to the free-thinking Jennifer. Their children were a weakness of Godfrey's, who saw them as the future of the Carson dynasty. There was university student Billy (Gregg Caves), music lover Sarah (Melanie Oppenheimer) and baby brother Sam (Edward Upjohn). To kick the series off, Jennifer wanted to return to the law career she had begun as a young woman and abandoned after marrying Bill.

Bill was supportive of Jennifer but Godfrey was aghast at the notion of a housewife and mother returning to the workforce. Jennifer's first noble cause didn't help matters. A young girl had been molested and killed, and she was suspicious about how quickly police had nabbed a suspect. She protested to Bill that every man deserved a proper defence, and they both agreed to represent the accused, George Royston (Trevor Kent). Godfrey

Gerard Kent
(Noel Trevarthen).

was horrified that they would drag the family firm into such a scandal, and blamed Jennifer for her dubious influence over his eldest son.

As the family arguments raged, Bill flew off in search of a witness but never came home, dying in a small plane crash. Viewers were shocked at this early plot development, even though it set up many story possibilities for the series. Had Crawford's realised their reaction, they probably wouldn't have dispatched Bill quite so quickly, but there was no room in the quality soap for a return from the dead or a long lost twin.

After the funeral, Jennifer carried out her promise to defend Royston. When she lost the case, the accused hanged himself before the state could. Jennifer was left devastated, wondering if it had all been worthwhile, and when Bill's finances were revealed to be worthless, she found herself penniless as well. 'Many of the cases were based on real court cases of the time, particularly the Royston story,' Bayly remembers. 'It was unusual for the so-called heroine to lose cases – Perry Mason never did – but I thought that was wonderful.'

A large sum of money had also gone missing from Carson & Carson which Bill was to be blamed for. Jennifer insisted on clearing her husband's name and refused any financial assistance from Godfrey. She started up her own practice with clerk Arthur Simpson (Patrick Dickson), but it would be some time before viewers would discover that it was the slimy Tommy Carson who was pilfering money from his father.

Carson's Law also drew inspiration from *Upstairs, Downstairs* by focusing on the Carsons' hired help. Eileen Brennan (Irene Inescort) was Jennifer's bossy-boots Irish housekeeper, while the seemingly sinister Gerard Kent (Noel Trevarthen) was Godfrey's driver and manservant. In a clever twist, Gerard turned out to be one of the good guys, while Tommy Carson went slowly off the rails, cheating on his fiancé and racking up huge gambling debts while always keeping one step ahead of anyone trying to expose him. The writers even introduced a real-life criminal to tangle with Tommy, underworld heavy Squizzy Taylor. Tommy's dangerous affair with Squizzy's mistress Eva (Anna Jemison) would prove to be fatal for several characters.

Jennifer, meanwhile, was kept busy defending the underprivileged and fighting off prospective suitors. These included Major James Dolman (Gerard Kennedy), David Cartwright (Neil Fitzpatrick) and Russell Burns (Hu Pryce), but she remained steadfast until fellow lawyer Christopher Dalton (Tony Bonner) returned to woo her again in the final episodes. Jennifer Carson's career was usually the undoing of her love affairs, as she fought to be taken seriously in a man's world and ended up taking on the cases most of them refused to touch.

Felicity became pregnant and gave birth to Edward, while her father and Godfrey became partners in a new investment, 'moving pictures'. In a sly dig at what was happening to the Australian film industry in the 1980s, an American actress (played by Natalie Mosco) was brought to Melbourne to star in a movie about the real-life Australian champion of women's rights, Caroline Chisholm. The Carsons, however, were shocked by the actress's script changes, tantrums and – an absolute no-no for polite society of the time – cocaine habit.

Recently widowed, Amy (Christine Harris), Godfrey's only daughter, wasn't up to being Sarah's maid of honour when Jennifer's daughter decided to marry Arthur. At the wedding reception, Tommy revealed some of his dirty deeds to his sister and, appalled, she ran outside. Tommy chased after her, terrified that she would blow the whistle on him. As they argued on the street, one of Squizzy Taylor's henchmen, aiming for Tommy, instead gunned down Amy. She fell dead into her brother's arms.

Jennifer's kids – Sarah (Melanie Oppenheimer), Sam (Edward Upjohn) and Billy (Gregg Caves) – disappeared never to be seen again.

This shocking moment was just the prelude to a complete series overhaul. In the next episode, the action had moved forward 17 months. Carson & Carson's faithful secretary Mrs Brooks (Marion Heathfield) had resigned and been replaced by a much younger secretary. Most disturbingly, Jennifer's entire family had vanished. Her father, Vic Brown (Gordon Glenwright), had gone off to work as a country cop; Billy was also out bush, working on the land; Sarah was off-screen, happily married; and poor little Sam had been sent away to a boarding school. Even Jennifer's housekeeper, Eileen, had been given the flick, although she stayed on in the series working at Godfrey's mansion now that Jennifer had sold her family home and moved into a new art deco apartment.

This was all a misguided attempt by Ten and Crawford's to improve ratings for *Carson's Law* in Sydney. Once again, the Melbourne-based show did blockbuster business in its home town and everywhere else but failed to ignite in Australia's other key television market, even after moving from 7.30pm to 9.30pm in that city. Despite the sumptuous locations, authentic detail and above average acting, Sydneysiders apparently needed 'racier' storylines. The show even opened a Sydney office of Carson & Carson and briefly tried to set the action in both Sydney and Melbourne. Well, it worked for *Sons and Daughters*.

Yet before the overhaul had gone to air in May, Crawford's announced that the series would wind up filming in July and finish on air in November. The revamp had all been for nothing and long-term fans felt betrayed, particularly when Jennifer's children were never seen again. So much for Lorraine Bayly being Australia's favourite mother.

'The change in direction was a mistake,' admits Lorraine Bayly today, 'because the reason it didn't rate in Sydney was because of constant time-slot changes. At the time, there were rumours of the Sydney/Melbourne rivalry thing going on which was causing all the messing around with the Sydney schedule. I don't know for sure. Everywhere else it rated well, but in Sydney it was all over the place.'

Now with more of a crime focus, Tommy's dirty dealings took centre stage. When Gerard and Russell tried to keep Tommy out of more trouble, their involvement backfired severely. Russell disappeared, only to turn up dead months later, while Gerard copped the blame for the killing of a policeman. Concerned that the increasingly frail Godfrey might not survive knowing the truth about his son, Gerard spent the 17 months the

Wayward Carson son Tommy (Chris Orchard) begs for mercy from manservant Gerard (Noel Trevarthen).

show conveniently skipped incarcerated in jail. Of course he was released just as the show did its time leap, only to find he had been replaced by Carlos (Tony Alvarez).

Tommy had spent that time poisoning his father's mind against Gerard, and Godfrey, who had originally promised to hold Gerard's job for him, was now refusing to have anything to do with his former manservant. Determined to clear his name, Gerard revealed a dark family secret – he was in fact Robert and Tommy's bastard half-brother, the product of an affair between Godfrey's first wife and a mystery man. Towards the end of the series, after Sir Humphrey died, Felicity found letters proving that her father was Gerard's father, meaning she and Gerard were also siblings. Gerard received a full inheritance, but it was made worthless almost immediately when Wall Street crashed in the final episodes.

First though, Gerard had to prove his innocence, and as he closed in on Tommy so too did Godfrey, unaware that the task force he was leading to clean up the city would expose his own son. As a last resort, Tommy kidnapped his own baby brother Edward, before finally being arrested. Escaping from custody, he tracked down Godfrey and Felicity who were in hiding at a secret country estate. Cornered, he shot himself in front of the entire shell-shocked family.

A weary and devastated Godfrey began to lose the plot, and as his judgement failed, he unwittingly allowed the firm to be ripped off by a shyster. Wall Street crashed and it looked like the old man would too. It was left up to 'the bane of his life' to drag him out into the hard streets to view first hand the beginnings of the Depression. Jennifer's plan worked and Godfrey rallied at a family gathering to announce that Carson & Carson would be re-built. Felicity was pregnant again and Robert and Margery were planning to adopt an abandoned little girl. Episode 184 ended with the soap's two protagonists, Jennifer and Godfrey, working side by side again despite all the tragedies of the past. Finally, there was mutual respect between them, and despite the obvious hardships ahead, family would prevail.

Was it the failure to capture a large enough Sydney audience that killed off *Carson's Law*? Possibly, but Lorraine Bayly admits today that both she and Kevin Miles had gone to Hector Crawford to advise him that neither had the stamina to continue past their two-year contracts. Bayly, who had prepared herself for another punishing schedule similar to *The Sullivans*, hadn't counted on the extra dialogue she would need to learn playing a solicitor. 'There were all these long speeches to learn that opened and closed a case,' Bayly shudders today. 'We'd start on location first thing in the morning, then head into the studio, sometimes till midnight. I would go home and have to learn my lines for the next day. Sometimes I'd get five hours sleep, other times none at all. I'd just shower and go straight back to work. It's a wonder I didn't conk out much earlier.'

Both actors were astonished at having to explain to Hector Crawford how much time it took them to learn their lines. 'He looked at our schedule and said, "What's the problem?"' recalls Bayly. 'He made out that he'd never thought of how much time it took to learn our dialogue and he was stunned at all the hours we used to put into learning the scripts. Odd, hey? He'd figured out that the Godfrey Carson character was based on him, but he'd never considered learning the lines took more time than filming them? They didn't call him the "silver fox" for nothing!' In the end, both Lorraine Bayly and Kevin Miles agreed to work one extra week past their two-year contract so the writers could give the show a proper ending.

Executive Producer Ian Crawford told *TV Soap* after *Carson's Law* had ended that 'of all the scores of dramas we have produced for television, none has received such an overwhelming appeal by viewers wanting it to be brought back once it was axed'. For a while there was talk that Gerard might get his own spin-off, after research on how to improve ratings had shown that the sinister manservant had quite a fan following. Sadly it was not to be.

With casting by *Number 96*'s Bunney Brooke, the cast was distinguished to say the least. Guest stars included John Hargreaves, Peter O'Brien, Sheila Helpmann (sister of ballet legend Sir Robert Helpmann), Chard Hayward and Simone Buchanan. Most of the Melbourne-based cast of *Prisoner* also donned 1920s gear as soon as they had traded in their denims, including Anne Phelan, Maggie Millar, Carol Burns and Caroline Gillmer. Not surprisingly, Lorraine Bayly's old workmates Vikki Hammond, Reg Gorman, Vivean Gray and Gary Sweet also popped in from *The Sullivans*.

Carson's Law deservedly won a swag of awards including five for the scriptwriters alone, while Lorraine Bayly (Jennifer), Kevin Miles (Godfrey), Christine Amor (Felicity) and Ross Thompson (Robert) were all recognised for their fine acting. Crawford's had no trouble selling the show to audiences all across the world, including Angola, Bulgaria, Israel, Swaziland, Italy and the Netherlands. In both New Zealand and Spain, after it had finished its first run on one network, a rival bought the show and re-screened it.

If ever a quality soap deserved a wider audience it was this one. Having set a new benchmark for authenticity with *The Sullivans*, Crawford's raised the bar even further with *Carson's Law*. Unlike the suburban Sullivans, the Carson women were decked out in the lavishly re-created costumes of the 20s while swanning around sumptuously decorated sets. Had the series been screened on the ABC, it probably would have been hailed as a classic. As a lead-in to *Prisoner* though, it seemed out of place. Despite Ten's good intentions, its audience hadn't realised what they had until it was too late.

25

STARTING OUT

PREMIERE: **1982** EPISODES: **85** NETWORK: **NINE** FINALE: **1983**

The staff and students of Thornleigh House.

The cancellation of *The Young Doctors* was unfortunate for Grundy's and Nine because even though Sydney ratings had bottomed out, the show was still doing well in Melbourne. With Sydney's 6.30pm news bulletin ailing, the network desperately needed another strong lead-in series. Nine wanted to make it up to Grundy's so they asked them to come up with a new five-nights-a-week series. Reg Watson already knew a soap about doctors was a winner, so he decided to set his new one in a medical university called Thornleigh College.

Starting Out would revolve around a boarding house on the college grounds. To keep the cast even younger than *The Young Doctors*, the majority of characters would be spunky teenage students who would be quite willing to slip into skimpy swimsuits and lie around the uni pool. To hook in an older audience, who would hopefully stay around for the news, there would be a housekeeper, groundsman and lots of professors. Grundy's went into production in 1982 and stockpiled months of episodes while waiting for Nine to program and launch the show.

Without any fanfare, Nine slipped it quietly into the schedule on 18 April 1982. So quietly that *The Sun-Herald* couldn't help noticing that 'stung by the failure of *Taurus Rising* and *Waterloo Station* Nine is launching this one with not so much of a bang as a whimper. Never before has a new Australian soap been launched with less ado.' Critics weren't even allowed to see the first episodes. Instead they were sent a compilation tape of the first five episodes that made understanding the plot or characters nearly impossible.

Starting Out opened on a farm where Craig Holt (Peter O'Brien) was working and romancing a local girl. Back in Thornleigh, his disappointed parents Dr James Holt (John Hamblin) and Dr Judith Holt (Jill Forster) were running the local surgery. Determined to talk his son into following in the family tradition of becoming a doctor, Dr Holt was driving to the farm when he was killed in a car accident. Feeling guilty, Craig decided to honour his father and go to medical college.

The school joker, Peter Nolan (Paul Williams), quickly scored a part-time job working for gardener Mac Rankin (Maurie Fields). Unlike roommate Jason (John Higginson) he got on well with everybody, including Will Brodie (Yves Stening) and Paul Harding (David Reyne).

Margot Fallon-Smith (Nikki Coghill) was an orphan pretending to be from a well-to-do family, hence the made-up surname. She secretly worked nights washing dishes in a restaurant and the only person who knew her secret was mechanic Ben (David Clencie) who had grown up in the orphanage with her. However, Thornleigh House's crusty house-keeper Mrs Lynch (Marie Redshaw) had also been a cook in the same orphanage, and it was only a matter of time before she was going to recognise Margot and blow her cover.

Overseeing this motley group was Russell Dean (Colin Vancao) who was also the Dean of the college. His niece Agnes, or as she preferred to be known, Aggie (Leander Brett), was a student and quite a handful, and was quickly faking exam papers and being arrested for armed robbery. What a pity she hadn't used her spare time investigating what had happened to the Dean's wife, her Aunt Carol. She had disappeared the previous semester, leading some students to wonder if the Dean had murdered her.

Instead, spooky Carol Dean was in an upstairs attic. Was she the mysterious prowler who stalked the corridors of Thornleigh House late at night? Was the Dean's wife mad, disfigured, or just determined to stay out of sight until Nine's publicity department promised a TV photographer would visit the set? Actually, she was just suffering from agoraphobia and it was Mrs Lynch who was sleepwalking because she couldn't get over the death of her mother.

Starting Out already had one disfigured student, mousy Michelle (Rowena Mohr), the daughter of new tutor Dr John Rivers (Gerard Maguire). He was unhappily married to stylish Yvonne (Suzy Gashler) and carried with him the guilt of the accident that had scarred their daughter for life. Yvonne was bored with school life and spent her time trying to get her daughter a boyfriend.

At the local hairdressing salon run by gossipy Mrs De Soosa (Anne Phelan), Trixie Sheldon (Totty Goldsmith) tried to make out she was cool and sexually experienced when in reality she was naïve and conservative. At least she could cut hair. As nobody could stand Mrs De Soosa ruining a rinse or blabbing their business all over town, the salon was in danger of closing down, but then Yvonne decided to buy it so she could make a life for herself away from the school. That put her in conflict with Trixie as both ladies had the hots for locum Dr Greg Munro (John Grant).

Actor and occasional *TV Week* critic Frank Thring was left permanently confused after receiving Nine's compilation tape of the first few episodes. He was hardly a fan of soap and regularly slammed the genre, but even after watching more episodes as they went to air, he still couldn't distinguish one character from the next. 'The Dean's daughter or niece (one loses track), in the flick of an eyelash, electrocuted someone trying to work a spin-dryer without paying while standing (where else?) in a pool of water.'

His stinging attack on *Starting Out* was published just after the show was unceremoniously yanked from Nine's schedule. 'Despite the cancellation of Grundy's latest assault on our senses,' Frank Thring wrote, 'I see no reason to alter (apart from tenses) a word of it other than to commiserate with the cast who, in a fit of exuberance, became involved with such drivel. It had to go and it did.'

Starting Out may have had some shaky opening moments, particularly with some of the inexperienced cast, but which soap hasn't taken a while to settle down into a rhythm? Storyline-wise, there were many interesting moments brewing, and apart from a maudlin theme sung by Simon Gallaher, and the odd dormitory set that looked like it had been retrieved from *Class of '75*, production values were good. Its departure does seem rather premature, particularly given the lack of notice to alert viewers it was 'starting out'. Did nobody at Nine remember that they had cancelled *The Young Doctors* after 13 weeks, only to give it a last minute reprieve and end up with a six-year hit? By 20 May, *Starting Out* had finished up, replaced by a nervous Nine with repeats of *Diff'rent Strokes*.

Starting Out ended up banished to the summer silly season when ratings finished that November. It joined *Waterloo Station* and *Kings* (another failed drama about a working class family) and was screened irregularly whenever the cricket allowed. Nine never did get around to airing all 85 episodes until a middle-of-the-night repeat many years later. And, bizarre as this seems, Grundy's did sell the show, 20 years after production wrapped, to, of all places, Vietnam. What they made of it is anyone's guess.

In *Starting Out*'s final episode, Mrs Lynch's sister Eleanor Harris (Caroline Gillmer) was determined to reveal to poor little orphan Margot that she was her real mother, but Mrs Lynch was ready to reveal that Eleanor was a murderess, so she quietly left town and said nothing. New cast members Rod Turner (Gary Sweet) and seductress Laurel Adams (Antoinette Byron) joined the farewell party at Thornleigh House where Ben (David Clencie) found love with Tessa Staples (Julie Nihill), and Will (Yves Stening) hooked up with Michelle (Rowena Mohr). Whether or not any would graduate as doctors seemed beside the point.

'The Dean's daughter or niece (one loses track), in the flick of an eyelash, electrocuted someone trying to work a spin-dryer while standing (where else?) in a pool of water.'

26

NEIGHBOURS

PREMIERE: **1985** EPISODES: ... NETWORK: **SEVEN/TEN** FINALE: ...

Jason Donovan and Kylie Minogue celebrate the greatest soap wedding of all time.

In 1980, the Seven network announced they were commissioning two family-friendly pilots in a supposed bid to 'clean up' Aussie soaps after the sex-obsessed excesses of the 70s. *A Special Place* was to be the story of an elderly woman who opened her home up to underprivileged kids, while *People Like Us* was about five families living together in the one suburban street. Neither pilot was picked up, although several years later the second concept resurfaced in a new guise. Grundy's had an idea for a serial about a suburban cul-de-sac but they couldn't quite decide on a title.

Would it be known as *Living Together*, *One Way Street*, *The People Next Door* or *No Through Road*? Could it be named after the region, like America's *Knots Landing* or the UK's *Brookside*, two soaps already being made about cul-de-sacs? Eventually it was decided to call the show *Neighbours*, even though one network executive was convinced it would flop because people hate their neighbours.

That comment was exactly why Reg Watson wanted to make the show. He was now the head of TV drama at Grundy's and had been responsible for hits such as *The Young Doctors*, *Prisoner* and *Sons and Daughters*. Those shows had blazed their way onto international TV screens, despite being created purely for an Australian audience. Watson wanted his new soap to have built-in international appeal, particularly for the UK where he had once worked his magic on the long-running soap *Crossroads*. The

BBC were approached about becoming a production partner with the promise that much of the cast could be English migrants living in Australia. They passed, and would eventually get the show at a fraction of the cost of co-producing it.

Watson had returned to Australia in the early 70s to work for Grundy's on the daytime soap *Until Tomorrow*. Like *Neighbours*, it was set in a suburban street, but with next to no budget, it disappeared within the year. Watson was convinced, though, that a neighbourhood setting could work, and wanted to avoid the melodramatic aspects of most of the soaps he had created for Grundy's. 'I wanted to show three families living in a small street in a Melbourne suburb who are friends,' Watson revealed in a tie-in book, *Neighbours – Early Days*. 'Humour was to play a big part in it and the other important thing was to show young people communicating with older people.'

Nevertheless, he found it difficult to start writing about 'normal' life. 'We had dispensed with rape and murder and contriving shock-horror situations and were left with a very ordinary situation with ordinary people,' he told *Time* magazine in 1988. 'It was immensely difficult, dramatically. And we were doing *Neighbours* simply to entertain. It would have been wrong to do another *Country Practice*.'

While Reg Watson struggled with his gentle premise, location scouts found a quiet cul-de-sac in the middle-class Melbourne suburb of Vermont. Bemused residents were told *Neighbours* would probably only last a couple of years, if that, and as they were being offered regular money just to film the outside of their houses, everybody signed up. For television, however, Pin Oak Court was re-named Ramsay Street. After a year of planning, production began in January 1985, with interior sets constructed at Seven's brand new HSV studios in Melbourne.

Gwenda Marsh was working as a consultant for *Neighbours* but admits that doing 'two and a half hours a week of TV was making me nervous. So when Crawford's offered me a half-hour series called *Zoo Family*, I grabbed the opportunity.' Unfortunately for Grundy's, *Zoo Family* also grabbed a new actress they were hoping to sign for *Neighbours*. 'Reg Watson was cool about me going,' says Marsh, 'but he flipped out about losing Rebecca Gibney because he wanted her to play the part of Daphne.'

Casting director Jan Russ ended up signing Elaine Smith to play Daphne, the saucy stripper with a heart of gold. The rest of the cast were a mix of new actors and well-known faces. Now famed as the woman who discovered Kylie Minogue and Jason Donovan (not to mention Guy Pearce, Radha Mitchell, Natalie Imbruglia, Holly Valance, Daniel McPherson, Delta Goodrem, etc, etc), Russ explains that she is always searching for 'looks, self-confidence and personality. There is also an indefinable thing I've sometimes described as a third eye.' Russ's third eye was definitely working when it came to picking *Neighbours*' original cast, many of whom were chosen for their comedic talents.

The press was describing *Neighbours* as an Australian version of *Coronation Street* as its premiere date approached. The truth was, they were grabbing at straws, for Seven was underwhelming them with information about their new soap. Producer John Holmes remembers Seven's head of promotions saying to him, 'Oh that's right, you go to air in a couple of weeks. We better do something about some promos.' Holmes was staggered at the lack of on-air advertising, especially given Seven's investment in the new production, said to be $8 million for the first year.

Set for a 6pm timeslot around Australia, Seven decided to experiment in the Sydney market as the nightly news there was going to expand to a full hour, bumping *Neighbours* back to a 5.30pm start. Executives knew the timeslot had once attracted record viewers for Ten's dating show *Perfect Match*. With that show fading, *Neighbours* was touted as the program to bring the masses back to early evening television.

On Monday, 18 March 1985, it all began with a noisy bachelor party thrown by Des (Paul Keane) which was keeping everyone awake in Ramsay Street, Erinsborough. Maria Ramsay (Dasha Blahova) tried to stop her hot-headed husband Max (Francis Bell) from calling the police, while their eldest son Shane (Peter O'Brien) was across the road ushering in the 'special entertainment' for Des.

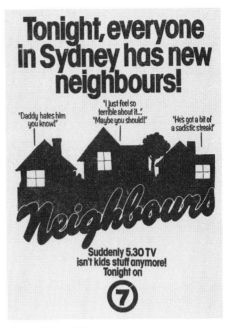

First night ad, intimating it was somewhat raunchier than it actually was.

Max stormed over to confront the revellers just as stripper Daphne (Elaine Smith) began her routine. He shut the party down, Daphne told him to 'drop dead' and a drunken Paul Robinson (Stefan Dennis) was helped home to father Jim Robinson (Alan Dale) and grandmother Helen Daniels (Anne Haddy). Jim was a widower with four kids, while stylish Helen was the mother-in-law who had moved in with the family after her daughter died.

Des's future bride Lorraine (Antoinette Byron) was having a sleepover with Jim's eldest daughter Julie (Vikki Blanche), who had previously been engaged to Des. After Julie spent all night discussing Des's shortcomings, Lorraine decided to call off the wedding the next day. As Des sank into despair, Daphne showed up to search for a lost watch and ended up moving in to help out with his mortgage. Max was horrified that a stripper was living in Ramsay Street (he felt it was 'his' street because it was named after his grandfather).

Over at the Robinsons', youngest daughter Lucy (Kylie Flinker) provided cute relief while other son Scott (Darius Perkins) was best mates with next-door neighbour Danny Ramsay (David Clencie). Their friendship was about to be tested over Scott's burgeoning relationship with shy schoolgirl Kim Taylor (Jenny Young), who was rebelling against the overprotective ways of her strict parents.

Newspaper ads for the opening over-emphasised its raunchier aspects – 'Suddenly 5.30 isn't kids' TV anymore!' While it's hard to imagine anything in *Neighbours* ever giving the censorship board cause for concern, it's true that it was far edgier in its first year than in its second, more wholesome incarnation on Ten. Scott's romance with Kim had him making a joke about being a 'rapist', while she went to a doctor and asked to go on the Pill. Despite being one of the 'mature' characters, Jim Robinson spent an inordinate amount of time gardening without a shirt on, while Shane practised diving routines in his Speedos (ironically, actor Peter O'Brien had also spent much of his time in failed Grundy's soap *Starting Out* wearing the same skimpy bathing suit).

The early episodes also had undercurrents and subtexts that didn't remain in the show. There was a light-hearted suggestion of wife-beating when annoying neighbour Mrs Armitage (Marion Heathfield) said of her husband, 'I put ice in his beer and he still hits me!' As for the constant tension between Max Ramsay and son Danny, was it possible that Danny was struggling to come to terms with his sexuality? While his father got on famously with Danny's elder brother Shane (the all-Aussie sporting champ), Danny got on best with his mother, with whom he could dance and be 'theatrical'.

The Sydney Morning Herald wrote that 'occasionally there comes to television a soapie so charming in its simplicity that to pronounce it a winner seems inadequate. *Neighbours* is such a series. Its startling premise is that everyday life is not about murders, rapes and bombings. By all indications, it is destined for a long and popular life and will steal much of the thunder of its 5.30pm rival *Perfect Match*.' Early ratings for *Neighbours* were encouraging all around Australia, except for Sydney. It barely held its own against the dating show or Nine's unfortunate remake of another quiz favourite, *Blankety Blanks*.

'In Melbourne at 6pm it was scoring 22s but in Sydney it was wallowing in single figures,' remembers producer John Holmes. 'It was in all sorts of trouble because it wasn't designed for a 5.30pm slot and it had become a huge financial commitment for the network since it wasn't being screened in prime time in one of TV's major markets.'

As the weeks wore on, Maria Ramsay admitted to Max that Danny wasn't really his son (supposedly Max had always suspected girlie Danny wasn't a real Ramsay). Max moved into a bedsit and hired a female plumbing assistant called Terri (Maxine Klibingaitis). Feeling unloved, Danny and Scott both ran away (no, they weren't eloping) and headed to the country to hide out at the farm of crusty old Mrs Forbes (Gwen Plumb). Des's mother Eileen (Myra De Groot) arrived unexpectedly and took an instant dislike to Daphne, while art collector Douglas Blake (James Condon, real-life husband of Anne Haddy) wanted to collect more than just art from budding artist Helen.

Julie Robinson fell in love with her boss at the bank, Phillip Martin (Chris Milne), but backed off when she found out he was married with two kids. When his alcoholic wife was killed in a car accident, the usually selfish Julie surprised everyone by leaving Erinsborough to take care of Phillip, who was now paralysed, and his children. Maria Ramsay, aware her marriage to Max was irreparable, also fled the neighbourhood, while

Helen discovered that Douglas was a con man after he stole all of her money. And plumber Terri, who married Paul Robinson after just one date, tried to shoot him dead. Grundy's had insisted that *Neighbours* would not be 'melodramatic' but, following a great soaps tradition, bad ratings led to gunfire – especially to catch the attention of Sydney viewers.

The extra drama didn't increase the Sydney ratings though, and rumours began to swirl that *Neighbours* was on the way out. Actor Peter O'Brien (Shane) was drinking in a Melbourne pub when he overheard two television executives saying they were in town to axe the show. Seven already had two soapie successes, *Sons and Daughters* and *A Country Practice*, and *Neighbours* was almost superfluous to their needs, especially with a Sydney news department unhappy about the disappointing lead-in audience the serial delivered to its all-important nightly news bulletin.

When Seven announced on 12 July 1985 that it was evicting *Neighbours* after just 170 episodes, it was front page news in the city where supposedly nobody watched it. The network cited financial concerns for its demise rather than ratings, which were now healthy everywhere except the harbour city. Fifty placard-waving kids wearing black armbands demonstrated outside Seven's Melbourne studios to no avail. While many other cancelled soapies had been forced to shut down production immediately, *Neighbours* would at least be given a dignified send-off, even if the cast and crew were disappointed.

What nobody knew was that, behind the scenes, Grundy's boss Ian Holmes was quietly flogging *Neighbours* to another station. The announcement that the Ten network would pick up *Neighbours* caused shockwaves in the corridors of Seven. They would not comment about the deal, which was the first time in Australian history that an axed TV drama had been picked up by a rival network. 'We feel *Neighbours* fits our needs,' Ten's Melbourne program director Tom Warne told *TV Star*. 'We have for some time. I think a lot of programs have been cancelled prematurely. *Neighbours* will continue basically as it appears on television at the moment.'

Well, not exactly. When Ten tried to collect the sets, they were told by Seven that they had all been 'accidentally' destroyed in a fire. 'It was very tribal back then,' says John Holmes. 'There was no way Seven was going to co-operate. The word "injunction" was flying around a lot.' Amazingly, Seven continued to screen their remaining episodes until the bitter end while Ten decided how best to revamp the show.

With new sets having to be built, it was decided to freshen up the show's look and make it more colourful. A new outside location was added, with Ten finally finding a use for their old *Holiday Island* resort which was rotting away on the backlot. The once-freezing swimming pool was turned into a pond surrounded by *Neighbours*' new Lassiter Hotel complex. It was also decided to up the comedy factor even further so that *Neighbours* would be 50 per cent drama and 50 per cent comedy.

There was also one re-casting, with Jason Donovan replacing Darius Perkins in the role of Scott Robinson. Donovan had originally been offered a role in the show a year earlier but actor dad Terence Donovan had convinced him to finish high school first. *Neighbours* came calling again after Donovan graduated, and this time he signed up. Darius Perkins was left unemployed and with a sullied reputation.

Several months later, the 'fallen idol' spoke to *TV Week* about some of the stories being spread about him. 'I don't think I was ever unco-operative,' Perkins said. 'I might have been late a couple of times but I didn't understand then just how much money it cost if they were held up.' As for reports that he smoked too much marijuana, the actor shrugged them off. 'How much is too much? Yes, I smoked dope. But I didn't go out raging. I didn't like going out at all when I was in the show – I got hassled too much. I blew it – it's that simple. I was too young and inexperienced to handle it. I was like a restrained monster.' It would be 18 months before Perkins would be seen again on television, in a one-off guest appearance in *The Flying Doctors* and then a small role in *Home and Away*.

On 20 January 1986, *Neighbours* premiered – again – on Ten. The stakes were even higher with a new timeslot of 7pm every weeknight. As part of the promotional push for viewers to 'Meet Your New Neighbours', Ten's head of publicity, Brian Walsh, unveiled the first of many publicity stunts. 'I wanted to physically move the show from one network to another,' Walsh recalls, 'and I did it in Sydney because that was the weaker market. We hired two toploader trucks and had Ten's props department build rooms that resembled the Ramsay Street sets. I flew up some of the cast – Anne Haddy, Alan Dale, Stefan Dennis and poor old Myra De Groot – and they all perched precariously on the back of the truck at 5.30am.'

Parked outside Seven's Epping studios, Walsh bribed the security guard with $100 to allow them to drive inside Seven's complex. 'I told him we were just doing a photo stunt to demonstrate the show was moving networks and he thought that was fine. Unfortunately he lost his job that afternoon.' At 7.15, Ten's *Good Morning Australia* crossed live, with a helicopter overhead, to watch the two trucks with waving cast members pulling out of Seven's driveway. Each bore massive banners which read 'We're moving *Neighbours* to a new home!'

The Sun newspaper labelled it 'one of the most bizarre show business gimmicks ever seen' before going on to report that the travelling circus had ended up at Algie Park, Haberfield, which backed onto a real-life Ramsay Street. Hundreds of guests were treated to a free breakfast and the chance to meet the stars. 'We got a mountain of publicity,' says Walsh.

Next came a series of breakfast radio promotions all round Australia where randomly picked streets were turned into Ramsay Street each morning. Five thousand homes were letterboxed with invitations to a free sausage sizzle breakfast, pony rides for the kids and meetings with the cast. Next came the 'Nominate Your Neighbour' promotion where people nominated their own neighbours as good citizens. Thousands of entries poured in, with various stars hand delivering portable TVs every weekend to the winners. 'The cast were literally streetwalking every weekend,' says casting director Jan Russ.

Reg Watson had told Brian Walsh that *Neighbours* was appealing to a strong teen demographic, so Walsh knew the younger actors were the key to its success. 'Grundy's were very open to giving cast time off for publicity,' says Walsh. 'It was a pretty unique situation and I still don't know of any other production which would halt filming because the actors had a shopping centre appearance. It was almost a regular thing for them to exit Nunawading on Fridays and jump on planes to fly all over the country. We worked them from Saturday morning until they returned to the set on Monday.'

The new and improved *Neighbours* had several new characters, particularly older actors who could keep the show ticking over while its teen stars were gallivanting around the countryside. There was Clive Gibbons (Geoff Paine), a doctor who was moonlighting as a gorilla-gram; Zoe Davis (Ally Fowler), who would win the hearts of both Jim Robinson (Alan Dale) and his son Paul (Stefan Dennis); Mrs Mangel (Vivean Gray), an annoying busybody; and Madge Ramsay (Anne Charleston), Max's domineering sister who moved in to look after him after Maria left her family.

New network,
New *Neighbours*.

Max (Francis Bell) and Danny (David Clencie) soon departed Erinsborough, leaving Madge in charge of the family home. Madge was on the run from an adulterous husband and had left two teenage children behind in Coffs Harbour. Daughter Charlene (Kylie Minogue) arrived on 18 April 1986. *Neighbours* was about to become a fully-fledged pop phenomenon.

Kylie Minogue was a little-known actress who had briefly appeared in *The Sullivans*, *Skyways*, *The Henderson Kids* and *Zoo Family*. Her biggest claim to fame was that she was the sister of *Young Talent Time*'s Dannii Minogue, or as she was called then, Danielle. In fact, *TV Week*'s first ever mention of Kylie was in 1983 just after 11-year-old Danielle had joined the pre-pubescent variety show. The magazine actually misspelt the older sister's name as 'Cahle'. They would never get it wrong again. By 1986, 17-year-old Kylie's first interview for the magazine was mostly about her singing and dancing sister instead of *Neighbours*. 'Being known as Danielle's sister didn't worry me but I will be glad to finally establish my own identity.' *TV Week* reported that Kylie had been signed for 12 weeks, with an option to continue.

It was Scott Robinson (Jason Donovan) who saw Charlene first, and he thought she was trying to break into the Ramsay house. When he ran to stop her, tomboy Charlene smacked him in the mouth (as did Kylie

Madge (Anne
Charleston) and
tomboy daughter
Charlene (Kylie
Minogue).

when her punch connected with Jason for real). Before long, Scott and Charlene were dating and encouraging their neighbours and fellow students at Erinsborough High to do the same.

Mike Young (Guy Pearce) was a troubled boy being bashed by his father. He moved in with Des and quickly attracted the interest of Mrs Mangel's niece Jane Harris (Annie Jones, who had originally auditioned for the role of Charlene). Jane 'Superbrain' begged Charlene to give her a makeover, and when her new look caught Mike's attention, they began to double-date with Scott and Charlene.

Despite the teen romances, Ten executives were privately wondering if they had made the right decision in taking over *Neighbours*. Seven had axed the show for only rating 12 at 5.30pm; now Ten was watching their evening ratings crumble as *Neighbours* could only manage 8 at 7pm. In desperation, they poured money into daily newspaper ads, turning every storyline into a lurid headline.

'Is your fiancé still in love with her old boyfriend?' accompanied a shot of Daphne (Elaine Smith), Des (Paul Keane) and Shane (Peter O'Brien). 'Can you work for the girl who's dropped you for your dad?' had Zoe (Ally Fowler) staring lasciviously at Jim (Alan Dale) while son Paul (Stefan Dennis) sulked in the background. And 'Who is his real father?' concerned new character Bradley (Bradley Kilpatrick) who was, according to his mum Andrea Townsend (Regina Gaigalas), Des's love child.

The extra advertising didn't help ratings but Brian Walsh refused to give up as he watched the increasing crowds at shopping centres all over Australia. The kids were also becoming more and more hysterical. Walsh couldn't convince the press that the show was turning into a fair dinkum hit so he sent Ten news crews to film the wild crowd reactions. The footage was then shipped out to newspaper editors, TV writers and radio DJs. Ignore the ratings, it said, and look instead at the video evidence – *Neighbours* was becoming a teen sensation in the suburbs.

After a meltdown at the Royal Easter Show, where thousands of kids stampeded the stage and injured five children, the tabloid newspapers couldn't ignore the show any longer. The incident became front page news and when Easter Show officials banned any more appearances from *Neighbours* cast members, it was almost as if they were playing right into Brian Walsh's hands.

Even with the extra press, the ratings remained unremarkable, and Walsh was told by Ten executives that they were on the verge of dusting off all those *M*A*S*H* repeats as a replacement. With just a few weeks to improve the ratings, he held an emergency meeting with Grundy's and suggested they do some filming in Sydney. 'I was down on Manly Beach watching filming and I thought this is my only chance,' says Brian Walsh. 'I phoned Roy Miller, who was the editor from *The Daily Mirror*, and I said I had these two young kids in school uniform and, fair dinkum, they're doing a sex scene down here.'

A photographer was quickly dispatched so the afternoon paper could have a front page headline of 'TV Shock – Teen Sex on Ten!' The accompanying story, which intimated that promiscuous teenage sex was about to start beaming into lounge rooms, had the desired effect. *Neighbours'* ratings began to rise.

It turned out that Roy Miller's teenage daughter, Jackie, had recently backed up the publicist's claims that all the kids at school loved *Neighbours*. '*The Daily Mirror* really got behind the show at that point and I think if we hadn't had that, or the co-operation from the show's producers, *Neighbours* wouldn't have lasted six months,' says Brian Walsh. 'Let's not forget the work done by all the cast members, although sometimes I now read stories about how they were constantly tired. There were good times too – we were very supportive of their extra efforts and made sure they got holidays to the snow or the Barrier Reef whenever possible.'

There was a bit of extra friction from the older cast members who didn't think they were getting recognised at a network level. 'They didn't necessarily make it known to those younger actors but they certainly made their feelings known to me about only promoting the young pretty ones. I was very upfront with them and said this is how the show is being marketed and now it's rating, you've all got jobs for a while.'

It might have been upsetting some of the older actors, but *Neighbours* would have been dead in the water if it hadn't capitalised on the rising popularity of Kylie Minogue and Jason Donovan. As their on-screen relationship hotted up, rumours began about what went on when the cameras stopped filming. 'I credit *Neighbours* becoming a hit to Brian Walsh,' says producer John Holmes. 'Of course, the Scott and Charlene storyline was gold for a publicist like Brian. Two actors having a relationship on screen, as well as possibly off screen, turned into tabloid fodder that took the show to a different audience.'

Kylie and Jason were indeed boyfriend and girlfriend, but Walsh instructed his two biggest stars to never admit that they were an item off-screen, knowing it would create endless speculation about what was really going on. The strategy worked – and in the UK too, where *Neighbours* fever was about to begin. The soap had quietly premiered on BBC1 at 1.30pm on 27 October 1986 (with a repeat the following morning at 9.05am). It was considered to be just a nice, cheap little daytime filler.

Back in Australia, the show was finishing its first year on Ten with continued ratings success. Jack Lassiter (Alan Hopgood), who turned out to be the real father of Bradley, sold his luxury hotel to the Daniels Corporation, a conglomerate run by Paul, Helen and Helen's adopted daughter Rosemary (Joy Chambers, wife of Reg Grundy). Des and

Daphne finally married while Zoe (Ally Fowler) fled after miscarrying Jim's baby.

Over at the Ramsay house, Madge was kept busy with her estranged husband Fred Mitchell (Nick Waters) who had come back begging for forgiveness. After he was shown the door, Charlene appeared with a baby, claiming it was hers, but Madge was horrified to learn the mother was actually Susan Cole (Gloria Ajenstat), Fred's mistress. Susan moved into the street and went on to romance Clive (Geoff Paine) and Paul, while Madge coped with the arrival of her parents, Dan Ramsay (Syd Conabere) and Edna (Jessica Noad), who re-married after discovering that their 50-year union hadn't really been legal.

Nineteen eighty-seven was the final year for Peter O'Brien (Shane) who left to travel round Australia. For years afterwards, his swimming trophies sat on Aunty Madge's shelf, and sometimes she would even pick up the phone and ask for his help on some odd job – which he always gave, but off-camera of course.

Shane was replaced in the Ramsay household by Madge's son Henry Ramsay (21-year-old Craig McLachlan), who was just out of prison after serving time for car theft. McLachlan was a former plumber's assistant and fitness instructor who had also made a demo tape of music. 'It went off to a major music publishing company but I didn't hear a lot about it,' McLachlan said in his first interview for *TV Week*. 'But we'll try again.'

Scriptwriters had meticulously constructed a back story for this next wave of the Ramsay family, and with Henry and Charlene now back with their mother, all Madge needed was a bit of romance. Enter Harold Bishop (Ian Smith), Madge's first boyfriend from her teenage years in Brisbane. Widower Harold opened up a health food shop and began boarding with Mrs Mangel (Vivean Gray), leading to many comic moments as the two women, already the worst of friends, bickered for Harold's affections.

In May, *TV Week* ran a controversial contest to capitalise on the Scott and Charlene romance. Viewers were invited to write in with their opinion of whether or not the teenagers should become live-in lovers. Thousands of entries poured in, with close to 70 per cent requesting to see them shacked up together. Mrs Lyn Parkes won a holiday to Singapore for writing, 'This presents an ideal opportunity to illustrate the social, moral and financial problems faced by young couples in this situation today. Teenagers would be more inclined to heed advice from viewing this program which is so popular. Advice from parents tends to be ignored!'

It had all been another giant publicity stunt as Grundy's had already taken the easy way out and filmed the school kids marrying. TV's 'Wedding of the Year' (and the most popular moment ever in Aussie soap history) went to air in June.

Charlene had tried to assert her independence by moving into a caravan (which later exploded, as all caravans on Aussie soaps do). Madge drew the line at allowing her daughter to move in with Scott so he pro-

Charlene had tried to assert her independence by moving into a caravan (which later exploded, as all caravans on Aussie soaps do).

posed at the garage where Charlene worked as a mechanic (a nice role reversal which inspired young girls in the 80s that they too could do anything and still land the man of their dreams). Jim wasn't too keen on his son marrying so young until mother-in-law Helen reminded him that he had married her daughter at around the same age. Putting aside the Robinson and Ramsay feud, Charlene became Mrs Robinson while Aussie rocker Angry Anderson warbled the ballad 'Suddenly', which suddenly shot straight into the pop charts after the episode screened.

A happy soap couple is considered the kiss of death, so temptation was soon thrown at the young newlyweds. Scott was the first to stray, sharing a kiss with Jane while she helped him study for his high school diploma. Meanwhile, there was another wedding in the Robinson family when Gail Lewis (Fiona Corke), Paul's assistant manager, became his wife. It was actually a marriage of convenience to secure a business deal, but by the end of the year the couple had fallen in love.

The biggest event ever in Aussie soap history.

Daphne gave birth to a boy, Jamie, and her estranged father Allen (Neil Fitzpatrick) turned up at the christening with a huge cash gift for his new grandson. When Daph found out her father was dying, she left to look after him. Des was left to deal with the return of his father, Malcolm (Noel Trevarthen), who had deserted him 20 years earlier, and half-sister Sally Wells (Rowena Mohr), who took over the running of the coffee shop and had a fling with Henry (Craig McLachlan).

Meanwhile, *Neighbours* mania was on the rise in the UK. The BBC was under siege from parents and schoolteachers who claimed students were missing classes to watch it. It all got a bit too close for comfort for BBC1 controller Michael Grade when his own daughter, 16-year-old Alison, admitted she and her friends risked detention every day to sneak into their school's computer room which had a television set.

In January 1988, BBC1 finally gave in to viewers' demands and moved *Neighbours* to 5.35pm, with a repeat the next day in the old lunchtime slot. Within a month, the Aussie soap had 16 million viewers (nearly the entire population of Australia) and was beating the 28-year-old *Coronation Street* in the ratings. *The Sunday Mirror* ran a competition for a winner to fly to Melbourne and watch the soap being made, and a million entries were received in three days. Twenty extra staff had to be hired to deal with the sackloads of mail.

Aussies were used to locally made soaps like *Prisoner* becoming cult shows in overseas markets, but nobody could quite understand the Brits' utter fascination with *Neighbours*. The demand for information caught everyone off guard as the UK tabloids headed down under in search of dirt. 'They'd be following actors from studio to home and offering money to their friends,' remembers Jan Russ. 'They were very aggressive and everyone was looking for stories along the lines of "Stars' Sordid Sex Lives".'

The UK press were quick to jump on the are-they-or-aren't-they relationship between Kylie Minogue and Jason Donovan. When they couldn't get the confirmation they needed, some went so far as to accuse the Australian press of being involved in a conspiracy to protect their privacy. Others just made up stories, claiming the pair were already living together in a 'love nest', while others said they were just about to marry. Kylie's reported favourite was from the newspaper that insisted she was actually an alien!

Another piece of fiction had Kylie breaking the heart of Greedy Smith (from rock group Mental As Anything) after he had supposedly been paid £25,000 ($63,000) to appear in one episode of *Neighbours*. In fact, Greedy had a girlfriend and never appeared in the show. As for the money paid to the actors, the truth was that, despite their new 'superstar' status, most were only paid $600 a week, while a handful received up to $2,500. All up, each episode of *Neighbours* only cost around $55,000 in the early years, which was quite the bargain by international standards.

UK Police next began warning '*Neighbours* addicts' that they risked up to two years imprisonment and a £2,000 ($5,000) fine for selling or buying pirated copies of episodes yet to screen in the UK. Obsessed fans were reported to be shelling out £100 ($250) for new episodes and it wasn't 'seedy underworld figures' behind the scam, it was apparently London cabbies. 'As soon as I hear someone talking about the show in the cab,' one told *TV Week*, 'I ask them if they'd be interested in buying the tapes. I do a roaring trade.'

Even most of the residents of Buckingham Palace were supposedly avid watchers of *Neighbours* at its peak, although Prince Charles had to be told what the show was about when he met Kylie Minogue at the Royal Bicentennial Concert in Sydney in 1988 ('I'll have to make a point of watching it,' he said). The Queen, Princess Di and Prince William were all said to be hopelessly hooked like the rest of the British populace, even the ones in comas. One unconscious teenager woke within 24 hours of hearing a special videotape message Ian Smith (Harold) had been asked to make, while another young girl woke up to demand that her parents switch back on the Jason Donovan music they had been playing non-stop.

Out in the country, it was singer Barry Crocker who was the farmers' favourite. One reported that his cows gave better milk if they were played the *Neighbours* theme song. Crocker's version never got to number one, but it did remain in the UK Top 100 Singles Chart for over a year.

As *Neighbours* turned into the biggest Australian TV show of all time, Channel Seven executives could only sit back and shake their heads in horror at what had happened to a show they had originally commissioned and then axed. Ron Casey, the general manager of Seven's Melbourne office, was upfront in admitting that 'obviously my timing was a little out but at the time, putting more money into *Neighbours* would have been like betting for a place in a one-horse race. It's a nice enough show, I suppose, but for the life of me I can't understand why it's done so well in Britain.' Determined to get a piece of the UK pie, Seven was already hard at work developing a new soap of their own that would forever be seen as a rival to *Neighbours*. It was to be called *Home and Away* and would also become a smash hit on the other side of the world.

Back in Australia, Ramsay Street's most eligible bachelor, Jim Robinson, married new doctor Beverley Marshall (Lisa Armytage) while Paul and Gail used the ceremony to renew their vows. Beverley's niece Katie (Sally Jensen) and nephew Todd Landers (Kristian Schmid) came for the wedding and ended up moving into 26 Ramsay Street, along with Jim's daughter Lucy (now played by Sasha Close).

Charlene (Kylie Minogue) in a typically embarrassing 80s moment.

Next door at number 28, Daphne (Elaine Smith) returned to Erinsborough when her sick father died but, on the way back from his funeral, she was involved in a car crash. After lingering for months in a coma, she died of cardiac arrest leaving Des devastated and alone with baby Jamie.

Over at number 24, Madge and Harold broke off their engagement and she ran off to Brisbane to visit her parents. On her return, Harold was mortified to discover that she had been dating another man, his former arch-enemy Lou Carpenter (Tom Oliver, who later admitted he played Lou as an older version of *96*'s Jack Sellars, complete with that dirty laugh). Lou and Harold fought endlessly to win Madge's affections, but in the end she married Harold with daughter Charlene as her brides-maid and Harold's son David Bishop (Kevin Harrington) as best man.

The tropical heat in Brisbane also had an adverse effect on Charlene who had an affair there with driving instructor Steve Fisher (Michael Pope). Charlene's constant trips away were now a necessity as Kylie Minogue's singing career was threatening to overtake her acting. Ironically, when Scott and Mike tried to break into music in *Neighbours*, 'old rocker' Monk McCallum told the boys to stick to writing songs for their charismatic back-up singer Charlene, whom he thought showed true talent.

Then the same thing happened in real life. When the cast of *Neighbours* were asked by actress Paula Duncan to sing at a Fitzroy foot-ball club variety night, it was Kylie who shone with her cover version of 'Locomotion'. That led to Mushroom Records releasing the track two weeks after Scott and Charlene's record-breaking wedding. Publicist Brian Walsh advised Kylie against recording because it would split her focus between acting and music. Fortunately, Kylie ignored him and the record was number one for seven weeks and went on to become the high-est selling single of 1987 in Australia.

Kylie flew to the UK to record her next track with Stock, Aitken and Waterman, the team responsible for best-selling singles from Bananarama, Rick Astley, Dead or Alive and Divine. They had no idea who Kylie was, and only wrote 'I Should Be So Lucky' when told she was waiting in reception. Kylie nailed the track in one take and flew back to Australia. The song was another smash, topping charts in Australia, the UK and most of Europe, eventually selling an amazing 1.7 million copies worldwide.

In March 1988, Kylie won an unprecedented four Logies, including the Gold Logie for Australia's Most Popular Television Personality. Yet within weeks, the press was speculating that Kylie would soon have to

Paperback books.

decide between TV and singing. By June, *Neighbours* fans were devastated to learn she had filmed her final episode. When it aired a few weeks later, Charlene was last seen driving north to Brisbane where a new house awaited her and Scott, courtesy of her grandfather. Kylie teased that she was only taking 'a break' while rumours swirled that a rival Australian television network was wooing her with a $2 million contract to switch channels. Hollywood was also supposedly calling, but by now journalists would write anything to get Kylie on the cover of their magazines.

Back in Ramsay Street, Scott had promised to follow his wife to Brisbane, but only if he could get a job in journalism like the one he had in Erinsborough. Grundy's were desperate to keep at least one half of their super couple around and offered Jason Donovan an 'unusual contract' to stay. The UK press, of course, tried to suggest that Donovan had 'demanded a $7,000 a week salary or he would leave'. He didn't leave, even though his own musical career had started to fire.

Jason had actually been offered a recording contract by Mushroom Records before Kylie, but having turned them down once, he wasn't about to say no again. He also headed to London to record with Stock, Aitken and Waterman. They palmed off a track that Rick Astley had rejected, 'Nothing Can Divide Us', and it instantly went Top Five in the UK and Australia. The second single, 'Too Many Broken Hearts', overtook Madonna on its march to the top slot and then sold a million copies worldwide, even in countries that didn't screen *Neighbours*.

While Kylie flew to the UK leaving Jason behind in *Neighbours*, the press desperately tried to keep track of their relationship. *TV Week* reported that Donovan was 'polite and patient, but he does give the impression that he has fielded the question about his relationship with Kylie Minogue almost once too often. "She can still be my friend without being my lover. No offence to Kylie, but if I was to come home and see her every night and be with her 24 hours a day, I couldn't cope for very long".'

'We went on holiday together because my mates didn't have any time off, but Kylie had the same schedule as me,' he continued, referring to the Bali trip the two had taken one Christmas. Kylie and Jason, both topless, had innocently posed for a tourist on the beach, but when the photographers figured out who the couple was, Kylie's boobs quickly found their way onto the front pages of tabloids all over the world.

While Kylie and Jason continued to dominate the pop charts with hit after hit, the Australian music industry turned their backs on them. Radio refused point blank to play their songs even though they were the best-selling records in the land. Soap stars, apparently, weren't allowed to also have successful music careers, especially if they hadn't done the hard slog in pubs and clubs across the country like all good rock'n'rollers.

Only in Ramsay Street, where all social issues of the day were conveniently shunned, was the soap singer debate not a topic of conversation. Over at number 32, Jane reunited Mrs Mangel with her estranged son Joe (Mark Little), who arrived back just in time to walk his meddlesome mother down the aisle. Divorcee Nell wed bowling colleague John Worthington (Brian James) after being driven to the church with her insanely popular pooch Bouncer. By the end of 1988, Joe's son Toby Mangel (Finn Greentree-Keane) had moved in with dad.

Come 1989, Harold reunited with his estranged (was there any other kind?) daughter Kerry (Linda Hartley) who now had a daughter of her own called Sky (Miranda Fryer). Kerry, much to Harold's horror, struck up a close friendship with Joe Mangel and ended up marrying him. Gail (Fiona Corke) had IVF treatment and became pregnant with triplets, but her marriage suffered because husband Paul was too obsessed with his business. Before the year was out, Gail had fled to New Zealand.

Dr Beverley Robinson (Lisa Armytage) went off to Perth on a work conference and came back a blonde instead of a brunette (and was now played by Shaunna O'Grady). Husband Jim was already cosying up to another woman, Madeline (Natalie Bate), while son Scott was being hit on by Greek girl Poppy Skouros (Lenita Vangellis). Suddenly Scott came to his senses and took off to Brisbane to live happily ever after with Charlene.

Jason Donovan had lasted another ten months after Kylie's departure, but the lure of a music career had proved too fabulous to ignore. The couple had sold close to a million copies with their Christmas duet 'Especially For You', but they had recorded their parts separately on opposite sides of the world. Still denying they were anything more than just good friends, Jason flew to London the morning after finishing up on *Neighbours*, not realising he and Kylie had already grown apart from each other. Kylie would never publicly admit to her first big love affair, and it was only confirmed by Jason in 1993 when he admitted live on BBC Radio One that he had been in a relationship with Kylie for four years.

Craig McLachlan (Henry) and Stefan Dennis (Paul) were keen to repeat the musical success of Kylie and Jason and headed for the recording studios. McLachlan reformed his three-piece band Y-Fronts and tried to avoid the soap singer tag with a series of pub gigs. Unfortunately, the stigma of *Neighbours* followed him, and McLachlan revealed to *TV Week* that he could hear a 'chorus of poofter chanting' while he sat backstage in his dressing room. Undaunted, the band changed their name to Check 1-2 and enjoyed some success with a single, 'Mona', and an album which managed to get into the UK Top 10. Stefan Dennis was less fortunate, releasing a dire disco track called 'Don't It Make You Feel Good'. It certainly didn't feel good when he only peaked at number 16 in the UK charts, and a second single sank without trace. No album followed and his failure proved that *Neighbours* wasn't a sure-fire recipe to break into music.

Meanwhile in Erinsborough, three-times-wed Betty Bristow (Abigail) tried to steal Harold away from her school buddy Madge, who quickly became a former buddy. Lucy Robinson (now played by Melissa Bell) returned from boarding school and proved to be a handful. Henry

Mike (Guy Pearce) and
Jane (Annie Jones).

became a radio DJ and took off for New Zealand (Craig McLachlan was actually crossing over to rival soap *Home and Away*) while Mike (Guy Pearce) left to look after his mother.

For the show's 1,000th episode, Jane (Annie Jones) and Des (Paul Keane) were celebrating their engagement, but when Jane found out that her grandmother, Mrs Mangel, was ill in England, she flew out to look after her. She later rang to say she wouldn't be coming back, leaving Des desperate again, and the last in a long list of men she had had disastrous love affairs with, including Mike (Guy Pearce), Shane (Peter O'Brien), Scott (Jason Donovan) and Mark Granger (Colin Handley).

In the 1989 finale Madge won the lottery, so when the show returned in 1990, she and Harold travelled to London. It was the first time the show had gone on location to the UK and it included appearances from Rosemary Daniels (Joy Chambers) and Lord Ledgerwood (Derek Nimmo), whom Madge and Harold thought was an eccentric gardener. UK fans loved seeing the soap on home soil, and when Madge returned to Australia, she had traded in her big 80s red hairdo for a stylish blonde bob.

Young Toby Mangel (now played by Ben Geurens) moved back in with his dad Joe (Mark Little). Then Joe's wife Kerry (Linda Hartley) copped a stray bullet while protesting against duck shooting. After she tragically died in his arms, Joe lost custody of Kerry's daughter, Sky, to her real father, Eric Jensen (John Ley), but the nervous dad eventually let Sky stay with Joe.

New Erinsborough High headmistress Dorothy Burke (Maggie Dence) moved into number 30 along with nephews Lochy (Amber Kilpatrick) and Ryan McLachlan (Richard Norton). Next door at number 28, the Willis family arrived, comprised of Doug (Terence Donovan, father of Jason), wife Pam (Sue Jones) and kids Cody (Amelia Frid) and Adam (Ian Williams). And Jim and Beverley Robinson finally called a halt to their endless bickering and divorced.

Paul Robinson hired a new worker called Linda Giles to replace Gail at the Daniels Corporation, but he couldn't figure out why her work ethic fluctuated wildly from day to day. Eventually it came out that Linda Giles was actually twins Christina and Caroline Alessi (Gayle and Gillian Blakeney) who were pretending to be one person as part of an elaborate ruse to hide from a stalker. After he was caught, serious Christina got engaged to Paul while flighty Caroline played Adam Willis and Jim off against each other, eventually settling on Adam.

For the 1990 summer cliffhanger, Glen Donnelly (Richard Huggett) turned up and told a shocked Jim that he was his long-lost son (well at least he wasn't estranged). In 1991, Lucy (Melissa Bell) came back from another boarding school spell and swapped spit with Glen, even after discovering he was her half-brother! Helen (Anne Haddy) wasn't much of an example to her wild granddaughter, marrying her late husband's cousin, Michael (Brian Blain), before discovering he was already married.

After Paul and Christina wed, she gave birth to a baby, Andrew. Then Paul, always a class act, started making goo-goo eyes at twin sister Caroline. Behind the scenes, Gayle and Gillian Blakeney were the next to enter a recording studio, reminding *TV Week* that they had previously been best known as singers from a Brisbane kids' TV show. They 'cringed' when told they were being sent to work with Kylie and Jason's hitmakers, Stock, Aitken and Waterman, but then decided that they were 'the best at what they do. It would have been crazy not to work with them.' And even though they didn't like Mushroom Records demanding they record under the group name of 'The Twins', they were determined to do whatever it took to get themselves a hit.

When their first single 'All Mixed Up' didn't fire, they waited until they left *Neighbours* and tried again in the UK in 1993. After two singles flopped, plans for an album were abandoned. Perhaps they should have teamed up with former on-screen lover Stefan Dennis (Paul) and created a *Neighbours* super group. Then again, Stefan Dennis should never be allowed back into a recording studio.

While the UK and 24 other countries were still eating up all things *Neighbours*, Grundy's couldn't resist seeing if America might learn to love it too. The first 65 episodes were sold to channels KCOP in Los Angeles and WWOR in New York for a 5.30pm weeknight slot. 'It's a strategy that we've come up with because it's summer here and there are more teenagers home at the moment, so we can test the show out,' Grundy's American vice-president of marketing and sales Bob Lloyd told *TV Week*. *Neighbours* might have still been rating in the Top 5 in the UK, but it barely made a ripple in the US and quickly disappeared.

Back in Oz, Joe married Melanie Pearson (Lucinda Cowden), then relocated to England to be near Mrs Mangel.

Doug (Terence Donovan) and Pam (Sue Jones) also jumped on a plane to rescue son Brad (Scott Michaelson) after he was falsely accused of smuggling drugs. Daughter Gaby (Rachel Blakely) rushed home from Japan, and when Brad was brought back to Ramsay Street, the new Willis kids replaced Adam, who moved to Newcastle (hey, at least it wasn't Brisbane) with Gemma Ramsay (Beth Buchanan) and Cody (Amelia Frid) who left to study in America.

Madge (Anne Charleston) and Harold (Ian Smith) decided to drive around Australia but they only got as far as a deserted beach when Harold was swept off the rocks and disappeared. At the time, Ian Smith was reported to be leaving because he was unhappy with the direction of his character. It wouldn't be until 2004 that he would admit to *The Daily Telegraph* that he was sacked. 'Oh yes, I'm not supposed to say that, but I was.'

On the day that Harold's disappearance was filmed, even nature seemed to conspire against his untimely demise. 'We were filming that day at a part of a beach that is usually rough, so rough. But when we went down there to shoot the final scene, it was like a millpond. They had to throw rocks in to get a ripple.'

Natalie Imbruglia.

Devastated at her loss, Madge moved to Brisbane to be with Scott and Charlene. As the show was finishing for the year, Glen (Richard Huggett) fell from the roof of The Waterhole and became a paraplegic. As 1992 dawned, he called off his romance with Gaby and left Ramsay Street with his former girlfriend Karen (Fiona Jarvis). Gaby was left with only her clothes boutique in the Lassiters arcade until it exploded later that year, as boutiques tend to do.

Neighbours had gone through a major overhaul, and there was even a new version of the theme music. The Tony Hatch song was re-recorded with Greg Hind. Script producer Barbara Angell told *Neighbours: The Perfect Blend* website that the show took on a darker, more adult tone during 1992. 'We were deliberately appealing to a much wider audience. We were conscious that the show was being seen all over the world in all languages, and we tried to convey Australian suburbia as interesting and diverse.' In other words, *Neighbours* was languishing in the ratings in Australia, its glory days well and truly behind it.

New characters included Caroline and Christina's cousins Rick (Dan Falzon) and Marco Alessi (Felice Arena), and their parents Benito (George Spartels) and Cathy (Elspeth Ballantyne), who moved into number 22. Within a year, the entire Alessi family had disappeared, leaving only Rick behind.

Neighbours' hot new love triangle involved Beth Brennan (Natalie Imbruglia), Lucy (Melissa Bell) and Brad (Scott Michaelson) until Lucy dumped Brad to run away and become a model. After a siege in which Brad was shot, Beth admitted her love for him and put behind her the abuse she had suffered at the hands of her stepfather. Christina (Gayle Blakeney) found out about Paul's affair with her sister as Caroline (Gillian Blakeney) fled to Milan. After forgiving her sister, Caroline left with Paul to live in Hawaii, before fleeing to Rio to avoid a fraud charge.

Phoebe Bright (Simone Robertson) fell pregnant to Todd (Kristian Schmid) but decided to have an abortion. While rushing to stop her, Todd was hit by a car and killed. Phoebe decided to keep the baby after the ghost of Todd returned to say he would always look after his little girl. Later, while visiting Todd's grave, Phoebe met Stephen Gottlieb (Lochie Daddo) who had also just lost the love of his life, so (naturally) the two started dating.

Todd's funeral brought back the eldest Robinson girl to Ramsay Street. Julie (now played by Julie Mullins) had married Phillip Martin (now played by Ian Rawlings) but she was no less annoying than when she had been single. While stepdaughter Hannah (Rebecca Ritters) was cool about having a new mother, stepson Michael (Troy Beckwith) wasn't and he embarked on a terror campaign to send Julie crazy. For the Christmas cliffhanger, his evil plans went awry when Hannah and Beth ended up trapped in a burning cottage.

Naturally, they were rescued just in time during the first episode of 1993, but Michael continued to make everyone think Julie was going mad. After drugging her so she nearly drowned in a spa and then spiking her drinks at Phoebe and Stephen's wedding, Michael was caught out and shipped off to a youth detention centre. Since one dog had been put away, it was also decided to retire Bouncer the Labrador, the wonder dog who could answer a phone and bark if there was an emergency. Bouncer left just in the nick of time too, for the beloved dog really did die from cancer just a few weeks later.

Brad (Scott Michaelson).

Luckily, there were still a few dirty dogs left in Ramsay Street. Brad (Scott Michaelson) started sleeping with Lou's daughter, Lauren Carpenter (Sarah Vandenbergh), even though he had become engaged to Beth (Natalie Imbruglia). Lou (Tom Oliver) was going through a mid-life crisis and had started dating Annalise Hartman (Kimberley Davies), who was more than 30 years his junior, while Jim (Alan Dale) started dating Annalise's mother Fiona (Suzanne Dudley).

While *Neighbours* was still garnering impressive figures in the UK, its ratings in Australia continued to be a real worry. According to producer Forrest Redlich, Ten was even thinking of cancelling it and stripping his *E Street* in *Neighbours*' former timeslot. Redlich refused to move his show to Melbourne, giving Ramsay Street a stay of execution.

Tom Oliver spoke out to *TV Week* and insisted 'the future of the show is brilliant. *Neighbours* keeps plodding along with what it's always done.' It was an unfortunate choice of words, since many Australian viewers had tired of all the plodding, but Oliver was quick to offer a suggestion on how to improve the ratings. 'People would love to get back to what the title is all about – look over your fence, get to know all your neighbours.'

Ignoring Oliver's advice, *Neighbours* introduced an Asian family from Hong Kong, the Lims, and when Julie (Julie Mullins) looked over her fence, she didn't want to know them. Instead, she abused them, claiming they had – wait for it – eaten a neighbourhood dog! After that stunning piece of racism, there wasn't really anywhere left to go for Raymond Lim (T.S. Kong), Jenny Lim (Diane Baker-Coleclough) and their three kids. Even though it wasn't her fault, actress Julie Mullins was abused and threatened in the street by Asian viewers, and by the time her character had seen the errors of her ways and made friends with the new neigh-bours, the Lims were dispatched after their 'six week guest stint' to go horrify some other redneck Australian suburb. Ramsay Street went back to being a strictly Caucasian enclave.

Without a foreign family to harass, Julie concentrated on berating her father over his ongoing affair with Fiona. After Jim (Alan Dale) gave his new girlfriend a pair of earrings that used to belong to his first wife, even

Daniel McPherson on
the UK panto circuit.

Helen (Anne Haddy) turned on him, and moved out to live with Julie. Left all alone in number 26, Jim had a heart attack. Money-hungry Fiona found him collapsed on the floor but left him there to die. After an off-screen funeral, Helen moved back into the Robinson home and found a letter from her dead daughter Anne revealing that Julie wasn't Jim's daughter, but the product of a rape. Julie went in search of her real father only to end up nearly getting raped by his son.

In the hope that even more melodrama might lift the ratings, another explosion rocked *Neighbours*. This time The Waterhole blew up, leaving Stephen (Lochie Daddo) an amnesiac in a wheelchair. His estranged brother Mark Gottlieb (Bruce Samazan) arrived, and by the 2,000th episode Stephen was taking his first steps again at the re-opening of the pub. Stephen and Phoebe moved to the neighbouring suburb of Anson's Corner while Mark stuck around to work as a chef at Lassiters.

Also new to Ramsay Street was Cheryl Stark (Caroline Gillmer) who moved in with her son Brett (Brett Blewitt) and daughter Danni (Eliza Szonert). Cody Willis was also back (now played by Peta Brady), returning just in time for Brad and Beth's wedding. The couple, who had already cancelled one wedding due to Brad's cheating ways, married in a registry office and tried to sneak away to Perth without any fanfare. Brad's mother Pam (Sue Jones) chased the bus down and insisted they repeat their vows back in Ramsay Street in front of family and friends.

With that, Scott Michaelson and Natalie Imbruglia left the series. Michaelson would continue to be associated with the soap for many years afterwards, managing the careers of future *Neighbours* starlets Kimberley Davies, Nicola Charles, Krista Vendy and his most controversial client, Holly Valance. Imbruglia went straight to London to star in the pantomime *Snow White* and then disappeared, re-emerging in 1997 with a massively successful debut single 'Torn'. Even more unusual for a *Neighbours* singer, her first album, *Left of the Middle*, was critically acclaimed and became a big seller all over the world, including America. 'She had refused to do *Home and Away* after *Neighbours*,' reveals casting director Jan Russ. 'Natalie was a very intelligent girl who realised she had to re-invent herself. She had no pretence about herself at all.'

Actors from *Neighbours* (and *Home and Away*) could earn up to $20,000 a week on the UK panto circuit, which was quite a profitable way to spend Christmas breaks from their shows. Anne Charleston (Madge) probably appeared in the most pantos and made quite a career for herself playing villains such as the Wicked Queen from *Snow White and the Seven Dwarfs*, which she played on more than one occasion. Kym Valentine (Libby Kennedy) told *TV Week* that *Neighbours*' producers were happy to 're-work the schedules if anyone needed to get to the UK early', but Actors Equity in the UK campaigned heavily in an attempt to stop Aussies stealing acting gigs from locals.

As *Neighbours* finished up for 1993, newly licensed pilot Gaby (Rachel Blakely) was crashing a plane with Annalise (Kimberley Davies) as her frightened passenger. Returning for its 1994 season, nobody was surprised to learn that both girls were unharmed. The Ten network had already promised *TV Week* that their struggling soap would have a 'younger, livelier look with six regular characters under the age of 18'. New to the show was Mark's hippie sister Serendipity Gottlieb (Raelee Hill) and Stonefish Rebecchi (Anthony Engelman).

As for Julie (Julie Mullins), she became more and more unhinged as the year went on, and her marriage to Phillip crumbled. After a murder mystery party, she fell off a tower roof and was found dead the next morning. Given her incessant whining, it was almost a relief to viewers. It was also time for the Willis family to disappear, clearing the way for the Kennedys – Dr Karl (Alan Fletcher), teacher wife Susan (Jackie Woodburne), daughter Libby (Kym Valentine) and sons Malcolm, aka Mal (Benjie McNair) and Billy (Jesse Spencer).

Lou (Tom Oliver) and Cheryl (Caroline Gillmer) had an on-off relationship that culminated with Cheryl having a baby, Louise, better known as Lolly. Cheryl discovered the woman living across the street from her, Marlene Kratz (Moya O'Sullivan), was actually her mother. Next, she wondered if Lou was having an affair when she spied him kissing a young Asian woman. Ling Mai Chan (Khym Lam) turned out to be Lou's daughter from an affair many years ago in Hong Kong. And yes, because she was Asian, Ling Mai quickly left never to be seen again.

Meanwhile, Lou's former girlfriend Annalise (Kimberley Davies) was getting married in an end-of-year cliffhanger, only to be jilted at the altar by Mark (Bruce Samazan) because he suddenly decided he wanted to be a priest. In 1995, Mark became the street's resident Christian and began lecturing everybody about their loose morals. He tried to save Lucy Robinson (Melissa Bell) when he discovered her working as a go-go dancer, her dreams of becoming a famous model long shattered (not to mention a hint of alcohol and drug abuse on her part). Mark's sermonising caused Lucy to run away (again) and she ended up in New York with Rosemary (Joy Chambers). By the time Mark fell off a roof and slipped into a coma, most residents were relieved he couldn't lecture them any more. When he eventually recovered, he went off to become a famous television chef instead.

Everyone's favourite grandma, Helen Daniels (Anne Haddy), still didn't have much to do in the show except paint, so she found herself in the company of the distinguished Reuben (James Condon in his second role in the show). He was perfect except for one small problem – a terminal illness. He died just days after marrying Helen, and she never seemed to notice that he was the spitting image of Douglas Blake, the con man who had ripped her off during the first year of the show. Given the continuing dramas since then, it's no wonder Helen had gone a bit senile.

Ratings were still iffy in Australia, even though the show was celebrating its 10th anniversary with a two-hour prime time special. Ten used the opportunity to begin a new advertising campaign – 'Get Back to Ramsay Street'. Front and centre of the campaign was sex symbol Kimberley

Over in the UK, magazines were getting fed up with what they described as the 'greedy Aussie soap syndrome'.

Billy (Jesse Spencer).

Davies (Annalise) who was practically turning into her own industry off-screen with provocative magazine spreads and a line of lingerie (all managed by Scott Michaelson).

When Annalise discovered her real dad was a female impersonator named Tarquin Hartman (Michael Carman), she got herself a blonde-bombshell-in-training kid sister, Jo (Emma Harrison). By year's end, she was having a secret affair with Stonefish (Anthony Engelman) even though she was also dating Sam Kratz (Richard Grieve). Stonie's mullet-haired brother Jarrod, aka Toadfish or Toadie (Ryan Moloney) and mother Angie Rebecchi (Lesley Baker) were now living in Ramsay Street, and the year finished with Angie catching Annalise and Stonie in bed together.

When the show came back in 1996, the scandal came to a swift conclusion as Kimberley Davies had quit the show. Annalise fled Ramsay Street as a scarlet woman, never to return. Nervous *Neighbours*' producers then had to cope with Caroline Gillmer getting sick and having to be temporarily replaced in the role of Cheryl by *Prisoner*'s Colette Mann. Writer and broadcaster Clive James dropped by to cameo as a postman, and Lassiters was rocked by another explosion when the doctor's surgery became the latest place to be blown sky high.

Sam got over his break-up with Annalise by posing nude for an advertisement. He started dating Cody Willis (Peta Brady) until she was shot during a drugs raid, later dying in hospital of a heart attack. Helen suffered a stroke while Phillip (Ian Rawlings) began writing romance novels under the pseudonym of Philippa Martinez. And Billy (Jesse Spencer) fell for Anne Wilkinson (Brooke Satchwell), the teenage daughter of Helen's physiotherapist Ruth (Ailsa Piper).

Cheryl was kidnapped in Colombia while trying to get son Brett (Brett Blewitt) off (another) trumped-up drugs charge. On her return, she had a nasty split-up with Lou just before being run over by a car outside her house. Dr Karl Kennedy (Alan Fletcher) injected her with morphine, unaware it would react with prescription drugs she was taking. Cheryl died in hospital while son Darren Stark (Todd MacDonald), just released from (another) youth detention centre, blamed the doctor for his mother's death.

Over in the UK, magazines were getting fed up with what they described as the 'greedy Aussie soap syndrome'. Despite *Neighbours*' enduring popularity, they wrote to the Aussie actors' managers asking for a stop to increasing demands for money. *The Daily Mirror* had just refused to pay $60,000 to a top soap star for a three-hour fashion shoot, while *TV Quick* magazine was outraged by Kimberley Davies' asking price of $12,000 for a photo shoot. 'They wouldn't budge on the price,' *TV Quick* editor Lori Miles told *TV Week*. 'It was, "Take it or leave it". They wanted half up-front and the rest at the photo session.'

While the UK press tried to pull *Neighbours*' stars into line, back in Australia the show was plotting a storyline that would have been unheard of in the early days. An amnesiac Harold (Ian Bishop) was found alive and well in a Salvation Army shop working under the name of Ted. He had no memory about being washed off the rocks five years earlier, so Madge (Anne Charleston) left Scott and Charlene (and her grandson) behind in Brisbane to reunite with her husband.

Actor Ian Smith told *Inside TV* that he thought the storyline 'stretches credibility a little, but it doesn't stretch it to breaking point. Harold was just picked up by a ship. It wasn't a Harold Holt type of situation,' he said, referring to the Australian Prime Minister who went missing while swimming in 1967. Smith insisted he was only returning to the show because he 'never got the chance to say goodbye properly the last time because my departure was a bit rushed. I've signed on for 15 weeks so I'll be able to say goodbye to the silly old bugger – only this time I'll do it properly.' Famous last words.

TV's greatest ever mullet – 'Toadie' (Ryan Moloney).

The truth was, and still is, that young actors come and go, but it's the older characters that become the most enduring and therefore vital to the show's continued success. 'The most popular characters in recent years have been Madge, Harold and Lou,' said casting director Jan Russ. 'The young viewers really want them as their own grandparents.'

Once again, *Neighbours* finished the year with a regular character suffering an injury while working at the pub. This time it was Mal (Benjie McNair) and, as the show broke for the summer, Dr Karl needed to perform an emergency tracheotomy or watch his son die. Karl, who had given up medicine after the Cheryl/morphine incident, quickly got over his fears and saved Mal.

Back for 1997, Madge and Harold remarried and Phillip fought his attraction to Ruth by convincing himself that he was allergic to her, just as she discovered that newcomer Ben Atkins (Brett Cousins) was the son she once gave up for adoption. As for Ramsay Street's last remaining original resident, it was time for a sad farewell.

Actress Anne Haddy (Helen Daniels) had often struggled with the never-ending grind of soap production, and having had two rounds of open heart surgery, was more than due for retirement from the industry. So Helen invited neighbours Harold and Madge around to watch a video of Scott and Charlene's wedding. After re-watching *Neighbours*' most famous moment, Helen obviously realised the good old days were never coming back, so she slipped off to sleep and never woke up.

Once upon a time, love Ramsay-Street-style led to splashy weddings (before the newlyweds were dispatched to Brisbane). By the time of the 1997 cliffhanger, however, the street had become the home of adultery and high-speed car chases. Married Dr Karl stole a kiss with his spunky receptionist Sarah Beaumont (Nicola Charles) while Anne (Brooke Satchwell) caught boyfriend Billy (Jesse Spencer) in a passionate embrace with Caitlin (Emily Milburn). Phillip proposed to Ruth only moments before her son Ben flipped his Holden racing car which burst into flames. The crash left Ben – where else? – in a coma for Christmas.

The good news for *Neighbours* was that it was finally enjoying a ratings resurgence in Australia, and they rose even further in 1998 with the addition of two new spunks, Drew Kirk (Dan Paris) and Joel Samuels (Daniel McPherson). Country boy mechanic Drew came to work at Lou's garage and fell hard for Libby (Kym Valentine), while triathlete Joel moved in with the Kennedys and trained a lot (while wearing not very much).

Sarah struggled to stay away from Dr Karl by resigning from the surgery and running off to a caravan park down the coast. While wife Susan (Jackie Woodburne) was working late at school, Karl drove down and convinced Sarah to return to Erinsborough. On the way back, his car conveniently broke down, forcing the couple to stay overnight in a motel. When they arrived back late for Phillip and Ruth Martin's wedding, Susan finally twigged and threw Karl out of the house, even though he swore he had only kissed Sarah. Sarah kept her distance, qualified as a nurse and eventually married Dr Peter Hannay (Nick Carrafa in his second role in *Neighbours*, having originally played Tony Romeo in the early years). She stole one final kiss from Karl (inside the church, no less) and left the series.

By the end of year, Karl redeemed himself when he was once again called on in an emergency situation – yes, it was another Christmas cliffhanger. This one had Anne driving off in a rainstorm after a fight with Billy and her car ending up in a river. Joel arrived to help push the car clear, but it rolled further into the lake, trapping him in the rising water as Dr Karl frantically tried to figure out how to keep him alive.

In 1999, Joel was – believe it or not – saved in the nick of time (must have been all that triathlete breathing practice). Now happily married, Phillip, Ruth and the rest of the Martins were sent packing and a new family quickly replaced them, the Scullys. Joe (Shane Connor) was a builder and wife Lyn (Janet Andrewartha) was a hairdresser. Daughter Stephanie (Carla Bonner) was a tomboy while sister Felicity, aka Flick (Holly Valance) was a glamourpuss.

Youngest Scully child Michelle (Kate Keltie) was a spoilt brat whose irresponsibility caused the 1999 cliffhanger. Michelle was supposed to be babysitting Lolly (Jiordan Anna Tolli) but left her alone in the house to pop in on the end-of-millennium street party outside. As the new century dawned for Ramsay Street, Lolly's playing with matches set the Scully house alight and Drew, who had just proposed to Libby, had to rush in and save her.

The year 2000 also saw a new English teacher at Erinsborough High, Tess Bell (Krista Vendy), who was on the run from an abusive husband, Brendan (Blair Venn). When he died after a motorbike accident, she started falling for Susan's nephew Dr Darcy Tyler (Mark Raffety). Problem was, Dr Darcy was mixing work with pleasure and also seeing nurse Dione Bliss, aka Dee (Madeleine West). When Dee spied the pair kissing, she waited until all of Ramsay Street was celebrating Dr Darcy's partnership with Dr Karl before she exposed the cad and poured champagne over his head.

In 2001, soccer player Jack (Paul Pantano), the eldest Scully boy who had been talked about but never seen, finally arrived in Erinsborough from the UK. Jack insisted he was through with soccer, but after a few days of working for dad on his building site, Jack decided Barnsford Football Club wasn't so bad after all. Meanwhile, Tess got cold feet about marrying Darcy, especially when she found out he was planning to take over Dr Karl's surgery and turn it into a 'superclinic'. She put off the wedding, made up with Dee and headed for Sydney.

For every wedding that was cancelled, *Neighbours* always had another one up its sleeve. The wedding of Drew (Dan Paris) and Libby (Kym Valentine) was a joyous occasion until Madge (Anne Charleston) discovered she had pancreatic cancer. She developed septicaemia and went downhill quickly, dying at home in Ramsay Street with Harold and her new 'children' – almost foster child Paul (Jansen Spencer) and his best friend Tad Reeves (Jonathon Dutton).

Missing from her deathwatch were real children Charlene and Henry and 'fans were very upset that no other family members returned for Madge's death,' says casting director Jan Russ. Rumours abounded that Kylie Minogue had offered to do a cameo while in Australia in 1998 for her 'Live and Intimate' tour, but – according to local legend – *Neighbours* never got back to her in time.

Madge (Anne Charleston) dies with Harold (Ian Smith) by her side, although her two children (Kylie Minogue and Craig McLachlan) were apparently too busy to attend.

Harold didn't cope too well in the aftermath of Madge's death and threatened to sell up and move away. Paul, Tad and Lou threw a surprise barbecue to show how much he was loved and Harold decided to stick around. Paul, however, got an offer to play for an AFL team, the Adelaide Crows, so he left Ramsay Street. Meanwhile, Lou was heartbroken when he lost custody of Lolly to her real father, in a storyline that twisted previously established continuity.

Supposedly, Cheryl had been having a secret affair behind Lou's back that had never been revealed to the audience. When John Allen (Adrian Mulraney) was proved to be Lolly's real father, a custody battle ensued and Lolly went off to her new father's home. No doubt, she will return when she has sprouted boobs and is ready to cause some trouble.

As the show neared the end of 2001, the action shifted to the Oakey rodeo where an old mate of Drew's was about to be introduced to the show. Earlier in 2000, *Neighbours* had been the lead-in for the first series of Australia's *Big Brother*. While Grundy's was heard to say they wouldn't be interested in hiring any of the new 'reality stars', they did an about-face by signing runner-up Blair McDonough to play country boy Stuart Parker. Ironically, Blair and eventual winner Ben Williams had been shown on *Big Brother* talking about how hot they thought Flick (Holly Valance) was on *Neighbours*. Blair would soon find out for himself how hot Flick was.

Flick (Holly Valance) and Joel (Daniel McPherson).

With the show about to break for Christmas, a pregnant Libby went into labour in a stable (or should that be a manger?). Miles from the nearest hospital, Libby had a difficult birth, and by the time they got her to a medical centre she had flat-lined on the table. Fortunately, she was revived in 2002 and named her new baby boy Ben. Unfortunately, husband Drew was killed a few months later after being thrown off his horse.

Steph (Carla Bonner) fell in love with Lassiters' new assistant manager, Marc Lambert (David Karakai) and was engaged to him within a matter of weeks. She failed to notice that Marc also had feelings for her sister Flick. At their wedding, Marc became tongue-tied halfway through his vows and finally blurted out that he couldn't marry her. When Flick was unmasked as the other woman, she was disowned by her family and fled to Sydney.

Meanwhile, Stuart had also fallen for Flick, so both he and Marc charged up to Sydney to claim her for themselves. Flick chose to go back with Marc so Stuart joined the army, but when the continued disapproval of her family finally caused her to crack, Flick called it quits with Marc and re-considered Stuart, who was so thrilled he quit the army.

Lou and Harold were also fighting over a woman again, this time Reverend Rosie Hoyland (Maggie Millar). Forced to choose, Rosie picked Lou, while Harold's confidence was shaken when Lyn's aunt (or was she?) Valda Sheergold (Joan Sydney) mistakenly believed Harold was gay.

Ramsay Street soon got to know Rosie's grandchildren Summer (Marisa Siketa) and Boyd Hoyland (Kyal Marsh). They were joined by their father Max (Stephen Lovatt), who arrived home from working on an oil rig. Max moved into number 32 and found himself falling for Steph. While she considered a new relationship, she still couldn't bring herself to forgive Flick, so Flick flicked off on an American holiday (in fact, actress Holly Valance went off to record her first single, 'Kiss Kiss').

Irish backpacker Connor O'Neill (Patrick Harvey) moved in with the Scullys but didn't let on he was illiterate. Jack Scully returned (now played by Jay Bunyan), and when his girlfriend Lori Lee (Michelle Ang) arrived a week later, the truth about Jack's soccer career came out. Having been dropped from his UK club, he had been hiding out in New Zealand with Lori's family. Jack wasn't too overjoyed that Lori had followed him back to Australia, and began to think about replacing his Kiwi girlfriend with Nina Tucker (Delta Goodrem).

Nina was a painfully shy schoolgirl who wrote songs and Connor entered one of them into a talent contest at UniFM. Nina won first prize and also a consolation prize in her first boyfriend, fellow student Taj Coppin (Jaime-Robbie Reyne, son of James), before realising she was also in love with Jack. Meanwhile, Flick got engaged to Stuart just before taking off on the world's longest modelling assignment (as Holly Valance took off on her post-*Neighbours* singing career, firing manager Scott Michaelson in the process).

While the show was again losing one of its most popular stars to a music career, it was already developing its first in-house singer, Delta

Goodrem. Already signed to Sony Music before joining the show, Delta's first single, 'Born to Try', was incorporated into *Neighbours* and became the number one single in Australia within weeks. Avoiding the bubblegum pop sound favoured by other cast members, Delta's original ballads were an unexpected success.

Back in Ramsay Street, Susan (Jackie Woodburne) slipped on the kitchen floor, banged her head and got amnesia, which wiped 30 years of memories. She couldn't remember Karl (Alan Fletcher) or any of her children and, even more disturbing, thought she was still a teenager. It took her months to warm to Karl, but it was all ruined when she had a recollection of slapping him during the Sarah affair of 1998. Concerned her 'family' might be hiding more incidents from her, she decided to divorce her husband.

By the end of the year, though, Susan had fallen in love with Karl again and the couple renewed their wedding vows during the final episode for 2002. While reciting her vows, she found herself remembering the first time she had married him, and was instantly cured of her amnesia. The episode ended with Joe (Shane Connor) discovering a pregnancy test kit in his garbage. He feared he had a pregnant daughter until wife Lyn (Janet Andrewartha) owned up and admitted it was she who would be having the baby.

In 2003, Dee (Madeleine West) and Toadie (Ryan Moloney) had fallen for each other, but were unaware that Dr Darcy (Mark Raffety) was using every nasty trick he could think of to break them up and snatch Dee for himself. He was also gambling and, after racking up $70,000 in debts, he broke into the Kennedys' house to steal an antique ring. As he tried to make his getaway, he slammed into the pregnant Lyn who fell down the back stairs. Darcy then proceeded to the hospital, signed on for work and treated Lyn's injuries when she was wheeled in.

Darcy was relieved when Lyn couldn't remember who her attacker was, and thrilled when Dee told him she wanted to give their relationship another go. However, after she discovered the stolen ring in Darcy's apartment, Dee dobbed him in to the police and the evil doctor was carted off to jail. Dee reunited with Toadie and they got engaged.

Dee was thrilled to be married in the grounds of a historic estate. As the couple drove away from the reception, Toadie surprised her with honeymoon tickets to the Maldives, but as Dee threw her arms around him for a kiss, Toadie drove over a cliff into the ocean. Despite looking like he wouldn't be able to swim one length of a 25-metre pool, Toadie somehow made it back to shore while athletic Dee was never found and presumed drowned (although it's still possible she was picked up by that same fishing boat that once saved Harold, particularly if Madeleine West's planned singing career sinks as fast as Toadie's car).

Lyn had another shock waiting for her when she discovered that Aunt Valda (Joan Sydney) was really her mother. After initially pushing her away, Lyn bonded with Valda, but she had more trouble bonding with her new baby boy, Oscar, while suffering postnatal depression.

Shy schoolgirl
singer Nina Tucker
(Delta Goodrem).

Meanwhile, the *Neighbours* love quadrangle was hotting up. Taj (Jaime-Robbie Reyne) and Lori (Michelle Ang) had no idea their partners had fallen in love with each other, and Lori was so clueless she even wrote a play full of kissing scenes for Nina and Jack. Just before Jack could tell Lori that he wanted to break up, she slipped on wet pool tiles and woke up in hospital unable to feel her legs. Guilt-ridden, Jack stayed by her wheelchair until the truth eventually came out about who he really fancied.

As soon as Lori got the use of her legs back, she had a one-night stand with Connor and fell pregnant. She asked Connor to take her to a clinic for an abortion but, once inside, Lori realised she couldn't go through with it. Letting Connor think she had gotten rid of the baby, Lori returned to New Zealand to have it.

By now, Delta Goodrem was an absolute superstar. Her first three singles and debut album had rocketed to number one in Australia and number two in the UK. She won the Logie for Best New Talent and was planning an assault on the American charts. Still contracted to *Neighbours* for another year, the soap was happy to work around her busy schedule. It appeared that the 18-year-old had the world at her feet until a bombshell was dropped in July. Diagnosed with Hodgkin's disease, she was written out of *Neighbours* to undergo immediate treatment.

Nina had been facing some competition from new blonde troublemaker Izzy Hoyland (Natalie Bassingthwaighte), the sister of Max. To keep her man, she slept with Jack, but then realised she might have feelings for Connor. Just after her mother Trixie (singer Wendy Stapleton) dropped in for a visit, Nina's disappearing act took effect. Trixie was left to tell her daughter (over the phone) that she was illegitimate. Ridiculous, I know, but Nina needed to be traumatised enough to run away. That left one last unseen Nina phone call in which she apparently said she was off to Bombay with her father for an Indian summer. Next stop, Bollywood.

In September 2003, real life once again threatened to become more titillating than any *Neighbours* storyline. Scott Michaelson was suing former client Holly Valance for $400,000 for dismissing him as her manager. Valance had flicked Michaelson by fax on the brink of releasing her smash hit single 'Kiss Kiss', with 15 months of their management agreement still to go.

Scott Michaelson told the Supreme Court that he had discovered Holly Vukadinovic when she was a 15-year-old model, helped choose her stage name of Valance (after a bed sheet) and secured her a role in *Neighbours*. Former cast mate Kym Valentine testified on behalf of Scott

Michaelson, causing Holly Valance to later shoot back in the courtroom, 'I can precisely remember not having that conversation [with her].' It was Erinsborough High all over again!

Holly Valance complained that Michaelson had marketed her in a 'titillating' and 'salacious' way, and she was 'sick of only being given *FHM* shoots' to do. Apparently, she had failed to notice that Michaelson had successfully managed several previous *Neighbours'* starlets in exactly the same way. And if she didn't want to be 'titillating' or 'salacious', why had she danced naked around a few beams of light for her first video clip?

Justice Clifford Einstein ruled in favour of Scott Michaelson. Holly Valance had, according to the judge, shown a 'calculated disregard' for Michaelson's rights as her manager. Valance and her mother were found to be 'unreliable witnesses' and the judge felt there was not a 'shred of substance' to their allegations of misconduct.

Holly was 'disappointed at the outcome. However, I want to put this behind me and get on with making my music.' A few weeks later, she unveiled her second album. In the video for the first single, 'State of Mind', she writhed around a filthy nightclub floor, peeled off her sweat-drenched Ramones T shirt and then appeared to be 'pleasuring' herself in a revolving bed overlooking LA. The single and album flopped in both the UK and Australia (where it sold just a measly 3,000 copies).

Kym Valentine admitted in *Who* magazine the following year that she 'didn't volunteer to be put into that situation and it broke my heart. Holly is my friend, but I had no choice. I had [an] obligation to tell the truth.' When asked if Valance understood that, Valentine paused before answering, 'No.'

Neighbours' next courtroom episode would feature Shane Connor (Joe Scully), who had been sacked after four years and escorted off the set. In 2004, he sued Grundy Television for $209,514 in lost wages ($210,000 would have just been silly). Joe Scully also remained lost, off-screen visiting some (apparently very) sick relatives a long, long way from Ramsay Street. He was replaced by Lyn's mum Valda (Joan Sydney) and forgotten about.

He wasn't missed because characters from the past were coming back to revitalise the show. New producer Ric Pellizerri was dipping back into *Neighbours'* rich history with the return of some of Harold's missing family. Sky Mangel (Stephanie McIntosh, half-sister of Jason Donovan) moved in with her grandfather while Harold's son David Bishop (Kevin Harrington) moved in across the street with wife Lilijana (Marcella Russo) and teenage daughter Serena (Lara Sacher).

Steph and Max's relationship was put to the test when she was diagnosed with breast cancer and bad head scarves while Connor fell for Carmella (Natalie Blair), the daughter of shady underworld figure Rocco Carmeniti (Robert Forza). Widowed teacher Libby fled her school after a disastrous affair with student Taj (Jaime-Robbie Reyne) so actress Kym Valentine could take time out to have a baby. Dad Karl began secretly drinking and flirting with sexy Izzy.

Who is Neighbours'
most famous graduate
– Kylie Minogue or
Delta Goodrem?

Neighbours' final episode for 2003 was full of Christmas cliffhangers and a fitting end to a very controversial year. Susan walked out on Dr Karl. Trixie and Lou married at Melbourne's Her Majesty's Theatre, despite an objection from Lou's old flame Valda (Joan Sydney). Outside, Harold (Ian Smith) slumped to the ground after suffering a stroke.

When the show returned in 2004, Harold woke up from his coma a changed man. Formerly a vegetarian teetotaller, cranky Harold became a meat-eating drinker who started pinching girls' bottoms in the coffee shop. Lou poured all his money into an Asian theatrical tour of *Hello Dolly* for Trixie, which failed along with his marriage. Connor jumped from mafia princess Carmella back to long-time love Michelle Scully (Kate Keltie) until Lori (Michelle Ang) returned with Maddy, the baby girl he didn't know had been born.

Meanwhile, Sky (Stephanie McIntosh) had it out with the duck-shooter who had killed her mother years before, and Toadie got over the death of Dee by reuniting with former girlfriend Sindi (Marisa Warrington), who filmed a reality series with the Scullys and was also the mistress of Mafia gangster Rocco (Robert Forza). And loopy Gus (Ben Barrack) began stalking Max (Stephen Lovatt) and sleeping with Izzy (Natalie Bassingthwaighte) while she made goo-goo eyes at Dr Karl (Alan Fletcher).

To celebrate the ten-year anniversary of the Kennedy family, the family was put front and centre for the 4,500th episode in June 2004. Izzy lied to Karl, telling him he was the father of the baby she was expecting by Gus. Libby (Kym Valentine) returned to be suitably shocked about her dad's new 'family', but an even bigger shock was in store from her mother. Deserted wife Susan (Jackie Woodburne) read the riot act to Karl but started her own mini-scandal just a few weeks later when she admitted being in love with Catholic priest Father Tom (Andrew Larkins), the brother of permanently missing-in-action Joe Scully.

Once upon a time, the Ramsays were the backbone of the show, but even though the Kennedys now seem to dominate the action, *Neighbours* is still essentially the same show it was when it first started 19 years ago. When it celebrates its 20th anniversary, there will no doubt be a huge party and retrospective, causing writers all over the world to look back and pon-der on who is *Neighbours*' most famous graduate. Is it Kylie Minogue, the enduring princess of pop who is a genuine superstar in every country in the world except America, or will it be up-and-comer Delta Goodrem?

Goodrem eclipsed John Farnham's long-standing record for having the longest charting Australian number one album of all time when *Innocent Eyes* spent its 26th week on top of the ARIA charts. Grundy's refused to believe she was gone forever, keeping her name in the credits for months after her departure. Finally, Goodrem was well enough to go back to work. She made her first feature film, *Hating Alison Ashley*, then returned to the Nunawading set for one week in May 2004. There was still about a year of her contract to go but Nina Tucker wouldn't have time. Next stop, America.

Before discovering Delta Goodrem, however, the USA would be re-introduced to *Neighbours*, 13 years after its last try-out. Sixty-five episodes were sold to American cable network Oxygen to run at 1pm weekdays. Much was made of the fact that it would follow repeats of *Roseanne* (is that good?). It began with the arrival in Ramsay Street of Holly Valance's on-screen Scully family, but within months the show was screening at 1.30am. So much for 'the hottest Aussie import since Russell Crowe'. Perhaps they should have started it from the episode where he played a hothead during the Scott and Charlene days.

If *Neighbours* hasn't hypnotised the Yanks, it is still seen in about 57 countries. During 2003, it averaged 3.6 million viewers in the UK up against Iraqi war coverage, and according to recent newspaper reports, the BBC pays $290,000 per episode, which is about half what it costs them to make an episode of *Eastenders*. It's a far cry from the rock-bottom prices they paid in the early days but the extra cost gives them a bigger say in its current content. And they seem to like it safe, inoffensive and still suitable for families to watch, although the times seem to be changing.

Two thousand and four has gone down as a watershed year for controversy, what with Susan (Jackie Woodburne) sleeping with her priest, Jack (Jay Bunyan) doing drugs in seedy nightclubs (OK, it wasn't that seedy and only on *Neighbours* could a nightclub have a pot plant in the corner) and the first-ever regular gay character, schoolgirl Lana (Bridget Neval), falling for Sky Mangel (Stephanie McIntosh). It's impossible to imagine a lesbian or a rogue priest in Ramsay Street back in the 80s, when a groundbreaking storyline had Charlene (Kylie Minogue) entering a man's domain by becoming a mechanic.

While it's impossible to ignore the appeal of Kylie Minogue and her fellow actors in the early days (not to mention the always uncanny casting from Jan Russ), *Neighbours*' early appeal may also have been due to the way it harked back to a simpler way of life. In the 70s, *The Sullivans* had struck a chord with its nostalgic look back at Australian suburban life. Even though *Neighbours* is set in the present day, its suburban street was also based on a bygone era where neighbours looked after one another, mothers stayed at home and cooked, and children were safe playing outdoors (even the opening titles had the Robinson family playing cricket on the road).

While other 80s soaps played up the 'greed is good' materialism of the decade (think *Return to Eden* and *Sons and Daughters*), *Neighbours* played it down, with the exception of the Daniels Corporation and JR-like businessman Paul (Stefan Dennis). This was a show that relied on simple stories about families, school and romance, and it cornered the teenage market. Reg Watson's original vision for the show – young people communicating with older people – translated into both groups watching, and it still has a multi-generational audience today.

While it never quite reaches the figures *Home and Away* racks up half an hour later at 7pm, nearly a million viewers still watch every night in Australia. It doesn't hurt that its competition on all three rival networks are current affairs shows, so *Neighbours* is the only spot of escapism

It's impossible to imagine a lesbian or a rogue priest in Ramsay Street back in the 80s.

Radha Mitchell
(Catherine) and
Anthony Engelman
(Stonefish).

on television screens at 6.30pm weeknights. It is an institution on Australian screens and seems stronger than ever at time of printing, although it would not have survived a couple of lean years if it hadn't been for that fanatical UK fan base.

A real-life English family who migrated to Australia on the basis of the show were bitterly disappointed that their neighbours never dropped in like they did on *Neighbours*. To this day, backpackers still make pilgrimages to the real-life Ramsay Street they secretly wish they lived in. No other Aussie soap has ever inspired such devotion or fanaticism, and it's doubtful there will ever be another success like it.

So what is it that British viewers still love about the show? And what first entranced them nearly 20 years ago? Is it the exotic swimming pool lifestyle under seemingly endless sunny skies, without a housing commission high-rise in sight? Could it be a preponderance of pimple-free, middle-class, Caucasians seemingly untouched by multiculturalism? Or is it just the nostalgic memory of that simpler time when neighbours really did become your friends?

Perhaps what really attracted the teenagers of the 80s to the show was a traditional family lifestyle that was rapidly disappearing during this period. For many, both parents were working and the overtime was increasing, and for many more their family was disintegrating through breakdown or divorce. In *Neighbours* they found a safe and secure haven few would ever know in real life.

Like many other actors, Radha Mitchell (Catherine O'Brien) can never escape the ghost of Ramsay Street, no matter how many Hollywood movies she makes. 'I was on top of a mountain at a rave party in India,' she told *Empire* magazine. 'The whole place was dark, and someone was like, "You're from *Neighbours*, aren't you?"'

Ian Smith (Harold) has never made it to the top of an Indian mountain, but the former associate producer and writer on *Prisoner* once admitted that he couldn't see the potential for *Neighbours*. 'I'd heard about a show in production about people living in a street,' he told *TV Week*. 'I said, it will never, ever work!' *Neighbours* is now the longest running Australian drama of all time.

POSSESSION

PREMIERE: **1985** EPISODES: **52** NETWORK: **NINE** FINALE: **1985**

Another Nine soap, another fancy launch, another massive failure.

In 1984, the Nine Network was trying to choose between three pilots for possible production the following year. Crawford's had offered *Hospital* starring Belinda Giblin, Vikki Hammond and Jon Sidney. Casting director Bunney Brooke (*Number 96*'s Flo) told *TV Week* it was to be about 'real people in a real hospital and not whether they are in love with the doctor around the corner. It's not full of glamorous young men running around with stethoscopes in their pockets. It's about a hospital and that's why it is called *Hospital*.' In other words, it wasn't going to be *The Young Doctors*.

PBL Productions had shot a two-hour pilot called *Skin Deep* about 'beauty, bedrooms and boardrooms'. Briony Behets played former model Barbara Kennedy who was now running a modelling agency, photographic studio, health centre and exclusive nightclub (typical 80s overkill). Vanessa Corey (Carmen Duncan) was another ex-model and long-time nemesis who would be plotting to take over Barbara's empire. Vanessa would also have a penchant for younger men like beach boy model Grant Johnson (David Reyne), although she enjoyed hitting the sheets with ruthless lover Cliff Hudson (Jim Smillie) because he was Barbara's fiancé.

The fashion industry soap's dream cast also included Kate Fitzpatrick, Bartholomew John, Antoinette Byron, Maureen O'Shaughnessy, Liz Harris and Angelo D'Angelo, not to mention a frizzy-haired Nicole Kidman playing an underage model murder victim with the unlikely

In a world of money, power and intrigue, friendship is their most valuable possession.

Possession

Two Hour Series Premiere Tonight. 7.30. ⦂⦂⦂ 9

name of Sheena Henderson. Written by *The Young Doctor*'s Anne Lucas, who had moved from acting into scriptwriting, *Skin Deep* was more *Skin Shallow*. It was one hell of a ridiculously complicated story, and all the big hair and big earrings in the world couldn't make it look big budget. Neither did everyone calling each other 'darling'.

Finally, there was Grundy's *Possession*, which was to start with a convoluted government espionage plot before revealing itself to be a soapy saga about rich bitches and long lost children just like *Skin Deep*. Being an in-house production, *Skin Deep* should have had the inside edge, but it must have been obvious to all at the network that the pilot was a stinker. After passing on *Hospital* and *Skin Deep*, Nine decided to go with *Possession*, despite a long list of Grundy Production failures a few years beforehand that still haunted both partners.

Possession went into production and Nine began hyping its premiere in on-air promos from the start of 1985. In Sydney, 14 January was billed as 'the moment all of Sydney has been waiting for!' It began in a locker room where men in black were arming themselves with rifles and donning scary Halloween masks to hide their identities. Reg Watson had based the opening concept on a real-life event, and a serious voice-over made clear that this latest Nine/Grundy's production wasn't going to be another *Taurus Rising*, *Waterloo Station* or *Starting Out*.

'On November 30, 1983, just after 8pm, members of ASIS (Australian Secret Intelligence Service) carried out a raid at a hotel in Melbourne which stunned the world. The following story represents a fictitious account of how the events of that night may have affected the lives of certain Australians. The characters, events, corporations and firms depicted in this photoplay are fictitious. Any similarity to actual persons either living or dead or to actual corporations or firms is purely coincidental.'

Phew! After an opening like that, it was going to be hard to take anything that followed seriously, but the two-hour pilot for *Possession* was actually a gripping set-up for what should have been an intriguing serial. Kathleen Dawson (Tracey Callendar) and best friend Jane Andrews (Tamasin Ramsay) were visiting the big city (Melbourne) in preparation for Kathleen's wedding to spoilt rich boy Greg Macarthur (Lloyd Morris). Unfortunately for Jane, Kathleen left her in the company of Greg's father, high-powered businessman David (Bruce Barry). They were making small talk in his hotel room just as the ill-fated raid began. In the melee, David was bashed and found himself a marked man. And unknown to Jane, she had just been through the experience with her real father.

In hospital, doctors discovered that David was dying. He immediately tracked down his former lover, Louise Carpenter (Darien Takle), who was recuperating from a facelift she had undergone in a desperate attempt to hold onto her toy boy, Gerry Foster (Eric Oldfield). David wanted to acknowledge their daughter and thought Louise should too. Years before, in the country town of Kingsmere, already-married David had deserted Louise when she fell pregnant, forcing her to marry John Andrews (Norman Yemm) on the rebound. Three years after giving birth to Jane, she had deserted her child and husband to run away and build a public relations empire with Claudia Valenti (Maggie Millar).

Louise's vanity prevented her from admitting that she had a 22-year-old daughter, but David was determined to right things from his end. He told his cold-hearted wife Elizabeth (Anne Charleston) that Jane was his illegitimate daughter and he was about to make her a beneficiary of the family fortune. Elizabeth went berserk at the news and Jane didn't cope too well either – she was having a bad couple of days. Upset by his confession, Jane ordered him outside, unaware an assassin was about to shoot her newly-discovered father dead with a high-powered rifle. When suspicious police wondered if the two had been having an affair, Elizabeth jumped on the lie and tried to use it to force Jane out of town and away from her inheritance.

Meanwhile, Detective Vince Bailey (David Reyne) arrived to investigate the murder and immediately fell in love with Greg's fiancé, Kathleen. All-knowing and watching in the wings was Kathleen's mother, Iris Dawson (Lyn Collingwood), who was the only person in town to believe Jane hadn't been having an affair with David. After crashing her father's private funeral and being ordered away by Elizabeth, Jane marched off, vowing to track down her mother and clear her reputation. Unbeknownst to her, Louise was watching the whole scene from the privacy of her chauffeured vehicle, refusing to reveal herself to any of the mourners.

The Sydney Morning Herald thought it had a theme song 'guaranteed to cut right through your head with possible brain damage resulting. But at the end of the first two hours, it has to be said that *Possession* is a ripping yarn and, although no lover of soaps, I can't wait to see the third hour this Thursday. It is something of a calculated cross between *Sons and Daughters* and *A Country Practice*.' When it came to Nine programming the show in a 7.30pm timeslot, *Possession* had to go head to head with at least one of those two shows on Seven, and in Sydney it screened on Mondays up against Grundy's own *Sons and Daughters*. *The Sun Herald* couldn't imagine 'S and D fans deserting the Channel 7 soapie in droves at a time when we are all waiting to find out just how Pat the Rat will make her departure'. In some cities, viewers had to decide between *Possession*, *Sons and Daughters* and *Carson's Law*.

The two-hour premiere was a classy affair that featured several strong performances (and several strong superbitches) but Aussie audiences never could quite grasp the secret agent bit. Writer Bevan Lee and execu-

The Sydney Morning Herald *thought it* had a theme song 'guaranteed to cut right through your head with possible brain damage resulting'.

tive producer Don Battye had concocted a delicious mix based on what was firing American daytime soaps of the mid-80s. Shows like *Days of Our Lives* were mixing traditional melodrama with thriller type storylines, particularly those that involved spies. 'I wondered if the Luke and Laura phenomenon (*General Hospital*'s iconic secret agent romance that had climaxed with Elizabeth Taylor appearing at the wedding) could work here in Australia,' says Bevan Lee. 'The audience responded with the view that that sort of stuff doesn't happen in this country. Making cups of tea for each other is apparently preferable. If Aaron Spelling had lived in Australia, he never would have had a career in television.'

'What the show ultimately suffered from, though, was being overly ambitious. Nothing looks cheaper than when your scripts are actually unshootable so you settle for what you can get away with.' Some of the actors also thought it was cheap. At the glitzy Hunters Hill mansion launch, David Reyne spoke unfavourably about his character to the press, saying it was 'verging on the unreal' and the detective was 'James Bond in a Commodore'. He did, however, acknowledge that soap was harder than it looked. 'I am really wondering whether I can do it or not. I see people in a soapie and I realise that if you are good in a soapie, then you must be very, very good, because your back is against the wall from the start.'

David Reyne, the brother of Australian Crawl's James, seemed unhappy that the series had been picked up at the expense of his music career. He didn't want to be there and Bevan Lee didn't want him there either. 'He was utterly miscast,' says Bevan Lee. 'He was too young. He was meant to be a rugged Clint Eastwood bloke.' *The Sydney Morning Herald* found it 'difficult to swallow that this beefy blond has the years or nous to have attained the rank of detective. Reyne's acting can only improve, but the teeny boppers will not have their critical facilities in top gear as they drool over him.'

'*Possession* was heightened reality and I don't think some of the actors got that,' Lee says. Not surprisingly, neither did the critics. 'Critics always bitch that Australian drama never tries anything different but when you do shake it up, they never give you credit for it.' Apart from *The Sydney Morning Herald*'s Geraldine Walsh, no other critic was prepared to admit the show was a 'possible winner'. Instead, it was much easier to circle like vultures, especially when ratings showed that it wasn't able to maintain its reasonably good opening night audience.

'Poor old Nine's previous soapie efforts bombed early on in life, making this attempt highly courageous and worthy of some support. [But] it's not charity week and there's no avoiding it – Nine's blown it again,' said *The Sunday Telegraph*. 'Flash cars, glamorous clothes, swept-up sets, intrigue, drama and passion were promised. Only the cars arrived. The clothes are over-the-top dreary, the set design's early nothing and the storyline's incredibly bad. In the space of two weeks, they've managed to cram in an international spy ring, a successful murder, an unsuccessful murder attempt, plastic surgery, mass infidelity, suicide, a rape and Russian roulette.'

The Russian roulette scene also puzzled another journalist who begged someone, anyone, to explain what Vince and Greg had been doing playing with a loaded gun. Actors David Reyne and Lloyd Morris composed a letter of reply, joking that neither of them had the slightest idea what it was about when they filmed it. Morris didn't realise that Reyne intended to post the letter and was horrified when he saw their reply in print.

What it was all about was that Greg, driven mad by Kathleen's rejection of him for the Commodore cop, had raped his fiancé. Tough guy Vince decided to get even with the rich boy and teach him a lesson. 'The way I originally wrote it was that Vince would fuck Greg's mouth with the barrel of his gun, in effect raping him so he'd know what it felt like,' Lee reveals today. 'Greg would think he was going to have his head blown off and shit his pants. Unfortunately, that was considered far too strong for television. It was re-written as Vince forcing Greg to play Russian roulette and I had to fight to get that in too.'

Darien Takle as superbitch Louise Carpenter.

Actor Lloyd Morris winces at the memory of the backfired joke letter (and the looks from the production office crew after the newspaper slagging from two of its own). 'I loved *Possession*. It was my first continuing role on TV but the spy story at the beginning got very confusing.' Also confusing was Greg's love life, since he got engaged three times in the short-lived series but never once made it to the altar. Mother Elizabeth had more luck, or thought she did, marrying scheming politician Oliver Hearst (Bryan Marshall), except he was really out to get her money. Elizabeth turned – briefly – from arch bitch to vulnerable victim as the marriage floundered alongside *Possession*'s ratings.

Meanwhile, Jane arrived in the big city, and in one of those convenient soap opera twists, was hired by Claudia to work for Louise. The mother continued to ignore her daughter until an accident forced her to come clean. Another bitch was mellowing. 'I wanted the Louise character to be written as a woman who had the same attitude to sex as that of a man,' says Bevan Lee. 'She had a little black book and was unapologetic about it. She didn't want to connect or have relationships because she had been so badly damaged.' Relieved of her secret, Louise fell for a priest, Alan Kennedy (Kit Taylor), until a looming bankruptcy proved she still really did love her money more.

While Jane went off to train as – wait for it – a spy, falling in love with fellow trainee Larry (Joe Petruzzi) along the way, Vince was faking his own death for an undercover mission. Grief-stricken, Kathleen married Brendon Parker (Larry Turnbull), who then began two-timing her by having an affair with the dubious Sylvie Bryant (Kerry Mack). Elizabeth finally twigged that Brendon was the assassin who had killed her husband back in the first episode, so he went on the run, leaving a pregnant Kathleen in court on a charge of aiding and abetting him.

Still unable to lift its ratings, the show began to be drastically re-tooled. Eve Cambridge (Briony Behets) arrived with her bratty child star actor while two posh visitors from England, Lady Shannon (Maggie Dence)

Jane Andrews (Tamasin Ramsay) probably should have stayed at home in bed with her stuffed toys.

and her daughter Nicola (Ally Fowler), moved in on Elizabeth. Despite appearances, they were flat broke and – like everyone else in the show – really out to get her money. 'Everyone decided it should become more "normal" which is why the little kids and wacky English folk arrived,' Bevan Lee says. It still didn't help.

By now, Nine would have already dispossessed *Possession* except for the fact that they still needed to meet their local drama content. They asked the Australian Broadcasting Tribunal to extend the quota time past 10pm. As soon as the tribunal agreed, they dumped *Possession* into a graveyard timeslot where it slid into oblivion after just 52 episodes.

Nine had established a new loophole for them to dump any future soap that didn't make the grade in prime time. Even so, they continued to point the finger at the Tribunal, which had decreed each Australian network make 104 hours of first-run drama per year. Ron Haynes, Nine executive vice-president of programs, told *TV Star* that 'they're just interested in quantity, not quality. You get to the stage where you can't keep on making expensive miniseries like *The Flying Doctors*.'

'The week after Nine had finally met their drama quota for the year, microphones and cameras started disappearing to go to the sports department,' remembers Lloyd Morris. 'They were slowly dismantling the sets around us. It was obvious they had made the decision to end the show. I was actually in the toilet at the urinal when one of the writers walked in and said he'd just finished writing the last episode. Actors are always the last to know.'

Producer Phillip East was philosophical about what had turned off audiences. 'We were moving away from the action-spy drama,' East told *TV Star*, 'and we were also making the program a little lighter so it wasn't so deadly serious. It's a great shame Nine has not persisted with it because the program did have a following.'

'It started off as a gripping and interesting show but in changing its identity to become more "kitchen sink", it became a "nothing" show,' says Bevan Lee. '*Possession* sold itself out in an attempt to keep going. Australia wasn't ready for an "out there" show. Sometimes Aussie audiences disappoint me.'

A disillusioned Darien Takle blamed the show's failure on unfavourable publicity and the program being mislabelled as a soap opera. 'It wasn't soap, it was a high-quality drama series,' she insisted. Someone really should have told David Reyne, who was still joking around right up to the end. After his character was shot and he was told to start limping, he deliberately switched legs from day to day to see if anybody noticed. Nobody ever did. He and Lloyd Morris had a good laugh about it afterwards though.

PRIME TIME

PREMIERE: **1986** EPISODES: **60** NETWORK: **NINE** FINALE: **1986**

David (Chris Orchard) and Diana (Julianne White) on the *Assignment* set.

Most Australian soaps are made to screen in 'prime time', so eventually someone was going to make a TV show using that as a title. Soap veteran Diane Craig and her husband Garry McDonald (Norman Gunston) starred together in a 1984 comedy pilot called *Prime Time* for the Seven Network. It was to be about two married actors who starred together in a soap opera but, sadly, it was never made into a series, which was a shame as the premise would have made it vastly superior to the show that eventually took the title. In 1986, Crawford's and Nine debuted their own *Prime Time* which was billed as 'a gripping look at the behind-the-scenes activities of a television production company'. Lockhart Productions made a weekly current affairs show called *Assignment* and its 'sensational exposés on crime, politics, rackets and public outrages' would supposedly keep soap audiences riveted from week to week.

David Lockhart (Chris Orchard) was in charge of the company as well as being the lead on-air anchor. He had a neglected teenage daughter, Sandy (Jane Hall), who wanted to live with him now that his former wife Judy was remarrying and moving away. Harry Jones (Tony Hawkins) was *Assignment*'s executive producer and happily married to Georgina (Sonja Tallis). Their over-enthusiastic teenage son Bart (Ben Mendelsohn) worked in the production office alongside Jamie (Totti Goldsmith).

Fifteen-year-old Jane Hall and 17-year-old Ben Mendelsohn were interviewed together for *TV Week*, probably in a desperate bid to snare a

The cast of *Prime Time*.

teenage audience. Naïvely, they both insisted the show would work, despite production chaos and unfavourable reviews of the early episodes. 'I think *Prime Time* has got much more appeal than other glossier shows that lack a down-to-earthness,' said Mendelsohn, obviously referring to the year's other big soap hope, *Return to Eden*. 'I am sure people will be able to relate to the characters.'

It was also the first long-running TV role for theatre actor Peter Kowitz, signed up to play hotshot reporter Jim Donnegan. Since Nine's high-rating *60 Minutes* was obviously the inspiration, Kowitz was put into the care of real-life reporter Mike Munro for a week to observe him up close. 'In those days he was a real larrikin and the stories about the lengths he would go to for a story were legendary. I ended up using a lot of him in the character of Jim Donnegan.'

Unlike *The Box*, Crawford's first behind-the-scenes of television soap, the business of making TV in *Prime Time* was somewhat pretentious and way too serious. Instead of Channel 12's blustering Sir Henry, *Prime Time* had an ineffectual station executive at the fictional Channel 5 called Charles Garrett (Peter Whitford, who nonetheless subtly tried to send up pompous network executives hovering around *Prime Time*). Unlike *The Box*, a soap which had no agenda, *Prime Time* had one and it didn't allow for any wackiness, nudity or bisexual reporters. Nine wanted its soap to be about noble and responsible journalists who considered people and their feelings more important than the story or ratings. As if!

Magazine reporter Kate McArthur (Nina Landis) came to interview David Lockhart in the first episode. She worked for the real-life magazine *The Bulletin* in what was obviously a cross-promotional plug for another Kerry Packer-owned enterprise. Kate exposed John Balenko (John Hannan) as an unscrupulous reporter and when he was thrown off the show, David asked Kate to stick around and become a much more caring and sharing replacement. She also provided the series with a bit of continuing unresolved sexual tension because, God knows, there wasn't much else going for it.

It was actress Nina Landis's first series and despite the show's oh-so-serious tone, she insisted to *TV Week* that 'luckily there is quite a lot of humour written into the script'. She also denied that her character was based on *60 Minutes'* real-life reporter Jana Wendt. 'I have a challenge to portray [Kate] as a believable character.' Sadly, the character and show would prove to be neither believable nor amusing.

The first two episodes cleverly tried to overcome the Sydney-Melbourne rivalry by setting the action in both cities, but one hearing of the dreadful theme music would have sent viewers in both cities changing the channel. Far-fetched storylines about an American millionaire (who naturally sat down on a barstool right next to an *Assignment* reporter) and a refuge for delinquent kids (who were really just misunderstood) didn't help.

Peter Kowitz was initially thrilled at getting paid about $2,500 a week until the overtime began to clock up and he found he had to break the speed limit when driving himself from location to studio to arrive on time. 'I called my agent and said they were killing me so they upped my money by another $500 a week. It was bizarre, but I just kept working and stayed on that awful treadmill.'

Unfortunately, *Prime Time* was not breaking any records on the ratings treadmill. 'We went from being feted to being pariahs pretty quickly once it became obvious the show wasn't getting the expected audience,' says Kowitz. The search for higher ratings, however, did not extend to telling it the way it really was. If *Prime Time*'s reporters were portrayed as anything less than upstanding, Nine demanded re-shoots which played havoc with the drama and storytelling.

'Because the only way you could have a story was to be a reporter, they ended up making all the characters reporters,' says Kowitz. 'And it became very weird, because the actors playing 'real' reporters began to resent the ring-ins.' So, Charles Garrett's niece Kylie Garrett (Antonia Murphy), who joined as *Assignment*'s new receptionist, was soon running after her own stories and new reporter Craig Lawrence (Gary Sweet) turned out to be a spy from another network.

After years of foot-in-the-door reporting from Nine's tabloid current affairs shows, it was naïve to imagine Australian audiences would believe reporters were always polite. In the end though, whether or not the audience would buy such malarkey was a moot point, because Nine consigned the show to a timeslot that virtually guaranteed its failure. Avoiding going head-to-head with other soaps like *Sons and Daughters* and *A Country Practice*, *Prime Time* premiered on the graveyard nights of Thursday and Friday. Late night shopping and the end of the working week meant that no regular audience would be at home to watch a continuing serial.

The deathwatch for *Prime Time* was so widely reported in the Melbourne newspapers that Peter Kowitz even remembers a bank teller casually asking if his show had been axed yet! After a move to Saturdays at 9.30pm, and another pep talk from Nine ('We are still behind you 100%! We feel there's an untapped audience on Saturday nights!'), the inevitable was confirmed. After just 60 episodes the series came to a close, not surprisingly, with a wrap party as *Assignment* was also laid to rest.

In 1994, comedy team The D-Generation premiered *Frontline* for the ABC, and just like *Prime Time* it was set behind the scenes of a mythical current affairs show. This time around, however, it was a biting and savage satire on tabloid television news shows, with the reporters being portrayed as selfish egomaniacs. *Frontline* was a massive ratings success and is still considered to be one of Australia's cleverest sitcoms. *Prime Time* was a misguided disaster and is deservedly forgotten. Its only claim to fame in soap history is that it was the last Aussie soap to be shot on film when on location while switching back to video for all interior studio scenes.

29

RETURN TO EDEN

PREMIERE: **1983** EPISODES: **28** NETWORK: **TEN** FINALE: **1986**

Scheming sisters Jilly (Peta Toppano) and Stephanie (Rebecca Gilling).

Return to Eden is probably the most successful Australian miniseries ever made, having attracted over 300 million viewers worldwide. Together with the series that followed, it is constantly repeated and is now a huge seller on DVD. It's so popular there has even been an unofficial Bollywood rip-off, and if you think the 28-hour serial stretches credibility, you've obviously never seen it done as an Indian musical.

The tale of a spurned woman seeking revenge on the traitors who tried to kill her has struck a chord with audiences everywhere it has been shown, but it had a rough journey to the screen. Twin producers Hal and Jim McElroy, best known for the cinema classic *Picnic at Hanging Rock*, first saw the treatment for *Return to Eden* after getting to know writer Michael Laurence. Hal took it home to his wife Di, who devoured it in one sitting and declared it would be a big hit. 'Feeling wonderfully confident, I gave it to 12 Australian directors, including many famous names, and they all, without exception, turned it down,' Hal McElroy remembers today. 'They were completely contemptuous about it, as were most of the agents.'

After getting the same response in England, in desperation McElroy flew home via the U.S. to meet with an American director. Karen Arthur had begun her entertainment career as a hoofer in Las Vegas, went on to be a choreographer and stage director, and eventually became an Emmy award-winning television director. Not only was she qualified for the job, but McElroy had finally found a director who loved the script. He applied for a visa for the American, citing how many others had declined the project to prove she was the only person available to do the job.

Return to Eden was to open on the wedding day of Stephanie Harper, a mining magnate's daughter. Stephanie was naïve and rather plain looking. Having been married twice before, she was now getting hitched to the much younger Greg Marsden, a sleazy tennis pro. This was her first big mistake. Her second was allowing best friend Jilly Stewart to join their honeymoon at the family homestead, Eden, in the Northern Territory, where the restless Jilly immediately embarked upon a torrid affair with Greg. Mistake number three was heading out with them on a night-time crocodile hunt, where she was thrown into a croc's jaws and left for dead.

Of course Stephanie didn't die. She was rescued and nursed back to health, but needed major plastic surgery to repair her hideous scarring. She emerged looking younger, more beautiful and just different enough to take on a new identity. And this was even before botox! As Tara Welles, she became a famous model who then sought out Greg and Jilly to exact revenge, leaving behind the heartbroken plastic surgeon who had fallen in love with her.

'Almost all the directors we'd spoken to said you must have two actors to play the title role, one to play ugly, one to play beautiful,' McElroy recalls. 'Nobody thought that it was possible with the same actress.' Enter Rebecca Gilling and an extraordinary make-up job. At 29, she was best known for her revealing nude scenes in the *Number 96* movie and the lightweight *Young Doctors*. But *Return to Eden* would transform her into a worldwide superstar.

'I did a particularly good screen test, probably the best ever,' remembers Rebecca Gilling. Acting opposite James Smillie, who would go on to play Stephanie's fourth husband, plastic surgeon Dan Marshall, they did the scene where her facial bandages were removed for the first time. 'I looked into my new "beauty" in the mirror and the tears just started rolling beautifully down my face,' Gilling says. 'I've never cried easily on camera before but the chemistry with James Smillie and director Karen Arthur was just right.'

With brown contact lenses, a prosthetic nose, a bridge to change her upper lip line and lots of padding, Gilling looked frumpy enough to play Stephanie, the 40-ish mother of two teenagers, but she also needed

Stephanie is attacked by the crocodile.

further inspiration. 'I drew a lot on my own mother, her body language, her niceness, and with a different exterior appearance, it changed what was going on internally for me,' recalls Gilling. With just a bit of glamming up, Gilling was effortlessly re-born as the stunning Tara and was now beautiful enough to turn the tables on her adulterous husband, Greg Marsden.

Hal McElroy was determined to find the perfect actor for the Greg Marsden role, and finally discovered him staring back from a record cover. 'I'm a rocker from way back,' McElroy confesses, 'and at home we had the most recent release from Australian Crawl. James Reyne's face just jumped off the cover. It was all about charisma.' Two screen tests later the lead singer of one of Australia's biggest bands had proved he had the necessary attitude, self-confidence and narcissism essential to the role. Writer Michael Laurence, who used to be an actor, was appalled at the choice, but director Karen Arthur was keen.

The final major casting was Jilly. 'This was a more straightforward role but she still had to show why a woman would fall in love with her best friend's husband, then try to kill her,' says McElroy. Acclaimed actress Wendy Hughes, seen briefly in *Number 96* but better known for a string of popular and successful movies (including *Newsfront*, *My Brilliant Career* and *Careful He Might Hear You*), signed on. The ambitious shoot in Sydney, Orpheus Island and Arnhem Land in the Northern Territory began under the watchful eye of cinematographer Dean Semler (later to win an Academy Award for *Dances With Wolves*).

Once completed, Ten's publicity department pulled out all the stops to make sure everybody would know about the show. After an extraordinarily expensive launch, complete with a giant stuffed crocodile in the foyer, *Return to Eden* aired on the Ten Network in September 1983. 'Some critics got it but the majority said you've got to be joking,' remembers McElroy. 'It was so different from everything else Australia was doing in miniseries at the time, being a bold, unabashed melodrama instead of a historical period piece or social realism.'

Once again, the critics would be proved wrong. The first night's ratings turned out to be better than even the most optimistic predictions. 'It was a phenomenal hit and night two was even bigger, which is very unusual in miniseries.' By night three, when the revelation of Tara's true identity had led to Greg crashing his plane in a fireball and Jilly being sent to prison, *Return to Eden* had set record ratings in Australia.

Talk of a sequel started within just a couple of months. *TV Week*'s sources suggested that Greg might survive the plane crash, get a bit of plastic surgery and plan his own revenge. They were wrong – Greg was definitely dead – but 'Return to' *Return to Eden* would eventually come to fruition. With the miniseries being sold for over $4 million to Worldvision for American distribution, it then started to travel the world, being seen in Britain, Italy, Finland, the Netherlands, Switzerland, Malta, Monaco, Panama, Ecuador, Chile, Israel and Jordan. Everybody wanted more.

Worldvision and Hal McElroy joined forces and eventually pre-sold a new 22-part series to America and England – unheard of at that time for an Australian show. The $8 million production began shooting in Sydney on 29 April 1985, in a specially converted studio at Five Dock. More than $2 million was spent on the elaborate sets while luxury cars were bought rather than leased. Meanwhile, a string of designers, from Carla Zampatti to Susan Hannaford (who played Kitty in *The Sullivans*), began whipping up high fashion threads for wardrobe supervisor Miv Brewer (Naomi Watts's mother).

The new serial picked up seven years after the original. Stephanie was now Australia's wealthiest woman and still happily married to Dr Dan (James Smillie). Her children from her first marriages were now grown-up. Hothead playboy Dennis (Peter Cousens) worked for Harper Mining while concert pianist Sarah (Nicki Paull) dreamed of being a designer for Harper fashion house Tara's. Their lives were about to be rudely inter-rupted by the release from prison of murderess Jilly Stewart. With Wendy Hughes declining to return to the role, a new actress was needed. This worked rather well since the character was no longer a needy alcoholic, but bitter, twisted and out for some revenge of her own. Enter Peta Toppano as Jilly.

The former star of *Class of '75*, *The Young Doctors* and *Prisoner* told *TV Week* she had been 'typecast as a sweet, girl-next-door type' and was 'grateful to be given the chance to play a conniving character'. Given that Stephanie needed a reason to allow her traitorous friend back into her life, episode one of the new series began with the revelation that Jilly was really Stephanie's half-sister. 'Two beautiful sisters fighting each other is much better than two beautiful women!' McElroy told *Cinema Papers* at

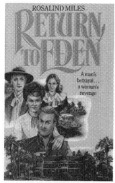

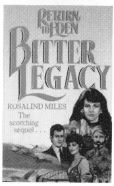

Hardcover books.

the time. Jilly wasn't just back in Stephanie's life, she was back in her house, a lavish waterfront mansion named Eden.

When offered $5 million to give up any future claims on the family fortune, Jilly told Steph that all she wanted was her trust and love. In reality, she was already scheming with corporate pirate Jake Sanders, who had his own agenda for revenge – he was the brother of Greg Marsden. James Reyne wasn't interested in returning to the series, so the role was offered to his real-life brother David Reyne. Sadly, David had just done his share of Aussie soap with the appalling pilot *Skin Deep* and doomed serial *Possession*. Running out of Reynes, British actor Daniel Abineri was signed. 'Jake is a real smoothie and wraps women around his finger,' Abineri told *TV Week*. His enthusiasm for the role would quickly wane.

'He had his own issues,' says Hal McElroy, 'and a need to subvert and demonstrate his working-class credentials to the audience. It diminished his character somewhat.' One example was Abineri's refusal to wear his tie properly adjusted. 'His character was a high powered businessman and when his tie was askew it reduced his credibility.' After a few 'sharply worded' memos, Abineri told *TV Week* that he made sure he straightened it up right in the middle of a scene, while throwing Jilly around a bedroom where she could be regularly found peeling off her over-the-top designer gear.

Like all good 80s soap superbitches, Jilly was slutting her way around town with anyone that would help her amass a fortune and destroy her enemies. Apart from regular raunchy scenes with Jake, she even schemed her way back into the life of former husband Phillip (John Lee), who re-married her. Upon learning he was being conned so she could get control of his shares in Harper Mining, he committed suicide. Jilly played the grieving widow to the hilt to elicit everyone's sympathy.

Just like in the original, killing Stephanie became a familiar pastime. At one stage she was shot at while horse riding by Olive Down (Suzanne Roylance), a prison friend of Jilly's now out on parole and bribed into carrying out Jilly's dirty work. Olive also attempted to kill Jilly using a snake, but ended up dead after it bit her. Jake and Jilly were forced to dispose of her body.

After diving into her swimming pool, only to discover a live crocodile had been slipped into the water overnight courtesy of Jilly, Stephanie had a breakdown and began to re-live the past, thinking she was Tara Welles again. While Jake and Jilly scrambled to use her breakdown to their advantage, Stephanie's son Dennis assumed control of Harper Mining.

While Dennis fell for Harper's spy Cassie (Megan Williams), Stephanie's daughter Sarah fell pregnant to Tom McMaster (Warren Blondell) only to later discover he might be her brother. After running into the arms of boxer Angelo Vitale (Angelo D'Angelo) and marrying him, she ended up losing the baby, then found out Tom wasn't her brother after all.

Meanwhile, plastic surgeon Dan found himself a new charity case in Jilly's niece Jessica (Saskia Post), who had a few hideous scars of her own. In another case of history repeating itself, he turned Jessica into a beautiful woman and began to fall in love with her. After finding Dan in Jilly's bed, however, Stephanie fled, faked her own death (again), and went into hiding with a former lover, millionaire Sheik Amahl (Robin Ramsay) and his sister Princess Talitha (Tamasin Ramsay, Robin Ramsay's real-life daughter). Jake and Jilly took control of her mansion, business and fortune.

Not surprisingly, Stephanie wanted revenge. Hanging out with her Arab friends proved very useful as Stephanie was able to slip back into Sydney pretending to be Princess Talitha while hiding her face behind a veil. In another nod to the original miniseries, she made a triumphant return to high society while striding down a fashion runway as Jilly screamed 'No!' in disbelief.

By now, the repetitive plots were proving to be a turn-off. The expensive series wasn't breaking any ratings records and comparisons to *Dynasty* and *Dallas* proved to be disastrous. Hal McElroy had sensibly pointed out at the beginning of the new series that American night-time soaps cost more than five times as much as *Return to Eden* but audiences weren't buying it. 'We did pitch it like *Dynasty* Down Under,' admits unit publicist Victoria Buchan, 'but we were trying to show it was a much more sophisticated product than *Prisoner* or *Neighbours*.'

Despite loving the original miniseries, it now became apparent that Australian audiences preferred their shows to be more downmarket and weren't interested in *Return to Eden* every week. It was camp and outrageous with a very Aussie sense of humour running through it, but viewers didn't even seem interested in buying the discarded designer dresses, which languished in a second-hand boutique. Aware that the series was tanking, many of the actors, with the exception of Rebecca Gilling, began to slag it off to the press.

Peta Toppano revealed to *TV Week* in the series' dying days that she led a rebel group of actresses who made a formal complaint about the endless sex scenes. 'We all loathed it,' she seethed. 'We felt we were being exploited and we didn't enjoy it.' Oddly, Toppano then complained that the problem was having to wear skimpy underwear. 'It would have been more honest for us to have done nude scenes than to run around in a pair of lace knickers. Maybe they thought that sex and naughtiness would sell *Return to Eden*. But I think it's quite tedious.'

What was tedious was Toppano's tirade. Despite admitting that she 'had very good feedback from the series' and that 'it has been good for my career and with the money I've earned I've been able to renovate our house overlooking Sydney Harbour', the actress whined about having to film a boardroom table sex scene against her will. 'It was 8 o'clock at night. I was very tired and just wanted to go home.'

Ten felt the same way about *Return to Eden*. While the series would garner big ratings overseas, Australian figures didn't justify more episodes. 'I was very unhappy with Ten's decision to re-schedule it in two-hour blocks up against the football. Our worldwide distributor, Worldvision, was devastated by Ten's decision to axe it,' McElroy declares.

Peta Toppano revealed ... that she led a rebel group of actresses who made a formal complaint about the endless sex scenes. 'We all loathed it.'

Jilly (Peta Toppano) and
Jake (Daniel Abineri).

'It could have been a huge franchise.' Since the series had ended with a humdinger of a cliffhanger, the McElroys decided to film a proper ending for overseas fans at their own expense.

Originally episode 22 had ended as all good night-time soaps did when finishing their season – with everything up in the air for a water-cooler-talk cliffhanger. Jake, by now besotted with Stephanie just like his brother Greg had been, agreed to race his horse against Steph's in the Melbourne Cup – winner take all. Jilly, who had just married Jake (and been given her own Swiss bank account as a wedding gift), screamed 'No!' in disbelief. Again. After Jilly unsuccessfully tried to jab a hypodermic needle into Steph's horse Tara's Pride, it went on to beat Jake's filly Revenge. (Well, what else did you expect it to be called?)

Crashing Steph's celebratory party at Eden, a pregnant Jilly pretended to be sick so Jake and Steph would help her to a bedroom. Once there, she pulled a gun from her purse, determined to kill Stephanie once and for all, but in the tussle, Jake ended up getting shot. As he staggered downstairs to die in front of the party guests, a blood-splattered Stephanie followed, now holding the murder weapon, as Jilly screamed out that her sister had just shot her husband dead.

When it became obvious that the torrid saga couldn't end like this, Rebecca Gilling and Peta Toppano were lured back for a new ending so Stephanie could be cleared of any wrongdoing. Much stranger though was the new-look Dennis (Peter Cousens). In the original version of the episode, mop-topped Dennis was last seen being abducted, but as Cousens now had short hair, Dennis became the victim of the world's strangest kidnapping hairdresser. In one of the newly filmed sequences, he was tied to a chair with his hair in clumps at his feet. 'This may seem like a silly question,' Dennis asked, 'but what the hell's going on?' Indeed you might ask.

Dennis's kidnapper turned out be – rather conveniently – Amahl and Stephanie's abandoned son Chris (Graham Harvey). Upon realising that his mother had been arrested for murder, Chris decided against asking for a ransom for his half-brother Dennis. Instead, he would prove his mother's innocence by revealing he had been – wait for it – out on the balcony when Jilly shot Jake. Even better, Chris had been taking photos at the time that could prove his mother's testimony.

As Jilly made one of her usual ludicrously dressed entrances into her sister's prison cell, Stephanie asked, 'Do you know how ridiculous you are?' Was this an ending or a giant in-joke from the writers and actors? In swept Stephanie's two sons, the shorn Dennis and long lost Chris, as Jilly looked on in disbelief (she really should have been used to this sort of thing by now). Jilly screamed 'No!' one last time as the authorities led her away. 'If you fell into a bucket of manure you'd come up smelling of roses, you bitch' was her final insult to her sister Steph, who emerged from prison to stare out over Sydney Harbour for the final scene.

Meanwhile, Daniel Abineri kept mouthing off about the show, admitting to *TV Week* that for the last ten weeks of filming, he had been playing it strictly for laughs. 'About halfway through it got really silly,' he said. 'Keeping a straight face for the last ten episodes was unbelievably hard for all of us on the show. We were getting the scripts a day or two before shooting and peals of laughter would ring out from all the actors.'

Abineri also revealed he was slipping in his own little moments to keep his spirits up. When Jilly kissed Jake at their wedding, Abineri turned to the camera and wiped her kiss onto his sleeve.

Even in the final episode the in-jokes kept coming. As Jake was driving off to the party where he was about to be killed, Abineri was whistling 'My Way'. 'I wanted to die with a smile on my face but they wouldn't let me,' he added. Amazingly, despite his attitude and permanent exit from the show, Abineri insisted that the producers had offered him an option to come back should another series go into production. 'I told them once was enough. Let Jake rest in peace.'

A year later, Daniel Abineri was still bitter. 'That was a gross, ill-conceived waste of money. Selling it to the United States was like taking coals to Newcastle,' he told *TV Week* as he travelled around Australia playing Frank-N-Furter in *The Rocky Horror Show*. Although he had come to fame playing the sweet transvestite, it helped in his post-*Eden* career that Abineri bought the rights to stage *Rocky Horror* himself. Not surprisingly, he continued to play the lead role.

Even Nicki Paull (the tortured Sarah Harper) maintained, 'It was the most intense experience I'd had. The show underwent such a change from what we were originally told. I'm someone who really needs a very clear and definite idea of the role I'm expected to play. I'd be very wary about anything like that happening again.'

However, the true star of the show, Rebecca Gilling, didn't have a bad thing to say about it all. In 1986, in response to her fellow cast members' comments, she told *TV Week*, '*Return to Eden* wasn't the most demanding material to work on but we were all on a good wicket and succeeded in entertaining people in a tongue-in-cheek way. If you've taken on a job, I think it helps if you support the project.' Today she is just as positive about it. 'I had a good experience on it, the scripts were good, it was well directed (Kevin Dobson, Tim Burstall, Jim Power, Rod Hardy amongst others) and I couldn't fault the commitment to quality on all sides.'

As countries around the world fell under the spell of *Return to Eden* all over again, Rebecca Gilling became an unofficial ambassador for Australia. In 1988 she was named Actress of the Year in Yugoslavia. And after a staggering 22 million Polish fans out of a population of 37 million got hooked on the crocodile-filled soap, polling booths changed their hours during the general election so people could stay home to watch it. Rebecca Gilling and her husband were flown to the then communist-controlled country for personal appearances at the invitation of Polish Airlines.

'I appeared on Polish television every night of the week on the news,' Gilling remembers. 'At one point, I said how I would have gone into training had I known how much I'd be eating and drinking and they all yelled "Cut! You can't say that on TV – there are people out there queuing for potatoes on the street!" Meanwhile we were eating beluga and having the best Polish vodka for lunch.'

In 1987, when relations between Indonesia and Australia were shaky, the Australian Government asked Rebecca Gilling if she would visit the country on a goodwill tour. However, they severely underestimated the response to bringing Stephanie Harper to town. 'I stepped off the plane to see 5,000 people trampling over cars to get a glimpse of me! I was three months pregnant with my first child and only had three security guards to protect me from this surging sea of people,' shudders Gilling. After a week of pandemonium throughout Jakarta, Gilling tried to unwind in Bali but was chased by paparazzi from one end of the island to the other. 'That week I felt like I was one of the Beatles.'

In the wake of *Return to Eden*, Rebecca Gilling made another McElroy miniseries, *A Dangerous Life*, but now with two small children, she retired from acting to bring them up. She found a new career as a television presenter on Nine's long-running lifestyle series *Our House*, and today works for Planet Ark environmental foundation.

Peta Toppano, once tagged as the nice girl, found herself typecast as a superbitch after screaming 'No!' so many times as Jilly. In the miniseries *Fields of Fire*, she stood by her comment to be naked rather than wearing lingerie and went topless for a memorable nude scene. She played nasty one more time in *E Street* before hitting that age where soap mothers beckoned on *Heartbreak High*, *Above the Law* and *Home and Away*.

Despite 80s fashion severely dating both series, the show lives on in endless repeats. '*Return to Eden* is one of the most profitable television productions ever made in this country,' says executive producer Hal McElroy, 'and to this day it continues to be re-licensed. It's a perennial favourite for audiences all over the world.' Having said that, there are no plans for a *Return to Return to Return to Eden*. After all, one woman can only fake her death so many times after a crocodile attack.

30

HOME AND AWAY

PREMIERE: **1988** EPISODES: ... NETWORK: **SEVEN** FINALE: ...

Grant (Craig McLachlan) farewells Summer Bay and Bobby
(Nicolle Dickson) as Donald (Norman Coburn) looks on.

Axing *Neighbours* proved to be a disastrous business decision by the Seven network, which watched the Ten network turn the show into a massive hit in Australia and then the UK. Desperate to get back into the soap market, Seven's head of drama, Alan Bateman, was trying to figure out how to launch a rival show that wouldn't be a copycat of Ramsay Street. He unexpectedly found his inspiration when he stopped in a small country town in Southern New South Wales to buy ice creams for his family. While chatting to the locals, he discovered they were up in arms over the construction of a home for foster kids from the city.

'I saw then the outline for a serial,' Alan Bateman said in the book *Home and Away: Behind the Scenes.* 'Nobody in the community wanted them to move in and I began to wonder how streetwise city kids would adapt to the new lifestyle. Suddenly I thought, there is my slice of life in a community.' Bateman went to work on the story outline and located it at a mythical beach to be known as Summer Bay. Seven executives were unconvinced, but audience research revealed the show could be a winner. Originally called *Refuge*, it was given the friendlier title of *Home and Away* as production got under way.

Alan Bateman gathered a team of soap professionals around him, starting with producer John Holmes, who had set up *Neighbours* twice, once for Seven before turning it into a blockbuster on Ten. Holmes, in turn, brought in Bevan Lee (*Sons and Daughters*) to fine-tune the script for the opening telemovie, which everyone agreed seemed to be missing something. Actors had already been cast and the sets were built, so Lee had to devise changes that could still work within that framework.

'The idea of the family coming to the seaside was fantastic but the way it was done was all wrong,' Bevan Lee recalls. 'The most interesting character in the original draft was Sally's imaginary friend Milko. Shooting was delayed for three weeks for me to write a whole new opening with completely different plot mechanics of how the family got to Summer Bay and what they did with each other. The character of Bobby (Nicolle Dickson) was not an outsider in the original script, arriving with the Fletcher family having already been fostered in the city. That didn't provide enough conflict and I thought how much more interesting it would become if the new family embraced an outsider from the community they were moving into, thereby making them double outsiders. It also made Bobby a potential time bomb being planted into the middle of that family. I therefore say I co-created *Home and Away* because I re-created it and stayed on as the head writer for the first fifteen months.'

'*Home and Away* was always set up in a way that we could rejuvenate the show when necessary,' says John Holmes. 'To this day, the show has been able to return again and again to its original concept which is ready-made for lots of soapie conflict.' Not only could its revolving door of young delinquents be expected to suffer from a multitude of problems, but their troubled families also provided plenty of shady relatives, many of whom could arrive with problems of their own. A cast of new television faces was assembled to play them, while Carol Willesee was hired for the pivotal role of foster mother, and earth mother, Pippa Fletcher.

Casting the wife of Mike Willesee, Australia's best known current affairs show host, was a publicity dream. 'She had just started acting and was pretty raw, but she had a warmth about her,' remembers John Holmes. Filming began, but Seven was nervous because Carol Willesee hadn't signed a contract. Willesee later maintained to *TV Week* that she had been given a 'verbal assurance' that she could get time off for school holidays, as well as late starts and early wrap-ups so she could spend time with her real-life family. This just wasn't workable for a five-episodes-per-week schedule, so Seven decided to re-cast and re-shoot the footage Willesee had already appeared in.

'Everybody got a bit of a shock but I think it showed that we were pretty serious about the show,' says John Holmes. 'It would have been irresponsible of me to allow an unsigned artist to keep filming when they could have walked out at any time.' In the days before mobile phones, Holmes left a tearful Carol Willesee and her agent sitting on the crew bus while he walked down the road to a public telephone box. First on his short list to take over the role was Vanessa Downing, and she would be required to be on set the very next day. For the next three weeks, until filming of the pilot was completed, a surprised but happy Downing worked 20-hour days, since she was already committed to appearing in a nightly all-girl a cappella show.

By the time the telemovie screened around Australia in January 1988, Seven was already in production of the spin-off series. It was decided to screen the new soap each weeknight at 6pm, pushing Seven's nightly news bulletin back to a 6.30pm start. *Home and Away*'s biggest competition would be Nine's news. It was a risky move and, given that Seven's news had not been able to beat Nine's, quite an ask for a brand new serial to do the job. An early good sign was a surprisingly positive reception from critics.

The Australian said it had 'first-class production skills and good acting'. *The Sydney Morning Herald* thought it was 'easily the best five-night serial in years', while *The Daily Telegraph* agreed there was 'something about the Fletchers and Summer Bay that pulls at the old heartstrings'. *TV Week* found it 'thoroughly enjoyable' while James Oram (who went on to write *Home and Away: Behind the Scenes*) was good-natured enough to admit that he had been one of the few TV journalists to question the show's potential. Writing for *The Sunday Telegraph*, he thought that 'caravan parks are hardly places of high drama'. Oram may well have had a point, but while scriptwriters struggled to come up with compelling caravan park stories, the biggest drama nearly turned out to be the early cancellation of the show.

'The telemovie rated pretty well on the Sunday night, but it wasn't a blockbuster,' says John Holmes. 'The first Monday night was OK but over the next few weeks, the show slipped down to very shaky ground.' The gradual acceptance of the new soap by the Australian public mirrored what was happening with the Fletcher family and their new neighbours in Summer Bay. It was touch and go for a while, but eventually both would be wholeheartedly embraced.

Home and Away began with a flashback to 1978, and the first actor heard was Bruce Venables as a cop who was chasing young Franky (later Venables would wed series regular Judy Nunn the same week her character Ailsa got married). Childless couple Tom (Roger Oakley) and Pippa Fletcher (Vanessa Downing) wanted to foster children, and keeping young Franky out of trouble seemed like a good place to start. Ten years later, Frank (Alex Papps) was just one of five foster kids that now included Carly Morris (Sharyn Hodgson), Steven Matheson (Adam Willits), Lynn Davenport (Helena Vozich) and Sally Keating (Kate Ritchie), not to mention little Sally's imaginary friend Milko (who had magically survived Bevan Lee's rewrite).

When Tom was retrenched from his city job, he and Pippa worried that the welfare department might try and take the kids back, so they decided a change in lifestyle was necessary. They bought a rundown caravan park and house in Summer Bay from widower Alf Stewart (Ray Meagher), who had a minxy teenage daughter of his own, Ruth, better known as Roo

'Caravan parks are hardly places of high drama.'

The affair that saved the show.

(Justine Clarke). The Fletchers soon met Alf's girlfriend Ailsa Hogan (Judy Nunn), who ran a little shop, and long-term caravan park residents (and former circus performers) Neville (Frank Lloyd) and Floss McPhee (Sheila Kennelly).

The breakout star of *Home and Away*, on-screen and off, was rebellious Bobby Simpson (Nicolle Dickson). Bobby was the town troublemaker discovered hiding out in the caravan park after being expelled by Summer Bay High's nasty deputy headmaster Donald Fisher (Norman Coburn). By the end of the opening telemovie, Bobby had moved in with the Fletchers to be their sixth foster child. Fisher, who wasn't pleased to find himself living next door to the dreaded Fletchers ('the bad blood brood'), was livid about having Bobby as a neighbour as well. A delicious mix, then, but why didn't the opening audience keep watching?

'We began *Home and Away* with noble intentions,' says Bevan Lee. 'We were trying to de-soapify the show and see each week as a bit more self-contained, with stories that would conclude each week. Unfortunately, that means there was no narrative imperative for the audience to come back night after night.' As the ratings stagnated, network executives came close to cancelling the show. 'Alan Bateman was wonderful in keeping the dogs at bay, and he managed to keep us on air for the six months it took to gain some traction,' says John Holmes. 'In our bones, we always felt it was going to work.'

In a last-bid effort to save the show, Bevan Lee went back to some soap basics – a psycho and a love triangle. The Summer Bay Nutter, who sneaked around peeping into windows, turned out to be the school headmaster (Owen Weingott), who had been sent mad by a classroom prank gone horribly wrong. His exit cleared the way for pompous Fisher to be promoted (and given the nickname of 'Flathead' by the students). As for the star-crossed lovers, Bobby fell in love with Frank, but he had already fallen in love with Roo.

Alan Bateman had always wanted the show to tackle serious social issues such as drugs, alcoholism and domestic violence. Wanting a harder edge than (what was then) the much softer *Neighbours* meant that *Home and Away* would tackle teenage pregnancy and rape within the first couple of months. A pregnant Roo told Frank he was the father of her child even though she knew the real culprit was city boy Brett (Gerry Sont). That lie led to *Home and Away*'s first wedding being abandoned when a guilt-ridden Roo fled the ceremony and a distraught Frank crashed his car. Even though some viewers complained such stories were too racy for an early evening timeslot, the ratings were beginning to climb.

Next, Carly (Sharyn Hodgson) was raped while hitchhiking, and although the word 'rape' was never actually uttered, savvy viewers caught on. In the aftermath of her 'assault', she began to drink heavily and the ratings continued to grow. From a low of 9, *Home and Away* slowly built its audience until the show was scoring a 25 by the end of its first year. The serial was finally a hit.

The rating figures were even more interesting in Perth, which was the only city where *Home and Away* went head-to-head against *Neighbours*. Amazingly, the new soap won resoundingly, scoring a 37, while the three-year-old *Neighbours* floundered with just a 3. *Neighbours* was quickly shifted to a different timeslot and the two shows have never been screened head-to-head in Australia since.

Home and Away began screening throughout the UK on ITV stations from 12 February 1989. The show wasn't an instant success there either, but just like the Aussie experience, British kids were soon wagging school to watch it. Eventually the show became so popular that students from the Bramdean school in the English village of Exeter insisted that their uniform be replaced with replicas from Summer Bay High.

Back on Aussie screens in 1989, Roo's baby was put up for adoption while Frank and Bobby married. Their union didn't last long, for 'TVs newest heart-throb' had tired of the grind and wanted a rest (Alex Papps was also hosting ABC-TV music show *The Factory* every Saturday morning). Instead of taking a break though, Alex Papps followed Alan Bateman as he switched networks from Seven to Nine and ended up in Nine's more prestigious *The Flying Doctors* (so considered because it was a one-hour drama on film rather than a five-nights-a-week video soapie). Consequently, Bobby and Frank's marriage foundered and he moved to the city to be with Roo. Triangle complete. Well, not really. One thing you can always rely on in Summer Bay is that everybody comes home for a visit if they're popular enough.

Momentarily single, Bobby went in search of her real parents, only to discover that hideous Donald Fisher (Norman Coburn) was actually her father. Even worse, High Court judge Morag Bellingham (Cornelia Frances) was her mother. Morag was the snooty sister of both Alf and prudish Celia Stewart (Fiona Spence). With Fisher already softening up to become a much more sympathetic long-running character, Bobby decided she hated her new mum but took to Dad and her newly discovered family. Unfortunately, Fisher's son Alan (Simon Bossell) died from a brain aneurism and daughter Rebecca (Jane Hall) ran away from home (was it something Bobby said?). Rebecca would come and go over the years, sometimes being played by Danielle Spencer, and eventually by Belinda Emmett.

In 1990, Bobby's original foster father, Al Simpson (Terence Donovan), was released from jail and headed straight to Summer Bay. He came to blackmail Fisher over a long-ago shooting incident that Fisher blamed himself for. Instead, Bobby was able to prove (yay Bobby!) that Al had actually pulled the trigger, so back to jail he went, leaving behind his illiterate daughter Sophie (Rebekah Elmaloglou) to be fostered by Tom and Pippa.

Meanwhile, Carly battled alcoholism while dating a string of hunky boyfriends including Matt (Greg Benson) and Adam Cameron (Mat Stevenson). Finally, Italian-Australian army boy Ben Lucini (Julian McMahon) proposed within two weeks of meeting Carly, and the happy couple began preparing for their wedding.

'He's always wary of
turning his back on
me thinking he will
end up with a steak
knife in his back!'

In between, *Home and Away* took full advantage of its beachside location by making Ben an ironman who frequently trained and competed in skimpy bathing togs, alongside unorthodox teacher Grant Mitchell (Craig McLachlan). While the Australian army never did get Ben back into its ranks, the score was evened when town yobbo Lance Smart (Peter Vroom) joined up, leaving behind equally dim-witted mate Martin Dibble (Craig Thomson) and his ditzy blonde fiancé Marilyn Chambers (Emily Symons).

Alf and Ailsa finally married after their engagement party had been ruined by Roo's announcement that Ailsa was a former jailbird convicted of manslaughter. Long-hidden secrets like this were constantly spilled in *Home and Away*'s early years, but justice and a good reputation would always prevail. Once Ailsa explained that her father was a drunkard who used to bash her mother, everyone accepted her again, especially the foster kids who identified with her disturbing home life.

'Just when I thought I'd been playing this rather nice woman,' Judy Nunn told *Soap World*, 'I had to take a different approach when Ailsa's dark past was revealed. Now, whenever Ray Meagher (Alf) and I play a kitchen scene, he's always wary of turning his back on me thinking he will end up with a steak knife in his back!' Afterwards, Nunn received a script where the Fletcher kids wanted Ailsa to help them organise a 60s night and reminisce about how much fun the decade had been. Fat chance, thought Nunn, given that Ailsa was in jail at the time!

After the Fletchers' latest foster kid, Brian 'Dodge' Knight (Kelly Dingwall), turned out to be very dodgy by burning down Ailsa's grocery store, Ailsa and Bobby went into business together to open up a Summer Bay institution, The Diner (which, in turn, housed the iconic hamburger phone). Alf rebuilt the grocery shop while Ailsa gave birth to baby boy Duncan, before suffering post-natal depression and nearly smothering him with a pillow. She recovered and turned into a 'bonza mum', but sadly, there would always be another breakdown just waiting round the corner for poor old Ailsa.

Another mid-life baby was even more unexpected, given that Pippa was fostering all those kids because she supposedly couldn't get pregnant. Baby Christopher was a surprise but the Fletchers' happiness was short-lived when Tom (Roger Oakley) died after a heart attack at the wheel of his car. Roger Oakley wasn't the only actor tiring of the grind, and Vanessa Downing also fled soon after.

Since the foster kids needed at least one of the Fletchers to hang around, the role of Pippa was re-cast with Debra Lawrance. Ironically, the new Pippa seemed to inspire everybody else in Summer Bay to start fostering their own children. Alf and Ailsa took in Karen (Belinda Jarrett), her brother Blake Dean (Les Hill) and then punk chick Emma Jackson (Dannii Minogue), not to mention Emma's rough-as-guts mum Bridget (Paula Duncan). 'I was so excited when Dannii joined the show because I was a diehard *Young Talent Time* fan,' remembers Kate Ritchie (Sally). 'I wanted to crimp my hair just like her. She was so lovely to me.'

Nineteen ninety-one ushered in a new generation of foster parenting when Bobby took in seven-year-old Sam (Ryan Clark) and then fell in love with his dad, Greg Marshall (Ross Newton). Donald's stockbroker nephew David Croft (Guy Pearce) was only in town for seven weeks, but that was long enough to impregnate teenage Sophie (Rebekah Elmaloglou). Meanwhile, widowed Pippa (Debra Lawrance) married Michael (Dennis Coard) and within a year, reel-life had crossed over into real-life with the news that both actors had secretly married during a weekend break in filming.

Frank and Bobby.

Smart actors who left the show were quick to head over to the UK and take advantage of its popularity there. While many followed *Neighbours* stars into pantomime, Julian McMahon, Sharyn Hodgson, Mouche Phillips and Justine Clarke joined up to do a two-hour concert, *Home and Away: The Musical*. 'The audiences are so enthusiastic, it's like being at a rock'n'roll concert,' Julian McMahon told *TV Week* at the time. 'It wasn't an officially sanctioned show and they wouldn't be able to do that today, since the network is a bit more sensitive about what the brand is used for,' says John Holmes, not to mention Seven wanting its cut. 'It was rubbish but the actors had a great time doing it.'

For the 1991 cliffhanger, Frank, freshly separated from Roo (and Alex Papps freshly separated from *The Flying Doctors*), returned to once again declare his true love for Bobby (Nicolle Dickson). When the show returned in 1992, however, Bobby decided that she really wanted to marry boyfriend Greg (Ross Newton). Meanwhile, Blake (Les Hill) fell in love with leukaemia-stricken Meg Bowman (Cathy Godbold) who later died in his arms at sunrise. *Home and Away* always loves a tragic romance.

The Summer Bay police station was now manned by Constable Nick Parrish (Bruce Roberts), and to give him a bit of conflict at home, his troublemaker brother Shane Parrish (Dieter Brummer) arrived. After just a few months, it was obvious that Dieter Brummer was the biggest heart-throb since Alex Papps. Shane had a brief fling with one of the rare Asians to stumble into Summer Bay, Kelly Chan (Theresa Wong), but producers were already seeking to capitalise on his popularity with a longer-term girlfriend. *Home and Away* wanted a soap supercouple to rival *Neighbours'* Scott and Charlene, and you know what? They got one.

After auditioning hundreds of hopefuls for the coveted role, Perth's teenage model of the year and 16-year-old champion rollerskater Melissa George won it. Runaway street kid Angel Brooks was taken in by Donald just as she was on the verge of malnutrition. She first met Shane when she sold him a fake concert ticket and, from that point on, the couple argued and bickered with each other. In soap land, that meant they were perfect for each other, so when Shane was framed for a robbery in the 1992 cliffhanger and sent to a youth detention centre, a hysterical Angel was left wailing outside the gates.

Left in the wake of Shane and Angel's massive popularity were Roxy (Lisa Lackey) and unconventional teacher (in soaps, is there any other kind?) Luke Cunningham (John Adam). Adam had already been in *Home and Away* three years earlier, playing Dave, the sleazy army buddy of Ben (Julian McMahon), but this time round he was cast in a good guy leading role.

Meanwhile, horny teacher David (Guy Pearce) was killed when Karen (Belinda Jarrett) and Revhead (Gavin Harrison) drove their car into him. Sophie (Rebekah Elmaloglou) moved away to bring up baby Tamara and be closer to David's mother Mary (Jan Kingsbury). Revhead felt bad, especially since he already had a sister in a wheelchair, Julie Gibson (Naomi Watts before Hollywood stardom).

Pippa gave birth to her second boy, Dale, as actress Debra Lawrance was having a child in real life. However, in one of *Home and Away*'s most unfortunate storylines, Pippa's on-screen baby died of Sudden Infant Death Syndrome (SIDS). Lawrance had to film 21 consecutive scenes in one day dealing with the tragedy. *TV Week* reported that Lawrance 'couldn't ignore her own maternal instincts and three times checked her own four-month-old baby, Grace, to be sure she was alive. "I defy anybody to look at a small white coffin and not be moved. We got through it but it was really so hard",' Lawrance told the magazine.

'Bobby was killed after Adam drove his speedboat into a floating log. Well, at least it was a novel way to kill someone off.'

In August 1993, *Home and Away*'s original troublemaker Bobby (Nicolle Dickson) was killed in a boating accident after Adam (Mat Stevenson) drove his speedboat into a floating log. Well, at least it was a novel way to kill someone off. Bobby died in hospital after failing to wake up from a coma. The insanely popular character had matured from a surly brat into a responsible wife and mother and the fans had loved every moment of it. 'The teenagers liked Bobby because she wasn't glamorous,' Dickson told *TV Week* as she filmed her final scenes. 'When you're a teenager, there's a lot of pressure put on you by gorgeous girls on TV shows, so [the unconventional-looking] Bobby made them feel at ease. And the older generation thought it was fantastic when Bobby became nice. They used to say to me, "I'm so pleased you're not that awful person anymore".'

Awful people still streamed into Summer Bay and the latest was the mother of Finlay (Tina Thomsen) and Damien (Matt Doran). Their drunken (and occasionally violent) mother Irene Roberts (Jacqui Phillips) was later reformed and replaced with a different actress. The new Irene (Lynne McGranger) got herself off the grog and tried to be a better mother, particularly to errant eldest son Nathan (David Dixon).

Against the backdrop of another surf club fancy dress party (pretty much all Summer Bay nightlife had going for it), the 1993 cliffhanger had naughty Nathan trying to deflower the virginal Sarah (Laura Vasquez), Alf and Ailsa's latest foster child. Meanwhile, Shane discovered that Angel was the mother of a three-year-old child (she was, like, so dropped). Roxy and Luke were also left on shaky ground thanks to her growing friendship with James (Simon Baker-Denny).

Nineteen ninety-four reunited Shane and Angel as they teamed up to search for her son, Dylan (Corey Glaister). They found him, got engaged and then started fighting about their upcoming wedding, which didn't actually happen till 1995 thanks to Alf's bad driving putting Angel into a wheelchair. She only regained the use of her legs on her wedding day (it's a miracle!) in Aussie soap's best wedding hobble.

New schoolteacher Beth Armstrong (Toni Pearen) wowed the students at Summer Bay High while new foster kids Curtis (Shane Ammann) and Shannon Reed (Isla Fisher) pretended to be brother and sister to keep their much closer relationship under wraps. Jack (Daniel Amalm) decided to improve his physique with the help of steroids and Laura (Claudia Buttazzoni) was killed running across the train tracks at a level crossing.

One of *Home and Away*'s strangest moments occurred in mid-1995 when Bobby (Nicolle Dickson) was brought back to the show in a blaze of publicity. Viewers waited breathlessly to see how she would return from the dead, only to see her emerge from a refrigerator and start chatting to Ailsa (Judy Nunn). After being held up at gunpoint at The Diner, Ailsa was suffering another mental breakdown, and this bizarre hallucination was only there to steal attention from the debut of *Echo Point* over on Ten. It worked, but thankfully Bobby went back to the deep freeze just like The Blob and has never been defrosted again.

'As always, Home and Away was about its younger stars, and as fast as one lot left the Bay, another motley crew arrived.'

Another breakdown happened when a much talked-about *Home and Away* feature film was shelved. *TV Week* reported that the film was going to 'rely heavily on young stars', leaving its fans wondering exactly who else it would rely on. As always, *Home and Away* was about its younger stars, and as fast as one lot left the Bay, another motley crew arrived.

After Shannon's romance with 'brother' Curtis faltered, she moved on to Eric (Daniel Goddard) and Marcus (David Price). The revelation that she had been sexually abused by a family member explained why Shannon wasn't having much luck with men, but undeterred, she started spending a lot of time 'babysitting' Dylan at Shane and Angel's place while she plotted her seduction of Shane. It didn't happen, although *TV Week* got a few lurid covers out of the potential scandal and it was probably just as well, as Dieter Brummer's cover days were over when he quit the show.

In the 1995 cliffhanger, Shane was involved in a motorbike accident but, miraculously, he survived into 1996. But not for long. On a picnic with Dylan and newly-pregnant Angel, Shane collapsed and died of septicaemia caused by an infected scratch on his arm sustained in the crash. (At least he didn't die of a brain condition.)

A devastated Angel was left alone to give birth to their daughter, whom she named Shane. With Melissa George now planning her own exit (hello, Hollywood), Angel met an English millionaire philanthropist, Simon Broadhurst (Julian Garner). After an inconvenient romantic triangle involving conniving school friend Joanne (Kimberley Joseph), Simon proposed and whisked Angel and her two kids away in the 2,000th episode.

As new doctor Kelly (Katrina Hobbs) worried she might have been infected with HIV in a work-related incident, *Home and Away* acquired another blonde ingénue to torture. Selina Cook (Tempany Deckert) fell pregnant, had a miscarriage and suffered an identity crisis before joining a wacky commune where cult leader Saul (David Ritchie) tried to have his evil way with her.

While a bushfire had threatened Summer Bay the year before, 1996 had multiple natural disasters. First a flood swept Michael (Dennis Coard) away, leaving poor Pippa a widow again, and then an earthquake struck, giving Alf a heart attack and all the kids another near-death experience as Summer Bay High collapsed round them. The State Emergency Service, headed up by Travis (Nic Testoni), jumped into action, and when the tiny town was discovered to be sitting right on top of a fault line, the SES remained on standby for future tremors and other disasters.

Meanwhile, the unlikely union of ditzy Marilyn (Emily Symons) and the much older Donald Fisher (Norman Coburn) led to marriage. Marilyn, who had left the show once before to marry Phil Bryant (Vince Martin), had returned as a daffy divorcee who originally spurned Donald's advances in favour of Haydn Ross (Andrew Hill). Fisher, who had been married once before to Alf's sister Barbara (Barbara Stephens), faced a battle convincing his newly-returned daughter Rebecca (Belinda Emmett) that Marilyn was the right woman for him.

'Theirs isn't a sexual relationship,' Emily Symons told *TV Week*. 'There's a deep respect and friendship between them, and that's the basis for Marilyn wanting to marry him. She's made up her mind she doesn't want to be hurt any more.' After the wedding (filmed on the coldest day in Sydney for over a century), Symons predicted viewers would get a giggle from the couple's home life, since it was going to be something 'straight out of a Fifties sitcom, complete with twin beds'. This unexpected union also had an unconventional ceremony when the couple couldn't agree on a church to get married in. To keep everyone happy, they married on the side of the road, exactly halfway between the Catholic and Anglican churches.

For the 1996 cliffhanger, a new Summer Bay stalker was on the loose and reformed drug addict Chloe (Kristy Wright) was his target. As the show began its 10th year in 1997, Chloe fought back and bad Brad (Bruce Samazan), the supposedly trustworthy counsellor, had his leg stuck in a pig trap. Things began looking up for Chloe when new doctor Lachlan Fraser (Richard Grieve) arrived.

Pregnant Irene (Lynne McGranger) carried a surrogate baby for Finlay (Tina Thomsen), while Curtis (Shane Ammann) left to join a pro-surfing tour under the guidance of former champ Snowy James (Patrick Ward). Drug addict Justine Welles (Bree Desborough) went cold turkey after some needles had been discovered under a bed. She recovered off-screen and returned a few months later as a foster child of Pippa's.

Meanwhile, it was time for Sally (Kate Ritchie), the last remaining original foster kid, to become a woman. So far she had made it through puberty without any drug-taking or molestation, and her most embarrassing moment had been when she had to ask if anybody noticed that she was now wearing a bra. The answer was yes, it was pretty hard to miss.

While a bushfire had threatened Summer Bay the year before, 1996 had multiple natural disasters – first a flood, then an earthquake.

Sally had indeed grown up, and grown out. With her hot new figure, she ended up in the back of a panel van with Scott Irwin (Heath Ledger before Hollywood stardom). One-off sexual encounters like this usually led to pregnancy in Summer Bay, but perennial nice girl Sally was spared such humiliation, although Scott did ignore her the next day.

Another deflowering had a more tragic ending when illegal immigrant Stephanie Mboto (Fleur Beaupert) slept with Liam (Peter Scarf). Despite having survived the massacre of her Somalian village and a United Nations war crimes trial, she died the morning after losing her virginity when she slipped off a cliff while bushwalking. It was a short-lived attempt to show that Summer Bay could be a multicultural community, but after an emotional graveyard burial for Stephanie, it was back to being all about the white kids again.

Steven (Adam Willits), now a teacher, returned and caused a scandal when he decided to marry student Selena (Tempany Deckert). Unfortunately, the bride was kidnapped on her wedding bay when demented cult leader Saul returned and tried to burn Selena alive (or, as he put it, giver her 'immediate enlightenment through the purification of fire'). Budding bad boy Jesse McGregor (Ben Unwin) turned up and saved Selina.

After another failed relationship with a man, this time Dr Lachlan (Richard Grieve), Shannon (Isla Fisher) decided to move to Paris with writer Mandy (Rachel Blake). Although never spelt out, the inference was clear that the two were lesbian lovers, sparking a storm of controversy in Australia about what was suitable to screen in a G-rated timeslot. Producer Russell Webb slammed the Commercial Television Industry Code of Practice, which was administered by the Australian Broadcasting

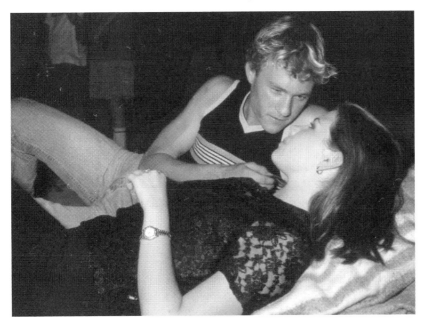

Scott (Heath Ledger) deflowers Sally (Kate Ritchie).

Authority, because it prevented *Home and Away* being socially responsible while allowing *Heartbreak High* to be racier, simply because it screened on a non-commercial network.

'If we wanted to do a story on teen sex we could not mention the word condom or show a condom-vending machine,' Webb told *TV Week*. 'I find it extremely frustrating that *Heartbreak High*, which is in an earlier time-slot, is able to tackle stories in more specific detail because it is on the ABC and therefore not subject to the same code.' In the UK, the self-imposed censorship by ITV was even more severe, with every bit of lesbian subtext between Mandy and Shannon completely removed when the show was screened there. Apparently, UK viewers couldn't cope with Shannon going to 'Gay Paree' with her 'special friend' Mandy.

Isla Fisher (Shannon) refused to buy into any of the gay controversy. She was avoiding the usual ex-soapie star route of pantos and personal appearances, choosing instead to study mime in Paris. She did, however, have a swipe at *Home and Away*'s scriptwriters for their lack of originality in sending her character to the same destination. 'I was just furious they were sending Shannon to Paris, because they knew I was going and, in fact, they could have sent her anywhere,' Fisher fumed to *TV Week*. 'The public thinks that you copy your character rather than the writers tending to base a lot of stuff on you.'

ITV's butchering of *Home and Away* was often bizarre, to say the least. An entire website was devoted to the subject and it reported that scenes disappeared if language as mild as 'you utter cow' was used. While part of the show's appeal was its Aussie slang (such as 'strewth', 'flaming heck' and 'stone the flaming crows' – thank you, Alf), English viewers were forbidden from hearing the expression 'ruddy'. In one instance, a sex discussion was cut because a character mentioned that she wanted her 'first time to be special'.

Desperate to prove it was still a family show at heart, *Home and Away* finished the year with a surprise heterosexual wedding between Travis (Nic Testoni) and Rebecca (Belinda Emmett), although the beachside nuptials took three attempts to film over a one-month period due to unseasonably cold weather and high winds on Palm Beach. Winter might sometimes get chilly in Sydney, but in Summer Bay, it's always summer.

In 1998 Chloe (Kristy Wright) found out she was pregnant to Lachlan (Richard Grieve), but his interfering mother plotted to send him away to America for work. After baby Olivia was born, Lachlan died overseas of another of *Home and Away*'s brain aneurisms (was it something in the water supply?), clearing the way for brother James (Michael Piccirilli) to move in on his deserted girlfriend.

Romance was also in the air for former lovebirds Jesse (Ben Unwin) and Kylie Burton (Roslyn Oades) who reunited. Harrowing times were ahead though, with daughter Rachel (Kelly Glaister) being abducted in a shopping mall by two boys. Given its unfortunate resemblance to the tragic real-life abduction of James Bulger in the UK, this storyline was, understandably, removed from the ITV episodes.

'The public thinks that you copy your character rather than the writers tending to base a lot of stuff on you.'

Meanwhile, the best-known foster mum of them all, Pippa (Debra Lawrance), finally called it a day and left with a new beau, Ian (Patrick Dickson). Since the Fletcher house was the centrepiece of the show, a new family flew in from Hong Kong, and as Alf would say, 'Strewth!' Was Summer Bay finally turning multicultural and getting an Asian family?

Fat chance. They were middle-class Caucasians just like everyone else in the Bay (and *Neighbours'* Ramsay Street). Joel Nash (David Woodley) was Travis's brother and they hadn't spoken in 17 years until Joel became the new town cop. Also in tow was wife Natalie (Angelica La Bozzetta, later Antoinette Byron), son Tom (Graeme Squires) and daughter Gypsy (Kimberley Cooper).

When bad boy Robert (Tony Poli) was released from jail and wanted to exact revenge on Joel for putting him away years earlier, he kidnapped Gypsy and locked her in a shed for the 1998 summer cliffhanger. When the show returned in 1999, Gypsy had been rescued but was deeply disturbed by the experience. She wasn't the only one to come unstuck that year.

Marilyn, who had undergone risky surgery in a bid to become pregnant with Fisher's baby, gave birth to a boy they named Byron. Unfortunately, Byron was diagnosed with cancer, Marilyn didn't cope, the marriage fell apart and she left for America where Byron eventually died.

Meanwhile, Vinnie (Ryan Kwanten) was also diagnosed with cancer (testicular, and thankfully, not the same kind as little Byron). Tragically, behind the scenes, actress Belinda Emmett found out she had breast cancer. As she left for three months of treatment, *Paradise Beach*'s Megan Connolly took over her role of Rebecca until Emmett was well enough to return.

Irene took in new street kid Will Smith (Zac Drayson) and eventually his sister Hayley (Rebecca Cartwright) arrived, followed by younger brother Nick (Chris Egan). Chloe (Kristy Wright) left after a disastrously short marriage to James (Michael Piccirilli) and it was also bye-bye to Travis (Nic Testoni) and Rebecca (Belinda Emmett) who departed on a round-the-world boat trip.

During 2000, Leah Poulos (Ada Nicodemou) arrived and brought an army of Greek relatives with her. For the new millennium, Summer Bay was finally evolving into a more multicultural community. Sexy lifesaver Shauna Bradley (Kylie Watson) tried to fend off the advances of a newly-returned Adam (Mat Stevenson), just as she discovered she was adopted and her real mum was Ailsa. Shortly after this revelation, Judy Nunn became ill and Nancye Hayes had to step in and play Ailsa. Producers sent Nunn a bunch of flowers with a card asking her to stop turning her life into a soap opera!

Jesse (Ben Unwin) got into more trouble with the law and had to flee town while Sam (Ryan Clark) took a more traditional route out of Summer Bay when he went away to become a professional surfer (let's face it, Summer Bay doesn't provide many other career options, apart from foster parenting). There was also a new family, the Sutherlands, who

For the new millennium, Summer Bay was finally evolving into a more multicultural community.

would become the most tortured lot in the history of the soap. Rhys (Michael Beckley) and Shelley (Paula Forrest) had three daughters, Dani (Tammin Sursok), the eldest, and fraternal twins Jade (Kate Garvan) and Kirsty (Christie Hayes). Or were they?

In September, *Home and Away* took a two-week break so that Seven could turn the network over to 24-hour coverage of the Sydney Olympics. Writers came up with a new natural disaster – a freak landslide caused by torrential rain. Shot over four nights at the bottom of a quarry, Ailsa's birthday party was interrupted by the mudslide, which flattened her alongside kids Duncan (Brendan McKensy) and Shauna (Kylie Watson). Jade (Kate Garvan) was also trapped, and the alarm was raised by Kirsty who could 'sense' that her twin sister was in danger, even though she was across town at the newly-opened drop-in centre.

A series of highly dramatic promo spots ran incessantly throughout the Olympics and by the time *Home and Away* was ready to return to its regular timeslot, even the most unlikely viewers were wondering 'Who Will Die?' As it turned out, all the major characters were pulled out alive (leaving just one bit player to bite the dust) but there was heartache ahead for Summer Bay's favourite daughter.

Sally (Kate Ritchie) hadn't been having a good year, what with an obsessive compulsive disorder and a dodgy fiancé, Kieran Fletcher (Spencer McLaren), whom she had met on an archaeological dig in Ireland. Returning to the Bay for her wedding were Sally's former foster siblings Frank (Alex Papps), Carly (Sharyn Hodgson) and Steven (Adam Willits), her first boyfriend Jack (Daniel Amalm), old caravan park friends Floss (Sheila Kennelly), Martin (Craig Thompson) and Lance (Peter Vroom), and foster mum Pippa (Debra Lawrance).

'I always love it when they bring back the old characters,' says Kate Ritchie. 'Actually, I had been thinking about leaving the show, but when I made the decision to stay, I decided I didn't want Sally to be married at 19. There are so many other options for young girls rather than just marriage and motherhood and I thought Sally needed to at least have a career before going down that path.'

Consequently, a tortured Gypsy announced to the congregation that Kieran had been trying to crack onto her, so that was the end of Sally's wedding day. Eventually Sally got a new man when Dr Flynn (Martin Dingle-Wall) arrived, and she started work as a teacher at Summer Bay High.

With just a couple of months to go until another end-of-year cliff-hanger, it was time to farewell one of the last remaining original cast members. Having just survived her house collapsing around her, Ailsa (Judy Nunn) didn't realise she was now suffering from a heart defect, and slumped to the shop floor just as the show shut down for summer. When 2001 started, her grief-stricken husband was scattering her ashes in the Bay.

Producers farewelled Judy Nunn with a party and a special gift given only to original cast members, a leather-bound copy of the original *Home and Away* pilot episode. Afterwards, Nunn reminisced about her 13 years on the show in her regular column for *TV Week*. Admitting she was short-sighted in the extreme, and couldn't wear contact lenses in bright sunshine, she had once asked Ray Meagher, 'Who the hell is that big bloke up on the hill? He's been watching us for ages and he hasn't moved an inch.' Meagher took a 'quick squiz' before telling her she was staring at the lighthouse!

Meanwhile, Ailsa's daughter, Shauna, proposed to Jude Lawson (Ben Steel) while a Scottish kilt-clad Vinnie and Leah married in a big fat Greek wedding. Leah fell pregnant straightaway but another pregnancy wasn't as welcome when Gypsy discovered she was single and expecting. Dani was 'assaulted' by Kane Phillips (Sam Atwell) and Noah Lawson (Beau Brady) became the Bay's latest teenage alcoholic. Leah's brother Alex (Danny Raco) smashed his car while driving home from the end-of-year formal, killing Miles (Steven Rooke) and injuring Brodie Hanson (Susie Rugg).

Over in the UK, *Home and Away* had been off air for over a year. ITV's request to pay less for the soap had resulted in its Australian distribution company, Southern Star, hiring a British research firm to find out exactly what sort of appeal the soap still had. 'It showed it was making ITV money,' Southern Star Sales chief executive Catherine Payne told *The Australian*, and armed with this research, they set about finding a new network to screen it (at a new price).

Enter the UK's youngest network, Channel 5, which was struggling to find a popular show to anchor its programming. Despite ITV enforcing a contract stipulation that prevented a new network from screening the soap for 12 months, Channel 5 signed up in a deal reported to bring Australia's Seven Network up to $20 million a year in revenue. Five now owns the series for as long as Seven continues to make it.

Like ITV before it, Channel 5 screened *Home and Away* twice a day throughout Britain (at 12.30pm and 6pm) with a new omnibus edition which repeated all five episodes every Saturday afternoon. Channel 5 began screening the series in July 2001, and *Home and Away* immediately became their top-rated show, not to mention a healthy lead-in for the audience-starved UK soap that followed it each day, *Family Affairs*.

Seven wisely decided to combine a location shoot with the necessary promotional push needed to tell everyone *Home and Away* was back. Nine cast members flew into London, but only five were required for the over-seas storyline that had the gang travelling abroad for the launch of a book by Donald Fisher (Norman Coburn), 'Letter to Byron', a tribute to the infant son he briefly had with the now-departed Marilyn (Emily Symons). Accompanying Fisher were Irene (Lynne McGranger), Nick (Chris Egan), Hayley (Rebecca Cartwright) and Will (Zac Drayson).

While Nick bumped into Jenny Frost and Natasha Hamilton from the pop group Atomic Kitten (unfortunately Liz McClarnon was sick and unavailable for the cameo), Fisher, sightseeing from a double-decker tour bus, spotted missing wife Marilyn walking down a street. When he also

Channel 5 signed up in a deal reported to bring Australia's Seven Network up to $20 million a year in revenue.

caught her ducking out of his book launch at London's Tate Gallery, he kept searching the streets until he found her. After all, London is just like Summer Bay, and when you need to find someone you just walk the streets.

When Marilyn was conveniently located, she brought closure to their relationship by telling Donald she couldn't return to the Bay because of the bad memories there. The truth was, actress Emily Symons had no need for another *Home and Away* stint. She was one of the few Aussie actresses to cross over to a UK soap, and was now playing barmaid Louise in *Emmerdale*.

For its 2001 summer cliffhanger, Leah (Ada Nicodemou) and Gypsy (Kimberley Cooper) were both giving birth. Leah delivered baby boy V.J. (in a boring hospital bed) while Gypsy squatted by the side of the road and squeezed out baby girl Lily. Helping out was proud father Will (Zac Drayson), who was so overcome by the experience he proposed to Gypsy on the spot. Unfortunately for Leah, her baby's father, Vinnie (Ryan Kwanten), was arrested for fraud and escorted straight to jail (turns out hospital rooms weren't so boring after all). Come 2002, Vinnie was incarcerated while Gypsy and Will left the Bay to start a new life together.

After the unexpected success of the first series of Australia's *Big Brother* (stripped opposite it at 7pm weeknights), *Home and Away* producers carefully prepared for the next assault in 2002. Scriptwriters came up with a 150th anniversary of settlement in Summer Bay celebration. It brought back to the show Frank (Alex Papps), Carly (Sharyn Hodgson), Blake (Les Hill) and Sophie (Rebekah Elmaloglou), while Pippa sent a video message (actress Debra Lawrance was filming *Blue Heelers* in Melbourne).

Not satisfied with this star-studded reunion, everyone was then boarded onto a ferry boat and sent out to sea for a night cruise. Naturally, a freak storm hit so promos could scream 'Who Will Survive?' *Big Brother 2* crumbled against the competition but critics failed to give credit to Seven's soap, preferring to invent their own reasons for the reality soap suddenly faltering.

While Dani fell for newcomer Josh West (Daniel Collopy), her sister Kirsty started getting up close and personal with the (apparently reformed) teen who had raped Dani, Kane Phillips (Sam Atwell). Dani was horrified at her sister's betrayal but her parents were too busy suffering their own crisis to offer much support. When devious schoolteacher (and first love) Angie Russell (Laurie Foell) arrived to tell Rhys (Michael Beckley) that he had an illegitimate son, Dylan (Brett Hicks-Maitland), Rhys's marriage didn't survive. Nobody seemed to notice his wife Shelley (Paula Forrest) leaving the family though, for they all had a new little nephew to play with, Max Sutherland (Sebastian Elmaloglou, brother of Rebekah), who turned out to prefer the company of doddery old Colleen (Lyn Collingwood).

Jesse (Ben Unwin), who had been languishing in jail alongside Vinnie, headed straight to the Bay on his release after promising to look in on

Returning for the
reunion. L-R: Steven
(Adam Willits), Floss
(Sheila Kennelly), Celia
(Fiona Spence), Matt
(Greg Benson), Sophie
(Rebekah Elmaloglou),
Sam (Ryan Clark),
Sally (Kate Ritchie),
Carly (Sharyn Hodgson)
and Blake (Les Hill).

Vinnie's family. Leah (Ada Nicodemou) had just learnt that V.J. was deaf,
and when Vinnie died in a prison fire, Jesse moved right in to help out, in
more ways than one.

Producers had originally been toying with putting Summer Bay in the
path of another bushfire for that year's summer cliffhanger, but they
decided to avoid another natural disaster (although it's a distinct possibility that one day a volcano will erupt under someone's house). While
the fire idea was extinguished, in a sad coincidence, a real bushfire raced
through many parts of Sydney that summer, and the house that was used
as the show's main residence went up in flames in December 2002.

'I will always call it the Fletcher house and I think it is integral to *Home
and Away*,' says Kate Ritchie (Sally). 'See, you need a central family
living there to give the show its stability. There's nothing wrong with
stories about broken homes or single parenting, but you need that house
with a family unit to anchor the show. I do get a bit sentimental about it
though!' While the burnt-out remains of the historic Jackaroo Ranch at
Kenthurst were eventually sold for over $1.5 million, the Seven network
constructed a replica on their backlot at Epping.

Instead of a bushfire, *Home and Away* finished its 14th year with an
absolute clanger when Alf discovered his dead wife Ailsa (Judy Nunn)
alive and well in his kitchen. When the show returned for 2003, Ailsa was
revealed to be a figment of Alf's imagination (he was slowly going wacko
because of a growing brain tumour). Alf was the only person who could
see Ailsa and she was written as a slightly malevolent force trying to tempt
him over to the other side.

As Alf's tumour worsened, he upset his friends by announcing that he
didn't want surgery if it meant he was going to lose Ailsa again. When he

A ghostly Ailsa (Judy Nunn) brings back a clinically dead Alf (Ray Meagher) to Summer Bay as an Aboriginal (David Ngoombujarra).

flatlined on a hospital operating table, doctors were left wondering if they should revive him or let him die as he had requested. While they argued, Alf floated off to soap opera heaven where everything was white and everyone had one last chance to decide between the hereafter and Summer Bay. Ailsa decided to transport Alf into the future to show him how things would end up if he died before his time.

Summer Bay, ten years down the track, had turned into an over-developed yuppies' paradise with an ugly underbelly of crime and drug abuse. Upset that he couldn't catch up with his former friends, Alf asked Ailsa to put him into a temporary new body. When he looked into the mirror, by crikey, he was an Aboriginal (played by David Ngoombujarra). Ailsa stood by with a sly smile on her face and quipped, 'It's good to step into someone else's shoes.' By the end of the landmark episode, Alf had decided to return and save his beloved Bay, so after a final farewell to Ailsa (well, it seems permanent this time, but she's always welcome back), Alf Stewart returned to the land of the living.

Home and Away, now under the control of producer Julie McGaurin and script editor Coral Drouyn, was on fire. In its 16th year of broadcast, it was winning its timeslot with an average 1.3 million viewers every night. A second generation of teenagers had begun watching the show, and it appeared from the figures that many of the show's original viewers had been enticed back.

Reunions seem to be a key ingredient in bringing back the lapsed. As former viewers tune in to see how the old favourites are ageing, the nutty storylines seem to draw them back in. Take, for example, Sophie (Rebekah Elmaloglou), who returned after the ferry disaster to carry a surrogate baby for the childless Sally (Kate Ritchie) and Flynn (now played by Joel McIllroy). After having their fertilised egg implanted into her, Sophie discovered she was already pregnant to Blake. Would she have twins? No, she miscarried just one baby – Sally's.

As Dani fell for handsome horse-riding-on-the-beach boy Scott Hunter (Kip Gamblin), teacher Angie Russell (Laurie Foell) became even more of a psycho bitch, making enemies with just about everybody in the Bay. Her shenanigans took *Home and Away* to even greater heights, setting an Australian ratings record of 1.49 million viewers. 'During the Angie stuff, all of the actors – including me – were coming in to work saying, "Oh my God, did you see that last night?" If we're doing that, the audience must love it,' says Kate Ritchie.

With a long list of suspects, Angie was murdered just in time for the debut of *Big Brother 3*, prompting a murder mystery competition (with

Sally finally marries
Flynn (Joel McIllroy).

$20,000 prize money) to keep the reality series at bay. Viewers couldn't decide if the killer was student Nick (Chris Egan), whom she had been torturing with twisted mind games, former hot-head lover Jesse (Ben Unwin) or humiliated Rhys (Michael Beckley), whom Angie had called a 'pathetic, middle-aged loser' in front of everyone at the Surf Club just before she died. Eventually, the murderer was revealed to be her ashamed son, Dylan (Brett Hicks-Maitland).

With the departure of Donald (Norman Coburn) to live in Queensland, *Home and Away* had just two remaining original characters – Alf (Ray Meagher) and Sally (Kate Ritchie). While Alf looked like being a widower for a while, the time had finally come to marry off Sally. Viewers had watched her grow up before their eyes since she was just eight years old, so her TV wedding on 25 June 2003 was such an event it even spawned a spin-off, *Home and Away – The Wedding Special*. This time, Sally finally got her man, Flynn (Joel McIllroy), although bridesmaid Sophie went into labour and Sally and Leah found themselves dumped by the side of the road after their horse-drawn carriage came loose.

'It seemed charming except that it looked as if it was filmed outside the local tip,' commented *Sydney Morning Herald* TV writer Michael Idato. 'Summer Bay might boast nice beaches, but the hinterland is screaming out for redevelopment. Or, at the very least, gutters. In the end, the wedding was finally had in the hospital, somewhere between casualty and renal, with the bride and groom clad in bathrobes and the bed-bound Sophie wheeled in to witness proceedings.'

Another milestone was quietly slipped into *Home and Away* at this time when the show finally managed to utter the word 'gay'. Pippa brought along son Christopher Fletcher (now played by Rian McLean) and remarked to Irene that he hadn't yet come to terms with his sexuality. After trying to kiss Seb (Mitch Firth), he returned to the big city with his progressive mum, but not before bare-chested Nick (Chris Egan) overcame his homophobia to jump into Chris's arms as a farewell present.

Some viewers may have then wondered if Summer Bay's newest resident, Tasha (Isabel Lucas), might be a lesbian, but alas, it seemed she was just a mermaid who had washed up on the rocks and only spoke pig Latin. Isabel Lucas had been spotted on a street in Far North Queensland and, lacking acting experience, was slowly introduced into the action by not having to say much. Sadly, Tasha didn't turn out to be a mermaid. Or a lesbian. Yet.

Tasha (Isabel Lucas) was (apparently) a mermaid who had washed up on the rocks and only spoke pig Latin.

Meanwhile, Sally and Flynn were thrilled when Leah fell pregnant with a surrogate baby for them. Colleen (Lyn Collingwood) struggled with cancer and wore a lot of bad wigs. Alex (Danny Raco) was caught trafficking in steroids (that old chestnut again), threatening his relationship with Hayley (Bec Cartwright). Hayley was still harbouring feelings for old boyfriend Noah (Beau Brady), who was counselling (in more ways than one) the Bay's newest teenage alcoholic, Kit (Amy Mizzi), the sister of Scott (Kip Gamblin). Kit and Scott's mother, Beth (Clarissa House), moved into the Sutherland house and into the bed of Rhys (Michael Beckley), who barely had time for romance given his teenage daughters' complicated love lives.

Kirsty and Kane's forbidden relationship was tearing her family apart (and was 'so hot' it spun-off into a tie-in paperback novel, CD soundtrack and DVD called *Home and Away: Hearts Divided*). Despite once 'violating' Dani, Kirsty insisted that Kane was her soulmate. Dani was furious and threatened to break the relationship up, so when she accidentally ran Kane over in her car, she was found guilty of attempted murder, thanks to the return of the judge everybody loved to hate, Morag (Cornelia Frances).

Dani had a brief spell in jail, where she ran afoul of its top dog, Guvnor (*Prisoner*'s Maggie Kirkpatrick), who seemed to take delight in tormenting the newly-arrived 'princess'. Maggie Kirkpatrick refused to re-hash her Joan Ferguson role and insisted on creating a completely new character. Strangely, her appearance, which should have been hailed as a camp cult cameo, was never publicised and the Summer Bay jailhouse rock petered out within the week. *TV Week* readers later complained about putting 'poor Dani' into such a hostile environment, apparently having no appreciation of soap irony whatsoever.

Home and Away finished its 16th year on air in 2003 with most of the Sutherland family trapped in a mine cave-in, while mermaid girl Tasha was revealed to be the secret daughter of superbitch Angie. Kirsty (Christie Hayes) and Kane (Sam Atwell) ran away to get married. Kirsty pretended to get pregnant, pretended to miscarry, then realised she really was going to have a baby, then really miscarried and needed a kidney. Really. Unfortunately, she had just found out that Jade was not really her twin sister, even though Jade had just used her 'twin psychic powers' to tell rescuers that Kirsty had been trapped down the mineshaft.

A 'hospital mix-up' meant that Laura (Christie Hayes with red hair extensions) was really the other Sutherland twin and she was therefore

There's never quite been another super couple like Melissa George and Dieter Brummer (Shane and Angel), pictured here with Lloyd Morris.

able to donate a kidney. Jade coped with her shock new identity by ingesting drugs with Alf's delinquent son Duncan (Brendan McKensy). It led to a car going off a cliff (just as *Big Brother 4* was starting over on Ten). Jade's boyfriend Seb (Mitch Firth) was left paralysed while Jade was feared drowned until she floated back alive to shore, as all good unconscious soap heroines in the ocean do.

Duncan's delinquency brought back to Summer Bay his useless guardian Morag (Cornelia Frances), and Donald (Norman Coburn) also popped back to take Seb home to Brisbane to recuperate. Original character Floss (Sheila Kennelly) also returned to ask Sally to help her die if her terminal cancer got the better of her. Miraculously, though, Floss went into remission.

Sally's willingness to overdose Floss with her husband's morphine caused problems in her marriage, but then Flynn (Joel McIllroy) was already making a mess of it with his growing fondness for pregnant Leah (who was strangely attractive to him even with braces on her teeth). After Leah (Ada Nicodemou) and Joel shared a forbidden kiss (maybe the doc secretly wanted to become a dentist), Jesse (Ben Unwin) told Leah it was over between them, causing her waters to break. Leah handed over her surrogate baby to Sally as agreed, but her relationship with Jesse was definitely kaput. In a nod to Summer Bay's original foster mother, Sally named her baby girl Pippa (played by baby boy Noah Fraser before being replaced by four-month-old Isabella, the daughter of *Neighbours'* veteran Melissa Bell).

Meanwhile, another Summer Bay triangle was under way with Tasha trying to make up her mind between Beth's nerdy son Robbie (Jason Smith) and 'hunky newcomer' Kim Hyde (Chris Hemsworth), the son of

Kate Ritchie
Best Wishes
love Kate Ritchie
xxx
⑦ Home and Away

Summer Bay High's tyrannical new headmaster Mr Hyde (Ivar Kants). Tasha also began having nightmares about her dead mother Angie (Laurie Foell) before discovering her real father was Ian Osborne, one of the wealthiest men in Australia. He insisted upon Angie's look-alike cousin (and former brothel madam) Josie (the return of Laurie Foell as a regular) moving to Summer Bay to help him decide whether Tasha was worthy of being officially recognised as his daughter and heir.

The 2004 season saw Bevan Lee, one of its original co-creators, back at the helm as script producer, and his stories began airing from May. He insisted he would move away from the increasingly frenetic storytelling of recent months, which made for attention-grabbing promos but had started to exhaust the audience. Lee decided to give Summer Bay's oldies some more screen time, starting with the break-up of the marriage of Rhys (Michael Beckley) and Beth (Clarissa House) when he fell back in love with ex-wife Shelley (Paula Forrest).

Despite the show's restrictive timeslot, Lee also exposed a growing drug problem with a crystal meth addiction story. Dani's demented stalker Felix (Josh Lawson) was revealed to be a user but when he was bashed and died, his enraged girlfriend Sarah (Luisa Hastings Edge) pointed the finger of blame at Dani and Scott (Kip Gamblin). It led to another memorable Olympics cliffhanger as Sarah fired a gun into a room crammed full of Summer Bay regulars. When the show returned after the Athens Games, Noah (Beau Brady) lay dead, leaving behind his new bride Hayley (Bec Cartwright).

Home and Away has always been a magnet for psychos but it's also had its fair share of celebrities, and particularly sporting stars thanks to Seven's long association with broadcasting the Olympics. Somehow, Aussie champions Ian Thorpe, Kieren Perkins, Clint Robinson and Susie O'Neill have all ended up in Summer Bay, even if their storylines were pretty naff (like when Thorpey couldn't train at the beach because it was closed). Other celebs who have dropped in for a cameo include *Monty Python*'s Michael Palin, supermodel Annelise Braakensiek and singer John Farnham, who came by in 1988 to give a private concert to Sally (Kate Ritchie).

Merchandising has come full circle and is now big business again for the long-running hit. After a series of early paperback tie-in books to cash in on its UK fans, *Home and Away* became a hot property again after the ratings resurgence of 2003. As well as *Hearts Divided*, the forbidden Dani and Kane romance (that came with a brand new, but ultimately inconsequential, episode on DVD), Dani's trial and brief jailing resulted in two more books during 2004, not to mention those ubiquitous CD soundtracks.

Home and Away could be with us for a long time, especially given that Channel 5 now funds more than half of the production costs for the show (not to mention having creative and editorial influence). While its former network, ITV, could only classify *Home and Away* as an acquisition, Channel 5 is able to count the Aussie soap as 'originated' programming, and 130 hours of it a year provides a substantial amount of its necessary quota requirements for UK broadcasting.

In 2003, they even considered a spin-off series to be known as *Away From Home*. It would be for an older audience (and later timeslot) and would follow *Home and Away* characters as they moved to the big city. Former actors such as Zac Drayson (Will) were tapped as potential regulars, but when Channel 5 eventually decided they didn't have enough money to do it, Seven was unable to proceed without their support.

However, after *Home and Away* returned in 2004 and became Seven's top-rating drama, the beleaguered network decided to resurrect the spin-off. Now called *Campus*, it will follow a group of Summer Bay High's alumni as they move away to university. If all goes according to plan, it could be on air in 2005.

Throughout the world, *Home and Away* has a nightly audience of more than 60 million in over 150 countries including Afghanistan, Bangladesh, Fiji, Iraq, Jamaica, Mongolia and the People's Republic of China where they made their own version called *Ba Ba Ma Shi Laowei*, which roughly translates to 'Mum and Dad are Foreigners'.

So what is its lasting appeal? Is it the sunny lifestyle, the delinquent rehabilitations or the hamburger phone in The Diner? '*Home and Away* is the ultimate Aussie soap,' says Kimberley Cooper (Gypsy). 'Its characters have become icons and the beach always provides the ultimate location to watch, probably more so than *Neighbours*' suburban street. The only thing I've ever found strange about the show is that it's so Aussie and yet Summer Bay doesn't have a pub.'

'Watching *Home and Away* is handed down from older kids to their younger sisters and brothers,' says Kate Ritchie (Sally). 'I've kept one letter from a grandmother who wrote that she watched me grow up alongside her daughter and now she watches the show with her granddaughter. I definitely have an emotional attachment to it because I came onto it so young. I just love it.'

It's obvious that producers would like Sally to go full circle and become the new Pippa. Kate Ritchie realised it the day she got the script that revealed Sally was going to have a hysterectomy. 'I saw [producer] John Holmes in the corridor and said, "Don't think I don't know what you're doing here, mate!" Maybe Sally can start fostering kids just like Pippa did, but only if she's still on the show in ten years time. I'm just not ready for that yet.' Ritchie probably shouldn't worry. In Summer Bay, there's no such thing as not being able to have children, as Pippa has proved again and again. In Summer Bay, anything is possible.

31

RICHMOND HILL

PREMIERE: **1988** EPISODES: **92** NETWORK: **TEN** FINALE: **1988**

Ivy (Maggie Kirkpatrick), Anne (Emily Symons) and Dan (Ross Higgins).

With *Neighbours* firmly entrenched as a prime time hit at 7pm week-nights, the Ten Network decided they needed one more Australian drama to anchor their night-time audience. Given the international sales of *Neighbours*, Grundy's were keen to make a new show, this time a 'soft' police drama with human interest stories. Reg Watson came up with *Richmond Hill* which appeared to put a *Country Practice* type spin on their previous cop soapie *Waterloo Station*. Given the quick failure of the latter, it probably wasn't the wisest combination.

Set in an outer city suburb, *Richmond Hill* spread its action over a police station, a real estate office, a pub and a farm for troubled kids. Producer Phillip East refused to label it a police show, possibly trying to divert attention away from the lame cop action which was never a Grundy's specialty. '*Richmond Hill* tried to be too many things to too many people and I think the show suffered because of it,' says Brian Walsh, who launched it in January 1988 amidst much fanfare, then ran into trouble keeping the momentum going.

Walsh had been the publicity supremo who turned *Neighbours* into a hit with his promotions and stunts, but his reputation preceded him with the cast of *Richmond Hill*. 'A lot of the "serious actors" feared that I was going to do a *Neighbours* on them,' says Walsh. 'Some of them were concerned about appearing in shopping centres and the like, so for that reason they never really embraced the idea of publicity and I think the show suffered because of it.'

There was also a lot of suffering planned for the residents of *Richmond Hill* with early storylines big on misery and implied violence. Single mum and brassy barmaid Connie Ryan (Amanda Muggleton) had a 14-year-old son, Andrew (Marc Gray), whom she always tried to pass off as her brother. When her yobbo ex-boyfriend Mick (Perry Quinton) turned up at the back door, Connie threw Andrew out the front door and told him to go live in a refuge. Within minutes of being alone with his woman, Mick started to smack Connie around.

Down at the pub, Constable Tim Shannon (Robert Sampson) discovered that his girlfriend Anne Costello (Emily Symons) was sleeping with his partner Constable Neil Travers (Serge Lazareff). Amoral Anne tried to blackmail Neil about the affair by threatening to tell all to his wife and her father, Sergeant Dan Costello (Ross Higgins), who was also Neil's boss. Daddy Dan had no idea his 'little girl' was a scheming seductress, but wife Alice (Rona Coleman) was beginning to catch on, until she caught herself an incurable disease and died.

Newly single Tim decided to ask neurotic real estate agent Jill Warner (Dina Panozzo) out on a date. He took her out to the farm where he had grown up and introduced her to crusty old Mum Foote (Gwen Plumb). Mum looked after troubled kids, and Tim was one of her success stories. As Tim reminisced about his childhood, he flashed back to the day a teen psychotic had threatened to kill Mum. Right on cue, said psycho (now grown up) arrived on a plane from New Zealand and immediately embarked on a campaign of terror against the do-gooders by burning down Mum's chicken shed. Given the unromantic location the lovers were getting to know one another in – even with the smell of roasting chickens in the air – Tim and Jill's romance was doomed.

This unpleasant tone was cemented with *Richmond Hill*'s very first cliffhanger. Janet (Paula Duncan) was already unhappily married to by-the-book (read: boring) Senior Constable Warren Bryant (Tim Elston), but within hours of arriving in the new suburb she was raped by another nutter who escaped from the back of an unlocked police van (yes, the cops there really were that inept). After the attack, Warren wouldn't allow incarcerated son Marty (Ashley Paske) to visit his mother, so the teenager ran away from his delinquent school, only to hitch a ride in a stolen car and end up in an accident.

The rape storyline was unfortunate for actress Paula Duncan, as she had just been raped in *Prisoner*. 'I hated my *Richmond Hill* character,' says Duncan today. 'She was always crying and it used to exhaust me. I couldn't see anything wonderful in being a complaining wimp, but the public liked her because they identified with a woman who was stuck at home.'

Light moments were few and far between, even with a bevy of spunky young cops. Constable Susan Miller (Felicity Soper), Constable Mark

There was a lot of suffering planned for the residents ... with early storylines big on misery and implied violence.

Johnson (Warren Blondell) and Constable Rick Reid (Martin Maddell) did little apart from looking good, answering the phone and attending to Mrs Jennings (Thelma Scott, real-life live-in companion of Gwen Plumb), a lonely old lady suffering senile dementia who hung around the police station front desk claiming prowlers were following her.

Down at the real estate office were the dodgy Alderman Frank Hackett (Robert Alexander) and his stuck-up wife Ivy (Maggie Kirkpatrick). When Ivy discovered that Frank was having it off with trailer trash Connie, she called the police and told them a rape was in progress, an unfortunate ploy given that a real rapist was on the loose. Consequently, the cops smashed their way into Connie's fibro shack only to find two very willing, but surprised, participants. Frank then slunk around his mansion pretending nothing had happened, while Ivy plotted her revenge with best friend Mavis Roberts (Betty Lucas).

'I loved doing the comedy,' says Maggie Kirkpatrick today. 'It was real *Golden Girls* stuff with Betty Lucas. Grundy's, God bless 'em, specifically created a character as far removed from *Prisoner*'s Joan Ferguson as possible. I was so grateful for that because I was never typecast.'

Apart from the nasty stories unfolding, it was disconcerting for viewers having to get used to their favourite actors playing against type, even if Grundy's were trying something different. After years of playing the politically incorrect and bumbling Ted Bulpitt in the sitcom *Kingswood Country*, Ross Higgins was now a humourless police chief. And while Maggie Kirkpatrick relished the chance to erase the memory of *Prisoner*'s 'The Freak', it was odd seeing her in pearls and shoulder pads while playing it for laughs, even if the actress was having a ball. 'I'd done the Jenny Craig thing and stripped the weight off so I loved looking glamorous,' Kirkpatrick laughs.

A much more successful casting was Amanda Muggleton as tarty Connie. It would not have been a surprise if one day Connie had revealed she was actually Chrissie Latham, on the run from *Prisoner*'s Wentworth Detention Centre. From the mouthy attitude to the desperate bids to better herself, Connie and Chrissie were one and the same.

Gwen Plumb (Mum Foote) was another acquisition from a previous Grundy's show. Creator Reg Watson specifically wrote the part for Plumb after her spookily similar guest appearance as *Neighbours*' Mrs Forbes, who also ran a farm and took in Scott and Danny when they ran away from Ramsay Street. Plumb's portrayal apparently moved Reg Grundy and wife Joy Chambers to tears so it was a no-brainer to get her back for *Richmond Hill*.

Gwen Plumb had already given her word to Reg Watson to do *Richmond Hill* when the Seven Network asked her to play town gossip Mrs Peters in the *Home and Away* pilot. She managed to do both but when it came time to commit to a long-running job, she would have preferred

Home and Away because it was being shot in her 'Palm Beach backyard'. However, a deal was a deal, so she stuck it out with *Richmond Hill* and travelled every day to Mona Vale where Mum's farm was created within a disused tomato nursery.

Clad in overalls (and a bad wig) and with faithful blue cattle dog Zorro by her side, Mum turned her farm into a market garden in a bid to keep troubled Marty Bryant (Ashley Paske) on the straight and narrow. Ironically, actor and soon-to-be teen heartthrob Paske only ended up in *Richmond Hill* after he failed an audition for *Home and Away*.

When Marty's real mum, Janet (Paula Duncan), finally developed a backbone and stopped crying (after the rape, the depression and the bad marriage), she defied her husband by getting a job as a doctor's reception-ist. Warren (Tim Elston) walked out on her and fell into an affair with Janet's new best friend, Jill (Dina Panozzo). Jill and Janet didn't stay friends for long but, in typical soap fashion, they made up again very quickly.

Mum (Gwen Plumb) with Tim (Robert Sampson) before the BBQ chook incident.

Given that Jill was one of the few remaining characters not to have been stalked by a psycho, she was duly abducted by an insane real estate agency customer (David Whitney), proving what Janet already knew – having a cop for a boyfriend or husband was of no help in keeping the loonies away in *Richmond Hill*. Jill found herself in a demented mock wedding ceremony, with her madman playing the multiple roles of priest, photographer and bridegroom. While this might have proved to be a truly memorable married couple in the show, Jill was rescued by Warren before the honeymoon could be consummated.

Janet found solace in the arms of the lawyer defending her rapist, Craig Connor (Michael Long), until she decided she preferred being with her chauvinist husband. Warren and Janet reconciled and reaffirmed their wedding vows, just before Janet discovered she was pregnant. With parents like that as an example, Marty embarked on his own disastrous love affairs, beginning with barmaid Fiona (Angela Kennedy).

A much-repeated plot device was the rocky relationship of Connie (Amanda Muggleton) and teenage son Andrew (Marc Gray). Time and time again, Connie would throw her son over for an ill-suited lover, only to realise her error and beg Andrew for forgiveness. They would set up house again until the next hopeless loser walked into the pub and caught Connie's eye. Theirs was the only truly interesting interaction in *Richmond Hill*, particularly when conman-in-training Andrew had to play the parent role to get Connie out of another jam.

As *Richmond Hill* began to lighten up, love was in the air. Connie found brief happiness with Bob Russell (John Howard), while Marty and Nicki (Danielle Carter) began dating. Ivy fell head over heels for sleazy real estate manager Lawrie Benson (Tom Richards) and now-widowed Sergeant Dan (Ross Higgins) found himself drawn to Inspector Evelyn Thomas (Jan Kingsbury).

Mum (Gwen Plumb) got rather chummy with old mate Clarrie Brennan (Kevin Leslie) and decided to go on an outback road trip with him. Connie hit the big time when she decided to track down Andrew's truckie father, Ben Brown (Dennis Grosvenor). He was now a millionaire who fell in love with Connie all over again and asked her to marry him. Unfortunately, *Richmond Hill* abruptly ended, before Connie could give Ben an answer, after just 92 episodes.

Although the show wasn't a runaway success, its ratings had been consistent, and by October it was overtaking the much more expensive *The Flying Doctors* in the key market of Melbourne. So it was all the more shocking when Ten announced it was to be discontinued, leading *TV Week* to suggest that the show could go down in history as one of the highest rating programs ever to be axed.

'It was rating very well in the 26s and 27s,' says Paula Duncan. 'It was a mystery to me why they took it off. You know when you're in a successful series because the public tell you. It was a devastating cancellation.' The shell-shocked cast were told on a Friday night they weren't needed the following Monday, with the official reason being that ratings had not improved after a final publicity and promotional push.

Ten were actually looking to cut costs after spending $10 million on the recent Seoul Olympics and had also just committed to a 'more cutting edge' soap. 'Valerie Hardy [Ten's head of drama] was determined that *Richmond Hill* make way for *E Street*,' says Peter Pinne, then head of production at Grundy's, 'even though it ended up rating worse than *Richmond Hill* for many, many months afterwards.' Dumping *Richmond Hill* proved to be even more of a costly exercise when it became known that one unfortunate executive had renewed key cast members' contracts just a month before the axe fell.

Richmond Hill had always faced an uphill battle, particularly being launched in the same month as *Home and Away*. Viewers could only commit to so much soap per week, and they decided they preferred *Home and Away*'s recipe for teenage delinquents rather than *Richmond Hill* (Gwen Plumb was none too happy that she had picked the wrong show and was now out of a job). Ten was quick to move Ashley Paske over to *Neighbours* as he had proved to be *Richmond Hill*'s only breakout star, while Emily Symons (who played bitchy Anne) dyed her hair blonde and found fame in *Home and Away* as ditzy Marilyn. *Richmond Hill* also discovered a few other actors who were still to hit it big, including David Wenham, Gavin Harrison, Melissa Tkautz and Toni Pearen.

As for overseas sales, Grundy's did sell it to the UK where the ITV Network started screening it in October 1988, every Wednesday and Thursday at 2pm. Its arrival on British screens caused a storm of controversy. *Richmond Hill*'s two one-hour episodes a week now meant Brits were watching 24 hours of Aussie soaps every week, and critics and producers began to howl about being taken over. UK viewers, however, lapped it up.

'You know when you're in a successful series because the public tell you. It was a devastating cancellation.'

32

ALL THE WAY

PREMIERE: **1988** EPISODES: **32** NETWORK: **NINE** FINALE: **1989**

Swinging 60s sisters Madelaine (Diana Davidson),
Lorna (Maggie Millar) and Elaine (Rowena Wallace).

After covering the 1940s (*The Sullivans*) and 1920s (*Carson's Law*), Crawford Productions decided to set a series against the backdrop of another tumultuous period in Australian history – the 1960s. Taking its title from the expression used by Prime Minister Harold Holt when declaring Australia's support for American involvement in Vietnam, *All the Way* started life as a six-hour miniseries.

It all opened (quite ridiculously) in November 1963, on board a flight from London to Melbourne. Journalist Alan Scott (Martin Sacks) had just broken the news story of the year in the UK – the Profumo scandal – and was returning home to visit his family. As he alighted from the plane, he learnt that President Kennedy had been shot. In yet another world scoop, he managed to phone the hospital in Texas and then relay the news of JFK's death to Prime Minister Robert Menzies. As *The Sun* newspaper reported when reviewing the first episode, 'there aren't enough editions in a day' for this hotshot reporter. Alan barely made it home before stumbling upon his next scoop – a political murder mystery.

Alan's clan was headed by three sisters, with widow Madelaine Vaughan (Diana Davidson) the eldest and most conservative. Her younger sister, Lorna Scott (Maggie Millar), had her hands full with opinionated taxi driver husband Ray (Dennis Miller) and their three kids, Alan, Christine (Lisa Hensley) and Barry (Dominic McDonald). Christine

Joy Smithers looking very 'mod'.

and Barry were both obsessed with four mop-haired boys from Liverpool, and just like *The Sullivans*, the action would switch from colour to black and white so they could be spliced into real footage of Melbourne's screaming kids greeting the Beatles.

Sister number three, Elaine (Rowena Wallace), was the tortured one. Unhappily married to ruthless politician Phillip Seymour (Peter Sumner), she fell for her husband's trade union opponent, Mike O'Brien (Grigor Taylor). She struggled to hide the affair from Phillip, son Lindsay (Ben Mendelsohn) and her unbearably snobby daughter Diana (Jacqueline McKenzie). The six-hour miniseries ended with Elaine walking out on her family to be with Mike.

Airing the week after Ten's hugely popular miniseries, *The Dirtwater Dynasty*, *All the Way* suffered when viewers didn't seem interested in committing quite so quickly to another Aussie saga. When the lacklustre ratings came in, Nine realised they had commissioned more episodes too early and were now stuck with 26 hours of yet another soapie dud. They dumped the continuing serial into the TV dead-zone of summer where it was burnt up as quickly as possibly in two-hour blocks (but only when the cricket wasn't on). Amazingly, with all these stops and starts, the series did actually improve its ratings, but nobody could be bothered making more.

As the first episode of the serial opened, Elaine was still fleeing in her taxi to be with Mike when she heard about his suspicious shipyard death on the car radio. Confused and in shock, she had no choice but to return to her family, where she didn't notice that her daughter was now called Penny (and was now played by Dannii Minogue. Actress Jacqueline McKenzie had decided to study at NIDA rather than do the series, which proved to be a wise choice for her future Hollywood movie career.) To take advantage of Ms Minogue's *Young Talent Time* popularity, the new Penny did a lot more go-go dancing.

In need of more characters for a continuing soapie, *All the Way* had Alan Scott move in with fellow journalist Teri O'Rouke (Nikki Coghill) while he continued to investigate Mike's death. Also working at the newspaper was Gillian Porter (Joy Smithers) who tried getting Alan's attention by wearing increasingly over-the-top psychedelic outfits and miniskirts.

Also bumped up to regular status was Christine's fiancé Joe Bianchi (Vince Colosimo) who was seduced by the new and bitchier Penny (still go-go dancing) before realising she was Christine's cousin. In denial about the fling, Joe married Chrissie. Penny was left pregnant and seeking an abortionist while Chrissie struggled to conceive.

ALL THE WAY
DANNII MINOGUE

Maddie was reunited with her supposedly-dead husband Keith (Noel Trevarthen) who had been missing in action since World War II. Meanwhile, Phillip was warned by his political cronies to make son Lindsay register for national service (cue the black-and-white footage of American President Johnson on his turbulent tour of Australia amidst violent anti-Vietnam demonstrations). Drafted by his dad, Lindsay went on the run and disappeared, just as the show did, too.

Perhaps it was too early in the 80s to be reflecting back on the 60s. Critics complained that far from looking 'mod' or 'swinging', the show seemed terribly old-fashioned. Unlike the rich, atmospheric sets from *The Sullivans* and *Carson's Law*, the homes in *All the Way* seemed ridiculously kitsch, particularly Elaine's supposed Toorak mansion. Mentions of old-style currency seemed laboured and the 'sound-alike' soundtrack only painfully exposed the lack of authentic music from the era.

Rowena Wallace remembers the show with a laugh, particularly because her character's wardrobe was based on Jackie Kennedy. She remembers laughing hysterically when seeing herself in rushes dressed in a pale pink Jackie O outfit. 'I looked like a crate of apricots on two sticks! It was hideous,' she shudders today. 'Ironically, years before, I'd had a reading with a clairvoyant who said "You're going to marry a politician and have to wear gloves and hats and you will hate it!" And I did!' If only the same clairvoyant had given Crawford's and Nine a reading about the chances of *All the Way* going all the way.

33

THE POWER, THE PASSION

PREMIERE: **1989** EPISODES: **168** NETWORK: **SEVEN** FINALE: **1989**

Crazy Kathryn (Tracy Tainsh) threatens dad Gordon (Kevin Miles)
when one of her multiple personalities returns for a visit.

Despite having failed four times before with daytime soaps (*Autumn Affair, The Story of Peter Grey, Motel, Until Tomorrow*), Seven tried one last time to get the genre to work. In April 1988 they announced they were going into production with *Love, Passion and Desire*. Seven's head of drama, Alan Bateman, announced to *TV Week* that it would be 'larger than life. There will be lots of beautiful young people with a solid core of very professional actors. I believe an Australian daytime soap will be massive because a locally-produced soap will always out-perform an international version.'

It took till 1989 for the show to get on air and by then its title had changed to *The Power, the Passion*. It was to be part of an ambitious attempt to dethrone the then reigning king of daytime, Ray Martin, over on Nine. *Midday with Ray Martin* had daytime sewn up between midday and 1.30pm, so Seven hired another Aussie TV legend as part of a two-pronged attack. *The Bert Newton Show* would air from midday, followed by *The Power, the Passion* at 1pm. At the very least, the new soap might entice some viewers across who had watched the first hour of Ray and might now be ready for something different.

Creator Bevan Lee wrote the serial's first five episodes before being headhunted and taking off to the Nine Network along with Alan Bateman. The scripts he wrote before leaving were an outrageously delicious mix of intrigue, lust and twisted family secrets. It played to the audience with a knowing wink, but once he left the show, he felt the scriptwriters made fun of its audience rather than bringing them in on the joke.

Des Monaghan, who came in to replace Alan Bateman as Seven's head of drama, became the new executive producer of *The Power, the Passion* while Oscar Whitbread (*Bellbird*, *Carson's Law*) took over as producer. The production schedule was designed so that each episode of the show could be shot in sequence over the week – unusual for soap production.

The Power, the Passion centred on powerful businessman Gordon Byrne (Kevin Miles), who was returning home to Australia after five years overseas. His return was most unsettling for his three shoulder-padded daughters, Anna (Suzy Cato), Ellen (Olivia Hamnett) and Kathryn (Tracy Tainsh) who all held various grudges against him for his past behaviour.

Kane (Julian McMahon) strips down for his bucks night.

Anna was unhappily married to former widower Justin Wright (George Mallaby) who had two kids of his own – Rebecca (Libby Purvis) and Samuel (Danny Roberts). Samuel was an ambitious misogynist, bitter about his mother's death. When he caught his stepmother in bed with toy boy Nick Cassala (Nick Carrafa), he used the incident to his advantage. Since the money-hungry Anna was determined to work Daddy over, Samuel blackmailed her into taking him along for the ride.

Ellen was happily married to Dr Andrew Edmonds (Alan Cassell) and had four children – there was upstanding medical student Kane (Julian McMahon in his television debut), sports-mad Adam (Neil Grant), druggie Danielle (Lucinda Cowden) and adopted daughter Talia (Susan Ellis).

Kathryn worked as a psychologist and was the most disturbed – to put it politely – about the return of her monstrous father. Five years beforehand, he had whisked the love of her life away to be his protégé and only now was Ryan McAlister (Ian Rawlings) returning home. Kathryn had previously been unable to have sex with Ryan because she was frigid but the romantic Ryan had promised her he would and could wait. She also suffered from that strange soap opera affliction known as split personality syndrome, and when another psychiatrist tried to cure her, it unleashed a third persona known as Diana.

Back at the Toorak mansion, Ryan's mother Sarah McAlister (Jill Forster) was preparing for the master's return. She had been very close to the deceased Martha Byrne and flashbacks revealed that Gordon's wife

L-R: Kathryn (Tracy Tainsh), Ellen (Olivia Hamnett), Anna (Suzy Cato), Gordon (Kevin Miles), Ryan (Ian Rawlings), Sarah (Jill Forster).

had begged Sarah to make him suffer for the many indignities he had put her through. It appeared Gordon was walking back into a house of vipers but what nobody realised was that he was fully prepared for all of them. 'Let the games begin,' he remarked that first week with a devilish smile.

Over at the university, drug dealer Sonny Davis (John Higginson) was pushing pills to the students. 'Shoot through, shoot up and shut up – and not necessarily in that order,' he snarled to Danielle, who decided to take advantage of the fact that nobody was glad to see her grandfather back in town. She thought Gordon would be a pushover to get money for more drugs, but he was quick to see through her fake smiles. Meanwhile, Kane's girlfriend Susan Walsh (Jacqui Gordon) overdosed and blew her chance to marry into the Edmonds family.

Instead, *The Power, the Passion* had its first wedding when Rebecca married Kane after just one week's engagement. Like all good soap weddings, the honeymoon was thwarted when a detective arrived to arrest Kane for the murder of Sonny. Investigating policeman David (Gerard Maguire) turned out to be an old sweetheart of Ellen's and admitted he was still in love with her. Meanwhile, tabloid journalist Carla (Jane Clifton) wormed her way into Gordon's bed.

Sadly, nobody – and I mean nobody – was watching by this stage. Daytime audiences were still glued to *Days of Our Lives* and *The Young and the Restless* and weren't at all interested in watching an Aussie version. 'My main headache with it was that it was caricature and the American soapies were so sincere,' says producer Oscar Whitbread. 'There were also too many kids in it. The audience wanted more mature stories.'

The ultimate insult was when *The Ray Martin Show* started their own spoof soap called *A Town Like Dallas*. According to the host, ratings for his show actually rose at 1.15pm every Friday when the send-up aired. 'After a couple of weeks we were rating 17 and *The Power, the Passion* was on a two,' Martin told *TV Week* when the tongue-in-cheek romp reached 50 episodes.

Before the year was out, Seven admitted defeat, axed *The Bert Newton Show* and moved *The Power, the Passion* to 11.30pm weeknights. After 168 episodes and two bad timeslots, it was all out of power and passion. It's quite possibly the lowest-rating Aussie soap ever to have been made and it's a shame it was never seen by a wider audience.

'Before we began, everyone was shaking my hand and Christopher Skase (the then big-spending owner of the Seven Network) gave me a big hug,' Oscar Whitbread remembers. 'When the ratings came out, he stopped talking to me. We never threw in the towel though, and we continued to make the best show we could. It was a most enjoyable experience and the cast were great.'

'It never surprised me that it didn't work because the 80s were ending,' Danny Roberts (Samuel) says today. 'It was such a funny time to be at Seven. You had Bert Newton parking his Jaguar wherever he wanted to and Christopher Skase running all over the buildings trying to get away from the authorities who started to close in on his "activities". Maybe if they had made *The Power, the Passion* five years earlier in the decade of greed, it might have worked rather well.

'I swore I was never going to do television again but Skase met with me, sold it to me and put me on a retainer and contract right there and then – which is unheard of today. Skase told us we were going to make Australian television history – he was very convincing.' Less convincing was Samuel's sexuality, which Roberts played up, given that the character wasn't bedding the female cast. 'I played it very camp all the way through because Samuel was obviously gay. I always hoped the writers would pick up on it. And maybe they did – his one girlfriend was very masculine!'

Viewed today, the wardrobe is a little dated but certainly much more restrained than the over-the-top wardrobe of prime-time shows like *Return to Eden*. Fashion coordinator Michael Chisholm told *TV Week* that it was the most glamorous wardrobe he had ever assembled and estimated the show went through $1.5 million in clothes alone. The sets were great and many of the performances outstanding, particularly Kevin Miles playing an even more morally corrupt version of his *Carson's Law* character.

When asked to nominate the most outrageous thing he ever wrote in his long history of soap, Bevan Lee doesn't hesitate in recalling what he put his demented psychologist Kathryn through. Waking up in her office chair one day, she was horrified to see that her dual personality was back and had left her a note. It read: 'I'm back you frigid bitch!' The line became such a catchphrase, crew members wore T-shirts emblazoned with it. It's unknown whether this was also the favourite line of dialogue for overseas fans, since the show was eventually sold to countries like France and Zimbabwe, but one would assume that moment brought a smile to anyone watching no matter where they lived.

It's quite possibly the lowest-rating Aussie soap ever to have been made.

E STREET

PREMIERE: **1989** EPISODES: **404** NETWORK: **TEN** FINALE: **1993**

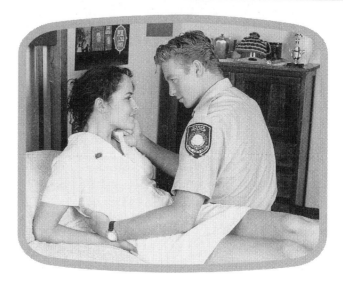

Rebecca Rigg (Amy) and Simon Baker (Sam)
met on set and married in real life.

In 1988 actor Harry Michaels stepped behind the camera to make a pilot called *Somerset Street*. It was about life in the Sydney suburb of Balmain and the cast were all soapie stalwarts. The core family consisted of Liz Collins (Judy McBurney), her oversexed sister Chrissie (Sarah Lambert) and warring parents Joe (Doug Scroope) and Ruth (Sheila Kennelly). Michaels played almost exactly the same character he had in *Number 96*, but instead of Giovanni and Aunt Maria, it was Alexis and mother Maria Spirou (Nancy Caruana) running the local delicatessen. Despite being shot entirely on location, *Somerset Street* didn't push any boundaries, and in trying to cover all bases it ended up covering not much at all. The worst insult, however, came when cast and crew discovered another soap pilot called *Westside* was being filmed in the same suburb. *Somerset Street* turned into a dead end while *Westside* became better known for the street it was set in. Eden Street, in the fictional inner-city suburb of Westside, was known to the locals (and future television viewers) as 'E Street'.

E Street was the brainchild of Forrest Redlich, a writer/producer who had written the 1977 movie *High Rolling* before spending three months in America cutting film trailers alongside director Jonathon Demme. During the 80s he worked on *A Country Practice* as part of an award-winning team that included Bruce Best and James Davern. '*A Country Practice* was the best time of my life,' says Forrest Redlich today. 'Jim was a good boss, Brucey looked after the production and I was responsible for story and edit.'

The early intention of *E Street* was to make it an urban version of *A Country Practice* with even harder social issues. 'My criteria was that it air in a later timeslot so that I didn't have to pull back on telling fair dinkum stories,' says Redlich, who also stipulated that his new show never air against his old one, *A Country Practice*. Discussions were held with the ABC but Ten made a better offer and Westside Productions began pre-production. 'We were totally autonomous with our own studios and over a hundred staff,' says Redlich. 'My brief was to deliver two hours of tape to the network each week for $350,000.'

In September 1988, *TV Week* reported that *A Country Practice*'s phenomenally popular Penny Cook might be returning to television. Cook told the magazine that 'it's a big decision to return to two hours a week television and it's one that simply can't be rushed'. Negotiations had broken down as the magazine went to press, but the lure of a part written especially for her proved to be too tempting. Cook signed on to play Doctor Eleanor Fielding. Elly, as she would be better known, was the chief medical officer at Westside Medical Centre, recently divorced from David (Noel Hodda) and bringing up precocious tomboy daughter Claire (Brooke 'Mikey' Anderson).

The community would also include legal aid officer Sarah McIllop (Katrina Sedgwick), district nurse Martha O'Dare (Cecily Polson), local publican Ernie Patchett (Vic Rooney), his son Chris (Paul Kelman), Sergeant George Sullivan (Les Dayman), Constable Paul Berry (Warren Jones), naïve wife Rhonda (Melanie Salomon), and a girl 'from the wrong side of the tracks', Lisa Bennett (Alyssa-Jane Cook). *E Street*'s most unorthodox character, however, was a former street worker turned minister, Reverend Bob Brown (Tony Martin).

With scripts written 15 weeks in advance, the Ten network decided that *E Street* would air at 7.30pm on Wednesday and Thursday nights, jettisoning *Richmond Hill* in the process. Consequently, Forrest Redlich needed to drastically rewrite to tone down the stories for the earlier timeslot. After a lavish media launch in Sydney, where 200 people dined and danced in a specially constructed treehouse estimated to have cost $100,000, *E Street* premiered on 19 May 1989.

In the first two episodes, Anglican rector Jimmy McCabe (Basil Clarke), who had taken in juvenile delinquent Bob years earlier, was retiring and wanted to leave his parish to the younger minister. Reverend Bob soon discovered his old mentor was actually dying of stomach cancer.

Meanwhile, Sarah's first legal case put her into conflict with Elly over the rights of a retarded girl left pregnant by local thug Mario (Ben Oxenbould). It was left to Reverend Bob to step in and remind both women to forget their own egos and remember who the real priority was. Elly wasn't used to being talked to so bluntly (especially by a man in a clerical collar) and despite her initial outrage, the two began a slow dance towards love and marriage.

The early intention of E Street was to make it an urban version of A Country Practice with even harder social issues.

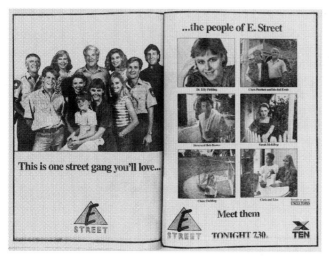

This is one street gang you'll love...

...the people of E. Street

Dr. Elly Fielding   Chris Patchett and Michael Kosic

Reverend Bob Brown   Sarah McKillop

Claire Fielding   Chris and Lisa

Meet them

STREET   TONIGHT 7.30.   TEN

E Street got off to a shaky start in the ratings with just a 13 share in Melbourne and not much better in Sydney. Ten might have wondered about the wisdom of cancelling the higher-rating *Richmond Hill*, but the beleaguered network had much more serious problems. The high-flying 80s were coming to an end and Ten was in serious trouble. American Bob Shanks, who had a proven track record in rescuing ailing stations in the US, was flown down under to make the network more profitable. Unfortunately, his new programming plan did nothing but dumb the channel down even further, including an uninspiring rip-off of *Candid Camera* and a prime-time version of kids' show, *Double Dare*, that was so stupid Ten couldn't even find families to appear on it. 'We all thought he was turning Ten into K-Mart TV after our first meeting with him,' remembers actor Paul Kelman. 'He told us that Ten was now the "no frills-station". It was a bit scary because on several occasions, I expected to arrive at work and find the station gates chained up and Ten closed for business!'

Rather than axe the low-rating drama, Shanks saw potential in *E Street* and halted production for three weeks. 'He stopped the show and only aired an hour a week so we could finally catch up with our script rewrites,' says Forrest Redlich. 'We came out of that with a more settled show but then they liquidated the network. The funny thing is that through all this nobody suggested taking it off the air. In fact, Nine even tried to poach us.'

Ten's research into *E Street* also revealed an audience that most Aussie soaps strive to achieve. 'We had no children watching because it was too hard-hitting and no grannies because it was too hip,' says Redlich. 'We had men and women under 40, and particularly a large male viewership, 14–35, which was an untapped group. I began writing the show for a male-skewing audience. Everyone said we were crazy but I knew exactly what I was doing.'

The new *E Street* had characters like Stanley 'Wheels' Kovak (Marcus Graham), who had earlier appeared in a one-off guest role as a misfit in a wheelchair and now returned as a regular, while George's hippie daughter Alice (Marianne Howard) also came on board. Elly got herself a new airline pilot boyfriend, Daniel Windsor (Chris Orchard), who came with four kids of his own, including the adorable Toni (Toni Pearen). While ex-husband David dealt with pushy TV talk show host Micki Fallon (Peta Toppano), Daniel proposed to Elly for the first year cliffhanger.

E Street was now a smash hit with its 'Generation X' audience. When the cast travelled in a boat to Darling Harbour for a promotional appearance, nobody could get off because a huge crowd of 60,000 was surging forward. 'When Gary Rice came in to run the network, he said to me, 'I don't care what you do, Forrest, just keep this thing working because I'm setting up this network for someone to buy it.' Even with a rating of just 15, we were making the network a fortune because the advertisers had a targeted demographic.' Despite the revenue and the hip young audience, however, Ten was slashing costs across the board and *E Street* was told to cut its budget by 25 per cent.

Bad Boy Sonny Bennett (Richard Huggett).

Ratings were steady the following year, when Daniel's affair with Jennifer (Virginia Hey) was revealed. Elly sent him packing to Switzerland with sick son Tommy, but Toni hung around to be near her boyfriend Harley (Malcolm Kennard), Reverend Bob's newly discovered son. Aunty Vi (Bunney Brooke) was busy trying to thwart brother Ernie from marrying Abby Rossiter (Chelsea Brown). Lisa was raped by Sam Bulmer (Serge Lazareff), the boyfriend of her mother Margaret (Briony Behets), and, traumatised, broke off her engagement to Chris, freeing him up to marry runaway mum-to-be Megan (Lisbeth Kennelly).

At the wedding, Wheels shocked everyone in the church by getting out of his wheelchair and walking down the aisle. Recovered from her rape ordeal, Lisa decided that if Wheels's legs were working, so might another important piece of his anatomy, and in the show's most steamy scene to date, she slid naked into his bathtub where the suds were very strategically placed for its early evening timeslot.

E Street was now positioning itself as a much grittier show than *Neighbours* or *Home and Away*, and the buzz for it started to build. '*E Street* evolved into a warmer, friendlier, less issue-based program and began to strongly feature music in the mix,' says writer Rick Maier. 'It was always a fantastic show for a writer because the scope was broad, comedy was important and encouraged, and the writers were encouraged to play with style and form.'

Comedy was certainly encouraged for the new character of Constable Max Simmons. Bruce Samazan was cast after being spotted bringing his girlfriend in for an audition. She went home empty-handed and he became a star and a pin-up for female viewers.

Forrest Redlich, however, was still determined to keep his male-skewing audience, and began to write darker storylines for them. First up was Lisa's bad seed brother, Sonny Bennett (Richard Huggett). Bitter over years spent in jail for robbery, amphetamines fiend Sonny freaked everyone out with his psycho antics. After weeks of a terror campaign, he was carted away to jail for trying to kill Max.

As the show's ratings began to rise, so did the sex factor. 'What we are trying to do is make the show as identifiable as possible,' Forrest Redlich told *TV Week* at the time. 'We've had no trouble with the Australian Broadcasting Tribunal at all, because what we've done has been within the context of the story. I think, seriously, that a bit of good ol' sex is much more favourable a thing to be putting on screen at 7.30pm than violence.' With that, schoolgirl Toni and patient boyfriend Harley went all the way (in a hayloft) and Lisa got herself a new man, newspaper heir Michael Sturgess (Graham Harvey).

With no publicity department pushing his show, Forrest Redlich knew he had to stir the pot and tell the press whatever they needed to hear to get *E Street* into the mags. His declaration about 'good ol' sex' being preferable to violence was said just for a headline. A few months after upping the raunch factor, violence was back at 7.30pm when Sonny Bennett escaped from jail to go on another Westside rampage. After shooting Kimberley Talbot (Rebecca Saunders) dead, the show prepared for what fans would forever remember as the *E Street* 'Christening Massacre'. Sonny planted a bomb under Reverend Bob's car but its faulty timer meant nearly every cast member rode in the vehicle as it travelled back and forth from Chris and Megan's baby ceremony. As the explosive $350,000 episode reached its climax, Chris (Paul Kelman), Megan (Lisbeth Kennelly) and Abby (Chelsea Brown) were blown to bits. It was the most talked-about bomb since the *Number 96* deli went sky high.

The explosion left Ernie Patchett a widower again, as well as killing off his newly married son and daughter-in-law. Getting married on *E Street* that year had proved to be a bad career move for actor Paul Kelman. 'For a young 22 year old on a TV show, what are you going to do after you get married? It's like the kiss of death,' says Kelman. 'For a while I wondered if I had done something wrong to get written out.' Luckily for Kelman's sanity, he was quickly snapped up for *The Flying Doctors*.

After Sonny leapt to his death, he had one last surprise planned for Reverend Bob by rigging his car door with a shotgun. Unfortunately, Elly took the brunt of the gunshot and was rushed to hospital. In a pleasant surprise for soap fans, neurosurgeon Susan Franklin (Anne Tenney)

Elly (Penny Cook) and Reverend Bob (Tony Martin) check that Sonny really is dead.

drilled a hole into Elly's head to save her life. Anne Tenney and Penny Cook hadn't been seen on-screen together since Molly Jones died in *A Country Practice* and Vicky the Vet had sobbed over losing her best friend. Both actresses admitted to getting the giggles at seeing the tables turned five years after Wandin Valley.

Ratings-wise, the show was now a firmly entrenched hit. In November 1990, *E Street* climbed to a ratings peak of 22 and outperformed *A Country Practice* for the first time. Soon it would be the third most watched show in Sydney behind the news and Rugby League.

When the show returned in 1991, Elly had survived her brain operation but *E Street* was down six characters. 'I think *E Street* will become even more upmarket and we'll be honing it to become more slick and hip than ever before,' Forrest Redlich told *TV Week*. He brought on a new group of regulars: Craig Jones, or C.J. for short (Adrian Lee); Martha's deserted niece Nikki Spencer (Melissa Tkautz) and her brother Zac (Daniel Knight); WTV8 television owner Sheridan Sturgess (Kate Raison) and Dr Virginia Travers (Julieanne Newbould).

E Street also brought on 'Dog Boy', a young guy called Dylan (Adam Lloyd) whom Reverend Bob had found chained up under a house like a dog. When Dog Boy's father Gus (Rob Steele) was found murdered, Reverend Bob became the prime suspect and was carted off to prison. Meanwhile, the once heroic Constable Paul Berry (Warren Jones) lost the plot and became a loopy vigilante. He developed an unhealthy fascination for Toni (Toni Pearen) and held her hostage while she was recovering in hospital from a miscarriage (the result of that roll in the hay).

Penny Cook, meanwhile, filmed her final scenes in March, and they aired in May with Elly farewelling Bob as he languished in jail. Determined to marry off Bob and Elly, Redlich decided to re-cast, so Elly returned to town, now played by Diane Craig, to tie the knot with the Reverend.

By now, rich bitch Sheridan was having a hot and heavy affair with toy boy Harley and the shit was about to hit the fan between Network Ten executives and *E Street*'s producers. When Harley was introduced to cocaine by a friend of Sheridan's, he grabbed two girls for a threesome before collapsing from an overdose. Ten refused to air the offending episode at 7.30pm and Redlich raged to *TV Week* about their objecting to a storyline about cocaine. 'You read about it in the newspapers all the time, about all the time lost on the factory floor due to alcoholism, but they forget about the cocaine in the boardroom.' Ten screened the controversial episode at 8.30pm as part of a two-hour block of *E Street* to go head-to-head with the usually unassailable State of Origin Rugby League telecast.

Cocaine in the convertible was another outrageously over-the-top moment as Harley's much-ballyhooed exit from the show put him into a coma. By now, many were wondering if *E Street* would do a storyline about ecstasy, the latest party drug that was flooding the nation. *E Street* indeed! It never did make it into the show but everything else you could snort or

Cocaine in the convertible was another outrageously over-the-top moment as Harley's much-ballyhooed exit from the show put him into a coma.

shoot up did. Heroin addict Laurel Ferguson (Melissa Kounnas) jabbed Max with a syringe she said was full of her HIV-infected blood, which led to a tasteless search through needle disposal units by Toni and Nikki to prove otherwise.

'We cover social issues but they are not our prime motivation,' Redlich told *TV Week* on the occasion of the show's 200th episode. 'Soap not soap-box is our motto.' The show everyone thought wouldn't last six months had been sold to Belgium and Holland. And in England, where it was about to debut on the Sky Network, double decker buses were driving around with the tagline, 'Your New Neighbours Are Moving In!'

Music had now become an integral part of the show. 'Forrest Redlich was the first producer to pay rights to APRA (Australian Performing Rights Association) and get some decent music playing in the background,' says actress Kate Raison (Sheridan Sturgess). 'Sheridan's first appearance in the show was edited together beautifully with the sound track. It was very cool.' Redlich had specifically created the role for Raison, having previously cast her as *A Country Practice*'s shy and retiring Cathy Hayden. 'His exact words to me were that he wanted to see Kate Raison grow up on Australian television,' Raison recalls, 'and I grew up into a superbitch!'

Forrest Redlich had always liked cutting *E Street* montages to music, so doing video clips was a natural progression. 'There was always a very 50s rock'n'roll sensibility to characters like Wheels and Sonny,' admits Redlich, who eventually spun off a music arm of his production company, Westside Records. Groups such as Radio Freedom, Honeymen and Boys in Black signed to the label hoping they would have an advantage by getting their songs played in the background every week on *E Street*.

The cast of *E Street* fool around and flash their bits during a photo shoot.

Jo-Jo (Kelley Abbey) was often belting out a tune in Patchett's Pub and Toni (Toni Pearen) sang up a storm whenever she was handed a microphone, but it was Nikki who would have the show's biggest spin-off single.

Melissa Tkautz had arrived on the set of her favourite TV show as an innocent 17-year-old Catholic schoolgirl to play Nikki. Forrest Redlich (with a nod of approval from his daughter) decided to film a video clip with Tkautz and use it in the show. 'It was just a publicity thing to get her profile up,' remembers Redlich. 'We thought we might be able to get her onto *Video Hits* and maybe into the Top 20.' Tkautz recorded the track and faced the wrath of some of the other 'singing' actresses on the show. 'There was a bit of competition on that show amongst some of the girls,' says Kate Raison. 'There wasn't much camaraderie amongst the younger crowd.'

Toni (Toni Pearen) and Nikki (Melissa Tkautz).

Polygram Records decided to release 'Read My Lips' and the video was premiered on the soap on 29 May. 'Nikki was sitting on a park bench daydreaming and they played the film clip,' Tkautz says. 'Next thing Mum was picking me up from the studio and it was playing on the car radio. It all happened so quickly, it was like a dream sequence in itself for me.' 'Read My Lips' went on to become the biggest selling single of 1991.

When Melissa's second single, 'Sexy is the Word', also became a hit, the actress found herself in a constant whirl of publicity and singing engagements. 'I didn't think it would ever end or go bad. Only Cecily Polson pulled me aside and said, "Listen, Mel, don't let them burn you out. When you're tired you speak up and say you've got to go home to learn your lines." I thought, whatever, but she turned out to be spot on with her advice. I would do interviews by myself all day in a room with no windows, and the phone would ring and ring non-stop. I was young and didn't know any better.'

By November, the pressure had grown too much and, although contracted to Westside for three years, Tkautz quit the show and Nikki was packed off to New Zealand. 'I had to leave because I could not physically tour and record and do the show as well,' says Tkautz. After a national tour, three Top 10 singles and an Australian Music Award for Most Popular Dance Act, bad management stopped Tkautz's singing career dead in its tracks. Her record label approached old boss Forrest Redlich to see if he would consider taking her back to *E Street*.

'I let her go because that's what she wanted to do and then a year later when her album stiffed, Polygram asked for a favour because we were in a joint venture with them,' admits Forrest Redlich. 'Forrest was surprisingly cool about me leaving in the first place,' says Tkautz, 'so I had no hesitation in going back.' Given that her dodgy management team had also squandered all of her royalties, Redlich's job offer helped to get Tkautz back on her feet.

Nikki's reappearance a few months later was not unusual by *E Street* standards, since the only thing that changed more than the characters was the wardrobe. The most outrageous outfits came courtesy of Lizzie Gardiner who, along with Tim Chappell from the *E Street* wardrobe department, would go on to win Academy Awards for Costume Design for

1st Mr Bad (Vince Martin) threatens Sheridan (Kate Raison).

The Adventures of Priscilla, Queen of the Desert. 'Lizzie was so talented and amazing,' remembers Tkautz, 'it never surprised me that she won an Oscar. I could go down to Lizzie and talk with her and know it wouldn't get back to everybody else.' Kate Raison also spent a lot of time in wardrobe chatting to the girls and Tim. 'They had such a vision right down to the last touch, everybody looked like individuals,' says Raison. Eventually, Lizzie Gardiner moved into *E Street*'s script department.

Adrian Lee was another fan of *E Street*'s unique character looks, and remembers well what was laid out at his first audition. 'Forrest explained the character to me and then he showed me the wardrobe. Within a couple of months, people in the street were copying C.J.'s look.' In creating a new Hollywood down under, soapie style, *E Street* had the stars, a look and a sound all of its own. Now all it needed was a jaw-dropping storyline to really make it the talk of the nation.

Enter Mr Bad, the serial killer who took the show to new heights. Architect Stephen Richardson (Vince Martin), an old friend of Reverend Bob's, was romancing Virginia. Then, he began romancing Sheridan (Kate Raison) and she began having nightmares about a childhood incident where a friend had been murdered by a boy who painted his face half black and half silver. Somehow, and please don't ask me how, Sheridan ended up psychically connected to Stephen and he began to unravel into his murderous alter ego again.

Mr Bad's first victim was Virginia (Julieanne Newbould, who was conveniently pregnant and wanting to leave) whom he buried in remote bushland. Stephen moved in with Sheridan, which unnerved her brother Michael (Graham Harvey) because she turned from a power-hungry TV station owner into a neurotic basket case. When Michael became overly suspicious, Mr Bad bashed him and buried him next to the rotting remains of Virginia.

E Street was now at its craziest and ratings rose to record levels. When a stray dog sniffed around the two dead bodies in the bush, viewers fell off their seats in shock when Michael burst out of the dirt (he'd actually still been alive when buried). He didn't stay alive for long though because after struggling for days to get to a major road, a semitrailer rounded the corner and flattened him.

After an end-of-year cliffhanger in which Mr Bad escaped from a psychiatric prison, the storyline dragged on into 1992. Actor Vince Martin spoke to *TV Week* about the controversial role. 'I asked for a little more character development and what the writers came up with was just more death – which wasn't what I wanted. I think there has been a lot of unmotivated killing.' Forrest Redlich was unrepentant. 'Shakespeare burnt out people's eyes and he's art. It's all very well to limp along with things that are safe, but the Ten network has a lot of problems and we have to work three times as hard for anything to rate at all. We have to take a bit of a punt.'

So, Mr Bad locked Lisa (Alyssa-Jane Cook) in a freezer as bait to lure Sheridan and Wheels (Marcus Graham) to come looking for him. As they all ran around a closed shopping centre, Mr Bad left the dead bodies of security guards for them to find on escalators. Finally, Sheridan psychically contacted Stephen and lured Mr Bad to a rendezvous point where Westside's inept police force was finally able to grab him. Sheridan pumped five shots into him, was arrested, escaped from jail and hit the road with Wheels, later discovering she was pregnant.

Wheels, who had moved in with Sheridan to protect her from Mr Bad, repeated his previous bath seduction by getting it all off again for a sexy shower scene with Kate Raison. 'The difference between *E Street* and other serials is that it takes risks,' Marcus Graham told *TV Week*. 'If Forrest wasn't doing it, nobody would be. Even the network doesn't want us to do it. If it wasn't for Redlich, I wouldn't be here. I'd leave.' *TV Week* thought Westside Productions were planning to spin Wheels off into his own series, to be called *Midnight City*. It was true they were working on a police action drama featuring Graham (although he wasn't going to be playing Wheels) but Nine, who were supposedly keen on seeing a pilot, never greenlit the project.

2nd Mr Bad (Olav Evanson).

'Both Marcus and I had decided to leave but Forrest sold us the idea of doing a road movie,' remembers Kate Raison. 'The storyline was fun and Forrest was right, it tied up the two characters neatly. It was a good time to go though, because the Mr Bad stuff was just too weird. It was impossible to play because nothing was based in truth.' Forrest Redlich disagrees. 'It was all thought out to the max,' he insists today. 'It was all good Freudian stuff that used new technology for the day like pencil cams.'

Vince Martin was gone but Mr Bad would live on as he recuperated from gunshot wounds in a hospital bed with his head swathed in a badly stitched leather face mask that revealed just one eye. Olav Evanson was now playing the role, and although he allegedly couldn't speak English too well, it didn't matter because his eye was the right colour to peek out from the mask. All Mr Bad now did was grunt occasionally while his demented nurse Amy Preston (Rebecca Rigg) began secretly injecting him with a mystery drug that would get him up and killing again, this time on Amy's behalf.

Toni Pearen told *TV Week* that the Mr Bad storyline was good because 'it's something that no other soap has done before, so viewers have really taken to it'. When *TV Week* pointed out to her that *Number 96* had its pantyhose murderer, she was genuinely surprised. 'Wow! Okay, so I wasn't around then. This serial killer storyline is new to my generation then.' Hopefully Chantal Contouri, who played *96*'s pantyhose strangler, explained all when she joined *E Street* as Dr Julia Preston, Amy's mother.

In the middle of all of this mayhem, Valentine (Larry D'Ercole), a guitarist who shared a house with Jo-Jo and had never uttered a word during the entire series, suddenly started talking. 'No wonder his music is so good,' Toni reported once on her current affairs TV show. 'It's his only form of expression.' No, Toni, Valentine's music was terrible, but yes, he did only have one form of expression – it was raising one of his eyebrows and looking stupid.

'Wheels' (Marcus Graham).

It turned out Valentine was the secret DJ Doctor Rock who had been taunting Mr Bad over the radio. Another *E Street* gimmick had run its course as Valentine kept talking (and some fans wished he'd kept quiet). Now it was time to put an end to the Mr Bad era.

After being sprung from hospital and escaping from the even crazier Amy, Mr Bad was befriended by a retarded boy who found him hiding in a warehouse, still wearing his stupid Hannibal Lecter-inspired head-piece. The once scary killer finally committed suicide by jumping into Sydney Harbour holding a rock, in a homage to *Cape Fear*.

E Street writers pondered about which Hollywood movie to plunder next. Forrest Redlich later told *Who* magazine that at this time there was 'a push from the network to get older viewers – so we introduced gangster storylines.' Today he realises it was a mistake. 'The gangster stuff didn't work as well, I admit that,' says Redlich, 'but I didn't want to do insipid new age males either.' Reverend Bob's brother, mobster Jack Brown (Andrew Williams), arrived, while Elly's sister, photojournalist Laura Fielding (Antoinette Byron), tried to uncover his murky past.

Meanwhile, fashion designer Penny (Josephine Mitchell) was busy searching for her kidnapped daughter Charlie, prompting the return of the tyke's dad (Craig Pearce). Ernie got a new love, Sally McKinnon (Joanna Lockwood), while original regular Claire Fielding was sent away to America to live with her father David. Ten-year-old Brooke 'Mikey' Anderson told *TV Week* she 'cried on the inside' at being axed, while producer Andrew Saw admitted that 'we had a lot of trouble finding storylines for her without blowing her up'.

The days of happy stories in *E Street* were a thing of the past. After a romantic wedding where the temporarily blind C.J. regained his sight in time to see Toni walk down the aisle, the couple returned from a Hamilton Island honeymoon to heartbreak and addiction. C.J. became yet another *E Street* regular to develop a drug problem (speed, just like Sonny) while Toni had an affair with Constable Sam (Simon Denny). When Reverend Bob died in a car accident in March, the press turned nasty and decided *E Street*'s days were numbered.

When Max turned into a werewolf, the tabloids seized upon this as evidence that *E Street* was running out of ideas. 'We didn't use prosthetics. We just worked with a base of make-up and hair and glue,' Bruce Samazan told *TV Week* as he posed for the magazine with long nails, fang teeth and what looked like pubic hair stuck to his face. The werewolf story has become *E Street* folklore since, but Forrest Redlich likes to point out that it was only done for a dream sequence. Still, it caused much drama at the time, especially with his leading men. Samazan, who was supposedly critical of the stunt, didn't go so far as telling the boss. When co-star Scott McRae did, he was shown the door after an 'allegedly heated argument'.

McRae, who played nerdy Jamie Newman, told *TV Week* he'd been singled out 'because I'm the most expendable. I don't mean that in acting ability, but in pin-up status. My character does not appeal to the people who are pushing the merchandising and hype side of the show. It is therefore easier to get rid of me. They wouldn't dare give anyone else the boot.'

'What would be lovely,' he added with a grin, 'is if I get Best New Talent at the Logies this year. Then I can say, "There you go, stick that!"' As it happened, Scott McRae lost that year's New Talent Logie to co-star Simon Denny, while Bruce Samazan was nominated for the biggest award of the night, the Gold Logie. Ironically, Samazan and Denny were the 'heartthrobs' *TV Week* had referred to as being the most vocal about the stupid werewolf story. A bigger irony was that *E Street* was axed the night before the Logies.

'What has happened is a disgrace,' Bruce Samazan fumed to *TV Week* at the Logies. His co-star was just as nervous about what the future held. 'One minute I'm winning this award and being placed into a star category but in ten weeks' time I'm going to be unemployed,' said Simon Denny. Unaware he was about to be snapped up by *A Country Practice*, Denny may have been concerned about on-screen and real-life girlfriend Rebecca Rigg who was pregnant with their first child. Denny, who had been 'discovered' dancing bare-chested in music video clips for Euphoria and Melissa Tkautz, later moved his family to Hollywood. Simon Denny became Simon Baker-Denny, then Simon Baker, and, after the critically acclaimed movie *LA Confidential* with *Neighbours*' Guy Pearce, got his own American TV series, *The Guardian*.

More off-set *E Street* romances kept the tabloids on their toes during the show's final months. Twenty-six-year-old Andrew Williams played down the controversy of living with 17-year-old *Family and Friends* actress Melissa Thomas. After many *TV Week* stories, she joined *E Street* as Rebecca, who decided she wanted to lose her virginity, not to Jack, but to Max.

Even actress Melissa Bell was dating someone from the show but he wasn't an actor – he was the producer's son and *E Street*'s musical co-ordinator, Jason Redlich. Bell, who originally played Janine in *E Street* before leaving to play Lucy in *Neighbours*, returned to Westside as eco-crusader Bonnie Tait. Jason Redlich would eventually reveal intimate details of his sex life with Bell to an English tabloid for an alleged $2,000. Describing her as a 'naïve lover', 'the world's worst actress' and 'an uppity star', the couple broke up but later reconciled, married and had a son Dylan before eventually divorcing.

In between slagging Bell off to the English press and remarrying her, Jason Redlich announced his engagement to another *E Street* actress, Teen Queen Kelly Hoggart, after a two-month 'whirlwind romance'. The Teen Queens were supposed to be Westside Records' supergroup and they had been appearing regularly in the final months of the show. One rumour held them responsible for the death of *E Street*.

All three Teen Queens had performed at Toni and C.J.'s wedding before Forrest Redlich tapped them for their own sitcom pilot. It was to be set in 1962 and have the girls winning a church talent quest, then moving to the big city in search of fame. Some thought that when Ten passed on the Teen Queens pilot, Redlich gave them an ultimatum – no Teen Queens, no *E Street*. Today, Redlich denies they had anything to do with it. 'The Teen Queens pilot was made for an English company. I just decided I didn't want to make *E Street* anymore. And this is the reason why. Towards the end, I had been subsidising the show out of my own money to the tune of about $20,000 to $30,000 a week. When Canwest took over the Ten network, we were supposed to renegotiate. Instead, they said they wanted to 'rationalise' by moving our production to Melbourne.

They were going to axe *Neighbours*, give us their studio and strip us five nights a week.

They were going to axe *Neighbours* (which was in a ratings hole), give us their studio and strip us five nights a week at 7pm. We considered it for a moment but then realised it was bullshit. We had already established *E Street* as being in a Sydney suburb and there was no extra money being offered for set-up costs or for the extra half-hour of television required to be made every week.

'Ten didn't understand anything about the show except it made money for them. It had just been nominated for nine Logies and was still rating in the 20s. I didn't want to tell everybody that I couldn't afford to make it anymore and that the network wanted to move us to Melbourne, so we just wrapped it up eight weeks early. It was just so fucking sad,' Redlich reveals today.

As the final episode of *E Street* approached, talk turned to how the saga would be wound up. One rumoured end was a bomb blast at Patchett's Pub that would kill off three characters. After that, a bald-headed extra, Reg, who was always seen in the bar but never heard, would be shown watching the explosion on TV and saying, 'I didn't think it was that bad!' Instead, the pub caught fire, nobody died and Bonnie (Melissa Bell) woke up from her coma as everyone gathered around her bedside. On that happy note, the show returned from its final commercial break with a ten-minute clip package of highlights from its 404-episode run.

Amazingly, *E Street* wasn't ready to disappear just yet. Disappointed fans packed an 'End of *E Street*' dance party in Sydney to hear departed cast member Toni Pearen sing hit songs from her *Intimate* album, including 'I Want You', 'In Your Room' and 'Walkaway Lover'. Joining her on stage was Bruce Samazan who had just recorded his first rap single, 'One of a Kind', and filmed an accompanying video with Teen Queen Kelly Hoggart (who eventually ended up singing and dancing her way through kids show *Hi-5*). Samazan could also be heard performing 'E Street (We Outta Here Mix)' on the *E Street* soundtrack which arrived in stores several months after the show had ended.

Inside the CD sleeve was a message from Forrest Redlich. 'In its five years, *E Street* broke all the rules, yet won every major drama award and was hailed as "The best show of its type in the world". It created a whole generation of stars and injected much-needed new blood into the Australian television and music scene. *E Street* has gone but the music lives on. This album is a fitting memorial to the television show that has become a legend.' As usual, Redlich's claims raised eyebrows, especially given the show was now just a fading memory. Looked at in retrospect though, no Australian soap that followed in *E Street*'s wake would ever again match its buzz or success. 'It was crazy and so out there,' says Melissa Tkautz. 'People couldn't stop watching it. I think that's why it worked, because it was so different to anything else.'

Unfortunately, the music did not live on, for Westside Records crashed and burned along with *E Street*. Even its biggest act, Melissa Tkautz, never recorded a follow-up. 'I thought I had a music career so I didn't give a shit about the show's axing, to tell you the truth, but I felt really sorry for the crew,' Tkautz remembers. 'I had a new manager who got paid $1,000 a week, they picked me up every day in a limo and I sat in his office from nine to five doing nothing except being taken out to lavish lunches. Later I figured out all the money being flashed around was mine. And then I got a bill from a limo service even though I'd never asked for it.'

E-Street CD.

The Honeymen were another act left high and dry by the demise of the Westside empire. The independent group had been getting airplay on radio station Triple J when Westside came after them. 'They promised we would be on page three of *Smash Hits* within three weeks if we signed up with them – and we were,' remembers frontman Sean Sennett, now a critically acclaimed solo performer. 'Westside spent a fortune on our first video clip but the demise of *E Street* also coincided with the end of pop music for a few years as harder bands like Nirvana arrived and changed the musical landscape.' The music was over and so was *E Street*. It truly was the end of an era.

Today the show is remembered for its outrageous storylines rather than for showing Ten how it could re-establish itself as a force to be reckoned with. Throughout the 90s, the network positioned itself as the hip channel of choice for its 18- to 35-year-old consumers. Ten still came third in the overall ratings, behind Nine and Seven, but with the kids it was number one and therefore quite a profitable channel. *E Street* had been the trailblazer.

'I never wanted to do something sentimental like *Sons and Daughters*,' says Forrest Redlich today. 'That would have been easy. I could have still been making it now. Everybody worked really hard on *E Street* and under the most abnormal conditions – we had no network most of the time, there were accountants running the joint! People say that I was some sort of drug-crazed megalomaniac but I always knew exactly what I was doing. I sat in on every edit and every script conference and I always had the show planned out six months in advance.'

E Street ended up being seen in about 15 countries, including Canada, Greece, Israel and Africa. Using the original scripts, there was even a German production that lasted 40 episodes and another version, in Flemish, that ran on Belgian TV for three years. It is unknown whether or not Mr Bad survived the translation.

35

FAMILY AND FRIENDS

PREMIERE: **1990** EPISODES: **96** NETWORK: **NINE** FINALE: **1991**

Pasquelina (Rebecca Rigg) sets her sights on the Rossi family.

By the start of the 90s, Ten had *Neighbours* and Seven had *Home and Away*, but Nine once again lacked a home-grown soap to anchor their night-time programming. Undeterred, they threw a lot of money at the creators of *Home and Away* and convinced them to leave Seven and work their magic for them instead. Alan Bateman, Seven's Head of Drama, led the exodus, which also included John Holmes and Bevan Lee. In short, Nine now had the entire creative team behind *Home and Away*, and they wanted another hit just like it.

Bateman came up with *The Family*, later re-named *A Family Matter* and finally known as *Family and Friends*. It was to follow the lives of an Australian family intertwined with an Italian one and examine the cultural differences between them. John Holmes and Bevan Lee would development produce and script edit respectively. Lee, struggling to figure out a premise for the show, told the assembled writers to 'do a *Romeo and Juliet* but not tell anybody because the audience is bored shitless with that story'. Unfortunately, Nine's publicity department thought they had discovered a fabulous concept to promote the show, and when a huge publicity campaign about *Romeo and Juliet* for the 90s started, Lee began to quietly worry that the show was now doomed.

Producer Bruce Best wasn't in the mood for another soap after falling out with Forrest Redlich over *E Street*, but Alan Bateman convinced him that *Family and Friends* would be 'an easy little show, no stress'. A pilot had already been shot which Best thought 'wore its ethnicity very uncomfortably because there were no Italians in it, acting-wise or even in the crew. As far as I knew, nobody knew anything about the Italian way of life so it was pretty forced right from the start.'

Real Italians or not, *Family and Friends* was being talked up as the serial that would finally break the dreaded soapie curse from which Nine appeared to suffer. The network couldn't have had a better opportunity to promote it ad nauseam than during their exclusive coverage of the 1990 Commonwealth Games. Not everyone was convinced however. Nine's Programming Manager, Ross Plapp, resigned before the show premiered, amidst rumours that Alan Bateman's new position afforded him a say in where his new drama should air in Plapp's schedule.

Rooted in the ratings from night one.

Finally it came time for the show's February premiere and it was placed directly opposite *E Street* on Wednesday and Thursday nights. Ten's soap was still on shaky ground in its second year and struggling to be called a success. Nine obviously thought the timeslots were ripe for a takeover but they had misjudged very badly. 'One of the worst moments in my life was when I was told it had premiered with a disastrous rating of just eight,' remembers John Holmes. 'I knew on that day it was rooted. You can never claw back from that.' Bruce Best remembers a distinct change in mood from Nine. 'We went from being the feted children where nothing was too much trouble to being pariahs after opening night.'

They carried on, even though nobody was watching. The pilot had introduced the warring Chandler and Rossi families and started the story back in 1951 to set up their long-standing feud. It involved Giovanni Rossi who, after being caught spying on a Chandler woman undressing, was attacked and killed while riding his bike home. The story then jumped forward to the present where bitter Italian matriarch Antoinetta (Dinah Shearing) was still waging a war against the family that killed her husband.

Antoinetta's son, Joe Rossi (Robert Forza), ran a construction business and he and his wife, Luciana (Anna-Maria Monticelli), had several children. There was Marco (Adrian Lee), Claudia (Rachel Beck) and Robert (Renato Bartolemei), who was about to fall in love with a dreaded Chandler girl.

The Chandler family had just moved back into the town of Westmead after being transferred to the nearby air force base. Greg Chandler (Sean Myers) and Pamela (Diane Craig) had their own brood which included pilot Damien (Simon Westaway) and schoolboy Toby (Dominic McDonald). Toby was still going to the school where his sister, Jennifer (Roxane Wilson), was just beginning her teaching career alongside Brother Ignatius (Jonathan Hardy).

Pamela Chandler's sister, Dawn (Anne Phelan), had split family loyalties when she married a Rossi, but was now widowed. She had a young son, Mikey (Mario Rossello), and ran the local café where the dopey Gloria (Klibingaitis) waitressed when not romancing the even dopier Thommo (Ross Newton). Meanwhile, Gloria's dressmaker mum, Doreen Stubbs (Abigail), was, according to Nine's publicity department, going to give new meaning to the phrase 'mutton dressed as lamb'.

That other big cliché was the *Romeo and Juliet* scenario. Robert and Jennifer's ill-fated romance resulted in a first night cliffhanger accident that temporarily paralysed Marco Rossi. While he was rushed off to hospital where he met a randy nurse (Justine Clarke), Grandmother Antoinetta declared war on the Chandlers, even though she was the only Rossi member interested in reviving the feud.

More interesting was the war behind the scenes. Nine weren't about to leave the show floundering in prime time so it was moved to 5.30pm weeknights. Bruce Best remembers 'just hacking it up' with an editor to re-format it so it could be stripped five nights a week. Its new timeslot, however, made it a lead-in for the all important 6pm news bulletin, and when *Family and Friends* continued to deliver lacklustre ratings, the wrath of the news department came down upon the ailing soap.

Nine's publicity department tried desperately to make it appear that they were still committed to the show. They snared their one and only *TV Week* cover with the announcement that *Sons and Daughters*' Alyce Platt would come on board as psychologist Stephanie Collins. The actress was already appearing on the quiz show, *Sale of the Century*, but as that only took up one day a week, she had plenty of time left over to romance Damien Chandler and reveal her own deep dark secret (something which soap psychologists always seem to have).

Psychologist Stephanie (Alyce Platt) treats Damien (Simon Westaway) but has a worse problem herself.

In April, Nine announced to *TV Week* that a major re-launch was being planned. Six actors were being dropped as well as the series' major storyline – the Chandler/Rossi feud – which 'hasn't proved popular with viewers. It's the start of a whole new look for *Family and Friends*,' said the Nine spokesperson. Joining the cast were red-hot temptress Pasquelina (Rebecca Rigg) and school-kids Renato and Blondie (Gavin Harrison and Kym Wilson), and negotiations were supposedly under way with *Neighbours*' Rachel Friend and Cameron Daddo to come on board.

Bruce Best had just finished telling the cast which actors were about to be culled when he had to tell everybody that the show had been canned. 'I remember being told quite early in the shooting week that it was over but I decided to complete post-production that week even though it wasn't needed. I'm a Virgo and it felt like we had a bit more dignity that way.' All around them, the studio was still being built and the facilities were never properly finished before the show ended. They eventually would become the new home of SBS Television.

Ill-fated 'Romeo and Juliet' couple Jennifer (Roxane Wilson) and Robert (Renato Bartolemei).

Family and Friends was yanked from the schedule and replaced by the umpteenth repeat of *The Bugs Bunny Show*. The final episodes weren't played until 11.30pm weeknights when ratings finished for the year in November. The final week was the start of the show's re-invention. Driving drunk, Robert had a head-on collision with his father-in-law, Greg. Now that a Rossi had finally killed a Chandler, Antoinetta found it in her heart to declare the feud over. The shock of losing her husband sent Pamela into early labour. Cradling the newborn baby in her arms, sister Dawn smiled and said, 'New start, eh?'

Not really. Alan Bateman 'parted company' with Nine on 22 June. (Ironically, he returned to the Seven Network in 1995 as managing director of ATN 7, where he was happy to renew *Home and Away* for another year). John Holmes moved over to become Ten's Head of Drama. Bevan Lee remained at Nine to give birth to more troubled soap children, *Paradise Beach* and *Pacific Drive*. 'We always knew from day one that *Family and Friends* was this bizarre hybrid show that didn't have a good premise,' Lee now admits. 'It was a really sad experience because we worked twice as hard to make it work but it was just awful. It just goes to prove that good people with the best will in the world can still fuck up.'

'They were a great cast, very professional, who always approached it all with enormous discipline even though we were all swimming like crazy to stay afloat,' says Bruce Best. '*Family and Friends* was talked up way beyond its ability to deliver but I actually enjoyed working on it. It was one of the more poignant shows I've worked on.'

36

CHANCES

PREMIERE: **1991** EPISODES: **127** NETWORK: **NINE** FINALE: **1993**

Jeremy Sims, nude and naughty.

How did a family saga about winning the lottery evolve into the strangest Aussie TV show of all time? What were Nazis and Egyptian sun goddesses doing in downtown Melbourne? And why was there a never-ending display of bare buttocks and breasts every week?

In 1988, while working at Nine as head of drama, Lynn Bayonas came up with the original concept for *Chances*. Nine desperately needed a popular local drama so they commissioned her idea as a telemovie which would introduce the Taylor family. Housewife Barbara (Diane Craig) and husband Dan Taylor (John Sheerin) had three kids – ambitious advertising executive Alex (Marcus Graham), about-to-be-married Rebecca (former Miss Australia Natalie McCurrey) and youngest sibling Nikki (Mouche Phillips).

Other characters included Dan's best friend and next door neighbour, pot-smoking Bill Anderson (Michael Caton), who had fought with him in Vietnam, and Dan's saucy sister Sharon (Mercia Deane-Johns). The telemovie would start with Rebecca's tragic wedding day and end with what *TV Week* described as 'an event that turns their comfortable middle class existence inside out'. That event was winning $3 million in a lottery.

The movie sat on the shelf for a couple of years until Nine decided to get *Chances* on air as a serial for the start of the 1991 ratings season. It was Beyond International's first foray into drama and they found, not surprisingly, that several of the cast weren't available after the two-year break. 'We were disappointed that we couldn't get Marcus Graham back,' remembers Lynn Bayonas, 'but he couldn't have been any better than Jeremy Sims,' who was eventually cast as 'resident bastard' Alex Taylor, the show's most memorable character.

John Sheerin, Mercia Deane-Johns, Michael Caton and Natalie McCurrey had all filmed the original pilot in Sydney, but with production moving to Melbourne, they had to pack up and move south to stay with the show. McCurrey had raced back from a European holiday when she got her callback only to discover that something had changed with the show's concept. Despite playing a kindergarten assistant, the actress was now required to strip since *Chances* was going to be a raunchy adults-only drama a la *Number 96* and *The Box*. 'I'm not happy about doing nude shots but it's part of the job,' she told *TV Week*. 'As long as it isn't gratuitous and is done with some class, it's all right. But if it's nudity for its own sake then it really degrades the show.' Famous last words.

As the show neared its Australian debut, producer Lynn Bayonas confirmed to the press that most cast members had been required to sign a contractual nudity clause stipulating they be prepared to bare fronts, backs or both at the producer's request. 'The first bare backside in the show belongs to Jeremy Sims (as Alex) and I'd say by the end of the first month, it will be seen from here to breakfast,' she told *The Sunday Telegraph*.

TV Week was told that *Chances* wouldn't deal with social issues. 'We'll leave that to *A Country Practice* and *GP*,' Bayonas said. 'We have personal issues. We've got older women and younger men, marriage break-ups, affairs with secretaries and women desperate for love and racing off with everybody.' While the lottery win was a great start for a new series, research had shown that what happens next is pretty boring. Lynn Bayonas and story editor Gwenda Marsh were ordered to take full advantage of the adult timeslot of 8.30pm every Tuesday and Thursday night.

Although at the time everyone scoffed at the suggestion, Bayonas admits today that Nine did indeed demand that the show be spiced up to cause as much controversy as possible. After a string of drama flops over nearly a decade (*Taurus Rising*, *Waterloo Station*, *Starting Out*, *Possession*, *Prime Time*, *All the Way* and *Family and Friends*), Nine had no intention of ordering another disaster. 'It was at their insistence that we put nudity and sex into the mix. When we were filming the first episodes in Melbourne, I kept getting calls from Sydney saying they weren't seeing enough flesh and I realised they had tapped into the studio feed. We had many boardroom arguments with the powers that be at Nine about the amount of nudity and sex.'

In retrospect, Bayonas now feels such moments didn't fit into *Chances*' early episodes. 'It made the actors uncomfortable because it looked gratuitous,' she says. 'Later on it fitted perfectly and nobody was embarrassed. Although it always makes me laugh that "top" actresses will only drop their tops if you're filming on 16 or 35mm.'

Chances debuted on 29 January 1991 in a two-hour premiere. Television ads trumpeted 'TV Sex is Back', and revealed that a Taylor

'The first bare backside ... belongs to Jeremy Sims ... and I'd say by the end of the first month, it will be seen from here to breakfast.'

family member would win the lottery. To find out who, you had to watch the show. As before in the telemovie, Rebecca's wedding to David Young (Rodney Bell) introduced viewers to the rest of the Taylor family tree. Father of the bride Dan beamed alongside wife Barbara (now being played by Brenda Addie) even though privately he was experiencing financial woes not helped by having to pay for the splashy wedding. Youngest daughter Nikki (now played by Cathy Godbold) was getting stuck into the champagne while advertising whiz-kid Alex was conniving to get the groom away on an urgent business deal.

As well as his younger sister Sharon, Dan had two other siblings, Connie and Jack. Nurse Connie Reynolds (Deborah Kennedy) was separated from her husband and had reared two sons, gym instructor Chris (Mark Kounnas) and little brother Sam (Simon Grey). Ex-cop Jack (Tim Robertson) had a volatile marriage to Sarah (Anne Grigg) and also two kids of his own. Daughter Philippa (Leverne McDonnell) had followed her dad into the police force while younger son Ben (Rhys Muldoon) had disappointed the old man by becoming a hairdresser. Everyone, particularly his dad, wondered if he was secretly gay, but Ben was really a heterosexual womaniser who just didn't like commitment.

Disaster struck when Alex was driving the groom back to the reception in his Porsche. He lost control, killed David and then blamed the accident on the dead man. As the family began to implode amidst the ensuing accusations, a nasty argument spilled into the front yard just as a bunch of television crews and photographers descended upon the Taylor suburban home where $3 million had just been won.

With an encouraging opening night rating of 31, most viewers returned for the next episode to discover that Dan (John Sheerin) was the lucky winner. Unfortunately, the lottery winner payoff possibly saw the series peak too quickly, for audiences swiftly dropped away leaving *Chances* struggling between 13s and 16s. On Tuesday nights, it competed against Beyond International's other show, *Beyond 2000*, as well as *LA Law*. On Thursdays it struggled against established drama series *Police Rescue* and comedy show *Fast Forward*. *The Sydney Morning Herald* described it as 'an exercise in Australian content cannibalism'. Wags, however, began referring to *Chances* as *Buckley's*.

While the series was lacking in viewers, it certainly wasn't lacking publicity. The tabloids were more than happy to talk up the sexy nature of the show, particularly when one of the actors began to complain about the nudity. *Flying Doctors* star Tammy MacIntosh (who played randy receptionist Mandy Foster) told *TV Week* that she had refused to do a naked shot. 'I was really very nervous about it,' she claimed. 'What we ended up doing was film me wearing a silk shirt and underpants. It's much better than just seeing your bum. It's better if you can use your imagination.'

Three weeks later, nervousness turned to fury. MacIntosh was splashed across the front cover of *TV Week* underneath the headline 'I was treated like a piece of meat.' The actress and the producers had fallen out and she was refusing an offer to come back for another 12-week guest stint.

According to the magazine, MacIntosh was unhappy with another nude scene when it went to air and had stormed off the set. A *Chances* source claimed she had 'exaggerated the seduction scene during the first take, then when it came to doing the scene a second time, Tammy didn't go as far – and refused to'. When the first take was used for broadcast, Tammy decided she'd be taking no more chances. Today though, Jeremy Sims laughs about it. 'What better set of breasts to start the show with than hers?' he asks, adding that the two became lifelong friends from that moment.

The naughty nonsense continued when *TV Week* reported that another actress would call for ice cubes during nude scenes to enhance her 'performance', and that a stripper was hired to help the cast 'work out various moves and positions in the delicate scenes'. Mercia Deane-Johns, who had made her television debut in *The Box* playing a nymphomaniac, couldn't help noticing the irony in playing another nympho (Sharon) two decades later. She told the press that she had given up bleaching her hair and resorted to wearing a blonde wig to have some anonymity away from the set since 'men thought I was a really easy pick-up because of the sort of character I play'.

Further cult success awaits *Chances* with the release of its craziest episodes on DVD.

As *Chances* pressed on, Dan distributed the fortune from the lottery win around the family. Connie got his old house when he and his family moved to a bigger place, and she began dating doctor Gary Duncan (Eric Oldfield). Nikki (Cathy Godbold) was grounded for popping out to nightclubs, and for popping pills, so she simply got her boyfriend Adam (Brenden Carter) to climb in the window for a bit of rumpy-pumpy. Soon she had developed anorexia and was falling in love with Gary, the doctor hired to treat her illness. Barbara's mother Hettie McGlasham (Yvonne Lawley, one of the few actresses who didn't have a nudity clause in her contract) collapsed and was taken to hospital where she bumped into a former lover, Aubrey Nash (Alwyn Kurts). She later married him and returned home to New Zealand.

Slutty Sharon slept her way into a job at Alex's ad agency before brother Dan bought her a business down at the marina which became Shazza's Bar. Sarah threw Jack out of the house before scandalising the family by sleeping with nephew Chris, whose shady father Eddie Reynolds (Dennis Miller) had raced back to town the moment news broke about the lottery win. He slithered his way back into Connie's bed, but kept quiet about his secret other wife Cheryl (Louise Siversen), all the time blackmailing Barbara about another long-held secret – that Jack, not Dan, was the father of Alex. Meanwhile, Ben fell for Charlie Gibson (Kimberley Davenport) after she had had an affair with Alex, and when she gave birth to a baby, both men stood by wondering who was the father.

More naughty moments came courtesy of Bill when he hired himself a prostitute, 'Mistress of Fantasies' Brandy (Tiffany Lamb), who dressed up as an air stewardess, policewoman and cowgirl to keep him interested (and paying up big). But it was a *Chances* double whammy that really caused viewers' jaws to drop – and nobody was even naked at the time. Outside a hospital, Barbara walked under a speeding car. When Jack wandered outside to look for her, he was hit by another one. Barbara ended up in a coma and Jack was also badly injured. She eventually recovered, but he required the services of Dee Dee Nelson (Lynda Stoner) to get back into the *Chances* swing of things. 'My character was based on a real sex therapist,' remembers an embarrassed Stoner, 'and Jack recovered so she was obviously worth it!'

'I remember one morning I was fully dressed sitting on top of Jeremy Sims, who was completely undressed, and I thought, what a way to earn a living!' Stoner says. The *Chances* cast 'wasn't a company that was as close as the ones I'd been used to and I think a lot of that came from the pressures that were put on them to do nude scenes. I never had it because I said upfront I wouldn't do that, but even though I was working with some fine actors, there was always that underlying tension. I saw people break down in the green room because they couldn't cope with it.'

Chances kept trying to get the ratings up, even launching a big murder mystery about who killed Eddie. Half the cast had a motive and six separate endings were filmed. When the killer was finally revealed to be his wife Connie, a torturous court case followed, and she was eventually acquitted on the grounds of self-defence. Unfortunately the viewing jury wasn't quite so kind to *Chances*. Nine announced that they would cease broadcasting the show twice a week and move to just one screening each Tuesday night at 9.30pm.

The reduced budget meant that executive producer Brendon Lunney had to begin whittling down the original cast of 17 to just six regulars. 'I'm sorry to lose good actors but bringing the show down to an hour is a difficult and very painful process. It was too tough, too big an ask of an audience,' Lunney told *TV Week*, blithely ignoring how many other soaps had successfully aired two hours a week before *Chances*. 'So we decided to shift the emphasis and attack more contemporary issues. Watch us and you will be rewarded. It is meant to be deliberately controversial.'

'The tail wagged the dog from the word go with *Chances*,' Jeremy Sims says today. 'They started with a concept that would bring in a certain audience and when that didn't happen, they just started trawling for any audience they could. The ratings would determine whatever demographic or niche they decided to go for. Every other week there was another change in style or tone. I was flattered that the show was all about Alex. They said they'd pay me for the extra workload and it turned out to be $200 a week more for 10 extra hours of overtime every week.'

When the new *Chances* began with episode 60, the story had jumped forward a year in time. The Taylor family believed Alex had died in a plane crash but he was really alive with amnesia. While working on a farm he met Paris (Annie Jones) and went with her on a trip to the big city where his memory slowly began to return. Meanwhile, Alex's sister Rebecca married prime ministerial hopeful Steve Harland (Peter Kowitz) and left the show after a splashy wedding. *TV Week* wondered if actors were leaving by choice or because new contracts were being negotiated that required more nudity.

Given its later timeslot, producers decided to go for broke with something they felt hadn't been done on Australian TV before – high camp and outrageous storylines. 'We knew we had the cast to do it and the writers to set it up,' says Lynn Bayonas. 'It was a great time. Everyone embraced it and the nudity just became part of it. Now we had people calling to see if they could be in the show.'

'All the actors wouldn't have minded doing high camp from the very beginning,' says Jeremy Sims. 'What pissed us off early on was the attempt to do *Home and Away* with the odd cutaway dropped in of some tits, sometimes without even a head attached! We were all grown-up theatre actors and quite happy to get naked but we wanted it to be sexy rather than stupid. Everyone had their miserable moments but the only time everyone had a ball on that show was during the last six months when we all got on famously and laughed and laughed making some of the silliest TV ever.'

Photographer Madeleine (Karen Richards) turns into an Egyptian sun goddess – as you do.

When the show began its new season in 1992, Alex was in hiding after a double murder in his apartment, and under the control of the evil Dr Kray who was supposedly helping him uncover the lost year of his life. Instead he got Alex hooked on drugs. Meanwhile, Alex's wealthy parents were off walking on the wild side. A bored Barbara, now living in a mansion, spotted a sexy pool cleaner next door. Cal Lawrence (Gerry Sont) became Barbara's toy boy and they embarked on a passionate affair until it was revealed he was a jewel thief. Cal hung around after the affair fizzled so he could get around to screwing all the other women in the show.

In March, *Chances* began on BSkyB and the UK network pulled out all the stops with its publicity campaign. As well as offering trips to Monte Carlo, billboards around the country featured a page three model who was gradually losing her clothes each day, alongside the tagline 'To get the full picture, watch *Chances*'. She was down to her bra and knickers when it became too much for councillors in Southwark, South East London, who complained that the posters were sexist and covered her up.

The brother of story editor Gwenda Marsh was working as a tour guide in Britain around the time the soap was launched there. He was telling a bus full of passengers about the wonderful show his sister wrote when, to his horror, they passed a billboard with a naked woman advertising it. He had no idea that *Chances* was that sort of show, or that his sister was now the producer responsible for steering it into even murkier waters. New story editors Barbara Bishop and Keith Aberdeen were letting their

Bogart (Lawrence
Mah) tortures
Cal (Gerry Sont).

imaginations go wild in plotting sessions, always assuming that Marsh would knock back their outrageousness. 'But every week I would say "Great!" and their faces would fall because it meant they now had to write it,' Marsh remembers.

Jeremy Sims was recruited to publicise the show in England and he didn't mince words about his infamous role. 'Personally, I find it worse to insult people's intelligence with mundanity and bad scripts than insult them with naked bodies. I'm sure there are other guys who are happy doing their bits in *E Street* and *Home and Away*, but I would be bored out of my mind doing that stuff.' Sims was already a publicist's dream because of his real-life relationship with *A Country Practice* regular Kym Wilson and his *Chances* character's bed-hopping antics. As Lynn Bayonas had once said, his bare bum was going to be seen from here to breakfast within the first month, and after more than a year of outrageous nude scenes, it had also probably flashed both cheeks to lunch and dinner as well. 'My backside must be the only recognisable one in Australia,' Sims told *TV Week*. 'Tits and bums are the most amazing subjects. You can get endless publicity over the fact you show a part of your body on television.'

While the show would only become a moderate success in England because of Sky Network's smaller audience reach, *Chances* became a bigger hit in Russia. If the ostentatious wealth of *Dallas* had been partly responsible for the fall of Communism in Eastern Bloc countries, leaders weren't too happy about the sexual shenanigans of *Chances* giving the population any more ideas. Fast cars and money were one thing but when the clothes started coming off, questions were asked in the Russian Parliament as to why everyone was watching *Chances* instead of local programs. It was soon the number one show in town.

'I didn't even know it screened in Russia until I went to London years later to make *Kangaroo Palace*,' says Sims today. 'We were in this hotel and on the floor above was the cast and crew from *The Saint* movie with Val Kilmer. There were all these Russian actors playing the bad guys and they recognised me and told me what a huge cult *Chances* was there. Apparently it was re-run all the time.'

Back on Australian screens, two more *Chances* regulars were about to disappear – the frequently nude Stephanie Ryan (Molly Brumm) and Jack Taylor (Tim Robertson) – when they were involved together in a drug-related disaster. Stephanie killed Jack by pumping him full of heroin, but Jack returned as a ghost, out to avenge his own death. By now, Alex was back in business with long-time nemesis Angela Sullivan (Patsy Stephen) in a new advertising agency called Inspirations.

As the show began to get hammered in the ratings by, of all things, Australian TV's first reality soap, *Sylvania Waters*, *Chances* fought back with even more craziness. Alex was now 'the chosen one' for the fifth richest man in the world, Crowley Lander (Barry Hill), who, it turned out, had been manipulating everything up to that point (including the family winning the lottery at the beginning of the series). Lander wanted Alex to donate his DNA so the squillionaire could live forever, as well as impregnating his mute daughter Imogen (Ciri Thompson).

With the hiring of Australian soap's first ever sex symbol, *Chances* paid homage to the show that had blazed the way for them back in the 70s, *Number 96*. Abigail joined the cast as former call girl/porn star Bambi Shute who hosted a revealing TV talk show about sex. It was a sly reference to Nine's own explicit and even more controversial series *Sex*, hosted by Sophie Lee, and later Pamela Stephenson.

Abigail's final soap role as former call girl/porn star Bambi Shute.

Chances' stylish and confident sex show host got most of the Taylor family blabbing on national television about their sex lives. Bambi even tried to cure Dan (John Sheerin) of impotence, but when Barbara (Brenda Addie) revealed her sexual fantasies on the show, it was the final straw for the Taylors' crumbling marriage. After separating, Dan discovered that Barbara had been working in a high-class brothel (doing the accounts, actually) which belonged to dead brother Jack. He took over the running of it, as well as trying out the employees.

Bambi wrote a book called 'Gender Bender' about transsexual Juanita, whom Bill fell for, but despite all the sexy talk, Abigail's days of nude scenes seemed to be in the past. Such skin-baring was left to younger actresses like Katherine Li, who played nymphomaniac Asian moll Lily, prompting an offer from *Australian Playboy* to strip for the magazine (which she sadly declined).

Abigail, who had already disrobed for *Playboy* in the 80s, eventually left *Chances* and retired from acting. 'She was a very good actress. It's a shame she didn't do more things afterwards,' says Jeremy Sims. Abigail was only ever seen again on Aussie screens doing weight loss commercials, while America tried in vain to buy her final soap. 'The Playboy Channel chased us for years,' says Lynn Bayonas, 'but we felt that *Chances* wasn't soft porn and we just felt that we didn't want to do that. Ultimately, that wasn't what it was all about.'

By now, the show had been shuffled off to an 11pm slot. Along came a long-lost relative of Crowley Lander's who turned out to be Imogen's mother *and* her sister (don't ask), even though she looked younger than her daughter. Alex kidnapped a pregnant Imogen and got his father to marry them at sea. When the ship got back to shore, Imogen hid away in a convent as a group of Asian Triad gangsters and Nazis invaded Melbourne. Yes, 'Heil Hitler' saluting types called Sieglande (Lorena Garcia) and Dietrich (Peter Webb) really did arrive to play sex games on a bed beneath a giant swastika.

While her father Bogart Lo (Lawrence Mah) plotted with the Hong Kong mafia to stop the Chinese takeover of the British colony coming up in 1997, Lily found herself hostage (in her underwear of course) in a cage during the search for a supernatural necklace that had once belonged to Eva Braun (yes, Adolf Hitler's mistress). Photographer Madeleine (Karen Richards) found it first and fell under its spell, turning into an Egyptian sun goddess. She tried to seduce Alex, which would have proved catastrophic for the world, but luckily Cal, wearing work gloves because it was too hot to touch, managed to rip the necklace off her and save Alex. And the world.

Virginal receptionist Wanda Starcross (Danielle Fairclough) was the only woman in the show not sleeping with everyone in sight, so that meant root rat Sean Becker (Stephen Whittaker) couldn't rest until he got her. 'Chances is exploitation TV at its finest,' actor Stephen Whittaker told *TV Soap* when he joined the show. 'It explores modern issues in a superficial and satirical fashion.' Meanwhile, a new Cal arrived when actor John Atkinson took over the role from Gerry Sont. Apparently, make-up artists had tired of spending up to four hours allegedly disguising a nasty skin condition of Gerry Sont's, not the most convenient thing for an actor required to be frequently nude.

'The more bizarre the better as far as I'm concerned,' Jeremy Sims told *TV Week*. 'If you believe any of it, to start with, you're a fool. The best day we have is when we get the scripts and do a read-through. It's just hysterical.' Sims wasn't joking. Read-throughs with the production crew always ended with someone asking if anybody had a clue what this week's episode was about. Nobody ever did, but they always left the room smiling.

Chances served up voodoo, vampires, reincarnation, man-eating plants, Israeli secret agents and angels on motorbikes before it all came to an end after 127 episodes. Crowley Lander, who had tried to metamorphose into Alex, had ended up as a younger version of himself (now played by Peter Webb). It turned out that Lander was responsible for unleashing AIDS, and just after threatening to control the world with a computer virus, he fell to his death from a cliff. Alex was dragged off with him but was metaphysically transported to the Melbourne library where a higher being told him he could go back to earth. Was God really making an appearance in *Chances*' final show?

Back at Shazza's Bar, everyone was celebrating the death of Crowley Lander. Shazza (Mercia Deane-Johns) was accepting Bill's marriage proposal, having just decided they were in love, and Sean had pledged true love to Wanda as a prelude to finally deflowering her. In walked Alex who told them he had inherited Lander's fortune. And he had bought them all a present – lottery tickets. 'You never know,' he said. 'Some win…'.

'We had a real cult following,' says Lynn Bayonas. 'In America, that would have kept us on air for years but Australia doesn't have the population to sustain it. Executives at the ABC used to tape and watch it with their morning coffee. The ABC wanted it but they didn't dare court the controversy.'

Gwenda Marsh has only ever been able to make children's television since *Chances* ended. '*Chances* spoilt me and the only other place to

L-R: Brenda Addie, John Sheerin, Mercia Deane-Johns, Tim Robertson, Patsy Stephen, Jeremy Sims, Michael Caton, Natalie McCurrey, Gerry Sont.

let your imagination go totally free is kids' shows.' Lynn Bayonas also wishes she could have gone on making *Chances*-type programs, 'anything a bit different to shake people up'. So how would Bayonas want *Chances* to be remembered? 'Innovative and outrageous, the most fun show ever to make.'

'I went straight from drama school to *Chances* and everyone said "I thought you were going to be a great actor" and I was like, I will be but first I'm going to make a wage and learn the entertainment business,' Jeremy Sims reveals today. 'I had to have some balls to trust that I could do all that and then come back as a serious artist but at least I have a breadth of vision now that maybe some pretentious theatre wankers have no image of at all. I've now got a very broad palette for the theatre.' Sims did indeed return to the stage, as a respected actor, director and producer, not to mention starting up his own theatrical company, Pork Chop Productions. And while TV viewers will always remember his bare bottom, Sims isn't concerned in the slightest. 'Baring my bum on *Chances* cured me of shame. I could do anything now and not feel humiliated.'

So what was *Chances*' craziest storyline? Jeremy Sims remembers 'becoming Joseph Stalin and meeting Marilyn Monroe. That was pretty cool.' Lynn Bayonas declares it has to be that divine moment from the final show. '*Chances*' most outrageous scene? Finding God in the Melbourne city library.' As you do.

37

PARADISE BEACH

PREMIERE: **1993** EPISODES: **260** NETWORK: **NINE** FINALE: **1994**

Lisa (Tiffany Lamb) crowns Tori
(Megan Connolly) Miss Paradise Beach.

Queensland's Gold Coast is Australia's playground, the home of holidaymakers, retirees and teenagers celebrating the end of school. Its long stretches of beautiful surfing beaches, coupled with sparkling high-rises, always seemed the perfect location to film a television series.

In 1979, a $100,000 pilot was shot on the Gold Coast called *Paradise Village*. Filmed in and around the Chevron Hotel, it concerned a glamorous blonde named April Thackeray (Suzy Gashler) who bought a hotel/motel/disco. Each week would feature a slew of visiting guest stars, with the pilot offering Lynette Curran, Joan Bruce and Christine Broadway.

The show also featured Peter Sumner, Olga Tamara, Anne Haddy and Bill Kerr. There were no teenagers, although *TV Week* couldn't help running before and after shots of 15-year-old extra Abigail Van Ooy in a school uniform and a skimpy bikini. Producers talked up a cameo appearance by John Cleese that never eventuated, while they desperately tried to shoot their sun-drenched show in unseasonable non-stop rain. So rough were the conditions, Suzy Gashler 'narrowly escaped death in pounding surf' after being hit in the head by a surf ski. Ironically, she was rescued by *Chopper Squad*'s Dennis Grosvenor.

Despite supposed interest from Seven and the support of the newly created Queensland Film Commission, the pilot didn't make it to a series. One factor may have been the lack of infrastructure, particularly when it came to studios or crews. It was one of the reasons why *Holiday Island* raced back to Melbourne in 1981 after filming establishing shots for their own surf 'n' sand serial.

That all changed in 1988 when Warner Roadshow Movie World Studios opened a few miles north of the Gold Coast. The Queensland Government was a major supporter of developing a local film and television industry and the site did seem to offer a myriad of possibilities. Within just half an hour of the studio facilities, productions could film on location at beaches, rainforests, theme parks and luxury waterfront homes on canals. Within just a few months, a revival of the American TV series *Mission: Impossible* was doing just that, disguising locales to make the Gold Coast and Brisbane look like different parts of the world every week.

Meanwhile, *Neighbours* and *Home and Away* had become the toast of English and European television but neither was deemed appropriate for American consumption. Not surprisingly, the US showed little interest in watching Australian TV dramas except for a brief fascination with *Prisoner* in 1980. As it turned out, they also had no time for any American series that filmed in Queensland. While *Mission: Impossible* lasted two years, environmental action series *E.A.R.T.H. Force* lasted just two weeks and *Dolphin Cove* not much longer.

Undeterred, *Paradise Beach* was ambitiously created to become a breakthrough soap on American TV. It was a co-operative venture between three production partners – the Nine Network, Village Roadshow and New World International. With the demise of *Chances*, Australia's highest-rating network still didn't have a locally made serial to help them reach their drama content quota. Given that they were an equity partner in the Gold Coast studios along with Village Roadshow, everyone agreed that a long-running TV series could be the backbone of the studios. The Queensland Government provided financial support and incentives in exchange for employing a certain number of local cast and crew members.

New World International was a US-based distribution company that had already had great success selling American soaps *Santa Barbara* and *The Bold and the Beautiful* all over the world. They had identified a niche for a new soap targeted purely at teens, who were then being largely ignored by American daytime TV. Filmed on location, *Paradise Beach* could also offer higher production values than American soaps which re-created everything inside a studio. They boldly predicted that *Paradise Beach* had the potential to reach a worldwide audience of 50 million people.

Armed with a promotional reel that consisted of scantily clad models alongside footage lifted straight from Queensland tourism videos and Aussie movie *The Coolangatta Gold*, *Paradise Beach* was pre-sold to America, Europe, Asia, South America, New Zealand and the UK. Buying the show, sight unseen, before it had been cast or any footage filmed, proved to be an unwise investment for many of the international networks.

They boldly predicted that Paradise Beach had the potential to reach a worldwide audience of 50 million people.

RAELEE HILL (Loretta Taylor)

MEGAN CONNOLLY (Tori Hayden)

New World convinced more than 150 American stations (85 per cent of the syndication market) that *Paradise Beach* was just what they needed for a late afternoon or early evening timeslot. And this was despite the fact that no soap screened anywhere in America after 3pm, while there had been no successful new soap there since *The Bold and the Beautiful* in 1987. *Paradise Beach* would be launched during the 1993 American summer break, when its target audience would hopefully be enticed by the show's tagline of 'where teenagers from everywhere converge to cut loose, find the perfect wave and fall hopelessly in love'.

Press kits even came with their own marketing plan, urging broadcasters to launch the series with the slogan 'Win a Trip to Paradise' as each network would receive free round-trip tickets to Australia for use in on-air promotions and competitions. New World also produced a complete catalogue of pre-approved, licensed merchandise, and suggested clothing from the 'Paradise Beach Line' could be previewed throughout various international cities as the 'Paradise Beach Fashion Show'. Before the clothes got made though, the show had to start filming.

Veteran producer Jock Blair (*The Box*, *The Sullivans*, *Skyways*) relocated to the Gold Coast and soon realised this would be unlike any production he had worked on before. 'I had never walked into a studio with only four walls and no infrastructure,' Blair recalls. 'So we just slowly started to put it all together. I ended up with a very young, raw, inexperienced team both in front of the camera and behind it, but they had an enthusiasm that I had never seen on any other show. All they wanted to do was learn and get it right.'

Nowhere did this apply more than to the cast. Yes, they were enthusiastic, but many were inexperienced and most had never acted before, although everyone looked great in swimming costumes. University student Kimberley Joseph was waiting for a friend to finish auditioning when she was spotted in the foyer by executive producer Nick McMahon. He convinced her to screen-test and, impressed, then had to convince her to drop out of uni. She signed up to play marine biologist Cassie, the sister of bad boy ironman Kirk (Jon Bennett) and the daughter of ruthless businessman Tom Barsby (Robert Coleby).

Paradise Beach would kick off with best friends Sean Hayden (Ingo Rademacher) and Roy McDermott (John Holding) fleeing their suburban home for a holiday up north. Sean's kid sister Tori (Megan Connolly) insisted on going with them so she could stay with penpal Cassie. Tori became immediately smitten with Kirk while Sean fell for Cassie. Roy, meanwhile, became the target of Cassie's best friend, Loretta Taylor (Raelee Hill).

Also new to the beach was American photographer Cooper Hart (Matt Lattanzi), who was looking for his childhood sweetheart, Lisa Whitman (Tiffany Lamb), unaware that she was already shacked up with tyrant Tom Barsby. The feared entrepreneur also had a younger brother, Nick (Andrew McKaige), who ran a surf shop next door to Anna's Beach Café. Anna (Deborah Coulls) had a teenage son, William 'Grommet'

Ritchie (Tony Hayes), who was something of a con man and desperate to hang out with the older crowd to avoid being around his abusive father Craig (Eric Oldfield).

Missing the fact that all the characters' surnames came from players in the Queensland Sheffield cricket team of that year, the Australian press zeroed in on (as he was always billed at the start of the show) 'special guest star' Matt Lattanzi, husband of Olivia Newton-John. He warned *TV Week* his family wouldn't stay 'if Livvy gets stressed out by paparazzi and that type of thing. She needs anonymity.' The Aussie icon had been battling breast cancer and the collapse of her clothing company, Koala Blue, and warranted special treatment. The visiting American, however, did not, and once critics got an eyeful of his supposed acting chops, the knives came out in force.

Paradise Beach's naïve newcomers were unaware they were also headed for a similar mauling from the press, particularly since they were all being led to believe they were about to make it big in America. 'We've talked about how this could be a really big thing and we could get pretty famous but we're NOT going to change,' Ingo Rademacher told *The Sunday Mail*. 'John Holding and I share a flat and we go grocery shopping every Saturday afternoon. We're still going to do that.' But the boys would never be in danger of being mobbed at the supermarket, and as for changing, while John Holding remained a down-to-earth local lad, crew members soon nicknamed his mate 'Ego Runamucker'.

'We've been told to brace ourselves,' Jon Bennett told *TV Week*. 'We've been told it is going to be huge overseas, especially since the surfing culture of Australia is very much flavour of the month right around the world. At the moment it feels like we are aboard the Starship Enterprise and sort of going out into the unknown.'

Despite being produced at a rock bottom price to ensure maximum profit, some investors hadn't been able to stop themselves talking it up beyond its capabilities. Amongst others, Village Roadshow president Greg Coote had been describing the show as a 'slick, glossy *Beverly Hills 90210* meets *Neighbours* meets *Baywatch*'. A few weeks before the show's premiere, Nick McMahon tried to backpedal from his colleagues' claims. 'It's unfair to draw the comparison of *Baywatch* and *90210* to *Paradise Beach*,' he told *The Sunday Mail*. 'They are American shows with huge budgets and ten days to produce one hour of drama. We produce two and a half hours of TV in five days, so the comparison is an odious one.' What *were* odious were the first episodes filmed, which McMahon had probably watched by this stage.

As the first episodes of *Paradise Beach* began to air in Australia, the show turned into a laughing stock overnight. Its production values were shaky, with the lack of post audio production giving it an unnaturally eerie silence that only highlighted the childish dialogue that trailed away to nothing or occasionally overlapped into following scenes. As for its performances, the show became every critic's favourite whipping boy as they tripped over themselves trying to come up with smart new titles for it.

There was *Stupidity Beach*, *Paradise Lost* and *Paralysed Speech*, which referred to the stilted delivery of all the lines. This was intentional and meant to assist international audiences in understanding the Australian accents. Unfortunately, it also rendered the dialogue stagey and made many cast members sound like yobbos who were popping tranquillisers.

No amount of rapidly edited MTV-style musical sequences could disguise the show's substandard storylines as clichés piled upon clichés. Most embarrassingly, there were corporate tie-ins to Village Roadshow's Gold Coast theme parks, Movie World, Sea World and Wet'n'Wild, which did little to help the show's credibility. *Paradise Beach* was accused of being nothing more than an extended television commercial. At this point, the only good thing about it was the snappy credits sequence.

Writer Bevan Lee believes the show had no identity at all. 'It was like Channel Nine and New World gave birth to this bastard kid that nobody wanted. It set out to be something it didn't have the money to be and in trying to be everywhere, it ended up being nowhere. *Paradise Beach* was the low point of my career.'

Launched almost simultaneously in America and Australia, it escaped critical reaction in the US by sliding in under the radar and not making any impact at all. In Los Angeles, despite early reports that it was headed for the prime time slot of 7.30pm, it was dropped into the 'black hole' of 3–4pm, notorious because it meant competing against *Oprah*. Producers were still optimistic, explaining that a minimum 3 rating would still return US$18,000 for a 30-second commercial in syndication. In LA, *Oprah* had ten times the audience of *Paradise Beach*, and across America its ratings flatlined at 1.2. Not surprisingly, the show did not complete its test run and was yanked off air before the summer was over.

In Australia, its timeslot of 5.30pm weeknights as a lead-in to Nine's all-important 6pm News proved to be another miscalculation. Premiering at 18, it had slumped to 11 by the end of the first week and began to affect ratings for the News. As arch-rival Seven came within striking distance, Nine demoted *Paradise Beach* to 5pm and replaced it with repeats of *Graham Kennedy's Funniest Home Videos*. The show also bombed on Britain's Sky One channel and ended up being moved around the schedule several times, never quite capturing the audience it needed.

Former game show hostess Tiffany Lamb begged *TV Week* readers to give the show a go. 'If Robert De Niro had to do as many scenes as we do in the same amount of time, I doubt he could make them all sensational either. The acting will improve as time goes by. At the moment, it's such a tough workload for a small cast.' Lamb, who had copped a barrage of criticism for her fake American accent, was no doubt relieved when the show failed to ignite in the U.S. Overnight, Lisa stopped talking like a Yank.

Behind the scenes, there was also pressure to improve the show's image, particularly the performances. 'There was a huge push to get rid of about four of the younger actors but I resisted that very strongly,' says Jock Blair. 'I believed in those kids, we got in a drama coach and it made a big difference. Plus we re-worked the story to showcase their abilities.' *The Young Doctors'* John Dommett came in as a 'dialogue coach' while more established names were also brought in to help with the workload.

The first was Melissa Tkautz who came on board to play 'Paradise Bitch' Vanessa Campbell, the former girlfriend of Sean. Four months down the track it had turned into a PR nightmare as a dieting Tkautz lost an alarming amount of weight and was denying to the press she was suffering from anorexia. Her new on-screen boyfriend, Jon Bennett, was also going through some bad press of his own, having been booked by police on a charge of wilful and unlawful damage.

Proving he was just as hot-headed as his on-screen character, Bennett got into trouble after finishing filming on location in Main Beach. He was waiting to cross the street to his high-rise apartment when one of the occupants of a passing car taunted the actor by calling him names. Chasing the car, the 23-year-old Bennett kicked its doors and punched his fist through the window. A severed tendon resulted in a 6cm scar on his right hand which affected his ability to play the piano. A Gold Coast magistrate's court recorded no conviction but ordered him to pay $700 for the damage he caused to the car.

Jon Bennett as hothead ironman Kirk.

'I think my achievements deserve a degree of respect,' he told *TV Week* at the time. 'When the taunting started, I felt I'd been stripped of respect and the pride I have for myself. Marlon Brando said, "If you play a pig, the public will think you're a pig". I don't want the image of a bad boy off-camera. Kirk's only a character.'

Desperate for some positive publicity, Matt Lattanzi and Olivia Newton-John's seven-year-old daughter was trotted out for *TV Week*. Chloe Lattanzi made her dramatic debut as an extra in a night-time beach singa-long, even though her appearance supposedly wasn't planned (that *TV Week* photographer was just walking past at the time). 'Before anyone knew it, Chloe was part of the party, roasting marshmallows and singing along with the cast,' a spokesman said. A month later, as Matt Lattanzi filmed his final scenes, *Paradise Beach* finally scored the ultimate cameo from Chloe's elusive superstar mother.

At Coolangatta Airport, as Cooper prepared to leave for good on an overseas photographic assignment, Chloe's second appearance in the show included dialogue as she revealed that she and her mum were travelling on the same flight that he was boarding. At this point, the camera pulled back to reveal a radiant Olivia Newton-John beaming at her real-life husband.

With all traces of its Americanisation now gone, producers decided to go back to some soap basics. Tori and Sean's parents, Joan (Paula Duncan)

Ingo Rademacher
(before *General
Hospital*) and
Megan Connolly.

and Ken Hayden (Michael Caton), arrived and took over the running of the Beach Café when Anna was killed by a taxi in New York. They insisted Tori go back to school (Paradise High) where she promptly had an affair with her teacher, Chris (Scott Michaelson), as well as getting herself a school friend, Robyn Devereaux.

Robyn (Isla Fisher) was the daughter of Natalie, the long-gone mother of Kirk and Cassie, who had fled Paradise Beach after having an affair with Tom's brother Nick. Robyn told her new family that Natalie had died and tests eventually revealed that Tom was her dad, not Nick. Re-living the past love affair revealed why the brothers had originally fallen out, and why the hatred continued to simmer between them.

Loretta, traumatised by Roy having an affair with her author mother Paula (Zoe Bertram), turned instead to pro jet-skier Harry Tait (Jaason Simmons). When neither couple could make it work, Loretta and Roy turned to each other and had sex on the beach, which left Loretta pregnant. After much to-ing and fro-ing, the couple finally admitted they loved each other and began to plan for their wedding, as did Nick and triathlete trainer Brooke Bannister (Gabrielle Fitzpatrick).

Paula Duncan, who had married John Orcsik when the pair worked together on *Cop Shop*, had broken up with him before *Paradise Beach*. Unbeknown to her, Orcsik signed to the cast and didn't tell her that they would soon be playing opposite one another again. 'I got this script and Joan was going to learn ballroom dancing and I asked who's going to be the dance teacher?' Duncan laughs. 'Darling Joy Blair (wife of the producer) had to teach us how to dance and found herself in the middle of this love affair being recreated. John and I were holding each other and looking into each other's eyes and bingo, we were on again!'

Slowly but surely, *Paradise Beach* improved, and by the time filming began for the second series it was a completely different show. No longer did it chew up and blow off good storylines as the scriptwriting team found their groove. More importantly, they had been transferred up from Sydney so they could actually experience the Gold Coast lifestyle rather than just imagine it.

The technical ineptitude of the first series was overcome and performances had improved but there was still a cultural cringe from the industry down south. 'Nobody wanted a TV industry to work up here,' insists Blair. 'Melbourne people in particular had a problem with Queensland culturally and the Gold Coast particularly inspired snobbery.'

It was a different story on the Gold Coast as locals got behind the show and offered unprecedented support. The Gold Coast City Council allowed the production to film anywhere they wanted free of charge, even though some Sydney local councils charged thousands of dollars per day to film on their beaches. For once, one of the predictions about the show's success came true, as overseas tourists arrived and began asking directions to where *Paradise Beach* was being filmed.

Despite its lack of success in the UK and America, the show had taken off in Europe, particularly in countries with cold climates. 'The majority of European channels were requesting more when they were only halfway through the first series,' says Jock Blair. 'It was also a huge hit in South America.' Bemused cast members were amazed to finally see their likenesses on European merchandise like pencil cases and T-shirts, not to mention a soundtrack CD featuring background songs from the early days by Aussie artists such as Ratcat, Russell Morris and Boom Crash Opera. In Australia, however, the press still treated them as pariahs despite the rise in audience figures. When it came to renewing the series for a third time, Nine was unforgiving.

'One of the great ironies was that it is possibly the only serial to get cancelled after it had improved its ratings,' states Jock Blair. 'Nine's news department were concerned that the more the show rated, the more we brought in a younger audience – and of course they were switching off when the news started.' It was even rumoured that a public relations company had been employed to continue bagging the show and, whether it came from Nine's News or from rival station Seven, it had the desired effect. *Paradise Beach* was axed and dumped to make way for another revival of *The Price is Right*. 'Quiz shows bring in the over 40s which the news team prefers,' says Blair.

When the show returned at 11pm during the non-ratings period, it was at its creative peak with a swag of new soap stalwarts on hand. Sean broke up with Cassie to date pro surfer Emily Harris (Melissa Bell), leaving Cassie free to be deflowered by environmental activist Sam Dexter (Richard Huggett). Tori ran away from home to live briefly in a seedy caravan park with wild child Karen Wolfe (Rebekah Elmaloglou). Lisa ripped off Tom and threw her money away on Brooke's jailbird brother Angel (Lochie Daddo), while Brooke fell into an affair with Tom, unaware she was being used as payback for Nick's affair with Tom's wife years earlier.

There was also *Paradise Beach*'s most bizarre moment – the shooting of Kirk's girlfriend, Pam So Oy (Theresa Wong), by a Chinese firing squad. The unfortunate Pam, who got everyone to raise money for Amnesty International so people could protest peacefully in her country of birth, returned to China only to find herself arrested for treason. 'Nine had a huge problem with it but I wanted to do it within a serial,' explains Blair. The truth was, Blair was determined to re-claim the sequence having originally done a similar scene in *The Sullivans* only to notice it being ripped off in the movie *Breaker Morant*. After *Paradise Beach*'s odd foray into execution, no filmmaker has dared to steal the sequence back.

Paradise Beach ended with a cyclone the night before Roy and Loretta's barefoot beach wedding. Then, after one last ironman competition where

Sean beat Kirk, Tom was knocked down by a hit and run driver. As he struggled for life in hospital, it became apparent that the demented driver was Lisa, who had gone psycho and would try to murder him again. But before she could, Robyn was telling a mysterious caller that Tom Barsby was dead and she had killed him.

Had the series continued, Tom's supposedly dead wife Natalie (to be played by Chantal Contouri) was going to sweep back into town to claim the family fortune, while Loretta's baby would be born deaf. 'The show could still be going now,' insists Blair. 'New World really wanted it to continue because they were making so much money off the show internationally, but without Nine, we couldn't get the finances to make it work within Australia. There's nothing more exciting than getting the green light to start a show and there's nothing worse than getting a cancellation.'

Paradise Beach can hold its head high for setting a new high-water mark in soap production. 'We did a lot of things that other serials hadn't done before,' remembers Blair. 'There were five days a week of location filming, major water sequences including underwater, all on a budget of far less than everybody else and a never say never crew.' Indeed, at 20 per cent exteriors per episode, *Paradise Beach* had set a new world record in television production. 'It was one of the happiest productions I ever worked on,' says Jock Blair.

As for the Nine Network, they were so embarrassed by the experience they used up their two repeat screenings of *Paradise Beach* in the dead of night. However, in 1996 they got back into bed with Village Roadshow and New World International for a spin-off of sorts to *Paradise Beach*, *Pacific Drive*. In 2003 they also revived *The Price is Right*, yet again, as the lead-in to their 6pm News, and to prove that some things in television

BACK L-R: Deborah Coulls, Matt Lattanzi, Tiffany Lamb, Robert Coleby, Kimberley Joseph, Ingo Rademacher, John Holding, FRONT: Andrew McKaige, Tony Hayes, Jon Bennett, Megan Connolly, Raelee Hill.

never change, they even brought back the same host they had used in 1994.

Meanwhile, many of the actors and crew members from *Paradise Beach* proved that, although *Paradise Beach* was their first break in television, they had long careers ahead of them in the medium. Kimberley Joseph hosted *Gladiators* and starred in *Home and Away* and *Tales of the South Seas* before starring in the British drama series *Cold Feet*. Raelee Hill skipped from *Neighbours* to *Shark Bay* to *Water Rats* before starring in cult sci-fi favourite *Farscape*. 'None of us take ourselves too seriously today because we were put down so badly during *Paradise Beach*,' says Kimberley Joseph. 'It did bring the cast and crew much closer together,' agrees Raelee Hill.

Isla Fisher, who moved on to *Home and Away* and the box office smash *Scooby Doo*, is thrilled that the tight-knit cast are still the best of friends. 'There was never any competition among the girls and *Paradise Beach* is the only show I can honestly say that about.' Tragically, the group lost one of their favourites when Megan Connolly died in 2001 after a long battle with heroin addiction.

Robert Coleby, whom Jock Blair credits with helping the younger actors, always believed his co-stars had potential. Anthony Hayes went on to appear in the acclaimed Australian movie *The Boys* and the miniseries *Changi*. John Holding retired from acting and went behind the scenes, while Jon Bennett starred opposite Claudia Karvan in the miniseries, *The Violent Earth*. Even Ingo Rademacher, once the butt of crew members' jokes, settled down to become a nice guy, on and off screen, in long-running American daytime soap, *General Hospital*.

As for those crew members, assistant producer Jo Porter went on to helm *All Saints* and *Always Greener*, director of photography Mark Wareham became an AFI-nominated cinematographer, while music editor Mandy Rollins became one of Australia's best known DJs. And *Paradise Beach*'s locations manager? Well, it was my first job in television and now I'm writing this book.

> 'There was never any competition among the girls and Paradise Beach is the only show I can honestly say that about.'

38

ECHO POINT

PREMIERE: **1995** EPISODES: **100** NETWORK: **TEN** FINALE: **1995**

Gordon (Alan Lovell) catches daughter Edwina
(Jessica Napier) with Zac (Martin Henderson).

In 1995, *Home and Away* on the Seven Network was flailing in the ratings and perceived to be vulnerable, so Ten decided to move in and see if they could kill off *Neighbours*' rival show for good. Together with Southern Star Productions (best known for cop drama *Police Rescue*), they planned something that was supposed to be fresh. Originally known as *Back Home*, with the setting a country town in the 60s, the title was then changed to *Bells Point*. It was now described by Ten as combining the 'cool, funky inner-city style of *E Street* with the relaxed bayside lifestyle of *Home and Away*'. The small community was to be a 'trendy settlement nestled just across the bay from a thriving metropolis'. The catch-line for the series was 'a cool place to be'.

By the time it had evolved into *Echo Point* the show was being described as 'intrigue and romance set against a backdrop of shady trees, fishermen, funky music and sunsets'. Another press release described it as '*Neighbours* with edge'. Filming began on location around Middle Harbour. It was the first soap from Southern Star and creators John Edwards and Sandra Levy were convinced they could pull it off.

Echo Point was to have four core families – the Lomans, the Brennans, the O'Connors and the Amadios. The Loman family was headed by Trish (Victoria Nicolls) and Neville (Sean Scully). Their three kids were intelligent Frannie (Rebecca Murphy), schoolboy scammer Dean (Diarmid

Heidenreich) and high-spirited Lisa (Hayley Phillips). Trish ran marina café 'The Shed' while Neville was a travelling salesman who regularly cheated on his wife.

Trish's surfie brother Hopper Hadley (David Woodley) was the local town heartthrob destined to give up his wild ways for single mum Coral O'Connor (Roxane Wilson). She worked at a bakery and had a 15-year-old daughter, Belinda (Rose Byrne). Belinda had been told her father had died when she was young, but there were hints of a dark secret surrounding her birth. Her 'adopted dad' was local baker Maurie Bernard (John Clayton).

Nurse Holly Winton (Kimberley Davenport) was madly in love with timberyard owner Gordon Amadio (Alan Lovell) but she had to deal with his bitchy daughter Edwina (Jessica Napier). Edwina's rebel ex-boyfriend Zac Brennan (Martin Henderson) would return to town in the first episode determined to win her back, although he had an alcoholic Vietnam War veteran dad, Darcy (Mick Innes), distracting him from the cause.

Holly also found herself having to look after her daggy niece and nephew from the country after a family tragedy. Budding psycho Shelley (Louise Crawford) and sensitive Marty Radcliffe (Jack Ellis, son of writer Bob Ellis) watched their mother die of cancer before their grief-stricken father fled town. 'It was my first television role and I was thinking it was all so glamorous,' remembers Louise Crawford, 'and there I was having to wear a tracksuit, sloppy joe and no make-up.' Shelley's clothes got funkier, but she turned nutty after becoming obsessed with budding artist Dave Campbell (Tom Long).

Echo Point's big opening mystery was supposed to be the return of Daniel Blake (Philip Gordon), back to reclaim his inheritance after a long absence. As he walked into his childhood home in the first episode, he had flashbacks to a mysterious violent event from the past, complete with overturned bookcase, people struggling and gunshots. What had happened the night his parents were killed? Did Daniel do it? He had been arrested for the crime but never charged and the incident was now Echo Point folklore.

The young actors were upbeat about the show's chances of success when *TV Week* interviewed them in May. 'We've managed to keep an edge to it,' said Tom Long. 'They intend to make it hip and fashion-orientated, so in terms of young people it is certainly going to appeal. It has a colour and vibrancy to it. It is upbeat and not typical soap.' Such talk had already fired up Seven who, given six months warning, had responded to the threat by rejuvenating *Home and Away* with new story editors Ray Harding and Greg Haddrick. By the time *Echo Point* was ready to launch, Summer Bay was gunning for them.

Ten's decision to air weeknights at 7pm directly in competition with *Home and Away* was considered aggressive programming. However, the decision to begin the week of 5 June proved to be suicidal programming. Not only did Seven schedule a 'watch and win' competition, with the prize

The show was now being referred to as Suicide Point or What's the Point?

being a trip to the Atlanta Olympics, there was also the highly publicised return of two fan favourites. Daffy blonde Marilyn (Emily Symons) was sweeping back into Summer Bay, very much alive, while a very dead Bobby (Nicolle Dickson) was emerging from a refrigerator to freak out an emotionally fragile Ailsa (Judy Nunn).

Despite *Echo Point*'s huge launch at Shelley Beach, complete with fireworks and denim jackets for the press, the timing could not have been worse. When national youth radio station Triple J asked its normally talkative listeners all across Australia to phone in about *Echo Point*, the switchboard was unusually quiet. Amongst its target audience, not one single person who had watched the premiere episode could be found.

Even with *Neighbours* as its lead-in, first night ratings revealed *Echo Point* (with 501,000 viewers in Sydney) captured fewer viewers than the *Roseanne* repeats it had replaced, while *Home and Away*'s audience (1,019,000) had increased. *Echo Point*'s audience slumped to 339,000 on its second night. It was the worst soap debut since Nine's *Family and Friends* in 1990.

Predictably, even though insiders were already comparing it to their other big soapie disaster *Arcade*, Ten went on the offensive. 'The [ratings] figures are what we expected,' publicity head Catherine Lavelle told *TV Week*. 'But we have great faith in the show. It's not the first day or first week that counts. You have to look six months on.'

Sadly, all anybody could see if they looked was one of the worst sets in soap history. 'The Shed' was set on the water but filmed inside a studio. To replicate the ocean bay, a colour photograph of water was the backdrop outside the windows. This is common practice in many Aussie soaps, but most designers make sure their backgrounds don't feature

Dave (Tom Long)
sketches stalker Shelley
(Louise Crawford).

anything that needs to be moving. Like water. No wonder the show was now being referred to as *Suicide Point* or *What's the Point*?

Still, the hype machine kept going, even if they only had a theme song to get excited about. Written by Human Nature (before they hit the big time) and sung by Nick Howard (who now writes music himself for TV productions), the *Echo Point* theme was relegated to B-side status when the single was released. It was, however, supposed to appear more prominently on an *Echo Point* sound-track album which was due in shops that August. Not surprisingly, the idea was quietly dropped.

TV Week moved in for the kill, reporting that an internal memo had been sent to the actors telling them to start turning up for work freshly showered (it was alleged that certain cast members were stay-ing out all night partying). 'Boys will be boys,' laughs Louise Crawford. 'All the young guys moved in together. Give them a bit of money, a bit of glam-orous lifestyle and what do you expect to happen?'

Martin Henderson.

Next, *TV Week* supposedly overheard two female cast members (one they nicknamed 'Princess') bitching about the media ignoring them to focus instead on cameo appearances from *E Street*'s Melissa Tkautz, *Paradise Beach*'s Ingo Rademacher and socialite Kate Fischer (as naughty nurse Gillian out to seduce the much younger Dean). After ratings actually dropped for Fischer's much ballyhooed appearance, Ten moved *Echo Point* to the less prestigious timeslot of 6pm weeknights.

Still the cast kept expanding. Julie McGregor came aboard as nutty Narelle, while Ben Oxenbould played surfie boy Wacka and Rowena Wallace dropped by as Coral's mother, Elizabeth O'Connor. Ratings remained dire and it shouldn't have been much of a surprise when the axe fell, but when it did, the cast were shocked. They wrote a letter com-plaining that nobody from the network was brave enough to visit the set and personally deliver the news. 'I remember being called up into the rehearsal room on a Friday night and it was only John Edwards and Sandra Levy there,' says Louise Crawford. 'We all felt very bad. Ten had spent such a lot of money on the show.'

Ten sent the disgraced show off to the graveyard slot of 11.30pm. Those few loyal viewers still watching saw Edwina have an abortion after falling pregnant to Zac. Ten had thought they would have to play these episodes at 7.30pm to avoid controversy, but it was a moot point at mid-night. Meanwhile, Shelley moved on from stalking Tom to stalking Hopper, slashing his tyres, cutting her wrists and pretending to drown so he would save her.

The series finished with the long running mystery of the murder of Daniel Blake's parents being resolved – their accidental killer was Zac's

CATCH AUSTRALIA'S
HOTTEST NEW STARS.

From the creators of Police Rescue, a major new Australian television series.
Echo Point. Weeknights at 7.00 on Ten. One address...a million secrets.   ten

mother who returned to confess. There was also the wedding of single mum Coral and Hopper, while Shelley, who was hitchhiking out of Echo Point, was picked up by Dave and driven into the sunset. She shouldn't have been hitchhiking, and he shouldn't have been re-uniting with his stalker ex-girlfriend, so they really did deserve each other. Just over 100 episodes had played out over four months in three different timeslots.

Eventually it was sold to Germany and was so successful there it led to a very short-lived rumour that *Echo Point* could be revived in Australia to help Ten with their local drama content. Not surprisingly, Ten had no plans to make the same mistake twice. The Germans went into mourning.

While everyone had initially laughed at the newspaper ad that had described it as having 'Australia's Hottest New Stars', *Echo Point* did have several famous graduates. Rose Byrne revealed in 2004, while doing publicity for blockbuster movie *Troy* (alongside a nude Brad Pitt), that she had got pretty caught up in her first TV role. 'I used to get home and take on my character's voice and mannerisms. I loved it. Fame kind of got me. Then everyone left and I had to go back to where I was before, back to high school. It was a really good lesson. It made me realise how fleeting fame is.'

Martin Henderson also hit the Hollywood big time with movies such as *The Ring* and *Torque*. Looking back on *Echo Point*, he admitted to signing up only because he thought the show was going to be another one-hour drama like Southern Star's other big production, *Police Rescue*. He hadn't wanted to do another soap after years spent in New Zealand's *Shortland Street* but the penny dropped about his Aussie debut when a truckload of scripts arrived. Had he known what lay in store with *Echo Point*, he might never have left *Shortland Street*.

Other famous *Echo Point* graduates included Tom Long (who went on to star in *SeaChange* and *The Dish*) and Jessica Napier (*McLeod's Daughters*) but despite the pedigree of its cast, the show is forever remembered as a monumental disaster. Years later, one newspaper described it as one of Australia's greatest ever failures, along with the Leyland P76 car and the Dennis Lillee aluminium cricket bat. Even with such an honour, the series has never been repeated on Australian television.

39

PACIFIC DRIVE

PREMIERE: **1996** EPISODES: **390** NETWORK: **NINE** FINALE: **2001**

Amber (Christine Stephen-Daly) and Georgina (Kate Raison) have
a screaming match as their useless men stand by and do nothing.

Even though *Paradise Beach* had tanked in Australia, it continued to turn a tidy profit for its backers, particularly when many stations in Europe and South America re-bought it to repeat again and again. Executive producer Nick McMahon knew there was a market for some sort of replacement show and planning began. One early version, revolving around an apartment block, was called *Breakers*. Later it was re-named *Sunset Beach* and was going to be a 'scorching new serial' about violent ex-cops, restless teenage kids and ruggedly handsome heart-breakers. Although it eventually evolved into *Pacific Drive*, television proved it was constantly bereft of ideas when both working titles were used for other soaps – Australia's *Breakers* set in Bondi and Aaron Spelling's *Sunset Beach* set in California.

Nick McMahon and New World's Brian Frons (before he became ABC's president of daytime soaps in America) agreed on a rough concept that could target the 'hip viewing audience in their twenties and thirties, the key demographic audience for every international television market from Australia to Zanzibar'. After the Nine Network came on board as a partner, script executive Bevan Lee refined the concept with writer Coral

Drouyn and came up with a show called *Pacific Drive*, a title Drouyn thought was much more evocative of what it would be about. Producer Bruce Best and writer Ro Hume came on board to elaborate on the idea. Best wanted social realism, Drouyn thought it should be wacky. Lee, mindful about going too far 'out there' (after the failures of *Possession* and *The Power, the Passion*), thought it should fall somewhere in between.

New World wanted the template to copy the style of then successful *Melrose Place*. 'A lot of people later said it was a direct rip-off of *Melrose*, but let's face it, it's not like they cast the mould,' says Bevan Lee. '*Melrose* is a rip-off of *Dynasty* which itself is a clone of *Peyton Place*. My feeling was to go for broke and try and do something Australian that would be flagrantly, outrageously melodramatic and high camp.'

Pacific Drive was to open with the murder of a rich socialite, followed by an investigation that would introduce everybody who lived on the golden strip of beachfront. Casting got under way and several well-known soap faces auditioned for the 14 regular characters. 'I remember fighting tooth and nail about the casting,' says Bruce Best, 'and pushing back production for two weeks because I refused to make it with a cast of models.'

New World particularly objected to the casting of unknown actress Christine Stephen-Daly as the crucial bitch character, Amber. Best stood his ground and was later proved to be right. New World continued to complain, insisting the male characters were 'all weak'. To better explain what they wanted, they suggested the Gold Coast-based show look at their very latest 'international' serial. *Valley of the Dolls* was a tacky new version of the Jacqueline Susann bestseller that ended up not selling in many territories because of its semi-nudity. That put an end to the odd early glimpses of nudity in *Pacific Drive*. Adrian Lee (Joel), who had shot two versions of the same scene, one nude and the other wearing flesh-coloured underpants, would forever live to regret the latter going to air.

Debate even ensued when it came to casting the very minor role of Sonia Kingsley, who only appeared briefly before being run over by a four-wheel drive. A suggested stunt casting was to use *Cop Shop*'s Lynda Stoner for the crucial opening sequence, until one wag suggested viewers would expect the vehicle to bounce off her voluptuous curves. After casting an unknown actress, it was re-shot with a stuntwoman. Despite two attempts, the opening moment never quite achieved what the writers had in mind.

'It was meant to be this beautiful woman happily jogging along the beach at sunrise when a recreational vehicle appears out of nowhere and slams into her,' says associate producer Jo Porter. 'Instead, Sonia ended up on the bonnet of the car, squawking like a seagull, while holding onto the windscreen wipers. The supposedly shocking opener was laughable – not a good start.'

After Sonia's dead body (thankfully, not squawking anymore) was found dumped in a sand dune, a long list of suspects emerged. Top of the list was her much younger husband, an egotistical radio shock jock called

Trey Devlin (Lloyd Morris). Sonia's bad seed daughter Amber Kingsley (Christine Stephen-Daly) materialised, hoping to collect a huge inheritance, but told she had to wait until she turned 30, Amber decided to take matters into her own hands.

Within weeks, Amber had dumped her hustler boyfriend Joel Ritchie (Adrian Lee) and was 'consoling' stepfather Trey. Meanwhile, Sonia's long-suffering sister Georgina Ellis (Kate Raison) found herself falling in love with Martin Harris (Joss McWilliam), the police detective investigating Sonia's murder.

Unfortunately, Martin had to end the affair and enter into a pretend marriage with his fugitive sister Laura (Simone Buchanan) in an effort to keep her hidden from stalker ex-boyfriend Flood (Brian Vriends). Laura wasn't quite so restrained when she met lifesaver Luke Bowman (Steve Harmon), falling for him even before he was revealed to be the illegitimate son of Sonia Kingsley and consequently an heir to the Kingsley fortune and businesses including a fashion house and radio station.

Meanwhile, male gigolo Brett Barrett (Erik Thomson) tried to shake allegations that he had killed his most regular customer, Sonia Kingsley. Brett entertained his clients on board a floating bordello and he soon recruited naïve Canadian backpacker Tim Browning (Darrin Klimek) into his lifestyle. Brett fell in love with paramedic Callie Macrae (Danielle Spencer, who later married Russell Crowe), who was busy coming to terms with the 'coming out' of her gal pal Zoe Marshall (Libby Tanner).

To complicate matters even further, Callie also had a disastrous affair with loser real estate agent Rick Carlyle (Andre Eikmeier), who had just dumped his supermodel girlfriend Bethany Daniels (Melissa Tkautz) the instant she revealed she had contracted HIV from a former boyfriend.

Quietly, Nine asked the Australian Broadcasting Authority to let them air *Pacific Drive* at 3.30pm five days a week, so it could count as part of their annual quota for Australian drama. The ABA refused, insisting local shows needed to screen in prime time, so Nine announced it was bound for late night viewing, twice a week. Filming began on 16 October 1995, amidst pre-sales to over 20 overseas countries such as Sweden, Germany, Thailand and Mexico.

Early publicity promised it was going to be cutting-edge, sexy and sophisticated, with half of every episode filmed on location. Instead of the standard soapie practice of three fixed cameras covering the action from three-walled sets, *Pacific Drive* would be filmed with single cameras, often hand held, as used in more expensive productions. Digital cameras were to be used for the first time in a bid to create a 'filmic' look. However, this meant that each scene needed to be shot from several angles before it could be edited, and this all added to a very busy shooting timetable.

This style of filming allowed for every set to be constructed just like a real apartment, with a few clever tricks that allowed adjoining apartments to share the same bedroom set. Bruce Best had always wanted to make a soap this way and the actors were initially thrilled to be trying something different. 'It's really quite a breakthrough in television and it is different from anything else being produced in Australia at the moment,' actress Kate Raison told *Woman's Day* as the premiere date loomed.

The first episode of *Pacific Drive* went to air, before ratings began, on 29 January 1996 at the one-off time of 9.30pm, and 1.7 million viewers across Australia tuned in. Despite the absence of voiceover or promotion at the end of the first episode, a second episode, screening after the news at 11pm, also exceeded expectations. It quickly sank in the following weeks though, and within months was attracting just 135,000 viewers and being referred to as *Pacific Drivel*.

Well, actually that's what many critics named it after the first night. *Time* magazine thought it all began 'with a whiff of self-parody' but was soon languishing somewhere between 'neither great trash nor clever satire'. *The Sydney Morning Herald* thought it 'painfully clumsy', *The Age* described it as 'monumentally crass', *The Herald Sun* insisted it was 'the worst Australian drama ever made', and *The Courier Mail* thought 'the *Melrose Place* creators should sue'.

TV's first ever lesbian love triangle with Virginia Hey, Libby Tanner and Clodagh Crowe.

The only thing anyone could agree on was how banal the initial dialogue was. The scriptwriters were singled out as being responsible for the clichés, and sadly for actor Lloyd Morris, most of them emanated from his character, Trey Devlin.

TREY: 'Don't be a bitch, Georgina, it doesn't become you. You're too young for Joan Collins and far too thin for Roseanne.'

And then came this oft-quoted exchange:

TREY: 'They think Sonia was cheating on me. Was she?'
GEORGINA: 'Trey, she loved you. How can you doubt that?'
TREY: 'She loved vanilla ice cream too, but she'd still sometimes order chocolate!'

Iconic Aussie comedians Roy and H.G. were just one comedy team who started poking fun at the new soap. When asked what he would do if he knew he was going to die, Roy told *The Courier Mail* that he would 'stay home and watch *Pacific Drive* to see who killed Trey's wife'. Greig Pickhaver, who played H.G., spoke about the '*Pacific Drive* phenomenon' to *The Age*, insisting such programs that 'don't give a hoot' about how Australia really is are only made for export. 'The things that sell in it are laughed at in Australia.' Years after the show had finished, comedians still knew it could get a laugh. When *TV Week* asked Kath and Kim in 2002 what they were watching that year on television, their response was still funny, even years later: '*Pacific Drive* repeats – and *Big Brother*.'

The only group who saw some potential were the gay press. Promised they were soon to see an HIV story (with Melissa Tkautz as Bethany) and Aussie TV's first 'positive depiction' of a lesbian (Libby Tanner as Zoe), they crowned both new gay icons. Within a few months, the *Sydney Star Observer* noted that it was 'kind of cool that Zoe is probably the most promiscuous character' because, in a show all about revolving bedroom doors, the gay character was finally having as many love affairs as the straight ones.

In a refreshing change, actress Libby Tanner didn't want to be known for always proclaiming her heterosexuality. Instead, she insisted that her then husband never be mentioned to the press, and if people thought she was gay, so be it. Tanner quickly became the breakout star of the show, and her character its most popular. 'I don't find anything offensive about two women in love,' she told *TV Soap*. 'It's rewarding when I meet real-life lesbians who tell me I'm doing it right.'

Danielle Spencer and Libby Tanner's 'controversial' screen kiss.

There had been gay girls before on Aussie soaps, but the portrayals were rarely flattering. *Number 96*'s Karen Winters (Toni Lamond) was a devil-worshipper, *The Box*'s Vicki Stafford (Judy Nunn) a rapacious bisexual who seduced an underage schoolgirl, and who can forget the butch bitches in *Prisoner*? Zoe Marshall wasn't a witch, a predator or a criminal – she was just a new, guilt-free dyke who, the *Sydney Star Observer* noted, didn't have to go through 'some kind of angst ridden crisis of conscience and confidence' in coming out. She was, though, still too much for one magazine, which refused to run a shot of her tentative kiss when she told best friend Callie she loved her (Callie did not return her affections). Instead, the photo ended up on the cover of *Lesbians on the Loose*, under the headline 'TV's Lesbian Kiss – Too Hot for *Woman's Day*'.

Zoe's first lesbian affair was with 40+ ex-model and international lipstick lesbian Margaux Hays (Virginia Hey). After Margaux jetted out, Zoe discovered Kingsleys' new lawyer, Dior (Clodagh Crowe). TV critic Kevin Dickson gushed, 'As a gay man, I am green with envy – why can't us boys have a fabulously attractive and only marginally uptight same-sex couple in a TV show?' Imagine his surprise when Margaux returned to the Drive and Australian television had its first ever lesbian love triangle. And it was all with a nod from the Nine Network, totally supportive of promoting it to a gay audience.

Keith Howes, from gay monthly mag *Outrage*, noted that the casting of Libby Tanner as a new lesbian icon was 'inspiring. In the hands of Libby Tanner, there is a spitfire quality, a quick fuse, much spontaneity but also great certainty and intelligence. Just get me some decent frocks, scrub the tinny music and bring in a few more sexy queers and I for one will swear eternal allegiance,' he concluded.

Yes, the tinny music was a worry and never did improve. While filming scenes inside a nightclub, actors were told to yell to each other as if they were in a real club with pumping music. However, in an effort to disguise how horrendous the musical score was, it was played as quietly as possible when eventually added during editing. Ultimately, the actors were left screaming, on screen and off.

By now, Nine had started to repeat *Pacific Drive* every weekday at 3.30pm. Amidst all the cross-dressing footballers, Manpower strippers (including Jamie Durie) and never-ending drug abuse, Nine's censor played on the side of caution and edited the girl-on-girl kisses. 'We had to cut the first smooch down,' Richard Lyle said, adding he was 'astounded' at the number of calls from women objecting to the scene. The next day's episode, however, where Zoe stated that she'd just had the best sex in her life, had men phoning. 'They obviously felt threatened by Zoe saying that.'

Pacific Drive quickly began to rate better in its afternoon repeats than it did when everyone was asleep. 'Did anyone from Nine ever watch it?' Bruce Best asks today. 'It was a pretty bold move but they must have known from the blurb that it wasn't appropriate for that timeslot.' Soon afterwards, there was a call for the show to be banned from daytime TV after Tasmanian Liberal Party politician Chris Miles said he had received several complaints. The Federation of Australian Commercial Television Stations said they were looking at revising their code of practice. Nine was not breaking any of their guidelines, so the show remained in its 3.30pm to 4pm, post-school timeslot. And Zoe's journey of discovery continued on its merry way.

After Margaux and Dior got together, and dumped Zoe, she was despondent until her always-helpful place of employment, Kingsleys, hired another girlfriend for her – interior designer Kay West (Brigid Kelly). Bisexual Kay was being forced by her voyeuristic husband to bring back fresh talent and perform while he watched from inside a closet. When Kay fell in love with Zoe and confessed all, sleazy Roger committed suicide but made it look as if Zoe was his killer. She was eventually proved innocent, but at the expense of her relationship with Kay.

Another twisted storyline involved lifesaver Luke (Steve Harmon), now a Kingsley, going in search of his real father, and finding him to be crooked politician Bill Garland (Chris Haywood). There was also a half-sister, Liza (Rebekah Elmaloglou), but she was a mess, hiding the fact that Dad had been molesting her for years. When she revealed all to her new brother, Bill gassed himself in the garage. Liza turned to drugs and dropped dead in Joel's (Adrian Lee) nightclub after popping ecstasy.

In an unpleasant coincidence, another Elmaloglou popped up within weeks as a different victim of sexual abuse. Tim (Darrin Klimek) discovered that surf lifesaving nipper Dale (Dominic Elmaloglou) was being interfered with by *his* father, Wes Sondergard (John Orcsik). When both were swept out to sea in a rip, Tim rescued Dale but let Wes drown.

Amidst all of this, a group of Vietnamese producers visited the set as part of a CARE International initiative to spread an AIDS safe sex message through serial television programs. Despite *The Courier Mail* describing the local show as being 'steeped in immorality', the Vietnamese observed *Pacific Drive*'s production techniques for a week, with a view to making their own. If it ever got made, can you imagine what it must have been like?

Nine had started to repeat Pacific Drive every weekday at 3.30pm ... and edited the girl-on-girl kisses.

Of particular interest to the Vietnamese was the HIV positive character of Bethany (Melissa Tkautz) who, in another Aussie soap first, was learning to live with her diagnosis, combination therapies, new boyfriends and pregnancy, accidental and then planned. Bethany wasn't about to get sick or develop AIDS and die – it was always to be about her living with the virus. That also left her open to constant attack from blonde bitch Amber, who didn't appreciate Bethany being 'comforted' by her ex-boyfriend Joel.

AMBER: 'So the bimbo's got the plague? Get over it.'

Melissa Tkautz spent time at the AIDS Council researching the role, and ultimately became a poster girl for them, travelling regularly around the country for fundraising events. 'I was at a service station in Sydney,' Tkautz told the *Sydney Star Observer*, 'and this guy said, "Are you that actress that's got HIV on the show?" I told him I was and he freaked! He pulled his hand away so quickly. I just looked at him and said "You pathetic human being, I am an actress and even if I wasn't, just because I've got HIV, you pull your arm back?" He was lucky I didn't smack him out.'

Another group applauding the show for its bravery were real-life prostitutes. Cast from *Pacific Drive* even attended a black-tie ball alongside the entire Gold Coast sex industry. 'It's great for sex workers to be represented by non-stereotypical characters like Brett and Tim,' a spokeswoman told *New Weekly*. The mainstream press, however, wasn't quite so impressed, and refused to name the event in their social pages. Instead of the Roses and Ribbons Ball, organised by the Queensland AIDS Council and SQWISI (Self Health for Queensland Workers in the Sex Industry), Melissa Tkautz and Erik Thomson were pictured as being at the 'Travelodge Surfers Paradise Ball'.

The press enjoyed promoting the more lurid details about the show. New Zealand actor Erik Thomson (Brett) was horrified when his first mention in the Australian press was a leaked news item about his being 'well-endowed', and 'how the wardrobe manager had to select especially loose pants for him. It's just too distracting.' Thomson later admitted to *New Weekly* that the canal-side house he shared with fellow actor Adrian Lee had been nicknamed 'the Batcave' after he had been followed home by 'a car load of female fans' and had to 'duck into someone else's driveway and kill the lights to lose them'. Perhaps the column about his manhood wasn't that damaging after all.

Housemate Adrian Lee, also always on the run from the girls, later lost his licence for drink driving. Rather than resorting to taxis for his early morning starts, Lee began navigating a dinghy through the network of Gold Coast waterways. He found he was able to get himself to most of the locations used on *Pacific Drive* as long as he kept to the speed limit – six knots.

Meanwhile, actors Christine Stephen-Daly (Amber) and Andre Eikmeier (Rick), occasional lovers on-screen and off (it was hard keeping

Pacific Drive *was the first Aussie soap to have its own website.*

up), went to Europe on a whistlestop tour to promote the show. 'It was crazy, really,' Stephen-Daly told *TV Soap*. 'The airport doors in Finland opened at 11.30pm at night and we found ourselves caught in the glare of television cameras. There were people everywhere.' Well, at least someone was watching, because when the show debuted on UK's Sky 2 at 9pm weeknights, it quickly sank without trace.

Back on the show, did anyone still care who Sonia's killer was? It was finally revealed to be another of her secret lovers, Adam Stephens (Mark Constable), and he was quickly sent off to jail. Securing Grant Bowler to play Adam's brother Garth Stephens, fresh from his role in Australia's number one drama, *Blue Heelers*, was a sign that *Pacific Drive* had a few more tricks up its sleeve. The show went on to recruit a number of other well-known soap faces, including Grant Dodwell, Hazel Phillips, Mouche Phillips, Angelo D'Angelo, Danielle Carter, Tony Bonner and Vic Rooney.

Pacific Drive was the first Aussie soap to have its own website. Within four weeks of going online, hundreds of emails were flooding in, proving that the show, despite its tepid ratings, had a cult following. It became obvious after reading the voluminous emails that there were characters people loved to hate, characters they loved to love and, in between, characters who elicited no response or emotion whatsoever.

One such waste of time was Laura (Simone Buchanan), the sister of bumbling cop Martin (Joss McWilliam), who had earlier been passed off as his wife. After the death of her stalker boyfriend Flood, Laura had nothing left to do except be the boring girlfriend of lifesaver Luke (Steve Harmon), a storyline which was dragging both characters down. Producers didn't want to lose Buchanan so writer Bevan Lee suggested a storyline he had been wanting to do for years.

Lee wanted Buchanan to play a doppelganger, but not in a re-hash of the 'long-lost twin' that soaps were infamous for. Instead, look-alike (and trailer-trash) waitress Anna would be unrelated to Laura but quick to take advantage of their resemblance when she saw her picture in the social pages. Anna decided to move in on Laura's life and see if she couldn't get herself a piece of the Kingsleys' pie. After Anna began impersonating Laura, she was kidnapped and suffered amnesia, gaining the sympathy of Laura's loved ones. Laura stormed off in a huff and neither her brother nor her boyfriend ever mentioned her again. It was now all about Anna.

Simone Buchanan loved playing the inept social-climber and began to improvise bits not written into the script. She kept waiting to be told it had to stop, but when nobody said anything she just became funnier and funnier. Unfortunately, the double-character play was marred by an unfortunate piece of casting. Another actress, around the same height and with the same hair colour, was needed to play opposite Buchanan for Anna-to-Laura conversations. The stand-in would only ever be shot from behind, and then both actresses would switch clothes.

The non-speaking role went to Sarah Monahan, but nobody realised she had played Simone Buchanan's cute baby sister in hit sitcom *Hey Dad* some years before. Buchanan was embarrassed and Monahan became increasingly un-cooperative having to play second fiddle. Someone had to go, and it wasn't Buchanan, although she had in no way wanted the situation to end with the dismissal of her former co-star.

Meanwhile, Canadian backpacker Tim discovered he was about to be deported, so Zoe agreed to marry him. They had a cliff-top wedding that left even *TV Soap* agog: 'A lesbian and a prostitute marry in what must be TV's most bizarre wedding!' Zoe's parents, Vince (Sean Scully) and Jill (Barbara Stephens), discovered their only daughter was gay and then learnt that the wedding was a sham. Zoe, however, had bigger problems – husband Tim really was in love with her.

Zoe loved Tim, and slept with him in the hope that she might be satisfied in the relationship, but she had to be honest and admit she still preferred women. In what would become *Pacific Drive*'s happiest marriage, however, they stayed together but looked outside the marriage for other partners. Unfortunately, they both fell for the same girl, Sondra (Helen Dallimore).

Serial killer Trey Devlin (Lloyd Morris) tries to make Bethany (Melissa Tkautz) his final victim.

Another tortured character was Georgina (Kate Raison), who disastrously fell in love with Martin, only to lose him because of his sister's problems. Then she fell in love with Adam, only to discover that he was her sister Sonia's murderer. Consequently, it wasn't too difficult for naughty niece Amber to convince her that she was going insane. Stooping to a new low, Amber pretended to be the ghost of her dead mother, and skipped around late at night after pumping Georgina full of hallucinatory drugs.

Next, Amber filled Georgina's bathroom nozzles with blood in a creepy *Psycho/Carrie*-inspired shower scene. Georgina, understandably, lost the plot, and found herself locked up in a sanatorium thanks to crooked psychologist Dr Josh Michaels (Peter Kowitz). Always scheming over some deal or takeover, Amber had decided to wrest control of Kingsleys from her agonised aunt.

Being showered in blood was one thing, but actress Kate Raison got more than a little upset over a bedroom scene. Noticing during playback that a nipple had inadvertently popped out, she insisted the scene be cut before it went to air. When it wasn't, she slammed her 'old friend and mentor' from *A Country Practice* days, producer Bruce Best. The offending scene was quickly removed from future daytime repeats and all overseas versions of the show.

Raison never got over the incident, and when she fell pregnant she saw it as her chance to leave early. As it turned out, scriptwriters were planning a long-running serial-killer tale and they needed some victims.

Before marrying
Russell Crowe,
Danielle Spencer
played good girl
turned junkie Callie
McRae, who became
the first victim of the
serial killer.

Producers were desperately trying to inject some life into Callie (Danielle Spencer) by turning her good girl character into a pethidine-stealing junkie, and eventually they decided to kill her and Georgina off. Both were gruesomely murdered, along with Tim and Zoe's gal pal Sondra, and rock star Nick Kelly (Salvatore Coco).

Psychic Phillipe (Paul Kelman) predicted there were more deaths to come, but he couldn't pick the killer. Bethany's new boyfriend Cameron (Malcolm Kennard) became suspect number one when he disappeared and his fingerprints started turning up on victims. He was found dead, stuffed in a fish freezer, missing one severed hand. That meant the real killer was … Trey Devlin, of course, the 'Voice of the Coast'. (See what breakfast radio does to you?)

Trey (Lloyd Morris) had been slowly unravelling for months, starting with his disastrous marriage to stepdaughter Amber (Christine Stephen-Daly) in a graveyard during a thunderstorm. While Amber loved Trey in her own twisted way, she was also getting revenge on her dead mother and her manicured hands on her mother's money. Trey had quickly tired of her antics, falling in love with Bethany (Melissa Tkautz) instead.

What pushed him over the edge, though, was the arrival of mysterious jazz singer Mara De Villenois (Rowena Wallace). Trey tried passing her off as his mother, but it soon emerged that Mara was actually his first wife. He now had two battling superbitches out for his money, so who could blame the poor guy for deciding to start killing them all?

When Georgina realised she was a possible victim, she turned to new boyfriend Brett (Erik Thomson), who was off 'the game' and using his bordello boat for charter cruises. They got married and slipped away on honeymoon to a 'secret' Kingsley mountain hideaway where Trey had no trouble tracking them down. He crept in while Brett was occupied and stabbed Georgina to death. Her exit came in the nick of time, as actress Kate Raison was finding it harder to hide a growing pregnancy behind huge handbags and wedding bouquets.

Pacific Drive's first series came to a close with Trey about to kill his last and most important victim, Amber (and she bloody well deserved it, too). However, he was overpowered after taking her hostage inside the radio station, so series one ended with the madman being led away by police. The cast and crew broke for a production break, unaware if the show would return for a second series. New World had recently been taken over by the Fox Network, and nobody wanted or needed an Australian-based soap anymore.

The second series only got the green light after Nine decided to step in and shoulder 50 per cent of the cost, thereby also getting half of the lucrative profits they still hoped for from overseas sales. Village Roadshow agreed to distribute the new series into territories where it hadn't already been sold.

When episode 261 began, Bethany was convinced Trey had just had a nervous breakdown and hired her sister Sam (Rebecca Macauley) as his defence lawyer. Sam promptly fell in love with Bethany's old boyfriend Joel (Adrian Lee), but then found herself defending Trey against her former boyfriend, prosecutor Alistair (Robert Taylor), in front of a no-nonsense magistrate (Carmen Duncan). Back at the police station trying to put together a shaky case was hopeless Martin (Joss McWilliam) and a new partner/lover, Detective Angela Dickenson (Katy Charles), named after *Policewoman*'s Angie Dickinson.

Scriptwriters toyed with turning Martin gay for the second series, especially since it had once been planned as the initial reason Martin's sister would pose as his wife (thereby keeping his homosexuality a secret in the police force). Instead, Martin turned into one very strange puppy after realising he was in love with his own sister. Naturally, he tried to replace Laura with Anna, although by this time actor Joss McWilliam was begging scriptwriters to turn his character gay. The producers felt there was already quite enough gay content in the show however, so Martin's great coming out fizzled out.

Meanwhile, trashy Anna (Simone Buchanan) was desperately trying to hold onto Luke (Steve Harmon) by pretending she was pregnant. She was being blackmailed by David (Geoff Paine), a doctor in on the baby scam, but she needed a confidant like Dr Josh Michaels (Peter Kowitz). The strange psychologist, who had once tried to lock up Georgina, was now a reformed regular but still just as nutty, in that *Pacific Drive* sort of way.

After the critical pasting the show had received in its early days, it was interesting to note that even *The Sydney Morning Herald* finally gave the show a 'thumbs up', saying it was 'immeasurably improved in looks, acting and writing'. *The Sunday Telegraph* named it one of the '10 Best Shows on TV' for 1997, saying it was 'cheesy and more than a little over the top, but it's clever and it does have Rowena Wallace delivering what could be the performance of her career as superbitch Mara. She's not Pat the Rat, but she is typical of this show's richly textured characters, trapped in overwhelmingly silly storylines.'

Rowena Wallace, who had just finished filming soap spoof *Shark Bay* before relocating to the Gold Coast for *Pacific Drive*, wasn't in the best of shape, physically or mentally, for another long-running gig. She was alone, despondent over not being close to her ailing parents and tortured by chronic back pain. After filming one night, she bought a bottle of vodka and accidentally overdosed on pills, leading to paramedics breaking down the door of her high-rise unit to get her to hospital.

Producers were quick to hush the incident up so Wallace could recuperate without the media glare. Although the incident was leaked to the press, who went into a predictable frenzy, the official word from *Pacific Drive*'s production office remained the same – Wallace had been admitted to hospital suffering a back complaint and the show would shoot around her till she was better.

Wallace later told all to *Woman's Day*, denying she had been trying to kill herself. 'If it had been a suicide bid, I would have done a proper job,' she said. 'It was more a desperate cry for help than anything else. Spiritually, emotionally, physically and mentally, I was exhausted, so I went on a kind of binge.' She could remember a paramedic slapping her across the face and 'saying something like "Rowena, say something, you're one of my favourite stars", and I was thinking if you stop slapping me, I might be able to say something! But they were truly fantastic, so kind, and I probably owe them my life.'

Scriptwriters, forced to re-write and replace Mara in several weeks worth of episodes, remembered a recent memorable guest turn by Arthur Dignam as an older (and extremely camp) benefactor called Marcus. The character was quickly re-invented as an old theatre acquaintance of Mara's, and he slotted effortlessly into the action in her place. It was completely believable too, since a bored gay man was perfectly positioned to amuse himself with Mara's affairs and other people's business (and businesses).

Wallace eventually returned to work and things got back to normal. Well, *Pacific Drive* normal, that is. Trey was (wait for it) found innocent of the killing spree after faking several multiple personalities and (wait for it again) successfully defending himself in court. Bethany, who thought Trey was sweet (hopefully, complete stupidity wasn't a by-product of her virus), fled the Drive with him to get away from all the accusations. Holed up in a hotel resort room down the coast, Trey revealed that he had indeed been the serial killer – and it had all been for her. Trying to drown Bethany, Trey slipped and electrocuted himself in the bath. Bye-bye, Trey.

Anna was still trying to ingratiate herself into the rich community but without much success.

Another wacky wedding. L-R: Dr Josh (Peter Kowitz), Bethany (Melissa Tkautz), Anna (Simone Buchanan), Tim (Darrin Klimek), Luke (Steve Harmon), Amber (Christine Stephen-Daly) and Mara (Rowena Wallace).

ANNA: 'Luke and I are looking for an investment. A business I can make a go of.'

AMBER: 'Good for you. Pacific Drive needs a good pie shop.'

Anna was also keeping up her pregnancy ruse (thanks to strategically placed pillows under her skirt) and was pretending just long enough to get Luke's ring on her finger. Another wacky *Pacific Drive* wedding ensued, with a reluctant Kingsleys' dress designer making the frock.

AMBER: 'Do you know how difficult it's been making a dress for a munchkin that won't make her look like a toilet roll holder?'

By now, Mara's long-lost son Grant (Les Hill) had turned up. He started dating Bethany and scheming for money, just like mother. When Rowena Wallace's health continued to deteriorate, producer Bruce Best released her from the show and insisted the production pay for any treatment she required. Wallace eventually made a full recovery, and to this day she is grateful to Bruce Best for his kindness. Actress Olivia Hamnett took over her role, and to explain Mara's sudden 'change of character', Mara was hit by a car and woke up suffering from amnesia.

Zoe, meanwhile, had met a crabby marine biologist, Gemma (Katherine Lee). They decided to have a baby together, only to be rejected by a homophobic artificial insemination board. Tim offered to sleep with Zoe so she could get pregnant, but when Gemma found out she went ballistic, only to be caught out having a secret affair with her college tutor. Zoe showed Gemma the door (thank goodness – she was Zoe's least believable girlfriend) and she and Tim began to prepare for the arrival of what would now be 'their' baby.

Nine now decided that 'their' baby, *Pacific Drive*, had a better future in a daytime-only slot, so they asked for the content of the show to be toned down. The pregnant Zoe was to have a break from girl-on-girl action, and HIV-positive Bethany off-handedly remarked on how well her combination therapies were working, so that the virus could never be mentioned again. Nine was once again lobbying the Australian Broadcasting Authority about the new daytime-friendly *Pacific Drive*.

'If quality Australian drama programs can compete with American soaps in the afternoon, then they should be able to qualify for local content quotas,' Nine's head of drama, Kris Noble, told the press. Since production of the series was now a full 18 months ahead of what was screening on air, Nine announced a six-month production break. 'By pulling the plug and at the same time renewing its quota campaign, Nine hopes to turn necessity into virtue, gaining political clout with the ABA by drawing attention to the drastic action of cancelling (albeit temporarily) a program it cannot find the time to screen,' reported *The Sydney Morning Herald*.

Noble went on to say that *Pacific Drive* was a success in its 3.30pm timeslot, 'consistently drawing a 40 per cent national audience share and 70 to 80 per cent share of its target audience: women aged 18 to 39.' The soap was then removed from both its timeslots, and when the ABA again announced that it would not change its rules, *Pacific Drive*'s production break became permanent.

The serial then came and went, at Nine's discretion. Sometimes it was once a week, other times every night, but usually in non-ratings periods and only when the cricket wasn't on. Cult fans, and there were plenty who were quite unhealthily obsessed, somehow kept up until 6 April 2000, when the final episode was supposedly airing at 11.35pm.

Bethany (Melissa Tkautz) was calling off her wedding to Grant (Les Hill) after Mara, now recovered from her amnesia and back to her manipulative ways, revealed to her that he was only marrying the modelling agency owner for her money. Anna (Simone Buchanan), dumped by Luke (Steve Harmon) in light of her fake pregnancy scandal, admitted she had fallen for Dr Josh (Peter Kowitz), and promised she would try and behave herself in future.

Joel (Adrian Lee) was in on an undercover drug scam to finally put his menacing brother Shane Ritchie (Brett Climo) behind bars, but things didn't go according to plan (any operation involving the local police force rarely did). When Shane tried to kidnap Zoe (Libby Tanner), Tim (Darrin Klimek) ran to her defence and was pushed head first onto a concrete jetty below. Shane sped off in a speedboat just as Zoe ran to Tim's lifeless body – and then a voiceover announced that that was the final episode.

Jim Schembri from *The Age* couldn't believe it. 'That was it? But what happened? We may never know and I'm sort of sorry. RIP *Pacific Drive* and all who sailed in her. I shall miss you. And if anyone knows the ending – or whether one was even done – please write. I need to know if Zoe's baby has a dad.'

Luckily, the show's former publicist saw the article and contacted Schembri. OK, it was me (the author of this book), and I knew there was one more half-hour episode that brought the saga to its rightful ending. Nine insisted no more existed and that they had played all 390 episodes made.

It took over a year, but someone at Nine finally figured out what had happened. When the first one-hour episode had screened all those years ago, the first three half-hour episodes had been cut down into a snappy one-hour premiere. This was why the episode numbering was out. Being good sports, Nine aired the finale in November 2001 as a one-off. It had taken nearly five years to screen all the episodes, but had the show been allowed to run without interruption, it would have played out in just 18 months.

In the (real) final episode, Tim died in hospital after a final declaration of love to his pregnant wife Zoe. She blamed luckless policeman Martin (Joss McWilliam) for her husband's death and said she would never forgive him. The drug-laden speedboat was caught and Shane hauled off to prison. That left Amber (Christine Stephen-Daly) to bring it all to an end.

She decided that she was really in love with Brett (yes, the male gigolo who had slept with her mother Sonia and her aunt Georgina), and as he had left the Drive several months before, she threw in her corporate lifestyle and drove off in her convertible to search for him. With that, a helicopter shot pulled back to reveal Amber driving away from Kingsleys – the radio station, the marina and, as the helicopter kept flying higher, eventually the entire Gold Coast coastline in all its sparkling glory. It was a final budget blow-out and if it had been done at the beginning of the show, viewers might have had a better sense of where *Pacific Drive* was located.

'We broke the mould in every sense, that's why I was a little disappointed it didn't get more credit for being innovative,' Bruce Best says today. 'I was always slightly bewildered that the network never understood that they had a show that attracted a twenty-something male audience as well. They could have capitalised on that since that's the audience everyone aims to get. We were just building an audience at 11pm and making the storylines work when suddenly it was going out in the middle of the day. It was just crazy, but at least filming on the Gold Coast was a very pleasant experience.'

It had taken nearly five years to screen all the episodes, but had the show been allowed to run without interruption, it would have played out in just 18 months.

40

BREAKERS

PREMIERE: **1997** EPISODES: **430** NETWORK: **TEN** FINALE: **1999**

Monique (Simone Robertson) with triathlete sister Xanthe (Melinda Kennings) and mum (Paula Duncan).

Scottish-born Jimmy Thomson never had any intention of writing soap. His move from journalism into TV writing was supposed to result in the great Aussie sitcom. However, when he received a tip-off that a new production company was looking to do a serial, he decided to give it a shot. Thomson thought he would try something new by blending the typical Aussie suburban soap with the edgier feel of British serials like *EastEnders*. He decided to set it in Bondi on the suggestion of his wife, who thought the iconic beach was the perfect location for a drama called *Breakers*.

Thomson decided right from the start that *Breakers* would tackle some heavy issues. In particular, he had always been alarmed by Australia's high youth suicide rate, so stories were created to offer options for what seemed like hopeless situations. There would also be representations of drug abuse, homeless youth, HIV, anorexia nervosa and homosexuals. Producer Andrew Howie told the press that he wanted *Breakers* to have 'a real edge to it, some social relevance. A little grittier than what we've been used to.'

While the UK was obviously in the producer's sights, an Australian network was just as vital to its initial success. The Ten Network decided to come on board and repeat the programming strategy that Nine had just abandoned with *Pacific Drive*. Recognising that a late night audience did exist for soap, *Breakers* would run every weeknight at 11.30pm with a repeat the following day at 4.30pm. Perhaps burnt by how much money they had spent on their last soap (flop), *Echo Point*, Ten was decidedly more low key this time round. There was no splashy launch and, as the network had a policy of not promoting shows screening out of prime time, *Breakers* never received a single on-air promotion during its entire run.

A pink and white apartment block on the Bondi esplanade was picked as the exterior location for the *Breakers* building. Instead of just apartments, though, it would also contain a trendy café, a newspaper office, a youth drop-in centre and a modelling school. 'To be absolutely honest, we created those things for the show, then went down to Bondi and realised everything was there already. Within 50 metres of our location building, there was a modelling school, and half a block away there really was a drop-in centre,' says Jimmy Thomson.

Casting included lots of new faces as well as several well-known actors who had never committed to a long-running soap before. Helen O'Connor wanted some regular work and running a café on *Breakers* proved to be a breeze, as she had already worked in them for years in between acting jobs. Classical ballet dancer Simon Munro was trying to decide between acting and dancing when he was offered the role of Vince. Getting hit by a car just before filming began helped him make up his mind, as the snapped ligaments in his right leg meant he couldn't pirouette for at least six months.

Meanwhile, Louise Crawford had been in hospital with a serious wound infection and arrived at her audition direct from her hospital bed. Underweight and washed out, she proved to have just the look the producers wanted for the character of Lucy, a recovering anorexic. Crawford would soon find herself re-living many situations she had been through in *Echo Point*, for both characters would be unlucky in love and emotionally unstable.

Executive producers Bob Campbell and Des Monaghan had left senior positions at Seven and teamed up to create Screentime, and *Breakers* was planned to be a long running show for the new company. Producer Andrew Howie, who had previously worked on the very Caucasian and middle-class *Home and Away*, told *TV Week* that *Breakers* would be the new face of Aussie soap because it would show more of Australia's multicultural face. 'Visually our show reflects much more of the types of people that we now see in the street. Reuben was not created as an Aboriginal character and Maggie was not an Australian-Chinese, but when we saw their auditions we had no doubt they were the ones for the characters. I think *Breakers* is much more representative of what Australians are all about now.'

According to the press kit, *Breakers* would be 'set amid the cosmopolitan bustle of Bondi Beach. It is all about what happens to young people when they are offered both opportunity and temptation – having to learn that the best choice is rarely, if ever, the easiest.' *The Sydney Morning Herald* was quick to rip the show apart after this florid description, insisting that

> Breakers never received a single on-air promotion during its entire run.

would mean it would be 'deliciously blatant' with 'a lot of young spunks getting their togs off'. They were also 'sceptical about the cosmopolitan aspect of Bondi's café strip, but the idea of a bustle is enticing'.

Breakers would revolve around two sisters, ambitious newspaper owner Eve Simmons (Julie Haseler) and idealistic Kate Markham (Helen O'Connor) who ran the local café. Eve had two kids – Danny (Ben Tate) and Terri (Emily Perry) while their laid-back father and Eve's ex-husband Paul (Richard Healey) lived on a lower floor of the building and ran the BMS modelling agency in partnership with Monique (Simone Robertson). Monique had a baby daughter, Lara (played by twins Ebony and Samantha Barnes), but had never revealed who her father was. Because of her close working relationship with Paul, many suspected he might be the father.

Kate's downstairs café was the local hangout and she loved playing the 'earth mother' to her many customers. She was an optimistic soul, despite having been dumped and left pregnant while still a teenager. Her baby boy Alex had grown up into a wild child and run off to live in England with his father a few years beforehand. *Breakers* began just as Alex (James Stewart) was waltzing back into Bondi. Kate was ecstatic but everyone else who remembered the way he used to be were a bit wary, particularly his fragile ex-girlfriend, and supposedly the *Breakers'* bitch, Lucy Hill (Louise Crawford). She worked as a reporter on Eve's newspaper, *The Breaker*, alongside Maggie (Ling Hsueh Tang).

Alex's constant womanising and abrupt departure had resulted in Lucy becoming anorexic, which she had only just recovered from as the series began. When Alex returned, it seemed as if he had changed for the better, but before too long he was involved in a love triangle with Lucy and her best friend Jaime (Miranda Chance). Lucy stopped eating and nearly succumbed to the slimmers' disease again.

Cooking up a storm behind the counter of Kate's Café was an imposing chef and ex-sailor, Boris McCann (Jean-Marc Russ). He was soon joined by his brother Jack (Preben Warren) and a motormouth waitress, Fiona 'Fee' Motson (Ada Nicodemou), whose popularity made her the small-town nemesis of Nina (Christen Cornell).

As *Breakers* began, Steve Giordano (John Atkinson) was setting up a homeless kids' refuge in the back of the building to be known as 'Against The Tide'. Since he had a shady past, some of the regulars were worried about him, but they soon came to realise that he was the perfect person to help kids in need. Eve still thought he was too good to be true, but this just hid the fact that she was falling for the younger man.

Steve's right-hand man turned out to be another reckless lad, Reuben Neeson (Heath Bergersen), who had been saved from going to jail by Kate. Reuben was desperate to get ahead but was often in danger of reverting back to his former lifestyle whenever the pressure got too much for him. The arrival of his old street friend Cheree (Angela Keep) didn't help. She couldn't cope with Reuben's transformation as Steve's helper, and caused as much trouble as possible before doing a runner. When she returned some time later, she carried a terrible secret. Her needle-sharing boyfriend was HIV-positive, and when friends finally convinced her to get a test, she was horrified to learn she also had the virus.

Young Vince Donnelly (Simon Munro) arrived on the show as a newly signed model at BMS, but freaked out when he discovered that school-mate Danny was the son of one of its owners. Vince begged Danny not to tell anyone he was modelling, but the friendship would soon be tested by an even bigger secret when Vince admitted that he was gay. Vince got a crush on dancer Bruno (Marco Venturini) but found his affections weren't returned. By this stage though, all of his friends were cool about his sexuality, and in one episode, they all traipsed off with him to the Sydney Gay & Lesbian Mardi Gras parade. Producer Andrew Howie said at the time, 'We don't want to do it in a salacious way. It's an emerging sexuality story in the context of any teenager having to deal with love. The twist this time round is he's gay.'

It was a different story though once the BBC bought *Breakers* and the British press got hold of the controversial plotline. Paul McCartney's former publicist was hired to launch the show in the UK and began pitching it as the most outrageous soap ever to come out of Australia. 'Being a former journalist, I lived by the adage that there's no such thing as bad publicity,' says Jimmy Thomson. 'I now realise that's not true! We had Mary Whitehouse and a member of parliament saying it was a disgusting show before anyone had ever seen a minute of it.'

Despite the show not having any nudity, violence or bad language, the character of Vince was seized upon as leading to the decline of civilisation. Although Vince would never kiss or sleep with another man during the entire run of *Breakers*, it was a bold plotline to have him coming out at

The lesbian affair – Kelly (Gabrielle Maselli) and Lucy (Louise Crawford) – that shocked a politician.

just 15. 'One of the newspapers I worked on in Glasgow did a number on me when I told them that it would be an edgy show with a young gay guy,' remembers Thomson. 'That ended up with a picture of me looking very happy and a headline that said "The Man Who Wants To Bring Underage Gay Sex To Afternoon TV!"'

Actress Louise Crawford was one of several stars flown over to London to promote the new 'sexy soap', but the trip turned out to be somewhat of a waste. A regime change at the BBC saw the show unceremoniously taken off air, even though *Breakers* brought in higher ratings than the show that replaced it. On an unofficial *Breakers* website, one fan fumed. 'During the last week or so of my Summer Holiday this year, I really got into BBC One's new daytime soap *Breakers*. Imagine my horror when I sat down to watch it and found [it replaced by] *Quincy*. I guessed that the BBC planned to restart the series to try and capture the youth audience during Half-Term week. Surely the BBC cannot just abandon a new series after less than two months, even *Eldorado* [a flop BBC soap set in Spain] got a stay of execution!'

The producers were secretly hoping that the postponement was temporary, so they continued to keep making *Breakers* a 'safe' show for an English daytime timeslot. They later regretted the move and wished they had gone for broke and considered the Australian market more. 'Given that the show was attracting two audiences at home, during the afternoon and late at night, we should have taken advantage of our PG timeslots and made it much sexier and quirkier,' says Jimmy Thomson. As far as the UK market was concerned, only Ireland continued to screen the show. When two Irish fans won a trip to Australia to visit the set, they were surprised to learn that the show wasn't screened in prime time like it was at home (although TV3 eventually moved it from its 7pm timeslot to a daytime one).

Breakers was unique among Aussie soaps in that often an episode would feature only one storyline – not that there was any shortage of goings-on in the busy Bondi apartment block. Steve's romance with Eve hotted up, while daughter Terri reacted badly and sought revenge, almost causing the closure of her mother's newspaper. After cancelling wedding plans with Eve, Steve went on to romance Lily (Megan Connolly) despite a conflict of interest from her little brother Titch (Brendan McKensy). Terri got over involving herself in her mother's romances, and became involved instead with Boris's brother Jack, until her big mouth and big attitude ruined the relationship.

Nina acquired a French-Canadian boyfriend called Serge (Jason Crewes), but then discovered he was already engaged and just using her to get Australian residency. Alternative therapist Crystal (Anja Coleby) turned out to be an imposter and skipped town (along with some very bruised male egos). Cheree wrote a book about her life on the streets and was excited about it being published – until she discovered she would have to work closely with loser publicist Benjamin (Andre Eikmeier).

Meanwhile, the mystery of Lara's father was revealed – he turned out to be *Breakers* 'root rat' Alex. The news that he was a father caused the rebel to reform and reunite with Monique, but tragedy was just around the corner. Lara drowned in the ocean after wandering away from a picnic, leading to a heart-wrenching funeral. After discovering that she had fallen pregnant before Lara's death, Monique and Alex found their way back to each other, and married in a splashy wedding attended by Monique's mother Karen (Paula Duncan) and her triathlete sister Xanthe (Melinda Kennings), who stayed on in Bondi afterwards.

Bondi was – and still is – a favourite hangout for actors, and often the cameras would catch them in the background of shots. When the unemployed actors asked what was being filmed, they would run in the other direction and beg not to be seen in the show. *Breakers* did not have the best reputation amongst the acting fraternity and the production often had trouble getting thespians to join up.

During the making of the wedding episodes, soap legend Paula Duncan was horrified by what she saw some of the teen set getting away with. 'Young people would be late on set, two days running, by five to six hours,' Duncan recalls. 'I couldn't understand why it was tolerated. Hector Crawford would have sacked them immediately. Nobody is indispensable.' Not long afterwards, James Stewart was replaced by Don Hany in the role of Alex. *TV Week* reported that James had 'decided to take a break from the popular Network Ten soap' and, consequently, a very different looking Alex returned from his honeymoon to find his mother Kate in a coma, no job and home loan worries.

While Vince never got any boy-on-boy action (although he did pick up a nipple ring along the way), *Breakers'* most controversial moment turned out to be between two girls. Lucy fell in love with newcomer Kelly (Gabrielle Maselli) and went away on an idyllic trip to the Blue Mountains with her. When the girls actually kissed, Ten didn't feel the need to cut the smooch for the afternoon repeat the next day at 3.30pm (the show had been moved back from 4.30pm since its premiere). Nine had not been as brave with *Pacific Drive*, and had always censored lesbian Zoe's sapphic moments from afternoon replays at the same time.

Paul, who hadn't been too keen on son Danny having a best friend who was gay, was somewhat more understanding (or turned on) when it came to Lucy, while Eve shocked herself by discovering she had more of a problem with lesbians than gay boys. Sadly for Kelly, her dopey actor brother Andrew turned up and, after a crack about a 'seafood platter', a confused Lucy decided she wasn't really gay and moved back to boys. The romance ended on air just as the tabloid newspapers went into overdrive after a politician complained about the gay storyline to the Australian Broadcasting Authority.

Liberal Senator Karen Synon thought it 'inappropriate' that *Breakers* depicted a lesbian relationship as 'normal' in the afternoon when kiddies could be switching over from the ABC's long-running pre-schoolers show *Play School*. Synon asked the ABA to provide her with information on its afternoon guidelines. In response to her complaint, an ABA spokesman told *The Daily Telegraph*, 'I would say a lesbian relationship is

'Young people would be late on set, two days running, by five to six hours. I couldn't understand why it was tolerated.'

The *Breakers* cast.

normal.' He also reminded the wowsers that *Breakers* was classified PG (Parental Guidance Recommended) and therefore allowed to be screened in the 3.30pm timeslot before the more restrictive G (General) classification came into effect at 4pm.

'I met Natasha Stott Despoja [the then leader of the Australian Democrats] once,' says Louise Crawford, 'and she sent me the transcripts of everything that was said about it in Parliament. The storyline had been running for three months and suddenly, in the last two weeks, someone objected. I always thought why not portray that as a normal relationship so we don't have discrimination and prejudice about it? We actually said the words "gay" and "lesbian" where *Home and Away* couldn't.'

Unfortunately, the publicity came too late to save the show as it had just been announced that *Breakers* would cease production within a few months, leaving a backlog of episodes that would continue through to the end of 1999. A group of people protested outside Ten's Sydney office, while 50 fans went on a protest march through Adelaide's Rundle Mall. It was all to no avail. Despite sales to 17 overseas countries, the failure to re-secure the UK had sounded its death knell. 'The program has consistently won its timeslot over recent months, but despite Ten's continuing support, the Australian television industry generally is experiencing problems with international sales – as evidenced by programs such as *Wildside* and *State Coroner* – and *Breakers* is currently a victim of the same circumstances,' Des Monaghan told *The Daily Telegraph*.

As the show wound down, Alex found himself attracted to India (Tirana Hassan) and was caught kissing her by Monique. She fled with baby Flynn (Kylie and Blake Lisk) and was heading back to Queensland to stay with her mother until Alex begged for forgiveness and insisted he would remain faithful. Lucy introduced herself to a famous producer (a cameo from creator Jimmy Thomson) she met outside the café, in the hope it might lead to a movie career.

Danny, meanwhile, was spending a lot of time around hospitals as his girlfriend Sam (Jessica Hill) was dying of brain cancer. Before Danny could say goodbye to her, actor Ben Tate had a serious car accident in real life. A hastily re-written scene had a bashed-up Danny, on crutches and in plaster, downplaying his own 'accident' and commenting on how handy it had been for him to be able to slip downstairs to the emergency ward. When Sam died, it was hard to tell if Danny was upset or actor Ben Tate was just in serious pain from his injuries. Ironically, *Breakers* was also ending the same way it had begun, with Tate's accident mirroring what had happened to actor Simon Munro at the start of filming.

Steve, who had discovered he had a long lost son, Cameron (Paul Pantano), was thrilled when the young boy announced he would be sticking around to get to know his dad. It was also looking like Cameron might get himself a new stepmother. Despite missing out on happiness with Eve, Steve now seemed to be moving towards a relationship with Eve's sister Kate, who certainly deserved a bit of happiness as the show ended.

Breakers' final scene, however, was very unsatisfying, opting for a cliffhanger ending that would never be resolved. Cheree, who had been living in fear of a psychotic stalker called Gabriel (so called because he considered himself Cheree's angel and planned to take her to heaven), was posing for artist Stuart (Adrian Jarrett). As they left to have dinner together, Stuart's notebook fell to the ground and the sketch revealed he was the stalker. And with that, *Breakers* ended, after 430 episodes.

At the cast and crew wrap party, each cast member received a video of show highlights and funny clips along with a favourite character prop. Louise Crawford received the rubber duckie from the bath her character had tried to commit suicide in. As most of the actors headed back to the unemployment office, fiction turned into reality when actor John Atkinson found volunteer work at a real-life drop in centre. As the kids all knew him from *Breakers*, he was once again the perfect guy to help them with their troubles.

41

ABOVE THE LAW

PREMIERE: **2000** EPISODES: **30** NETWORK: **TEN** FINALE: **2000**

Olivia (Alyssa-Jane Cook) and bodyguard Bill (Scott Burgess).

In 1999, the Ten Network began searching for a local version of *Melrose Place* that would appeal to the coveted 18-39 demographic. However, it would need to be produced at a fraction of the cost of the American model. They turned to the new production partnership of Columbia Tri-Star and McElroy Television. Writers Tony Morphett and Inga Hunter had come up with a concept after reading about a community police station being built into an apartment block in Bondi. When the beach suburb proved too difficult to film in, the location was moved west so the show could be set somewhere around Parramatta.

Hal McElroy, no stranger to soap after *Return to Eden*, screen tested over 250 actors before signing a mix of well-known names and new faces. Filming began at Global Television Studios in North Ryde, formerly the home of another legendary television disaster, *Arcade*. The new soap would use state-of-the-art digital cameras and Columbia Tri-Star would handle what was hoped to be major international TV sales. 'We were ordered in July, shooting in October and on air in February. With the benefit of hindsight, we should have said we needed six more months to get it right," says McElroy. Ten, however, wanted to premiere the new series during the first week of the 2000 TV season.

Ten's press kit promised that The Metro apartment block would be a 'towering art deco converted warehouse'. Unfortunately, the 'latest in digital television technology' only resulted in a fake-looking building. On the top floor was a (supposedly) sumptuous penthouse apartment owned by 'Vegas' Pete Murray, an illegal bookmaker with shady business dealings. Hence the show's punning title – as the underworld criminal lived on top of a police station, he had the irony of being 'above the law'.

The series began with the unseen Pete Murray being sent to jail, leaving his right-hand man Bill Peterson (Scott Burgess) to alert his estranged daughter. Corporate headhunter Olivia Murray (Alyssa-Jane Cook) was meant to be Australia's answer to *Melrose Place*'s Heather Locklear, but the only things they had in common were short skirts and lingerie. As far as street smarts went, Olivia was just plain clueless, which hardly endeared her as the series' complex female lead.

Why had Olivia, a smart businesswoman, never enquired as to where her family fortune came from? Wasn't grunting, pistol-packing henchman Bill a clue? And what about the all-knowing but hardly-speaking housekeeper Sunny Rodriguez (Meme Thorne), who came with the penthouse? It was hard to take Olivia seriously from night one.

Alyssa-Jane Cook did her best to ignore her character's failings as the publicity machine began. 'It's a new direction for Australian drama and tackles something that has never been done before,' she told *TV Week*. 'It's got the apartment, the police station, the paramedics coming and going, a restaurant … there's so much to tap into, storywise.' Cook had obviously never seen *Number 96*, *Cop Shop* and *The Young Doctors* before, but worse was to come. Publicists were also proclaiming that *Above the Law* was basing itself on *The Sopranos*. Without the big American budget, of course.

Olivia moved into the 'funky inner city block' where Bill could watch over her and continue in his other job as chief of security at The Metro. The downstairs Italian café, oddly named 'Us2u', was run by Matt Bridges (Nicholas Bishop), and it wasn't long before he was slipping upstairs to deliver home-cooked meals to Oliva, who was, of course, unlucky in love and just waiting to begin a torturous relationship with him. Matt single-handedly ran the busiest café in Parramatta until he hired model Chloe Richards (Kristy Wright).

'To be working on an adult drama is so different,' Wright, formerly of *Home and Away*, told *TV Week*. 'It will be a huge challenge – and as an actor, it's great to know you are going to be secure for a while.' It wasn't long before the story had Chloe on the run from a demented stalker (a jealous schoolgirl from her past) and after that, Chloe flew to London to 'recover from the traumas of the last few months'. The truth was that Wright had flown to the UK to appear in the pantomime *Peter Pan*, so the show cleverly got Chloe to send back video postcards to keep her presence up.

Running the community police station were two young and spunky officers – country girl Debbie Curtis (Bridie Carter) and naïve Con

Publicists were also proclaiming that Above the Law was basing itself on The Sopranos. Without the big American budget, of course.

Stavros (Jolyon James). They regularly ran into party girl Vicki Giovanelli (Ingrid Ruz) as she was part of a crack paramedic team often involved in the same cases they were. Vicki was having an affair with her married partner Sean (Tim McCunn), who was hit by a car in the first episode and left a quadriplegic. When he begged her to switch off his life support, she refused, but when someone did put an end to his suffering, Vicki was suspect number one.

Vicki lived in The Metro with her law student dropout brother Skeez (Teo Gebert). He was now working the dance music scene as a DJ and was meant to be wild and kooky. Unfortunately, he came across as annoying and childish, particularly when he channelled his creative side into writing gibberish all over his bedroom walls.

Premiering on 1 February 2000 (in the old *Melrose Place* timeslot of 8.30pm Tuesday nights) wasn't an auspicious start as it was slap bang up against the season return of two already established Aussie dramas, *Water Rats* and *All Saints*. The following week, Ten moved it an hour later to 9.30pm, insisting that the show would take advantage of the more adult timeslot. Sadly, this only translated to the script using words such as 'dick', 'screw' and 'shit'.

While some of the performances and plotlines weren't up to scratch, *Above the Law* looked lavish, which was quite an achievement considering it was done on the cheap. The sets were moody, while the soundtrack music proved to be the one funky thing in the series. 'We were instructed to make a low-cost show and we delivered the cheapest show on television at the time,' says Hal McElroy. 'Then the network wondered why it was so

BACK L-R: Teo Gebert, Meme Thorne, Nicholas Bishop, Ingrid Ruz, Scott Burgess, Jolyon James FRONT: Kristy Wright, Alyssa-Jane Cook, Bridie Carter.

cheap. With a low budget, if you don't get it right there's no more money to throw at it to get it right. And if you've got high expectations and a low budget, you have problems.'

Ten's expectations were obviously high ratings, but *Above the Law* didn't deliver anywhere near a satisfactory result. 'We were told to get the 18-39 audience,' recalls McElroy, 'but what we discovered is that they are the most elusive audience to get. It is in fact the 40+ females who are the early adopters of Australian TV dramas. They're the ones who will give it a go so you've got to get them first and not alienate them.' *Above the Law* failed to hook them or the young groovers.

The show struggled on as familiar soapie faces came and went, including Peta Toppano as Vicki and Skeez's mother; Mark Raffety as sleazy Scott; and Ned Lander as drug dealer Donovan, who got Matt hooked on amphetamines. Housekeeper Sunny turned out to have twin daughters, Isobel and Teresa, who were kidnapped so that tough guy Bill could keep brandishing his gun and running around looking important. And Debbie's closeted (but virtuous) gay brother Michael came out to her by announcing he wanted to marry his boyfriend. Debbie discovered she was quite homophobic but she managed to get over it during a commercial break.

'We had a mix of storylines that wasn't quite right,' admits McElroy, 'The storytelling wasn't as good as it should have been.' Realising the biggest stumbling blocks were those laughable gangsters involved with Olivia Murray and her imprisoned father, producers began to phase the mob out. Chloe, Vicki and Debbie were also being moved into the one apartment, but the chick hijinks would never make it to air as the show was dumped to 10.30pm just before being pulled from Ten's schedule altogether at the beginning of May.

Although 30 episodes were made, only 19 were screened, so viewers never got to see the show attempt to overcome that age-old problem in Australian television, the Sydney-Melbourne rivalry. In the last episode to be made, which didn't tie up any of the stories, Olivia announced she was moving to Melbourne to keep strolling through parks with new love Chris Clark (Ditch Davey), Chloe's cousin.

Despite its good intentions, *Above the Law* was never going to work with its projected 20-something audience, particularly as many of its scriptwriters were 40-something or above. Ten would eventually strike it lucky and get their desired audience with *The Secret Life of Us*, but only after a much longer script development process and some hip young writers. *Above the Law* was just *Below the Par*.

42

SOMETHING IN THE AIR

PREMIERE: **2000** EPISODES: **260** NETWORK: **ABC** FINALE: **2001**

Jeremy Lindsay Taylor, Nina Liu, Mariel McClorey and Sullivan Stapleton.

In 1999, the ABC was desperate to stop the decline in their evening ratings. With their 7pm national news bulletin losing ground, a call was put out for a new half-hour soap to air at 6.30pm Monday to Thursday for a minimum of 40 weeks. From all the responses received, seven production companies were short-listed and asked to write the first four episodes. On the basis of those scripts, Simpson Le Mesurier was awarded the tender and *Something in the Air* was born.

The production company, run by writer/producer Roger Simpson and producer Roger Le Mesurier, was best known for its *Halifax f.p.* telemovies starring Rebecca Gibney, the cult series *Good Guys, Bad Guys* with Marcus Graham, and the undercover police series *Stingers* with Peter Phelps. They had never made a soap before, so in figuring out a strategy for *Something in the Air*, they looked at what had previously worked on the ABC in that time-slot. The only soap was *Bellbird*. 'There hadn't been a rural soap since *A Country Practice* and there was no need for a city-based show like *Neighbours*,' remembers creator Roger Simpson. 'We also knew at the time that the ABC was very sensitive about their regional viewers not being serviced.'

Executive producer and commissioning editor for ABC drama Sue Masters, who had produced *Prisoner* and commissioned the phenomenally successful *SeaChange*, was equally convinced they were onto a winner. 'In our hearts we felt that a rural-based serial would give us great freedom to create a new TV world audiences would warm to – and we liked the idea of tipping our hats to the ABC's rich tradition of long-running country dramas,' Masters explained in an official press release at the time. 'We have real hopes that *Something in the Air* will become the sort of show that families grow up with.'

'The rural recession was a big problem at the time so we set it in a town which the railway didn't run to anymore and that became a metaphor for the show,' explains Roger Simpson. 'The theme song referred to the line being closed but you can still hear the train – which harked back to the good times when the bush was profitable. The new guy to arrive from the city would become a pied piper in leading them all to the rebirth of their town. So there was a strong political agenda behind it, even though the first thing you do is bury that within the drama because that's not why people watch soaps.'

Len (Ray Barrett) and Mon (Anne Phelan).

The 'pied piper' was self-righteous radio king Tom Dooley (Colin Moody). When the first episode aired on 17 January 2000, Tom was arriving in Emu Springs fleeing from a disastrous radio stunt that had gone wrong in the city. Faking a nervous breakdown to avoid defamation writs, he found himself irresistibly drawn to 'The Voice of the Springs' – 3ES, the local radio station which was housed in the former railway station. Tom began to wreak havoc when he hit the airwaves as a talkback provocateur and, as the press kit promised, when he barked, the local townsfolk obligingly bit back.

Emu Springs was once a thriving gold-mining town now struggling to hold onto its provincial viability. The most popular pub in town was the Station Hotel run by ex-cop Stuart McGregor (Frank Holden), who was now the town's guidance counsellor, bookie and honorary sheriff. A thrice-divorced father of five, Stuart was a former NSW copper who had probably been on the take and had quit before any underhand dealings had been discovered. Living with him was his feisty 17-year-old daughter Megan (Mariel McClorey), who worked at the radio station, desperately awaiting her big break at a city radio station.

Mon Taylor (Anne Phelan) ran the general store while her husband Len (Ray Barrett) sat outside on the verandah watching the world go by. A hard drinker and heavier smoker, the former football hero now coached the spectacularly unsuccessful Emu Springs footy team while Mon washed the jerseys. By week two, Len found out he was dying from emphysema and hit the bottle even more than usual. When son Wayne (Sullivan Stapleton, brother of *Neighbours*' Jacinta Stapleton) was released from prison after serving two years for car theft, he arrived home to discover everyone had been told by his parents that he had been away in the army. When it turned out he was now an accomplished footballer, Len went to his grave a happy man, dying in week nine of the series.

Ex-city banker Helen Virtue (Ulli Birve) had returned home to Emu Springs with her 12-year old-son Harry (Thomas Blackburne) after the death of her husband. As manager of 3ES, she hired Tom to be her controversial new radio personality and then discovered he drove her crazy. As she fought with him, sacked him and then reinstated him, Helen was alarmed to realise that he was the reason she was staying in the town. She and Harry lived with her sister Sally (Danielle Carter), a schoolteacher married to her high school sweetheart, farmer Joe Sabatini (Eric Bana).

Station 3ES was part owned by Senator Doug Rutherford (Roger Oakley) and his feminist wife Julia (Kate Fitzpatrick). She hosted a show called 'Rural Roundup', moved into politics herself and eventually fell pregnant with a late-in-life baby. However, conservative Doug turned out to be one of the town's most surprising residents when he was revealed to be a cross-dresser. Julia tolerated it in the privacy of their own home but worried about what would happen to both their political careers if it was ever leaked to the press.

Dr Eva Petrovska (Melita Jurisic), who had set up her clinic at the back of Mon's store, travelled around the area on the unused railway line, using a motorised trolley decorated with an umbrella to shade her from the sun. Local 30-something Catholic priest Father Brian (Steve Adams) was sports mad and had his own radio spot called 'Fess Up'. Ryan Cassidy (Jeremy Lindsay Taylor) played on the local footy team and harboured his own dreams of hosting the breakfast radio show. And finally, there was the town mascot, an emu who wandered in and out of proceedings whenever he felt like it.

Stories quickly sprung into action with such an interesting group of people. Tom stirred up the sports-mad town by organising an anti-football crusade. Stuart upset his regulars with the introduction of poker machines and a healthy new menu. Harry considered becoming a priest when he grew up, and Mon wondered if Len was sending her messages from the grave. She took over the coaching of the football team while Tom insulted everyone when he poked fun at their annual festival, the Emu Springs Travelling Earthworm Display.

Despite *Something in the Air* being ABC TV's biggest ever first-series commitment to local drama at a cost of $14.5 million (including an investment of almost $5 million from Simpson Le Mesurier), the belea-guered network still had no idea how to publicise itself or a hot new show. Ratings were encouraging though, and viewers were warming to the series and writing in to say so. Behind the scenes, however, everything was about to change. The Government appointed Jonathon Shier as the head of the ABC, and he brought in Gail Jarvis as his new head of television. Sue Masters hightailed it off to the Ten Network and it was the beginning of the end for *Something in the Air*.

'We had our first meeting with the new guard,' recalls Roger Simpson, 'and one said straight out, "I don't like the show". It was the worst meeting in 30 years of television I've ever had, aggressive and unpleasant.' When asked to explain why, Simpson was told they didn't like one of the actors. 'It didn't seem to be based on any intimate knowledge of the series or its aims. From that day on there was extreme disinterest from the ABC. Morale was appalling and the whole place became a mess.'

With the 2000 Paralympics needing the 6-7pm timeslot for an hour of highlights each night, the ABC pulled *Something in the Air* from their schedule and kept it off. 'Their contempt for the audience and the Australian taxpayer was astounding,' says Roger Simpson. 'At one point they threatened to never show it again if we didn't co-operate over re-programming the next series.' The ABC had never been comfortable when *Bellbird* and *Certain Women* became too successful as they felt popular success was a bit too 'commercial'. Now they hated a soap because it wasn't commercial enough.

'The first rule of ABC programs is to satisfy the audience you've got, which usually skews old,' says Simpson. 'The second rule is to grow the audience.' The serial was now going to chase a younger demographic, and to bring in younger characters, so some older ones had to go.

'We didn't know who to write out and no actor volunteered to go,' says Simpson, revealing how happy his cast were even after a year of non-stop production. 'It was very difficult because we really loved all of the characters but in the end we wrote out the doctor and the priest because they didn't have family.' Dr Eva was replaced by Dr Annie (Nina Liu). Father Brian mysteriously disappeared after admitting he had feelings for Helen, leaving room for Mon's son Wayne to return to the cast as a regular.

The second series got under way but its return to the ABC schedule in March 2001 didn't please fans who wanted to see it back in its former timeslot of 6.30pm each weeknight. Two episodes of *Something in the Air* were now being played back to back on Saturday nights at 7.30pm. As one episode of *Something in the Air* ended, another would begin, meaning Saturday night viewers were subjected to two renditions of the unbearably long theme music. Why weren't the episodes re-cut into one show? 'They tried to take the credits off the end of the first episode and masquerade it as a series instead of a soap,' Simpson recalls, 'and we said, "Legally you can't do that because of different people working on different episodes".'

Something in the Air's other producer, Roger Le Mesurier, feels that the real issue here was that he wasn't about to let them recut and try and butcher the show into a series, when it had been ordered, structured and made as a serial. 'They ordered a serial and that's what we delivered,' Le Mesurier says.

Regular viewers complained and ratings were lukewarm. The more favourable weeknight 6.30pm slot was now the home of *Dimensions*, a lifestyle/current affairs hybrid that was the brainchild of the new regime. *Something in the Air* was demoted to be its lead-in at 6pm, which totally destroyed any chance of regaining its audience. 'It was far too early,' Anne Phelan fumed to *The Age* after the show had gone. 'I went to a function once where five generations were there, and five generations were watching *Something in the Air*. But you have somebody in Sydney making these

'Their contempt for the audience and the Australian taxpayer was astounding.'

Cross-dressing
politician Doug
Rutherford (Roger
Oakley).

decisions, somebody who doesn't even bother to find out that in the country everyone watches their local news at 6pm. That's why it worked at 6.30pm. They would watch their local news at 6pm, us at 6.30 and the ABC news at 7pm.'

By now actor Eric Bana had exploded onto Australian cinema screens in *Chopper* and Hollywood came beckoning. He asked to be released from his contract and the two Rogers agreed to let him go to make *Black Hawk Down*. The ABC thought it was 'weak producing' to release Eric from his contract. 'But down at the rock face where we work with actors and writers and crews every day, we know that the business doesn't actually operate like that,' said Roger Le Mesurier. 'We depend on goodwill and fair play, and if Hollywood was calling – which to be honest is a very rare event – then we needed to make an exception.'

'Eric loved the show and was such a gracious guy so we wished him well, even though the ABC kicked up a huge stink. You don't get any brownie points from the rest of the cast or anybody in the business by standing in the road of somebody whose career is taking off.'

Producers decided to take full advantage of his departure and kill Joe Sabatini off. 'Then the project dates were advanced and Bana had to leave early. The scripts had already been written so we had to re-cast. If we were going to go the re-cast route in the first place, we wouldn't have written out the character,' says Simpson. 'That was simply bad luck for everyone – but we managed to turn that to our advantage as well. Because we were only looking for a limited commitment, we managed to get Vince Colosimo, who was, ironically, also on the comeback trail thanks to starring alongside Eric Bana in *Chopper*.' Colosimo agreed to the seven-week stint and Joe died as scripted – the result of a tractor accident.

In a five-week guest role, *Something in the Air* also got a dose of the soap superbitch when Lisa Cambridge (Kristy Wright) started working for Tom and began torturing Megan. The actress raved about her latest role to *TV Week*, insisting that 'In *Home and Away* you don't have to worry about continuity because it's always about the storyline and not the character. There's more analysis of the character in *Something in the Air* and that's something I'm loving.'

Dr Annie's abrupt manner caused a few problems at first, and Megan and Wayne got it on even though he was discovered to be illiterate. Proving that things really had changed since *Bellbird*, there was a lesbian called Esther, a friend of Ryan's who turned out to be gay, and politician Doug found himself splashed across newspapers in drag. Into the mix were thrown beauty contests, fundraisers, nude calendars, Elvis look-alikes, dance competitions, and even an earthquake that got some old springs gushing and had everyone in a frenzy thinking a resort could be built.

The new ABC had no intention of commissioning a third series and the show was finally axed, although the announcement was delayed in deference to the second series which was still on air. 'I don't think I've been more upset by a cancellation in my life,' says Simpson. 'People who watched it loved it and if it was still on now it would be a major force. I get very sad when I think about it because it should have been one of our finest hours, in fact I would have liked it to have been my last credit. It should have run seven to eight years and that's the highest compliment I can think of to say about it.' Anne Phelan told *The Age* she thought it could have run for ten years if the ABC hadn't messed with it.

For the final episode, something was in the air all right – love. In one of the most beautifully crafted soap finales ever, the wedding of Helen Virtue (Ulli Birve) to Dave Gorman (Jeremy Callaghan) was the catalyst for most of the cast. Sally Sabatini (Danielle Carter) was in love with Mark (Grant Bowler), Megan (Mariel McClorey) was enjoying her first kiss with Ryan Cassidy (Jeremy Lindsay Taylor) while Dr Annie (Nina Liu) was making eyes with Wayne (Sullivan Stapleton).

Eric Bana *as Joe Sabatini*

Eric Bana's fan card – before *Hulk* and *Troy*.

The last line was Ryan broadcasting over 3ES, 'All is right with the world here in Emu Springs on another perfect day.' Not quite. In an attempt to lure tourists to the town, construction of 'The Big Emu' had begun, with one giant leg now straddling the main street. When the real emu (and town mascot) wandered through town, the giant leg came crashing down to the ground to the tune of Daddy Cool's 'Eagle Rock'.

Tragically, the series has hardly been seen overseas. 'We made a strategic error because we could have sold it to ITV but they only wanted to buy a year's worth because they were making their own soap called *Night and Day*. We thought long and hard about it and thought after a year we wouldn't be able to sell it to any other English broadcaster. So we decided to wait and see if we could sell it elsewhere. Had we known that *Night and Day* was going to be a complete disaster, an ITV audience might have demanded more after watching the first series, but by then the news was out that we were doomed. The ABC had killed off any potential to sell it overseas so it was a double disaster.'

43

GOING HOME

PREMIERE: **2000** EPISODES: **130** NETWORK: **SBS** FINALE: **2001**

BACK: Rhonda Doyle, Khristina Totos, Arthur Angel,
Brian Meegan, Camilla Ah Kin, Lyn Pierse.
FRONT: John Gibson, Jason Chong, David Callan.

After the failure of *Above the Law*, producer Hal McElroy was looking to re-invent the wheel. The worldwide television market was shrinking, particularly since many European countries were now making their own dramas and didn't want as much Aussie product. McElroy needed to come up with a format that could be sold to other countries so they could make their own versions. It would have to be cheap, able to be made quickly and not rely on conventional scriptwriting.

'I had an irritation with the writing process since a typical drama episode takes 22 weeks from conceptualising an idea to actually making the episode,' says McElroy. 'Obviously, you can't refer to anything topical or it's out of date by the time the show airs.' He began to realise that the solution to this problem was to get actors to improvise some of the dialogue and create an 'instant drama'. 'If we could shoot it fast and get it to air quickly then we could also make it topical. Actors are way smarter than a lot of writers give them credit for. With the right actors creating improvised interpersonal drama, we realised it could also be very funny too. A daisy chain of possibilities began to connect.'

Together with his wife and partner, Di McElroy, they came up with *Going Home*. It would be about a group of regular train travellers on their daily commute home from work each evening. Together with the unfolding dramas in their lives, they would also discuss the news stories of that day. It would be a hybrid of a weeknight soap and a current affairs chat show. *Going Home* would also utilise an Internet site so viewers could interact and comment about where they wanted the show to head.

McElroy Television took the unusual concept to Nigel Milan and Peter Cavanagh at Australia's multicultural network, SBS. 'They loved it straightaway,' says McElroy. 'It was the quickest sale we ever had. It required a huge leap of faith for a broadcaster to go for it because nobody knew whether or not we could pull it off. We thought we could, but we actually didn't know for sure.'

Next, McElroy needed to find a story editor who could cope with much of the dialogue being improvised. Ro Hume, who had plotted some of *Pacific Drive*'s stranger moments, quickly signed on. 'It required a writer to think a different way and Ro was up for it,' says McElroy. 'It was wonderful working with her.' Every actor would receive a script outline and then be required to fill in the blanks themselves.

Casting began and only actors who could improvise were auditioned. The characters everyone ended up playing arose out of the casting process. 'We didn't go out looking for preconceived characters,' says McElroy. 'We found actors, then decided what character they might be.' McElroy and the actors workshopped the life stories of their characters, and a cast was gradually assembled. Once chosen, each actor began to work closely with the scriptwriters. 'The opportunity for an actor and writer to work together is a wonderful thing for everyone because you get a true collaboration happening,' says McElroy. 'It also forced the actors and the writers to be better at their jobs because good improv is based on truthful characterisation.'

'Improvisation was a requirement of the audition,' says actor Brian Meegan. 'Hal and Di McElroy had only a basic outline of the type of characters they wanted, everyday people the audience could relate to. Luckily, I wanted to be a middle-class, right-wing kind of guy and they loved that. Colin Thompson was created from those discussions and he soon became a protagonist for a lot of the drama.'

Two weeks of test shooting were done with a full crew and cast to see if the show could indeed be written, shot, edited and broadcast on the same day. Wary of the nightmare of failure – not getting to air on time – Hal and Di also made a couple of generic shows just in case something ever went wrong in the future. Fortunately, they were never needed. SBS introduced its unique train carriage to the public on 22 May 2000.

On board that 6.36pm homeward bound train every night were nine regular characters. Poppy Savvas (Khristina Totos) ran her own beauty salon and was questioning her seven-year affair with a married man. Travel agent Pam Coughlan (Lyn Pierse) had a builder husband whose business was going bad. Already in her mid-forties, and the mother of

'Nobody knew whether or not we could pull it off. We thought we could, but we actually didn't know for sure.'

Colin (Brian Meegan)
and Najette (Camilla
Ah Kin).

three growing kids (one in prison for drunk driving), Pam was shocked to discover she was pregnant again.

Chinese-Australian advertising executive Kwan 'Davo' Lee (Jason Chong) was climbing the ladder of success while Mike Cortez (John Gibson) was struggling with a small business amidst Australia's then slowing economy. Storeman Stefano Pappadopoulos (Arthur Angel) loved to talk about soccer while hotel receptionist Tiffany Parker (Rhonda Doyle) was more interested in the latest celebrity scandal.

Lift technician Noel Johnston (David Callan) had a troubled family life, with a father retreating into alcoholism after the murder of Noel's brother. Interpreter Najette Malek (Camilla Ah Kin) was fighting to gain custody of her young son Halim in the wake of her failed marriage to a Lebanese man. Finally, there was conservative Colin Thompson (Brian Meegan), the (supposedly) happily married financial consultant.

'In terms of being stimulated, it was an actor's dream,' says Brian Meegan. 'Because it was improvisation, it could go off on a completely different tangent. If you felt strongly about a particular subject, it usually ended up on the screen.' Each actor arriving for the 6am start each morning would be greeted with a handful of newspapers and a researcher who would fill them in on overnight world happenings. 'I had to go to bed by 9pm to be on the ball the next morning. It was exhausting and probably much like doing breakfast radio every day.'

Going Home aired at 7.30pm, with a 4.30pm repeat the next day. During the show's first season, its website garnered over 60,000 emails, with devotees not shy about suggesting future story ideas for the characters. The risky experiment became a cult success, not to mention a world first as the fastest-made drama on TV. Finding enough viewers to justify its cost, however, proved more difficult. 'How do you promote a show when critics can't review it in advance?' asks McElroy. 'We didn't really crack that side of it. We over-delivered on the show and the website but we under-delivered on the publicity side.'

Still, SBS were impressed enough to order a second 13-week series in May 2002. In the months that the show had been off air, many of the characters' lives had changed dramatically. Poppy had ended her affair only to watch her beauty salon go up in an electrical fire. Forced to work for somebody else while the insurance money came through, she was shocked when arson was revealed to be the cause of the blaze.

Pam's mid-life baby had resulted in a role reversal in her family. Her whingeing husband was now at home looking after the baby. Poor Pam had been forced to go back to work, and was even knitting sweaters for a designer to make extra cash. Then she was thrown for a loop when her eldest son was released from jail and moved back home.

Ad exec Davo had been promoted and given a hefty pay rise, which led some of his fellow commuters to wonder what he was doing still catching the train. Sure enough, Davo had a secret gambling problem, and he was soon bashed by debt-collectors after gambling away the equity in his own apartment.

Mike, whose business had gone belly up, was back on the commute, now working in a junior position at a big manufacturing firm and answerable to a much younger man. Noel had been all ready to move out with a new girlfriend until his mother was diagnosed with incipient Alzheimer's.

Najette had only just won custody of her child when her ex-husband kidnapped the boy and whisked him away to Lebanon. One trip to recover him had been unsuccessful and Najette was desperately trying to get the Australian authorities to help. Wanting to make sure the local Lebanese community supported her, she worried that her increasingly passionate relationship with Brian might jeopardise her reputation.

Brian's marriage had finally collapsed after he caught his wife in bed with his own brother. Brian had feelings for Najette, but when her husband returned, Najette struggled to keep the marriage together for the sake of their son. Brian's wife was also sniffing around for a reconciliation.

Tiffany had won a sexual harassment case and was hoping for a promotion at work, but a barrage of psychological tests revealed that she was addicted to shopping. As she curbed her spending habit, she replaced it with an Internet relationship with a man she had never met – a black soldier stationed in Pearl Harbour. Tiff debated whether to take the relationship further, but became confused when she and Noel unexpectedly kissed one night on the train.

Rhonda Doyle and Arthur Angel filming.

Going Home's biggest in-joke happened when Tiffany's fellow travellers remarked on how much she looked like the girl in the *Yellow Pages* TV commercial. At the time, actress Rhonda Doyle and *Chances'* Deborah Kennedy had coined a national catchphrase: 'Not happy, Jan!' and *Going Home* couldn't resist having a gentle dig at the ad's popularity.

For SBS, fading advertising revenue, rather than low ratings, could not justify another series, but the cast and crew didn't realise they were gone when they filmed the last episode. The finale was a fancy dress party to celebrate Stef's first wedding anniversary to Mei-Lin, Kwan's cousin. Unfortunately, a gunman was on board, out to avenge his father being laid off from work, a decision that Stef was being held responsible for. As the madman threatened everyone in the train carriage, Brian tackled him from behind and the shotgun went off. Who copped a bullet? The audience never found out.

Brian Meegan (Colin) got a shock when he had to return to his previous job and start commuting again on trains. 'People would come up and start chatting to me all the time. 'What do you think about that?' they'd ask, thinking I was really Colin. When people watched *Going Home*, they didn't see actors, they saw real people.'

Undeterred, McElroy Television went to work selling the format overseas. 'The cast mix can be skewed for any audience demographic a network wants to attract,' says Hal McElroy. 'It's a very powerful piece of drama because it can be so targeted, economic and directly responsive to an audience via the website. Every senior executive of every US network thought it was amazing.' The first overseas sale was to Canada. Renamed *Train 48*, it wasn't a favourite of TV critics when it premiered in 2003, but audience response kept it on air for a second season.

Just like *Going Home*, *Train 48* kept the soapie stories going alongside the daily chit-chat about the news. Filmed in Toronto, it scored well with young (and key) demographics when it screened across Canada on the Global network. Just like its Aussie parent, it was repeated the following day. Unlike *Going Home* though, viewers weren't invited to be quite so interactive. The one exception was deciding the fate of lesbian couple Dana and Sue. Despite the province of Ontario's recent decision to legalise gay weddings, *Train 48*'s audience voted via the show's website against the girls marrying. In 2004, a French version began airing on Canal+.

Going Home's concept was also optioned in Britain, Europe and the US. Plans were made for an American version to be called *Bar Car*, where the setting would be the saloon carriage of a New York commuter train. The series was pitched to the Showtime network as '*Sex and the City* meets *Cheers* on wheels', and the raunchy pilot was directed by Karen Arthur, who also directed McElroy's original *Return to Eden* miniseries.

Back in Australia, the McElroys tried another interactive series called *Twentyfourseven*, which was set in the offices of an entertainment magazine. This time, in another world first, the audience could vote (via SMS text or email) on one of a choice of three storylines for each upcoming episode. Unfortunately, without the daily topics for the cast to improvise about, the show struggled to find the audience that had loved *Going Home*. 'Many people believed that *Going Home* was filmed with real people on a real train,' says Hal McElroy. 'The simplicity of it gave it a hypnotic quality. And the audience would find somebody in the show that they identified with. It was talk radio on television in a way, giving viewers the opportunity to eavesdrop in on a conversation with different points of view.'

'If *Neighbours* and/or *Home and Away* are ever cancelled,' suggests McElroy, 'no network is ever going to have the courage again to wait for a replacement show to find its audience. *Neighbours* took 18 months to work and *Home and Away* a full six months before it fired. Maybe future drama is going to have to be cheaper, very local and smarter in terms of audience participation. Maybe *Going Home*-type shows will be the future.'

44

THE SECRET LIFE OF US

PREMIERE: **2001** EPISODES: **86** NETWORK: **TEN** FINALE: **2005**

Deborah Mailman and Claudia Karvan.

As the 21st century began, Australia had still not come up with a local version of *Melrose Place* (USA) or *This Life* (UK), the dramas that had redefined the night-time soap for a younger, hipper audience. Ten wanted to do such a show. So did producers John Edwards and Amanda Higgs who had approached the network about a 'morally ambiguous' show in 1999. Ten worried that it would appeal to too narrow an audience, and besides, it had just committed to *Above the Law*. To allay their fears, Edwards and Higgs suggested that they commit to a two-hour pilot that could be a telemovie if they didn't like it, or 'insurance' if the other drama failed. When *Above the Law* went down the gurgler, the Southern Star production began to look a whole lot more interesting.

John Edwards realised that the glory days of selling Aussie episodic drama internationally were over. Shows that worked domestically weren't selling overseas, and in many cases were actually losing money. Edwards wanted to make a cheap 'quality drama' that would grab people's attention by trying something new and different. In other words, not another *Echo Point*.

Obvious soap clichés were to be avoided. Instead, the action would move into 'grey' areas – the mess of life where the real fun was. 'That's where the "morally ambiguous" concept came from,' says John Edwards today. 'Historically, nobody had ever tried to do a prime time soap that had these thematic aspirations. We were trying to make our mark by truthful storytelling.'

This appealed to the UK's Channel 4 and they took out an option to invest in the two-hour telemovie, then decided to co-invest in an entire series. Suddenly, the show didn't need to be so cheap anymore. Briefly known as *Fast Times*, *The Move* and *Nine Lives*, the more inspired title of *The Secret Life of Us* was chosen and the new production was off and running.

'What surprised us is that when Channel 4 first read the script, they said, "This is great, we've never had a show about middle-class people that is so optimistic," John Edwards told *The Bulletin*. 'We didn't set out to do an optimistic show but I think there is something in our nature [in Australia] that makes us tend to be optimistic, even though the show is about a much more morally grey place.'

The original episode was penned by Christopher Lee, a first time writer for television, and Judi McCrossin (cousin of ABC journalist and comedienne Julie McCrossin). Lee told *The Sydney Morning Herald* that what they were trying to avoid was 'what you could almost call the television of last century: blokey cops, doctors and lawyers, a plot-driven show with superficial characters. On *Secret Life* there's no plot, as such. There's just the depth of the characters and the questions we ask them. The problems that we put in front of them. We treat each episode thematically: there's a theme we deal with, and we use that theme to dig into the characters, rather than working out some sort of three-act structure where a plot is developed.' Such a show was well overdue, but its concept would enrage some viewers and critics in the years to come.

Ten's executive producer of creative development, Rick Maier, suggested setting the show in the cool Melbourne beachside suburb of St Kilda rather than Sydney's Bondi Beach as had originally been planned. He reasoned that a Melbourne audience would be much more prepared to stick with a new show if it was set in their backyard. After all, Sydneysiders had hardly been kind to the last soap set in Bondi, *Breakers*.

All that was left to do was bring together a talented cast. While settling on a mix of unknowns and not-quite household names yet, the producers were determined to get one big name – Claudia Karvan. Disillusioned by 1988 flop *The Last Resort* for the ABC, Karvan had never done regular TV since, but the script for *The Secret Life of Us* intrigued her, as did her 'deliciously flawed' character. Assured she could walk from the project after just four episodes if she was unhappy with its direction, Karvan eventually hung around for 53.

The opening telemovie was shot in just three weeks, on film rather than videotape, and for $1.2 million (still a bargain when most two-hour TV flicks clock in at about $2 million plus). In an unusual move, *The Secret Life of Us* premiered in the UK two weeks before it aired in Australia, and the rapturous response it received from English critics gave the show instant street cred back home. London's *Observer* newspaper noted that it 'cherry picks the best bits of *Friends*, *This Life*, *Cold Feet* … and then, quite extraordinarily, has constructed something better than any of them.'

The Guardian thought it looked 'American but feels Australian in the sense that it's both artier and sexier than the networks in the States would allow'. They were no doubt referring to the nudity, farting, urinating, vomiting, oral sex, tampons, marijuana and ecstasy use all seen in the first two hours. 'In reality, Melbourne is no Sydney, but the location scout or director of photography has found the most glittering bits. Paradise seems to lie outside the window of the flats.'

Richie (Spencer McLaren) and Miranda (Abi Tucker).

The series began with Evan Wylde (Samuel Johnson), one of its two narrators, waking up in bed beside two topless girls, then wandering through the streets of St Kilda to the apartment block where he lived. As he walked past Flat 9, his neighbours inside also had threesomes on the brain. Will McGill (Joel Edgerton) was a scaffolder, flatmate Miranda Lang (Abi Tucker) an aspiring actress, and Richie Blake (Spencer McLaren) was Miranda's boyfriend and Will's best friend. 'I don't want to have sex with a guy,' Richie insisted in the first spoken line of dialogue about the merits of threesomes, yet in an ironic twist, he was about to spend the next three years doing just that.

Upstairs in Flat 6, budding novelist Evan and his surgeon-in-training muse Alex Christensen (Claudia Karvan) were interviewing potential new flatmates Andrena (Tempany Deckert) and Kelly Lewis (Deborah Mailman). Andrena was blonde and fell into bed with Evan. Kelly wasn't blonde and Evan didn't want to sleep with her, so she got to move in despite having just quit her dead-end job and being on the run from a married boyfriend. *The Secret Life of Us* now had a second narrator – its female voice.

The male/female narrators were crucial for differing points of view in the story. However, this fundamental push and pull, 'he said/she said' dynamic was also repeated, right across the board, behind the scenes. 'Amanda Higgs was a younger female producer and I was the old fart bloke,' admits John Edwards. 'We also decided on a fundamental rule that if an argument in any department came to an impasse, the chicks would prevail.'

Finally, there was the upstairs flat where plenty of arguments were about to take place, and yes, the chick there was going to win every time. Political staffer Gabrielle Kovitch (Sibylla Budd) lived with her disenchanted lawyer boyfriend Jason Kennedy (Damien de Montemas). Gabrielle had been Alex's best friend since primary school but their friendship was about to hit a very sticky patch when Jason went down on Alex on their building rooftop (while a shocked Kelly, who was hanging out her washing, tried not to look). It was not until after he had nailed Alex properly on his and Gab's lounge that Jason felt any guilt about the affair. Before the two-hour telemovie was over, Gab had said yes to Jason's surprise proposal, but then figured out that her new husband and

best friend had cheated on her. The opener ended with both relationships in tatters.

Ten did not want its relationship with *The Secret Life of Us* to end the
same way, and at the Melbourne launch, chief executive officer John
McAlpine happily proclaimed it 'the best product in drama we have ever
produced. To be perfectly honest, we haven't had a good track record in
Australian drama. You have to go back as far as *Number 96* and *The Box*
to find anything lasting. We've relied very heavily on US imports like
Seinfeld and *Mad About You*, but those guys have lost the plot and they're
not making anything we want any more.' Ten gave it the best timeslot
possible for its premiere on 16 July 2001, straight after the nation-
stopping finale of the first *Big Brother*. Some TV writers harped that *The
Secret Life of Us* had only kept half of its massive lead-in audience, but Ten
wasn't concerned – they knew that 1.3 million of their core demographic
had stuck around to watch.

As the regular series kicked off, the focus switched to some of the other
characters. Miranda's acting career stalled as Richie's began to take off,
but that wasn't all he wanted to take off. After a late night of filming his
first movie, Richie lost his pants in a same-sex encounter with Simon
Trader (David Tredinnick), the wry bartender at local watering hole
The Fu Bar. Richie began to withdraw from Miranda before admitting
he was really gay, while shell-shocked Will sidestepped his best friend's
new lifestyle by hanging out with new girlfriend Samantha Conrad
(Jess Gower).

Heartbreaker Evan (narrator number one) got a taste of his own
medicine when he was dumped by 'older woman' Carmen (Catherine
McClements). Meanwhile, the hot new actors were courted by the press in
both England and Australia. 'Let's hope we can make the Brits forget
about *Home and Away* and *Neighbours*,' Samuel Johnson told *The Daily
Telegraph*. 'It's about time we showed them what we can actually do.'

Lovable Kelly (narrator number two) got disastrously involved in a
pyramid selling scheme, worked for a dating agency and also began
pulling beers at The Fu Bar alongside Simon. Deborah Mailman was
happy to be playing a character looking for love and happiness rather
than making a political statement about her Aboriginal heritage. 'It is just
refreshing to know that I am here working on a character who is not specific to anything – who's just this Kelly girl. I'm very, very happy to play
that,' Mailman said.

Sibylla Budd wasn't too sure that she would be friends with her character in real life, especially after Gabrielle forgave Alex for sleeping with her
husband and resumed swimming laps with her former girlfriend. 'If
someone cheated on me I would never take them back again, no way,' she
told the press. When Jason began stalking Gabrielle in an effort to get
their marriage back on track, Gab ran off into the arms of rock musician
Mac (Damian Walshe-Howling).

Unfortunately, viewers of *The Secret Life of Us* were also running, with
some apparently preferring to watch a groovy American show, *Sex and the*

City, over on Nine. When episode nine of *Secret Life* focused an entire hour on a pasta dinner where its characters reminisced about their childhood (Will's mean teacher, Alex's rollerskating triumph and Kelly's pet mouse), one TV critic, Debi Enker from *The Age*, asked why the audience might be drifting away. She thought the show was 'adult and witty and has a sense of community and vitality. Many of the characters are beautifully cast and there's a great chemistry between the actors. There's also a stylistic playfulness that's really appealing.' However, a 'veteran television scriptwriter' had told her that, in his opinion, the show's first few weeks were disappointing and 'the characters hadn't seemed to go anywhere; they hadn't developed much since we first met them. There was no sense of a journey.'

Enker compared the show to *This Life* and wondered if that was a more successful concept because it integrated its characters in the same professional setting. Alex's hospital was a hotbed of medical intrigue but nobody else in the show shared it, except hearing about it during drinking sessions after hours. 'Richie got his big break, but we've never seen him at work; we have no idea if he's a good actor or a lousy one. Ditto for Miranda, who keeps getting knocked back at auditions; is she an untapped talent, or should she be considering a career in the hospitality industry? All we know about Will's work as a scaffolder is that he's easily persuaded to take a sickie. Jason is feeling unfulfilled by community law and considering trading up to the big bucks of corporate work, but he looks like he'd be miserable anywhere he went. A series can depict confusion without getting mired in it, and a sense of stasis is something no production can afford.'

It was one of the only negative things written about the show in its first year and its amazed producers half expected more criticism. 'We knew we would cop it with that whole issue of resolving stories, but for the sake of truth, we thought we had to do it that way,' says John Edwards who was pleased to read an immediate response from broadcaster Sian Prior the following week in *The Age*.

'One of the things I enjoy most about *The Secret Life* is the way it sneaks those wholemeal moments into the whitebread diet. Recently, Claudia Karvan's character, Dr Alex, was confronted with a medical ethics dilemma. Without so much as a coy euphemism, we were told about a baby born with an enlarged clitoris, which made the issue of gender assignment confusing and traumatic for her parents. Now when did you last hear the word clitoris used on Australian television?'

Well, probably on *Sex and the City*, and as the American comedy bowed out for the year, *Secret Life*'s audience slowly began to drift back. Nine and Seven were always keen to point out that it never got huge ratings, particularly in rural areas, but Ten were more than happy with winning their key demographic. *The Secret Life of Us* became the number one Australian drama for the 16–39 audience, with an average of 900,000 regular viewers. For much of its first year, it was also very clever, funny and incredibly moving.

Rex (Vince Colosimo) and Alex (Claudia Karvan).

Gabrielle and Jason officially dissolved their stormy marriage just before he discovered he had impregnated cello player Caitlin (Alice Garner) in a one-night fling in Sydney. After a hiccup in the form of Will's gold-digger ex-girlfriend Leah (Tasma Walton), he admitted he was in love with Sam (Jess Gower) just before she was killed by a bus. As Will struggled with his grief, Richie struggled with the gay scene and moved into a flat with Simon, unaware that Simon was secretly in love with him.

Meanwhile, Alex and Evan danced around the growing attraction they felt for each other. Evan bedded half of St Kilda while Alex had a brief (read: one episode) flirtation with Miranda's lesbian friend Pandora (Susie Porter). After Alex finally shared a drug-fuelled pash with Evan, she discovered she had a job in London. Evan retaliated by applying to a writer's colony in New York, which backfired on him when Alex was dropped from the surgical program and he made it through. In the first season cliffhanger, the couple finally admitted their love and kissed each other in the taxi all the way to Melbourne airport. Evan flew off to the other side of the world leaving Alex behind in St Kilda.

Would Evan and Alex become lovers in the second series? Not likely, since even *The Secret Life of Us* knew that unresolved sexual tension was one television tradition that worked a treat in keeping viewers watching. Enter 'Sexy Rexy' (Vince Colosimo), a handsome doctor, to offer Alex an attractive alternative. Colosimo told *The Courier Mail* he was already a fan and felt that the 'socially aware' bar had been raised by the show. 'I think that's why people like it and I think that's probably why people don't like it as well because it goes too far sometimes. People have had a lot of things to say about this show but I think that only makes it more popular.'

Deborah Mailman (Kelly) admitted to *The Age* that people also had a lot of things to say about her character, and not everybody was as thrilled as she was about Kelly's background being ignored. 'I find it odd that people criticise the fact that her Aboriginality is so subtle. And a lot of this is coming from non-Aboriginal people. They say, "Is she really a blackfella? Where's her family?" But, as Deb Mailman, I don't wake up every morning with my family. I don't always have a political agenda.'

'A lot of people see Kelly as a bit ditsy and they're saying, "Finally we have a black woman on screen and she's like this!" But I love the fact that Kelly's drive in life is to fall in love. Why can't she have a sexuality? Schoolgirls from North Sydney to Fitzroy Crossing can relate to her, and that makes a difference.' For season two, Kelly would try to keep both camps happy by continuing to obsess over her love life and then getting advice from her aunty when things got tricky with Jewish boyfriend Nathan Lieberman (Todd MacDonald).

The popular actors soon discovered they could stop traffic when they returned to St Kilda to resume filming for the second series. While they had made much of the first series under relative anonymity, crowds of 300 were now watching. 'It's bizarre,' Damien de Montemas (Jason) told *The Australian*. 'We're filming a television series but when we're on location it feels like we're giving a theatre performance.'

Back on air in February 2002, the action picked up three months after the last episode. Evan, having finished his writer's stint, was travelling through Cuba with Gabrielle. When Gab returned with a video Evan had made for her, Alex was devastated at the 'empty postcard' and no mention of their budding love affair. Feeling unloved and vulnerable, she responded to the attention being showered on her by the new doctor she had met in Accident and Emergency, Anthony 'Rex' Mariani (Vince Colosimo).

Richie now had a role in top-rating soapie *The River* and was under the thumb of ballbreaker producer/publicist Peta (Debra Byrne). She wanted to push him as the show's new heartthrob but only if he kept his new-found sexuality under wraps. 'Part of being a soap star ... is being a sexy straight actor that every 5 to 15 year old wants to go out with,' Peta told Richie. 'A tiny, tiny, tiny piece of it is acting. If you think acting is just about acting then you better wake up.' Richie toed the network line and became a closeted star, and when the group gathered to watch his first TV appearance, he was suitably macho, cooing to a female co-star, 'Can I come in for a cuppa?'

After a particularly unconvincing 'appearance' on chat show *Rove Live*, Richie let the fame go to his head and turned into a wanker. He begged his soapie producer to make his character more 'three dimensional with angst and depth and maybe give him a spiritual quest', to which Peta replied: 'It's a soap – people get knocked up, knocked out, falsely accused of things and find long-lost siblings and parents. Bye now.' Richie was duly sacked but got his spiritual quest. Now a shaven-headed monk wanting to be known as Mookatarno, he exited *The River* by asking, 'Can I come in for a herbal cuppa?'

Secret Life had made their views on traditional soaps quite clear with this storyline because they felt they were redefining the genre. 'We were trying to be anti-soap by subverting some Aussie drama conventions,' says John Edwards. 'That's why our characters weren't always likable and the show's first wedding (Gabrielle and Jason) happened off-screen rather than end up as a *TV Week* cover. We wanted to go against the conventional wisdom of what soaps were.'

Miranda also needed a bit of wisdom when it came to her acting career. She advertised acne strips as the 'Pores Afresh' girl, made a B-grade film called 'Panther Girl', then starred in a one-woman play about anorexia while admitting that she used to suffer from it herself. She also became increasingly infatuated with Will, leaving Richie to feel like the outsider as

The show won the inaugural Boozies Award from the Australian Drug Foundation for the most gratuitous promotion of alcohol on television.

his former girlfriend and best friend became lovers. Richie turned, as did Evan when he returned from Cuba and discovered that Alex hadn't waited and was now dating Rex.

Gabrielle got a new job at a trade union and embarked on an improbable affair with her married boss, Dominic (Jacek Koman). Pregnant Caitlin (Alice Garner) came down to be with Jason but the outsider didn't fit in with his tight-knit, left-wing group (just in case it wasn't clear to viewers, Caitlin even hinted she had voted for Liberal prime minister John Howard). After giving birth to baby son Angus, and still refusing to become one of the gang by playing soccer in the park, Caitlin realised Jason didn't love her and took her baby back home to Sydney.

In April 2002, *The Secret Life of Us* won the Logie for the Most Outstanding Drama Series and Deborah Mailman won Most Outstanding Actress. The show also won the inaugural Boozies Award from the Australian Drug Foundation for the most gratuitous promotion of alcohol on television. 'The entire first series appears to have been scripted by the alcohol industry,' said foundation director Geoff Munro. '25% of all scenes in the whole series featured alcohol consumption or visual references to alcohol,' compared to 3.4 per cent in *Blue Heelers*. *The Bulletin* pointed out that while it was OK for the regular characters to chug booze, none of them appeared to smoke cigarettes.

There was more controversy when Alex, having broken up with Rex over her unresolved feelings for Evan, discovered she was pregnant and decided to have a termination. Abortion often resulted in soap heroines going loopy afterwards, but Alex would not need to have a breakdown in order to show that it had been an emotionally harrowing experience. In fact, no Aussie drama had ever dealt with abortion in this way, particularly the confronting detail of having Alex undergo the process alone.

Outraged anti-abortion activists waited till the show had screened before begging viewers to protest to Ten. The network replied that they had only received congratulatory calls about the episode. 'It's almost like the last taboo,' Claudia Karvan told *The Age*. 'I think what's interesting about *Secret Life* is that we haven't dealt with it in a moralistic way or passed judgement on Alex. It's not as if she's a bad person for doing this.'

Yes, but was she a bad person because of her ongoing attraction to Evan, a hopeless slacker who continued to have beautiful women fall over him? Journalist Jemima Taylor (Diana Glenn), who quite rightly pegged him as an 'arrogant, self-obsessed wanker' when she interviewed him on the occasion of his first book being (inexplicably) published, nevertheless slid into his unkempt bed before the episode was over. Good or bad, the girls just couldn't resist Evan.

Will announced he was going to travel around Australia and asked Miranda to go with him, but she stayed behind to further her acting career (yes, Miranda really was that stupid). The show waved its first regular character goodbye as actor Joel Edgerton went off to concentrate on his burgeoning movie career. Will was replaced the next week when Evan started chatting to landscape gardener Christian Edwards (Michael

Dorman) in a bowls club, and quick as a flash, Christian was Miranda's new flatmate. This rushed and forced introduction for the show's first re-cast shouldn't have worked, but Christian was adorable enough to fit right in. Unfortunately, it would set a dangerous precedent in the months and years ahead, as more regulars would depart to be replaced less success-fully each time.

Meanwhile, Miranda and Richie came to blows when he left one of their sex videos lying around and it ended up on the Internet. Dominic left wife Francesca (Daniella Farinacci) to move in with Gab but she rebelled about having to come second to his deserted children and broke off the affair. Kelly and Nathan's relationship also bit the dust when she decided she could never pass for the nice Jewish wife he really wanted.

Will (now with a beard since Joel Edgerton was making *Ned Kelly*) returned briefly for a wild party at Simon's and nearly had a threesome with Kelly and Miranda who were both off their faces (as were the rest of the revellers). Tragically, it ended up with Richie, who now had a boyfriend called Nick (Murray Bartlett), in hospital, although only *Secret Life* could gay-bash Richie because he had momentarily switched sides and slept with a girl. Meanwhile, Alex had a secret one-time-only fling with Christian and was conveniently around to diagnose him as an epileptic when he suffered a fit. By the end of season two, Alex and Rex were reuniting at a swimming pool carnival in an uplifting finale.

The second series had continued to be a major hit with its 16–39 audience and the timeslot change from 9.30pm to 8.30pm hadn't affected the stories it could tell. Nevertheless, Ten had put pressure on to get more traditional, self-contained stories onto the air. 'We said to the network, please leave it to us because theme is what separates us from the other shows, so we continued to focus on that rather than individual plots,' says John Edwards. 'The one time we did a traditional self-contained ep (Richie coming out to his dad) was the one time the ratings dipped below a million and so we were vindicated.'

Unfortunately, Channel 4 wasn't as lucky with its ratings for their Aussie co-production and chose not to screen the second series in prime time. British viewers got double episodes, back to back at 12.30am on Wednesday mornings. Ratings-wise, *Secret Life* had died in the UK, suggesting viewers there definitely preferred their soaps done in the traditional style.

The first episode of the third season, which screened in Australia on Monday, 17 February 2003, was a wonderful experiment in backwards narrative, starting with the end before going back to the beginning. Evan was now off the dole and working in an advertising agency, Richie was trekking in Nepal and Miranda was single and working in a call centre where her boss was a lesbian called Chloe (Nina Liu). Kelly was studying at university where she was dating the obnoxious Jake (Torquil Neilson), fighting with beer-swilling student council rival Justin Davies (Sullivan Stapleton) and flirting and cheating on exams with teacher Frank Goodman (Rhys Muldoon).

Damien de Montemas.

Jason was gone, having begged Gab to move with him to Sydney so he could be near his baby son. 'There was increasingly less and less to like about Jason,' says Damian de Montemas. 'I was waiting for some previously hidden aspect of his personality that could justify two intelligent women (Alex and Gab) finding him attractive. For a lawyer, he wasn't particularly articulate, witty or capable. Despite the fact that I still loved the show, and working with such an excellent group of people, Jason just bored the hell out of me.'

Ten was also worried about boring the hell out of their audience, particularly now that they had to compete against the second series of American drama *24* over on Seven. *Secret Life* had been rushed into production early to get a head start on the Monday night audience, and it wouldn't help that two of the show's biggest stars were going to depart just six episodes into the new season.

Episode 50 saw the departure of Alex and Rex to London after an impromptu wedding on the building rooftop. While actors Claudia Karvan and Vince Colosimo became the new faces of clothing line Country Road, many critics wondered if *Secret Life* could survive without them. Replacing them was crucial and Marnie (Alexandra Davies), who moved into Alex's old bedroom, wasn't a good start. She didn't last the year but the new doctor who moved in with Gab, Tidy (Dan Spielman), was a bit more successful.

In May 2003, *The Secret Life of Us* came under fire from anti-drug campaigners when the characters were seen eating hash muffins. Ten defended the scene, saying that 'any portrayal of drug use is very incidental, it's never a focus or a major theme'. The National Drug and Alcohol Research Centre's information manager, Paul Dillon, thought the show was treading a fine line between reflecting social trends and setting them, although he admitted that 'it's not completely over the top' to *The Sun-Herald*.

It was, however, getting too over the top for writer Angela Pulvirenti, who pulverised the show in *The Daily Telegraph*. She thought it had become ludicrous and unbelievable and felt its fundamental flaw was the 'failure to patiently set up major storylines and evolve them slowly enough for the audience to become interested in them. Forcing utterly inconceivable sexual chemistry between other characters seems to be one of the show's fortes – especially in the case of Evan and Alex ... and Gaby's affair with married boss Dominic. How are we meant to will Gaby to cross a line we know she shouldn't, when we'd really rather spare her the process of sleeping with someone who, quite frankly, doesn't look enough like Tom Selleck (think Monica's lover in *Friends*). Evan's had more sexual partners than Kelly's had jobs; Jason's been an adulterer and a father; Miranda has slept with all her flatmates; Gaby's been the "wronged" and "other" woman; and Richie's been straight and gay. I don't believe him playing straight. I don't believe him playing gay and I certainly didn't believe him playing an actor. Unfortunately for *The Secret Life of Us* and its aggressively supportive network, the promos do not maketh the program.' *The Daily Telegraph* got 15-year-old work experience girl Rebel Sorensen to respond: 'If the show is as horrible as Pulvirenti says, why did she watch it for two seasons?'

At least the Ten network was still supporting its Aussie drama, even though sometimes the show couldn't help but under-deliver on those 'aggressive' promo promises. When the 'most shocking event ever' turned out to be Gab catching Tidy having a wank, many viewers simply shrugged. It didn't seem to bother Gaby much in the long run either, for she soon slept with him before deciding they were better off staying flatmates. And then she slept with him again and decided they did make good lovers after all.

Meanwhile, the only acting job Richie could get was wearing an animal suit in a kids' show for producer Luciana (Pamela Rabe), who then decided he was so good at working with kids, she wanted his sperm to make one of her own. Marnie was replaced by George (Gigi Edgley) who was soon wandering in and out of Evan's bedroom before the inevitable post-sex blues.

While the 'coming out' of Richie, and Miranda's protracted hysteria, had been one of the longest running storylines in the first series, Miranda's lesbian liaison in season three was fast, forced and caused nary a ripple of reaction from her friends. Even Vince Colosimo (Rex) 'cautiously expressed misgivings', even though he emphatically denied he was being negative about the show. 'For me, it became a tamer *Queer as Folk*. You had to sort of push the whole lesbian and gay thing, just in case you didn't think we were on the edge enough. And it was like, boring.' Abi Tucker fled the series in episode 56 to pursue a singing career while Miranda left behind the love of her life to pursue her acting career in the US. Yes, Miranda really was that stupid.

The series continued to cop it from critics like *The Courier Mail*, who decided it had 'not only jumped the shark but also has leapt from the aquarium and is lying on the table turning an unflattering shade of purple'. Yet *The Secret Life of Us* could still pack a punch and not surprisingly, Deborah Mailman, as the eternally lovable Kelly, was still the heart and soul of the show. Evan's stupidest ever moment was when he invited Kiwi backpacker Ken (Damien Richardson) to stay with him and Kelly. Ignoring her uneasiness with the new boarder, Evan refused to throw him out and eventually Ken assaulted Kelly. Deborah Mailman won the Most Outstanding Actress Logie the following year for her harrowing performance, beating fellow nominee Claudia Karvan (who had already won her Most Outstanding Actress Logie the previous year). Karvan, who had been back to Crawford's Box Hill studios to direct an episode, then returned as Alex for the season's final three episodes.

Evan moped around and Rex rushed back from overseas as Alex dithered, once again, between her husband, a 'clean-shaven, regularly-showered heart-throb with a future and a reasonable degree of emotional maturity,' as critic Angela Pulvirenti put it, and her former flatmate who 'looked like he never bathes or brushes his teeth and has the worst hair stylist since Kramer from *Seinfeld*'. Fortunately for Pulvirenti, Alex chose Rex and they both headed back to London to make babies. Unfortunately for *Secret Life*, the series three finale was also the last appearance of Richie (Spencer McLaren), Chloe (Nina Liu) and George (Gigi Edgley). Reunited with on-again, off-again love and flat-mate Tidy (Dan Spielman), Gab (Sibylla Budd) threw a rooftop party to celebrate her election victory, then she also disappeared without trace along with her man.

Claudia Karvan was still confident that the series could survive without her. 'I think the show's still got a hell of a lot of life in it and being the type of show that it is I think it could handle a whole new cast and a whole new set of storylines and just keep the character of St Kilda as one of the constants,' she told *The Sun-Herald*. Samuel Johnson was less com-plimentary, telling Perth's *Sunday Times* that he was sick of playing Evan. 'I have to decide: "Do I want to sit on it while it sinks or do I want to get off while it's still a cruise liner?" I'm so annoyed with [Evan] right now. He hasn't really grown a lot. I'd like to see him either not grow at all as opposed to just inch his way forward.'

The overhaul for the next series would also include replacing depart-ing co-creator Amanda Higgs and original writers Judi McCrossin and Christopher Lee. Ross Allsop, a former line producer, and Peter Millington, once a post production supervisor, both stepped up to become co-producers. They had a thankless task in front of them – to reverse the audience decline – and Ten was banking on a new cast to revitalise the show in the new timeslot of Wednesdays at 9.30pm.

When the show returned for its fourth year on 18 February 2004, Evan and Kelly were once again looking for a flatmate and decided upon the somewhat-younger apprentice hairdresser Bree (Brooke Harman). The 22-year-old character had obviously been created to snare a younger demographic in the hope of lifting the ratings. Sadly, all she was going to lift were stolen goods since she was a secret kleptomaniac.

Kelly's uni rival Justin (Sullivan Stapleton) was a new regular and now a firm friend of Evan's. Christian (Michael Dorman) had lost his long blonde hair and was also down a flatmate, until an old mate from Geelong, student nurse Stu (Stephen Curry), broke up with his girlfriend and moved in. 'The two of them … are pretty laconic,' said producer Allsop. 'It's not *Men Behaving Badly* but it's watching a couple of Geelong boys trying to find their way in the big city. It's just added such a great dimension to Christian's character and to the show.'

Not really, for delighted rival network executives began referring to new promos for the Geelong boys as *The Secret Life of Bogans*. What had happened to that original female/male, push/pull perspective? It cer-tainly wasn't apparent in the introduction of a never-seen-before flat, number 11. The producers told *The Age* they wanted to avoid some of the show's mistakes in the past where 'new and established characters became friends too quickly,' but instead of slowly introducing the new regulars, they were going to be launched with a 'full-on domestic barney.

We wanted to have that conflict right from the start.' It proved to be a major miscalculation.

In the season premiere, Kelly (Deborah Mailman) was under attack from the new nasty neighbours upstairs. When not hogging the communal washing machine, or snarling at her on the rooftop, they were slamming the door in her face when she went to complain that their cat was defecating on her bed. It all ended badly in the first episode cliffhanger when Evan and Kelly accidentally ran over the flea-ridden moggie. For episode two, they returned the dead cat to its surly owners on, wait for it, a dinner plate.

The unappealing Flat 11 residents included a womanising stockbroker, Adam (Nicholas Coghlan), whose lovemaking was so violent it caused the pictures on the wall to fall off. Adam's deeply neurotic sister was Lucy Beckwith (Alexandra Schepisi, daughter of director Fred) and she seemed to do nothing but mope around waiting for a backpacking boyfriend to phone home. Lucy and Adam shared with (stop me if you've heard any of this before) Lucy's best friend Anna Torv (Nikki Martel), a commitment-phobe who was secretly in love with Adam. By the time these newbies had kissed and made up with Kelly and her gang on the rooftop, it was too late. After just two episodes, the national viewership was less than half what it had been the year before.

Tasma Walton and Joel Edgerton.

Ten screened a third episode, which focused on workplace dramas with Adam and Anna. However, given their confrontations with the show's most-loved character the week before, there was zero care factor for their brash office attitudes. When Ten realised their daytime soap *The Bold and the Beautiful* was getting more viewers at 4.30pm, the network pulled the troubled drama from its prime time schedule.

Some long-term fans were devastated and wrote to *TV Week*. 'Airing three episodes doesn't give viewers enough time to get used to all the new characters. It was never given a chance!' said Katt via email, while Morgan lamented the loss of 'an original Aussie drama with a realistic basis that everyone could relate to. Are we so Americanised that we no longer recognise good drama?' More spot on, though, was a Deborah Mailman fan: 'The producers should have made *The Secret Life of Us* more about her than those bratty newbies. I will miss Deb; her smile made the world shine.'

How was Evan going to be written out (actor Samuel Johnson had only been contracted to three more episodes) and would he drive off into the sunset with the newly returned Jemima (Diana Glenn)? How would the show cope with only having a female narrator? What about the underutilised Simon (David Tredinnick) finally getting a hairdresser boyfriend

The first three series have become best-selling DVD collections.

called Jeff (Jonathon Dutton)? Who was Zelko (Ryan Johnson) and whose bed would he end up in inside St Kilda's busiest apartment block?

And would Aboriginal AFL footy player Corey Mailins (Aaron Pedersen) finally make an honest woman out of Kelly after she had had another disastrous love affair, this time with her uni teacher Frank Goodman (Rhys Muldoon)? The biggest question of all, however, was when would Ten return the once-popular show to its schedule. Would it end up in a black hole over the non-rating summer period or would it be banished to a late-night slot so the network could count it as local drama content? All of these questions remain unanswered at the time of writing, as Ten has still not screened the rest of the series.

The Secret Life of Us has now been seen in Sweden (where it's known as *Det Hemlinga Livet*), Amsterdam (*Ons Geheime Leven*), Israel (*Chayeynu Hasodyim*), Norway, Denmark, South Africa, Finland, Ireland, New Zealand and Iceland. It has inspired best-selling DVD collections, three soundtrack compilations and a paperback tie-in (supposedly the novel Evan wrote in the series but actually just a rehash of much of the show's dialogue).

Secret Life won the Logie for Most Outstanding Drama for three years running, three Australian Film Institute Awards (for Joel Edgerton, Samuel Johnson and Catherine McClements), two Australian Writers' Guild Awards and a Bronze World Medal in the 2001 New York Festival for Television Drama.

The Secret Life of Us deserved every one of its accolades but its early demise proved how fickle its young audience could be. Perhaps it could have afforded to be just a little bit more traditional and anchored itself down with an older soap-watching audience. Then again, maybe the show was destined to live fast and die young. Nevertheless, *The Secret Life of Us* pushed the boundaries of traditional soap storytelling for 86 episodes.

It's also worth noting that, after the success of *Number 96*, Ten managed to hit the jackpot again with another apartment block saga. As far as sex went, not much had changed in 30 years, with plenty of bed-hopping and same-sex encounters. Old people, however, were gone, apparently banished to suburbia and retirement villages so the trendy young folk could enjoy their inner-city lifestyle without a wrinkle in sight.

CRASH PALACE

PREMIERE: **2002** EPISODES: **65** NETWORK: **FOXTEL** FINALE: **2002**

Tory Mussett as Argentinian backpacker Inez.

When it was announced that Australian subscription television channels needed to invest at least 10 per cent of their programming budgets in new local productions, Foxtel already had an idea in mind for a new soap. The Fox family had a number of television outlets all over the world which were looking for a project they could contribute to and air within their respective markets. Fox 8 pushed for a show set in a Sydney youth hostel that would follow the travels of 16 young and spunky regulars. With all the characters being international travellers, their nationalities could depend on which countries invested in the production.

Having already created *Breakers*, Jimmy Thomson was developing projects at Fox Television in Sydney when the call went out for the international concept. Living in Kings Cross, in the heart of backpacker territory, was all the inspiration he needed for *Crash Palace*. 'It had the right elements from the business angle, but in terms of dramatic possibilities it had so much to offer,' says Thomson. Basing it on the real-life Original Backpackers Hostel in Victoria Street, he re-named it 'The Royal' and began hammering out storylines.

Crash Palace premiered at 8.30pm on 11 March 2002 on Fox 8, amidst full-page ads featuring actress Tory Mussett (Inez) wearing nothing but a

pair of red undies. Thomson told *The Age* that there would be swearing, sex and drug taking but 'more important than that are the attitudes we have allowed people to have. We are allowed to have young people who are really, really nasty and get away with it. You are not allowed to do that in your early evening teen drama [like *Neighbours* or *Home and Away*]. You can have nasty characters but they have to be punished.'

The nastiness was originally going to begin with a fire in an illegal backpackers' hostel. Unfortunately, the similarity to the real-life Childers hostel fire in 2000, which tragically killed 15 backpackers, many of whom were British, did not sit well with the show's British backers. So instead, the new soap began with Tina Clark (Stephanie Waring) and her best friend Kirsty (Rachel Aveling) arriving at Sydney airport. For once, a character in a soap admitted to being a soap addict, with Tina saying that she was travelling to Australia because of her love for *Home and Away*. Then, having mistakenly picked up the wrong backpack (it would turn out to be full of ecstasy tablets), she made a beeline for The Royal.

The hostel was run by George Jackson (Tim McCunn) and his Brazilian de facto Isabella Rocha (Lisa Bailey), and it was already a hotbed of sexual intrigue. Among the guests were an American couple, rich lawyer Wendy Greenham (Amelia Barrett, daughter of Carmen Duncan) and her much poorer boyfriend Ricky Deitz (Daniel Billet). Mother Penny Watts (Tandi Wright) and her naïve and virginal daughter Miranda (Jess Gower) had arrived from New Zealand and were already competing for the affections of part-time hostel caretaker and all-round good bloke Dave Collins (Dieter Brummer).

Also on holidays from the UK were the sleazy John Dickson (Warren Derosa) and his Londoner lackey Bryan Rossiter (Toby Truslove), who kept the hostel awash in party pills. There was also a sexually voracious

Scottish lass called Angie McIntyre (Simone McAullay) who was out to shag Ricky. From Argentina had come sultry (or slutty depending on which description you prefer) Inez Del Rey (Tory Mussett) and her best friend Carla (Victoria Hill), a lesbian who was secretly in love with her.

Inez was originally meant to be from Spain and Tory Mussett had been practising her Spanish accent by listening to Antonio Banderas in *The Mask of Zorro*. Aussie producers David Maher and David Taylor were thrilled at her dialect until a South American financier congratulated the team on finding an actress who could speak perfect Argentinean, leading to a quick rewrite of Inez's origins. Meanwhile, the American partners complained that Daniel Billet didn't sound convincing as an American until they discovered the actor really was from the USA. And the English were convinced that Aussie actor Toby Truslove was a Brit.

With accents finally sorted out, the game of sexual musical chairs began with Angie and Ricky getting physical on a bushwalking tour as John tried to have his evil way with Wendy back at the hostel. After being chased by drug dealers and police, Kirsty fled, leaving Tina free to dance on top of pub bars and screw everyone in sight. German doctor Klaus Miller (Julian Garner) rescued Angie and Ricky after they got lost in a national park, while Inez posed nude for sleazy photographer Leon (Paul Capsis). John began to exploit Ricky's gambling problem and pretty soon girlfriend Wendy discovered he had been emptying her bank account.

After being robbed, Penny turned to secretly working as a high-class hooker until client Aaron (David Woodley) freaked her out by bringing along a male friend for a threesome. Thinking that she and Dave were a couple, Penny got even more of a shock when she opened up the back of Dave's kombi van and found him inside bonking Tina. Jimmy Thomson remembers the scene well. 'In *Hollyoaks* Stephanie Waring was a little bit

Kirsty (Rachel Aveling) and Tina (Stephanie Waring) arrive in Sydney and meet Bryan (Toby Truslove).

Dave (Dieter
Brummer)
and Miranda
(Jess Gower).

overweight and had played a dowdy single mum,' he explains. 'Having worked hard to get her body into shape, she was up for any sex scenes. We were planning to use a body double for a panel van make-out with Dave but she said no bloody way. She wanted to be able to tell her friends that she'd got nude with Dieter Brummer!'

Nude moments in *Crash Palace* did occur, but it was mostly pretty discreet stuff. There were lots of naked backs and girls skinny-dipping while hiding their breasts behind folded arms. 'There were certain markets that would not have tolerated nudity,' Thomson says. 'We often spoke about doing what I called 'third button' scenes where a woman would be unbuttoning her top and it would stop there for some markets and continue further in others. But that idea got dropped because of economic viability.'

Another coy moment in the show came when Japanese surfer Junichi (Masa Yamaguchi) and Bryan took ecstasy together. *Crash Palace*'s mostly realistic depiction of casual drug use was undermined by Jun and Bryan's 'under the influence kiss', surely one of the most unconvincing lip locks in soap history. Luckily the show redeemed itself with a couple of unexpected story developments. Tarty Tina celebrated her birthday by flirting with every man in the hostel but after she went to lie down in her dorm room, a stranger entered and locked the door.

'Tina's rape was a very hard sell as a storyteller. This situation involved a very drunk girl and a very drunk guy getting down to it and she changes her mind,' says Jimmy Thomson. 'I'm sure a lot of the audience were saying she asked for it, but sex against her will was rape.' After hostel owner George was revealed as the rapist and finally accepted that he was in the wrong, he got his comeuppance by discovering girlfriend Isabella making out in a storage cupboard with new French tourist Luc (Damien de Montemas).

Next up was the death of Dave after a diving accident. Dieter Brummer was the show's best-known face, so why did he leave so quickly? It turns out that the role was always meant to be short term, having been originally written for Craig McLachlan. When the *Neighbours* and *Home and Away* actor became unavailable, producers decided to cast another iconic soap actor, but he still needed to be killed off for other planned storylines.

'There's an adage I live and write by, and that's never waste a good death on a bad character! So we made Dave a really nice guy. Dieter turned out to be ideal and then we kicked the audience in the nuts with a double whammy. Dave collapsed, we brought him back to life and then he died again. The audience wasn't prepared for that and it kept them always guessing as to what we might do next,' says Jimmy Thomson.

John's involvement in Dave's death resulted in so much scheming, it's a wonder he didn't grow a moustache to twirl. He was screwing Inez on the side while planning a seduction of Miranda, who had been left motherless after Penny fled town following a botched attempt to rob her escort agency. When Klaus tried to expose John's evil ways, the baddie threatened to tell Klaus's parents that the German doctor was really gay. There were more gay shenanigans with the arrival of Carla's former lover, Canadian Chris Sandford (Jenni Baird). But then an influx of Aussie characters seemed to put the brakes on the smorgasbord of dodgy accents. Along came sexy country singer Cassie (Penne Dennison), well-hung Queenslander Gary (Don Hany) and the mysterious Suze (Kristy Wright).

Location filming was regularly fraught with peril, especially on the streets of Kings Cross when real-life junkies and hookers unknowingly wandered into the action. Tory Mussett remembers filming a scene where she had to hand out flyers to a pretend nightclub. Dressed in a typically barely-there Inez outfit, she attracted more than just the paid extras, and no doubt a few confused souls went in search of an opening night that only existed on a TV show. As for the beach scenes, these were often shot at the crack of dawn in the middle of winter. Not surprisingly, the beach would be deserted except for a crew on standby waiting to throw hot water bottles and blankets over the shivering actors. 'It was once so cold sitting on the beach, my toes went numb and I didn't regain feeling in them till 4pm that afternoon!' reveals Tory Mussett.

After 65 half-hour episodes, *Crash Palace* was ending its first series and expecting to come back for a second, so every storyline finished up in the air for a traditional cliffhanger. Miranda had taken an overdose having finally figured out that John was bad to the core. Bryan, Tina and the newly returned Kirsty stole a boat and were basking in the afterglow of a threesome until the water police turned up. And Chris and Suze made a very silly decision when they pulled their kombi van over to pick up a weird pig hunter hitchhiker called Elvis (Raj Ryan).

'The Brits wanted to fund a second series without any of the other overseas partners and spice it up,' says Jimmy Thomson. As filming wrapped, producers were told a final decision would be made within two weeks. A year later they were still on hold, and after a regime change at Sky, everyone realised a second series of *Crash Palace* would never be made. 'Miranda was going to survive her suicide attempt but John was going to become even more manipulative and go to a very dark place before dying at the end of the second series. Angie was going to end up becoming a nanny for a psycho woman and poor old Bryan was headed back to square one, since both girls would want nothing to do with him after being arrested.'

How does creator Jimmy Thomson want *Crash Palace* to be remembered? 'Sex, drugs and rock'n'roll.' Instead, it may be remembered for avoiding endless clichéd shots of the Sydney Harbour Bridge and Opera House and focusing instead on the trashy backpackers' hangout of Kings Cross. 'My wife actually met two British backpackers who had come to Sydney because of *Crash Palace*,' insists Jimmy Thomson. Given that the show portrayed the inner-city 'burb as a drug-soaked, never-ending party town, British backpackers should still be swarming over Kings Cross as we speak.

46

REALITY SOAPS

The Donaher family before the media storm erupted.

Reality TV is now a staple on our screens but when it first started, nobody knew quite what to call it. Not surprisingly, the first big Aussie reality TV series was called a soap because it had so much in common with its fictional counterparts. *Sylvania Waters*, which premiered in 1992, had romance, drama and a bitch everybody loved to hate, and eventually paved the way for other reality soaps such as *Big Brother* and *The Block*. But was it a documentary, soapumentary, docusoap or real-life soap opera?

The Louds of Santa Barbara, California, had become the first family to let television cameras into their homes in 1973. Ten million viewers were astounded at the developments over 12 episodes of *An American Family*. Not only did parents Bill and Pat Loud decide to divorce on-camera, but 19-year-old son Lance became the first gay person to ever come out on American television. Before dying in 2000, Lance famously declared that TV 'ate' his family, and in particular, 'feasted' on him.

Across the Atlantic, documentary maker Paul Watson unveiled his own version, *The Family*, in 1974. Britain was fascinated by the working-class Wilkins family in what was described as a 'fly-on-the-wall' documentary serial. When mother Margaret later split from her husband, producer Watson and the UK tabloids were accused of breaking up her family.

In 1991, still flushed with the ongoing success of *Neighbours*, the BBC decided to make a real-life version of the hit Aussie soapie, so they recruited Watson to head down under and work his magic again. The ABC, at this time trying to be more competitive against Australia's three commercial networks, saw the potential of the controversial BBC idea and came on as co-producers. *Sylvania Waters* researcher Chris Pip would later admit in *The Age* that 'the brief was clear. We were making a series to go back to back with *Neighbours*.'

The ABC began to advertise for their real-life Ramsay Street saga: 'Any dramas in your house? We are looking for ... a lively family with something to say, who are willing to let us into their lives ... better than a soapie, this is real life.' Chris Pip even went onto 2KY to talk up the concept, and it was this interview that proved fateful for one NSW housewife.

Noeline Baker lived in the southern Sydney suburb of Sylvania Waters, along with de facto Laurie Donaher, daughter Joanne and teenage son Michael. In her book *The Sylvania Waters Diary*, written in 1993 after the show had been aired, Noeline admitted thinking that her family fitted the bill, especially when she thought she heard 'the amount of a million dollars mentioned'. She spoke to Chris Pip and suggested they 'should be the family to show the British how lucky we were to live in Australia'.

Chris Pip arranged to meet Noeline's clan, which also included Noeline's son Paul and his pregnant girlfriend Dione, who lived nearby. Laurie also had a son, Mick, married to Yvette, with two small girls of their own, Kristy and Lisa. After auditioning the family, Pip told the Bakers and Donahers that her bosses were 'besotted' with them and Paul Watson wanted to meet them. 'Everyone in the family was very intrigued, and yes, a sense of stardom had hit most of us,' Noeline wrote. 'We were going to be on television! Bear in mind that we thought we would be getting this huge amount of money and become instant movie stars. Oh dear, how stupid and naïve it was when I look back on it now.'

Paul Watson and BBC directors Kate Woods and Brian Hill took the family out to dinner the night before filming started so they could meet everyone in the crew. The whole deal nearly fell apart when Laurie discovered they were to be paid just $10,000 (although the family eventually received $13,999). Laurie's gut reaction was to call the whole thing off, but the others were in too deep (with stars in their eyes) to pull out at such a late stage. After being reminded that the television exposure might help in getting a sponsor for his racing car, Laurie relented and decided to 'accept the challenge'. Noeline's daughter Joanne remained unconvinced and, demanding never to be seen on camera, packed up and moved away that night. Filming began the next morning, 6 December 1991.

Like lambs to the slaughter, the family faced the constant glare of television cameras for the next five months. They became friendly with the cameramen and sound guys, and only occasionally objected to having certain incidents filmed, although they later claimed they were reassured such scenes would never be used. At other times they were led to believe the cameras weren't rolling. While they thought their conversations were

'We thought we would be getting this huge amount of money and become instant movie stars. Oh dear, how stupid and naïve it was when I look back on it now.'

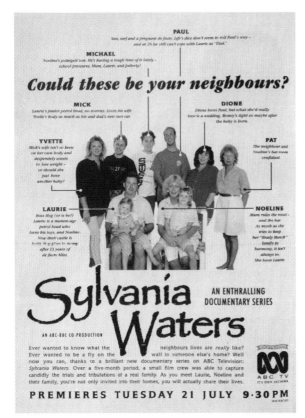

PAUL
Son, surf and a pregnant de facto. Life's dice don't seem to roll Paul's way – and at 26 he still can't cope with Laurie as "Dad."

MICHAEL
Noeline's youngest son. He's having a tough time of it lately – school pressures, Mum, Laurie, and puberty!

Could these be your neighbours?

MICK
Laurie's junior petrol head, no worries. Loves his wife Yvette's body as much as his and dad's new race car.

DIONE
Dione loves Paul, but what she'd really love is a wedding. Money's tight so maybe after the baby is born.

YVETTE
Mick's wife isn't so keen on her own body and desperately wants to lose weight – or should she just have another baby?

PAT
The neighbour and Noeline's bar-room confidant.

LAURIE
Boss Hog (or is he?) Laurie is a mature-age petrol head who loves his toys, and Noeline. Now their castle is theirs, thanks to no mortgage after 13 years of de facto bliss.

NOELINE
Mum rules the roost – and the bar. As much as she tries to keep her "Brady Bunch" family in harmony, it isn't always so. She loves Laurie.

Sylvania Waters

AN ENTHRALLING DOCUMENTARY SERIES

AN ABC-BBC CO-PRODUCTION

Ever wanted to know what the neighbours lives are *really* like? Ever wanted to be a fly on the wall in someone else's home? Well now you can, thanks to a brilliant new documentary series on ABC Television: *Sylvania Waters*. Over a five-month period, a small film crew was able to capture candidly the trials and tribulations of a real family. As you meet Laurie, Noeline and their family, you're not only invited into their homes, you will actually share their lives.

ABC TV
IT'S YOUR NETWORK

PREMIERES TUESDAY 21 JULY 9·30PM

innocent, history would prove that they were jaw-dropping enough to stop the nation. And to make sure the chit-chat stayed controversial, Noeline wrote later, director Kate Woods 'began setting up scenes, which might start with a question to keep the conversation going, like: "Do you think there are too many Asians in Australia?"' Stupidly, they were only too happy to answer.

Critics would later question whether it had been ethical to describe the series as a documentary, given that the filmmakers 'regularly intervened in the family's lives, asking them to do things which they sometimes felt were out of character'. Over a hundred hours of footage was filmed before it was all edited down to 12 half-hour episodes. Each show had a theme like 'Sex', 'Arguments' and 'Alcohol', but it soon become apparent these topics would be constantly referred to throughout the entire series.

Although the Bakers and the Donahers requested (and later demanded) to see every episode before it went to air, they never did see one until it screened each Tuesday night, along with the rest of the country. The only footage they were permitted to see was a 20-minute promotional reel, which consisted mostly of Noeline 'ranting and raving'. To her horror, she also discovered that teenage son Michael had been secretly taping the show's narration from the privacy of his bedroom. As publicity heated up for the series premiere, Noeline learnt that *The Family* was now to be known as *Sylvania Waters*. Finally, the penny dropped. 'The show was not going to be what we had expected.'

Sylvania Waters exploded across Australian screens on 21 July 1992 at 9.30pm. *The Daily Telegraph Mirror* predicted that by 10pm 'the family will probably be cringing in their pastel living room, wondering why on earth they participated. Judging by the scenes of drinking, racism, jealousy and bickering, the welcome mat outside their canal-front home soon will disappear. This is not going to be a glossy portrait of the Australian good life. Rather, it shapes up to be a vicious putdown of the nouveau riche – tailor-made for British audiences.' Just to make sure that Aussies got the picture, the paper went on to explain that close friend Trish Wick was 'puffing on a menthol cigarette at her front door' while defending her next door neighbours.

Richard Glover, writing for *The Sydney Morning Herald*, also felt the British filmmakers were pandering to clichéd Aussie stereotypes. 'In

Noeline and Laurie, every British preconception about the Aussies comes alive … Meet Australia's new ambassadors: a family whose members are variously materialistic, argumentative, uncultured, heavy drinking and acquisitive.' Brisbane's *Courier Mail* thought it all simply dreadful: 'Big-mouth, bad-taste real soap is really awful.'

By the next morning, Noeline was being described around the country as 'a racist, a drunk and a crass blonde', and those were the nice ones! Noeline had opened the series 'ranting' and 'raving'. 'Gawd, strewth, Lawrie, one of these days I'll pack me bloody bags and I'm going out of here. There's more drama living in this house than living out of it!' Drama was certainly the word for it.

Deep family rifts were exposed from the first night. At the core was surfie son Paul who resented, and had never accepted, petrol-head Laurie coming into his mother's life. Straightaway, a social divide had been revealed, accentuated each week with exterior shots of Noeline and Laurie's house (million dollar canal-front mansion) before cutting away to Paul and Dione's house (fibro shack on noisy main road). There hadn't been a juicier comparison since the well-to-do Hamiltons and the working-class Palmers traded barbs on *Sons and Daughters*.

Viewers lapped it up, with the first episode scoring a 20 in the ratings. This was an outstanding result for the ABC and they continued to milk the controversy, particularly through their own current affairs shows, for the rest of the series' three-month run. After the fourth episode had aired, Noeline was horrified to read that she was being described by the press as a 'brassy bottle-blonde who watches all the soap operas'. Bottle-blonde she could take, but Noeline felt the need to set the record straight in her diary afterwards: 'I don't watch this sort of stuff. Laurie and I did watch a few episodes of *Chances* but it became a little bit over the top.'

Ironically, the success of *Sylvania Waters* would damage *Chances'* ratings by airing directly opposite Nine's sexy (but struggling) soap. And despite her denials, Noeline now did feel that her 'innocent family' had indeed 'been chosen to do a soap series without the actors'. *Chances* might have been too over the top for her, but she and Laurie were too down to earth. They were just regular Aussies … who didn't much care for foreigners.

Night one had revealed Noeline's feelings about Asians ('The dreaded yellow peril! I reckon they should go back to their own country and stay there.'). A few weeks later, Noeline hired a 'very large, black, Negro stripper' to perform at a party and Laurie could barely contain his disgust ('They smell. They stink.'). Surfie son Paul kept his views on non-Aussies to himself, but let it rip about what he thought of homosexuals ('Each to their own, but it makes me sick, it makes me angry. That's where AIDS seems to be spreading at the moment. I think they're punching too many donuts without condoms on.').

Just as the second-last episode was going to air, Australia's deputy prime minister and federal minister for health, Brian Howe, dropped a clanger while speaking at a health conference in Canberra: 'Noeline admits she has a drinking problem, wants to give up smoking, has a close relationship with the TAB, and is constantly vacillating between Gloria Marshall [weight clinic] and creamcakes.' Noeline was furious and demanded that he apologise. When he did, she scoffed that it was a 'standard' letter of apology and that he should have 'apologised to me personally'.

The Donahers and the Bakers had now hired former *Neighbours* publicist Brian Walsh to handle their growing media commitments. The Howe incident got Noeline onto Nine's *A Current Affair*, charming host Jana Wendt in the process. Paul and Dione became favourites of ABC youth radio station Triple J and the entire family agreed to allow cameras from *Hard Copy* to film their reactions to the screening of the final episode. Reporter Renee Brack was instructed to get the family to 'exhibit every emotion possible', and on cue, Noeline cried as the credits of the final episode began to roll.

Brian Howe's attack upon Noeline was a turning point for the beleaguered mum. For once, the positive letters finally outweighed the negative ones. 'I have been watching *Sylvania Waters* from the start,' wrote Sheila from Moonee Ponds, 'and have become increasingly appalled at the hostility generated at you in particular. I've been prompted to write because of the unbelievable speech by Brian Howe. The Labor Party is supposed to represent the working class, not treat them as a lower species. I believe you are a very typical Australian family who work hard and earn your enjoyment. Of course you haven't got a drinking problem – if you have, then most of the country has.'

Moonee Ponds' most famous son (and sometimes daughter) also weighed in on the debate. Barry Humphries, in town to promote his autobiography, told *The Daily Telegraph Mirror* that 'Howe's mistake, poor man, is that he didn't know whether he was talking about a real person or Mrs Mangels [from *Neighbours*]. The borderline between fiction and fact is becoming very blurred, particularly in Australia, with the dream-time in which we all live.' Humphries went on to call for Noeline to be included in the next Queen's honours list. 'Move over Dame Edna! Here comes Dame Noeline! Edna must look to her laurels with a new housewife megastar in the pipeline, ready to step into her slingbacks.'

Noeline's 'drinking problem' was blamed on the fact that 'the crew came to our house most afternoons at about 4pm, and I do have a drink with Laurie before dinner'. Not to mention after dinner, on the boat and at the airport, as the happy couple boarded a plane in the final episode to fly to Monaco and get married. *The Courier Mail* noted that 'several fistfuls of drinks are consumed at the airport and … just in case the unsuspecting Europeans don't realise Laurie is an Australian, he is wearing an Akubra hat and a green and gold tracksuit top'.

Paul Watson, the filmmaker at the centre of the storm, was a guest on ABC-TV's late-night current affairs show, *Lateline*, the night *Sylvania Waters* finished its Australian run. He declared that what his team had produced was 'a serious look at contemporary life' through 'highlighted, edited editions'. In no way apologetic about the end result, he suggested that 'you have to be an absolute bastard to be a documentary filmmaker'.

According to Noeline, Watson never again had any contact with her family once the series started on air despite 'assuring us that they would keep in touch. What a load of rubbish,' she later wrote. As the storm slowly abated in Australia, things began to heat up again the following year as the show neared its on-air date in the UK.

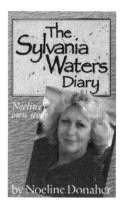

In May 1993, Noeline and Laurie travelled to London for the BBC's premiere. Once again, the newspapers tore them to shreds. *The Sun* headlined with: 'Meet Noeline. By Tonight, You'll Hate Her Too.' *The Guardian* shuddered at 'Noeline's bigotry and gruesome materialism,' while British TV critic Mark Stein thought it was 'like *Home & Away* gone mad – *Home & Away* on drugs!' *News of the World* described Noeline as 'the most hated woman in Oz'.

When Noeline touched down in London, she vowed to have a face-to-face showdown with the BBC but confessed she had no idea what she'd say or do. *The Daily Mirror* reported that Noeline was also hoping to meet Princess Di. 'With what I've been through lately, I've got a lot of sympathy for her. I think she's the most wonderful person. We are the same height and we're both blonde.'

When English fans lined up to get her autograph, Noeline was thrilled. 'After the fuss in Australia, this is a dream come true.' Not only did she have her book *The Sylvania Waters Diary* to flog, Noeline also had a single on the way called 'No Regrets', complete with an accompanying video shot on Sydney harbour with hunky lifesavers. While in London, she also guest hosted Seven's late-night news/variety show *Tonight Live* in a live satellite cross back to Australia.

It took till August 1993 for Noeline to have her showdown with the BBC, when she returned to the UK on an 'all-expenses-paid trip' to the Edinburgh Television Festival. 'For the past 15 months, I thought if I could commit suicide or leave my husband it would be better. I thought it was going to be like *The Brady Bunch* but instead our dream of being shown as a fantastic Australian family has been smashed. The editing was absolutely cruel and vicious.' *The Herald-Sun* reported that, 'as if her tribulations were not enough to bear, Mrs Donaher also was obliged to suffer BBC producer Kate Woods' patronising assurances. Miss Woods said "By far the most endearing quality about Noeline and Laurie has been their honesty".'

In one particularly contentious exchange, Noeline raged about being seen at the hairdressers while daughter-in-law Dione was giving birth. Claiming the scene was shot days beforehand in an obvious effort to make her look 'hard, harsh and unthinking', Woods responded that they were trying to show that Noeline was so proud to be a grandmother, she had to get her hair done to go the hospital. Paul Watson was a notable no-show.

Watson continued to make controversial documentaries in the UK for years afterwards. There was *The Dinner Party* (1997) where a group of Conservative voters revealed themselves to be just as racist and homophobic as the *Sylvania Waters* bunch, and *The Queen's Wedding* (2002) which followed the lives of several drag queens planning a gay marriage. In

neighbours
neighbours
neighbours
neighbours
neighbours

Blair
McD...

ten

Big Brother's Blair McDonough walked straight into a long-running role on *Neighbours*.

2003, *The Guardian* described his latest work, *Desert Darlings*, as a 'turkey. His signature touches were all over the place: revelatory personal interviews and wide establishing shots, but in all other aspects, *Desert Darlings* was just like any other dreary reality TV show.'

In 2001, Paul Watson appeared on Australian screens again when ABC current affairs program *Four Corners* examined the growing trend of reality television. Looking back on *Sylvania Waters*, Watson thought 'the point of it all was, though, that in the end, materialism won over maternalism. And for me that was the subtext of that particular woman and her relationship with that particular family.' When pressed again about portraying Noeline as a drunk, Watson was still unrepentant. 'They haven't been misrepresented. Absolutely and categorically not. Noeline is who and what she is. Um … we took very little advantage, if that's the word, of her being drunk.'

Responding to the worldwide phenomenon of reality shows like *Big Brother* and *Survivor*, Watson insisted he was different because he 'didn't make things up. I don't give people booze or drugs, I don't tell them lies about one person in order to get a reaction from them. And very many of those techniques are used in these new so-called reality series.'

Also appearing on that episode of *Four Corners* were *Sylvania Waters'* Mick and Yvette Donaher. When asked if she watched *Big Brother*, Yvette said, 'Definitely I do. I'm addicted.' She had to admit that, despite it happening to her, she was still fascinated by it happening to someone else. And she was far from being the only Aussie fascinated by *Big Brother*.

The Australian versions of *Big Brother* are unique because the nightly update show is screened on the Ten network each weeknight in the prime viewing time of 7pm (up against Seven's *Home and Away*). Everywhere else in the world, *Big Brother* is usually a late-night phenomenon. It was this bold programming initiative, suggested by Ten's Tim Clucas during an October 2000 trip to the Dutch headquarters of Endemol, creators of *Big Brother*, that sealed the deal when every Australian network was bidding for the rights.

'Apparently the others had, at one time or another, referred to *Big Brother* as a game show or 'reality' show when negotiating with Endemol. That's not how they saw their program,' says Clucas. 'When I said Ten saw *Big Brother* as a 'real life soap' and not a game show, their eyes lit up. When I said we [Ten] planned to run it early evening, straight after one of the world's favourite soaps, *Neighbours*, and make it accessible for the whole family, the deal was all but done. We had been the last Australian commercial network to enter the race for rights to *Big Brother* but we had suddenly become the front-runners … all because, as the Dutch still say, we "got" the concept.'

Australian *Big Brother* even finishes each night with a cliffhanger ending, just like *Sylvania Waters* did all those years ago. And the line between reality television and soap continues to blur today. *Big Brother*'s first series runner-up, Blair McDonough, went straight into a regular role in *Neighbours*. Nine's *The Block* – a mix of lifestyle TV and soap (a la *Number 96*) – was the smash hit of 2003 and the format was sold all over the world. Both *Home and Away* and *Neighbours* have reacted to this phenomenon by having their own characters appear on fictional reality TV shows within their soaps.

noeline. no regrets

Noeline's CD release, thankfully the only one.

Sylvania Waters' Dione Baker was last interviewed by *New Idea* in 1994. She admitted that *Sylvania Waters* had 'left her marriage in tatters and sparked a bitter rift with her mum-in-law Noeline Donaher'. She revealed that she had walked out on Paul, after two years of marriage, to bring up son Kane alone.

In 2003, Noeline and Laurie sold their home for a reported $2.2 million and moved to a smaller mansion (allegedly $1.5 million) on Queensland's Sovereign Islands. Once again, they invited the television cameras to film their every move, and once again, they were taken advantage of. *A Current Affair* just couldn't resist showing Noeline sweeping down her new grand staircase, in slow motion, to the theme music of *Gone with the Wind*. When pressed to update viewers about her family, Noeline revealed that baby Kane was nearly as tall as she was, while her son Michael was married and expecting his own child.

A decade before, Noeline had finished her best-selling diary with an open letter: 'To the people of Australia, I want it known that I did not undertake to do *Sylvania Waters* for notoriety or gain. It was innocently done and I say sorry to those I have offended. I am thankful for the support I have received and will go back to being Noeline Vera Donaher – 5 feet 10 inches tall with big feet, Laurie's wife and very proud and happy to be her. To my own children, whom I love, I say one final time that I am sorry for any heartbreak I have caused you. To my stepchildren also, I am sorry.'

Poor Noeline has every right to be sorry about *Sylvania Waters*. Today, the show lives on in repeats on subscription television in Australia. It is played, strictly for laughs, on The Comedy Channel.

47

SOAP SPOOFS

Shark Bay's Raelee Hill, Frances O'Connor,
Tina Thomsen, Lisa Baumwol, Kate Gorman.

Soaps, by their very nature, are perfect targets for sending up. With storylines already verging on the ridiculous, comedy writers have loved taking them to the extreme. America's *Mary Hartman, Mary Hartman* (1976-77) and *Soap* (1977-81) proved the joke could be sustained over several seasons, yet it was not until 1996 that Australia tried its own version. Before *Shark Bay*, however, there had been a long tradition of sending up local soaps, even if it was just one segment within another series.

The first was *The Checkout Chicks* which aired during the second series of ABC-TV's *The Norman Gunston Show* in 1975. The eight-part, three-minute spoof was written each week by Bill Harding and Garry McDonald, and in the spin-off book, *Norman Gunston's Finest Moments*, it was described as 'a raw adult Australian drama. From the outside it looks like any ordinary supermarket – that's just from the outside.'

The actors were all familiar soap faces, with most of the cast fresh from *Number 96*. Working the cash register on checkout one was Bobo Stassinopolos (Vivienne Garrett, who played *96*'s Rose Godolfus), the runaway daughter of a Greek shipping magnate who was also an undercover terrorist planning to bomb the embassy across the street. Whinge-ing cockney migrant Joan Bygraves (Abigail, *96*'s Bev Houghton) was also on the run, but she was hiding from a psycho ex-husband who was about to break out of jail.

Pot-smoking and occasionally nude hippie Jasmine Marlowe (Candy Raymond, *96*'s Jill Sheridan) had just returned after spending several years in a monastery in Tibet. She was 'nursing' her invalid brother amidst a suggestion of incest. Tea lady and general caretaker Minnie O'Dowd (Philippa Baker, *96*'s Roma Godolfus) had a heroin-addicted daughter and a supposedly incapacitated husband, until it was revealed he had really died years before on the Kokoda Trail.

Minnie's rough trot continued when she went blind, while pregnant co-worker Ruth Taylor (Anne Lambert, *96*'s Sue Marshall) was dumped by her boyfriend when he found out she was 'coloured' (part Maori). Then Minnie and Ruth won the lottery and threw a big party to celebrate (only after late night shopping, mind you). Ruth was despondent ('What's the good of money? Will it buy me a place in your rotten white society?') and, consequently, didn't notice setting her rubbish bin on fire with a careless cigarette.

In the over-the-top climax, the party came under siege from a bikie group, thanks to motorbike moll Randy Simpson (*The Unisexers*' Sonia Hoffman). Amnesiac and part-time lesbian Erica Daniels (Judy Lynne) had just discovered that she was wanted in connection with a mutilation murder in Adelaide and the shocking revelation turned her into a were-wolf! As she sprouted hair and started snarling, Bobo's stockpile of terrorist ammunition caught alight and blew the supermarket, and every-one in it, sky high.

In 1989, the Nine Network's daytime variety show *Midday with Ray Martin* decided to create its own soap send-up as a direct result of Seven's new daytime soap *The Power, the Passion*. *A Town Like Dallas* featured *Midday* regulars such as Geoff Harvey, Brian Bury and Shane Bourne; visiting international soap stars such as *Days of Our Lives*' Thaao Penghlis and *Dynasty*'s Emma Samms; singers John Denver, Angry Anderson and Doug Parkinson; football player Fatty Vautin and veteran actress Queenie Ashton. And just to keep the audience guessing, there was usually a last-minute rope-in from the studio audience.

The original concept, title and first 15 episodes were written by *Midday* regular Gretel Killeen (who went on to host the Australian version of *Big Brother*). She cast herself as the soap's matriarch, Sylvia Trotter, while Ray Martin played her hapless husband Raymondo, who was more obsessed with housework than the family pig farm. *Midday* audience warm-up guy Ross Daniels played their twin sons and would walk out one door as a lawyer and back in with a stethoscope around his neck to portray his iden-tical doctor brother.

'Any viewer watching it would see no logic to any storyline,' remembers Gretel Killeen. 'One minute someone would die and then the next week they'd be alive again. It was all very silly.' While continuity wasn't a feature, at least there were plenty of laughs. 'One of the principal preoc-cupations for the cast was to make each other laugh, and throw in lines

'What's the good of money? Will it buy me a place in your rotten white society?'

The Checkout Chicks.
BACK: Philippa Baker,
Sonia Hoffman, Candy
Raymond, FRONT: Judy
Lynne, Abigail, Vivienne
Garrett, Anne Lambert.

that would shock your fellow performers. The sets would break and people would lose their places or walk in at the wrong time, yet before too long, the ratings were actually starting to go up just for *A Town Like Dallas*. Audiences could clearly see that we were all having a good time doing it.'

Ray Martin ridiculed Seven for trying, unsuccessfully, to dethrone him with *The Power, the Passion*. 'Obviously networks regard lunchtime viewers as cretins,' he told *TV Week*, 'so we thought we'd give them a really bad soap. *A Town Like Dallas* has no plot and bad lines, but what it shows is people still like a break from homogenised, sanitised TV where nothing ever goes wrong.'

'It was good for Ray to do because he is a very well-respected journalist. Yet there he was every Friday wearing a smoking jacket and being a goose,' Gretel Killeen reminisces. 'His comic timing was appalling but it all added to the fun.' So much fun was had, in fact, nobody can quite remember how *A Town Like Dallas* ended, and in great soap tradition, it also ran for several years.

Around 1990, Artist Services were producing the popular night-time skit show *Fast Forward* for the Seven Network and they started up their own piss-take of soaps, *Dumb Street*. It was heavily influenced by the peaking popularity of *Home and Away* and *Neighbours*, so *Dumb Street* had Gina Riley playing Dannii (recalling Dannii Minogue's hair-flicking role as *Home and Away*'s Emma); Jane Turner was Bobby (think *Home and Away*'s Nicolle Dickson); Marg Downey was Shelley (a composite of soaps' many dumb blondes); while Magda Szubanski could barely keep a straight face every week as the face-slapping Nikki.

Steve Blackburn played Craig Donovan, a dopey surfie boy who never spoke. Loosely based on *Neighbours*' Craig McLachlan and Jason Donovan, neither actor took offence at the joke and, indeed, Jason Donovan even guest starred as Craig for one episode. When asked how real-life friend Craig McLachlan would react, Donovan told *TV Week*, 'He'd love it, that's the great thing about him. I have a few good Craig mannerisms I've been working on.'

Rounding out the cast were two final characters, both called Bob. Michael Veitch played Reverend Bob (just like the *E Street* minister) while Geoff Brooks was country bumpkin Bob Hatfield (*A Country Practice*). Neither had much to say, and in fact, *Dumb Street* is best remembered for what wasn't said. Instead, the cast would adopt open-mouthed expressions every time a new crisis befell them. And like any good soap send-up, there was always a crisis in *Dumb Street*. For example:

Let the Blood Run Free.

> BOBBY: Here you are Craig, one double choc milkshake. And Craig – your mum's dead.
>
> NIKKI: What's wrong mate? You got a little bit of polio today?
>
> SHELLEY: Wasn't it lucky about the deserted old mine shaft? I thought we were goners for sure until Nikki realised she had Bob Hatfield's portable phone in her pocket and that Dannii had his phone number and that earth moving machinery just happened to be there and he knew how to operate them!

Meanwhile, the Ten network was airing a strange comedy that same year called *Let the Blood Run Free*. Produced by Media Arts (*The Comedy Company*), and rejected by Nine for being too off the wall, the 'human cartoon' found a home on Ten, even if it didn't find an audience. It was definitely an acquired taste.

St Christopher's was a hospital where perky new nurse Pam Sandwich (Jean Kittson) worked alongside dribbling orderly Wozza Cronkshonk (Peter Rowsthorn) who suffered regular personality changes because of a failed medical experiment. Pam quickly fell in love with the evil moustache-twirling Dr Richard Lovechild (David Swan) while monstrous Matron Dorothy Conniving-Bitch (Lynda Gibson) ran around cackling and pointing her obscenely long fingernails at everyone.

'The show's not making huge statements, but it's a lot of fun,' Jean Kittson told *TV Week*. 'All the characters are those you see in soaps ... there's the nice character, the manipulative doctor and the lovesick mercenary. The more exaggerated they are, the better. The show works because the audience loves the characters.' Although the cheap budget and laboured gags resulted in low ratings, the show became enough of a cult hit in Europe to return with new episodes. 'There's a fanatical audience out there for *Blood*,' producer Ian McFadyen told *TV Week*. 'I think it's the funniest show since *Fawlty Towers*. Remember that a show like *Monty Python* rated an asterisk first time around.'

During the show's second series, Pam and Matron Conniving-Bitch found themselves incarcerated. And since the show was a Ten property, it was a nice tie-in to send the pair off to *Prisoner*'s Wentworth Detention

Shark Bay's Dieter Brummer and Tottie Goldsmith.

Centre. Forced to share a cell together, the pair fought off other butch prisoners (all played by men in dresses) before Matron escaped by flushing herself down the toilet. Sadly, the show then moved its action back to the hospital and also disappeared down the gurgler.

In 1995 cable television finally started in Australia and advertising was almost non-existent for the first few years. To fill in the gaps, Foxtel needed five-minute interstitials for every half hour of transmission. Artist Services, who had proved their comedy chops with *Fast Forward* (and *Dumb Street*) were commissioned to make *Shark Bay*. Created by Steve Vizard, Ray Kolle and Peter Herbert, it ran for five minutes each weeknight at 6.55pm, with all the episodes being re-packaged for a half-hour episode Friday nights at 7.30pm.

Shark Bay was set in Noosa, Queensland, but filmed in Melbourne's drab-looking Port Phillip Bay for comic effect. Its premise was that it had already been running for 24 years and was celebrating its 8,000th episode. Consequently, viewers were dropped into the middle of the action as super-superbitch Clarissa Delaney (*Sons and Daughters'* Rowena Wallace) was being held hostage in a warehouse while surrounded by explosives. After it blew up, her dysfunctional family gathered for her funeral, only to discover that Clarissa had survived the blast and was still very much alive.

'Initially, all of us found *Shark Bay* rather tricky,' Rowena Wallace told *The Courier Mail*, 'because quite how to play a spoof is difficult. You have to say such outrageous things, yet you have to play it for real. We had some terrific directors and some very funny scripts. Eventually we all got into the swing of it. No stone was left unturned.'

Clarissa owned Hammerhead International and had made her fortune from a string of surf shops and nine dead husbands. Since she was still the marrying kind, she quickly secured a new fiancé in toy boy Rupert (Doug Penty), unaware that he was struggling with voices in his head that commanded him to kill her. Back at the Hammerhead offices, Clarissa's sleazy stepson Justin Farraday (37-year-old Tiriel Mora playing a 22 year old) was scheming to take over her corporation, along with his devilish partner in crime Daphne (Lisa Baumwol).

Meanwhile, Clarissa's wimpy brother Peter Delaney (William Gluth) and his family struggled to make ends meet. Wife Kylie (Zoe Bertram) ran coffee shop Kylie's Korner while daughter Miranda (Kate Gorman) was a butch mechanic (a la Charlene from *Neighbours*). Speedo-wearing son Steve (real-life ironman Joel Williams) was training to compete in a 'gigathalon' which involved running along the beach holding barbecues in the air, while Peter and Kylie's third child, sexually illiterate computer nerd Brad (*Home and Away's* Dieter Brummer), struggled to be as popular as his spunky brother and was secretly in love with airhead waitress Debbie (Tina Thomsen).

When the kids realised mum Kylie was a closet kleptomaniac, she was sent off to psycho psychiatrist Dr Jane (Frances O'Connor) who promptly fell in love with Kylie's husband Peter. While they struggled to keep their affair a secret, Clarissa's secret hippie daughter Heather (Raelee Hill mocking her own *Neighbours*' Serendipity character), who had been kidnapped at birth by her French mime-artist father, left her commune and quickly found herself initiated into the evil world of big business by her nefarious mother.

Many soap actors were thrilled to get in on the fun, including *The Flying Doctors*' Peter O'Brien, *Dynasty*'s Kerry Armstrong, *Prisoner*'s Lois Collinder, *Home and Away*'s Roger Oakley, *Starting Out*'s Tottie Goldsmith, *E Street*'s Adrian Lee and *Neighbours*' Scott Michaelson (in a *Twin Peaks* send-up not many people got). 'I had so much fun on that show,' Michaelson told *The Sunday Telegraph*. 'I'd be sitting in the green room watching [the studio monitors] and I would be in tears [of laughter] by the time my scene came up.'

The series was shot at Network Ten's Melbourne studios, also the home of *Neighbours*. Cast and crew from both shows shared a canteen and the Ramsay Street regulars were widely reported as being the first fans of *Shark Bay* even though they knew they were being sent up.

Shark Bay cast: Doug Penty, Rowena Wallace, Joel Williams, Raelee Hill, Dieter Brummer, Tina Thomsen.

For once, the critics loved *Shark Bay*, if only because Aussie soaps were being skewered again. Sandra McLean from *The Courier Mail* thought that, 'despite the silliness of *Shark Bay*, the beauty of it is it's not that far from the real thing. After watching the preview tape, I happened to switch on to Nine's *Pacific Drive* and it was so similar, it was just spooky.' *Rolling Stone* thought it was a 'razor sharp piss-take … with drop-dead funny dialogue ("Oh, by the way, your sister dropped round and said she was going to destroy us")' and that it was 'so good that it makes you wish it was on a free to air channel.' Sadly, *Shark Bay* never did get seen by a wider audience.

In 2003, the soapie send-up tradition was re-established by the Nine Network's *AFL Footy Show*. *The House of Bulger* was described as *Dynasty* meets Bay 13, the infamous yobbo stadium at the Melbourne Cricket Ground. Conceived by *Footy Show* regular and footballer Shane Crawford, he followed Gretel Killeen's lead years earlier by casting himself as country football star Hank Bulger, the head of a major fashion empire.

At home in his *Taurus Rising*-like mansion were father George Bulger (Sam Newman) and his nymphomaniac mother Joybell (Billy Brownless in an inspired piece of drag casting). Despite, or because of, being married to George for 45 years, Joybell spent every episode having it off with an assortment of handymen and maintenance guys who came by the mansion for a quickie. Rounding out the cast was Bulger daughter Alexandra (Nikki McCarthy), Hank's right-hand man Joffa (Roland Rocchecciolli), fashion designer Chelsea Briggs (Renee Henderson) and arch-rival Heuston Crabbe (Garry Lyon).

The House of Bulger.

Over 26 weeks, Hank was jailed for murder, developed amnesia and got kidnapped by aliens. Heuston tried to steal the Bulger fortune by marrying Alexandra while she was in a coma before being 'killed', getting a twin brother Austin and then coming back from the dead as Heuston again.

In a live finale in front of thousands of fans for the final show, Hank married long time love Deirdre, only to discover it was Heuston underneath the white veil. It was, of course, a classic cliffhanger ending for the first season which had also included guest appearances from comedian Shaun Micallef, *Prisoner*'s Colette Mann, *E Street*'s Dermot Brereton, journalist Derryn Hinch, Gary Sweet (as Inspector Hector, the world's greatest 'detector') and music guru Molly Meldrum as Hank's long lost brother Frank.

The House of Bulger became so popular that it was released on DVD (just in time for Christmas). Within two weeks it had become a double platinum success story. When *The Footy Show* returned for 2004 so did its soap, but it was now called *Bulger MD*. Hank was now a 'former fashionista' who had returned to his first love, medicine, in what was now an inspired hospital soap send-up.

Shane Crawford had already garnered some flak for appearing in the show, particularly when the club he captained, Hawthorn, struggled in the footy competition. But it was nothing compared to the furore that erupted when another 'metrosexual' – this time Richmond recruit Nathan Brown – was hired to play a gay doctor in *Bulger MD*. Brown's club decided that playing Dr Pink didn't fit in with their idea of 'leadership' and the footballer was forced to withdraw after filming just two episodes.

'People are watching Nathan Brown,' said Richmond's humourless director of football Greg Miller, 'younger players are very impressionable about what you do, and how you act, and I wasn't keen for Nathan to be involved.' Dr Pink was quickly written out of *Bulger MD*, with *Footy Show* host Eddie McGuire stepping in to play the controversial doctor for his final appearance.

Meanwhile, the cameos kept on coming, including *The Bold and the Beautiful*'s Ronn Moss (playing Forrest Ridge instead of Ridge Forrester) and Tottie Goldsmith (as Elizabeth Taylor, and then Liza Minnelli, both after plastic surgery). Slutty Joybell gave birth to a baby girl, and blood tests later revealed that Heuston Crabbe was the father. He insisted the baby be called Whitney Houston while the Bulgers preferred Betty. Joybell wasn't bothered either way and swapped the newborn for a football medal on eBay.

Even though the show was now set in a medical facility, some fans seemed to prefer the original. In May 2004 when Hawthorn played Fremantle at York Park, a supporter was seen holding up a placard that read 'The Park of Bulger'. Regardless, the hospital remained the focus for a slew of health-related stories as Hank Bulger turned old before his time (a cameo from AFL legend Lou Richards) before going blind. The Bulgers look like they could be around sending up soaps for years to come.

48

KATH AND KIM

PREMIERE: **2002** EPISODES: ... NETWORK: **ABC** FINALE: ...

Kim (Gina Riley), Kath (Jane Turner) and Sharon
(Magda Szubanski) on Kath's wedding day.

Australia doesn't have a good record with homemade situation com-edies but every now and then (once a decade if we're lucky) one fires the imagination and actually takes off. *Kath and Kim* isn't strictly a soap spoof but here's the ultimate irony – in sending up suburbia, it's actually a much more realistic portrayal of Australia in the 21st century than *Neighbours'* Ramsay Street.

Kath and Kim has become the most successful comedy in Australian television history, and while our soaps are used to travelling the world, this time it looks like a locally made comedy is about to follow in their footsteps. And why not? Just like our serials, audiences respond to the lov-able, larger-than-life characters, the continuing storylines, soap staples such as weddings and births, and the liberal use of catchphrases and malapropisms. Creators and stars Jane Turner and Gina Riley first met at the age of 17 when they co-wrote and starred in a play at a Melbourne youth arts centre. While Turner did the odd guest role on *Cop Shop* and *Prisoner*, she and Riley found themselves gravitating towards the Melbourne comedy scene. By the end of the 80s, they were household names on Seven's *Fast Forward* along with future *Kath and Kim* regulars

Magda Szubanski and Glenn Robbins. As well as playing multiple characters on the sketch comedy show (including the riotous soapie send-up *Dumb Street*), it was also the beginning of *Kath and Kim*. 'I did a 21st speech as a sort of a mumsy character,' Jane Turner (Kath) revealed on *Enough Rope* with Andrew Denton, 'and I think [Glenn Robbins] was Uncle Kel or something.' A comedy team had been born, even if it was a variation of the same daggy couple. 'We've had each other's numbers for a while as those characters,' Turner would later tell *Filmink* magazine. After *Fast Forward* finished, the female comedians in the group reunited in 1995 for *Big Girl's Blouse*, which included the first appearance of the spoilt princess daughter, Kim. Gina Riley was inspired by pioneering reality shows such as *Sylvania Waters* and *Weddings*, particularly the latter where a petulant prospective bride had responded to every marriage option with 'I hate it'.

The first ever *Kath and Kim* skit on *Big Girl's Blouse* aired over eight episodes and began with Kim announcing her engagement and ended with her riotous wedding reception in the garage. Without any male regulars in the new troupe, Jane Turner had to stick on a false moustache to play Kim's hapless husband.

In 1998, the characters turned up again on the girls' next skit show, *Something Stupid*, and this time, Kim had a baby called Brittany. When the ABC came calling a couple of years later to see if the team had any ideas for a new show, Jane Turner and Gina Riley thought there was potential in this suburban mother and daughter act (although the baby was quickly dropped – for now).

After 18 months of development, with both stars writing all the scripts ('We've been a lot more generous than many male writers have been to us,' Gina Riley would tell *The Sydney Morning Herald*), both were ready to start filming. Unfortunately, the ABC wasn't, as it was going through another one of those 'dark' periods government channels are prone to. 'Nobody thought the show was going to work,' Riley told *Filmink*, and just two days before they were due to start production, the project was shut down. 'The ABC was in turmoil,' Jane Turner told *The Sydney Morning Herald*. 'Everyone was immobilised and we got caught up in that. We thank God that Sandra Levy took over as head of television and that Robyn Kershaw came into the drama department and things got back on the rails.'

Under the new regime, *Kath and Kim* finally went into production in 2002, and eight half-hour episodes were soon ready to be unveiled. 'Ours is not strictly a sitcom,' Jane Turner said. 'It's sort of a breaking-the-mould type of show. It's sort of reality-television-situation-comedy, but it's more a comedy show than a situation comedy. It's character comedy, in the way that *Absolutely Fabulous* is.'

Indeed, the early episodes were shot as if a reality TV crew was following the characters' every move. In the second series, it would move away from this 'reality', although it would never have a studio audience or laugh track and would continue to be shot with hand-held cameras for a more natural feel.

'I think it's real middle Australia,' Gina Riley told *The Age*. 'Everyone can relate to it. I think we all live, partly, those kind of lives. It's not one tiny little group we're poking a finger at. It's just a general, middle kind of suburb.'

Kath and Kim finally debuted on 16 May 2002 with perky, 40-something divorcee Kath Day (Jane Turner) enjoying her 'empty nest' lifestyle in her Fountain Lakes townhouse now that obscenely self-obsessed daughter Kim (Gina Riley) had finally left home to marry computer salesman Brett Craig (Peter Rowsthorn). Unfortunately for Kath, Kim didn't like coming second to Brett's pet Rottweiler Cujo ('I'm not a housewife, I'm a hornbag!') and stomped back home after two months of marriage, just as Kath was getting it on with 'great hunk o' spunk' Kel Knight (Glenn Robbins), a local butcher or, as he preferred to be known, a 'purveyor of fine meats'.

Popping in from next door to observe these antics was Kim's second best friend, the overweight and accident-prone Sharon Strzelecki (Magda Szubanski). Sharon's view on life seemed to be summed up with her statement, 'The sooner you realise that all men are bastards and develop an interest in sport, the happier you'll be.' (As for Kim's best friend Lisa, she was often referred to but never seen).

During the first series of eight episodes, Kim was sacked from her call centre job and sat around gorging on junk food while wondering if husband Brett had gotten it on with neighbourhood sluts Kylie and Dannii Bolton. Under constant pressure from her mother to lose weight, Kim attempted to lose weight via 'Celine Cuisine' (as in Celine Dion) but eventually took up smoking again, while Kath tried to find time to watch her videotaped episodes of *Sunset Beach*. Meanwhile, Sharon got it on (a nasty case of 'pash rash') with bush band fiddler Mark (Tony Martin), and when he lost interest in her, began stalking him.

Just like every good soapie, *Kath and Kim* based its first series around a big wedding, Kath and Kel's upcoming nuptials, although it's safe to say that even *Home and Away* wouldn't resort to the groom working overtime to create the perfect commemorative sausage. After the proposal inside an electrical store ('Kel and I have decided to make our beautiful, sensual relationship into a mere formality!'), Kath embarked on a strenuous exercise regime with her fiancé, while continuing to sneak the odd cigarette, with rubber gloves and fresh breath spray at the ready to hide the smell from her clueless man. During an uproarious hens' night, Kath and Kim were both drugged by spiked drinks, causing them to 'go off' to the pulsating beats of what they referred to as 'town house music'. Kath ended up pashing a taxi driver (a cameo from Jane Turner's real-life husband) while Kim underwent a complete personality change. After scaring Sharon and Brett witless by baking cakes and showing affection for Cujo, the dog she hated, the drugs eventually wore off and Kim was back to her 'gropable' self.

As the wedding loomed, Kel worried about being left at the altar (which had happened on his previous four wedding attempts), but Kath

'The sooner you realise that all men are bastards and develop an interest in sport, the happier you'll be.'

arrived in a Cinderella-like pumpkin coach for the backyard ceremony (a tarpaulin had been thrown over the clothesline). It all ended up with Kath in traction in hospital, a plate in her head and one leg now shorter than the other. Kim grabbed the opportunity to go on Kath and Kel's Bali honeymoon with Sharon, who (as in all previous episodes) returned with a nasty injury, this time a festering monkey bite.

The Age, which visited the set during the filming of the first series, couldn't believe that eight episodes had been filmed in just six and a half weeks, especially considering how often the cast broke up laughing at each other. The paper reported that series director Ted Emery, who had worked with the group on *Fast Forward*, knew it was useless to lose his cool, so instead he shot the giggling actors separately until the laughter was under control.

The ABC doesn't allow for product placements, so the rampant consumerism in *Kath and Kim* was carefully manufactured by the network's clever art department. They produced Glad Rap instead of Glad Wrap, ESP baked beans instead of SPC, and the biscuit that Kim was forever munching on, Dippitybix. Even with such subtle gags, there were still some people who failed to get the joke.

Just like many a soap before it, *Kath and Kim* attracted mixed criticism, especially from some viewers and TV writers who felt that suburbanites were being held up to ridicule for the entertainment of inner-city sophisticates who like to watch the ABC. The (elitist) *Sydney Morning Herald* was an early fan while the (populist) *Daily Telegraph* withheld a 'thumbs up' until it became obvious that suburbanites were flocking to the national broadcaster to watch characters they identified with.

Gina Riley told *The Herald Sun* that such critics 'jumped to conclusions and said, "Oh, it's just a send-up of a load of ugly Westies wearing moccies and tracksuit pants".' Jane Turner was quick to point out that Kath and Kim 'never wear moccasins. We are not bogans. You get Kath and Kims in Toorak, Frankston, Prahran – everywhere.'

Indeed, Jane Turner and Gina Riley also poked fun at another type of suburbanite with their snooty society dames Pru and Trude, who work in an upmarket homewares store. In one hilarious exchange, Kim began mimicking the over-enunciated way that Pru and Trude spoke, prompting Kath to chide her with, 'Kim! They can't help it!' 'Our script editor at the time said, "No, you cannot do that. You've got to give those characters to someone else". And we just couldn't!' Riley told *Enough Rope*. 'We love doing them,' said Turner.

After the runaway success of the new comedy, the ABC were quick to invite Jane Turner and Gina Riley back for more, even giving them an office to work in which they never used, preferring instead to work at Turner's house. 'She who types has the real power,' Riley revealed on *Enough Rope* and Turner agreed. 'If you don't like it, you just don't write it down.'

There was another brief pre-production hitch when Jane Turner broke her ankle, but filming eventually got under way on the second series.

'Great hunk o' spunk'
Kel (Glenn Robbins)
with Kim (Gina Riley)
and Kath (Jane Turner).

Since the show was such a hit, both Turner and Riley were embarrassed when told they might now need security guards, especially when filming at Australia's largest shopping centre which doubled as the characters' favourite hangout, Fountain Gate. 'Nobody came up to us at all,' Riley told *Enough Rope*. 'There was one stage where there were five security guards. Jane and I were just sitting at a table. No-one was near us and people were just walking past – it was so sad.'

It's quite likely that the pair blended too successfully into the shopping mall background, for when *Kath and Kim* returned to the ABC on 18 September 2003, the show was bigger than ever. Kath Day-Knight was now involved in a love triangle with Kel and his lecherous best friend Sandy Freckle (William McInnes) and Kim was expecting a baby. Brett was renovating and Sharon was still unlucky in love, while guest stars included Sibylla Budd from *The Secret Life of Us* (playing Lisa at Kim and Sharon's high school reunion) and Vince Colosimo (as Jarrod, a rival of Brett's for a computer shop promotion).

Just as Kim was going into labour, the show went into flashback mode to the 80s where it was revealed that 'new romantic' Brett had first been dating Sharon – until Kim stole him away. Soap fans also noticed a rare blooper for the show, as Kath talked about watching Kerry Armstrong in *Dallas* (it was in fact *Dynasty* in which the Aussie actress had appeared).

A great soapie tradition was given a nod when the second season finished with a cliffhanger just after Kim had given birth (very noisily) to baby girl Epponnee Rae. Kath's first husband Gary Poole (Mick Molloy) turned up and announced that since he had never signed his divorce papers, he and Kath were still legally married. This episode attracted over 2.15 million viewers and became the highest-rated Aussie sitcom since 1991.

Perhaps *Kath and Kim* also owes something else to an Aussie soapie. With the infamous malapropisms and exaggerated accents, one could be forgiven for thinking that *Number 96*'s Dorrie Evans was still mangling the language. A swag of expressions were now being repeated ad nauseum around the country by the show's fans, including wanting to be 'effluent' instead of affluent; 'I can feel it in my waters'; 'It's noice, it's different, it's unusual' and the ultimate stretched vowels catchphrase 'Look at moiye!'

For its third season premiere on 7 October 2004, the cliffhanger situation was resolved during the first episode. Kath worried she might end up going to jail for bigamy (prompting her to re-watch her *Prisoner* tapes) before discovering that she and Kel weren't legally married, thanks to unregistered marriage celebrant Marion (Marg Downey, another old mate from *Fast Forward/Dumb Street* days). By the end of the episode, Gary (Mick Molloy) had tricked Kim into mortgaging Brett's home unit and fled with the money, setting up a brilliant premise as Kim and family were forced to move back in with Kath and Kel (who quietly re-married off-screen in episode two).

As well as Epponnee Rae now making it onto the opening credits (alongside dog Cujo), writers Jane Turner and Gina Riley seemed to have overcome their earlier fear that 'babies aren't funny'. When needed, the 'bubs' was dumped onto Brett to allow the girls to continue their adventures (like a drunken day at the races where they got to horrify guest star Rachel Griffiths with their portaloo vomiting). When incorporated back into the story, however, Epponnee Rae was proving to be a winning new addition to the show, particularly when entered into 'Bubs Idol', a wry piss-take on *Australian Idol* (and yet another high-profile guest star, this time *Idol* judge Mark Holden).

The show has proved to be a cash cow when it comes to merchandise, with everything from *Kath and Kim* T-shirts, tea towels, aprons, oven mitts, calendars and tie-in books. It has also become Australia's biggest-selling television series on DVD. For the CD tie-in, *Kath and Kim*'s *Party Tape* (which included 'old grogan' bands such as Status Quo, The Commodores and The Captain and Tennille), Gina Riley and Jane Turner found the perfect song to sing in character – 'Lady Bump', the disco hit from the 70s which already had the lyric 'Look at moiye!'

Awards-wise, *Kath and Kim* has won two Logies for Most Outstanding Comedy Program, while series one also picked up three AFI Awards, including a Best Actress nod for Magda Szubanski. The 2003 Australian Comedy Awards singled out Glenn Robbins for Outstanding Comic Performance, and the show won Outstanding Australian Comedy. It's a pretty safe bet that there are more awards in store for as long as they keep making the show.

The hit series has now been seen in the USA (on gay-friendly cable channel Trio), Canada, South Africa, Ireland, Singapore, Fiji, Finland, Scandinavia and New Zealand but has received its best reviews from the UK. After acquiring a cult audience on boutique cable station Ftn, the show began screening on a bigger-reach pay TV station, Living, in April 2004. *The Evening Standard* described it as 'a kind of *Neighbours* meets The Royle Family' while *The Daily Telegraph* thought it resembled another classic Aussie soapie, *Prisoner*, 'but set in the prison of suburbia'. Others simply referred to it as '*Neighbours* on acid'.

By September, *Kath and Kim* was getting a third run on British TV and its biggest audience yet on the free-to-air BBC2 as part of its autumn comedy line-up. 'I think *Kath and Kim* will do well because it is not like anything else we are making at the moment,' the BBC's head of comedy entertainment Jon Plowman said of the purchase. 'The [UK] audience aren't stupid. They know that they are watching something that doesn't stem entirely from their culture.' Geez, do ya' reckon?

Not surprisingly, two of Australia's biggest soap superstars, Kylie and Dannii Minogue, both admitted to being huge fans of *Kath and Kim*, with Kylie even going so far as to publicly beg for a guest role. It worked and while the show was filming its third series, Kylie slipped into Melbourne, supposedly to play Kim's daughter Epponnee Rae in a flash-forward scene. Since Gina Riley also believes that her comedy is 'probably more realistic than *Neighbours*', it really would bring Charlene – and Kylie – full circle.

Unlike *Neighbours*' Ramsay Street, Kath doesn't socialise with her neighbours in White Horse Court. The most they get is a curt 'Hello' or 'Having a good look, are you?' if mother and daughter are attracting the attention of stickybeaks. Even worse, Kath is prone to sneak her rubbish into other people's garbage bins and Kim disposes of Cujo's dog poo by flinging it into somebody else's yard. It's a long way from the sharing and caring attitude in *Neighbours* and yet, sadly, a much closer depiction of what goes on in the real-life streets and towns of Australia.

Perhaps the secret to success in Australian TV for the 21st century is hybridising genres, in *Kath and Kim*'s case, the combination of reality TV, sitcom and soap. There will always be a place for *Neighbours* but it seems the characters of *Kath and Kim* and company are just as enduring and relevant. As Gina Riley observes, 'Quite a few people tell me, "God, I know a Kim." It's never themselves.'

We're all friends,' Riley told *The Age* about the tight group of Melbourne comedians who continue to entertain audiences more than a decade after they first appeared on *Fast Forward*. 'We all see each other socially, and yet we can work together. Often those things don't mix, but with us it just seems to. We just really, really spark off each other.'

49

CONCLUSION

The final bombshells...

The success of *Number 96* revolutionised Australia's television industry in the early 70s. In addition to many more soaps being made, actors finally dropped their British accents and spoke true blue Aussie. Serials became a barometer of changes in society, from sexual to multicultural. As in ancient Greek theatre, tragedy and comedy went hand in hand. Much of the humour was camp long before that aesthetic went mainstream, and soaps were multicultural and retro long before anybody had coined such terms.

Serial production in Australia peaked in 1979 when 13 hours of soap (*The Sullivans*, *The Young Doctors*, *The Restless Years*, *Prisoner*, *Cop Shop* and *Skyways*) were beamed into Australian lounge rooms every week. Back then, there was no competition from cable TV, computers or video games, and if a soap was ever seen in an overseas country, it was a bonus, not a lifeline.

During the 80s, international sales boomed and fan hysteria around the world was unprecedented. Aussie soaps (particularly *Neighbours*, *Home and Away*, *Sons and Daughters*, *Return to Eden* and *Prisoner*) became so successful that foreign networks began to copy the formats. Grundy's began to remake its serials for European territories, and UK production companies doubled their workloads to match the Aussie output. International audiences slowly found they had a whole lot more soap to watch.

Back in Australia, everyone wanted to make the next Aussie soap hit, but the demand was shrinking as the 90s dawned. *E Street* was the last true soap success for local audiences, but its minor success abroad proved the market was saturated. For the rest of the decade, some shows were made primarily for an overseas audience, and their producers then wondered why they couldn't crack the big time, here or abroad.

The dawn of a new century has seen a return to basics with a greater maturity amongst the two remaining stalwarts. As *Neighbours* and *Home and Away* approach their 20th anniversaries, both are determined to move with the times, despite the restrictions of their early evening timeslots. Once upon a time, drugs were ignored by both shows. Now morality tales about ecstasy in Ramsay Street and crystal meth in Summer Bay are being skilfully woven into stories about crooked cops and psycho killers. Once again, soaps are teaching and entertaining their multi-generational fans, the kids, their parents and grandparents who might all be watching under the same roof.

Rather than condemning these shows as fodder, maybe it's time to observe and value them for what they tell us about our changing society. It's only now, with the passing of time, that we can look back and realise how many soaps were groundbreaking and taboo-breaking, anticipating cultural shifts in our society. Australia needs to value its soap industry more and remember that soaps can discover the directors, scriptwriters and stars of tomorrow.

The television climate of today is much different from the past and new soaps don't appear nearly as often as they used to. Far be it from me to tell the networks how to run their business, but here's a checklist they might want to refer to in the years to come, based on what has gone before:

Keep making new Aussie soaps but don't get too clever. *The Secret Life of Us* was gutsy and innovative but ultimately alienated its audience with its non-traditional plotting and characterisation. This is a show that should have gone on for years and years and defined the generation that grew up with it. Instead, it's dead in the water after just three seasons.

Don't expect immediate success. Soaps take time to find their audience. *Neighbours* needed two networks, two timeslots and 18 months of pavement-pounding publicity. *The Young Doctors* was cancelled after 13 weeks but given a last-minute reprieve before going on to become a six-year hit. Sometimes it's worth persevering.

Nail a core concept. If you get it right, the show can return to its roots time and time again, as long as you respect your show's history. *Home and Away* has the most brilliant concept ever – look, here comes another troubled foster child with a whole heap of drama to play out! *Arcade* was arguably the worst – see, there was a whole bunch of shops … and people came to shop … and … and …?

Don't mess with success. *Always Greener* had a great concept – city family swaps lifestyles with their country cousins – and the highest ever opening night audience (2.1 million viewers) for a new Aussie drama. And what did Seven do? Through a series of programming mishaps, they stuffed it up. Confused audiences couldn't keep up with unscheduled changes, which saw the show moved from Sundays to Mondays and back to Sundays again. The critically acclaimed show was cancelled even though it had managed to retain a weekly audience of 1.3 million and a nomination for an international Emmy award.

Keep a good mix of comedy and drama. The most memorable soaps have always been the ones that made you laugh as much as they made you cry. Although *Kath and Kim* is a recent highlight, Aussies have never been renowned for their sitcoms, yet soap's comic characters prove we can laugh at ourselves when we need to.

Re-casts are crucial. Most actors eventually get tired and/or bored but a good soap should be able to withstand the loss of its most popular characters (like *A Country Practice* did after Vicky, Simon, Molly and Brendan left). Replacing them, however, is a true art form. Introduce the newbies slowly and, if possible, bring them onto the canvas before the key characters disappear. If they don't click, admit the mistake, get rid of them and try again. And finally, if a network executive insists it's time to lose the older characters to try and bring in a younger demographic, ignore them. *A Country Practice* only went down the gurgler after Seven insisted on putting Cookie and Bob out to pasture. Which leads me to…

Older people like soaps too. Unfortunately, these days, every new drama is aimed at their children (or grandchildren). Take *Fireflies*, the ABC's big drama hope for 2004. It was an exquisitely acted show that was supposed to find a wide audience, but what chance did it have with a bunch of sulky teenagers, spunky firefighters and middle-aged, pot-smoking hippies? There was just one lone, cranky, bitter old woman in Lost River and she ended up bedridden in a nursing home after a stroke. This is NOT what the over-50s want to see on their ABC, and since they were already the major existing audience, why go out of your way to alienate them? *Fireflies* might have made it to a second series if they'd made a token gesture to this continually overlooked audience and written in some well-adjusted, happy, vital, lovable older characters. And let's not forget there's a whole bunch of older, respected soap actors who were once household names and are now sitting around doing not very much. Isn't it a tragedy that they're being ignored in their later years rather than worshipped?

Respect the fans. Without fans there would be no soaps and no audience is more devoted. The Internet is a unique and instantaneous way to discover what they like and what they hate. The stuff in between that fails to rate a mention probably isn't working. And don't muck around with the scheduling of their favourite show unless it's absolutely necessary – people like the regularity of soap watching without any interruptions.

The ABC should have a soap. The BBC launched *EastEnders* in 1985 and it has regularly been the highest-rated show in the UK ever since. Here in Australia, our national broadcaster stuffs up *Fireflies* and prematurely kills off *Something in the Air* even though a high-rating soap could bring them the type of audience they so desperately crave. The ABC never got its head around the popularity of *Bellbird* which is probably why they could only be bothered preserving two year's worth of episodes from a ten-year run. Which brings me to...

Nine doesn't need a soap. After the double whammy of *The Young Doctors* and *The Sullivans* back in the 70s, Nine has had more soap flops than any other network. Apart from needing local drama points, the sports-mad network can't strike it lucky with a soap because it doesn't need to – it's been the number one channel in Australia for over two decades.

Preserve our culture. Unlike Americans, Australians are woeful at treasuring their TV archives. It's bad enough that we've already erased years of original broadcast tapes, but it's even worse to realise that whatever videotape does remain is slowly disintegrating with every passing year. DVD is proving there's a market for such material but Australian television stations refuse to ride the wave of nostalgia. Instead, the digital, multi-channel, subscription TV environment is awash with repeats of American shows. Couldn't one channel be devoted to transferring Aussie shows onto digital tape, thereby saving them for future generations while introducing them to today's viewers?

If just a few of these tips are followed, I might find myself writing a second volume of this book. Not to mention getting hours and hours of viewing pleasure.

Andrew Mercado
October 2004

PHOTO CREDITS

BIBLIOGRAPHY

Abigail, *Call Me Abigail*,
Maxwell Printing, 1973.

Beilby, Peter, *Australian TV: The First 25 Years*,
Thomas Nelson Australia, Melbourne, 1981.

Bourke, Terry, *Prisoner Cell Block H*,
Angus and Robertson, 1990.

Bowles, Kate & Turnbull, Sue,
Tomorrow Never Knows: Soap on Australian Television,
AFI Research and Information Centre, 1994.

Davies, Brian, *Those Fabulous TV Years*,
Cassell Australia, Sydney, 1981.

Donaher, Noeline, *The Sylvania Waters*,
Bookman Press, Melbourne, 1993.

Harrison, Tony, *The Australian Film and Television Companion*,
Simon and Schuster, Sydney, 1994.

Kingsley, Hilary, *Soap Box: The Australian Guide to Television Soap Operas*,
Sun Books, South Melbourne, 1989.

Lamond, Toni, *First Half*,
Pan Macmillan, Sydney, 1990.

Lane, Richard, *The Golden Age of Australian Radio Drama
1923–1960: A History through Biography*,
Melbourne University Press, Melbourne, 1994.

McDonald, Garry & Harding, Bill, *Norman Gunston's Finest Moments*,
Angus and Robertson and Australian Broadcasting Commission,
Sydney, 1976.

McKee, Alan, *Australian Television: A Genealogy of Great Moments*,
Oxford University Press, Melbourne, 2001.

Moran, Albert, *Moran's Guide to Australian TV Series*,
Allen and Unwin, Sydney, 1993.

Murray, Scott, *Australia on the Small Screen 1970–1995*,
Oxford University Press, Melbourne, 1996.

Oram, James, *Home and Away: Behind the Scenes*,
Angus and Robertson, Sydney, 1989.

Oram, James, *Neighbours: Behind the Scenes*,
Angus and Robertson, Sydney, 1988.

Plumb, Gwen, *Plumb Crazy*,
Pan Macmillan, Sydney, 1994.

Reid, Don & Bladwell, Frank, eds,
Close-Up: Scripts from Australian Television's Second Decade,
Macmillan, Melbourne, 1971.

Salter, June, *A Pinch of Salt*,
Angus & Robertson, Sydney, 1995.

Tulloch, John & Moran, Albert,
A Country Practice: Quality Soap,
Currency Press, Sydney, 1986.